sweet reason

A FIELD
GUIDE
TO
MODERN
LOGIC

sweet reason

A FIELD GUIDE TO MODERN LOGIC

tom tymoczko

jim henle

SMITH COLLEGE

W. H. Freeman and Company
NEW YORK

Library of Congress Cataloging-in-Publication Data

Tymoczko, Thomas.
    Sweet reason : a field guide to modern logic / Tom Tymoczko
    & Jim Henle.
        p.   cm.
    Includes bibliographical references and index.
    ISBN 0-7167-2430-8
    1. Logic, Modern—20th century.   I. Henle, James M. II.
    Title.
BC38.T86 1995
160—dc20   93-38476
                                                                  CIP

© 1995 by W. H. Freeman and Company

Printed in the United States of America

1 2 3 4 5 6 7 8 9 0   HG   9 9 8 7 6 5

To our colleagues and friends

Alexei
Dmitri
Fred
Julianna

contents

FORMAL LOGIC with & about logic *informal logic* curiosities & puzzles

3 STATEMENT LOGIC, FORMAL LANGUAGES, AND INFORMAL ARGUMENTS

6 DEDUCTION, INFINITY, AND A HAIRCUT

FORMAL LOGIC   with & about logic   *informal logic*   curiosities & puzzles

preface for the general reader

This book was written for both students and teachers of logic. Our goals were to

- promote literacy in logic
- communicate the beauty and excitement of logic
- present the fundamental ideas of logic concisely
- set out the variety and depth of the manifestations of logic
- **Literacy in logic**   The concept of logic literacy is a natural idea. As a discipline, logic has grown enormously in the last century. It is now an important constituent of philosophy, mathematics, computer science, linguistics, and the cognitive sciences. Each of these fields, at different times, has asserted that logic is its essence or core. Whatever the truth of these claims, it is clear that these fields need people who can read and write logical symbolism and who grasp both the deductive and the expressive powers of logic.

    This is what we mean by literacy in logic—not the mastery of exercises or algorithms but conversational, linguistic fluency. A perfect example is the ability to read (or hear) essays (or lectures) that use logical symbols and concepts, whatever the context.
- **Beauty and excitement of logic**   The pleasure of logic is evident to any serious logician. Logicians do logic because it's fun and frustrating. Examplars of logical fun and frustration are paradoxes and puzzles. It is not too much to say that modern logic was born in paradox—in Cantor's nearly paradoxical assault on infinity, for example, or Russell's shattering discovery in Frege's *Foundations*. The logical puzzles in this book vary from the enchanting constructions of Lewis Carroll and Raymond Smullyan to disguised versions of classical conundrums, such as the surprise exam and the incredible Miniac, where the playful and the profound are one and the same.

This is what we mean by logic's beauty and excitement. Logic is elegant. It is also subversive. We appreciate its capacity to surprise and entertain as much as its perfection of form. And beyond logic itself, we are in awe of the genius that brings it to us. As we savor logic, we admire the towering monuments of thought that mark its history.

- **Fundamental ideas of logic**   The fundamental ideas of logic are presented here with a minimum of fuss and a maximum of variety so that this book can be used for a variety of possible courses. The formal parts are compact: The core of logic is presented simply and directly. Readers will grasp the sense of predicate logic right away, although they may be unsure of the details. They will, we expect, benefit from engaging in what amounts to genuine logical conversations. We return again and again to the fundamentals, but we do conceive of logic as a language, and we emphasize its use as much as its grammar. And what a language it is! A vocabulary that is tiny, but powers of expression that liberate and astound.

- **Variety and depth of logic**   We present advanced topics as both challenges and rewards. There are at least a dozen extended logical essays, from the section on the Gricean theory of implicature to the busy beaver problem to mathematical impossibility to the paradox of the surprise examination.

  The accomplishments of logic are varied and profound. Logic is not an empty game. It is the engine of thought and the fruit of thousands of years of human endeavor. The opportunity to appreciate it in serious applications is both exciting and empowering. *Sweet Reason* attempts to provide this opportunity. Our goal is not algorithmic facility but logical fluency. The phenomenon of "memory dump" is not a great concern. In a year's time, one may forget when a term is free for a variable in a formula but retain, we believe, one's logical reflexes.

Sweet Reason would not have been possible without the help of numerous people. Colleagues near and far contributed much to the shape and content: Howard Adelman, Lee Bowie, Jill DeVilliers, Keith Devlin, Ruth Eberle, Randy Frost, Jay Garfield, Mike Henle, Fred Hoffman, Murray Kiteley, Roman Kossak, Joe O'Rourke, Judy Roitman, Bob Roos, Lee Sallows, Stan Wagon, Marlene Wong, and Andrzej Zarach.

We are especially grateful for the support of our course assistants Gina Cooke, Kira Hylton, Marti McCausland, and Cathy Weir, as well as the countless students who cut their logical teeth on primitive versions of "Buffalo Buffalo Buffalo," "*The Digestor's Digest*," and "Obscure British Novels of 1873."

We are indebted also to Smith College for its constant support— spiritual and material.

Finally, we appreciate the editorial feats performed at W. H. Freeman and Company in putting together a complex volume. The book hangs together, and thanks is due to the management of Penny Hull and the sympathetic and dedicated staff.

Tom Tymoczko
Jim Henle
June 1994

preface for logic teachers: how to use this book in logic courses

The Preface for the General Reader discusses some of the more unusual features of this book, so in this Preface for Logic Teachers we restrict ourselves to sketching various logic courses that might be based on the book. We present two basic courses with variations. One course is a general introduction to logic, formal and informal, for average students of logic—first-year students or students without a special background. The other course is an introduction to symbolic logic especially for very good students—students with a particular interest in philosophy, mathematics, linguistics, or computer science.

A General Introduction to Logic

The simplest course would have students read the first parts 1–4 and allows for students reading some sections more than once. (The material here is pithy. Our motto is "read again," not "keep reading.") Such a course would give students an overview of logic, including predicate logic, and an in-depth study of statement logic, as well as introducing them to several sophisticated topics (paradoxes) and practical topics (LSATs and writing paragraphs). An easy way to supplement the course is to assign Curiosities & Puzzles from parts 5–9.

   If students are able to cover the preceding subjects before semester's end, this course could be continued any number of ways depending on the goals of the teacher and the interests of the students. One continuation would stress informal logic. The practice of informal argumentation could be extended by analyzing presidential debates and senate hearings (parts 6 and 8) and by working on such practical exercises as the legal forms ("The W-4" and "Canadian Customs") in part 7 or the LSAT-like exercises of part 9. The discussion of traditional logical forms and of rabbinic logic in part 5 might be especially interesting to students.

A more traditional continuation would introduce students to the idea of formal argumentation by studying the idea of deduction for truth functions in part 6: Formal Logic (and perhaps skimming the outline of predicate logic in part 5: Formal Logic). An interesting complement to the formal argumentation is "Parliamentary Debates" in part 8: Informal Logic. Although the actual section is very short, we've found that it can be profitably used for one or two weeks. Students not only enjoy debating, they then analyze their own debates using the techniques of both formal and informal logic and the criteria applied to presidential debates.

A more unusual continuation of a basic logic course would introduce students to various topics of advanced logic. One such topic is infinity (covered informally in part 6: With & About Logic). Another topic is computers and programming (covered in parts 4 and 5: With & About Logic). The surprise exam puzzle contains considerable material that is both intuitively appealing and formally challenging; it appears in "Exam Warning" at the end of parts 2–9 and is discussed in part 8: With & About Logic ("From Puzzle to Paradox").

Obviously there are many other ways to trace basic courses through the book. Indeed, some teachers might prefer to teach out of their own notes and use *Sweet Reason* as a class resource — it repeats the essentials briefly and offers many different kinds of enrichment.

An Introduction to Symbolic Logic

This more advanced course presupposes that students need an understanding of first-order logic to progress in their majors — philosophy, mathematics, computer science, and so on. Naturally, it is the practice in informal argumentation that must give way.

The bare bones of this type of course include parts 1–6: Formal Logic. This material takes students through predicate languages, natural deductions, and interpretations over structures. But we encourage teachers not to skip all the Curiosities & Puzzles. And the With & About Logic sections are often valuable for appreciating formal logic. Those in parts 1 and 2, for example, introduce students to the important idea of paradox, and the ability to parse "buffalo" sentences (part 3) is a must for any linguistic analyst!

We call attention to parts 7–9 of *Sweet Reason,* which contain many virtually self-contained essays on advanced topics in logic: axiomatization, definite descriptions, Russell's paradox, Montague and Kaplan's version of the surprise examination, infinity, noncomputability, and so on. We've found that we can motivate good students by beginning the course with a lecture on one of these topics. Our challenge to students is to learn enough logic in the course to understand the initial lecture! Surprisingly, this works. Some students who wouldn't ordinarily care for logic want to learn enough logic to understand Russell's account of definite descriptions or the most plausible solution of the surprise examination puzzle. Other students are delighted to find that they can understand just enough of the first lecture to make them eager to sign up for a course that will teach them to understand the whole thing. We then conclude the course by reprising the original lecture so that students can see how much they've learned.

There is perhaps enough material in parts 1–6 for an entire semester, but some teachers have specific topics they want to cover, and we ourselves prefer to hurry over the details initially and develop logical skills by practicing on substantial topics. Thus the sections of part 7: Formal Logic naturally hang together: numerical quantification, functions, and definite descriptions. They are especially important for philosophy students since they introduce some of the great early successes of symbolic logic and paradigms of analytic philosophy. A marvelous course could be obtained by continuing through Frege's analysis of number and ending with the story of Russell's paradox (part 9: Formal Logic).

Mathematics students, on the other hand, might be better served by the discussion of completeness in part 8: Formal Logic. Mathematicians need to be aware of the interplay between models and formal methods. The discussion of the parallel postulate makes that point vividly, and the section on Boolean algebras raises the issue of axiomatization. We give just a hint of the proof of the completeness theorem, but any logic teacher who so desires will be able to fill it in.

Other important mathematical topics are infinity (part 6: With & About Logic), algorithms (part 5: With & About Logic), and non-computability (part 9: With & About Logic).

A third and novel variant would be to develop students' logical skills by focusing on the several paradoxes discussed in the book. Very early on (part 4: With & About Logic) is the deceptively easy "Miniac." Not many of our students have been able to articulate the flaw in the argument for Miniac's supposed success. In "Games" (part 5: With & About Logic) and "Hypergame" (part 9: With & About Logic), students are challenged by a novel paradox that is yet within their grasp. "The Paradox of the Heap" (part 9: Formal Logic) introduces students to an ancient conundrum and raises questions about the limits of logic. The surprise exam paradox (formalized in "From Puzzle to Paradox" in part 8: With & About Logic) takes students to the edge of Gödel's theorem. And "Russell's Paradox and Frege's Mistake" (part 9: Formal Logic) discusses the most famous paradox of logic. Many of these sections could be supplemented by other readings on the topics, giving students a fine opportunity to extend their mastery of logic and to better appreciate what they've learned from the course.

We've sketched at least six potential logic courses, from the most general elementary introduction to more specific, advanced introductions. *Sweet Reason* opens the possibility for many others. Indeed, *Sweet Reason* is an excellent supplementary text. For each topic it says what it has to say simply, with a mininum of jargon.

Tom and Jim

INTRODUCTION

How critical is Logic? I will tell you: in every corner of the known universe, you will find either the presence of logical arguments or, more significantly, the absence.

— V. K. Samadar

Logic is the study of reasoning and arguments.

Logic is concerned with what makes reasoning good and what makes arguments valid. We study the arguments for themselves alone. Unlike, say, psychologists, we do not seek to understand the authors of the arguments nor the effect of the arguments on others.

Arguments

An **argument** is a collection of statements called **premises** and a final statement called the **conclusion**. In formal arguments, the premises and the conclusion are clearly identified. In informal ones, the premises and conclusion may be difficult to determine; some of them may only be hinted at.

EXAMPLES
1. **Formal argument**   *Premises* The United States must either energetically support the development of solar-powered cars or else suffer increasing atmospheric pollution. The United States must not suffer increasing atmospheric pollution. *Conclusion:* The United States must energetically support the development of solar-powered cars.

2. **Informal argument**   Why do I have to study algebra? I'm going to be either a rock star or a mortician like my dad. He couldn't factor his way out of a wet paper bag.

The intended conclusion to the informal argument is unstated, but the conclusion is surely that the author need not study algebra. The premises are that she will be either a rock star or a mortician, that her father is a mortician, and that he is poor in algebra. We'll discuss later in the book the problem of identifying premises and conclusions.

We will be concerned with all sorts of arguments, and different sorts are evaluated differently. Formal arguments, for example, are either perfectly valid or perfectly invalid and hence completely worthless. Informal arguments, however, can be good, bad, or anywhere in between.

Formal Arguments

This is the traditional area of study for logicians. We examine idealized arguments, arguments whose formal structure completely determines their worth. A formal argument is **valid** (good) if and only if it is impossible for the premises to be true and yet the conclusion false. There is nothing to debate here. If an argument is valid and if the premises are true, then the conclusion *must* be true.

EXAMPLES

3. If Sophist College is an elite liberal arts college then it must require a semester of logic.
   Sophist College is an elite liberal arts college.
   Therefore, Sophist College requires a semester of logic.

4. If our government fails to control military spending, then it will suffer huge budget deficits.
   We are suffering huge budget deficits right now.
   Therefore, our government has failed to control military spending.

Argument 3 is valid because it is logically impossible for the premises to be true and the conclusion false. Argument 4 is not valid because it is possible that the government faces huge budget deficits because it spent trillions on drip coffee machines. In other words, it is possible for the premises to be true, and the conclusion false.

A **formal argument** is one that can be accurately translated into a **formal language** and analyzed by **formal rules**. Arguments 3 and 4 can be abstracted as follows:

EXAMPLES

   3. $P \Rightarrow Q$
      P
      $\therefore Q$

   4. $P \Rightarrow Q$
      Q
      $\therefore P$

Later we will see how formal logic helps us to understand why 3 is incontrovertible and 4 is worthless.

Formal reasoning is practiced by philosophers, insurance companies, lawyers, mathematicians, computers, and small children arguing with their parents. Its song is sung by logicians and poets.

Informal Arguments

An informal argument presents evidence for the conclusion, facts that support the truth of the conclusion. The worth of such an argument depends on the relevance and strength of the evidence presented. Two examples will illustrate this, both letters to *The New York Times* in response to a column recommending legalizing marijuana as a way of fighting alcohol abuse.

EXAMPLES

   5. From 1976 to 1980 I was assigned to some of the Shaeffer Beer concerts in Central Park. When we had a crowd in the park that was predominantly beer drinking, there were so many fights and other problems that we had our hands full. . . . On the other hand, when we cracked down on the beer drinking, marijuana smoke wafted overhead, and the few problems we encountered were usually the result of police officers arresting marijuana users.

      To spend enormous sums of money and tie up large numbers of police personnel to reduce the lesser evil of marijuana, but thereby increase the greater evil of alcohol among teenagers, seems so counterproductive.

   6. According to Government statistics, underage drinking is at its lowest level since 1974; accidents involving teen-age drunken drivers are down 39 percent since 1982; binge drink-

ing among high school seniors has dropped more than 20 percent in the last 10 years.

The solution to underage drinking is not easy. It involves the cooperation of parents, teachers, churches, the mass media, the Government and the industry. This approach is working—and will continue to work if it is not subverted by outlandish and facile proposals.

The first writer supports the column with his own experience. His evidence is not conclusive, but it is relevant and supportive.

The second writer attacks the column by claiming that current efforts to curb drinking are working. His evidence supports his claim, but the claim itself does not address the question of whether legalization of marijuana is actually good or bad. He describes it as "outlandish and facile," but this characterization does not add to the argument. The fact, incidentally, that he is president of the Distilled Spirits Council does *not* detract from the argument, as we shall see.

Informal reasoning is practiced by politicians, economists, historians, weather forecasters, insurance companies, lawyers, advertisers, and small children arguing with their parents. Its song is sung by statisticians and political analysts.

Language

This book is concerned with both formal and informal logic. Our purpose is to investigate what constitutes correct and incorrect reasoning. One factor that makes reasoning difficult is language. English, for all its power of expression, is limited, its words and phrases ambiguous.

EXAMPLES
7. Arthur is better than Boris.
   Boris is better than Cassandra.
   Therefore, Arthur is better than Cassandra.
   (This seems perfectly reasonable.)
8. Cold spaghetti is better than nothing.
   Nothing is better than peace and freedom.
   Therefore, cold spaghetti is better than peace and freedom.
   (This seems absurd!)

The arguments appear to have the same structure. Why is one good and the other bad? The simple answer is that the arguments do not have the same structure. While "Boris" is a name, "Nothing," as used in the second argument, is something completely different. As we will learn, it is a word of powerful and subtle logical significance.

To tame the unruly English language, it is necessary, on occasion, to take drastic steps. We have to choose between meanings, and restrict our study to selected sentence structures. Although we lose some of the richness of the language, we expose its logical content. The importance of this insight cannot be overstated.

Logic is the soul of language.

Common Sense

Fundamentally, common sense is behind all our analyses. In the course of our work we will use truth tables, predicate logic, probability theory, Venn diagrams, and deduction schemes, but they are merely tools, aids to our common sense. Whenever we are in doubt, we must ask ourselves, "What does it all *mean*?

Truth

We are ambivalent about truth. Truth is important, without question; we can hardly discuss arguments without reference and appeal to it. On the other hand, truth is not our goal. Consider, for example, the concept of a valid argument. In essence, a valid argument is a promise. If the premises of the argument are true, then the valid argument promises that the conclusion is also true. Well, what if not all the premises are true? What then?

Then nothing. The argument bears no responsibility. If the premises of a valid argument are false, or even if just one of them is false, then we can conclude nothing about the conclusion. The argument makes no promises. Furthermore, the validity of the argument is independent of the truth of the premises. Look again at example 3. The argument is valid. It doesn't matter whether or not Sophist is truly an elite liberal arts college or even whether it exists.

Logic is that which remains when truth is taken away.

A TASTE
OF
LOGIC

1

contents

FORMAL LOGIC
introducing the language of logic   8

with & about logic
paradox   17

informal logic
negation   21

curiosities & puzzles
quiz   24

FORMAL LOGIC

INTRODUCING THE LANGUAGE OF LOGIC

> During the First World War he [Ernest Harrison] was a naval officer and shaved his mustache. On visiting Cambridge, the Master (not recognizing him) asked him at a dinner whether he was related to "our dear Ernest Harrison." Adopting a certain philosophical view of relations . . . . he replied: No.
>
> —J. E. LITTLEWOOD

Before you begin to study logic seriously, we think you should practice manipulating the basic symbols of logic in a rough and ready sort of way. We think this because we view logic as an activity to be practiced rather than a subject to be memorized.

One traditional way to learn to swim is by being thrown into the water. As you struggle toward the shore, your body discovers the movements of swimming. One way to learn logic is by being thrown into the language of logic. As you struggle to meet logical challenges, your mind discovers the movements of logic.

At least that's what we hope will happen to you here. We'll challenge you with a number of exercises involving almost all the logical symbols you'll see in this book. After you've explored awhile and gotten yourself wet, so to speak, we'll take you through the precise rules behind the symbols. But the rules make more sense if you've had some experience first.

Our basic presupposition is that you and everyone else knows a considerable amount of logic. If you didn't, you couldn't even speak, let alone get along in the world. So our first goal is to make the knowledge you have more explicit, systematic, and precise.

Logical knowledge is particularly close to the surface in the area of kinship relations. Kinship relations are relations between people based on common ancestry and birth. Words like "father, grandmother, aunt," and so on express the thought that particular kinship relations hold between the speaker and the designated party. Anthropologists are especially interested in the kinship terms of various languages and cultures. A motivating idea behind our exercises is the possibility that kinship terms, at least those of English, are just logical combinations of a few basic elements. To lay our logical cards on the table, we're willing to bet that the kinship terms of any culture speaking any language are just logical combinations of a few basic logical primitive terms.

Kinship relations have fascinated all peoples. Just ask Oedipus, or recall the very old childhood riddle: "Brothers and sisters I have none, but that man's father is my father's son. What is my relation to that man?" To answer that old question, you need to use considerable logic (even if your use is only implicit).

We'll soon discuss kinship relations using the language of logic. But to be true to our wish to immediately throw you into logical waters, let us set you a few logical challenges. You try these exercises first, then we'll tell you what you need to know to do them! Be sure to understand that this is a no-lose situation for you. If you can't meet the challenge now, read on for some explanation and come back and try the challenge again. If you can meet even some of the challenges now, then you're ahead of the game! You're developing your hidden logical talents.

Let's set up a referential connection by supposing that

a refers to Jim Henle (a mathematical logician)
b refers to Madonna (a singer & dancer but ¬ a great actress)
c refers to Tom Tymoczko (a philosophical logician)
d refers to Aristotle (a philosopher, scientist & logician)
e refers to Adrienne Rich (a poet)

and that

Fx is "*x* is female" (We could express the same connection by saying *Fy* is "*y* is female" or that *Fz* is "*z* is female." All we are saying is that the symbol *F* _____ stands for "_____ is female.")

Gx is "*x* is male"

Myz is "*y* is married to *z*"

w = *u* is "*w* is identical to *u*" or, in other words, "*w* and *u* are one and the same thing"

Rxyz is "*x* and *y* together beget *z*" or "*x*, *y* are the parents of *z*"

Question 1 What is my relation to that man?

• Note on Challenges: The logical challenges in this book are not tests of previous material. We often challenge you to try something before we've told you how to do it!

CHALLENGE 1 **Interpretations and Examples** Write English sentences or phrases that express the meanings of these formulas.

1. *Fc*   2. *Mea*   3. *d* = *c*   4. *Racb*
5. *Rcab*   6. *Rabc*   7. *y* = *b*   8. *Fa* & *Ga* (guess!)
9. *Mxb*   10. ¬*Fx* (guess!)   11. *Fx* & *Gx*

CHALLENGE 2 **Translation and Logical Analysis** Using only the symbols that have been introduced, write formulas that express the meanings of these sentences.

1. Madonna is married to Aristotle.
2. Aristotle is male.
3. Aristotle is married to Madonna.
4. *x* is a child of Aristotle and Tom Tymoczko.
5. Jim Henle is Madonna.
6. Madonna is herself.
7. Adrienne Rich is not herself.
8. Aristotle and Jim Henle beget Adrienne Rich.
9. Jim Henle is male and Tom Tymoczko is female.
10. Tom Tymoczko is not married to Jim Henle.

How well did you do with those challenges? (The answers to the questions are printed in "Notes, References, Hints, and Some Answers" at the back of the book. You would do well to familiarize yourself with that interesting part.) If you had difficulty, you will probably appreciate the following explanations. If you had no difficulty, be sure not to let the following explanations confuse you!

There are two very basic logical–linguistic operations that underlie our language—reference and predication.

Reference

Language sets up certain conventional (arbitrary) connections between words and things. The best example of this conventional connection is the way proper names pick out (or connect to) things; for example, the English name "Jim Henle" picks out a certain professor at Smith College.

Analogously, the English name "Florence" picks out a city in Italy that is also picked out by the Italian name "Firenze"; "Mark Twain" and "Samuel Clemens," as can be easily verified, pick out the same man. The English name "London" refers to the same city referred to by the French name "Londres." The phrase "the United Nations" picks out a certain international institution even though the member nations of the institution aren't always united.

The basic thought is that a name, like "Jim Henle," *refers to or labels a certain object* (one Jim Henle, if the truth be known) without regard to any descriptive or connotative features of the name.

Question 2 Explain the difference between Jim Henle and "Jim Henle" in terms of the concept of reference.

This elementary connection between names and things is called **reference** or **denotation;** the names *refer to* or *label* or *denote* the things. There is nothing special about what name is chosen to refer to a thing. His parents could have named Jim Henle "Mortimer Snerd" (although until quite recently English speakers followed the convention of assigning the father's last name to a child). Similarly, we could be calling dogs "cats" and cats "dogs." In this sense the basic referential connections are arbitrary. But all speakers of a language share the same conventions and know that they do.

Any word or phrase that bears this simple referential connection to a thing is a **name** or, more generally, a **referring expression.** Examples of referring expressions: "Jim Henle," "Martha Washington," "Malcolm X," "New York City," "Mississippi River," "maples," "tigers," "arsenic," "H$_2$O," "FBI," "3." These all label things or at least they appear to (words like "maples" and "tigers" are sometimes said to label species or natural kinds; a word like "3" appears to label an abstract object).

Question 3 Is "Santa Claus" a referring expression? Give at least one reason for thinking it is and one for thinking it isn't. (*Warning:* Philosophers dispute this question. It's not clear that it has a right answer.)

Predication

Other words and phrases of English serve the logical function of attributing properties to things or attributing relations between things. The phrase "is red" when applied to the name "Jim Henle" forms the sentence "Jim Henle is red" and conveys the thought that a certain Smith professor (Jim Henle) is a certain color (red). Other phrases for attributing properties and relations are "is black," "is single," "is married to," "jogs," "learns from," "loves," "is a male," "is a female," "is a number," "is a tall, blond ghost."

Logicians use the term **predicates** for such expressions that *attribute properties to things or relations among several things.* Logical predicates are very much like verbs or verb phrases. A simple logical sentence is made up of names and a predicate, the names picking out what we talk about, the predicate ascribing some property to what we talk about. The sentence is true if the thing or things we're talking about have the stated property or the relation. Otherwise, the sentence is false. The sentence "Tom likes Jim" refers to the two referents of the names "Tom" and "Jim" and asserts that the referents fall under the relation "first likes second."

The simplest logical predicates are **one-place predicates.** They apply to one thing at a time. We could highlight this by writing blanks to indicate the places or positions in the predicate. For example "_____ is purple," "_____ is thin," "_____ is female." (In logic, we represent predicates by capital letters from the middle of the alphabet—*Px, Tx, Fx*.) These blanks might be filled in by the names we've already discussed. We can say "Jim Henle is female" or "Martha is female" but not "Jim Henle is female Martha" or "Jim Henle Martha is female." These word strings are *ungrammatical*.

Predicates that apply to two things at a time are **two-place predicates,** for example, "_____ loves _____," "_____ is smaller than _____." In logic, we represent two-place predicates by capital letters from the middle of the alphabet—*Lxy, Sxy*.) As before, we can fill in the blanks with referring expressions. "Malcolm X loves New York City" and "2 is smaller than 3" are both acceptable sentences.

It is logically crucial whether a predicate is one-place, like "_____ jogs," or two-place, like "_____ is heavier than _____," or three-place, like "_____ gives _____, as a gift, to _____." Important philosophical disputes turn on whether a given predicate is formalized a given way: Is "*x* is moral" a one-place predicate of actions or is it a two-place predicate ("*x* is moral in culture *y*") of actions and cultures? Hence we have to take special care when symbolizing predicates.

Reference and predication are standard features of English or any other language spoken by human beings. If you don't understand those semantic operations, neither we nor logic can explain them to you. Instead we must suppose our readers' familiarity with such notions. But since all of our readers can read, and presumably also speak, they all are quite experienced at reference and predication!

On the other hand, we won't presuppose farmiliarity with the technical details of logic. Instead, we'll gradually introduce them to you here and part 2. In the rest of the book, we'll go over the technicalities in more detail.

Symbols of Logic

Ordinarily, names and other referring expressions of ordinary language are represented in logic by symbols called **names** or **constants.**

These symbols are generally lower-case letters early in the alphabet: a, b, c, d, and so on. If we need lots of constants, we use primes a', a'', or subscripts b_1, c_2, d_{473}. (Later, when we learn to deduce conclusions from premises, we'll introduce a special category of temporary names indicated by asterisks, as in b^* and c^*.) We'll discover that it's controversial matter whether such an English expression as "the President of the United States in 1994" is really a referring expression (and so symbolized by a constant) or something completely different.

Predicates are represented by capital letters (usually from the middle of the alphabet) which we call **predicates.** Rather than use blanks to indicate the places in a predicate, we add lower-case letters from the end of the alphabet to the predicate letter. These letters, called **variables,** show the places in the predicate and so can be seen as place holders. For convenience, we almost always write the predicate letter first, e.g.,

$$Fx \qquad Gy \qquad Mxy \qquad Rxyz \qquad Fx_1x_2x_3x_4$$

We read the formula Fx as "F of x" or "x F's" or "x has the property F" (similarly for Fy, Gx, Gz, and so on). Of course if Fx is short for "x is female" then we read Fx as x is female"; if it abbreviates "x jogs" then we read Fx as "x jogs."

We read the formula Rzw as "R of z, w" or "z bears R to w" or "z stands in the relation R to w." Of course, if Ryu is the marriage relation, we read Ryu as "y is married to u"; if Ryu is the less-than relation, we read it as "y is less than u."

The simplest way to form statements from predicates and constants is to replace the variable letters (x, y, z) in the predicate by constants to get Fa, Fb, Rab, Rba, Raa, and so on.

Logical Operations

Logical operations allow us to combine simple statements, thereby making complex statements, and to combine simple predicates, thereby forming complex predicates. Suppose A and B are any statements. Among the logical operations we will be concerned with are the following.

Operation	Logical Expression	Reading
Negation	$\neg A$	not A; it's not the case that A
Conjunction	$A \mathbin{\&} B$	A and B; both A and B; A moreover B
Alternation	$A \lor B$	A or B; either A or B; A unless B
Conditional	$A \Rightarrow B$	if A, then B; if A is true, then B is true; if A, B; B, if A; (and oddly) A only if B
Biconditional	$A \Leftrightarrow B$	A if and only if B; A iff B; if A, then B and if B, then A

Another kind of logical operation, quantification, starts with *predicates* and *quantifies* them to form statements or other predicates. Suppose A is some predicate with variable x. We write it as Ax (Ax might be "x is female" or "x is married and a female"). There are two basic kinds of quantification in logic.

Operation	Logical Expression	Reading
Existential quantification	$\exists x Ax$	something is A; there is an A; there is something such that it is A; there is at least one A
Universal quantification	$\forall x Ax$	everything is A; all are A; everything A's; each thing A's

The choice of variable in the quantification doesn't much matter. Both $\exists x Ax$ and $\exists y Ay$ say the same thing and that is that something is A. Logicians tend to use x as the most common variable, but we could just as easily use $\forall y Ay$ as our base case or $\forall z Az$ and so on for any variable. The existential quantifier $\exists z$ when applied to Az asserts that Az is true of at least one object. The universal quantifier $\forall w$ applied to Aw asserts that Aw is true of every object.

When we're talking only about people, then we can read $\exists x Ax$ as "someone A's" or "somebody is an A"; we can read $\forall x Ax$ as "everyone A's" or "everybody is an A."

We use parentheses and brackets, ( ), [ ], { }, to group the operators. For example, "either A or both B and C" is "$A \lor (B \mathbin{\&} C)$" while "Both A or B and C" is "$[A \lor B] \mathbin{\&} C$."

CHALLENGE 3   Write the formulas that are *read* or pronounced as follows.

1. Both *Fx* and *Bx*.
2. Something is *G*.
3. It's not the case that either *Fd* or *Fe*.
4. Either not *F* of *d* or *F* of *d*.

5. *F* of *x* and that *x* bears the relation *M* to *a*.
6. There is something such that both *b* bears *M* to it and it is *G*.
7. Everything is either *F* or not *F*.
8. Either everything is *F* or everything is not *F*.
9. If not *F* of *a*, then *G* of *a*.
10. It's not the case that if *F* of *a*, then *G* of *a*.
11. Both *R* of *x, y, z* and either *M* of *x, y* or not *M* of *x, y*.

CHALLENGE 4   Write the formulas that *express the meanings* of these sentences (regardless of how they are pronounced).
1. Jim Henle is married to Aristotle and Aristotle is male.
2. There is someone Jim Henle is married to who is male.
3. There is someone Jim Henle is married to and someone is male.
4. Madonna has a husband. (*Note:* We don't have a simple predicate for husband, but you can convey the thought that Madonna has a husband by using the symbols that we do have.)
5. Tom Tymoczko is a husband.
6. *y* has a husband.
7. There is someone Adrienne Rich is married to.
8. Adrienne Rich and Madonna beget Jim Henle.
9. There is some *y* such that Adrienne Rich and *y* beget Jim Henle.
10. Adrienne Rich is a parent of Jim Henle.
11. Adrienne Rich is a father of Jim Henle.

CHALLENGE 5   Write English sentences that express the meaning of these formulas.
1. $\exists x Mcx$
2. $\exists y Mcy$
3. $\neg \forall z Mza$
4. $\forall x (Fx \lor \neg Fx)$
5. $\forall x Fx \lor \neg \forall x Fx$
6. $\forall z (Fz \Leftrightarrow \neg Gz)$
7. $\exists y (Rayc \,\&\, Gc)$
8. $\exists y (Rayc \,\&\, Ga)$
9. $\forall x (Mxa \Rightarrow Max)$
10. $\neg \exists z (Mza \,\&\, \neg Maz)$
11. $\exists z \neg Mza$
12. $\exists x \exists y \neg Mxy$
13. $\forall x \forall y (Mxy \Rightarrow \neg (x = y))$

CHALLENGE 6   (especially challenging because this problem raises some deep issues in logic and anthropology)   After the previous work it might occur to you that many other kinship terms could be defined using the basic predicates that we've set out.

EXAMPLES

x is the mother of *y*	$\exists z Rxzy$ & Fx
x is a grandmother of *y*	$\exists z(\exists w Rxwz$ & $\exists u Rzuy$ & $Fx)$

How far can you go with such logical definitions? Can you express such kinship relations as maternal grandmother, grandfather, brother, niece, and mother-in-law? Do you think that every kinship relation human beings use can be expressed using just *Fx*, *Gx*, *Rxyz*, and *Mxy* and the symbols of logic? Give yourself one point for every kinship term (like "uncle") that you can define in terms of the introduced symbolic expressions. Give yourself five points if you find a kinship term that can't be defined in terms of those expressions.

Here's a problem that interests anthropologists: Can all kinship terms be defined in terms of the introduced symbols? Can all kinship terms of English be so defined? Are kinship relations *universal* (common to all human beings) or are kinship relations *parochial* (relative to a culture)?

SUMMARY: Elementary sentences are formed by combining predicates with the appropriate number of referring expressions. Whole sentences, elementary or not, can be combined by such logical operations as negation, conjunction, alternation, conditional, and biconditional. The universal and existential quantifiers apply to predicates (the quantifiers "quantify" certain positions in the predicate) to yield sentences or complex predicates.

with & about logic

paradox

> There was only one catch and that was Catch 22, which specified that a concern for one's own safety in the face of dangers that were real and immediate was the process of a rational mind. Orr was crazy and could be grounded. All he had to do was ask; and as soon as he did, he would no longer be crazy and would have to fly more missions. Orr would be crazy to fly more missions and sane if he didn't, but if he was sane he had to fly them. If he flew them he was crazy and didn't have to but if he didn't want to he was sane and had to.
>
> —Joseph Heller, *Catch-22*

What is a paradox? As a first approximation, we might say that a paradox is an argument that arrives at a contradictory conclusion. But this can't be exactly right. Any proof by contradiction arrives at a contradictory conclusion, and we interpret that result as showing that one of the premises is false. As a joke we might say that a paradox is a proof by contradiction with no false premises! "But that's impossible!" you say. "If the premises are true and the argument is valid, you *can't get* to a contradiction." And you're right. But paradoxes *seem* to do this; paradoxes present the illusion of true premises, a valid argument, and false or even contradictory conclusions. The challenge of a paradox is to put it in proper perspective—to find the faulty premise or the flaw in the reasoning.

Why are logicians interested in paradox? Partly because paradoxes are challenges to our understanding. A paradox unresolved is an affront to our reason. The existence of a paradox shows that we have not grasped all there is to grasp about certain concepts and the logic that deals with them. Paradoxes almost always teach us something about the concepts involved. Finally, paradoxes are fun, like puzzles.

EXAMPLE 1 **Achilles and the Tortoise** Suppose a very slow Tortoise races a very fast Achilles, but the Tortoise is given a head start. Can Achilles pass the Tortoise? Common sense answers yes.

Achilles   Tortoise
o   o
starts here   starts here

But consider this. By the time Achilles gets to where the Tortoise started, the Tortoise will have gone a little further.

Achilles   Tortoise
o   o
now here   now here

And in the time it takes Achilles to go that little bit further, the Tortoise will have gone still further.

Achilles   Tortoise
o   o
here   here

In other words, it will always take Achilles some time to get to where the Tortoise *was*, and in that time the Tortoise will have advanced further. So Achilles will never catch the Tortoise.

That's a paradox.

It's a paradox because the conclusion (Achilles will never catch the tortoise) is absurd, but the argument for the conclusion is compelling. We can *resolve* the paradox either by finding a mistake in the argument (either a false premise or an invalid inference) or by reconciling ourselves to the conclusion (as Zeno did, believing that although things *appear* to move, *in reality* there is no motion!).

CHALLENGE 1 Can you resolve this paradox?

CHALLENGE 2
Who cuts the barber's hair?

CHALLENGE 3
Was what Epimenides said true or false? (This does have a definite answer.)

EXAMPLE 2 **The Barber Paradox** On my trip to France, I visited a town in which the barber cuts the hair of all and only those people who don't cut their own hair.

EXAMPLE 3 **Epimenides' Paradox** Epimenides said that all Cretans were liars. By this he meant that whatever any Cretan said was false. Epimenides, by the way, was a Cretan.

EXAMPLE 4 **A more serious Liar Paradox** "I assure you that I am now lying to you."

18

Did I just lie to you or tell you the truth? If I lied to you, then since I *told* you I was lying, I was really telling the truth. But if I told you the truth, then since I told you I was lying, I was really lying.

EXAMPLE 5   **The Revised Liar Paradox**   Is the following sentence true or false?

> This sentence is false.

If the sentence is false, then what it says is correct, so it is true; if it is true, then it must be saying what is correct, so it is false!

EXAMPLE 6   **Grelling's Paradox**   Let us call a word **autological** if it correctly describes itself and **heterological** otherwise. For example, the word "short" is a short word and so it is autological. The word "long," however, is not long, so it is heterological. "English" is autological (because "English" is English), but "French" is heterological (because "French" is not French, it's English). "Polysyllabic" is autological, but "monosyllabic" is heterological.

CHALLENGE 4   Is "heterological" autological or heterological?

Paradoxes are charming, but they present serious problems. We can't respect logic if it gives us contradictory results. Whether we are philosophers, mathematicians, or sanitation engineers, we cannot be completely happy until we either find a flaw in the reasoning behind the paradox or accept the paradoxical conclusion.

The paradox in example 2 is the easiest. The English sentence describing the town seems to be consistent. In fact, it turns out to be inconsistent: We discover from the description that the barber shaves himself if and only if he doesn't. This can't be.

One explanation for example 5 is that there are some sentences that are neither true nor false. The idea is not unreasonable, since sentences like "Wash the dishes" and "Please pass the watermelon pickle" are clearly neither true nor false. But of course these sentences express commands, and the sentence in example 5 seems to be a description. Well, perhaps what example 5 shows is that some descriptive sentences are neither true nor false.

Suppose we change the sentence to

> This sentence is not true.

What then? For if it's neither true nor false, then it seems that it must be true!

There is no universally accepted answer to that paradox. Indeed, there are many essays and books on the subject. Some people argue that no sentence can refer to itself. But the sentence you are reading seems perfectly decent, and it clearly refers to itself!

Another solution is that we have no coherent concept of truth. This seems very extreme. What are true–false quizzes about if there is no truth?

EXAMPLE 7 **Euathus** The story goes that Euathus studied law under Protagoras, who agreed to be paid only when Euathus had won his first case. Euathus completed the course of instruction but did not begin to practice law for some time. At length, Protagoras grew tired of waiting for Euathus to win his first case and sued for payment. Protagoras argued that either the case should be decided in his favor, in which case he would be paid, or else Euathus would win, in which case Euathus would have to pay him, because Euathus won his first case. Euathus, on the other hand, argued that either he would lose, and so would not have to pay yet, or else the judge should rule that he did not have to pay. What should the judge decide?

EXAMPLE 8 **Berry's Paradox** Since there is a finite number of English words, there is only a finite number of phrases consisting of fewer than twenty words. Some of those phrases describe positive whole numbers, for example, "one," "three hundred seventy-seven," "the square of ninety-nine," and "the first prime number greater than ten to the power forty-two." Since there is only a finite number of such phrases, there must be some positive whole numbers that cannot be described by an English phrase consisting of fewer than twenty words. Consider, then, the phrase "the smallest positive whole number that cannot be described by an English phrase consisting of fewer than twenty words." This phrase seems to describe a certain number, the smallest number that cannot be described by a phrase of fewer than twenty words.

CHALLENGE 5   Explain why the phrase yields a paradox. (*Hint:* How many words are in the phrase?)

EXAMPLE 9 **All numbers are interesting.** Some numbers are special for one reason or another. A number may be special or interesting because it is unique in some way. Examples are the number of platonic solids, the smallest prime number, and the largest number of queens that can be placed on a chessboard so that no queen is attacking another queen. A famous story recounts a visit the mathematician Hardy paid to the mathematician Ramanujan. Both were deeply involved in number theory. Hardy mentioned that the number of the cab he had just taken was 1729, not an interesting number. Ramanujan replied that it was indeed an interesting number; it was the smallest number that could be expressed as the sum of two cubes in two different ways (1729 equals 10 cubed plus 9 cubed, and it also equals 12 cubed plus 1 cubed).

Indeed, *all* numbers are interesting! To see this, suppose we imagine that there are numbers that are not interesting. Clearly 1, the first number, and 2, the first even number, are interesting, so what is the first non-interesting number? Whatever it is, it is interesting, because it *is* the first non-interesting number! The assumption that there are non-interesting numbers leads to a contradiction, and so there can be no non-interesting numbers.

We will often return to the notion of paradox in this book. Sometimes the paradoxes will be puzzles. Sometimes they will be profound challenges to reasoning. Sometimes they'll be both!

We believe that modern logic is inextricably linked to paradox and that understanding one requires understanding and appreciating the other. See what you think by the end of the book.

---

informal logic

negation

The Nothing Nots
—MARTIN HEIDEGGER

Negation is an elementary logical operation and perhaps the most important. In the words of an old logician, "If you can't negate, you can't think straight."

One statement is the **negation** of another if it is impossible for the two statements to be true at the same time *and* it is impossible for them both to be false at the same time. For example, what is the negation of the following compound statement?

> Mei-ling is at home and the sun is shining.

An answer often given is "Mei-ling is not at home and the sun is not shining." This is *wrong*: Although the statements can't be true simultaneously, it is possible for them to be false simultaneously. Suppose, for example, that it is a sunny day and Mei-ling is not at home.

To find the correct answer, imagine that you are in a court of law and you must prove that the statement "Mei-ling is at home and the sun is shining" is false. What do you have to do? It would be sufficient to show that Mei-ling is not at home. It would also be sufficient to show that the sun is not shining. Either one alone would work, although, of course, both together do, too. In short, you must show that either Mei-ling is not at home or that the sun is not shining. This actually tells us the correct answer:

Either Mei-ling is not at home or the sun is not shining.

Another example is

Every student has weird ideas.

What would you have to do to disprove this? All you have to do is find *one* student who doesn't have weird ideas. The negation, then, is the following:

Some student does not have weird ideas.

Informally, "negation" is often confused with "opposite." In logic, they do not mean the same thing. The opposite of "Every student has weird ideas" might be "No student has weird ideas," which is definitely *not* the negation.

EXERCISE Find negations for the following statements. Your answers should be in colloquial English. Furthermore, do not simply place "It is not true that" in front of the statement. This actually works—that is, it produces a correct negation—but it is too easy. You are asked here to think about what the statement means and to compose a negation based on the meaning. Some of these problems are a bit tricky. You might, in fact, not understand all of them until you have finished this book!

1. Jim Henle is bald.
2. Mad Max is the president of IBM.
3. Tom and Jim are bald.
4. Tom is bald and Jim is bald.

5. Either Tom or Jim is a rock star.
6. Either Tom is a rock star or Jim is a rock star.
7. Dick is married and Jane is married.
8. Dick and Jane are married.
9. All mollusks are female.
10. Some popsicles are ambidexterous.
11. No geology majors are amphibious.
12. Some vegetables are carnivorous.
13. Jean can outrun everybody.
14. Jean can outrun somebody.
15. Sue is a friend of every student at the university.
16. Every student at the university has a friend.
17. There is some student who is friends with everyone at the university.

curiosities & puzzles

quiz

To test your aptitude for studying logic

For each of the statements below, answer true or false:

1. My answer to statement 2 is different from my answer to this statement.

2. My answer to statement 3 is the same as my answer to this statement.

3. Wow! This book is off to an amazing start! These guys Jim Henle and Tom Tymoczko are awesome! What a great read! I'll bet this wins a Pulitzer or Nobel or Oscar, or whatever it is they give to obscure texts in logic! I can't wait to find out what happens in the next chapter! I want to sit here and read the whole thing! Wow!

You may grade the quiz yourself. After you have completed writing your answers, ask yourself whether each answer is correct. For example, if you answer T, T, and T to the three statements, respectively, then the answer to statement 1 is incorrect (your answer to 2 is not different from your answer to 1) and 2 is correct (your answer to 3 is the same as your answer to 2). Your own judgment is perfectly acceptable in deciding whether you have answered 3 correctly.

EVERYTHING ALL AT ONCE AND A WARNING

2

contents

FORMAL LOGIC: OVERVIEW

with & about logic

informal logic

curiosities & puzzles

GOAL: To get an overview of the basic concepts of logical theory and how they relate to each other. In the following sections these concepts are presented on an intuitive level. Later more precise and technical definitions will be given. You should try to develop your logical intuitions even if they're not always correct. You can use them as a standard against which to check the technical definitions.

FORMAL LOGIC: OVERVIEW

TRUTH AND FALSITY

What is truth? said jesting Pilate; and would not stay for an answer.

— FRANCIS BACON

The simple statement "Joan is female" is true (often abbreviated T) if and only if Joan is female (i.e., the human named "Joan" has two X chromosomes, secondary sex characteristics like breasts, and so on). Otherwise, "Joan is female" is false (often abbreviated F).

More generally, the expression Fc is T if and only if the object c has the property F. (From now on, we will frequently abbreviate the important phrase "if and only if" as "iff.") Otherwise, Fc is F. Similarly, "Ophelia is married to Tom" is true iff Ophelia is, in fact, married to Tom (the human named "Ophelia" participated in a legal ceremony of a certain type with the human named "Tom"). More generally, Mde is T iff the thing d stands in the relation Mxy (or $M\{\ \}[\ \ ]$) to the thing e. Otherwise, Mde is F.

(Predicates like "w is male" (Gw) or "z is married to u" (Mzu) are *not* true or false in and of themselves. Instead they are true *of* or false *of* things. For example, "w is male" (Gw) is true of all those things in the world that are male and false of every other thing. Philosophers often say that a given thing "satisfies" the predicate Gw (e.g., w is a toad") just in case the predicate Gw is true of the thing (e.g., it is a toad).

The **truth value** of a complex statement is determined by the truth value of its parts. ("Truth value" is just a general name for true and false [and true of and false of]). For example, consider statements formed using $\neg$:

"Jim is male" is true   so   "$\neg$(Jim is male)" is false
"Jim is female" is false   so   "$\neg$(Jim is female)" is true

In general, if A is a true statement, $\neg A$ is false; if A is false, $\neg A$ is true. Similarly, if Gx is true of some object, $\neg Gx$ is false of it; if Gx is false of something, $\neg Gx$ is true of it.

Question   In the world of human beings, are these statements true or false?

1. Each thing is either female or not female: $\forall y(Fy \vee \neg Fy)$.
2. Each thing is either female or male: $\forall y(Fy \vee Gy)$.
3. Either each thing is female or each thing is not female: $(\forall y Fy \vee \forall y \neg Fy)$.

We can summarize the story of negation in a table as follows:

A	$\neg A$
T	F
F	T

Indeed, we can give similar tables, generally called **truth tables** for the other operational symbols &, $\vee$, $\Rightarrow$ and $\Leftrightarrow$:

A B	A & B	A B	$A \vee B$	A B	$A \Rightarrow B$	A B	$A \Leftrightarrow B$
T T	T	T T	T	T T	T	T T	T
T F	F	T F	T	T F	F	T F	F
F T	F	F T	T	F T	T	F T	F
F F	F	F F	F	F F	T	F F	T

The tables for & and $\Leftrightarrow$ are straightforward. A conjunction is true iff both conjuncts are true. The operation $\Leftrightarrow$ asserts identity of truth value; $A \Leftrightarrow B$ is *T* iff *A* and *B* are both *T* or both F.

The only noteworthy thing about $\vee$ is that it means "either one or the other *or* both" (this is called the *inclusive* or). The $\vee$ does *not* mean "one or the other but not both" (this use is called the *exclusive* or).

The operation $\Rightarrow$ has a perplexing truth table. The important part is the first two lines. They ensure that when *A* and $A \Rightarrow B$ are both *T*, *B* must be *T*. Thus we can reason like this:

Given *A* and $A \Rightarrow B$, then *B*.

The confusing part of the table is the last two lines. They ensure that $A \Rightarrow B$ is *T* whenever *A* is F. Perhaps we should read $A \Rightarrow B$ as "if *A*

CHALLENGE 1

1. Calculate the truth table for $\neg A \vee B$ using the truth tables for $\neg$ and $\vee$.

A B	$\neg A \vee B$
T T	— —
T F	— —
F T	— —
F F	— —

Is this truth table the same as that for $A \Rightarrow B$?

2. Calculate the truth table for $\neg(A \vee B)$ using the truth tables for $\neg$ and $\vee$.

A B	$\neg(A \vee B)$
T T	— —
T F	— —
F T	— —
F F	— —

Is this truth table the same as that for $A \Rightarrow B$?

3. Calculate the truth table for $\neg(A \,\&\, \neg B)$.

A B	$\neg(A \,\&\, \neg B)$
T T	— — —
T F	— — —
F T	— — —
F F	— — —

Which basic truth table is the same as this table?

4. Calculate the truth table for $(A \Rightarrow B) \,\&\, (B \Rightarrow A)$. Which basic truth table is the same as this table?

is T, then B is T; if A is F, the whole thing is T."

So according to the truth table, the compound statement

Tuskegee is in France $\Rightarrow$ Tuskegee is in Africa

counts as true for us because "Tuskegee is in France" is false; Tuskegee is in Alabama.

This usage marks a difference between $\Rightarrow$ and some ordinary uses of if–then. One ordinary use is called the *contrary-to-fact* conditional or the *subjunctive* conditional because its verbs are often in the subjunctive mood. Thus the statement

If Tuskegee *were* in France, then Tuskegee *would be* in Africa

is false (even though Tuskegee is not in France) because France is not in Africa; it is in Europe. A true subjunctive statement is

If Tuskegee *were* in France, then Tuskegee *would be* in Europe.

However, the logical $\Rightarrow$ does not represent the subjunctive conditional. It represents something much more elementary. In general, if we're to achieve the simplicity and precision of a symbolic language, we're forced to compromise the richness and ambiguity of ordinary speech.

It will help you if you always remember that $A \Rightarrow B$ says the same thing as $\neg A \vee B$ (either not A or B), no more, no less. In other words, $A \Rightarrow B$ is F in only one case, namely, when $A \,\&\, \neg B$ is T.

Even in this introduction, we want to progress beyond the truth table operations to the quantifiers. These are harder to explain, but in a nutshell, $\exists x A x$ is T iff there is at least one object that has property A. (Many objects might have A; what matters is that at least one does). $\forall x A x$ is T iff every object has property A. (We mean *every*. If all but one object in the universe has A, then $\forall x A x$ is F).

To determine the truth values of $\forall x A x$ and $\exists x A x$, you need to specify what you're talking about. This is called stipulating a *universe* (or *domain*) *of discourse*. For instance, if the universe is just the natural umbers (the natural numbers are the whole numbers greater than or equal to 0), then

$\forall x A x$ is T   iff $A x$ is T of each and every number

Thus $\forall x(x$ is even$)$ is F and $\forall x(x$ is even $\vee \neg (x$ is even$))$ is T. Moreover, $\forall x \neg(0$ is less than x and x is less than $1)$ is T because no natural number is between 0 and 1, although in a universe including fractions, $\forall x \neg (0$ is less than x and x is less than $1)$ is false.

Similarly,

$$\exists x A x \text{ is T} \quad \text{iff} \quad A x \text{ is T of at least one number}$$

Thus $\exists x(x$ is even$)$ is T and $\exists x(x$ is even & $\neg(x$ is even$))$ is F. Moreover, $\exists x(0$ is less than x and x is less than $1)$ is false in the universe of natural numbers.

Analogously, if you say your universe is all people—living, dead, or yet unborn—then

$$\exists x(x \text{ is an 8-foot female})$$

is T iff there is or was or will be a woman 8 feet tall; otherwise, it's F. On the other hand,

$$\forall x \neg (x \text{ is an 8-foot female})$$

is T iff every human being who ever was or will be is *not* an 8-foot female. In other words, each such being either is male or is not 8 feet tall.

With this much of a background, try the following challenges.

CHALLENGE 2 Suppose the universe consists only of the students and the faculty at Sophist College. Assume that the usual facts about colleges are true of Sophist. (If you don't have enough information to answer a certain question, note what you'd need to know.)

Fy is   "y is a freshman"
Sz is   "z is a sophomore"
Tyx is   "y teaches x"

Finally, let c denote a person, Gina Cooke. All you need to know about her is that she is a sophomore at Sophist.

Which of these following expressions are T and which are F?

1. $\forall x(Fx \ \& \ \neg Sx)$ 2. $\exists y(Fy \ \& \ \neg Sy)$ 3. $\forall x(Fx \lor Sx)$
4. $\exists x \neg (Fx \lor Sx)$ 5. $\forall x(Fx \Rightarrow \neg Sx)$ 6. $\exists z Fz \Rightarrow Fc$
7. $\forall z Fz \Rightarrow Fc$ 8. $Sc \Rightarrow \exists x Sx$ 9. $Sc \Rightarrow \forall w Sw$
10. $\exists w(Fw \ \& \ Sw)$ 11. $\forall x Sx \Rightarrow \neg \exists y Fy$ 12. $\forall x Sx \Rightarrow \forall x Fx$

WARNING: Formulas containing $\Rightarrow$ are very tricky. Problem 7, for example, does not say that if everyone at Sophist *were* a freshman, then Gina Cooke *would* be a freshman. It says that if "Everyone at Sophist is a freshman" is true, then "Gina is a freshman" is true. Check the table for $\Rightarrow$. Problems 11 and 12 are similarly tricky.

13. $\exists y Tyc$ 14. $\exists y Tcy$ 15. $\forall x Tcx$
16. $\forall x (Tcx \lor \neg Tcx)$ 17. $\exists x \exists y Txy$ 18. $\forall z \forall w Tzw$
19. $\forall x \exists y Tyx$ 20. $\exists y \forall x Tyx$

WARNING: These could be tricky for a different reason. If x teaches y, must x have a Ph.D. or some other advanced degree, or might x be a student and y a professor? Let's agree that x teaches y iff x is a professor and y is enrolled in a class taught by x.

CHALLENGE 3   Suppose the universe consists only of natural numbers (0, 1, 2, 3, . . .). Assume the usual facts about natural numbers. (If you don't have enough information to answer a certain question, note what you'd need to know.)

Fy is   "y is an even number (0, 2, 4, . . .)"
Sz is   "z is an odd number (1, 3, 5, . . .)"
Tyx is   "$y < x$" (that is, y is less than x)

Let c denote 12, which is an even number.
Which of the following expressions are T and which are F?

  1. $\forall x (Fx \& \neg Sx)$ 2. $\exists y (Fy \& \neg Sy)$ 3. $\forall x (Fx \lor Sx)$
  4. $\exists x \neg (Fx \lor Sx)$ 5. $\forall x (Fx \Rightarrow \neg Sx)$ 6. $\exists z Fz \Rightarrow Fc$
  7. $\forall z Fz \Rightarrow Fc$ 8. $Sc \Rightarrow \exists x Sx$ 9. $Sc \Rightarrow \forall w Sw$
10. $\exists w (Fw \& Sw)$ 11. $\forall x Sx \Rightarrow \neg \exists y Fy$ 12. $\forall x Sx \Rightarrow \forall x Fx$
13. $\exists y Tyc$ 14. $\exists y Tcy$ 15. $\forall x Tcx$
16. $\forall x (Tcx \lor \neg Tcx)$ 17. $\exists x \exists y Txy$ 18. $\forall z \forall w Tzw$
19. $\forall x \exists y Tyx$ 20. $\exists y \forall x Tyx$

SUMMARY: The five basic truth tables and the conditions under which the two quantifiers are true or false determine the meaning or truth conditions of all the more complex sentence forms. Indeed, once you know the universe of discourse (the things we're talking about), together with the reference of any names and the interpretation of any predicate letters, you can, in principle, calculate the truth value of any sentence form.

LOGICAL FORM: THE KEY TO LOGIC

. . . form is the ultimate reality.
—PLATO, *REPUBLIC*, book 10

Suppose we asked you if *Fc* is T. You might well protest that the answer depends on the interpretation of *Fc*. For instance, at various times we have used *Fc* as short for

"Tom Tymoczko is female" (which is false)
"Gina Cooke is a freshman" (which is also false)
"12 is an even number" (which is true)

But suppose we asked you if $\forall xFx \Rightarrow Fc$ is T. You could still protest that it's ambiguous. It might mean, among other things,

"If everyone is female, then Tom T is female" (which is true)
"If everyone (at Sophist) is a freshman, then Gina is" (which is true)
"If every natural number is even, then 12 is even" (which is also (true)

Notice, however, that on every interpretation $\forall xFx \Rightarrow Fc$ comes out T. Even more, it is easy to see that for *any* interpretation, $\forall xFx \Rightarrow Fc$ *must* come out T. This is because any interpretation must pick out a universe of "all things" ($\forall x$), must assign some property to *Fx*, and must assign some object in that universe to *c*. So if everything in the universe has property *Fx*, then of course a particular object *c* must have property *Fx*. (On the other hand, if it's false that everything in the universe is false, i.e., $\forall xFx$ is assigned the value F, then the conditional $\forall xFx \Rightarrow Fc$ is still T.) We can never have a case of T $\Rightarrow$ F, but that is the only case in which a conditional is false.

We can sum up by saying that $\forall xFx \Rightarrow Fc$ is a *logical* truth. What makes any instance true is the **pattern** or **form.** It doesn't matter what *Fx* or *c* means or what we're talking about; what matters is the connection among the parts.

Let's try to explain this a little more slowly.

We first introduced logical symbolism by abbreviating ordinary speech: *Fc* was short for "Tom T is male" and $\exists yFy$ was short for "Someone is male." Later we started to use the same pattern of sym-

31

bols to abbreviate other things: *Fc* as short for "Gina Cooke is a freshman" and ∃*yFy* as short for "Someone is a freshman."

Now we want you to focus on the patterns themselves. We want you to see the patterns—or forms (the words mean the same)—as the primary object of attention. For example, *Fc* (or *Gc* or *Fd* or *Gd* or *He*) is the form or pattern common to all sentences involving simply a subject and a predicate.

EXAMPLES

"Jim Henle is female"   "God is good"
"169 is even"   "Gina is a sophomore"
"Paris is large"   "Jo jogs"

∃*x*(*Fx* & *Gx*) (or ∃*y*(*Fy* & *Gy*) or ∃*x*(*Hx* & *Jx*) or ∃*z*(*Hz* & *Jz*)) is the form or pattern common to all existential sentences that assert that something has a compound property or predicate.

EXAMPLES

"Someone is tall and silly"
"Some number is even and prime"
"Something is a wise virgin"
"There is a creepy crawler"

Again, *A* & *B* is the pattern common to all conjunctions, however simple or complicated each part might be. Logical sentences of the form *A* & *B* might have the more refined forms

∗ *Fc* & *Gc*   ∃*x*(*Hx* & *Jx*) & *Mde*   ∀*xFx* & (∀*xFx* ⇒ *Fd*)

These forms, in turn, have such English instances, respectively, as

"Tom is female and Tom is male."
"Someone is Haitian and Jewish and Dan is married to Edward."
"Everything stinks and if everything stinks, then Dallas does."

CHALLENGE 1

1. Give two more examples of English sentences having the logical forms of each form in line ∗.
2. Give three examples each of English sentences that have the forms
   a. ¬*A* ∨ *B*   b. *A* & (*B* ⇒ *C*)   c. ∃*xAx*

The ability to give concrete instances of abstract logical forms is a key to success in logic. It enables you to see the point!

Shortly we will give you precise rules for composing logical forms. Every precise set of rules for logical forms gives rise to a **formal language** whose **formulas** are precisely the logical forms determined by those rules. But for the moment, we want to rely on the intuitive notion of logical form just given so that we can provide you with an overview of logic. Logic is about logical form.

The most important class of logical forms is the **valid forms.** As we saw, a logical form (or pattern of symbols—remember these mean the same) is not, strictly speaking, true or false. Actual sentences having that form are true or false. Such sentences are called **instances** of that form.

While not true or false, logical forms have properties analogous to truth and falsity. The most important of these are validity, consistency, and inconsistency.

A logical form is **valid** iff every instance of that form is a true sentence.

EXAMPLES

$A \lor \neg A \quad \forall x Fx \Rightarrow Fc \quad (A \,\&\, B) \Rightarrow A \quad Ac \Rightarrow \exists z Az$

$[\forall y (Fy \Rightarrow Gy) \,\&\, \exists y Fy] \Rightarrow \exists y Gy \quad \neg \forall x Ax \Leftrightarrow \exists x \neg Ax$

WARNING: Spoken English sometimes uses the word "valid" differently. "Her statement was valid" can just mean that her statement was true. "That's a valid point" can just mean "that's a reasonable point." In logic, however, when we call a form "valid," we mean that it has only true instances.

CHALLENGE 2 List three other forms you think are valid, that is, whose every instance is true.

A logical form is **consistent** iff at least some instance of that form is a true sentence.

EXAMPLES

$Fc \quad Mcd \quad \exists x Fx \quad A \lor B \quad A \Rightarrow (A \,\&\, B) \quad A \Rightarrow \neg A \quad A \lor \neg A$

CHALLENGE 3 List three other forms you think are consistent, that is, have some true instances. By the way, is there any relation between valid forms and consistent forms?

A logical form is **inconsistent (contradictory)** iff no instance of that form is a true sentence.

EXAMPLES
$$A \Leftrightarrow \neg A \quad \neg(A \Rightarrow A) \quad \exists y \forall x (Rxy \Leftrightarrow \neg Rxx) \ [!]$$

C H A L L E N G E   4   List two other forms you think are inconsistent.

Two logical forms are **equivalent** iff any true instance of one form is a true instance of the other.

EXAMPLES
$$A \text{ and } \neg\neg A \quad A \vee B \text{ and } B \vee A \quad \forall x \neg Bx \text{ and } \neg \exists x Bx$$
$$\exists y \exists z Ryz \text{ and } \exists z \exists y Ryz$$

Obviously, equivalence is a very important notion. Statements that have equivalent forms say basically the same thing, as, for example, do A and $\neg\neg A$.

C H A L L E N G E   5   List three other pairs of forms you think are equivalent.

One logical form **implies** another iff any true instance of the first is a true instance of the second.

EXAMPLES
$$A \ \& \ B \text{ implies } A \quad \neg\neg A \text{ implies } A \quad \forall w Gw \text{ implies } Gc$$

Obviously, implication is a very important notion. If one statement implies another and we're sure of the first, we can be equally sure of the second.

C H A L L E N G E   6   List three other pairs of forms such that you think the first implies the second but the two are not equivalent. Obviously, if form A is equivalent to form B, then A implies B and B implies A.

A very big part of logic is learning which forms are valid or equiv-alent and learning techniques that enable you to classify a form as valid, consistent, or inconsistent. The valid forms can be seen as the **laws of logic.** These are the basic laws of thought. They are not quite analogous to the laws of nature. As the great logician Gottlob Frege put it, "The laws of logic are not like the laws of nature. They . . . are laws of the laws of nature."

SUMMARY: There is an important difference between state-ments and statement forms (or logical forms). Statements are true or false; logical forms are not, strictly speaking, true or false, but valid, consistent, or inconsistent. Statements instantiate logical forms; conversely, logical forms represent, well, the logical forms of statements. Equivalent forms say the same thing, as far as truth value goes. One form can imply another if whenever the first is true, the second is. These concepts should be committed to memory. They recur throughout logic.

ARGUMENT FORM: THE KEY TO REASONING

Behind every argument is someone's ignorance.
—LOUIS BRANDEIS

In English an argument is a set of sentences including premises and a conclusion. Sometimes this is all there is to an argument; sometimes there are other sentences that serve as intermediate conclusions.

Now look at these two arguments, one very bad and one very good.

EXAMPLES

(a) All women are mortal.
Ophelia is a woman.
∴ Ophelia is mortal.

(b) All women are mortal.
Ophelia is mortal.
∴ Ophelia is a woman.

35

Suppose you believed the premises of argument (a). Would you feel obliged to believe the conclusion? What about argument (b)? Consider:

The conclusion of (a) and the conclusion of (b) are both true.
Both premises of (a) are true.
Both premises of (b) are true.

So why is (a) a better argument than (b)? Because the logical form of argument (a) is valid but the logical form of (b) is not.

The logical form of an argument is obtained by replacing each sentence in the argument by its logical form.

EXAMPLES

(a) $\forall x (Wx \Rightarrow Mx)$
     Wc
     $\therefore Mc$

(b) $\forall x (Wx \Rightarrow Mx)$
     Mc
     $\therefore Wc$

An argument form is **valid** iff any instance of it that has true premises has a true conclusion. We get an instance of an argument form by substituting actual statements for the statement forms. Another way to define a valid argument form is to say that no instance of it has true premises and a false conclusion. We also say that an argument is valid if the premises *imply* the conclusion. An argument form is **invalid** iff some instance of it has both true premises and a false conclusion.

By these definitions, form (a) is valid; form (b) is not. However you replace the symbols W, M, and c of example (a), the result is an argument such that, if its premises are true, its conclusion is true:

EXAMPLES

All wombats are mammals.   All women are human.
Cher is a wombat.   Chelsea is a woman.
$\therefore$ Cher is a mammal. $\therefore$ Chelsea is human.

(To be sure, these two examples don't establish the truth of the claim that any instance of this argument form with true premises has a true conclusion. But they help to show why that claim is plausible.)

The case is altogether different with argument form (b). Observe that the following arguments of form (b) both have true premises.

EXAMPLES

All wombats are mammals.   All women are human.
Cher is a mammal.   Bill Clinton is a human.
∴ Cher is a Wombat.   ∴ Bill Clinton is a woman.

CHALLENGE 1   Find two other instances of argument form (b) that have true premises and a false conclusion.

Before attempting Challenge 2, look at a few more examples of valid and invalid argument forms and try to understand why each is valid or not.

EXAMPLES

Valid argument forms

$\neg\neg A$	$\forall z Gz$	$A \Rightarrow B$	$A \lor B$
$\therefore A$	$\therefore Gc$	$B \Rightarrow C$	$\neg A$
		$\therefore A \Rightarrow C$	$\therefore B$

Invalid argument forms

$\neg A$	Gc	$A \Rightarrow B$	Fc
$\therefore A$	$\therefore \forall x Gx$	$B \Rightarrow C$	Gd
		$\therefore C$	$\therefore \exists x(Fx \ \& \ Gx)$

Now try the challenge.

CHALLENGE 2   Which of the following do you think are valid and which do you think are invalid?

1. $A \ \& \ B$
   $\therefore B$

2. A
   $\therefore A \ \& \ B$

3. $A, A \Rightarrow B$
   $\therefore B$

4. $A, A \lor B$
   $\therefore B$

5. $\forall z(Fz \Rightarrow Gz)$
   $\exists z Fz$
   $\therefore \exists z Gz$

6. $\exists x(Fx \ \& \ Gx)$
   $\therefore \exists y Fy$

7. $\exists x Fx \ \& \ \exists x Gx$
   $\therefore \exists x(Fx \ \& \ Gx)$

8. $a = b$
   Fa
   $\therefore Fb$

Observe that we can write an argument in a row, such as X, Y ∴ Z, or in a column, such as

$$X$$
$$Y$$
$$\therefore Z$$

Particularly simple valid arguments are sometimes called **infer-ences.** An example is ¬¬A ∴ A. It is convenient to look at the inferences and valid formulas involving ¬, &, ∨, ⇒, and ⇔ together, and then to look at the inferences and valid formulas involving ∀, ∃, and =. A basic idea of logic is that all arguments, no matter how complicated, are formed by chaining together very simple inferences.

Validity measures the *logical connection* between the premises and the conclusion of an argument form. If an argument has a valid form, then the conclusion follows from the premises. Neither the premises themselves nor the conclusion must be true in an instance of a valid form. What must be true is that *if* the premises are true, *then* the conclusion is true.

If an actual argument has a valid form and its premises are true, then the actual argument is said to be **sound** or **correct.**

Question   What is the truth value of the conclusion of a sound argument?

Notice that *valid* is used in two different senses, one applying to argument forms and the other to statement forms.

SUMMARY: The difference between arguments and argument forms parallels the difference between statement and statement forms. An argument form is valid iff every instance of that form with true premises has a true conclusion (this definition requires nothing of instances with false premises).

with & about logic

paradox and W. S. Gilbert

How quaint the ways of paradox!
At common sense she gaily mocks!
—W. S. GILBERT
THE PIRATES OF PENZANCE

William Schwenk Gilbert, together with Arthur Seymour Sullivan, wrote a series of operettas in the late nineteenth century that have become some of the most popular works of the muscial stage. Gilbert wrote the words. His devastating wit and clever plots irritated Queen Victoria but amused millions. The twists in his plays often had logical content.

Gilbert's most famous plot device is from *The Pirates of Penzance, or the Slave of Duty*. Years before the start of the action, Frederic was apprenticed to a pirate captain (through an error by his nursemaid). A fiercely moral person, his sense of duty forced him to be true to the terms of the agreement, which was in effect until his twenty-first birthday. In the first act, he has just turned twenty-one and is about to leave the crew to join the other side (again, his sense of duty). Since the pirates are all his friends, he promises to make their deaths as "swift and painless" as he possibly can.

In the second act, however, as he is about to lead the police on a raid against the pirates, the captain finds him and explains to him a "startling paradox." The paradox is that Frederic was born in a leap year on February 29. Although he *is* twenty-one years old, he has had only five birthdays! As a consequence, his apprenticeship is not yet over. As logical as he is moral, Frederic soon agrees. He thus changes sides again, asking his newly beloved to wait some 63 years until he should be free to marry her.

This may not seem like a genuine paradox to you. However, in Victorian England the word could mean "puzzle" or "conundrum."

As a logical gem in the Gilbert and Sullivan canon, *Ruddigore, or The Witch's Curse*, is the best. For various reasons it was not as popu-lar, but it is a brilliant piece of work. Hundreds of years before the start of the action, a curse was laid upon the Baronet of Ruddigore and all those who should succeed to the title. The curse required the baronet to commit one crime or more every day—or die in agony. The curse was effective, and each baronet committed a crime a day until he could stand it no more and perished.

The hero of the play is Robin Oakapple. Robin is actually Ruthven Murgatroyd, who should have been the baronet but ran away some years previously; and so his younger brother had to assume the title. Robin loves and is loved by Rose Maybud as the play begins, though neither knows how the other feels. Rose would say something to Robin, but etiquette tells her not to speak "until spoken to."

At the end of the first act, Robin is accused of being the rightful baronet. He acknowledges it—and he doesn't. The song he sings will have echoes throughout this book.

> As pure and blameless peasant,
>   I cannot, I regret,
> Deny a truth unpleasant,
>   I am that Baronet!
>
> But when completely rated
>   Bad Baronet am I,
> That I am what he's stated,
>   I'll recklessly deny!

There are wonderful bits in the second act, but let us leap to the finale. How is it all resolved?

Robin realizes that to refuse to commit a crime is "tantamount to suicide." But suicide is, in fact, a crime! As a consequence, by not committing a crime, the baronet is satisfying the condition of the curse, which requires him to commit a crime a day. This argument turns out to be so powerful that the late baronet, Robin's father, and all the other baronets are persuaded that they shouldn't have died at all and come back to life!

EXERCISE *Ruddigore* ends leaving a logical loose end. It is possible to argue that refusing to commit a crime is *not* tantamount to suicide. Make this argument. Find a copy of the libretto and rewrite the ending, taking this into account.

The Orb and Post

July 28, 1988

Scientist Implicated in Steroid Probe

Mathematician May Have Used Illegal Drug to Aid Research

OTTAWA, July 27 (LPI) Hearings of the Parliamentary Commission on illegal steroid use reopened today with the startling revelation that a leading Canadian mathematician may have been aided in his major research successes by the use of steroids.

Scientists at the Northern Centre for Testing in Flinflon, Manitoba, reported to the Commission that they had obtained evidence that Prof. Thomas Viddersprook, a professor of mathematics at Sophist College, had used steroids to help him in his proof of the "trace formula," an important advance in theoretical mathematics. According to other mathematicians, the "trace formula" is used in number theory and in the study of Lie (pronounced "lee") groups. Prof. Vidder-

Prof. Viddersprook (LPI photo)

sprook's work in this area was regarded as unusually profound even by other mathematicians.

Nation Shocked

Commission members reacted with shock and horror. "This is a sad day for Canada," was a refrain repeated over and over again. "First Ben Johnson and now this," said one member who asked not to be identified. "Where will it end? Will we have any heroes left?" Earlier reports that Sergeant Preston and Yukon King of the Royal Canadian Mounted Police were undergoing

daily urine testing remained unconfirmed.

Scientists at the Northern Centre for Testing were willing to talk about their work, but only on a not-for-attribution basis. "The journals won't publish our papers on the new procedures if we give away too much to the press," one explained. They did seem genuinely excited about the new testing procedure. While the method is complicated, the essence of it is that they have new ways of detecting extremely small traces of steroids and other chemicals. "The odd thing about it," one scientist added, "is that the new protocol is based on applying Prof. Viddersprook's trace formula to the problem of detecting trace quantities."

Results in Doubt

Mathematicians declined to be quoted, but almost all were glum about the discovery. Most agreed that Prof. Viddersprook's

proofs would have to be invalidated. "We can't allow these sorts of activities in mathematics," one said. "It wouldn't be fair. Computers are bad enough." But some expressed doubts. "It's a complicated issue," an expert in forensic mathematics remarked. "If the trace formula is invalidated, then the theoretical underpinnings of the new testing procedure are knocked out. In that case, the tests don't prove anything. That clears Prof. Viddersprook of steroid charges and makes the trace formula valid again. But then the test is valid too, and proof of the trace formula is invalidated again. That means that the theoretical underpinnings of the test are again undermined. But then, of course, we would once again have to invalidate the test. That would mean that the evidence against Viddersprook vanishes as before, and the proof again becomes acceptable. Then, however, (continued on p. 7, col. 3)

paradoxes and psychology

Please accept my resignation. I don't want to belong to any club that will accept me as a member.

—Groucho Marx

Paradoxes figure prominently in this book, but most of them are purely intellectual. Paradoxical statements are apparent impossibilities that seem well supported by apparently good arguments. Interestingly, there are paradoxical commands as well as paradoxical statements. A very simple example is the command "Don't follow this command!" Whatever you choose to do seems to violate the command. In order to obey it you must disobey it, but in disobeying it, you seem to obey it.

Now, at first it might seem that such a command is rather silly and easy to ignore. But suppose you are in the army and the command is given by a superior officer, or you're a child and the command is given by a parent, or you're in love and the command is given by your lover. In short, imagine that the command occurs in a markedly unequal relationship. Second, suppose that you can't step outside the situation to point out the absurdity of the command. There is no judge that you can appeal to. Then you would be in a major bind indeed. You would be in what psychologists call a "double bind": Anything you do can and will be held against you.

Thus we see the three ingredients of a paradoxical command or double bind: (1) a strong complementary or asymmetrical relationship (officer–subordinate) (2) that can't simply be terminated (because of society, laws, and so on) and (3) an apparently meaningful but logically contradictory order.

A realistic example of a double bind is described by an old joke. An overbearing mother gives her son two shirts for his birthday. Trying to express his enthusiastic appreciation, the son rushes upstairs to try one on. As he comes down the stairs, the mother asks, "What's the matter? Didn't you like the other one?"

In their book *Pragmatics of Human Communication*, Watzlawick, Beavin, and Jackson give other examples of paradoxical commands or injunctions:

(a) "You *ought* to *love* me."
(b) "I *want* you to *dominate* me."

(c) "You *should enjoy* playing with the children."

(d) *"Do not* be *so obedient"* (parents to a child whom they consider too dependent on them).

Paradoxical commands, and paradoxical communications in general, have generated some interest among psychologists. Around 1960 several psychologists independently began looking at the family situations of "mentally disturbed" people. They found that many of these situations were filled with paradoxical commands and double binds. Indeed, it sometimes seemed as if mental illness was a perfectly rational response to an inherently irrational situation. Imagine living with a father who said things like this (quoted from a real-life interview by Watzlawick et al):

"My contribution to our problem is that I'm a habitual liar . . . a lot of people will use the expression—uhm—oh, falsehood or exaggeration or bull-slinger, many things—but actually it's lying . . . "

Or imagine living with a mother who talked about you like this (again, an actual quotation from Watzlawick et al.):

"He was very happy. I can't imagine this thing coming over him. He never was down, ever. He loved his radio repair work at Mr. Mitchell's shop in Lewiston. Mr. Mitchell is a very perfectionistic person. I don't think any of the men at his shop before Edward lasted more than a few months. But Edward got along with him beautifully. He used to come home and say (the mother imitates an exhausted sigh), 'I can't stand it another minute!'"

Paradoxical communication can cause as much—or more—cognitive distress as the theoretical paradoxes of logic. But paradoxical communication can cause deep emotional distress as well. However, paradoxes have proven useful in psychotherapy. Occasionally, a therapist can double-bind a patient by prescribing the very symptom that concerns the patient. Imagine, for example, a family in therapy. As the parents begin to work on a threatening problem, one of the children continually disrupts the therapy (by arguing and digressing).

EXERCISE **Explain why each of the commands is paradoxical.**

EXERCISE **Is the father telling the truth or not? Should you believe him or not?**

She announces that she won't cooperate in therapy in any way. Watzlawick records a case where

> . . . the therapist countered by telling her that her anxiety was understandable and that he *wanted* her to be as disruptive and unco-operative as possible. By this simple injunction he put her into an untenable situation: if she continued to disrupt the course of the therapy, she was co-operating and this she was determined not to do; but if she wanted to disobey the injunction she could do so only by *not* being disruptive and unco-operative, and this would make it possible to continue the therapy undisturbed.

The basic point is that psychological disturbances are often indirect and symbolic of something outside themselves. For example, they might express the patient's resistance, rebelliousness, or just plain evilness. Once the therapist orders the patient to act out the symptom as part of the therapy, it automatically ceases to function as a sign of resistance! More often than one might suppose, the patient simply loses the urge to act out in that particular way.

In fact, it has been suggested that psychotherapy itself is an essentially paradoxical situation. Again we quote Watzlawick:

> The paradoxical nature of psychoanalysis was realized by one of Freud's earliest collaborators, Hans Sachs, who is credited with saying that an *analysis terminates when the patient realizes that it could go on forever*, a statement strangely reminiscent of the Zen Buddhist tenet that enlightenment comes when the pupil realizes that there is no secret, no ultimate answer, and therefore no point in continuing to ask questions.

the title of the section on self-reference

All generalizations are dangerous, even this one.
—Alexandre Dumas (fils)

Something is **self-referential** if it refers to itself. Self-reference is the source of many paradoxes and contradictions. It is a literary and artistic device. It is a mathematical tool. It is an important type of procedure in computer programming. It can be a lot of fun.

Self-reference is ancient: The paradox of Epimenides (see "Paradox" in part 1) is thousands of years old. It is also modern: The use of self-reference in computer programs has blossomed in the last fifty years with the development of machines capable of implementing self-references.

In this section, we simply give you a number of examples to ponder and enjoy.

1. Literature

> Prologue
> . . . Admit me Chorus to this history;
> Who, prologue-like, your humble patience pray,
> Gently to hear, kindly to judge, our play.
> —William Shakespeare, *Henry V*

The "me" who speaks "prologue-like" is, of course, the Prologue.

On the page opposite this speech—which opens *Henry V*—in Jim's complete edition of Shakespeare is the final speech in *Henry IV, Part II*, where the self-reference goes on and on. You will see that it is a very natural way of speaking:

First my fear; then my court'sy; last my speech. My fear is, your displeasure; my court'sy, my duty; and my speech, to beg your pardons. If you look for a good speech now, you undo me: for what I have to say is mine own making; and what indeed I should say will, I doubt, prove mine own marring. But to the purpose, and so the venture.—Be it known to you,—as it is very well,—I was lately here in the end of a displeasing play, to pray your patience for it and to promise you a better. I meant, indeed to pay you with this; which, if like an ill venture, it come unluckily home, I break, and you, my gentle creditors, lose. Here I promised you I would be, and here I commit my body to your mercies: bate me some, and I will pay you some, and, as most debtors do, promise you infinitely.

2. Bumper sticker

If you can read this, you're driving too close!

3. Music (This is debatable, perhaps.) In a fugue, the composer begins with a theme. The theme reappears again and again, in different voices, in different keys. Sometimes (J. S. Bach does this) it appears backwards or upside down. In one sense, the piece of music is referring to itself, is quoting itself.

The idea of self-reference in mathematics, music, and art is thoroughly developed in Douglas Hofstadter's best seller, *Gödel, Escher, Bach: An Eternal Golden Braid.*

4. Logic The "Gödel" of *Gödel, Escher, Bach* is Kurt Gödel, mathematician and logician. His great incompleteness theorem is discussed in "Impossibility" in part 9. In the proof of the incompleteness theorem, Gödel mathematically constructs a sentence that is true but cannot be proved. The sentence is too long to print here, and it would be unintelligible, written entirely in the language of arithmetic. It does, however, code a very simple English sentence. In essence, the sentence says

This sentence cannot be proved.

Is it true? Well, if it weren't, then it could be proved. But then we could prove a false statement. This is not contradictory in itself — there are systems that can prove false statements — but it is one of the premises of the incompleteness theorem that this cannot happen. Thus the sentence is true.

Can it be proved? No, since it says it can't, and we have already established that it is true.

5. Art The "Escher" of *Gödel, Escher, Bach* was Maurits Escher, a twentieth-century artist of unusual imagination and daring. His works often demonstrate mathematical patterns, and he was something of an amateur mathematician. His works have gained great popularity in recent years. One of the more frequently reprinted pictures shows a pair of hands, each in the act of drawing the other. Is this self-reference?

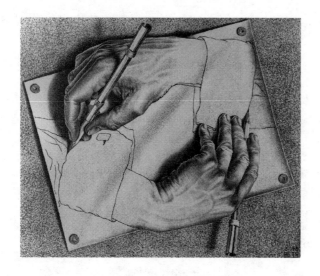

6. Graffiti Seen on a locker at Franklin Regional High School, Murraysville, Pennsylvania: "If you notice this notice, you'll notice this notice is not worth noticing."

7. Sign in the woods

Posted
No Hunting or
Trespassing
Violators will be prosecuted.

Legally, one can walk on any property unless the owner has marked out the boundaries and the prohibitions. Property that has been so marked is called "posted."

8. Puzzle How many errors are there in the following sentence?

> There are two errers in this sentence.

9. Paradox Most of the paradoxes in "Paradox" in part 1 have self-reference at their root. See if you can spot them.

10. Computer Science Self-reference is just one of the tools of the trade in computer science. One of its uses dates back thousands of years. It is used in something called the *Euclidean algorithm*, a procedure for calculating the greatest common divisor (GCD) of two natural numbers (excluding zero). A simplified version of the algorithm goes as follows:

Algorithm: *Euclid*

1. If the two numbers are equal, then print that number and quit.
2. Reduce the size of the larger number by subtracting the smaller number from it.
3. Apply the algorithm **Euclid** to the smaller number and the difference just obtained and then quit.

This is a procedure that refers to itself. The idea behind it is as follows:

a. If $x = y$, then the GCD of x and y is equal to x (or y).
b. If $x < y$, then the GCD of x and y is the same as the GCD of x and $y - x$ (this may not be obvious, but it is not difficult to prove mathematically).

Intuitively, finding the GCD of x and $y - x$ ought to be easier than finding the GCD of x and y, since one of the numbers is smaller. The procedure works by slowly reducing the size of the numbers involved until they are equal, at which point the answer is clear. Let us see how it works.

Suppose the two numbers are 24 and 15. To apply **Euclid,** we go to step 1.

1. The numbers 15 and 24 are not equal.
2. We subtract 15 from 24, so now the numbers are 9 and 15.
3. To apply **Euclid,** we go to step 1.
    1. The numbers 9 and 15 are not equal.
    2. We subtract, so now the numbers are 9 and 6.
    3. To apply **Euclid,** we go to step 1.
        1. The numbers 9 and 6 are not equal.
        2. We subtract, so now the numbers are 3 and 6.
        3. To apply **Euclid,** we go to step 1.
            1. The numbers 3 and 6 are not equal.
            2. We subtract, so now the numbers are 3 and 3.
            3. To apply **Euclid,** we go to step 1.
                1. The numbers 3 and 3 are equal, so we print "3" and then quit.
                3. And now we quit.
            3. And now we quit.
        3. And now we quit.
    3. And now we quit.
3. And now we quit.

It looks a little silly at the end, but the fact is that we must terminate each application of Euclid that we started. You may think of using **Euclid** as going into a box. In the example above, we went into a box inside a box inside a box inside a box inside a box. All those step 3's at the end represent getting out of the boxes.

11. Mathematics One of the trendiest areas of modern mathematics is the study of *fractals*. You undoubtedly have an idea of what "three-dimensional" and two-dimensional" mean. You may be a little fuzzy about "four-dimensional." The idea of more than three dimensions probably makes you very nervous. Fractals are even stranger. A fractal can have a fractional dimension, such as 2.57. They are very odd indeed.

Examples of fractals from the real world include the coastline of the United States. The usual mathematical examples are more interesting to us, however, since they are self-referential. Here is one called the "snowflake curve."

If you take one part of it

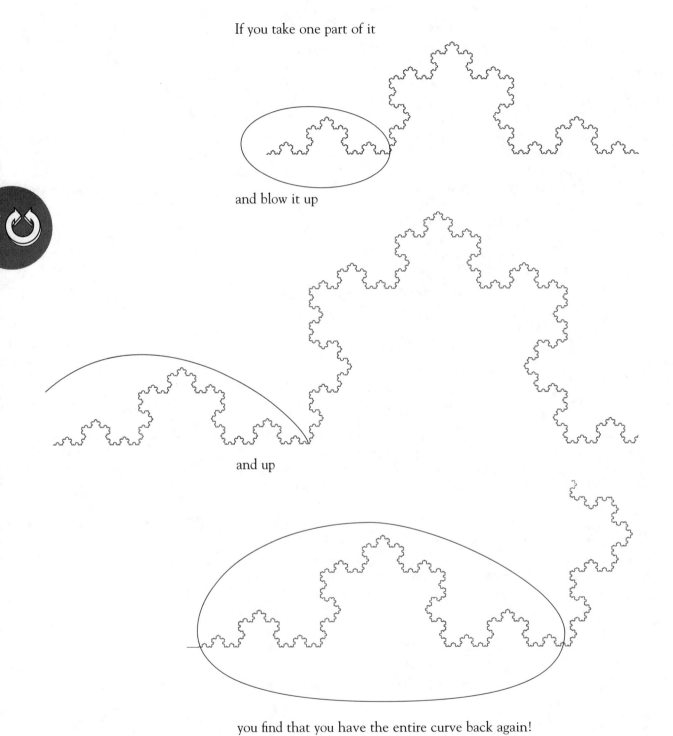

and blow it up

and up

you find that you have the entire curve back again!

This is true no matter how small a part you start with:

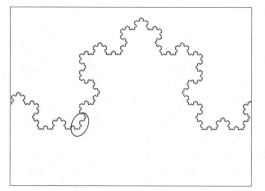 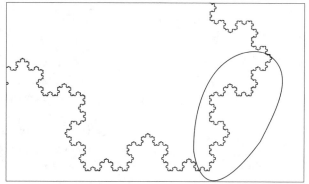

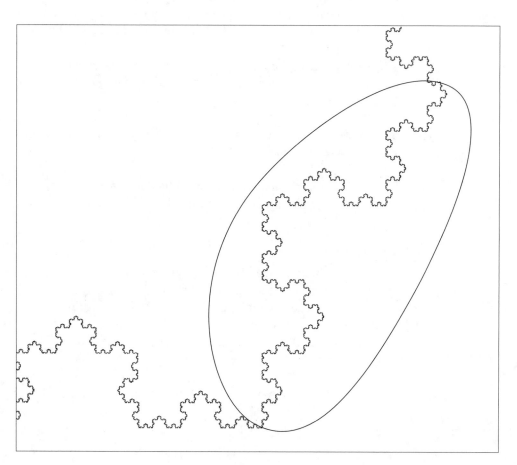

Each piece of the curve "refers" to the entire curve.

12. Academia at Play Academics have written many papers that are on the light side. Recently a paper by John Perez Laraoudogoitia from the Universidad del Pais Vasco in Spain entitled "This Article Should Not Be Rejected by *Mind*" was published in the philosophical journal *Mind*.

In the same year, David Moser, a research assistant in cognitive science at Indiana University, contributed a story to the *Whole Earth Review* of which nearly every sentence was self-referential. The title was "This is the Title of This Story, Which Is Also Found Several Times in the Story Itself." Following are a few sentences from the story, selected at random: "This sentence is introducing you to the protagonist of the story, a young boy named Billy." "This is actually the last sentence of the story but has been placed here by mistake." "A sentence fragment." "This sentence, in a sudden and courageous burst of altruism, tries to abandon the self-referential mode but fails."

13. Biology Every one of your cells contains your genetic code. It contains the information necessary to build you up again from scratch (this is what is meant by "cloning").

14. Miscellaneous In a classic "patter" song in the second act of *Ruddigore* (see "Paradox and W. S. Gilbert"), Sir Despard sings:

> This particularly rapid, unintelligible patter
> Isn't generally heard, and if it is it doesn't matter!

EXERCISES
1. Is example 13 really self-referential?
2. Is "I beg your pardon" self-referential?
3. Find further examples of self-referential . . . things.

informal logic

how to argue

"I can lick you!"
"I'd like to see you try it."
"Well, I can do it."
"No you can't either."
"Yes I can."
"No you can't."
"I can."
"You can't."
"Can!"
"Can't!"
An uncomfortable pause. Then Tom said:
"What's your name?"
— MARK TWAIN, TOM SAWYER

You are a freshman. You arrived two weeks ago at Sophist College, the ivy-draped liberal arts institution you have dreamed of for years. Two weeks, but you are still floating on air. The intellectual atmosphere . . . the intellectual giants who are your professors . . . the imposing architecture . . . the excitement of campus life . . . the opportunities you see ahead of you . . . the challenge of the courses you have just begun . . . everything is as new and as thrilling as you had hoped.

Above all, you are in awe of the older students. They are so confident, so accomplished, so wise, so *cynical*. Well, I suppose there is nothing great about being cynical, except that you have to know a lot to be cynical, don't you? In any case, you relish those bull sessions that last until three in the morning . . . that's where it's at, that's where the world really unfolds, that's where . . . .

But then one night the whole wonderful picture collapses. The discussion is about China. You just read that morning about the tight rein the government keeps on people. All you say is, "What they need is some democracy. If they would only let the people rule," and then Cathy jumps on you. Cathy, the junior whom you admire for her quickness, her assurance—and she seems to like you.

"What's so terrific about democracy?" she asks. "In a democracy, the people choose, but they make all the wrong choices! As soon as Eastern Europe gets democracy, they start shooting at each other. As soon as Iran gets democracy, they start executing people. We have democracy, right? But we don't protect the environment, our streets aren't safe, and our schools are rotten. If democracy is so wonderful, how come only 23 percent of the people vote here?"

You try to cut in. "But democracy has made us the most powerful, the most envied . . . ." But she runs right over you!

"Oh, brother! We're powerful and envied because we're rich, and all we do is abuse that power. And anyhow, we don't really have democracy. You know about Washington, D.C.? A city of millions, and they don't have self-government or representation in Congress. Why? Because it's a black city and we're all racists.

"Look at all the democracies in South America: all bankrupt. The only country down there with its act together is Chile, and it was the dictator Pinochet that put it on the road to recovery. You know what H. L. Mencken said? He called democracy a form of government that believes that the people know what they want and they deserve to get it—good and hard!"

You are devastated. Your deepest beliefs are in ruins! You can't say a thing because everything she's saying . . . sort of makes sense. But you still believe in democracy! You know it's right! But then, what's wrong with her arguments? What do you say?

You need to know how to argue!

One of the more important applications of logic is the analysis and construction of arguments. In a series of sections in the Informal Logic strand of this book, we will discuss this in detail. In outline, here it is.

I. Analyzing an argument
   A. What is the conclusion?
   B. What are the relevant statements?
   C. Which statements support which?
   D. What is being assumed?
   E. How can the argument be attacked?

II. Forming your own argument
   A. State your conclusion.
   B. Diagram the structure of your argument.

C. Cut your argument into bite-size pieces.

D. Write it.

E. Criticize your own argument (see I).

In this section, by way of introduction, we will analyze the argument we have just seen. In the next section, "Rebuttal," we will formulate a response.

Before we begin, let us emphatically note that the purpose of these skills is not to win, not to humiliate your opponent, not even to defend yourself from rampaging upperclassmen. The purpose is to find the truth. Argumentation is a critical step in the search for truth. Only when arguments are carefully presented and thoroughly criticized can we appreciate their value.

CHALLENGE 1   Before reading further, write down what you think are the weaknesses, if any, in Cathy's argument.

Now let's follow the analysis steps with Cathy's argument.

A. What is the conclusion?

The question is, What is point of the argument? To appraise a line of reasoning, we must know what it is trying to accomplish.

The chief conclusion in Cathy's argument is that democracy is not so great. All the other statements seem to support that conclusion (though they may not actually do so). A secondary conclusion is that the United States is not a democracy. This conclusion is out of place.

B. What are the relevant statements?

Statements that have no bearing on the conclusion are a nuisance and a serious weakness in any argument.

Most of the statements here look relevant, except perhaps those that argue that the United States is not a democracy. These may actually damage the argument.

What about the Mencken quotation? It really contributes nothing except to tell us that Mencken had a jaundiced view of democracy. In general, opinions count for very little compared to the facts.

An exception is when we have the opinion of an expert. Was Mencken an expert?

C. Which statements support which?

The structure of the argument is important for evaluating it. When we know how the pieces are supposed to fit together, we can examine how well they do it.

There appear to be three attacks on democracy. The first is that people make the wrong choices. This is supported by the examples of Eastern Europe, Iran, and the United States. The second attack is that few people participate in our own democracy, that is, vote. The third, contained in the third paragraph, is that democracy results in bad economic management. This is supported by the example of South America. We could draw a rough diagram.

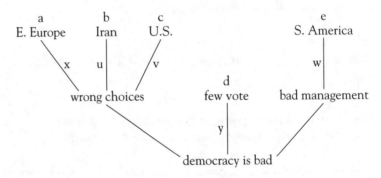

Diagramming your own argument is useful, but diagramming the arguments of others is tricky. One might argue, for example, that Cathy's third argument is really just part of the first, that bad economic management is another case of the people making the wrong choices.

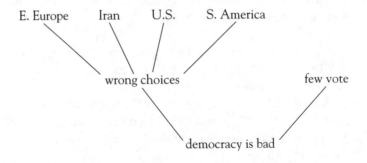

D. What is being assumed?

All arguments make assumptions. Sometimes they are clearly indicated; sometimes they are implicit. It is not wrong to make assumptions—unless the assumptions are false or improbable.

If you have diagrammed an argument, the assumptions or premises are those statements that no other statement points to. In this argument, there are quite a few (the letters refer to the first diagram in C):

a. Cathy assumes that Eastern Europe now has democracy, that Eastern Europeans are now shooting at each other, and that they didn't do it under communist governments.
b. Cathy assumes similar facts about Iran.
c. Cathy assumes that the United States is not taking care of the environment, that crime is a big problem here, and that the schools are rotten.
d. A premise of Cathy's argument is that only 23 percent of Americans vote.
e. Finally, Cathy assumes that Chile is prospering while the rest of South America is not, and that this difference is due to the dictatorship of Pinochet.

E. How can the argument be attacked?

There are two ways to attack an argument. First, we can attack the assumptions: Are they true? Are they plausible? Can they be supported? Second, we can attack the lines of support: Does P really follow from Q, as claimed?

Arguments—and this one is a good example—can be approached in many ways. We present a selection here, but you may find others.

There are some problems with Cathy's premises. There is truth in all of them, but there are distortions as well.

a. Not all of Eastern Europe is thoroughly democratic (as of September 1991), though most countries here had some free elections.

c. Although it is true that the United States has not done all it can to protect the environment, its record has some bright spots. The schools have received bad press, but there is a great deal of debate about their actual condition.

d. The figure 23 percent is clearly wrong. We made it up anyhow. The true figure varies from national to state to local elections. On the other hand, the true figure is still pretty low.

What about the lines of support?

x. There is a great deal of truth to the accusation here, but one can still rebut the argument. The alternative to democracy is to deny participation in government to most citizens. One can argue that such repression cannot succeed indefinitely.

u. While it is true that there are many times more public executions in Islamic Iran than before, this does not mean times are worse, since the previous regime was fairly brutal. One could also argue that the savage incidents occurring in the last ten years had their origins in the repression of the previous thirty.

v. While our record on the environment is spotty, the record is much worse in countries that have had authoritarian regimes.

v. True, crime is a problem here, but it is not a problem in many other democracies.

v. Even among those who agree that our schools are poor or that they have deteriorated, the reasons are much disputed.

y. True, voting rates are low, but can one be certain that this is due to despair and not to contented complacency?

w. Finally, perhaps Pinochet can be given some credit for economic well-being in Chile, but there were other dictators in South America who made no progress at all.

Informal reasoning follows the lines of formal reasoning exactly, but it involves some different considerations. A formal argument is valid if whenever the premises are true, the conclusion is true. A sound argument is a valid argument with true premises. Our goal, however we are reasoning, is to form sound arguments.

Informally, it may be difficult to determine the truth of the premises. Discussion of the premises can lead to ever more arguments. Formally, the truth or falsity of the premises is usually not an issue.

Informally, the validity of a line of reasoning can be debated. We must check both relevance and support. Formally, validity can often be determined mechanically, although there can be problems here too (for example, see "Valid Arguments" in part 4).

CHALLENGE 2   Before reading the next section, write your own rebuttal to Cathy's argument.

rebuttal

> An autocrat's a ruler that does what th' people wants an' takes th' blame f'r it. A constitootional ixicutive, Hinnissy, is a ruler that does as he dam pleases an' blames th' people.
>
> —FINLEY PETER DUNNE

Now, how do you answer Cathy? You would like to be able to fire back a withering reply, but it is too late for that. It is the morning of the next day, so as an exercise, you are composing a response on paper.

A. State your conclusion.

Writing is difficult, but it is more so if you don't know why you are doing it. You must first determine what the point of your piece is.

Originally you had the idea that democracy will solve all China's problems. Now that you are going into print, this claim seems pretty extravagant. Perhaps it is enough to parry the attack on democracy. Let's say your argument is just that Cathy has not shown that democracy is untenable.

B. Diagram the structure of your argument.

If you have difficulty composing and writing arguments, we recommend that you diagram them first. It helps you see what you have and where it should go.

What are your points? They may as well match Cathy's. You want to

a. rebut the charge on eastern Europe
b. rebut the charge on Iran

c. rebut the charges on the United States

d. correct her on the number of voters

e. address the issue of South America

Additionally, you may want to

f. dispose of H. L. Mencken

g. disentangle the business about America not being democratic (Cathy was a little inconsistent here—either the United States *is* democratic and she is wrong on that point, or the United States is *not* democratic and so she can't attack democracy by pointing out problems here.)

How do you organize your points? I suppose you could put points c and g together.

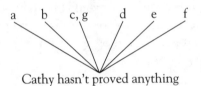

Cathy hasn't proved anything

But this still seems like a lot of points. Probably you should group more of them.

C. Cut your argument into bite-size pieces.

Just as arguments are difficult to write, they are difficult to read. The easier your argument is to understand, the more powerful it is. Smaller pieces are easier to digest.

First, you need a paragraph announcing your intentions. The points about the United States probably deserve their own paragraph. Shall we say a paragraph for Eastern Europe and Iran, and another for South America? Let's see how it might look.

D. Write your argument.

You can plan too much. At some point you have to start writing. Even if you expect it to be garbage, start writing anyway. You will have something to work with.

Dear Cathy,

You overwhelmed me last night with your stimulating comments on democracy. [It's not a bad idea to be polite.] I have only just now collected my thoughts. Of course, democracy is not the answer to everything, but looking back on what you said, I don't see any criticism that sticks.

Let's take the United States. First of all, I don't think you really meant that the United States is not fundamentally a democracy, because that would make your remarks on the environment and other things pointless. Now, what about the environment? Actually, we do a pretty good job compared to other countries. Our schools aren't so bad either. And you goofed on the percentage of people voting here. I looked it up and it was over 50% in every congressional election up through 1988.

Finally, you mention Chile and South America, but Chile is just an exception.

Also, I never heard of H. L. Mencken.

Best,

E. Criticize your own argument.

Arguments are always better for careful analysis, and we will never find truth if we don't try to see the other side.

Actually, your letter to Cathy looks pretty weak. You need to put much more into the arguments. You need specifics. Look at the second paragraph, for example. Can you say more about the environment and schools? Also, you left out crime. Perhaps the second paragraph should really be several paragraphs.

Let's take the United States. First of all, I don't think you really meant that we are not fundamentally a democracy, because that would make your remarks irrelevant. If we aren't a democracy, then our supposed faults in education, environment, and so on can hardly be blamed on our democratic principles.

Now, what about the environment? Actually, we do a pretty good job compared to other countries. The worst offenders, in fact, are the countries that have suffered from authoritarian regimes and central planning. I'm thinking of the Soviet Union (Chernobyl) and Eastern Europe (I have read that people in Poland with lung disease are treated in coal mines, where the air is cleaner!), as well as developing nations such as Brazil. Protecting the environment is actually a good argument for democracy—just look at the former East and West Germanies.

True, crime is a problem here, but is that the fault of democracy? If that were so, then Great Britain, Japan, and Costa Rica would be equally dangerous, but they are not.

Our schools aren't so bad either. And if they are, there is no generally accepted explanation. There are theories that the problem is actually <u>lack</u> of democracy! Some educators feel that parents should have more control of schools, and an experiment is under way in Chicago to test this. Others feel that teachers should have more control (rather than autocratic administrators), and this is being tested in Florida.

Finally, you goofed on the percentage of people voting here. I looked it up, and it's been over 50 percent in every congressional election up through 1988.

You can also expand the paragraphs on Eastern Europe, Iran, and South America:

It's true that under democratic governments some bad things have started to happen in Eastern Europe and Iran, but aren't those problems just as much the fault of years of repression? One can certainly argue that if democratic governments had been in place the last forty years, ethnic tensions would have had safe avenues for release. Nationalities yoked together in countries like Yugoslavia would not now be at each other's throats, but might have learned to live together, as they do in the world's oldest republic, Switzerland. It may be too late now. In the case of Iran, don't forget how ruthlessly the Shah's secret police dealt with dissent.

Chile may be something of an exception. Possibly Pinochet deserves some credit for the success of that nation's economy, but while he was in power, the rest of South America (except for Venezuela) was also governed by dictators. Those countries are in terrible shape, no thanks to the generals.

Finally, you don't have to admit your ignorance about Mencken.

Finally, the Mencken quote is great; I'm going to use it on my parents—but it's not really an argument, is it?

More criticism?

You parry the issue of crime well, but there is a rebuttal: Cathy could admit that democracy doesn't *cause* crime but still assert that it is powerless to *control* it. She can point to Colombia and the Philippines.

Your defense of schools is a little thin. If you didn't have a class in an hour, you might look for reports comparing our schools with those in other countries. Are the totalitarian countries ahead or behind?

You give no explanation of voter apathy, which is pretty marked in the United States (50% turnout at congressional elections isn't 23%, but it's pretty poor). Why don't more Americans vote, anyhow? Did *you* vote?

You tried hard with the ethnic tensions, but the reality still looks bad. Face it, they got democracy, they started shooting. It certainly gives freedom a bad name. If you want to counter this part of Cathy's argument well, you have to explain carefully why democracy is not the cause but the cure.

Your defense is usually that democracy is better than dictatorship, but Cathy's point is that democracy is not so great. You haven't actually shown that democracy is *good*.

Ah well, your letter is pretty decent all in all, and it will sure surprise Cathy. Wouldn't it be nice to end with a quotation of your own? Check out *Bartlett's Familiar Quotations* or maybe the *Oxford Dictionary of* . . . aha!

Finally, the Mencken quote is great; I'm going to use it on my parents—but it's not really an argument, is it? This quotation isn't an argument either, but I am fond of it: "No one pretends that democracy is perfect or all-wise. Indeed, it has been said that democracy is the worst form of Government except all those other forms that have been tried from time to time" (Winston Churchill).

CHALLENGE Suppose you are Cathy. What is your response?

law boards: reading comprehension

Logic is nothing more than a knowledge of words.
—CHARLES LAMB

The Law School Admission Test (LSAT), or "law boards," is a thoroughly logical exam. It features three parts designed to test important logical skills. A fourth section, now discontinued, tested yet another logical faculty. We will give samples of all four sections. The first, given in this chapter, is a test of reading comprehension. That may not sound like logic, but in fact it is critical for anyone using logic. Before you can analyze an argument, you must understand what it is saying.

*Directions: The questions in this section are based on short essays. After reading each essay, answer the questions based on what the essay says or implies. Always choose the **one** answer that is most appropriate.*

I think no one would quarrel with me if I said that number systems lie at the heart of mathematics. That being so, it is especially interesting to look at the history of numbers, because at this point in time, there is a curious symmetry.

The earliest systems, we must suppose, were finite. Even today there are primitive cultures where there is no number greater than 100. Babylonian and Egyptian civilizations developed sophisticated means of describing large numbers, but almost certainly their number systems were finite as well. Even ancient Greece, which we often regard as the first modern mathematical culture, had very limited means for notating numbers. The ancient Greeks did understand that there were infinitely many numbers, but it was not until much later that Hindu and Arabic mathematicians discovered a notation that could express them.

Despite its infinitude, the Greek number system was quickly found to be insufficient. The Pythagoreans discovered that some natural quantities, such as the square root of 2, are irrational; that is, they cannot be written as fractions. The Greeks did not regard these as *numbers*, however, because such quantities did not fit neatly into the theory they had developed. The collection of accepted numbers did not grow to include irrational numbers until much later.

The pattern has been repeated many times. Negative numbers were discovered, rejected, and then accepted. Ditto the complex numbers, ditto infinitesimals and infinite numbers. At each stage, the new concept, however useful, had to wait before it was granted the status of *number*.

It is hard to explain why mathematicians might accept or reject a number or system of numbers. The decision is usually made on philosophical grounds, but the underlying causes can be as much psychological. Numbers have an almost religious significance for mathematicians. They represent what mathematics values.

The number population reached its peak in the middle of this century when the mathematical world accepted virtually any object with the general characteristics of a number: quaternions, extended reals, surreals, hyperreals, supercompact cardinals, and so on. But then something odd began to happen.

A group of mathematicians felt that numbers had begun to lose their original intuitive meaning. A desire to sweep away the clutter and excess arose. In response, the *constructive real numbers* were invented. These were a severe limitation on numbers. Although most mathematicians continued to view numbers as liberally as before, this new number system represented a genuine retrenchment.

Then came the general realization that for all practical purposes, one need deal only with rational numbers. All our computations are fundamentally fractional approximations. The irrational numbers discovered by the Greeks were found to be (in some sense) unnecessary.

Most recently, the importance of computers and computing has forced us to realize that the only numbers critical to the scientist are those that can be represented on computers. How extraordinary! The computer number systems are actually finite! How far has civilization really advanced?

1. The purpose of this passage is to
   (A) outline a history of numbers.
   (B) describe the relationship between numbers and mathematics.
   (C) demonstrate that there are only finitely many numbers.
   (D) show that there has been no progress in number systems.
   (E) describe an interesting pattern in the evolution of number systems.

2. The "symmetry" in the essay refers to
   (A) the fact that number systems are symmetric.
   (B) the relationship between numbers and mathematics.
   (C) the fact that the size of number systems began small, grew large, then became small again.
   (D) the fact that numbers are symmetric.
   (E) the fact that number systems were always rejected and then accepted.

3. The author believes that the restriction to computer number systems is
   (A) progress.
   (B) not progress.
   (C) intriguing.
   (D) unfortunate.
   (E) the natural result of mathematical evolution.

4. It can be implied from the article that the constructive real numbers are
   (A) a smaller number system than the rationals.
   (B) a larger number system than the complex numbers.
   (C) a larger number system than the infinite numbers.
   (D) a smaller number system than the real numbers.
   (E) a smaller number system than computer number systems.

5. It cannot be inferred from the article that the recent changes in number systems
   (A) reflect significant changes in mathematics itself.
   (B) are toward smaller systems.
   (C) have the approval of the author.
   (D) are related to practical concerns.
   (E) are related to the attitudes of mathematicians.

We might call it the problem of confused minorities. All over the world there are ethnic groups demanding independence whose members are inconveniently distributed. Yugoslavia, as it began to fall apart in 1990, offers a classic example. The Croats were demanding freedom from the Serbs. Unfortunately, Croatia contained regions that were full of Serbs. Those Serbian regions contained Croatian enclaves which in turn harbored some Serbian families. At this stage, suppression of nationalist desire will not work. Separation without bloodshed is virtually impossible.

I would like to suggest a solution to such problems. It is techno-logical in nature, and I should say up front that I am no better in-formed about electronic gadgetry than the average reader and that I possess no special expertise. Indeed, I spent many years (at least four) in fog and confusion before I was made to understand that there really were several long-distance phone companies and that neighbors could subscribe to different ones. It still seems miraculous to me, but it has given me an idea: perhaps something similar could save the Bal-kans, East Africa, India, the Middle East, or Philadelphia.

Suppose a number of different nationalities could be recognized inside a loose confederation—nationalities based not on land but on individual free choice. In India, for example, you could be Muslim, Sikh, Kashmiri, Hindu, Tamil, etc., regardless of where you live; moreover, it would have political importance. Your taxes would be assessed by your own parliament. Services, obligations, national an-them, holidays, religious taboos, Olympic team, lotteries, and so on, all would be determined by you and your conationalists.

The greatest difficulty would be coordinating different economic systems. Machines would help enormously. Just as computers route phone calls, connect international telephone systems, and bill cus-tomers, they could monitor interstate economic transactions. Taking into account the citizenship of the contracting parties, software would allow or disallow deals, compute sales taxes, excise taxes, and import duties, and so on.

Even radically inconsistent systems could coexist. One nation could be capitalist. Its citizens would own businesses and go bankrupt. Another could be communist. Its citizens would have jobs and short-ages. Of course, you could choose your nationality (and change it later) for any reason, social or economic. Consequently, centrally planned economies would be forced to compete with market econo-mies in, of all places, a market.

Of course, there would still have to be some joint authority for roads, schools, and defense, but even in these areas there is room for autonomy. Although all governments would contribute to maintain a highway, for example, one might choose direct appropriations while another might collect tolls from its citizens.

I would even permit subnations to formulate their own foreign policies (that is, after all, the most fun a government can have). And if one subnation messes up, technology can step in again. It may soon be feasible, with especially smart bombs (or smart hackers), to wage war on the most thoroughly scattered ethnicities!

6. The point of this essay is to
   (A) propose a governmental structure for countries with minority populations that are not located in well-defined regions.
   (B) suggest a solution to the ethnic crisis in India.
   (C) urge the adoption of democratic political structures in autocratic nations.
   (D) suggest turning over the responsibilities of government to telephone companies.
   (E) urge warring nationalities to live in peace.

7. The essay implies that
   (A) India is ruled by a dictatorship.
   (B) the people of India favor widely differing economic systems.
   (C) there are different ethnic groups in India.
   (D) the Indian people are scattered all over the country.
   (E) there are foreign groups in India.

8. All of the following are mentioned in the article as possible responsibilities for nationalities in a confederation *except*
   (A) making highways.
   (B) taxation.
   (C) setting holidays.
   (D) carrying out economic policy.
   (E) designing T-shirt logos.

9. The author implies that without governments for each nationality,
   (A) ethnic groups would be confused.
   (B) ethnic groups would not get along.
   (C) countries would be unable to govern economic policy.
   (D) countries would still have roads, schools, and an army, but nothing else.
   (E) ethnic groups would live in ethnically mixed areas.

10. The essay suggests that technology will help
    (A) make foreign policy.
    (B) make economic policy.
    (C) design T-shirts.
    (D) build roads.
    (E) monitor sales.

Communism, as a paradigm of economic and bureaucratic control, is in retreat. All over the world, centrally planned economies collapse. Everywhere free markets triumph. Ironically, here in the United States, the greatest capitalist nation of all, a "communist" system still functions, though it, too, is beginning to crumble. Our communist commodity is art.

In the socialist state, the bureaucracy dictates prices and production. In this country, the art world has its own bureaucracy: the major critics. In music, art, literature, and architecture, critics control the market. They tell artists what to do, museums what to buy, symphonies what to play, and us what to like.

Economic communism was a response to perceived evils in the free market. Just so has artistic communism grown. The perceived evil in our case is the starving artist. The story is simple: A talented individual toils in obscurity producing masterpieces. Genius is recognized only when the artist is dead. Optional characters include an unsympathetic spouse and a greedy agent.

The starving artist story is a myth. It rests on the premise that the public is too ignorant to understand great art or to judge attempts at making it. In this view artists are the adults liberated by imaginative experience while we—their public—are the children trapped in the here and now. Only when we are a few hundred years older will we be able to share their visions.

To guarantee that society does not mistreat our geniuses by frivolously rejecting their visions, we have taken the market out of the hands of the people and given it to the critics—to extend the metaphor, to a select group of children wise beyond their years. Following their judgement, we have committed a significant fraction of our public resources to support starving artists. It has been a brave but presumptuous attempt to predict who are geniuses and who are merely starving. The result has been worse than failure.

For seventy years, artists have had very little incentive to produce great art. By our deeds, we have made it difficult for them to know what great art is. They are supported by us no matter how offensive and meaningless their work. One might even say that the more ghastly and confusing their work is, the more likely it is to attract attention and money.

As in communist countries, a black market has developed. When we don't get what we want at concerts and museums, we look elsewhere. We decorate our homes with calendars and movie posters. We read spy thrillers and historical romances. We listen to Elvis and John Williams.

Not surprisingly, as capitalism spreads around the world, it is making inroads at home. We see paintings now that contain recognizable objects. We hear music that is melodic. We read stories that are entertaining and relevant.

At the same time, the old communist apparatus is crumbling. Government support for the arts is in turmoil and dwindling. Perhaps in a few years, this will all be a memory, as artists strive once again to bring us beauty, insight, and pleasure. After all, it wasn't the public that was too ignorant; it was the critics.

11. The purpose of this piece is to
   (A) chart the history of art in this country in the last seventy years.
   (B) expose the myth of the starving artist.
   (C) draw a parallel between communism and the art world today.
   (D) expose the evils of communism.
   (E) expose the evils of critics.

12. In the view of the author,
   (A) today's critics are starving.
   (B) today's artists are geniuses.
   (C) today's artists are not geniuses.
   (D) today's artists are starving.
   (E) today's critics are geniuses.

13. Which of the following statements is inconsistent with the passage above?
   (A) Critics have preferred paintings without recognizable objects.
   (B) Elvis was a great musician.
   (C) Communism brought substantial benefits to social peace in Yugoslavia.
   (D) Most people today have not listened to the music of J. S. Bach.
   (E) Communists are winning elections in many Asian countries.

14. In the article, critics were accused of all of the following except
    (A) telling the public what art is good.
    (B) telling us which artists to support.
    (C) forming a "bureaucracy."
    (D) encouraging artists to produce art that is poor.
    (E) recognizing which artists are geniuses.

15. Which one of the following facts would best support the passage above?
    (A) evidence that great artists in the past were successful
    (B) evidence that many current artists are communists
    (C) evidence that many current critics are communists
    (D) evidence that the government bureaucracy is corrupt
    (E) evidence that inferior artists in the past were successful

curiosities & puzzles

The Digestor's Digest

The Digestor's Digest is a weekly newspaper devoted to reports on food for the benefit of consumers. Each issue carries product reviews by the *Digest* staff. The first issue is devoted to breakfast. Unfortunately, for financial reasons it must print advertisements as well. The situation is made worse by the fact that the advertisers make their ads look as much like articles as possible. To help readers tell the ads from the articles, the *Digest* requires every sentence in every ad to be false. A page may contain two ads, two articles, or one of each. Since every statement in every article is true, it should be easy to tell them apart. Or should it?

The Digestor's Digest

Vol. I, No. 1	Page 1

Scientists Report

Grittibits is good for you! Among all breakfast cereals on the market, Grittibits has the most protein. This is not an advertisement!

Scientists Report

Wheezies is good for you! Among all breakfast cereals on the market, Wheezies has the most protein. This is the only ad on this page!

exam warning I

A special feature of this book is the Surprise Examination. The exam is printed on one page, and it is clearly identified by the title "Surprise Examination."

The title is apt. *The exam will come as a surprise.* By this we mean that is impossible for you to know before you turn the page and see it that the exam is there. There is no way for you to deduce what page it will be on.

Of course, you might simply guess that it is on page 139, and it is possible that you might guess correctly, but *guessing* is not *knowing*. What we are saying is that there is no way that you can be *sure* what page the exam is on until you actually see it.

Philosophers have traditionally worried about what constitutes knowing. In general, however, for you to know that the exam is on, say, page 139, it must be the case that

1. the exam *is* on page 139.

2. you believe the exam is on page 139.

3. you have good reasons for your belief.

We are confident that you will not know the page of the exam until you come across it. By the way, it is not on page 139!

Study hard and be prepared for the Surprise Examination!

talking heads

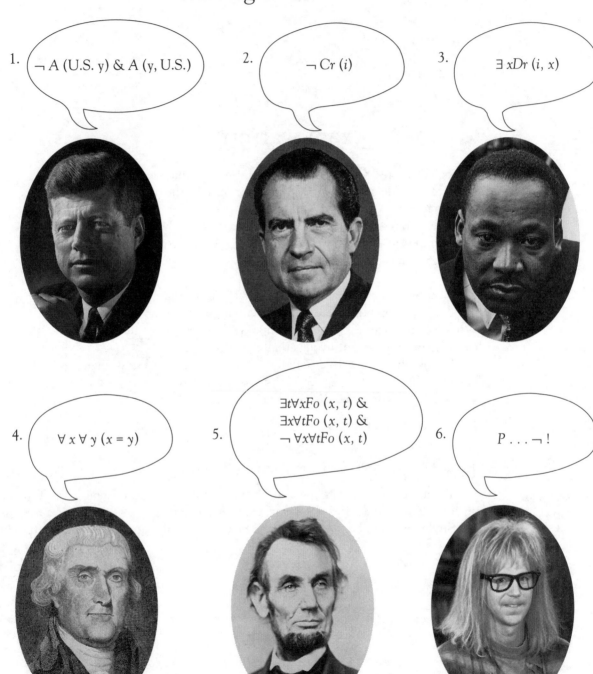

STATEMENT LOGIC, FORMAL LANGUAGES, AND INFORMAL ARGUMENTS

3

contents

FORMAL LOGIC: STATEMENT LOGIC

with & about logic

informal logic

curiosities & puzzles

GOAL: To master the technical apparatus of statement logic, also known as propositional logic, sentential logic, or truth-functional logic. This branch of logic covers the connectives ¬, &, ∨, ⇒, and ⇔. It begins with a formal language for symbolizing logical forms and then offers an interpretation of the connectives and the forms by means of truth tables. This gives rise to simple and precise definitions of validity and consistency.

FORMAL LOGIC: STATEMENT LOGIC

FORMAL LANGUAGES: SENTENTIAL

> The Symboles serve only to make men go faster about, as greater Winde to a Winde Mill.
>
> —THOMAS HOBBES

Formal languages are rules for generating *logical forms*. The more complicated the language, the more complicated are the forms that can be generated. Formal languages are also interesting as *models* of natural languages, and as you read about them, you might ask yourself how close the match is between a given formal language and natural languages.

Let's begin with an especially simple kind of formal language we'll call Sentential. ("Sentential" is a made-up word. We call this formal language "Sentential" because its formulas are analogous to sentences, the grammatical equivalents of statements.) Sentential deals with the forms generated by ¬, &, ∨, ⇒, and ⇔ and allows us to make some points in a very general way (these points also apply to more sophisticated languages).

Vocabulary: The basic symbols are grouped into three categories:
  Sentence letters: $P, Q, R, S, P_1, Q_1, R_1, S_1, P_2, \ldots$
  Connectives: ¬, &, ∨, ⇒, ⇔
  Parentheses: ( )
Grammar (or syntax): The basic definition of formula (or "well-formed formula," or "wff" for short)
Atomic (or basic) wff: Any sentence letter (P, Q, R, etc.) is an atomic wff.
Formula (wff):
1. Any atomic wff is a wff.
2. If A and B are any wffs (distinct or identical), then so are
  a. ¬A   b. (A & B)   c. (A ∨ B)
  d. (A ⇒ B)   e. (A ⇔ B)

EXAMPLES
wffs

P $\quad\neg P$ $\quad\neg\neg P$ $\quad\neg\neg\neg P$ $\quad(P \mathbin{\&} Q)$

$(P \mathbin{\&} \neg Q)$ $\quad(Q \vee (R \Rightarrow S))$ $\quad(P_1 \Leftrightarrow (\neg Q \vee P_1))$

non-wffs

$(P\vee)$ $\quad(R_1 \neg \mathbin{\&} P)$ $\quad P \mathbin{\&} Q \vee R$

"Abelard loves tofu." $\quad P \Rightarrow Q$

EXERCISE 1 **Which of the following are wffs?**

a. $\neg\neg P_3$
b. $P \vee Q \vee R$
c. $P = Q$
d. $(P \vee Q \vee R)$
e. $(Q \mathbin{\&} B)$
f. $((P \mathbin{\&} (Q\vee R) \Leftrightarrow ((P \mathbin{\&} Q) \vee R))$
g. $(R \Leftrightarrow (\neg @@P \Rightarrow R_1))$
h. $\vee\neg\neg\Rightarrow\mathbin{\&} PQRS$
i. $(P \mathbin{\&} (P \vee P))$
j. $\neg\neg\neg\neg\neg Q_{89}$

Some Comments About Sentential

The preceding definition of wff is called a **recursive definition.** Recursive definitions are very common in logic. A recursive definition has two parts:

1. A basis, in which certain identifiable things are specified to have the property in question (All sentence letters are declared to be wffs.)

2. A recursive part, which tells us how to use things that have the property (of being a wff) to get new things with the property (of being a wff).

Thus, the recursive clause tells us how to get new wffs from old ones. For example, if A is any wff, then so is $\neg A$. Since Q is a wff, $\neg Q$ is a wff; since $\neg Q$ is a wff, $\neg\neg Q$ is a wff; and so on.

CHALLENGE 1 Can you give the definition of "ancestor of Tom" using a recursive definition? In the base clause, say who Tom's immediate ancestors are (there are only two). Then in the recursive part, explain how Tom's other ancestors arise. (*Hint:* Use the parent relation Pxy, "y is a parent of x." Suppose that x is one of Tom's ancestors. Then what relatives of x are also Tom's ancestors?)

Parentheses

Parentheses are used to clarify wffs. Without parentheses, we wouldn't know whether $P \mathbin{\&} Q \vee R$ stood for $(P \mathbin{\&} (Q \vee R))$ or for $((P \mathbin{\&} Q) \vee R)$. Although the strict definition of wff requires us to enclose everything in parentheses, we occasionally omit the outermost parentheses, particularly in later sections. Thus, $(P \mathbin{\&} (Q \vee R))$ is written $P \mathbin{\&} (Q \vee R)$.

CHALLENGE 2 Construct truth tables for $(Q \Rightarrow (P \Rightarrow P))$ and $((Q \Rightarrow P) \Rightarrow P)$ and see whether they are the same. Do the same for $(P \mathbin{\&} (Q \vee R))$ and $((P \mathbin{\&} Q) \vee R)$. Do parentheses matter?

The Structure of Wffs in Sentential

Each wff is constructed in only one way from the sentence letters by the connective operations. The **main connective** is the last connective applied in the generation process. The main connective determines the logical structure of a wff. The construction of a wff can be represented by a tree structure, which we will call the **syntactic tree** for the wff. We draw lines from the main connective of a wff, and under them we write the smaller wff (or wffs) that the original was composed of. Then we apply the process to the main connectives of the smaller wffs until we come to simple letters.

EXAMPLE

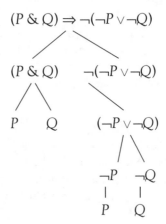

The **scope** of a negation symbol (or any other one-place logical operator) is the smallest wff following the negation symbol. In other words, the scope of a $\neg$ sign is the wff immediately under the lowest appearance of the sign on the syntactic tree. In the example tree, the scope of the first $\neg$ is $(\neg P \vee \neg Q)$; the scope of the second $\neg$ is P. The scope of a negation symbol tells us what is being negated by that symbol.

EXAMPLE

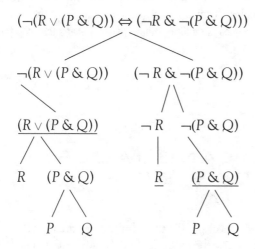

The scope of each negation symbol is the underlined formula beneath its last occurrence on the tree.

EXERCISE 2   **Draw syntactic trees for each of the following wffs and underline the scope of any negation operator.**

a. $\neg(P \,\&\, Q)$ b. $(\neg P \,\&\, Q)$

c. $(S \,\&\, (R \vee Q))$ d. $((S \,\&\, R) \vee Q)$

e. $(P \Rightarrow (Q \Rightarrow R))$ f. $((P \Rightarrow Q) \Rightarrow R)$

g. $\neg((S \,\&\, (P \vee \neg Q)) \Leftrightarrow (\neg S \vee (\neg P \,\&\, \neg\neg Q)))$

Compared to the predicate languages we will see later, Sentential is very primitive. Complex predicate wffs, such as *Fa, Mab, Mba, $\forall x Fx$,* and *$\exists y Mby$,* can only be represented by letters: *P, Q, R,* and so on. So all the relationships among atomic wffs in Sentential get washed out. Still, we can see Sentential as revealing part of the structure of predicate languages. Sometimes this revelation is useful, as when we want to explore the meanings and relations between $\neg$ (not), $\&$ (and), $\vee$ (or), $\Rightarrow$ (if–then), and $\Leftrightarrow$ (if and only if). Moreover, we can examine logical rules that apply to these connectives; for example, $A \& B \therefore B$ is valid, $A \therefore A \& B$ is not; and $\neg (A \& B)$ is equivalent to $\neg A \vee \neg B$. Finally, for present purposes, we can modify the rules to obtain different languages.

SUMMARY: The wffs (or formulas) of Sentential are built up from the sentence letters by (repeatedly) applying the connectives. The syntactic tree of a wff reveals the logical structure of that wff and defines the scope of any negation symbol in it.

FORMAL LANGUAGES: VARIATIONS OF SENTENTIAL

> Grammar, n. A system of pitfalls thoughtfully prepared for the feet of the self-made man, along the path by which he advances to distinction.
> — AMBROSE BIERCE

In this section we'll look at some languages very similar to Sentential. Each of these may look superficially different from Sentential. Our aim is to get you to see each of them as just a variation on a common theme. Consider, first, the matter of parentheses.

Polish Sentential

It is possible to do logic without parentheses. In the early part of this century, Polish logicians invented a system of notation in which the connectives are written before the wffs they connect, not between them. Thus the positions of the connectives themselves serve to clarify wffs and so eliminate the need for parentheses. This way of writing symbols is called **Polish notation.**

> **Atomic (basic) wff:** Any sentence letter (P, Q, R, etc.) is an atomic wff.

Formula (wff):

1. Any atomic wff is a wff.

2. If A and B are any wffs (distinct or identical), then so are

    a. $\neg A$ b. $\& AB$ c. $\lor AB$

    d. $\Rightarrow AB$ e. $\Leftrightarrow AB$

Thus $(P \& (Q \lor R))$ becomes $\& P \lor QR$, $((P \& Q) \lor R)$ becomes $\lor \& PQR$, $\neg(Q \Rightarrow R)$ becomes $\neg \Rightarrow QR$, and $(\neg Q \Rightarrow R)$ becomes $\Rightarrow \neg QR$.

EXERCISE 1 Translate these wffs from Polish Sentential to Sentential.

    a. $\neg \& PQ$ b. $\& \neg PQ$ c. $\neg \& \neg P \neg Q$

    d. $\lor \Leftrightarrow SQP$ e. $\lor S \Leftrightarrow PQ$ f. $\Rightarrow \& PQ \lor PR$

EXERCISE 2 Translate these wffs from Sentential into Polish Sentential.

    a. $(P \Rightarrow (Q \Rightarrow R))$ b. $((P \Rightarrow Q) \Rightarrow R)$

    c. $\neg(P \& (Q \lor \neg P_1))$ d. $((\neg P \& Q) \lor \neg P_1)$

    e. $((\neg P \lor \neg Q) \Leftrightarrow \neg(P \& Q))$

Syntactic trees are especially easy to construct for wffs in Polish Sentential. This is because the leftmost connective is always the main connective (this is not true in regular Sentential).

EXAMPLE

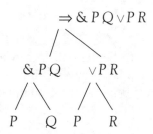

EXERCISE 3 Construct syntactic trees for the wffs in exercise 1.

The architecture of most computers and calculators employs Polish notation (also called "prefix") or something similar. Hewlett-Packard calculators, for example, use *reverse* Polish notation (also called "post-fix"): the user who wishes to add two numbers types one number, then the "enter" key, the second number, then the "+" key. Essentially, this is $ab+$ instead of $(a + b)$. In general, machines communicate with humans using standard notation and parentheses for the convenience of the human only.

Finally, we note that the Poles originally used capital letters for the connectives according to the following table:

¬	N (negation)	&	K (konjunction)
⇒	C (conditional)	⇔	E (equivalence)
∨	A (alternation)		

The Sentential wff $((P \Rightarrow Q) \Rightarrow (\neg Q \Rightarrow \neg P))$ would have been written CC*pq*CN*q*N*p* in the original Polish notation. Polish Sentential, of course, is equivalent to Sentential; it involves only a slightly different style of writing symbols.

Weak Sentential

Other variants of Sentential can be obtained by adding or subtracting symbols. For example, in Weak Sentential—just a proper subset of Sentential—the only connectives are ¬, &, and ∨.

Atomic (basic) wff: Any sentence letter ($P, Q, R,$ etc.) is an atomic wff.

Formula (wff):

1. Any atomic wff is a wff.

2. If A and B are any wffs (distinct or identical), then so are
   a. ¬A b. $(A \, \& \, B)$ c. $(A \vee B)$

Modal Sentential

We can also add symbols to Sentential. In Modal Sentential—the basis of modal topics, which are ways of thinking about what might have been and what must be—two new one-place connectives are added: □ and ◇.

□A is read "necessarily A" or "A is necessarily true."
◇A is read "possibly A" or "A is possibly true."

CHALLENGE 1
Compare Sentential to Weak Sentential. Is every wff of one a wff of the other? Explain. Do you think that we could paraphrase any wff in Sentential by a wff in Weak Sentential?

The idea behind these symbols is that $\Diamond A$ is true if A *could have been* true, regardless of whether A is in fact true or false. So, although "John Hancock was the first president of the U.S.A." is false, it could have been true—he might have been elected. So

$\Diamond$ (John Hancock was the first president of the U.S.A.)

would count as true.

$\Box A$ is true if A *could not have been* false. So although "George Washington was the first president of the U.S.A." is true, given what we just said,

$\Box$ (George Washington was the first president of the U.S.A.)

is certainly false. On the other hand, $\Box(2 + 2 = 4)$ is true.

But for now the important point is not the meaning of the symbols; rather it is the definition of the language of Modal Sentential. Observe that it has exactly the same structure as Sentential.

Atomic (basic) wff: Any sentence letter (P, Q, R, etc.) is an atomic wff.

Formula (wff):

1. Any atomic wff is a wff.

2. If A and B are any wffs (distinct or identical), then so are
   a. $\neg A$ b. $(A \& B)$ c. $(A \vee B)$
   d. $(A \Rightarrow B)$ e. $(A \Leftrightarrow B)$ f. $\Box A$
   g. $\Diamond A$

EXERCISE 4 Write out six wffs of Modal Sentential that are not wffs in Sentential. Define the scope of a $\Box$ symbol in Modal Sentential.

CHALLENGE 2 Write out in full the definition of wff in Tensed Sentential.

EXERCISE 5 Construct syntactic trees for the following wffs of Modal Sentential.

a. $\Diamond(P \,\&\, Q) \Rightarrow (\Diamond P \,\&\, \Diamond Q)$
b. $\Box P \Leftrightarrow \Box\Box P$
c. $\Box(\Box P \Leftrightarrow \neg\Diamond\neg P)$

CHALLENGE 3

1. Find a statement of English, R, such that PR is false but NR is true. Find an R such that NR is true but FR is false. Find a Q such that NQ is false but FQ is true.

2. What do the following wffs say (A is an arbitrary statement)? Do you think either of them should be valid in Tensed Sentential?

   a. PP$A \Rightarrow$ PA b. P$A \Rightarrow$ PPA

Tensed Sentential

Here is a final expanded Sentential language. In Tensed Sentential, we add the new connectives N, P, and F, which are read as follows. If A is any wff, NA is read "A is now true;" PA, "A was true;" FA, "A will be true." Tensed Sentential allows us to represent tenses. It could be that PQ is true (Q was true) but NQ is false (Q is no longer true). An example would be if Q is "Ronald Reagan is President."

SUMMARY: Many variations of Sentential are possible. However, each yields the same pattern of definitions for wff, major connective, resolution tree, and scope of one-place connectives.

TRUTH TABLES

> True and False are attributes of speech, not of things. And where speech is not, there is neither Truth nor Falsehood.
>
> —Thomas Hobbes

In order to recognize the laws of logic and valid arguments, we need some technique for recognizing when a logical form is valid, when two forms are equivalent, and so on. The simplest technique for Sentential is that of truth tables. Truth tables have an important theoretical disadvantage: They apply only to Sentential connectives like $\neg$, $\&$, $\vee$, $\Rightarrow$, and $\Leftrightarrow$, not to the quantifiers $\forall$ and $\exists$. But they give us a chance to see a whole system of logic working, so we start with them. Recall the basic truth tables for the logical operations.

A	$\neg A$
T	F
F	T

A B	$A \,\&\, B$	$A \vee B$	$A \Rightarrow B$	$A \Leftrightarrow B$
T T	T	T	T	T
T F	F	T	F	F
F T	F	T	T	F
F F	F	F	T	T

For the moment, do not worry why the tables have the values they do. Think of them as simply giving the meaning of the logical operations. Later, we'll ask how well these meanings match their English counterparts.

The crucial fact relating Sentential and the basic truth tables is this:

Every formula (wff) of Sentential determines a unique truth table.

The table for a wff includes each sentence letter that occurs in it. For every combination of truth values that can be assigned to the sentence letters of a wff, there is a row in the table that assigns exactly one truth value to the whole wff.

EXAMPLE

P Q R	$\{(P \Rightarrow (Q \Rightarrow R)) \Leftrightarrow ((P \& Q) \Rightarrow R)\}$
T T T	T
T T F	T
T F T	T
T F F	T
F T T	T
F T F	T
F F T	T
F F F	T

What this table shows us is that the wff (logical form)

$$\{(P \Rightarrow (Q \Rightarrow R)) \Leftrightarrow ((P \& Q) \Rightarrow R)\}$$

is valid (every instance must be true), or, as we sometimes say, that it's a *tautology*. Furthermore, this wff is also a useful tautology; it says, in effect, that you get the same result by chaining conditionals $(P \Rightarrow (Q \Rightarrow R))$ that you get by collecting the antecedents into one large conjunctive antecedent $((P \& Q) \Rightarrow R)$. Technically, the last two wffs are equivalent.

But let's back up a minute. How do we know that any wff determines a unique truth table? Here is a simple proof. Given a wff, construct its syntactic tree. At the bottom of the tree will be all the sentence letters in the wff. For any combination of truth values for those letters, write these truth values under the individual letters. Now use the basic tables to determine the truth values for the next higher node or nodes, then the next higher nodes, and so on, until you have one truth value for the wff at the top of the tree.

EXAMPLE

Start with the expression $\{(P \Rightarrow (Q \Rightarrow R)) \Leftrightarrow ((P \& Q) \Rightarrow R)\}$.

Step 1: Construct the syntactic tree and write the truth values.

$$\{(P \Rightarrow (Q \Rightarrow R) \Leftrightarrow ((P \& Q) \Rightarrow R)\}$$

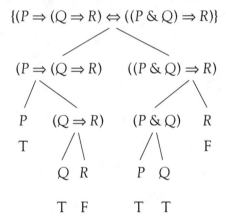

Step 2: Use the basic truth tables to calculate $Q \Rightarrow R$ and $P \& Q$, since we now know the values of P, Q, and R.

$$\{(P \Rightarrow (Q \Rightarrow R)) \Leftrightarrow ((P \& Q) \Rightarrow R)\}$$

Step 3: Use basic truth tables to calculate $(P \Rightarrow (Q \Rightarrow R))$ and $((P \& Q) \Rightarrow R)$; we now know the value of each component;

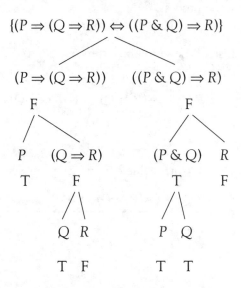

Step 4: Use the truth table for ⇔ to find the value for F ⇔ F.

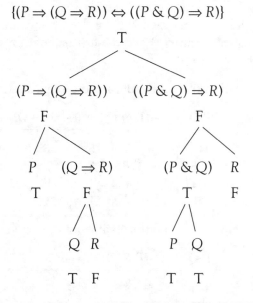

This corresponds to the second line of the table, T T F, and gives the final truth value T to the wff for this line.

An obvious drawback to this way of constructing tables is inconvenience: It takes too long and takes up too much space. Here is a way of shortening the process.

EXAMPLE

Step 1: List all the sentence letters of a wff to the left of the wff in alphabetical order.

P Q	¬(P & Q) ⇒ (¬P & ¬Q)

Step 2: List all truth value combinations under the letters.

P Q	(¬(P & Q) ⇒ (¬P & ¬Q)
T T	
T F	
F T	
F F	

(It's common practice to list them in this standard order in which the rightmost letter alternates between T and F, the next letter alternates between 2 T's and 2 F's, etc., until the leftmost letter has consecutive T's in the first half of its rows, and consecutive F's in the last half.)

Step 3: Fill in the truth values of the simplest sub-wffs first.

P Q	(¬(P & Q) ⇒ (¬P & ¬Q)
T T	T F F
T F	F F T
F T	F T F
F F	F T T

Step 4: Now fill in the truth values of the next simplest wffs.

P Q	(¬(P & Q) ⇒ (¬P & ¬Q)
T T	F T F F F
T F	T F F F T
F T	T F T F F
F F	T F T T T

Step 5: Continue in this fashion until truth values are assigned to the whole wff.

P Q	$(\neg(P \,\&\, Q) \Rightarrow (\neg P \,\&\, \neg Q)$
T T	F T **T** F F F
T F	T F **F** F F T
F T	T F **F** T F F
F F	T F **T** T T T

The last table is all that would appear on your paper. As you become familiar with the truth tables, you can invent your own shortcuts. When you have memorized the truth table for &, for example, you don't have to write it out; instead, you can go straight to $\neg(P \,\&\, Q)$. When you have memorized the truth table for $\Rightarrow$, you know that as soon as you get something of the form $F \Rightarrow A$, then the whole thing is T; you don't have to figure out whether A is T or F. Similarly, if you're dealing with $A \,\&\, B \,\&\, C \,\&\, D$, then as soon as one of the wffs A, B, C, or D is F, the whole conjunction will be F. And if the wff is $A \vee B \vee C \vee D$, then as soon as one of the wffs is T, the whole alternation will be T.

Of course, if you really want convenience, you can write a computer program to produce the truth table for any wff within limits. (The qualification "within limits" is necessary. Although each step of the truth table is perfectly mechanical, there is a "combinatorial explosion" in constructing truth tables. A wff with n sentence letters has 2^n rows in its truth table. If $n = 100$, no computer could handle the resulting truth table. Hence the idea of developing shortcuts is quite important.)

EXERCISE   Construct truth tables for the following wffs. Compare the tables of wffs on the same line to see which are equivalent and which imply which. Remember, two wffs are equivalent if they have the same truth table. One implies another if whenever the first is true, the second is also true.

1. a. $P \Rightarrow Q$ b. $Q \Rightarrow P$ c. $\neg P \Rightarrow \neg Q$ d. $\neg Q \Rightarrow \neg P$
2. a. $P \,\&\, (Q \,\&\, R)$ b. $(P \,\&\, Q) \,\&\, R$
3. a. $P \Rightarrow (Q \Rightarrow R)$ b. $(P \Rightarrow Q) \Rightarrow R$
4. a. $(P \,\&\, (Q \vee R))$ b. $((P \,\&\, Q) \vee (P \,\&\, R))$
5. a. $(P \Rightarrow Q)$ b. $(\neg P \vee Q)$
6. a. $(P \,\&\, \neg Q)$ b. $\neg(P \Rightarrow Q)$
7. a. $P \,\&\, \neg P$ b. P c. $\neg P$ d. $P \Rightarrow \neg P$

SUMMARY: Every wff of Sentential determines a unique truth table, and there is a mechanical method for constructing the appropriate table for any wff.

LOGICAL THEORY FOR STATEMENT LOGIC

Logic must take care of itself.
—LUDWIG WITTGENSTEIN

A basic result of sentential logic is that every formula of Sentential determines a unique truth table. This truth table determines the interesting logical properties of the associated wff. This enables us to give precise definitions for the logical properties we talked about in the subsection "Logical Form" in part 2 (it would be advisable to reread that subsection now). Here are some of the most important definitions.

Let A be any wff. Then

A is **valid** (or is a **tautology**) if in the truth table for A, the final column contains all *T*'s.

A is **consistent** iff in the truth table for A, the final column contains at least one *T*.

A is **inconsistent** (or **contradictory**) iff in the truth table for A, the final column contains no *T*'s.

These categories divide up wffs in the following way:

consistent wffs   vs.   inconsistent wffs

/ \

valid wffs   consistent but not valid wffs

WARNING: Notice that we use the same word, "valid," to talk about wffs and arguments. It is not used in the same sense, but by the end of this section, you'll understand the relationship.

Tautologies are like the laws of logic. They can always be relied on, but they don't tell us much about the real world. Propositions whose forms are contradictions should be avoided; they can never be true. Most of our communication consists of statements that are consistent but not tautological. They can be true, and when they are, they give us information about the real world.

• Notice, by the way, that the definitions aren't stated in the language Sentential. That is, they aren't expressed by wffs. Instead, the definitions are expressed in English and say something about wffs. For this reason, we call English a "metalanguage" for Sentential; it's the language we use to talk about Sentential. If valid formulas express the laws of logic, the following definitions and remarks express the laws of metalogic.

90

These definitions, and all definitions that follow, should be memorized. You can get a better feel for the concepts involved and their interrelations by answering the questions in Challenge 1. They show what is often the case in studying logic: that we sharpen our reason by reasoning *about* logic as well as by reasoning *in* logic. For example, we know that $B \vee A$ is valid whenever A is because if A is valid, A is T in every line of its truth table. Since $B \vee A$ is T whenever A is, $B \vee A$ is T in every line of its truth table, so $B \vee A$ is valid.

CHALLENGE 1

1. If A is consistent, is A also a tautology? (Remember, "tautology" means "valid expression.")
2. If A is a tautology, is A also consistent?
3. If A is a tautology, what kind of wff is $\neg A$?
4. If A is not a tautology, can you say what kind of wff $\neg A$ is?
5. If A is consistent, what can you say about $\neg A$?
6. If A is a tautology, explain why $B \Rightarrow A$ is also a tautology.
7. If A is a contradiction, explain why $A \Rightarrow B$ is a tautology.

More definitions: Let A and B be any wffs. Then

A **implies** B if in the joint truth table for A and B, whenever A is true, B is true.

A is **equivalent** to B iff in the joint truth table for A and B, whenever A is true, B is true and whenever A is false, B is false (in other words, A and B have the same truth values in the same circumstances).

Implication is a crucial logical concept. A implies B when there is some logical connection between A and B. If you know A and know that A implies B, then you know B. We use implication to deduce far-flung conclusions of a premise or premises.

Equivalence is just two-way implication. We can give an informal argument that it is by using the definitions. Suppose that A is equivalent to B. Then in the joint table for A and B, whenever A is true, B is true. But this is just to say that A implies B. Moreover, if A is equivalent to B, whenever A is false, B is false. But then whenever B is true,

A must be true (for if A were false, B would be too). But this is just to say that B implies A.

Now show that when A implies B and B implies A, then A is equivalent to B, and go on to show 2 and 3 in Challenge 2.

CHALLENGE 2

1. Show if A implies B and B implies A, then A is equivalent to B.
2. Show that A implies B iff the wff A ⟹ B is a tautology.
3. Show that A is equivalent to B iff the wff A ⟺ B is a tautology.

Last definitions: Let A, B, C, and D be any wffs. Then

A, B, and C **imply** D iff in the joint truth table for A, B, C, and D, whenever A, B, and C are all true, D is also true.

A set of wffs is **mutually consistent** iff in the joint truth table for the wffs, there is at least one line that makes them all come out true.

CHALLENGE 3

1. Show that the three wffs A, B, and C imply D iff the single wff (A & (B & C)) implies D.
2. Show that if A, B, and C imply a contradiction, they are not mutually consistent.

Tautologies are the basic laws of (statement) logic. They reveal the essential connections between the basic operations of negation, conjunction, and so on. When a statement has the form of a tautology, the statement is true; indeed, it can't be false.

Tautologies are also important because they include implications and equivalences. Implications capture the valid principles of reasoning with negation, conjunction, and so on. A & B implies A. A and A ⟹ B together imply B. Equivalences are important not only because they are two-way implications, but also because whenever A and B are equivalent, then one can be replaced by the other in any truth-functional context. For example, ¬¬A and A are equivalent and one can replace the other. In general, if A and B are equivalent, then they have the same truth tables, so both are true under exactly the same circumstances, and so both contribute the same thing to any wff in which they occur as parts.

Finally, consistency is important because when we make statements about the world, we intend to speak the truth. If we contradict ourselves, then regardless of what is really true, we must have told a falsehood. Inconsistent descriptions or theories cannot be true of anything.

SUMMARY: We have defined, for wffs of Sentential, the concepts of validity, consistency, and inconsistency. We have defined two relations among wffs, implication and equivalence. All the definitions are given in terms of truth tables.

SOME BASIC TAUTOLOGIES AND IMPLICATIONS

> "Is it very long?" Alice asked, for she had heard a good deal of poetry that day.
>
> "It's long," said the Knight, "but it's very, very beautiful. Everybody that hears me sing it—either it brings the tears into their eyes, or else—
>
> "Or else what?" said Alice, for the Knight had made a sudden pause.
>
> "Or else it doesn't, you know."
>
> —LEWIS CARROLL, *Through the Looking Glass*

Suppose that A, B, and C are any wffs of Sentential, whether simple or complex. Then each of the following formulas is valid, or a tautology. Any English statement that has one of these forms must be true. Read each one and ask if it seems intuitively valid. If it doesn't, check it by means of truth tables. Better yet, check it by means of the truth tables anyway.

$A \Rightarrow A$
Of course, if A is true, then A is true.

$A \Rightarrow (B \Rightarrow A)$
If A is true, then regardless of anything else, if B then A is true.

$(A \Rightarrow B) \Rightarrow ((B \Rightarrow C) \Rightarrow (A \Rightarrow C))$
This is a substantial law; it allows us to "chain" conditionals. It can be iterated $(A \Rightarrow B) \Rightarrow [(B \Rightarrow C) \Rightarrow ((C \Rightarrow D) \Rightarrow (A \Rightarrow D))]$. *Note:* A chain of conditionals is of the form $A \Rightarrow (B \Rightarrow C)$, *not* $(A \Rightarrow B) \Rightarrow C$.

$(A \Rightarrow (B \Rightarrow C)) \Leftrightarrow (B \Rightarrow (A \Rightarrow C))$
The order of the antecedents doesn't matter.

$(A \Rightarrow (B \Rightarrow C)) \Leftrightarrow ((A \,\&\, B) \Rightarrow C)$
The antecedents of a chain of conditionals can be collected into a conjunction that is an antecedent of one conditional.

$(A \Rightarrow \neg B) \Leftrightarrow (B \Rightarrow \neg A)$
Note the negation symbols. $(A \Rightarrow B) \Leftrightarrow (B \Rightarrow A)$ is *not valid*.

$(A \Rightarrow B) \Leftrightarrow (\neg B \Rightarrow \neg A)$
Replace B by $\neg B$ in the preceding formula and cancel $\neg\neg B$.

$\neg\neg A \Leftrightarrow A$
"Double negations cancel out," your grade school teacher may have once said.

$A \Rightarrow (\neg A \Rightarrow B)$
Since A and $\neg A$ can't be true at the same time, the whole conditional can never be false. It's the basis of the claim that contradictions imply anything.

$(A \Rightarrow \neg A) \Rightarrow \neg A$ $(A \Rightarrow (C \,\&\, \neg C)) \Rightarrow \neg A$
Neither wff is contradictory. In the first, the truth of the antecedent implies the falsity of A. The generalization forms the basis of arguments by *reductio ad absurdum*.

$(A \Rightarrow B) \Leftrightarrow (\neg A \lor B)$ $(A \Rightarrow B) \Leftrightarrow \neg (A \,\&\, \neg B)$
These laws just indicate the relations among the truth functions.

$\neg(A \,\&\, \neg A)$ $(A \,\&\, A) \Leftrightarrow A$ $(A \,\&\, B) \Rightarrow B$
$(A \,\&\, B) \Rightarrow A$ $A \Rightarrow (B \Rightarrow (A \,\&\, B))$
All of these are obvious. The first law is called the law of non-contradiction, one of the three basic laws of Aristotelean logic.

$(A \,\&\, B) \Leftrightarrow (B \,\&\, A)$ $(A \,\&\, (B \,\&\, C)) \Leftrightarrow ((A \,\&\, B) \,\&\, C)$
These laws mean that we can rewrite any conjunction in any order or grouping (so we can ignore the placement of parentheses in, say, A & B & C—all placements are equivalent).

$$A \vee \neg A \qquad\qquad (A \vee A) \Leftrightarrow A$$
$$A \Rightarrow (A \vee B) \qquad\quad B \Rightarrow (A \vee B)$$

All of these are obvious. The first law is called the law of the
excluded middle, one of the three basic laws of Aristotelean
logic.

$$(A \vee B) \Leftrightarrow (B \vee A) \qquad (A \vee (B \vee C)) \Leftrightarrow ((A \vee B) \vee C)$$

These laws mean that we can rewrite any alternation in any order
or grouping (so we can ignore the placement of parentheses in,
say, $A \vee B \vee C$—all placements are equivalent).

$$((A \vee B) \mathbin{\&} (A \Rightarrow C) \mathbin{\&} (B \Rightarrow C)) \Rightarrow C$$

This law is central to $\vee$ and underlies the argument by cases: We
have A or B. Case 1 is A, so C. Case 2 is B, so C. In either case,
we have C.

$$\neg(A \mathbin{\&} B) \Leftrightarrow (\neg A \vee \neg B) \qquad\quad \neg(A \vee B) \Leftrightarrow (\neg A \mathbin{\&} \neg B)$$

These laws are called De Morgan's laws. They show that $\&$ and $\vee$
are interdefinable in the presence of $\neg$.

$$(A \mathbin{\&} (B \vee C)) \Leftrightarrow ((A \mathbin{\&} B) \vee (A \mathbin{\&} C))$$
$$(A \vee (B \mathbin{\&} C)) \Leftrightarrow ((A \vee B) \mathbin{\&} (A \vee C))$$

These are called distributive laws, with $\&$ distributed over $\vee$ in
the first case and conversely in the second.

$$(A \Leftrightarrow B) \Leftrightarrow (B \Leftrightarrow A)$$
$$(A \Leftrightarrow (B \Leftrightarrow C)) \Leftrightarrow ((A \Leftrightarrow B) \Leftrightarrow C)$$
$$(A \Leftrightarrow B) \Leftrightarrow (\neg A \Leftrightarrow \neg B)$$

These are not obvious. They show that we can rewrite any biconditional in any order or grouping.

Some basic implications of statement logic are as follows.
We'll write A, and B imply C as

$$A, B$$
$$\therefore C$$

You'll notice that many of our comments on the preceding tautologies
apply directly to the analogous implications. This is no accident, as
you know. A implies B iff $(A \Rightarrow B)$ is a tautology.

$$\frac{A \ \& \ B}{\therefore A} \qquad \frac{A \ \& \ B}{\therefore B} \qquad \frac{A, \ B}{\therefore A \ \& \ B} \qquad \frac{A \ \& \ B}{\therefore B \ \& \ A}$$

$$\frac{\neg\neg A}{\therefore A} \qquad \frac{A \Rightarrow (B \ \& \ \neg B)}{\therefore \ \neg A} \qquad \frac{A \ \& \ \neg A}{\therefore C}$$

$$\frac{A, \ A \Rightarrow B}{\therefore B} \qquad \frac{\neg B, \ A \Rightarrow B}{\therefore \ \neg A}$$

$$\frac{A \vee B, \ A \Rightarrow C, \ B \Rightarrow C}{\therefore C} \qquad \frac{A}{\therefore \ A \vee B} \qquad \frac{B}{\therefore \ A \vee B} \qquad \frac{A \vee B, \ \neg A}{\therefore B}$$

$$\frac{A, \ A \Leftrightarrow B}{\therefore B} \qquad \frac{B, \ A \Leftrightarrow B}{\therefore A} \qquad \frac{(A \Rightarrow B), \ (B \Rightarrow A)}{\therefore \ (A \Leftrightarrow B)} \qquad \frac{(A \Leftrightarrow B), \ (B \Leftrightarrow C)}{\therefore \ (A \Leftrightarrow C)}$$

The Very Important Replacement Principle

The replacement principle is an enormously useful time-saving device. It allows you to utilize the logical truths you already know in order to discover new truths. Conversely, it allows you to verify that something is a logical truth without going through the trouble of constructing a truth table. Here's a simple case. Consider the law relating the antecedents of a conditional to the conjunction of the antecedents:

$$(A \Rightarrow (B \Rightarrow C)) \Leftrightarrow ((A \ \& \ B) \Rightarrow C)$$

We stated it for three wffs, A, B, and C, but we might wonder if it holds for four wffs, X, Y, Z, and W:

$$(X \Rightarrow (Y \Rightarrow (Z \Rightarrow W))) \Leftrightarrow ((X \ \& \ Y \ \& \ Z) \Rightarrow W)?$$

Of course, you could check this with a 16-line truth table, but look at this snappy proof.

The original tautology (with Y for A, Z for B, and W for C) tells us that

$$(Y \Rightarrow (Z \Rightarrow W)) \Leftrightarrow ((Y \ \& \ Z) \Rightarrow W)$$

so the two wffs on each side of $\Leftrightarrow$ are equivalent. So we can replace one by the other in $(X \Rightarrow (Y \Rightarrow (Z \Rightarrow W)))$, yielding the tautology

$$(X \Rightarrow (Y \Rightarrow (Z \Rightarrow W))) \Leftrightarrow (X \Rightarrow ((Y \& Z) \Rightarrow W))$$

But then the original tautology (with X for A, $(Y \& Z)$ for B, and W for C) tells us that

$$(X \Rightarrow ((Y \& Z) \Rightarrow W)) \Leftrightarrow ((X \& Y \& Z) \Rightarrow W)$$

is valid. Hence

$$(X \Rightarrow (Y \Rightarrow (Z \Rightarrow W))) \Leftrightarrow ((X \& Y \& Z) \Rightarrow W)$$

is valid.

> **The Replacement Principle** Suppose C and D are any wffs that are equivalent (i.e., $C \Leftrightarrow D$ is valid). Suppose W_C is a wff that contains C. Let W_D be the wff you get from W_C by replacing one or more occurrences of C in W_C by D. Then W_C is equivalent to W_D (i.e., $W_C \Leftrightarrow W_D$ is a tautology).

EXAMPLE 1
    C is $(Y \Rightarrow (Z \Rightarrow W))$
    W_C is $(X \Rightarrow (Y \Rightarrow (Z \Rightarrow W)))$
    D is $((Y \& Z) \Rightarrow W)$
    W_D is $(X \Rightarrow ((Y \& Z) \Rightarrow W))$

EXAMPLE 2
    C is $\neg\neg A$
    W_C is $\neg(\neg B \& \neg\neg A) \Leftrightarrow (A \Rightarrow B)$
    D is A
    W_D is $\neg(\neg B \& A) \Leftrightarrow (A \Rightarrow B)$

EXAMPLE 3
    C is $(\neg B \& A)$
    W_C is $\neg(\neg B \& A) \Leftrightarrow (A \Rightarrow B)$
    D is $(A \& \neg B)$
    W_D is $\neg(A \& \neg B) \Leftrightarrow (A \Rightarrow B)$

A simple proof of the replacement principle: Construct a truth table for W_C. On the top of that table, replace all occurrences of C by D to get W_D. *But since C and D are equivalent, they have the same truth table! Therefore, what you have is just the truth table for W_D.* Since their truth tables are obviously the same, W_C and W_D are equivalent.

EXERCISES

1. In examples 1 and 3, construct truth tables to verify that W_C is equivalent to W_D.

2. Use the replacement principle to show the following:
   a. $A \mathbin{\&} \neg\neg B$ is equivalent to $A \mathbin{\&} B$.
   b. $\neg(\neg A \mathbin{\&} \neg B)$ is equivalent to $A \vee B$. (*Hint:* Check the tautologies to see what $\neg(X \mathbin{\&} Y)$ is equivalent to.)
   c. $(X \mathbin{\&} (Y \mathbin{\&} (Z \mathbin{\&} W)))$ is equivalent to $(((X \mathbin{\&} Y) \mathbin{\&} Z) \mathbin{\&} W)$.

SUMMARY: Tautologies and implications reveal the true meaning of the truth table interpretation of the connectives. To someone who knows the basic tautologies and implications, statement logic is obvious; to someone who doesn't, statement logic is a mystery. Given the truth-functional interpretation of Sentential, the replacement principle is a straightforward consequence. This principle is enormously useful in logic.

with & about logic

buffalo buffalo buffalo

"When I make a word do a lot of extra work like that," said Humpty Dumpty, "I always pay it extra."

—LEWIS CARROLL, *THROUGH THE LOOKING GLASS*

"Buffalo" is an interesting English word. On the one hand, it is a noun denoting any individual animal of a certain species, as in "Look at that buffalo trample Bill." Moreover, it doubles as a plural noun, denoting any group of animals of that species, as in "Look at those buffalo trample Bill." On the other hand, the word "buffalo" is also a transitive verb meaning roughly "to intimidate or confuse," as in "Buffalo Bill buffaloes buffalo." More exactly, "buffalo" itself is a plural verb; thus "Many people buffalo buffalo" is a well-formed English sentence.

Since "buffalo" is both a plural noun and a plural transitive verb, the following sentence, though strange, is quite grammatical and meaningful: "Buffalo buffalo buffalo."

Because of other peculiarities of English, any transitive verb can be used with its object deleted, as in "Tom eats [something]" or "Jim buffaloes [someone]." Hence "Buffalo buffalo" is perfectly grammatical. Additionally, in the imperative mood, the understood subject "you" can be deleted, as in "[you] Eat!" or "[you] Buffalo!"

In summary, "Buffalo!" "Buffalo buffalo," and "Buffalo buffalo buffalo" are all grammatical and meaningful English sentences. Is this the limit of buffalo sentences? No, thanks to another special property of English. In relative clauses introduced by the word "that," the word "that" can sometimes be deleted. For example, "Dogs that kids like bark." can be shortened to "Dogs kids like bark." However, this happens only when the word "that" is not the subject of the relative clause. In the sentence "Dogs that kids like bark," the relative clause is of the form "kids like that [dogs]", so "that" is the object of the clause. When "that" is the subject of the relative clause, it cannot be deleted. Thus "Kids like dogs that bark" cannot be shortened to "Kids like dogs bark."

With this in mind, we can interpret "Buffalo buffalo buffalo buffalo." It cannot mean "Buffalo buffalo buffalo [that] buffalo," because here "that" would be the subject of the relative clause. But it can

EXERCISE What does the sentence "Buffalo buffalo buffalo" mean? Parapharase using "bison" as a synonym for the noun "buffalo" and "intimidate" as a synonym for the verb.

99

mean "Buffalo [that] buffalo buffalo buffalo," because here "that" is the object. Hence "Buffalo buffalo buffalo buffalo" is a legitimate English sentence, meaning "Bison [that] bison intimidate [also] intimidate [something].

CHALLENGES

1. Can you show that the following are legitimate English sentences? Paraphrase, using "bison" for the noun "buffalo" and "intimidate" for the verb. Show any "that" deletions.
    a. Buffalo buffalo buffalo buffalo buffalo.
    b. Buffalo buffalo buffalo buffalo buffalo buffalo.
    c. Buffalo buffalo buffalo buffalo buffalo buffalo buffalo.
2. Can you show that (or explain why) *any* sequence consisting of only the word "buffalo," no matter how long the sequence, is a legitimate English sentence?
3. A word S is called a star (∗) word if any sequence SSS . . . S is a legitimate sentence. (It's called a star word because the symbol $S∗$ denotes the set of sequences SSS . . . S.) "Buffalo" is a star word. Are there any other star words in English? A few minutes with a dictionary might help you to answer this.

artificial and natural languages

Colorless green ideas sleep furiously.
—Noam Chomsky

Sentential is called an artificial language because it is an artifact—we explicitly constructed it. We contrast **artificial languages** with **natural languages** like English, Mandarin, Urdu, or Hopi, which are actually spoken by human beings. The two principal kinds of artificial language are the formal languages of logic, such as Sentential, and programming languages for computers.

A key feature of artificial languages is their simplicity and regularity. In comparison, natural languages appear very vague and irregular. The rules of Sentential determine well-formed formulas precisely. Recall the rules:

1. Any sentence letter is a wff.

2. If A and B are wffs, then so are

$$\neg A \quad (A \mathbin{\&} B) \quad (A \vee B) \quad (A \Rightarrow B) \quad (A \Leftrightarrow B)$$

By contrast, it might seem that any collection of words makes up a grammatical English sentence.

Modern linguistics, however, is based on the assumption that this appearance is deceptive. As the founder of modern linguistics, Noam Chomsky, observed, each of the following sequences of words is nonsense, but one has the definite form of a grammatical English sentence.

Colorless green ideas sleep furiously.
Furiously sleep ideas green colorless.

Analogously, we can guess at the intention behind a word string like

Read book you a on modern music?

but we have no doubt that it is not a grammatical English sentence. On the other hand, a sentence like

The horse raced past the barn fell.

might first strike us as ungrammatical nonsense until we recognize its underlying structure (A certain horse fell. Which one? Note the deletion of "that" again.)

Examples like these convinced Chomsky that English, as well as all natural languages, possess the same kind of rigorous structure as artificial languages like Sentential. The major difference between artificial and natural languages, Chomsky suggested, is that the structure of natural languages is much more complex and less easily discerned. Let's spend just a little while considering Chomsky's claim. If it is correct, then artificial languages are more interesting than one might think. They're a good first approximation to English.

A basic tool of modern linguistics is a "rewrite rule." An arbitrary rewrite rule has the form $X \rightarrow Y$ and means that the expression X is to be rewritten as (or replaced by) the expression Y. Let's first give the grammar of Sentential in terms of the following rewrite rules (where the symbol W represents a wff).

$$W \rightarrow \neg W \qquad W \rightarrow (W \Rightarrow W)$$
$$W \rightarrow (W \, \& \, W) \qquad W \rightarrow (W \Leftrightarrow W)$$
$$W \rightarrow (W \vee W) \qquad W \rightarrow \{p, q, r, \text{etc.}\}$$

We can define a wff as any expression formed by starting from a single W and applying any of the above rules until no instance of

W remains. For example, here is the rewrite derivation of
$\neg(p \; \& \; (q \lor r))$:

$$W$$
$(W \; \& \; W)$	Rule 2
$(\neg W \; \& \; W)$	Rule 1
$(\neg W \; \& \; (W \lor W))$	Rule 3
$(\neg p \; \& \; (W \lor W))$	Rule 6
$(\neg p \; \& \; (q \lor W))$	Rule 6
$(\neg p \; \& \; (q \lor r))$	Rule 6

A language whose sentences can be given by a set of rewrite rules is said to have a *phrase-structure grammar*. Does English have a phrase-structure grammar? We will let the following abbreviations stand for the grammatical categories specified:

S	Sentence	N	Noun
Det	Determiner	VP	Verb Phrase
NP	Noun Phrase	V	Verb

Using these letters, we give a sample of rewrite rules for English:

1. S → NP + VP

2. NP → Det + N

3. VP → V + NP

4. Det → {a, the}

5. N → {man, boy, woman, girl, ball, etc.}

6. V → {hit, took, bit, kissed, fed, kicked, etc.}

A grammatical sentence is one obtained by starting with the symbol S and applying the rewrite rules until no more can be applied.

For example, using the rewrite rules for English, we can derive "the man kissed a dog" as follows:

S
NP + VP	Rule 1
Det + N + VP	Rule 2
the + N + VP	Rule 4
the + N + V + NP	Rule 3
the + man + V + NP	Rule 5

the + man + V + Det + N   Rule 2
the + man + kissed + Det + N   Rule 6
the + man + kissed + a + N   Rule 4
the + man + kissed + a + dog   Rule 5

EXERCISES

1. Construct derivations of the following sentences from the rewrite rules for English.
   a. A girl fed the woman.
   b. The man hit the ball.
   c. A dog bit the man.
   d. A girl took a ball.
   e. The ball kicked the dog.

2. Explain why the following sentences can't be derived by the rewrite rules for English.
   a. Hit the ball!
   b. Robbers took a dog.

The rewrite rules for English leave most English sentences unaccounted for (that is, underived). But linguists have come up with a great many other rules. For example, we can have

$$NP \Rightarrow \{NP_{sing}, NP_{pl}\}$$

in order to allow the alternative substitution of singular or plural nouns. Optional elements can be indicated by parentheses, for example,

$$VP \Rightarrow V + (NP)$$

which means that one can rewrite VP either as V or as V + NP. The interested reader can find out more from any introductory linguistics text.

Although Chomsky did not deny that English might be a phrase-structure grammar, he thought it advisable to introduce a new kind of rule altogether called a *transformation* (giving rise to transformational grammars). A crude example of a transformation is the passive transformation, which transforms "the boy hit the ball" into "the ball was hit by the boy." Chomsky argued that transformational grammars were especially simple, since the rewrite rules generate a stock of basic sentences that can be transformed into many variations. Lately, the whole idea of transformations has been seriously questioned.

Finally, it's interesting to note that Chomsky always argued that the sophisticated structure of natural languages reveals profound properties of the human mind or brain. In particular, he suggested that the human mind has a complex innate structure with a special ability to learn (human) languages. Common to us all is a "universal grammar" that enables each human to figure out the grammar of the particular language she is exposed to, whether it be English, Mandarin, Hopi, or Urdu. Not surprisingly, Chomsky's views have generated considerable controversy.

rewrite rules and finite automata

They have been at a great feast of languages, and stolen the scraps.
—William Shakespeare, *Love's Labour's Lost*

We've described how Sentential and some of its variants can be generated by "rewrite" rules. They can also be generated by a list of "productions" (rules) of the sort:

⟨nonterminal symbols⟩ →
⟨terminal symbols and nonterminal symbols⟩

(Nonterminal symbols are usually written as capital letters and terminal symbols as lowercase letters.) To build sentences in the language, one starts with a capital S (the start symbol) and then chooses rules and applies them, replacing any instance of the left-hand side of a rule with the right-hand side. One continues until all the letters are lowercase.

In "Buffalo Buffalo Buffalo," we discovered that any number of *buffalo*'s put together made a perfectly legitimate, albeit ridiculous, English sentence. If we call this sublanguage of English "Buffalo," then a set of rewrite rules for Buffalo is

$$S \rightarrow SS \mid buffalo$$

The | means "or." This is shorthand for two rules:

$$S \rightarrow SS$$
$$S \rightarrow buffalo$$

In trying to understand Buffalo, we worked with another sublanguage, something we could call "Bison." The basic forms of Bison are the sentences

Bison intimidate bison. [We'll abbreviate this as BIB]
Bison intimidate. [BI]
Intimidate! [I]
Intimidate bison! [IB]

More complicated sentences can be built by substituting for any noun "bison" the noun phrase "bison bison intimidate." Here is a set of rewrite rules for Bison:

$$S \rightarrow BIB \mid BI \mid I \mid IB$$
$$B \rightarrow BBI \mid bison$$
$$I \rightarrow intimidate$$

There is another way to describe some languages that has great visual appeal: finite automata. A **finite state automaton** (FSA) can be represented by a special sort of diagram mathematicians call a *finite labeled digraph*. It consists of nodes or states (circles) and edges (arrows) with labels.

EXAMPLE

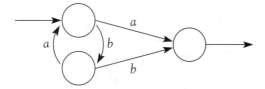

The language associated with a finite automaton consists of all "words" you can form by beginning at a starting node (a circle with a blank arrow leading in), then moving around the diagram in the direction of the arrows, picking up the characters that label the edges (internal arrows), then finally exiting from an exit node (a circle with a blank arrow leading away). For example, in the automaton above, there is only one starting node (extreme left) and one exit node (extreme right), but there are several possible words and corresponding paths.

EXAMPLES

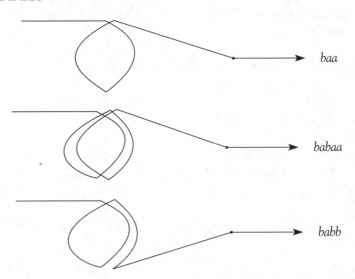

baa

$babaa$

$babb$

Any language that can be represented by an FSA is called *regular*. Unfortunately, the only language we have taken up that is regular is Buffalo!

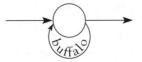

On the other hand, every regular language can be generated by a set of rewrite rules. This is easy to show: Simply take the finite automaton:

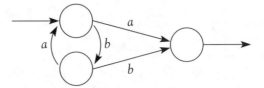

Put capital letters at the nodes:

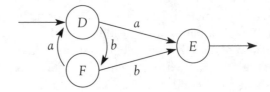

Then put an S at the start:

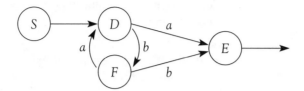

Now we can just read off the rules:

$$S \rightarrow D$$
$$D \rightarrow aE$$
$$D \rightarrow bF$$
$$F \rightarrow aD$$
$$F \rightarrow bE$$
$$E \rightarrow$$

i.e., simply remove E.

Why study FSA's? Researchers in linguistics attempt to understand the rules of natural languages. Artificial languages have many of the same characteristics. Any insight we gain into artificial languages may tell us something about English and other natural languages.

Why look at regular languages? Regular languages are especially nice because we can construct algorithms to determine important facts about them. Given an FSA, we can program a computer to tell us what strings of symbols are legitimate sentences in the language. This is very useful if we are trying to build a machine that can communicate. Languages defined by using rewrite rules do not always have the property that we can program a computer to recognize legitimate sentences.

Here is a particularly shocking example: Suppose we want to know if there are *any* legitimate sentences—any at all! Can we program a computer to tell us, given any set of rewrite rules, if there are legitimate sentences? The astonishing answer is no, we can't. For more things we can't do, see Algorithm in part 5.

EXERCISES

1. Construct an FSA for the language where the only words are x, yx, yyx, $yyyx$, ...

2. Find a set of rewrite rules for the language in exercise 1.

3. Construct an FSA for the language where the only words are abc, $abbc$, $abbbc$, $abbbbc$, ...

4. Find a set of rewrite rules for the language in exercise 3.

5. Can you construct an *infinite* state automaton that generates the language whose only words are: *xy*, *xxyy*, *xxxyyy*, *xxxxyyyy*, . . . ?

6. An automaton that allows several arrows with similar labels to leave the same node is called a *nondeterministic finite state automaton* (NFSA). It is an important result of formal language theory that if a language can be represented by an NFSA, then it can be represented by an FSA. Construct an FSA that represents the language described by the following NFSA.

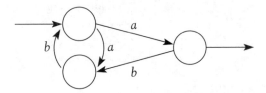

7. Suppose we use only the letters *a* and *b*. Can you construct an FSA so that the legitimate words are exactly
   a. those words with no *a*'s?

   [Answer: 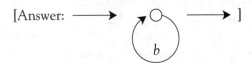]

   b. those words with exactly one *a*?

   [Answer: 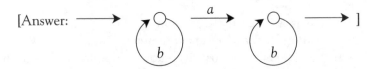]

8. Can you construct an FSA so that the legitimate words are exactly
   a. those words with no two *a*'s in a row?
   b. those words with no isolated *a*'s (e.g., *bab* is not allowed)?
   c. those words with an equal number of *a*'s and *b*'s?
   d. those words with at least one *a*?

WARNING: One of these is not possible!

loofah loofah loofah

People who like this sort of thing will find this the sort of thing they like.
—ABRAHAM LINCOLN

Are there any other words in the English language that have the same properties of "buffalo," that is (1) they can be plural nouns, (2) they are transitive verbs, and (3) they are not proper nouns? If so, such words can be used to form sentences of any length, as explained in "Buffalo Buffalo Buffalo." Our student, Gina Cooke, after extensive research, discovered 25 such words. We will let you determine the necessary meanings.

bear	duck	loofah	seal	squirrel
buck	fox	perch	shark	stag
char	hog	pig	shrimp	steer
clam	horse	pike	smelt	stint
crane	iron	rail	snipe	whale

informal logic

conclusions

Argument—Discourse, or an example of it, designed to convince or to persuade.
—WEBSTER'S INTERNATIONAL DICTIONARY, 2ND ED.

Arguments are an integral part of language, of logic, and of this book. Politicians want us to vote for them. Manufacturers want us to buy their products, newspaper columnists want us to agree with them, and friends want us to go to the movies. Their advertisements, editorials, and invitations contain one argument after another.

In "Valid Argument Forms" in part 4 we introduce a very precise definition of "argument" for Sentential and later for predicate language, but for the moment, let us think of an *informal* argument as any piece of language that purports to demonstrate the truth of some statement.

The first step in understanding an argument is to determine its *conclusion*, the point of the argument.

EXAMPLE

Sweet Reason is the only logic book that truly explores the ubiquity of modern logic. The authors are leading figures in their fields. The book is nicely printed with a stylish, glossy cover. It is clear, therefore, that *Sweet Reason* is the best logic book on the market.

The word "therefore" usually signals a conclusion. The point of this paragraph is simply the last sentence.

EXAMPLE

The man who signs a petition against higher taxes reveals a "meanness he would otherwise blush at."

Taxes are needed to protect the aged and the infant and to give liberty a land to live in.

The people of America are not a poor people, why should they appear so? We hurt our credit, our honor, our reputation in the world, by proclaiming ourselves what we are not.

—Thomas Paine, quoted in a letter to the *Boston Globe*, August 13, 1990

Paine is supporting the principle of higher taxes. The conclusion is that we should not oppose higher taxes.

EXAMPLE

"The new anesthetizer is giving way!" shouted an intern. "There is no one in the East who knows how to fix it!"

"Quiet man!" said Mitty, in a low, cool voice. He sprang to the machine, which was now going pocketa-pocketa-queep-pocketa-queep. He began fingering delicately a row of glistening dials. "Give me a fountain pen!" he snapped.

—James Thurber, *The Secret Life of Walter Mitty*

Well, not everything is or contains an argument. Our language, of course, is full of descriptions, questions, explanations, prayers, and so on, which are often free of any argumentation.

EXAMPLE

Let's go to the movies! You aren't going to get any work done tonight, and this is the last showing of *Archie and Jughead: The Movie*. The whole third floor is going.

What is the statement that the speaker wants the listener to believe? It isn't stated explicitly, but we are being asked to accept that we should go to the movies.

EXAMPLE

When is George Bush going to wake up? It's about time the phrase "national security" was understood in terms every American can viscerally understand.

Ask yourself what would make you, as an American, feel more secure—one more Stealth bomber, or the money to build that bomber used instead to take 5,000 violent addicts off the streets and give them the treatment that so many are desperately waiting for?

Our national psyche is permeated with a fear of drug-, race- or economically induced street crime. We as a nation could speak to the world community with a more assured, credible voice for peaceful change, if our national resolve weren't being sapped by the debilitating diseases from within our own communities.

It is time for a dramatic shift in national priorities. If George Bush truly believes Americans are the most productive workers in the world, he would not be frightened to make meaningful cuts in defense spending. Surely a motivated work force could whip us back into fighting shape in short order.

It's so exhilarating, but also saddening, to see the rest of the world taking on reality by the horns, while Bush has to be dragged, kicking and screaming into the 1990s.
—Letter to the *Boston Globe*, February 19, 1990

Conclusions, we emphasize, *need not be stated*, and understanding a passage such as this one can be difficult if we have to guess the author's intention. In this case, the point seems to be that we should spend less on defense and more on other needs. The writer mentions one other need, drug treatment, but the phrase "drug-, race- or economically induced street crime" suggests that it is not the only one.

EXERCISE Most of the following passages contain arguments. Which passages are they, and what are the conclusions?

1. Daniel Pipes (Op-Ed. Feb. 13) writes: "Turks are almost entirely Muslim; with a total population of some 108 million, they constitute the second largest ethnic group in Islam, following only the Arabs."

    Mr. Pipes overlooks the claim of the Muslims of South Asia to a position of primacy. Pakistan, almost entirely Muslim, has a population of 110 million; India, though predominantly Hindu, has 92 million Muslims in a population of 830 million, and Bangladesh has 85 million Muslims in its population of 110 million.

    Although inhabiting three countries, the Muslims of South Asia, who belong to the same stock and together number 287 million, constitute the world's largest ethnic group adhering to Islam.

    —Letter to *The New York Times*, March 6, 1990

2. Phoebe stared glumly at the sign over the gas pump, which read "1.49."

    "What happened?" she asked. "Last week you were satisfied with only $1.29 a gallon. Do you have large gambling debts?"

    "Oil crisis, lady," the attendant replied. "The price of crude went up ten dollars a barrel. When the gas in my storage tanks is gone, it's going to cost me more to replace it. If I didn't raise the price, I would lose money selling it to you. I can't stay in business long doing things like that."

3. [Background: The week before there was an air show at a nearby air base.] There is no rational reason why C-41s in a time of peace must be paraded around civilian homes in the Pioneer Valley for purely recreational reasons as was witnessed last weekend.

    These huge military cargo planes pose a great threat to human lives in heavily populated areas. If one crashed, it would cause a major disaster. Do we really need to waste tax dollars in a time of economic upheaval on such ridiculous shows of military might? I think not.

    —Letter to the *Daily Hampshire Gazette*,
      August 8, 1990

4. I was born in the year 1632, in the City of York, of a good family, though not of that country, my father being a foreigner of Bremen, who settled first at Hull. He got a good estate by merchandise, and leaving off his trade, lived afterward at York, from whence he had married my mother, whose relations were named Robinson, a very good family in that country, and from whom I was called Robinson Kreutznaer; but by the usual corruption of words in England we are now called, nay, we call ourselves, and write our name Crusoe, and so my companions always called me.

    —Daniel Defoe, *Robinson Crusoe*

5. Westinghouse Electric is building two 300-megawatt power plants for $300 million each. They use natural gas, were started in 1989 and will be ready in 1991. Texaco is promoting its Syngas fuel made from the gasification of coal. It is not only cost effective but also exceeds the Bush Administration's environmental requirements for the year 2000.

    "New Ideas Changing Nuclear Debate" (Week in Review, July 22) discusses ways in which nuclear power could be used. In view of the success of the examples, nuclear power should not be given any consideration at all.

    —Letter to *The New York Times*, August 5, 1990

6. In 1988 Associate Justice David H. Souter of the New Hampshire Supreme Court wrote an opinion supporting the overturning of a rape conviction on the ground that the rapist should have been allowed to present as evidence the victim's "open, sexually suggestive conduct in the presence of patrons of a public bar" just prior to his raping her.

    I have flirted with men in bars. Men have flirted with me in bars. I know a lot of men and women who flirt with each other in bars. Is flirting sexually suggestive? Of course. But all I know is, if I flirt with a man in a bar, I don't deserve to get raped.

    If a woman's conduct toward a man is sexually suggestive, but at the same time she tells him she does not want to have intercourse, the vast majority of men in that situation will not rape her. A man who would—and

113

in the process perhaps mutilate or strangle her—should go to jail.

—Letter to *The New York Times*, August 7, 1990

7. Phoebe stared glumly at the sign over the gas pump, which read "1.49."

"Hey, c'mon!" she said. "The crisis is over! Oil prices fell ten dollars a barrel last week. Why haven't you lowered your price?"

"Sorry, lady," the attendant replied. "Prices have gone down all right, but the gas in my storage tanks was bought at the old, higher price. If I lowered the price, I would be selling it for less than I paid. I can't stay in business long doing things like that."

8. Americans would risk their lives for freedom. President Bush risks their lives for cheap gasoline.

Sure, Saddam Hussein is a tyrant. The United States supports many tyrants around the world, and tolerates many others when it suits our interests. So let's not kid ourselves with high-flown talk about stopping aggression. This "crisis" is about the price of oil.

Speaking to the nation, Bush gave lip service to energy conservation. (We know what his lips are worth.) Were the United States to undertake comprehensive conservation measures, we could soon do without Gulf oil.

If we would sooner sacrifice our sons than pay a few more cents—or dollars—at the gas pump, what kind of people have we become?

—Letter to the *Boston Globe*, August 13, 1990

9. O Lord our God,

help us to tear their soldiers to bloody shreds with our shells;

help us to cover their smiling fields with the pale forms of their patriot dead;

help us to drown the thunder of the guns with the shrieks of their wounded, writhing in pain;

help us to lay waste their humble homes with a hurricane of fire;

help us to wring the hearts of their unoffending widows with unavailing grief;

help us to turn them out roofless with their little
children to wander unfriended the wastes of their deso-
lated land in rags and hunger and thirst, sports of the sun
flames of summer and the icy winds of winter, broken in
spirit, worn with travail, imploring Thee for the refuge of
the grave and denied it—
for our sakes who adore Thee, Lord.
—Mark Twain, "The War Prayer"

supporting statements

"Shut up," he explained.
—RING LARDNER

An informal argument is (usually) an organized network of statements. If the argument has force, then the statements must support
the conclusion.

When does one statement support another?

In one sense, this is a difficult problem. Volumes have been written about it, detailing types of support, specifying degrees of support,
cataloging false claims of support. It is, in fact, easy to phrase statements that can fool careless listeners and readers.

In practice, however, the task is not so formidable. If two statements are connected, and we are quite clear about what those statements mean, then it is fairly easy to see the connection. The difficult
part, perhaps, is deciding how strong the connection is.

Our procedure will be to write down what additional statements
are needed to bridge the gap. This will be clearer with some examples:

1. One acre of land can produce 165 pounds of beef, but that same
   acre can grow 20,000 pounds of potatoes.

2. Raising cattle is a very inefficient way of producing proteins and
   other nutrients.

There appears to be a strong relationship between these two statements: 1 supports 2. What statements are needed to make it solid? We
need a statement such as

3. There is a great deal more protein and other nutrients in 20,000
   pounds of potatoes than in 165 pounds of beef.

Notice that we are not defining support. What we are doing is recognizing it. You would have a hard time defining the taste of coffee, but it is easy to recognize it.

4. The weatherperson said this evening that we can expect showers tomorrow.

5. It will rain tomorrow.

Pretty clearly statement 4 supports statement 5. There is certainly a connection. Now we ask ourselves, "What additional statement or statements do we need to make the connection perfect?"

One statement that would certainly suffice is that the weatherperson is always right. To ask this of a weatherperson, however, is unreasonable. No weatherperson is always right. Should we then reject the connection? But most weatherpeople are very often right. A statement such as

6. The weatherperson has been right about 80% of the time.

is both reasonable and makes the connection between statements 4 and 5 strong.

7. Senator Smurf is in favor of higher taxes, but her favorite TV program is *Sesame Street*.

8. We don't need to raise taxes.

There is some connection, isn't there? The person who said statement 8 doesn't want higher taxes, and the person who said statement 7 has information about a supporter of higher taxes. What statements would close the gap? A statement saying that anyone who watches *Sesame Street* always makes wrong decisions about fiscal policy would do it. But this seems ridiculous. (After all, a five-year-old who watches *Sesame Street* would probably respond to a question on fiscal policy with "I don't know," which is what most economists say eventually).

Ultimately, nothing will work very well. It is hard to imagine a series of statements that would lead us to conclude statement 8 from statement 7. Whether we need taxes or not depends on the present level of revenues, national priorities, and so on, but not on the TV viewing habits of Senator Smurf.

9. Senator Smurf is in favor of higher taxes, but Smurf is under indictment for tax fraud.

10. We don't need to raise taxes.

This is slightly trickier, but it has many of the same problems as statements 7 and 8. To strengthen the tie between statements 9 and 10, we might try "People who are indicted for tax fraud are often guilty" or "Legislators who are guilty of felonies often support measures for personal gain and not for the good of the country." Unfortunately, even these equivocal statements are not enough. We would also need a fact such as "Proposals that are supported for private gain are usually not for the good of the country."

All this is too much—and not enough. The connection between statements 9 and 10 is extremely weak. Imagine, after all, that Senator Smurf is under indictment but has said nothing about taxes. Now she holds a press conference and calls for higher taxes. Does this change whether or not taxes are actually needed?

In fact, are there *any* circumstances under which a statement about Senator Smurf is relevant to whether or not the country needs higher taxes?

11. Over half of the farmland in the United States is devoted to beef production.
12. Raising cattle is a very inefficient way of producing proteins and other nutrients.

Statements 11 and 12 are relevant to beef production, but nonetheless, 11 does not support 12. It says nothing about efficiency. The best way to see this is to try to construct statements to make a connection.

13. If you reduce the amount of meat you eat, you can reduce your risk of heart attack.
14. We should grow less beef.

On the face of it, there is a connection. We shall see how strong. What is needed to complete the connection? First, we need

15. Growing less beef will result in less beef consumption.

This is not necessarily true, because we import more and more beef from South America. Second, we need

16. Reducing the amount of beef will not cause other health problems.

Technically, we might want a third statement:

17. Heart attacks are bad.

The method we suggest here has the advantage that we get some sense of how strongly one statement supports another, and not just whether or not it does.

EXERCISE   In each of the following pairs, decide to what extent the first supports the second.

1. a. High school students in the United States are far behind students in Europe and Asia in mathematical skills.
   b. We must reform our schools if we want to compete.

2. a. High school students in the United States are far behind students in Europe and Asia in mathematical skills.
   b. The school year should be increased to ten or eleven months.

3. a. For a being to be God, that being must be all-powerful and all-loving.
   b. If there were a God, then God would prevent the suffering of innocent children.

4. a. Drug use is rampant in this country, and no attempt to restrict it has been successful.
   b. Legalizing drugs and selling them in state stores would generate significant revenues.

5. a. It is evil to commit murder.
   b. We should abolish the death penalty.

6. a. My father's boss smoked for thirty years and died of lung cancer.
   b. Smoking is hazardous to your health.

7. a. My father's boss ate for thirty years and died of stomach cancer.
   b. Eating is hazardous to your health.

8. a. My father's boss is at risk because he has been smoking for thirty years.
   b. Smoking is hazardous to your health.

9. a. Persons who smoke two packs of cigarettes a day have a significantly greater chance of contracting lung cancer than those who do not smoke.
   b. Smoking is hazardous to your health.

10. a. Persons who eat two pounds of butter a day have a significantly greater chance of contracting atherosclerosis than those who avoid butter.
    b. Eating is hazardous to your health.

11. a. Smoking is hazardous to your health.
    b. The government should tax tobacco products heavily to discourage smoking.

12. a. Eating is hazardous to your health.
    b. The government should tax food heavily to discourage eating.

relevance

If you can't convince 'em, confuse 'em.
—HARRY TRUMAN

In "Supporting Statements," we learned how to go about detecting when statements are connected. We now put that to use in analyzing arguments. What we want to do is prune an argument down, removing statements that have no bearing on the conclusion so that we may pay attention to what is left.

EXAMPLE
[a] Let's go to the movies! [b] You aren't going to get any work done tonight, and [c] this is the last showing of *Archie and Jughead: The Movie*. [d] The whole third floor is going.

We decided in "Conclusions" that the point of this argument was that we should go to the movies. Now, which of the statements are relevant? Statement [a] is essentially the conclusion. What about statement [b]? It is relevant if you have work to do, if you really aren't going to make progress on it, and if you do want to go to the movie. This seems a little weak, but depending on the circumstances, it may be relevant. Statement [c] is relevant if you want to see the movie. Statement [d] is relevant if you like going with the crowd.

EXAMPLE

[a] The man who signs a petition against higher taxes reveals a meanness he would otherwise blush at."

[b] Taxes are needed to protect the aged and the infant and to give liberty a land to live in.

[c] The people of America are not a poor people, why should they appear so? [d] We hurt our credit, our honor, our reputation in the world, by proclaiming ourselves what we are not.

—Thomas Paine, quoted in a letter to the *Boston Globe*, August 13, 1990

We decided earlier that Paine is saying we should not oppose higher taxes. Is statement [a] relevant? Statement [a] says that to oppose higher taxes is to be stingy and also that stinginess is bad (something to blush about). It is clearly relevant.

Statement [b] is also relevant. It lists reasons why taxes are needed. Nonetheless, the connection isn't perfect. Why do we need *higher* taxes? The same comments apply to statements [c] and [d].

EXAMPLE

[a] When is George Bush going to wake up? [b] It's about time the phrase "national security" was understood in terms every American can viscerally understand.

[c] Ask yourself what would make you, as an American, feel more secure—one more Stealth bomber, or the money to build that bomber used instead to take 5000 violent addicts off the streets and given them the treatment that so many are desperately waiting for?

[d] Our national psyche is permeated with a fear of drug-, race- or economically induced street crime. [e] We as a nation could speak to the world community with a more assured, credible voice for peaceful change, if our national resolve weren't being sapped by the debilitating diseases from within our own communities.

[f] It is time for a dramatic shift in national priorities. [g] If George Bush truly believes Americans are the most productive workers in the world, he would not be frightened to make meaningful cuts in defense spending. [h] Surely a motivated work force could whip us back into fighting shape in short order.

[i] It's so exhilarating, but also saddening, to see the rest of the world taking on reality by the horns, while Bush has to be dragged, kicking and screaming into the 1990s.
—Letter to the *Boston Globe*, February 19, 1990

The conclusion here is that we should spend less on defense and more on other things. Is statement [a] relevant? No, it is merely rhetoric. It catches our attention. Statement [b] is similar. What about [c]? If we think about what [c] is actually saying, we see that it is relevant. It is in the form of a command, but it is really a statement that spending for drug rehabilitation would make us more secure. We need only the connective statement that security is important.

Statement [e] says exactly that, that our internal security is vital.

Statement [d] supports [c] in that it emphasizes how insecure we are domestically. Statement [g] also supports [c] by deemphasizing the question of defense. It is further supported by [h], which supplies the important statement that Americans are productive.

Statement [f] is for emphasis. It contributes nothing to the argument. Statement [i] is also only rhetoric.

Important note: We are busy throwing out irrelevant statements, but it is important to recognize that they have their place. Arguments are not easy to read. The reader needs all the assistance the writer can provide, and many sentences that have no content or relevance serve us well by pointing us in the right direction, leading us through the argument and motivating us to read further.

Insidious note: And of course those irrelevant statements can be very useful in constructing convincing arguments that are not altogether logical! "When is George Bush going to wake up?" allows you to infer that he is asleep without actually having to take responsibility for saying it. Referring to Democrats as "tax-and-spend liberals" allows you to plant ideas in the minds of your readers without making an argument. It passes as part of the language of discourse (unless an opponent challenges you and calls attention to it).

EXERCISE Identify the relevant sentences in the following arguments.

1. [a] Daniel Pipes (Op-Ed. Feb. 13) writes: "Turks are almost entirely Muslim; with a total population of some 108 million, they constitute the second largest ethnic group in Islam, following only the Arabs."

[b] Mr. Pipes overlooks the claim of the Muslims of South Asia to a position of primacy. [c] Pakistan, almost entirely Muslim, has a population of 110 million; [d] India, though predominantly Hindu, has 92 million Muslims in a population of 830 million, and [e] Bangladesh has 85 million Muslims in its population of 110 million.

[f] Although inhabiting three countries, the Muslims of South Asia, who belong to the same stock and together number 287 million, constitute the world's largest ethnic group adhering to Islam.

—Letter to *The New York Times*, March 6, 1990.

2. [a] Phoebe stared glumly at the sign over the gas pump, which read "1.49."

[b] "What happened?" she asked. "Last week you were satisfied with only $1.29 a gallon. [c] Do you have large gambling debts?"

[d] "Oil crisis, lady," the attendant replied. [e] "The price of crude went up ten dollar a barrel. [f] When the gas in my storage tanks is gone, it's going to cost me more to replace it. [g] If I didn't raise the price, I would lose money selling it to you. [h] I can't stay in business long doing things like that."

3. [Background: the week before there was an air show at a nearby air base.] [a] There is no rational reason why C-41s in a time of peace must be paraded around civilian homes in the Pioneer Valley for purely recreational reasons as was witnessed last weekend.

[b] These huge military cargo planes pose a great threat to human lives in heavily populated areas. [c] If one crashed, it would cause a major disaster. [d] Do we really need to waste tax dollars in a time of economic upheaval on such ridiculous shows of military might? [e] I think not.

—Letter to the *Daily Hampshire Gazette*, August 8, 1990.

4. [a] Westinghouse Electric is building two 300-megawatt power plants for $300 million each. [b] They use natural gas, were started in 1989 and will be ready in 1991. [c] Texaco is promoting its Syngas fuel made from the gasification of coal. [d] It is not only cost effective but also

exceeds the Bush Administration's environmental requirements for the year 2000.

[e] "New Ideas Changing Nuclear Debate" (Week in Review, July 22) discusses ways in which nuclear power could be used. [f] In view of the success of these examples, nuclear power should not be given any consideration at all.

—Letter to *The New York Times*, August 5, 1990.

5. [a] In 1988 Associate Justice David H. Souter of the New Hampshire Supreme Court wrote an opinion supporting the overturning of a rape conviction on the ground that the rapist should have been allowed to present as evidence the victim's "open, sexually suggestive conduct in the presence of patrons of a public bar" just prior to his raping her.

[b] I have flirted with men in bars. [c] Men have flirted with me in bars. [d] I know a lot of men and women who flirt with each other in bars. [e] Is flirting sexually suggestive? [f] Of course. [g] But all I know is, if I flirt with a man in a bar, I don't deserve to get raped.

[h] If a woman's conduct toward a man is sexually suggestive, but at the same time she tells him she does not want to have intercourse, the vast majority of men in that situation will not rape her. [i] A man who would—and in the process perhaps mutilate or strangle her—should go to jail.

—Letter to *The New York Times*, August 7, 1990.

6. [a] Phoebe stared glumly at the sign over the gas pump, which read "1.49."

[b] "Hey, c'mon!" she said. "The crisis is over! Oil prices fell ten dollars a barrel last week, why haven't you lowered your price?"

[c] "Sorry, lady," the attendant replied. "Prices have gone down all right, but the gas in my storage tanks was bought at the old, higher price. [d] If I lower the price, I will be selling it for less than I paid. [e] I can't stay in business long doing things like that."

7. [a] Americans would risk their lives for freedom. [b] President Bush risks their lives for cheap gasoline.

[c] Sure, Saddam Hussein is a tyrant. [d] The United States supports many tyrants around the world, and tolerates many others when it suits our interests. [e] So let's not kid ourselves with high-flown talk about stopping aggression. [f] This "crisis" is about the price of oil.

[g] Speaking to the nation, Bush gave lip service to energy conservation. [h] (We know what his lips are worth.) [i] Were the United States to undertake comprehensive conservation measures, we could soon do without Gulf oil.

[j] If we would sooner sacrifice our sons than pay a few more cents—or dollars—at the gas pump, what kind of people have we become?

—Letter to the *Boston Globe*, August 13, 1990.

premises

So convenient a thing it is to be a *reasonable creature*, since it enables one to find or make a reason for everything one has a mind to do.

—Benjamin Franklin

In the "Relevance," we stripped arguments of statements that have no bearing. What we have left is the conclusion (if stated) and the statements supporting it. Some of these statements are supported by other statements, but some are given no support at all. We call these unsupported statements *premises*, or *assumptions*. The argument may depend on these statements. In evaluating the argument, we will be paying attention to the premises and how likely they are to be true.

EXAMPLE

[a] Let's go to the movies! [b] You aren't going to get any work done tonight, and [c] this is the last showing of *Archie and Jughead: The Movie*. [d] The whole third floor is going.

What are the premises? Actually, every statement except the first is a premise. The first is the conclusion. None of the rest is supported by any of the others.

EXAMPLE

[a] The man who signs a petition against higher taxes reveals a "meanness he would otherwise blush at."

[b] Taxes are needed to protect the aged and the infant and to give liberty a land to live in."

[c] The people of America are not a poor people, why should they appear so? [d] We hurt our credit, our honor, our reputation in the world, by proclaiming ourselves what we are not.

— Thomas Paine, quoted in a letter to the *Boston Globe*, August 13, 1990

All are premises. None is supported.

EXAMPLE

[a] Ask yourself what would make you, as an American, feel more secure—one more Stealth bomber, or the money to build that bomber used instead to take 5,000 violent addicts off the streets and give them the treatment that so many are desperately waiting for?

[b] Our national psyche is permeated with a fear of drug-, race- or economically induced street crime. [c] We as a nation could speak to the world community with a more assured, credible voice for peaceful change, if our national resolve weren't being sapped by the debilitating diseases from within our own communities.

[d] If George Bush truly believes Americans are the most productive workers in the world, he would not be frightened to make meaningful cuts in defense spending. [e] Surely a motivated work force could whip us back into fighting shape in short order.

— Letter to the *Boston Globe*, February 19, 1990

It helps here to understand that the unstated conclusion is that we should spend less on defense and more on domestic problems. Statement [e] supports [d], which supports the conclusion, so [d] is not a premise, but [e] is. Statement [c] supports the conclusion but is not supported itself; it is a premise.

What about [a]? It's not even a statement. It is really a colloquial way of saying that we would feel more secure if we reduced defense spending in favor of domestic spending. Thus it supports the conclusion and is supported by [b]. The last premise is [b].

EXERCISE   Identify the premises in the following arguments.

1. [a] Daniel Pipes (Op-Ed. Feb. 13) writes: "Turks are almost entirely Muslim; with a total population of some 108 million, they constitute the second largest ethnic group in Islam, following only the Arabs."

   [b] Mr. Pipes overlooks the claim of the Muslims of South Asia to a position of primacy. [c] Pakistan, almost entirely Muslim, has a population of 110 million; [d] India, though predominantly Hindu, has 92 million Muslims in a population of 830 million, and [e] Bangladesh has 85 million Muslims in its population of 110 million.

   [f] Although inhabiting three countries, the Muslims of South Asia, who belong to the same stock and together number 287 million, constitute the world's largest ethnic group adhering to Islam.
   —Letter to *The New York Times*, March 6, 1990

2. [a] Phoebe stared glumly at the sign over the gas pump, which read "1.49."

   [b] "What happened?" she asked, "Last week you were satisfied with only $1.29 a gallon. [c] Do you have large gambling debts?"

   [d] "Oil crisis, lady," the attendant replied. [e] "The price of crude went up ten dollars a barrel. [f] When the gas in my storage tanks is gone, it's going to cost me more to replace it. [g] If I didn't raise the price, I would lose money selling it to you. [h] I can't stay in business long doing things like that."

3. [Background: the week before there was an air show at a nearby air base.] [a] There is no rational reason why C-41s in a time of peace must be paraded around civilian homes in the Pioneer Valley for purely recreational reasons as was witnessed last weekend.

   [b] These huge military cargo planes pose a great threat to human lives in heavily populated areas. [c] If one crashed, it would cause a major disaster. [d] Do we really need to waste tax dollars in a time of economic upheaval on such ridiculous shows of military might? [e] I think not.
   —Letter to the *Daily Hampshire Gazette*,
   August 8, 1990

4. [a] Westinghouse Electric is building two 300-megawatt power plants for $300 million each. [b] They use natural gas, were started in 1989 and will be ready in 1991. [c] Texaco is promoting its Syngas fuel made from the gasification of coal. [d] It is not only cost effective but also exceeds the Bush Administration's environmental requirements for the year 2000.

[e] "New Ideas Changing Nuclear Debate" (Week in Review, July 22) discusses ways in which nuclear power could be used. [f] In view of the success of these examples, nuclear power should not be given any consideration at all.

—Letter to *The New York Times*, August 5, 1990

5. [a] In 1988 Associate Justice David H. Souter of the New Hampshire Supreme Court wrote an opinion supporting the overturning of a rape conviction on the ground that the rapist should have been allowed to present as evidence the victim's "open, sexually suggestive conduct in the presence of patrons of a public bar" just prior to his raping her.

[b] I have flirted with men in bars. [c] Men have flirted with me in bars. [d] I know a lot of men and women who flirt with each other in bars. [e] Is flirting sexually suggestive? [f] Of course. [g] But all I know is, if I flirt with a man in a bar, I don't deserve to get raped.

[h] If a woman's conduct toward a man is sexually suggestive, but at the same time she tells him she does not want to have intercourse, the vast majority of men in that situation will not rape her. [i] A man who would—and in the process perhaps mutilate or strangle her—should go to jail.

—Letter to *The New York Times*, August 7, 1990

6. [a] Phoebe stared glumly at the sign over the gas pump, which read "1.49."

[b] "Hey, c'mon!" she said. "The crisis is over! Oil prices fell ten dollars a barrel last week, why haven't you lowered your price?"

[c] "Sorry, lady," the attendant replied. "Prices have gone down all right, but the gas in my storage tanks was

bought at the old, higher price. [d] If I lower the price, I will be selling it for less than I paid. [e] I can't stay in business long doing things like that."

7. [a] Americans would risk their lives for freedom. [b] President Bush risks their lives for cheap gasoline.

[c] Sure, Saddam Hussein is a tyrant. [d] The United States supports many tyrants around the world, and tolerates many others when it suits our interests. [e] So let's not kid ourselves with high-flown talk about stopping aggression. [f] This "crisis" is about the price of oil.

[g] Speaking to the nation, Bush gave lip service to energy conservation. [h] (We know what his lips are worth.) [i] Were the United States to undertake comprehensive conservation measures, we could soon do without Gulf oil.

[j] If we would sooner sacrifice our sons than pay a few more cents—or dollars—at the gas pump, what kind of people have we become?

—Letter to the *Boston Globe*, August 13, 1990

Cathy has breakfast

If you give me six lines written by the most honest man, I will find something in them to hang him.

—CARDINAL RICHELIEU

Remember Cathy in "How to Argue" in part 2? She's back.

"Hi, Cathy! Join us for breakfast?" You and your friends Matt and Wei have just started to eat. Full of excitement at the prospect of the classes ahead, you flash a cheerful smile at the drowsy junior.

"What's that stuff you're eating? It looks like Meow Mix."

"Cheerios! Breakfast of Champions! Or is that Fruit Loops?" Wei's mastery of late twentieth-century American culture has some gaps.

"Oh, brother! You're in big trouble. Cheerios are wrong, wrong, wrong!" As Cathy approaches, you shrink.

"Sugar. It's got sugar in it. Sugar is bad for you. You pump sugar into your blood. Your body has to counterattack with insulin. That drives down your blood sugar and so you get hungry before your eleven-o'clock class. It's bad!"

Wei picks up her spoon.

"Salt. Cheerios has more salt per ounce than potato chips. Salt is bad for you. It gives you high blood pressure. Would you pour milk on a bowl of potato chips and eat it for breakfast? Gimme a break!"

Wei puts down her spoon.

"You know, don't you, how the U.S. uses sugar to oppress third-world nations? It buys sugar at inflated prices from giant plantations. It's a bribe. It guarantees the power and wealth of the ruling class while discouraging industrialization. Those countries then sell us their raw materials cheap and buy our products. They might as well be colonies."

Matt covers his Pop Tart with a napkin.

"That's why they hate us. Even after the revolution. They seize our embassies, they support terrorists, and they call us the great Satan. Please don't eat Cheerios."

Wei gets up to go.

"They also have this real dumb shape."

EXERCISES

1. What is the conclusion of the argument? What statements are relevant to it?

2. Compose a rebuttal to Cathy.

curiosities & puzzles

The Digestor's Digest

Vol. I, No. 1	Page 2

Great News!

For those of you who need a high-fiber breakfast, the new cereal, Honey Hemp, has more than all others combined. In addition, three years of testing now shows conclusively that it can be eaten under laboratory conditions. The other item on this page is an advertisement.

Great News!

For those of you who need a high-fiber breakfast, the new cereal, Sani-Bran, has more than all others combined. In addition, three years of testing now shows conclusively that it can, with appropriate equipment, be eaten. This report is just as correct as the other on this page.

exam warning II

We warned you earlier that there would be a Surprise Examination in this book. Since we issued that warning, we have received numerous letters from excited readers. We found one particularly interesting and we are printing it below in its entirety:

Dear Jim and Tom:

I read the section "Exam Warning I" with interest. I thought about it a great deal, and it seems to me that whatever else happens, you can't possibly give the exam on the last page of the book. The problem is that if we have read all the way to the next-to-last page and there still has been no exam, then we will know that the exam will be on the last page, since it's the only page left. Since we can't know the page ahead of time, this is impossible!

Am I right about this? I don't see any flaw in my reasoning.

By the way, I really like this book! I find logic fascinating, but you guys are just immense. I mean GOSH!

Respectfully,
Lora Logic

Well, Lora, we think you may be right! We don't see a flaw in your reasoning either. Luckily, this book has many pages, and if we can't put the exam on the last page, there is still plenty of room for the Surprise Examination.

And thanks, by the way, for your kind words about our humble efforts!

a nonlogical puzzle

> We are symbols, and inhabit symbols.
> —RALPH WALDO EMERSON

In each of the following statements, you are asked to discover what words the initials represent.

EXAMPLES

52 = W in a Y   12 = I in a F
Answer: 52 weeks in a year.   Answer: 12 inches in a foot.

Your turn:

a. 26 = L of the A   b. 7 = W of the A W
c. 1001 = A N   d. 12 = S of the Z
e. 54 = C in a D (with the J)   f. 9 = P in the S S
g. 88 = P K   h. 13 = S on the A F
i. 18 = H on a G C   j. 32 = D F at which W F
k. 90 = D in a R A   l. 200 = D for P G in M
m. 8 = S on a S S   n. 3 = B M (S H T R)
o. 4 = Q in a G   p. 1 = W on a U
q. 5 = D in a Z C   r. 57 = H V
s. 11 = P on a F T   t. 1000 = W that a P is W
u. 29 D in F in a L Y   v. 64 = S on a C
w. 40 = D and N of the G F   x. 24 = Q in this P

self-referential puzzles

> The golden rule is that there are no golden rules.
> —GEORGE BERNARD SHAW

Cross-Number Puzzles

These are like crossword puzzles except that each square is filled with a single digit, not a letter. The leading digit in a number with several digits cannot be 0.

EXAMPLE

Across

1. 2-down minus 40
3. a large number

Down

1. a small number
2. 3-across minus 40

1	2
3	4

There is only one correct answer:

1	**5**
9	**5**

Note that

0	**4**
8	**4**

is incorrect since 1-across and 1-down must be two-digit numbers and hence cannot begin with 0.

1. *Across*
   1. 18 minus 1-down

   Down
   1. 1-across

1

2. *Across*
   1. less than 2-down
   3. 4 times 1-down

   Down
   1. less than 3-across
   2. less than 1-down

1	2
3	4

3. *Across*
    1. 9 times 3-down
    4. less than 2-down
    5. less than 2-down

    Down
    1. greater than 1-across
    2. 3 times 5-across
    3. less than 4 across

Reflexicon

This is a most unusual crossword puzzle invented by Lee Sallows. Each entry is to be a phrase of the form "five ds" or "three hs" (don't forget the space). When you are done, the phrases you have written should describe completely the letters you have used. For example, if you write "five ds" as one of the entries, then in the entire puzzle you should have used the letter *d* exactly five times. Furthermore, if you ever use a letter, then one of the entries must note exactly how many you used. This is not easy!

VALID ARGUMENTS, CONVINCING ARGUMENTS, AND PUNK LOGIC

4

contents

GOAL: To apply the technical apparatus of statement logic in order to clarify everyday thoughts in natural language. Simple English arguments are formalized and tested for validity. The meanings of some common English words are clarified by using the tools of statement logic.

• By the way, notice that the word "valid" has two different uses in logic. We talk about valid argument forms, as we do here, and we talk about valid statement forms, as we did in "Logical Form" in part 2. The uses are connected by the fact that the argument form A, B, C, ∴ D is valid iff the statement form (A & B & C) ⇒ D is valid.

FORMAL LOGIC: VALID ARGUMENTS

VALID ARGUMENT FORMS

If you will not hear Reason, she will surely rap your knuckles.
—Benjamin Franklin

We say that the argument form

$$A, B, C, \therefore D$$

is **valid** (in other words, the premises A, B, and C imply conclusion D) iff, in the joint truth table for A, B, C, and D, whenever the premises are true, the conclusion is true. This is a conditional assertion; we do not insist that the premises be true or that the conclusion be true, only that *if* the premises are true, *then* the conclusion is. Some examples should make this clear. Be sure to notice that the wffs A, B, C, and D will generally be composed of statement letters such as P, Q, and R. It is the latter that determine the lines of the truth table.

EXAMPLE 1

$P \Rightarrow Q$
$\neg Q$
$\therefore \neg P$

P	Q	$P \Rightarrow Q$	$\neg Q$	$\neg P$
T	T	T	F	F
T	F	F	T	F
F	T	T	F	T
F	F	T	T	T

This argument form is valid because in every line in which both premises are T (only the last line), the conclusion is also T.

EXAMPLE 2

$P \Rightarrow Q$
$\neg P$
$\therefore \neg Q$

P	Q	$P \Rightarrow Q$	$\neg P$	$\neg Q$
T	T	T	F	F
T	F	F	F	T
F	T	T	T	F
F	F	T	T	T

This argument form is not valid because there is a line in which both premises are T and the conclusion is F (the third line).

EXAMPLE 3

$P \Rightarrow \neg R$
$\neg(\neg P \,\&\, R)$
$\neg Q \Leftrightarrow R$
$\therefore Q$

P	Q	R	$P \Rightarrow \neg R$	$\neg(\neg P \,\&\, R)$	$\neg Q \Leftrightarrow R$	Q
T	T	T	F	T	F	T
T	T	F	T	T	T	T
T	F	T	F	T	T	F
T	F	F	T	T	F	F
F	T	T	T	F	F	T
F	T	F	T	T	T	T
F	F	T	T	F	T	F
F	F	F	T	T	F	F

This argument form is valid because in every line where each premise is T (lines 2 and 6), the conclusion is T.

The valid argument forms of Sentential help us to evaluate arguments in English and other natural languages. For example, the argument

If Jeff hates Akbar, Jeff insults Akbar.
Jeff does not insult Akbar.
∴ Jeff does not hate Akbar.

is a valid argument because it has the form of example 1, which we saw was valid. If the premises about Jeff and Akbar are true, then the conclusion is true.

On the other hand, the argument

If Jeff hates Akbar, Jeff insults Akbar.
Jeff does not hate Akbar.
∴ Jeff does not insult Akbar.

is not a valid argument because it has the form of example 2. Both premises can be true even when the conclusion is false (perhaps Jeff insults Akbar as a sign of affection).

In order to evaluate arguments in English, you'll have to learn to formalize English statements in Sentential. We'll discuss that in a later section. But now let's be sure you can recognize valid argument forms in Sentential.

137

CHALLENGES

1. Test these arguments for validity.

   a. $P \Rightarrow Q$ b. $P \Leftrightarrow Q$ c. $Q \Rightarrow R$ d. $S \Rightarrow (Q \Rightarrow T)$
   Q Q $R \Rightarrow T$ $S \,\&\, Q$
   $\therefore P$ $\therefore P$ $\therefore Q \Rightarrow T$ $\therefore T$

   e. P f. $Q \,\&\, \neg P$ g. P
   $\therefore Q \Rightarrow P$ $\therefore Q$ $\therefore Q \vee \neg Q$

   h. $P \vee Q$ i. $Q \vee P$ j. $P \Leftrightarrow Q$
   $\neg Q \vee \neg R$ $\neg R \vee \neg P$ $\neg (P \,\&\, Q)$
   $P \Rightarrow Q$ $R \Rightarrow \neg Q$ $\therefore \neg P \,\&\, Q$
   $\therefore \neg R$ $\therefore R$

2. Let P stand for "Our economic policy is the right policy," and let Q stand for "We have prosperity." Translate the argument form in problem 1a into English.

3. Repeat problem 2 but this time translate the sentence letters freely, using your own words. Embellish the argument without adding any new *relevant* statements. You may add statements that repeat or emphasize points, but do not change the argument structure. Make your argument as convincing and as plausible as you can.

SUMMARY: An argument form is valid iff any truth assignment to the sentence letters that makes each premise true also makes the conclusion true.

FORMALIZING FOR VALIDITY

> After a great pain, a formal feeling comes—
> —EMILY DICKINSON

Perhaps the main reason to formalize English statements in Sentential is to evaluate arguments for validity. So the translation process usually takes place in this context. For example, if one of the statements involved is "Calvin is a little brat," then whether you translate this as P or as $Q \,\&\, R$ (for "Calvin is little and Calvin is a brat") depends on the argument. If the words "brat" and "little" occur only in the context "Calvin is a little brat," then the two alternatives are virtually the same: One will have $Q \,\&\, R$ wherever the other has P.

On the other hand, if the argument also includes the statement that "Calvin is a brat" or that "Calvin is not a brat," then clearly

(Q & R) is the better choice, since by translating "Calvin is a brat" as R or "Calvin is not a brat" as $\neg R$, we reveal the logical connections involved.

The point is that formalization—or translation—is neither automatic nor mechanical. It requires some practice and a deft touch. To drive this point home, we invite you to consider negation. Granted that "Tom is male" is to be formalized as P, which of the following English statements could you formalize as $\neg P$?

> Tom is not male.
> It's not true that Tom is male.
> It's not the case that Tom is male.
> That's not male (said of Tom).
> Tom is female.

The first four statements can be translated as $\neg P$. But even if no male is female and everything is one or the other, it seems stretching things to consider "Tom is female" as $\neg P$. It would be much better to formalize the latter by some new letter Q and, if you insist, to introduce a new premise, such as "Tom is female if and only if Tom is not male," or $Q \Leftrightarrow \neg P$. The advantage of this approach is that everything is explicit and aboveboard. At least it allows the possibility of a challenge to the premise $Q \Leftrightarrow \neg P$ (perhaps Tom is a car [neither male nor female] or a hermaphrodite [both male and female]). Formalizing "Tom is female" by $\neg P$ rules out such challenges rather arbitrarily.

The reason translation is not mechanical is that there are no hard and fast rules for it. The English word "and" generally signals the conjunction &, but in "Calvin and Hobbes are buddies," the "and" cannot be represented by the truth-functional &.

Another case in point is supplied by negation. "Tom is not male" is the negation of "Tom is male"; "Calvin is not a brat," is the negation of "Calvin is a brat." But don't for a moment think that "S is not G" is generally the negation of "S is G." "Tom and Jim are not bald" is not the negation of "Tom and Jim are bald" (not in the usual reading), and "All readers of this book are not female" does not negate "All readers of this book are female."

This being said, let us give you a few useful hints for translating or formalizing. We list formulas and some common English signals of them.

1. **P & Q**: "P and Q," "both P and Q," "P, however Q," "P, moreover Q," "P, furthermore Q," $P . Q$" (That . is the ordinary period.)

All are obvious except the "*P*, but *Q*." We grant that the English "but" means something different from the English "and," but if you attend only to truth values, you'll see that they amount to the same thing. "She's rich, but she's honest" is true in only one case: when she's rich and honest.

2. **$P \lor Q$**: "*P* or *Q*," "either *P* or *Q*," "*P* unless *Q*"

   That $P \lor Q$ can translate "*P* unless *Q*" certainly seems strange. But suppose I insist that "Jim will come unless his car breaks down." It's clear that if Jim comes and his car doesn't break down or vice versa, I've spoken truthfully, and if he doesn't come and his car doesn't break down, I've spoken falsely. But what if he comes even though his car does break down? I think I can justly claim to have spoken the truth. After all, I wasn't ruling out the possibility that he might hitch a ride with Superman. I merely said that the only alternative to his coming (if he didn't come) was that his car broke down.

3. **$\neg(P \lor Q)$** or **$(\neg P \,\&\, \neg Q)$**: "neither *P* nor *Q*"

4. **$P \Rightarrow Q$**: "if *P* then *Q*," "if *P*, *Q*," "*Q*, if *P*," "*P* only if *Q*," "*P* is a sufficient condition of *Q*," "*Q* is a necessary condition of *P*," "not *P* unless *Q*"

   The first three are obvious (although the third is a bit tricky —as if English had the symbol $\Leftarrow$). The bits about necessary conditions and sufficient conditions can be taken as definitions of "necessary conditions" and "sufficient conditions." "Unless" was covered above, given the tautology

$$(\neg P \lor Q) \Leftrightarrow (P \Rightarrow Q)$$

"Only if" is another one of those strange cases that you can work out line by truth table line. If I insist that "Jim won't come only if his car breaks down," my claim is false only in the case that he doesn't come, but his car hasn't broken down ($T \Rightarrow F$).

5. **$P \Leftrightarrow Q$**: "*P* if and only if *Q*," "*P* iff *Q*," "*P* is a necessary and sufficient condition of *Q*"

CHALLENGE Try to formalize the following arguments in Sentential and assess them for validity. (WARNING: The mere fact that an English argument doesn't come out valid when formalized in Sentential doesn't completely show that the argument is invalid—unless Sentential is the only logic there is. But you already know that there is more to logic than Sentential.)

1. You can learn logic only if you study. You study. Therefore, you learn logic.

2. You learn logic if and only if you study. You study. Therefore, you learn logic.

3. You don't graduate unless you learn logic. Moreover, you learn logic only if you read this book. If you don't graduate, you don't get into law school. Therefore, if you get into law school, you learn logic.

4. Mrs. White did it and she did it either with the wrench or with the rope. But she did it with the rope iff the murder was committed in the hall. The murder was committed in the kitchen. Therefore, Mrs. White did it and she did it with the wrench.

5. Mr. Hoopsnider, if you advocate the legalization of drugs, you are sending a message to all our youth that drugs are not dangerous, that our young people can take drugs and enjoy them in safety. This is what they will think! Yesterday, however, you did exactly that, you suggested that the way to fight our drug problem is to decriminalize drugs. As a consequence, you have in essence told the young people of this city that drugs are OK.

6. Not both Jim and Tom are rock stars. Jim, however, is not a rock star. Therefore, Tom is a rock star.

7. If drugs are legalized, then there will be more money to treat addicts, there will be less drug-related crime, and the mob will lose its main source of income. Without that source of money, the mob will wither away and die. It is clear, then, that drugs will never be legalized, since the mob will never die.

8. $N + 1$ is greater than N. If $N + 1$ is greater than N, then N is not greater than $N + 1$. If N is the largest number, then N is greater than $N + 1$. Therefore, N is not the largest number.

9. Interest rates will rise unless both the Federal Reserve Bank intervenes and the stock market doesn't fall. If interest rates rise, many will lose their jobs. Therefore, if the stock market falls, many will lose their jobs.

10. If the world is round, then I can sail around it if I have a boat. I have a boat, but I don't sail around the world. Thus, the world is not round. (WARNING: What are your intuitions about the argument in English? Do they agree with your formal results?)

11. If the next president's drug policy is to legalize drugs, then it will reduce addiction. The next president, however, must decide either to legalize drugs or to oppose such a legalization. If she ultimately decides to oppose legalization, then her policy will clearly proclaim the danger of drugs to our society. If her policy either reduces addiction or at least proclaims clearly the danger of drugs, then it can be called a success. We can say, therefore, that the next president's policy, whatever it is, can be called a success.

12. A necessary and sufficient condition that humanity be free is that human beings are not bound by an essence. If God created humans, then we are bound by an essence. Yet clearly we humans are free. Hence, God did not create humans.

13. Back in 1995 when we raised taxes, there were many who wondered if it was the right thing to do. The country was in serious economic trouble. There was high unemployment, high inflation, and an extremely high rate of business failures. We were on the spot and we knew it, but there was hope. I believe everyone agreed that if we made the correct economic moves, the country would recover and recover quickly. Well, it has been three years since that moment, and the record speaks for itself. Inflation has cooled, prices are down, the market is up. People are back at work and the recovery is complete. If there was any doubt before about our policy, there can be none now. Raising taxes was the right thing to do.

14. All men love to be scratched behind the ears. Hobbes is a man. Therefore, Hobbes loves to be scratched behind the ears.

15. Clark Kent wears glasses. Superman is Clark Kent. Therefore Superman wears glasses.

SUMMARY: Arguments expressed in English (or other natural languages) can be formalized in statement logic and assessed for validity according to the technical definitions. Ordinarily the assessments agree with our intuitions, but occasionally they do not. The reason for the divergence is that English can employ logical reasoning that is not captured by Sentential.

A SHORTCUT FOR CHECKING ARGUMENTS

> If you call a tail a leg, how many legs has a dog? Five? No, calling a tail a leg don't *make* it a leg.
>
> —Abraham Lincoln

There are many shortcuts that can be used to abbreviate a full truth table, but one in particular deserves special mention. Suppose you want to test an argument form for validity, say

$$A, B \therefore C$$

where A, B, and C are complex wffs. You know this form will be invalid if any line in the truth table delivers the pattern T premises, F conclusion, that is,

A	T
B	T
$\therefore$ C	F

The essence of the shortcut is to search for such a line. If you find a line in the truth table with this pattern, the argument form is invalid. If you can't find such a line, the argument form is valid. The reason this process is a shortcut is that you focus on a single line or two in an attempt to get the pattern.

EXAMPLE

Given the argument form	find a truth assignment yielding
$P \& Q$	T
$R \lor \neg Q$	T
$\therefore R$	$\therefore$ F

Then R must be F, and since $P \& Q$ is to be T, both P and Q must separately be T. Notice that no truth assignment other than

$$P\,T \quad Q\,T \quad R\,F$$

can possibly make both premises true and conclusion false. But notice also that this assignment makes the second premise F:

$$R \vee \neg Q = F \vee \neg T = F$$

Therefore *no line of the truth table makes both premises true and the conclusion false*. Therefore, the argument form is valid.

EXAMPLE

Given the argument form	find a truth assignment giving
$Q \vee \neg S$	T
$Q \Rightarrow P$	T
$\therefore P \Rightarrow \neg S$	F

The only way $P \Rightarrow \neg S$ can be F is if P is T and $\neg S$ is F (hence S is T). Since $\neg S$ is F and $Q \vee \neg S$ is to be T, Q must be T. Thus the assignment

$$P\,T \quad Q\,T \quad S\,T$$

is necessary to make the first premise T and the conclusion F. What does this assignment do to the second premise $Q \Rightarrow P$? It becomes $T \Rightarrow T$, which is T. Thus we *did* find a line in the truth table that made all premises T and the conclusion F (namely P is T, Q is T, and S is T). Hence the argument form is invalid.

This technique can save considerable time, especially as the number of basic letters mounts up. Instead of constructing a 32-line truth table, for example, you try to zero in on the line or lines that show an argument form invalid. This technique will also be useful in later sections.

EXERCISE   Use the shortcut to test the validity of these argument forms.

1. $P \Rightarrow Q$
   $Q \Rightarrow R$
   $\therefore R \vee \neg P$

2. $Q \Rightarrow \neg P$
   $\neg P \Rightarrow \neg R$
   $(\neg Q \& \neg R) \Rightarrow \neg P$
   $\therefore P \Leftrightarrow R$

3. $S \vee R$
   $\neg S \vee T$
   $U \Rightarrow \neg S$
   $\neg U \Rightarrow (T \& S)$
   $\therefore U \& R$

4. $Q \Rightarrow P$
   $(R \vee S) \vee T$
   $U \Leftrightarrow \neg Q$
   $(R \& U) \Rightarrow P$
   $T \Rightarrow (R \vee P)$
   $\therefore (\neg P \& T) \Rightarrow (P \vee \neg S)$

SUMMARY: One can test whether an argument form is valid by focusing on the possibility that it is not and (exhaustively) checking the possibility of true premises and a false conclusion.

FORMALIZING ENGLISH WITH THE MEAGER RESOURCES OF SENTENTIAL

Get your fresh-picked ifs, ands and buts.
—NORTON JUSTER, *THE PHANTOM TOLLBOOTH*

Some logic textbooks devote considerable time to formalizing statements (or arguments) of ordinary English in the simple language of Sentential. We think this is a mistake. Sentential is woefully inadequate to express interesting English statements. (Remember how useful predicates and quantifiers were when we tried to formalize statements about kinship relations, Sophist College, and elementary arithmetic in parts 1 and 2?) Extensive practice formalizing in Sentential is like extensive piano practice with only the notes C, E, and G!

In this section, we'll use the little bit of logic we know to pose and tentatively answer some challenging questions about formalization. We want to investigate how well statement logic accounts for ordinary English; that is, how well &, $\vee$, and $\Rightarrow$ mirror the ordinary English operations expressed by "and," "or," and "if . . . then." It would be quite an accomplishment if we could show that the logical account captures the English usage. The truth table explanation of the connectives &, $\vee$, and $\Rightarrow$ is simple and precise; the English uses of "and," "or," and "if . . . then" seem complex and unruly. Wouldn't it be lovely if the latter mysteries reduced to the former simplicities?

& and "and"

Let's begin with English "and" and Sentential &. Of course, we know from the start that some uses of "and" aren't explained by Sentential &. Occasionally, "and" connects genuinely compound subjects, as in "Peter and Paul are brothers [of each other]." (Note that predicate logic can represent this use of "and" by a relation, as in Bcd.)

On the other hand, we know that the basic use of "and" as a sentence connective, as in "Jim whistles and Tom sings," is easily expressed by $P \& Q$. Moreover, we've seen how to paraphrase other conjunctions of words or phrases by &. Thus,

"Sinead and Tracy sing"   is just
"Sinead sings & Tracy sings"   or $S \& T$

Similarly,

"Sinead sings and whistles"   is just
"Sinead sings & Sinead whistles"   or $S \& W$

Now let us turn to a question that logicians dispute. Some logicians think that there is a special sense, or meaning, of the English word "and" that connects statements in a time-dependent way. From this point of view,

"Mel got bored and Mel left the party"

is not equivalent to and thus does not mean the same as

"Mel left the party and Mel got bored"

(Remember $P \& Q$ is logically equivalent to $Q \& P$, so if these logicians are right, this is a case when English "and" does not match up with Sentential &.)

We can paraphrase the issue thus. According to the critics, there is a special, temporal sense of the English word "and" that can be roughly expressed by the truth-functional & as

P and Q iff $P \& Q \& (P$ happened before $Q)$

The temporal sense of the English "and" includes the claim that the first conjunct occurred before the second. Such a sense of "and" would not obey the logical laws about &. For example, both

$(P \& Q) \Leftrightarrow (Q \& P)$ and $(P \& P) \Leftrightarrow P$

would fail for the temporal "and."

How can we tell whether the English word "and" has just the truth-functional meaning of & or whether it is ambiguous, sometimes meaning the truth function & but sometimes meaning the tensed "and"? Of course, the particularities of "and" are far less interesting than the general theoretical question, How can we tell what the meaning of a given English word is? (And notice the peculiarity of *that* question. As speakers of English, don't we automatically know what the meaning of an English word, a word in our language, is?)

So with very little logic, you have been plunged into a debate involving logicians, philosophers, linguists, and computer scientists. Does the ordinary English conjunction of sentences—P and Q—have a sense conveying temporal priority (P before Q) or not? Intuition supports the special sense of priority. There *seems* to be a difference between "Jim got sick and died" and "Jim died and got sick." But love of logical theory supports the idea that "and" is unambiguous, and so it always means &. "Mel got bored and left the party" *does* mean the same as "Mel left the party and got bored"; the suggested temporal order is irrelevant.

The philosopher Paul Grice suggested a solution to this dilemma by reconciling the simplest theory ("and" means &) with our counterintuitions. Roughly speaking, his idea was to distinguish between (1) *what a sentence means* and (2) *the information that an audience can get from a typical use of that sentence.* In more technical terms, Grice's idea was that we distinguish between the logical (semantic) implications of a sentence and the pragmatic implications of an utterance of that sentence. Grice called the latter "implicatures."

For example, suppose you tell me that your sister is looking for someone (male) to date and I tell you, "Boris is a bachelor." Ordinarily you would be justified in concluding that Boris is interested in meeting your sister and women in general. But this conclusion is based not just on the meaning of what I said but also on the circumstances of the conversation and the general protocols governing conversations.

One protocol or conversational convention is that what is said should be relevant to the conversation, and my statement would be most irrelevant if I made it knowing that Boris hated women or that he was away in the Antarctic for six months. Under those circumstances, it would be irrelevant to bring up Boris at all in the conversation we were having.

Nevertheless, the simple English statement

"Boris is a bachelor"

certainly does not imply that

"Boris likes women"   or that   "Boris is not in Antarctica"

However, it does imply (given the definition of "bachelor") that

"Boris is unmarried"

Grice suggested a nice way to distinguish real or logical implications from conversational implicatures. Grice said that the speaker can cancel implicatures by saying something further, but he noted that real logical implications can't be canceled.

So, for example, both

"Boris is a bachelor; unfortunately, he hates women"

and

"Boris is a bachelor; however, he's now in the Antarctic"

are acceptable English sentences that might be true. Their acceptability and possible truth show that, strictly speaking, the statement "Boris is a bachelor" does not imply that he doesn't hate women or that he's not now in the Antarctic.

Compare these sentences to the statement

"Boris is a bachelor; unfortunately, he's married"

This sentence is logically (semantically) contradictory. If I asserted it, you might well wonder if I spoke English (but if I asserted either of the previous two sentences, you would have no worry on this score).

To summarize, the meaning of an expression cannot be canceled or discounted. However, a natural association based on meaning can be canceled, according to Grice.

Now let's apply Grice's idea to conjunction. If it is an acceptable sense of "and" in "P and Q" that "first P happened and then Q happened," then we should not be able to cancel the implicature that P happened before Q. But if the suggestion that P happened before Q is merely a conversational implicature, merely a conventional inference based on expectations, then we should be able to cancel the implicature that the clauses were stated in any specific order.

Consider

"Mel left the party and got bored but not in that order"

Is that more like

"Boris is a bachelor, but he's in the Antarctic now"

or

"Boris is a bachelor, but he's married"?

Actually, it seems very much like the former, not the latter. We can apply this case to other apparent cases of the so-called temporal "and." "Jim died and got sick—of course, not in that order; he got sick first" is unusual but intelligible. This is strong evidence that there is no special temporal sense to English "and" and hence that "and" is well represented by the logical &. The evidence suggests that in speaking English, there is a pragmatic tendency to mention the conjunct that occurs first in any temporal conjunction, although this tendency can be canceled.

One student, Fei Xu, suggested several other examples that corroborate this point. Consider

"I visited Tulane and Davis on my trip. Indeed, I just flew in from Tulane"

is not at all odd. The second sentence merely cancels any implicature that I visited Tulane first, Moreover, if I say

"I saw both *Alexander Nevskey* and *Citizen Kane*"

there is absolutely no suggestion that I saw *Alexander Nevksy* first.

Finally, as Fei Xu points out, it would be downright odd to say that

"I read *Crime and Punishment* and *The Brothers Karamazov* but not in that order"

because no one would assume that I'm suggesting that I read them in that order. But if "and" had a temporal sense, that would be a perfectly legitimate supposition.

The moral of these reflections is what Grice would have supposed. It is that the meaning of the English sentential connective "and" is tense neutral and well captured by the truth-functional &. In particular contexts, the audience often supposes that the first conjunct happened before the second, but this is not because of a meaning of "and" but because of the general structure of human communication.

EXERCISES

1. Jim has applied to be chairman of the mathematics department at your college, and you ask me for a recommendation. All I tell you is that Jim is an excellent cook. Have I recommended him for the job? Does his being an excellent cook logically imply that he'd be a lousy chair? How might Grice explain this?

2. "Maria had a baby and got married." Does this cast any aspersions on Maria's sense of propriety? Explain how Grice might counter the claim that the original sentence logically implies that Maria had a baby before she got married.

∨ and "or"

The main worry about translating English or by the connective ∨ is in the first line of the truth table. Many people feel that P or Q should be counted false when both P and Q are true. In fact, there is a quite respectable truth function called the "exclusive or," which we can symbolize by $\veebar$. It has the following truth table (the table for ∨ is included for comparison):

P	Q	P $\veebar$ O	P ∨ O
T	T	F	T
T	F	T	T
F	T	T	T
F	F	F	F

Moreover, we can define either truth function in terms of the other:

$$A \veebar B \Leftrightarrow (A \lor B) \,\&\, \neg(A \,\&\, B)$$
$$A \lor B \Leftrightarrow (A \veebar B) \veebar (A \,\&\, B)$$

Which one is the better rendition of the English "or"? Once we understand the work of Paul Grice, we can see how to answer this. The best argument for ∨ is the simplicity of the resulting scheme. Consider this: "Neither P nor Q" is the English negation of "either P or Q." Now, "neither P nor Q" is equivalent in English to "not P and not Q." Moreover, $\neg(P \lor Q)$ is logically equivalent to $(\neg P \,\&\, \neg Q)$, but $(P \veebar Q)$ is not. This is a powerful argument for the traditional truth table for ∨.

Some people think that the exclusive "or" is needed to express alternations that can't be true at the same time, as in

"Either the Cubs or the Pirates will win the World Series."

But this thought is wrong. It is the world of baseball, not logic, that keeps two teams from winning the World Series. In the world of baseball, the top line of the truth table (T T) can't ever be realized. Thus we can legitimately translate the above as

"The Cubs win the World Series ∨ the Pirates win it."

If both won, as might be possible if the rules of baseball were changed, the alternation *would* be true, but the current rules of baseball prevent two teams from winning the same pennant and, hence, the same World Series.

Perhaps the strongest argument for the exclusive "or" is based on the following considerations. Suppose someone asks you who wrote this book, and you say, "Jim or Tom wrote this book." Now if it is discovered that *both* Jim and Tom wrote this book, and especially if it comes out that you knew this all along, your questioner might accuse you of lying or being misleading. "Look," your questioner might say, "if you knew that both Jim and Tom wrote this book, you shouldn't have said that either Jim or Tom wrote it." And because people do criticize each other like that, it is suggested that the best way of representing your statement is by the exclusive "or": "Jim wrote this book ∨̱ Tom wrote this book." This statement is false if both wrote the book, and that explains why your critic was mad at you.

This kind of argument seems less compelling after Grice. For Grice taught that there are conventions that govern conversations, and these conventions give rise to implicatures. One convention we saw was "Be relevant." Not only do we try to be relevant, but we try to interpret our conversational partners as relevant, too. Another convention is "Be as informative as possible (within reason)." When you told the questioner that "Jim or Tom wrote this book" she justifiably assumed that you were trying to be as informative as possible; therefore she assumed that at least you did not know that Jim *and* Tom wrote the book; otherwise, you would have said that. But according to Grice, it does not follow from "Jim or Tom wrote this book" that it is not true that both Jim and Tom wrote it, nor does it follow that the speaker does not know that both wrote it. But the latter is a natural conversational implicature. Your critic rounded on you because you did not give her all the relevant information you had. You didn't speak falsely, but you violated a convention of conversation.

Thus the truth-functional accounts of & and ∨ seem to hold up pretty well as accounts of the meaning of English "and" and "or" as statement connectives. The apparent difference between the truth tables and the English seem better explained by Grice's theory of conversational conventions and the resulting implicatures than by looking for new truth tables or non–truth table senses of "and" and "or."

EXERCISE "Either you clean up your room or you don't go out to play," father Homer says to child Bart. Does it follow that Homer spoke falsely if Bart cleans up his room but doesn't go out to play? Give a Gricean defense of Homer. (What if a hurricane hit in the meantime, or while cleaning his room, Bart broke his bed?)

⇒ and "if . . . then"

The most mysterious truth table is certainly ⇒'s, where F ⇒ T is T and F ⇒ F is also T. There are many ways to make this table more appealing. Consider, for instance, the colloquial negation "If you're right, then I'm a monkey's uncle." This is intended to be a true assertion, but it's obviously false that I'm a monkey's uncle. Thus, if the conditional is obviously true and the consequent is obviously false, the antecedent must be false and you must be wrong ($F \Rightarrow F$ is T).

But we must admit that we part company with Grice in our general attitude toward the English "if . . . then." Grice really thought the logician's conditional basically captured all the meanings of our English phrase "if . . . then."

We, on the other hand, are inclined to recognize non-truth-functional uses of "if . . . then" and to admit that no truth table can capture them. The easiest non-truth-functional use for us to explain is "implies." Often in English we express the thought that A implies B by saying "if A, then B." For example, given the usual meanings of "freshman" and "sophomore," we say that

If all students are sophomores, then none are freshmen"

is true both if "if . . . then" is interpreted as $\Rightarrow$ and if "if . . . then" is interpreted as "implies." But

"If all students are sophomores then all are freshmen"

is true if "if . . . then" is interpreted as $\Rightarrow$ (antecedent false) but false if "if . . . then" is interpreted as "implies." Given the usual meaning of "freshman" and "sophomore," "all students are freshmen" implies "none are sophomores," not "all are sophomores."

The word "implies," as we've often said, can be represented as the truth-functional validity of the conditional. "A implies B" iff $A \Rightarrow B$ is valid. This relation between implication and the conditional is enough to explain logicians' fondness for the conditional. But there are other reasons.

But first let us note that there are other non-truth-functional uses of "if . . . then." In addition to implication, there are causal connections: "If you're boiled in oil, then you die." Being boiled in oil causes one to die because of the extremely high temperature of boiling oil. A more pointed example is "If anything is taken to absolute zero on the Kelvin scale, all motion in it stops" (this is a true law of physics, although nothing has been observed at zero on the Kelvin scale). But "If anything is taken to absolute zero on the Kelvin scale, it will turn into a replica of Jimmy Cagney and sing "I'm a Yankee Doodle Dandy" is a false bit of physics, even though the antecedent is always false (and so the $\Rightarrow$ statement is true). We mentioned counterfactuals earlier. "If you had not read this book, you would have done something useful with your time" is neither a trivial truth (as it would be if the "if . . . then" were $\Rightarrow$) nor a statement of some causal law.

But if we want a representation of "if . . . then" in terms of truth tables—and we want this to relate it to &, ∨, and ¬—then the truth table for ⇒ is the best there is. One simple argument (due to Samuel Guttenplan) is just this: English speakers are inclined to accept that

"If A & B, then A"

is a logical truth (or tautology), true under any circumstances whatsoever. But then it follows that

"If Jim and Tom are teachers, then Jim is a teacher"

(this must be true, so "if T then T" is T) and

"If Jim is a teacher and Tom is a penguin, then Jim is a teacher"

(this must be true, so "if F then T" is T) and

"If Jim is a penguin and Tom is a teacher, then Jim is a penguin"

(this must be true, so "if F then F" is T). And, of course, we know that "if T then F" must be counted F. This justifies all four lines of the truth table for ⇒.

The fact that there are arguments like

"If Jim gets the job, Tim resigns"

(because they're the two candidates and Tim is a jealous sort) and

"If Tim dies, Jim gets the job"

(because they're the only two candidates)

"Therefore, if Tim dies, Tim resigns."

can be explained as hasty approximations. If the premises really are true, the conclusion really is true. But in fact, the first premise is false in just the way the conclusion is. If Jim gets the job, Tim resigns only if Tim is still alive (dead men don't resign), only if Tim is well enough to resign, only if Tim is not offered such a boodle of money that he changes his mind, and so on.

Whether or not our examples are convincing, our moral should be taken to heart. Think twice before you insist that something is part of the meaning of an English word or phrase. It might not be part of the meaning of English, but just, as Grice suggested, be readily concluded by English speakers who are aware of the usual contexts of use.

SUMMARY: The act of formalizing English in Sentential can raise some interesting logical questions. As you've seen, the questions concern some basic issues as to how well Sentential can represent the ordinary logic of familiar English words. In contrast, detailed questions about the formalization of specific arguments are less interesting.

with & about logic

Miniac

> Heads, it's this way!
> Tails, it's that!
> "The toss of a coin
> will solve the spat!
> Unquote!
> —CARL BARKS, "FLIPISM," WALT DISNEY'S COMICS AND STORIES, 1953

Computing has come a long way from the days when a single machine filled a large room with vacuum tubes, circuits, and wires. In 1985 a machine no larger than a typewriter could be more powerful, have more memory, and compute faster than the largest machines of 1970.

Today miniaturization has been taken to a new extreme. A computer that can answer any yes-or-no question will fit in the palm of your hand! That computer is the humble penny. It was discovered by Thomas Storer. Due to the ubiquitous nature of the machine,

Mr. Storer has made virtually no money from his epoch-making invention.

Here is how it works. The procedure is to ask a question, then flip the coin. For the benefit of interpreting the output, we will take heads to be a yes answer and tails to be a no. You may ask, for example, "Is George Bush president of Eastern Airlines?" and flip the coin. If the coin comes up heads, the preliminary answer to the question is yes; if tails, the preliminary answer is no.

Of course at this stage, the computer looks rather silly. In fact, as you can verify by experimenting, the computer coin comes up with the correct answer only about half the time.

Now we describe a modification that ensures that you can figure out the correct answer all the time! The trick is to ask the computer a second question, namely, "Does the answer to this question have the same truth value as the answer to the preceding question?" We claim that if the computer answers yes to the second question (the coin comes up heads), then the first answer is correct. And if the computer answers no to the second question (the coin comes up tails), then the first answer is incorrect. In other words, we now *know* the answer to the original question! Hard to believe?

For example, suppose we wish to know whether it will rain tomorrow. We first ask:

Question 1. "Will it rain tomorrow?"

Then we flip the coin. Suppose, for example, that it comes up heads (yes). We don't yet know whether it will rain tomorrow, since this answer may be incorrect. Consequently we ask:

Question 2. "Is the truth value of your answer to this question the same as the truth value of your answer to question 1?"

and we flip again. Suppose this time we get tails (no). Once again, we have no way of knowing whether this answer is correct. But as long as we get tails the second time, we know the correct answer to question 1 is no. How? Consider the two possible cases.

Case 1. The answer to question 2 is correct. If it is correct, then the truth value of Miniac's answer to question 1 is not the same as the truth value of the answer to question 2.

Question 2's answer was correct, and so question 1's answer was incorrect, and so it will not rain tomorrow.

Case 2. The answer to question 2 is incorrect. If it is incorrect, then the truth value of Miniac's answer to question 1 is the same as the truth value of the answer to question 2. Question 2's answer is incorrect, and so question 1's answer is also incorrect, and so it will not rain tomorrow.

In *both* cases, we conclude that it won't rain tomorrow. Since one of the cases must be true, we know that it won't rain tomorrow! We are able to extract this information from a penny.

We have followed what happens if we flip a tails on the second flip. If we flip a heads, we can show in a similar way that the correct answer to question 1 is yes (see the Exercise).

This system takes wrong answers into account. To find the correct answer to any question, we ask the computer two questions. The answer to either or both of the questions may be false; nonetheless, we can determine the correct answer from the computer's output!

EXERCISE **Complete the argument for Miniac's worth. Suppose we've flipped a coin once and then get heads on the second flip. We then consider two cases:**

Case 1: The answer to question 2 is correct.
Case 2: The answer to question 2 is incorrect.

1. Show that in case 1, the answer to question 1 is correct.
2. Show that in case 2, the answer to question 1 is correct. After two flips, we know whether the answer to the first question is correct.
3. Is the answer to the second question correct?
4. Is there anything wrong with this procedure? In particular, can you spot a flaw in the "proof" that the procedure always works?

flipism

From *Walt Disney's Comics and Stories* #149, 1952. Reprinted by permission.
© The Walt Disney Company

sets

Histories make men wise; poets, witty; the mathematics, subtile; natural philosophy, deep; moral philosophy, grave; logic and rhetoric, able to contend.

—Francis Bacon

We assume that you are familiar with the concept of a set as a collection of objects. There are many ways to picture sets, but perhaps the simplest is with circles or blobs on a page. Such pictures are called *Venn diagrams* for their inventor, John Venn. For example, if A is the set of letters in the word "mother" and B is the set of letters in the word "father," we can draw

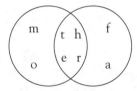

That is, $A = \{m,o,t,h,e,r\}$ and $B = \{f,a,t,h,e,r\}$.

The **union** of A and B, written $A \cup B$, are the letters in either set:

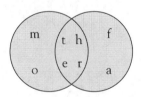

so $A \cup B = \{m,o,t,h,e,r,f,a\}$.

The **intersection** of A and B, written $A \cap B$, is only the letters that are in both sets:

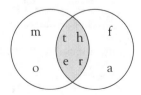

so $A \cap B = \{t,h,e,r\}$.

The **complement** of A, which we will write as A^c, consists of all things that are not in A:

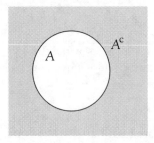

Actually, there are lots of things that aren't in A, including the letter *j* and the letter *z*, and also Marcel Proust, the People's Republic of China, and all members of the 1946 Boston Red Sox. Usually, however, we limit ourselves to some category. In this case, letters of the alphabet seem appropriate. Thus

$$A^c = \{a, b, c, d, f, g, i, j, k, l, n, p, q, s, u, v, w, x, y, z\}$$

There is a nice connection between this notation and our symbolic language. Let P and Q be propositions. Let p be the set of situations where P is true and q be the set of situations where q is true:

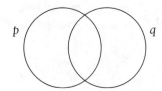

Now, what is the set of situations where $P \lor Q$ is true? The answer is $p \cup q$:

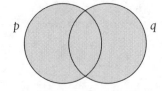

What about the set of situations where $P \ \& \ Q$ is true?

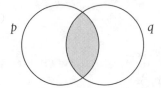

It is $p \cap q$. And the set of situations where $\neg P$ is true is p^c. The correspondence is especially nice when we tell you that mathematicians (as opposed to philosophers) prefer to use the notation $P \wedge Q$ instead of $P \& Q$.

This relationship can be seen in every tautology. Take, for example, $P \vee \neg P$. In terms of sets, this reads: $P \cup P^c$. The diagram for this is

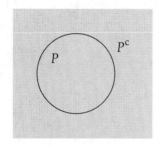

that is, everything. Every situation makes $P \vee \neg P$ true. On the other hand, for an inconsistent statement, such as $P \& \neg P$, we get $P \cap P^c$, or nothing at all. No situation makes $P \& \neg P$ true.

How do we interpret P implies Q? That statement says that everything in the set p is contained in the set q. We say in this case that p is a **subset** of q and we write $p \subseteq q$. The line at the bottom helps us to remember that p and q might be equal.

EXAMPLE

Here is a problem that we can tackle using Venn diagrams. Out of a total of 73 students, 31 have signed up for a course in Aristotle, 17 have signed up for both Plato and Aristotle, and 12 have failed to sign up for either. How many signed up for Plato?

To solve this problem, we can draw a Venn diagram as follows:

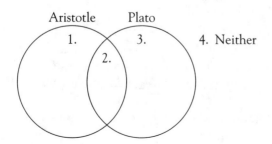

CHALLENGE The following questions pertain to these statements:

a. $P \vee \neg Q$
b. $\neg P \& Q$
c. $\neg(P \& Q)$
d. $\neg(P \vee \neg Q)$
e. $\neg P \vee \neg Q$
f. $\neg(\neg P \& Q)$

1. Write the corresponding expression with sets.
2. Draw the Venn diagram for each expression.
3. Note which diagrams are the same. What can you say about the statements that produced equivalent diagrams?

• The lovely correspondence we have been observing is marred here by the notation for implication that is used by some authors, namely, $\supset$. This leads to $P \supset Q$ iff $p \subseteq q$.

159

The problem says that there are 31 students in regions 1 and 2 combined and 17 students in region 2. Putting this information together, we have

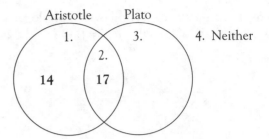

The problem tells us that there are 12 students in region 4.

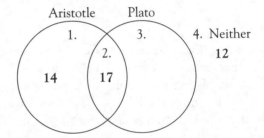

Altogether there are 73 students. By a little subtraction, we find that there are 30 students in region 3. Finally, the answer we seek is the number in 2 and 3 together, or 47.

EXERCISES

1. Out of 59 students, 13 signed up for both logic and "The Gothic Novel in Malibu"; 40 signed up for exactly one course, 21 signed up for logic. How many signed up for "The Gothic Novel in Malibu"?

2. You are thinking of running for the city council. You are especially cynical and have no firmly held opinions, and so you have decided to take positions on the three major issues that will give you the greatest advantage during the election. You make the reasonable assumption that voters who agree with you on at least two of the three issues will vote for you. The three issues are

(1) Should the city turn the high school into a mall?

(2) Should the city sell the mineral rights to downtown?

(3) Should there be term limits for meter maids?

A Venn diagram is helpful for classifying the voters:

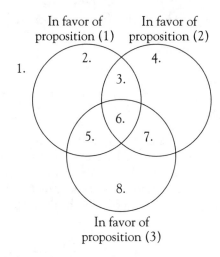

In favor of   In favor of
proposition (1)   proposition (2)

In favor of
proposition (3)

a. If you oppose proposition (1) and support (2) and (3), voters in which regions of the diagram will support you?

b. If you support proposition (2) and oppose (1) and (3), voters in which regions of the diagram will support you?

c. How many different combinations of positions are there?

d. Polls show that 46% favor proposition (1), 54% favor proposition (2), and 55% favor proposition (3). We also know that 22% favor both (1) and (2), 13% favor both (2) and (3), and 24% favor both (1) and (3). Finally, just 1% favor all three. What percentage of the population fall into each of the eight regions?

e. What positions should you take to maximize your vote?

3. In 1991, it rained on 57 days and snowed on 14 days, and the sun came out at least once on 280 days. There was no precipitation on 301 days. Whenever it snowed, the sun failed to come out, and there were only 3 days of both rain and sun. Use a Venn diagram such as the one in exercise 2 to answer the questions.

a. How many dry, sunny days were there?

b. How many dry, cloudy days were there?

c. On how many days was there rain or snow but no sun?

    d. On how many days was there just rain?

    e. How often was there both rain and snow?

    f. On how many days was there just snow?

4. The same weather statistics were true in 1992. What change did that make?

5. Can you draw circles (or any other shape) to show four sets with all possibilities represented?

logic circuits

> I had a feeling once about mathematics—that I saw it all, Depth beyond Depth was revealed to me—the Byss and the Abyss. I saw as one might see the transit of Venus or even the Lord Mayor's show—a quantity passing through infinity and changing its sign from plus to minus. I saw exactly how it happened and why the tergiversation was inevitable—but it was after dinner and I let it go.
>
> —WINSTON CHURCHILL

Communication inside a digital computer takes the form of streams of impulses. These impulses are of two kinds, which we can call yes and no, or true and false. Usually they are represented as 1 and 0.

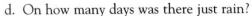

11010110

These streams are manipulated when they pass through *gates*. For example, the *not* gate

11010110

takes a stream and changes all the 0s to 1s and all the 1s to 0s:

00101001

There are several gates that take two input streams and produce one output stream. The *or* gate

162

is one. Whenever two streams enter, it checks to see if either one is a 1. If so, then it outputs a 1; otherwise, it outputs a 0.

Before

    101001
    110101

After

                                                        111101

Another is the *and* gate.

This outputs a 1 if and only if both streams have a 1:

Before

    101001
    110101

After

                                                        100001

At this point, you may see the connection to Sentential. The *or* gate, for example, has its own "truth table":

Input 1	Input 2	*or* Gate Output
1	1	1
1	0	1
0	1	1
0	0	0

which looks exactly like the truth table for the connective ∨.

We don't need a gate to correspond to ⇒ because we can construct a circuit that will have the same effect. Recall that $\neg P \vee Q$ and $P \Rightarrow Q$ have the same truth tables. We can then use a *not* and an *or* gate to create a *conditional* gate:

163

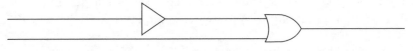

These gates are the computational heart of a computer. Theoretically, any machine or organism with these gates and with some sort of accessible memory can compute!

EXERCISES

1. What comes out of the following circuits when the streams 101001 and 110101 enter? How would you describe the action of the circuits in terms of our logical connectives?

   a.

   b.

   c.

   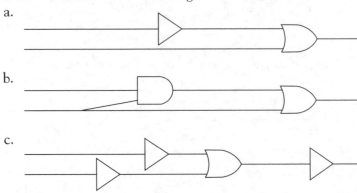

2. Design a circuit from *and*, *or*, and *not* gates that functions as a biconditional gate.

3. Design a circuit for two input streams and a single output stream that sends out a 1 if and only if two 0s enter.

Bertrand the First

He thought he saw an Argument
  That proved he was the Pope:
He looked again, and found it was
  A Bar of Mottled Soap.
  —LEWIS CARROLL, *SYLVIE AND BRUNO*

Bertrand Russell was one of the most influential philosophers and mathematicians of this century. His fame rests on his many contributions, essays, books, and his monumental work with Alfred North

Whitehead, *Principia Mathematica*. If he had done none of this, however, he would live forever for a small piece of conversation at a dinner.

The story is that Russell was dining with a group of people and discussing the principles of logic. He explained that from a contradictory proposition one can prove anything. One member of the party thought this was outrageous. He challenged the idea but said he would be convinced if Russell could take the proposition "$0 = 1$" and then prove that he, Russell, was the Pope.

Russell considered this briefly, and then said something like, "If $0 = 1$, then by adding 1 to both sides, we have $1 = 2$. I and the Pope are two, therefore I and the Pope are one."

---

informal logic

criticizing arguments

"Are they in the prisoner's handwriting?" asked another of the jurymen.

"No they're not," said the White Rabbit, "and that's the queerest thing about it." (The jury all looked puzzled.)

"He must have imitated somebody else's hand," said the King. (The jury all brightened up again.)

"Please your Majesty," said the Knave: "I didn't write it, and they can't prove I did: there's no name signed at the end."

"If you didn't sign it," said the King, "that only makes the matter worse. You must have meant some mischief, or else you'd have signed your name like an honest man."

—LEWIS CARROLL, *ALICE'S ADVENTURES IN WONDERLAND*

Criticizing arguments is essential. If they are arguments whose conclusions we disagree with, we must study them to expose their deficiencies. If the arguments are our own, we must learn about their weaknesses so that we can strengthen them. Most important, if we are actually seeking *truth*, then we want to deal only with arguments that are genuinely solid.

There are two basic reasons that arguments can be weak. The first is the premises. The logic of an argument can be impeccable, but the argument is worthless if the assumptions are wrong. From $0 = 1$, Russell argued with perfect logic that he was the Pope.

The second source is the structure of support or the inferences. We have seen how a statement may support another in a very weak manner. If the support requires other statements, and these in turn are doubtful, then the whole argument is flawed.

EXAMPLE

[a] The man who signs a petition against higher taxes reveals a "meanness he would otherwise blush at."

[b] Taxes are needed to protect the aged and the infant and to give liberty a land to live in.

[c] The people of America are not a poor people, why should they appear so? [d] We hurt our credit, our honor, our reputation in the world, by proclaiming ourselves what we are not.

—Thomas Paine, quoted in a letter to the *Boston Globe*, August 13, 1990

Are we being stingy when we vote against higher taxes? Perhaps, but not necessarily. It depends on the immediate situation. Certainly those who do oppose tax increases don't think so. They might argue that the money could be raised by making government more efficient. We are certainly not poor now, whether or not we were in Paine's time. Do we hurt our credit by not raising taxes? Possibly and possibly not. Altogether, this is not a strong argument. As we mentioned before, there is nothing to support *raising* taxes, although taxes themselves are supported.

EXAMPLE

[a] When is George Bush going to wake up? [b] It's about time the phrase national security was understood in terms every American can viscerally understand.

[c] Ask yourself what would make you, as an American, feel more secure—one more Stealth bomber, or the money to build that bomber used instead to take 5,000 violent addicts off the streets and give them the treatment that so many are desperately waiting for?

[d] Our national psyche is permeated with a fear of drug-, race- or economically induced street crime. [e] We as a nation could speak to the world community with a more assured, credible voice for peaceful change, if our national resolve weren't being sapped by the debilitating diseases from within our own communities.

[f] It is time for a dramatic shift in national priorities. [g] If George Bush truly believes Americans are the most productive workers in the world, he would not be frightened to make meaningful cuts in defense spending. [h] Surely a motivated work force could whip us back into fighting shape in short order.

[i] It's so exhilarating, but also saddening, to see the rest of the world taking on reality by the horns, while Bush has to be dragged, kicking and screaming into the 1990s.

—Letter to the *Boston Globe*, February 19, 1990

There are several weak points in this argument. The weakest may be the assertion that our productivity would save us in the event of a military challenge (premise h). This is actually what the whole argument is about. What do we require to be secure?

Another weak point is the question of how insecure our domestic troubles leave us. Some might contend that premise e is false. Still others might question premise d.

EXERCISES

1. Criticize the arguments in the exercise in "Relevance" in part 3.

2. Criticize this argument.

    [a] At the present time it is now true that either you will get a good grade in logic or you will not. [b] If it is now true that you will get a good grade, then studying for logic is pointless. [c] That would be like yelling to the tide as it goes out, "Go out, Tide"— pointless, it doesn't help. [d] On the other hand, if it's now true that you will not get a good grade, studying for logic is fruitless. [e] That would be like yelling to the tide as it comes in, "Go out, Tide"—fruitless, can't work. [f] Hence, studying for logic is either pointless or fruitless. [g] But the rational woman does

not do what is pointless or fruitless. [h] So the rational woman does not study logic.

3. Criticize this argument.

[a] The federal government should legalize all recreational drugs and sell them in government-run stores. [b] In the first place, drug use is rampant in this country and no attempt to restrict it has been successful. [c] By selling in state-run stores, the government will be able to put some curbs on use. [d] Moreover, the government could continue an educational campaign warning of the harmful effects of drugs. [e] And although drug use is harmful, people do many things that are harmful and we as a nation support their right to do harmful things. [f] In the second place, legalizing drugs and selling them would be an economic boon. [g] Vast sums of money now siphoned out of the country would stay in. [h] Many jobs would be created by manufacturing and distributing drugs. [i] The increased revenues would do much to reduce the national debt. [j] Finally, police departments across the country would be freed from the fruitless task of trying to interdict drugs. [k] They would be able to provide much better services to the people.

4. In *Ruddigore* (see "Paradox and W. S. Gilbert" in part 2), Robin begins committing his crimes, but his dead ancestors are unimpressed by his efforts:

Sir Roderick: Wednesday?

Robin (*melodramatically*): On Wednesday I forged a will.

Sir Roderick: Whose will?

Robin: My own.

Sir Roderick: My good sir, you can't forge your own will!

Robin: Can't I though! I like that! I *did!* Besides, if a man can't forge his own will, whose will can he forge?

Criticize this argument.

5. Criticize the argument in the quotation at the beginning of this section.

writing arguments

Reading maketh a full man; conference a ready man; and writing an exact man.

—Francis Bacon

Writing is extremely difficult. Our thoughts are complex; how can we convey them to someone else, with only words to help us?

Actually, words are extremely powerful, and that is part of the problem. Employed indiscriminately, they can be a danger to the user and anyone in the way.

Writing arguments presents special challenges, and while there is nothing easy about the task, some of the difficulties can be eased by the tools we have been studying.

Perhaps the most common mistake to make is to start without really understanding our own argument. If we are not clear about its structure, we can hardly expect the reader to be. To make the structure evident, we recommend diagramming it.

Suppose we wish to argue that [a] taxes should be raised.

What are our reasons? Well, for one thing, [b] our schools are in terrible shape, and we need to spend more on them. For another, [c] the state is in the midst of a giant budget crisis; we have a deficit of half a billion dollars. Anyhow, [d] we haven't had a tax increase in eight years.

How do we diagram this? The idea is to represent each statement by a letter:

$$b \qquad\qquad d$$

$$a \qquad\qquad c$$

Now draw arrows between them to indicate support:

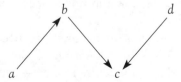

When two or more statements work together to support another, the arrows should be joined.

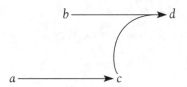

In the case of our present argument, the diagram might look like this:

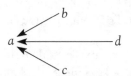

Now we attempt to write it.

EXAMPLE

[a] Let's raise taxes. [b] Our schools are in terrible shape. They need lots of money to get fixed up. Also, [c] the state is in debt. We have to raise an additional $500 million to pay what we owe. You shouldn't complain about it, because [d] taxes haven't been raised in eight years.

Not so good. It doesn't read very well and sounds sort of aimless. This is due in part to some clumsy wording, but in addition, we are putting too many ideas into a single paragraph. If we look again at the diagram, we see three reasons for our tax proposal. They are not closely related, so perhaps they should each have a paragraph of their own.

EXAMPLE

[a] We need to raise taxes. No one wants to pay more and no legislator wants to ask more, but we have no real choice. To be perfectly blunt, our state has obligations that must be honored. [c] We are now running a deficit of half a billion dollars. The debt must be paid.

If further reasons were required, we need only look at education. [b] Across the state our schools are in terrible shape. The problem will require money—quite a bit of it.

I can understand the reluctance of the citizens of this commonwealth to an increase, but it should be pointed out that [d] this is the first in eight years. That's not a bad record.

This is better. Notice that the diagram is exactly the same. The additional sentences are added to make the argument "user friendly"; they add nothing to the logical structure of the argument.

Now let us imagine an opponent examining the argument and looking for its weak points. What would she find?

Let us assume that we have our facts straight and [c] and [d] are not in dispute. The premises [a] and [b], however, could be matters of opinion. They might be weak points. In that case, we could improve our argument by adding detail to the second paragraph. Specifically, we could list areas where schools need money.

Related to this is the arrow from [b] to [a]; it could use additional support. We could include facts that show money is needed, not just better management. Further, we should show that the money we need is significantly more than what the state usually provides (otherwise education would not be a reason for raising taxes).

What about the support of [c] for [a]? Can that be attacked? Perhaps, if other parts of the state budget could be reduced instead of raising taxes. If, in fact, there is a lot of waste in the government or a few large inefficient programs, then perhaps we don't need to raise taxes and perhaps we should forget about writing this argument! If, on the other hand, every effort has already been made to trim the budget, then evidence of this fact belongs in the first paragraph to help the argument.

Finally, what about the support of [d] for [a]? If you think about it, you should see that it doesn't really support [a] at all. Statement [d] makes it look as if we are raising taxes out of boredom. The argument is useful only if someone has already complained about the frequency of tax increases. Since it contributes nothing, [d] should be deleted.

EXAMPLE

[a] We need to raise taxes. The facts are clear and well known. [b] The state is in debt now to the tune of $500 million, and [e] a year of budget trimming, belt tightening, and creative bookkeeping has failed to take care of it. [f] The Roxie Report, the considered judgment of a bipartisan committee that worked three months on the problem, is that an increase of 5% to the state income tax is both adequate and necessary.

If further reasons are required, we need only look at education. [c] For some years now, our schools have been deteriorating as [g] state support is frozen at 1980 levels. [h] A recent estimate puts the number of leaky roofs at 357. [i] Our president has recently set ambitious educational goals for the nation, goals that require effort above and beyond what is needed to repair a neglected system. A tax increase is a chance for us to raise the necessary revenue for our state school system.

This is much improved. The diagram now looks like this:

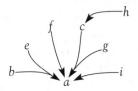

The argument could be made even tighter. We could continue the process, taking the new premises and arrows and examining them for weaknesses.

In general, it always helps to look at things from the other side. Another point of view can help you refine your reasoning. Also, you may discover you are wrong!

EXERCISES

1. Write arguments on the following questions. If you can, write arguments on both sides.
   a. Should capital punishment be abolished?
   b. Should students be "tracked" in high school, that is, placed in separate classes according to ability?
   c. Should women be allowed combat roles in the military?
   d. Should colleges have "distribution requirements" for graduation?
   e. Should drugs be legalized?
   f. Should public schools be federally funded?
   g. Should the national dish be turkey or pizza?
   h. Should the winner of the so-called World Series play the best baseball team in Japan for the world championship?
   i. Should surrogate motherhood (bearing children for a fee) be prohibited?
   j. Should grades be abolished?
2. Choose a topic of current debate in the newspaper and write a letter to the editor on the subject. Send it in!

a good paragraph

As for logic, it's in the eye of the logician.
—GLORIA STEINEM

Many things go into writing a good paragraph, but most analysts point to **unity** and **coherence** as the most important. The central problem is that reading is hard, and reading arguments is even harder. Anything you can do to help the reader is appreciated. In logic, we are interested in paragraphs that argue a point. This is a special sort of paragraph, and its special nature helps us by narrowing our choices.

"A paragraph is *unified* when all of its sentences answer questions generated by the paragraph's first sentence," writes Kenneth A. Bruffee in *A Short Course in Writing*. A very reasonable way to satisfy this in an argument is to put the conclusion in the first sentence (and have only one conclusion).

EXAMPLE

You should take calculus. You know your parents expect you to go to medical school and become a doctor. A semester of college mathematics is an important part of the premed curriculum. Philosophy isn't important. Later, when you have a private practice you can read metaphysics, and when you are retired you can read ethics.

A second method is for the first sentence to pose the question that your conclusion answers.

EXAMPLE

What's your fourth course going to be? You're already taking two science courses and a history course, so perhaps something in the humanities would be good for balance. You told me last semester you were interested in intellectual history—you should take philosophy.

"A paragraph is *coherent* when every sentence in it answers a question generated by the sentence (or sentences) that immediately precedes it," writes Bruffee. Coherence means essentially that a diagram of the paragraph is not too messy. A diagram such as this

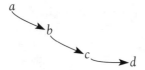

might represent a very natural paragraph, with each sentence leading to the next.

EXAMPLE

You should take vector calculus. You are planning to be a civil engineer. The most sensible major for that is physics. One of the required courses for the physics major is electricity and magnetism. Vector calculus is a prerequisite for electricity and magnetism.

A diagram such as this

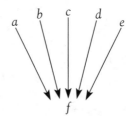

would be trickier, but still possible, if the connections were easy to get across.

EXAMPLE

What? You haven't decided yet? You *have* to take Brit lit! Everybody in the suite is taking it! It meets only two hours a week! There's no final! The term paper is limited to three pages, 1500 words, and 2000 syllables! Lancelot Tweedy is the professor!

The following diagram, however, is too complex for one paragraph:

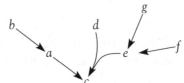

Consider the difficulties: You must make at least six statements. You have to show the arrows; that is, the purpose of each statement must be clear from your paragraph. On top of this, the reader should be led through the diagram in a logical way.

To make it simple, your first sentence could declare [c]. You might then say one reason is [a], and that follows from [b]. Now, you have to redirect the reader from this line and introduce another. If you follow with [f] and [g], you have moved quite a way from [a], [b], and [c]. You can't do [d] or [e] alone; you have to do them together. Once you have done that, you have to take on [f] and [g] in such a way that they apply to [e] and not [d].

Of course, this *can* be done, but at great cost to the reader. It would be much better to split this argument into several paragraphs.

Note that in analyzing arguments, we did not suggest diagramming them, although this is sometimes a good idea. The reason is that diagramming is very hard, and it is especially hard when the argument is not well written.

The point is that in a well-written paragraph, the structure is evident. The connections are clear. If you intend for [b] to support [c], then you have two obligations:

1. [b] really should support [c]
2. Your intention should be clear.

In other words, if the reader is trying to diagram your argument, the reader should be able to figure out that you are saying

and that you are justified in saying it.

EXERCISES

1. Consider the following argument.

   [a] Most workers in this state belong to a religion that considers Sunday a day of rest. [b] Most workers in this state are Christians. [c] It should be illegal for stores to open on Sunday. [d] It would be absurd and difficult to require stores to close any day except Sunday. [e] The government should ensure that all stores close one day a week on the same day. [f] Workers need at least one day of rest each week. [g] Employers cannot be counted on to give employees a day of rest if the government doesn't insist on it.

The structure of this argument follows the complex diagram on page 174. Rewrite it in two or more paragraphs.

2. Turn to the editorial or op-ed page of a newspaper. Choose a column or letter to the editor. Is the structure of the argument evident? Can you diagram it?

3. Repeat exercise 2.

4. Repeat exercise 3.

5. Choose a topic and write a letter to the editor. Send it in!

Cathy goes to war

In Italy for thirty years under the Borgias they had warfare, terror, murder, bloodshed, but they produced Michelangelo, Leonardo da Vinci and the Renaissance. In Switzerland, they had brotherly love, they had five hundred years of democracy and peace. And what did they produce? The cuckoo-clock.

—Orson Welles

Here is Cathy again, in a holiday mood.

Somebody was playing Christmas carols. It was an evening in December, and most of the first-year students were decorating a tree, when Maud breezed in.

"Hey!" she said. "Peace on earth!"

Cathy, who had been scowling in the corner for the past twenty minutes, snorted. "Baloney! Veggie baloney! Peace is the pits! Peace is stagnation. Peace is boring. In peace, the problems of the world only get worse." Cathy grinned as everyone looked at her in astonishment. "War may be hell, but it's progress. In war, the economy booms because everybody is working to make weapons and feed the troops. War forces important advances in science and technology. War inspires great music, art, and literature. In war, things get done!"

"But people die!" began Jennifer, who hadn't seen her family in three months and was beginning to wonder if an Eastern liberal arts college was a mistake.

"Yeah, and another problem with peace is overpopulation," Cathy continued. "Look, when we build a monument to somebody, that means that person is a hero, right? Well, we don't build monuments to peacemakers, so they're bums!"

EXERCISES

1. Write a rebuttal to Cathy.

2. Write Cathy's rebuttal of your rebuttal.

curiosities & puzzles

The Digestor's Digest

Vol. I, No. 1	Page 3

In Taste Tests

The latest laboratory tests show that the ever-popular Choco-lumps is the best-tasting cereal of all!

In Taste Tests

The latest laboratory tests show that Chem-treats is *not* the best-tasting cereal. Chem treats did, however, place second behind Flaky Corns. Actually, it placed third behind Flaky Corns and Tastiturf.

exam warning III

Since the last exam warning, we have had more mail. We are certainly pleased with the response! One reader has sent us a most intriguing letter, and we thought we would share it with you:

Dear Tom and Jim:

I just read "Exam Warning II" containing the letter from Lora Logic. It seems to me that her reasoning can go further. Can't you argue that it is impossible for the exam to be on the next-to-last page? I mean, suppose we get to the next-to-next-to-last page and there is still no exam. Then, because we now know that the exam can't be on the last page (Lora's argument), we know it must be on the only other page left, the next-to-last page. Again, this would be impossible, since we can't know the page ahead of time.

I think I'm right about this.

By the way, this book is absolutely the stup. . . . Just chill out, O.K.?

Teresa Truthtable

Well, Teresa, you are really on the ball. Maybe we don't have quite as much room as we thought we did to pull off our surprise. Nevertheless, we are confident about our Surprise Examination!

And thank you, Teresa, for your thought-provoking comments.

the family reunion

There is a popular sort of puzzle known as a logic puzzle. Generally, you are given a number of categories and a number of items in each category that have to be matched to each other. You are given a series of clues to help.

We give you three such puzzles in this book. The first is given below. The diagram on the next page is to help with the bookkeeping. You shouldn't have much trouble with this one; the other two are more difficult.

You belong to a large family—so large that you have trouble keeping the family members straight. To be honest, you don't care much for some of them and the rest don't care much for you. The problem is, there is going to be a family reunion next week and you want to avoid trouble.

Your mother tells you that among the guests are Edgar, Edwin, Eduardo, Edsel, and "Crazy" Eddie. You are not eager to see any of these specimens. One, for example, didn't invite you to his wedding. You don't recall which of them it was, however, except that it wasn't your nephew.

Another tried to borrow $1000 from you last year. Yet another is a cousin or stepcousin you haven't met but who is always being favorably compared to you. He is at Harvard and seems to get all A's.

Then there is somebody, either Edwin or Edsel, who is mad at you because you got him mixed up with Edsel or Edwin. Also, there is the one you disapprove of because he's living with this ex-nun (you aren't Catholic—you aren't even very religious—but you *are* something of a snob and kind of intolerant as well).

Altogether, there is a nephew, an uncle, a cousin, a stepcousin, and then someone whose relation to you no one wants to discuss. This is the one, in fact, who tried to borrow the money.

Edwin, you now recall, is somebody you dislike, which means that he's either the one who didn't invite you to his wedding or the one at Harvard.

The stepcousin is either Edgar or Edsel. Crazy Eddie, however, is your uncle, and Eduardo is your nephew.

Who are the others, and how do you feel about them?

The Family Reunion Worksheet

	wedding	$1000	Harvard	mixed-up	ex-nun	nephew	uncle	cousin	stepcousin	?
Edgar										
Edwin										
Eduardo										
Edsel										
Crazy Eddie										
nephew										
uncle										
cousin										
stepcousin										
?										

Name	Relation	Ugly Incident
Edgar		
Edwin		
Eduardo		
Edsel		
Crazy Eddie		

punk logic

Laura Logic, 1979

PREDICATES, PROGRAMS, AND ANTIQUE LOGIC

GOAL: To master the technical apparatus of predicate logic (also known as quantification theory or first-order logic). This branch of logic covers the quantifiers ∀ and ∃ and the identity relation = and their interrelations with the Sentential connectives.

We begin with a set of formal languages for symbolizing the logical forms, then we show how to interpret the quantifiers and the rest of the languages by what are called "structures" or "interpretations." This gives rise to precise definitions of validity, consistency and other basic logical notions. Finally we summarize the basic laws of predicate logic and some basic techniques for formalization. Lots of questions will remain, but if you press on understanding will come.

The overall structure of predicate logic is very much like the overall structure of statement logic—this is what we want you to see now. But predicate logic is more complex. Fortunately, the complexity pays off —predicate logic is much more powerful than statement logic.

FORMAL LOGIC: PREDICATE LOGIC

PREDICATE LANGUAGES

I believe that I can best make the relation
of my ideography to ordinary language clear
if I compare it to that which the microscope has to the eye.'
—GOTTLOB FREGE, *BEGRIFFSSCHRIFT*

Predicate languages are a kind of formal language. Like Sentential, the language of statement logic, they are devices for generating logical forms. One difference between predicate languages and the language of statement logic is that there are many predicate languages. Although all predicate languages contain a common core, their vocabularies can vary.

The common core of any predicate language includes

Vocabulary
Connectives (truth-functional): ¬, &, ∨, ⇒, ⇔
(Individual) Variables: $x, y, z, x_1, y_1, \ldots$
Quantifiers: ∀, ∃
Parentheses: ( )

Every predicate language must contain at least one predicate letter. In this book, we will consider only predicate languages that contain identity. When a predicate language includes the special identity predicate $=xy$ (usually written $x = y$), it is called a *predicate language with identity*.

The vocabulary, which can vary from language to language, includes

Predicate letters: $F, G, H, \ldots$

where each predicate letter is associated with a fixed number of *places*. When F is associated with one place, we can write Fx (or Fy); when H is associated with two places, we write Hxy (or Hyz); when R is associated with three places, we write $Rxyz$. If we need to be explicit, we can indicate the number of places with a superscript; F^1 applies to one thing (F^1x); M^2 applies to two (M^2xy); and G^n applies to n things ($G^nx_1x_2 \cdots x_n$). (Note that the choice of capital letter is arbitrary here.) Sometimes we use parentheses to make predicates more readable, as in $M(xy)$.

Moreover, a predicate language can contain

Names (or **constants**): $a, b, c, a_1, \ldots$

Finally, for convenience in formulating certain rules, we include a special category:

Temporary names: $a^*, b^*, c^*, a_1^*, \ldots$

We can now describe how the formulas of predicate languages are put together.

Syntax of predicate languages
Terms: Any variable, name, or temporary name is a term. We will represent terms by such symbols as $t, s, t_1, s_1, t_2, \ldots$

Notice that, strictly speaking, the predicate language does not contain a symbol t, just variables (x, y, z), names (a, b, c), and temporary names (a^*, b^*, c^*). We shall use t as shorthand for any old variable or name.

Recall that wffs (well-formed formulas) pick out the grammatically acceptable strings of symbols. We now define predicate wffs precisely.

Atomic (or basic) formula: Any n-place predicate letter followed by n terms (not necessarily distinct) is an atomic wff (Fx, Fy, $Mxy, Maa, Rabc, \ldots$). (This is a major difference from the language Sentential. In Sentential, the atomic wffs had no structure.)

Formula (wff):
1. If A is an atomic wff, it is a wff.

2. If A and B are wffs, so are
    a. $\neg A$ b. $(A \, \& \, B)$ c. $(A \vee B)$
    d. $(A \Rightarrow B)$ e. $(A \Leftrightarrow B)$ f. $\forall x A$
    g. $\exists x A$ where x is any variable

In this definition, the quantifiers function as one-place connectives.

Notice that we introduced symbols like A, B, and C to talk about wffs. The symbol A can stand for any arbitrary wff. But strictly speaking, the predicate languages do not contain the symbols A, B, and so on; they contain specific wffs like $\forall x(x = x)$ or $(Fc \Rightarrow \exists xFx)$, which we represent by the symbols A, B, C, and so on.

EXERCISE 1   Which of the following are wffs, assuming that F and G are one-place predicate letters and R is a two-place predicate letter? (Parts e and g are trick questions. Pay attention to the strict definition of a wff.)

a. $\exists z Fz$ b. $\exists z Gxz$ c. $\exists x(Fx \Rightarrow Gx)$
d. $\forall \exists xy \neg Txy$ e. $\forall a Ga$ f. $\vee FxGy$
g. $\exists y Fa$ h. $\forall x \exists y(\exists xRxy \Rightarrow \neg Ryx)$
i. $\forall z(Rxz \Leftrightarrow (\exists xRx \, \& \, Ga))$

We have defined wff or well-formed formula for any first-order language. A crucial feature of wffs is that each arises in only one way from the atomic wffs. The structure of the wffs is determined by the parentheses. The structure is also determined by the syntactic tree of the wff, which is just a way of mirroring the wff's construction.

EXAMPLE

$$\forall z \, (Rxz \Leftrightarrow \exists y(\exists xRxz \vee \neg Rzy))$$
$$|$$
$$(Rxz \Leftrightarrow \exists y(\exists xRxz \vee \neg Rzy))$$
$$\diagup \diagdown$$
$$Rxz \qquad \exists y(\exists xRxz \vee \neg Rzy)$$
$$|$$
$$(\exists xRxz \vee \neg Rzy)$$
$$\diagup \diagdown$$
$$\exists xRxz \qquad \neg Rxy$$
$$| \qquad\qquad |$$
$$Rxz \qquad\quad Rxy$$

186

Let's add a few more technical concepts.

Scope of Quantifiers

The **scope** of a quantifier in a wff is the smallest wff following the occurrence of that quantifier in that wff.

EXAMPLE

wff:	$\forall x Fx$	$\forall x Fx \,\&\, Gx$	$\forall z(Fz \,\&\, Gz)$	$\exists y(\forall x Fx \lor Gxy)$
Scope:	Fx	Fx	$(Fz \,\&\, Gz)$	$(\forall x Fx \lor Gxy)$
				Fx

Thus the scope of a quantifier is defined exactly as the scope of a negation symbol. As we did with negation, we can define the scope of a quantifier in terms of syntactic trees: The scope of a quantifier is the wff under the last occurrence of that quantifier on the tree.

EXERCISE 2   **Underline the scopes of the quantifiers in the following wffs:**

a. $(\exists w Fw \lor \exists w Fw)$ b. $\exists w(Fw \lor Fw)$ c. $Rya \,\&\, \forall y Gy$

d. $\forall y(Ryz \,\&\, Gy)$ e. $\forall x \forall y((Rxy \,\&\, Fz) \Rightarrow \exists z Rxz)$

A quantifier binds the variable with it and all *like* variables in its scope. ($\forall z$ can bind only the variable z, not x or y.). When (an occurrence of) a variable is *bound* by a quantifier, we say that the occurrence is **bound.** A variable in a wff that is *not bound* by a quantifier is **free.** (All variables start out free in atomic wffs. They get bound only if a quantifier with that variable subsumes them in its scope).

Free variables are just like placeholders. They mark a spot in a predicate where a subject term may be substituted. Bound variables are very different. Bound variables relate a spot to a quantifier, be it $\exists$ or $\forall$. Some logicians use different notations for bound and free (occurrences of) variables.

In the following, the free variables are underlined:

$$R\underline{x}a \lor \exists x Fx \qquad \forall w \forall z((Rwz \,\&\, F\underline{u}) \Rightarrow \exists u Rwu)$$

Note that if the second wff is changed slightly, there is another free variable:

187

$$\forall w \forall z (Rwz \ \& \ F\underline{u}) \Rightarrow \exists u R\underline{w}u$$

A wff with no free variables is **closed.** Closed wffs represent ordinary statements that are true or false. A wff with free variables is **open.** Open wffs represent complex predicates that can be true of things or false of things. For example, under one interpretation, the wff *Mxb* & *Fx* represents the predicate "wife of Jim Henle." The number of free variables in an open wff indicates the number of places in the complex predicate; for example, *Mxb* & *Fx* is a one-place predicate, since only the variable *x* occurs (though it occurs twice).

EXERCISE 3   Which of the following wffs are open and which are closed? For any open wffs, indicate which variables are free.

   a. $\exists y Fy \lor Gy$ b. $\forall y(Fy \lor Gy)$
   c. $\exists w \forall z(\exists y(Fy \ \& \ Rxy) \Rightarrow Rzw)$ d. $\exists x \exists y(Rxyz \ \& \ Fz)$

Substitution

We substitute only for the free variables of a wff. When we express a law such as $\forall x Ax \Rightarrow At$, At is supposed to be the formula that you get by first dropping $\forall x$ from $\forall x Ax$ and then replacing all free x in Ax by t.

In substitution, we can substitute any term t *so long as* t *does not become bound in the substitution.* Hence we can substitute any constant for a variable and also substitute any variable that remains free. More precisely, given any wff Ax with x free, we may substitute t for x and get At as long as

• Incidentally, we can write *any* wff as *Ax* (or *Ay* or just *A*). Writing a variable after a wff is just a technique for drawing attention to a possible free variable in the wff. So one and the same wff can be indicated by *A*, or *Ax* or *Ay* or *Axy*.

1. we substitute t for *every* free occurrence of x.

2. t isn't a variable that gets bound in the substitution.

EXAMPLES
   If Ax is $Fx \lor Rxy$, then Ac is $Fc \lor Rcy$.
   If Ax is $\exists x Fx \lor Rxy$, then Ac is $\exists x Fx \lor Rcy$.
   If Ax is $\exists y \neg(x = y)$ then Az is $\exists y \neg(z = y)$.
   If Ax is $\exists y \neg(x = y)$ then Ay is just Ax.

In the last example, the substitution has no effect. The free x cannot be replaced by y in Ax since the y would become bound. To see the reason for this, ask yourself what $\exists y \neg (x = y)$ says (it expresses a trivial property relative to x that any object satisfies in a universe of two or more objects). Ask yourself what $\exists y \neg (y = y)$ says (it expresses a logical contradiction).

EXERCISE 4   Find the substitution instances for the following.
 1. t for free x in
    (a) Rxy (b) $(\forall x Rxy \Rightarrow Fx)$ (c) $x = x$
 2. t for free x and z for free y in
    (a) Rxy (b) $\exists y Rxy$ (c) $\exists z (y = z)$

SUMMARY: Predicate languages determine a precise class of formulas, or wffs (the logical forms expressible in predicate logic). As in statement logic, the structure of a wff is determined by its syntactic tree. The scope of quantifiers is particularly important, since the scopes of quantifiers determine which occurrences of variables are free and which are bound as well as defining the difference between open and closed wffs.

VARIATIONS ON THE THEME OF PREDICATE LANGUAGES

We are symbols, and inhabit symbols.
—RALPH WALDO EMERSON

The most obvious difference between various predicate languages is that they can contain different predicate symbols and names. We can consider a predicate language with just the predicates and names that appeared in part 1's "Kinship Logic." Alternatively, we can consider a predicate language with predicates and names that represent mathematical concepts, or we can consider a predicate language with enough predicates and names to (partially) represent American English as of 1994.

Of course, we can modify the basic definition of predicate languages just as we modified Sentential. For instance, we could eliminate some symbols, as we did in Sentential when we eliminated $\Rightarrow$ and $\Leftrightarrow$. This is especially easy when we can duplicate the effect of the missing symbols. Just as we could define $A \Rightarrow B$ as short for $\neg A \vee B$, we could eliminate $\exists$ and define $\exists x Ax$ as short for $\neg \forall x \neg Ax$. How do logicians decide which symbols to keep in the basic vocabulary and which to define? It is largely a matter of convenience. The point is this: By eliminating symbols, we shorten our formal definition of wff, but we lengthen the individual wffs we want to express. Thus a full-fledged predicate language, which has recursive clauses for $\Rightarrow$ and $\exists$, has as a wff $Fc \Rightarrow \exists x Fx$. In an abbreviated predicate language, we don't need clauses for $\Rightarrow$ and $\exists$ (these are introduced as shorthand), but by the same token, the actual formula abbreviated by $Fc \Rightarrow \exists x Fx$ is, in unabbreviated form, $\neg Fc \vee \neg \forall x \neg Fx$. As your grandmother told you, "six of one, half a dozen of the other."

Furthermore, we can modify a predicate language by adding any of the symbols we discussed earlier, such as $\Box$, $\Diamond$, N, P, or F.

Finally, there is a most important addition to predicate languages that we should discuss. We can add to our basic vocabulary the category of function symbols. A **function symbol** is a lowercase letter, like f, g, or h, which, like predicate letters, comes with a fixed number of places. A function symbol applied to a term gives a new term. Thus fa is some object determined by a, gab is an object determined by a and b. For example, "father of" is a function symbol in the language of human beings; "father of Tom" picks out a human being. So "father of x" is the general functional relation that, given any x, picks out x's father. We could represent this as fx. Similarly, hx might be a function symbol picking out the weight of x (perhaps this should be a two-place function symbol, hxt, indicating the weight of x at time t). We are all familiar with $+$, a two-place function symbol; for any two numbers x and y, $x + y$ assigns a new number, their sum.

Let us be more explicit before we become more precise. In a simple predicate language, we begin with basic predicate letters such as Fy or Hwz and then go on to construct complex predicates such as $\forall x(Fx \Rightarrow Hxz)$ (which is really of the form Az), or $Fy \,\&\, \exists x Hxy$ (for example, "is a wife"). Function letters allow us to achieve a similar effect for names. We can have basic names like c or d (as well as variables) in a simple predicate language. But in an expanded predicate language with function letters, we can have complex names like fc, hcx, or even $hc(fx)$.

In order to incorporate function symbols into our languages, we must revise the definition of term as follows:

Term

1. Any variable, name, or temporary name is a term.
2. If f^n is an n-place function symbol and $t_1, \ldots, t_n$ are any n terms, then $f^n t_1 t_2 \ldots t_n$ is also a term.

EXERCISE If f is a one-place function symbol and g a two-place function symbol, then which of the following are terms? (Parentheses are used just for convenience.)

a. *gff*   b. *gxy*

c. *gcd*   d. *fffc*

e. $f(gxy)$

The definition of wff remains as before.

Not surprisingly, function symbols are needed to represent functions and functions are needed for everything under the sun, from mathematics—$\sin(x) = z$—to physics—$velocity(x, t, c) = v$, which states that the velocity of body x at time t according to coordinate system c is v—to medicine—$temp(x, t) = n$ which states that the temperature of body x at time t is n degrees Fahrenheit.

Later in the book, we will discuss functions in more detail. Here, we merely point out that the definition of substitution in a formula should be slightly modified if functions are included. This is because function symbols contribute to complex terms. Recall our original definition of substitution: For any wff Ax with x free, we may substitute term t for x and get At as long as

1. we substitute t for *every* free occurrence of x.
2. t isn't a variable that gets bound in the substitution.

Now we must modify the second stipulation as follows:

2′. t doesn't contain a variable that gets bound in the substitution.

For instance, suppose fx is to be interpreted as "the father of x." Then, forgetting about Adam and Eve, it seems clear that everyone has a father, that is, $\forall x \exists y (fx = y)$. So this must hold for any individual, say x:

$$\exists y (fx = y)$$

Clearly we can substitute any constant for x:

$$\exists y (f \text{"Jim"} = y) \text{ (Jim has a father)}$$

and for most variables:

$$\exists y(fz = y) \text{ (} z \text{ has a father)}$$

But just as clearly, we could not substitute y for x:

$$\exists y(fy = y) \text{ (someone is his or her own father)}$$

The term t must not contain a variable that gets bound in the substitution.

We will say more about functions when we discuss their semantics (meaning) as opposed to discussing their syntax (grammar).

We conclude this section with two other variations important to linguists, cognitive scientists, and philosophers: restricted quantification and second-order quantification. We define **restricted quantifiers** as follows. If Fx is any one-place predicate, then $(\forall x : Fx)$ and $(\exists x : Fx)$ are restricted quantifiers. We modify the definition of wff by allowing that if A is any wff, so are

$$(\forall x : Fx)Ax \qquad \text{and} \qquad (\exists x : Fx)Ax$$

These are read, respectively, as "every F is A" and "some F is A." The simple difference between restricted quantifiers and unrestricted quantifiers is that unrestricted quantifiers are read without restriction: $\forall xAx$ is "everything is A" and $\exists xAx$ is "something is A."

Later, after we've assigned meanings to these formal symbols, we can compare restricted quantifiers to unrestricted quantifiers. The basic idea here is that restricted quantifiers build into the notation certain logical facts that must be made explicit with unrestricted quantifiers. Naturally, this will seem mysterious until you learn some logical facts about unrestricted quantifiers. But when you do, you'll discover that

"All F are G"	can be represented either with
$(\forall x : Fx)Gx$	restricted quantifiers or with
$\forall x(Fx \Rightarrow Gx)$	unrestricted quantifiers.

Similarly,

"Some F are G"	can be represented either with
$(\exists x : Fx)Gx$	restricted quantifiers or with
$\exists x(Fx \,\&\, Gx)$	unrestricted quantifiers.

Last, we will explain the phrase **first-order language.** We could modify our vocabulary by allowing variables for predicates; for example, letting Xa indicate an arbitrary unnamed property of a, and Yab indicate an arbitrary unnamed relation between a and b. (This reveals an important point: Ordinary predicate symbols like F and G are like names and *not* like individual variables.) If we had property variables, we could introduce quantifiers for property and relation variables. For example, $\exists X Xa$ could be read as "a has some property," and $\forall Y(Yab \Rightarrow Yba)$ could be read as "every relation that a bears to b, b bears to a."

Quantifying functions is much like quantifying predicates. $\exists f(fx = x + 1)$ says "There is a function that takes x onto $x + 1$." Adding property or function variables gives us **second-order quantifiers** and hence second-order languages. Philosophers and logicians debate whether the distinction between first- and second-order languages is very significant.

SUMMARY: Predicate languages differ according to which predicate symbols and names (and function symbols) they contain. Moreover, we can vary predicate languages by adding logical symbols (e.g., $(\forall x : Fx)$) or deleting them (e.g., defining $\exists x$ in terms of $\neg$ and $\forall x$).

FROM STATEMENT LOGIC TO PREDICATE LOGIC

You can only find truth with logic if you have already found truth without it.

—G. K. CHESTERTON

Statement logic is interesting, but it hardly suffices for the detailed applications of logic to philosophy, mathematics, or cognitive science. With regard to the potential applications of logic, statement logic is best regarded as a preview of predicate logic or quantification theory. By itself, statement logic only introduces logical form. It is the quantifiers ∀ and ∃ and the identity =, as well as predicates, that give us the full power of symbolic logic.

To deal with predicate logic, we need to know how to assess wffs and argument forms for validity. In the next section, we'll present a way to do this. Then we'll approach the concept of predicate validity from another direction.

But first, to bridge the gap between statement logic and predicate logic, let's consider the relation between the quantifiers and the truth functions (the Sentential connectives ¬, &, ∨, ⇒, and ⇔). If there were only a fixed, finite number of things that existed in any universe, then the method of truth tables could be extended to predicate logic. In that case, the quantifiers could be seen as abbreviations for truth functions; ∀ would be short for &, and ∃ would be short for ∨. It is worth explaining why this is so, even though there is not a fixed, finite number of things in our universe. If you remember the connections between ∀ and & and between ∃ and ∨, then you will be able to use your understanding of sentential logic to learn predicate logic.

For example, suppose that only three things exist and they are named a, b, and c. Then when we say *all* objects have property P, we would mean a has P *and* b has P *and* c has P. Similarly, when we say *some* object has property P, we would mean *either* a has P *or* b has P *or* c has P. More formally, for any wff Ax, we explain

$$\forall x Ax \qquad \text{as short for} \qquad Aa \ \& \ Ab \ \& \ Ac$$
$$\exists x Ax \qquad \text{as short for} \qquad Aa \lor Ab \lor Ac$$

If Aa also involves quantifiers, we can continue to expand it according to these rules. For example,

$$\forall z \exists w Rzw$$

("Everything (z) is such that it R's something") becomes first

$$\exists w Raw \ \& \ \exists w Rbw \ \& \ \exists w Rcw$$

("Something is such that a R's it and something is such that b R's it and something is such that c R's it"). This follows by the rule for expanding ∀ applied to $\forall z(\exists w Rzw)$.

194

Next, each conjunct is expanded by the rule for ∃ applied to ∃wRaw, ∃wRbw, and ∃wRcw, respectively, giving

$$(Raa \lor Rab \lor Rac) \mathrel{\&} (Rba \lor Rbb \lor Rbc) \mathrel{\&} (Rca \lor Rcb \lor Rcc)$$

CHALLENGE   Suppose the universe consists of only *a*, *b*, and *c*. Expand the given quantified formulas in terms of truth functions. If not already given, be sure to specify what each wff says before expanding. Doing so will help you check your expansion.

1. ∀z(Fz ∨Gz) and ∀zFz ∨ ∀zGz (These formulas say, respectively, "Everything is such that either it *F*'s or *G*'s" and "Either everything *F*'s or everything *G*'s." Are they equivalent, that is, does one imply the other? [Remember, *A* implies *B* if whenever *A* is true, *B* is. *A* is equivalent to *B* if each implies the other.])
2. ∃z(Fz ∨ Gz) and ∃zFz ∨ ∃zGz
3. ∀x¬Fx and ¬∀xFx
4. ∀x¬Fx and ¬∃xFx (These formulas say, respectively, "Everything doesn't *F* and "Not even one thing *F*'s.")
5. ∀x(Hx & Jx) and ∀xHx & ∀xJx
6. ∃x(Hx & Jx) and ∃xHx & ∃xJx
7. P ⇒ ∀xFx and ∀x(P ⇒ Fx) where *P* is just a statement letter. (The formulas say, respectively, If *P* then everything *F*'s" and "Everything is such that if *P*, then it *F*'s.")
8. ∃xFx ⇒ P and ∃x(Fx ⇒ P)
9. ∀x∀yRxy and ∀y∀xRxy
10. ∃x∃yRxy and ∃y∃xRxy (These formulas say, respectively, "Something *R*'s something" and "Something is *R*'d by something.")
11. ∀x∃yRxy and ∃y∀xRxy

Ultimately the method of truth tables does not directly extend to predicate logic. Some objects simply don't have names (not every atom or star does, for example). Moreover, there is no limit to the size of even finite domains. But most crucially, there are infinite domains, such as the collection of natural numbers 0, 1, 2, 3, . . . , *n*, *n* + 1, ... Truth tables do not extend to infinity:

$$F0 \mathrel{\&} F1 \mathrel{\&} F2 \mathrel{\&} \cdots \mathrel{\&} Fn \mathrel{\&} F(n + 1) \mathrel{\&} \cdots$$

is not a wff. Indeed, we might say that the quantifiers are just the way logicians deal with infinite collections.

But how do we deal with quantifiers if not by truth tables? One way is by the method of structures, which we discuss next.

SUMMARY: ∀ is like a giant & and ∃ is like a giant ∨. Remembering this will enable you to use your knowledge of truth-functional tautologies to guess (if not to know) the valid predicate wffs involving quantifiers.

INTERPRETING PREDICATE LOGIC BY STRUCTURES

"The name of the song is called 'Haddocks Eyes.'"

"Oh, that's the name of the song, is it?" Alice said, trying to feel interested.

"No, you don't understand," the Knight said, looking a little vexed. "That's what the name is called. The name really is 'The Aged Aged Man.'"

"Then I ought to have said 'That's what the song is called'?" Alice corrected herself.

"No, you oughtn't: that's quite another thing! The song is called 'Ways and Means': but that's only what it's called, you know!"

"Well, what is the song, then?" said Alice, who was by this time completely bewildered.

"I was coming to that," the Knight said. "The song really is 'A-sitting on a Gate': and the tune's my own invention."

—LEWIS CARROLL, *THROUGH THE LOOKING GLASS*

In Sentential, or statement logic, we introduced the concept of a truth table for a wff and showed how all the theoretical concepts of logic could be defined in terms of truth tables. Unfortunately, the method of truth tables does not extend to predicate logic. Although it seems intuitive that universal quantification $\forall x F x$ should represent a conjunction over the universe of discourse, $F c_1 \& F c_2 \& \cdots$, and that existential quantification $\exists x F x$ should represent an alternation, $F c_1 \vee F c_2 \vee \cdots$, the fact is that we would need infinitely long wffs to represent such conjunctions and alternations, and there simply aren't such wffs in our formal language.

Structures for Predicate Logic

In order to interpret predicate languages, we need a more powerful analogue of truth tables. The basis for the analogy consists of structures (or interpretations or models). *A structure for a predicate wff is like a line in a truth table for a Sentential wff.* The basic idea is that a structure for any predicate wff determines a truth value for that wff, just as a truth assignment for the sentence letters determines a truth value for a wff of Sentential.

With this idea we can develop a logical theory of predicate languages analogous to our logical theory of Sentential. In Sentential, we defined a valid wff as one that was true in all situations—its truth table always takes the value true. If structures matched lines in a truth table, then we could define a valid predicate wff as one true in all situations—one true in every structure—and similarly for the other logical notions.

It's easy to explain structures informally. A rigorous explanation was first given by the great Polish logician Alfred Tarski in the early 1930s. His explanation laid the foundation for that branch of logic known as model theory as well as initiating a torrent of philosophical commentary.

Let's try to explain exactly what a structure is and how it makes each closed wff true or false. A **structure** for a predicate language comprises

1. a (nonempty) universe or domain D of objects
2. an assignment to each name c of the language of a single object from the universe D (so we say c refers to that object)
3. an assignment to each one-place predicate letter F of the language of a property or set of objects in D (the property or set can be empty)
4. an assignment to each n-place predicate letter F^n of the language of an n-place relation or set of n-tuples of objects in D (the relation or set can be empty)

A structure is like a line in a truth table. Given a closed wff in a predicate language and a structure for that wff, the structure makes that wff true or makes it false (given any open wff and suitable number of objects from the domain, the structure makes that wff "true of"

• *Note:* Philosophical logicians often stress the converse of the "true of" relation. Instead of saying that a wff is true of an object, they say that the object *satisfies* the wff.)

or "false of" those objects.) Thus *a predicate wff is valid iff it is true in all structures, consistent iff it is true in some structure*, and so on. Moreover, given an open wff and a structure, the structure makes that wff *true of* any object in (the domain of) the structure or *false of* that object.

The precise explanation of how a structure assigns a unique truth value to any closed wff requires some sophisticated mathematics, but the intuitive idea is clear. The truth of a wff A in a structure is defined by induction on the syntactic tree of A. For atomic wffs like *Fc*, the clause is simply

> The structure makes *Fc* true iff the object that the structure assigns to *c* has the property that the structure assigns to *F*.

(That is, a structure makes "Snow is white" true iff what the structure makes "snow" refer to has the property that the structure assigns to "white.") Identity ($=$) is always interpreted as real identity: $c = d$ is true iff *c* is *d*.

For truth-functional compounds, structures follow the truth tables according to Tarski. Suppose the truth or falsity of A and B in a structure S has been defined. Then

CHALLENGE 1 Explain when S makes $A \lor B$ true and when it makes $A \Leftrightarrow B$ true.

S makes $\neg A$ true iff S does not make A true.
S makes A & B true iff S makes A true and S makes B true.
S makes $A \Rightarrow B$ true iff S makes A false or S makes B true.

CHALLENGE 2 Explain when S makes $\forall x A x$ true.

Lastly, for the quantifiers, we have

> S makes $\exists x A x$ true iff S makes Ax true of at least one object in the universe of discourse, that is, the property or set that S assigns to Ax is not equal to the null set.

Although the actual definition is more complicated, it is not much more edifying. Philosophers and logicians debate whether Tarski's work has great philosophical significance or is a mere technical trick.

EXAMPLES OF STRUCTURES   Consider a language with a name *c* and a predicate symbol *Lxy*.

Structure 1 (S1)
Domain: natural numbers 0, 1, 2, . . .
c refers to 0
Lxy is $x \leq y$ ("x is less than or equal to y" or "y is greater than or equal to x")

Structure 2 (S2)
Domain: natural numbers 0, 1, 2, . . .
c refers to 0
Lxy is $x \geq y$ ("x is greater than or equal to y" or "y is less than or equal to x")

Structure 3 (S3)
Domain: all negative numbers -1, -2, . . .
c refers to -1
Lxy is $x \geq y$

Structure 4 (S4)
Domain: all integers
c refers to 0
Lxy is $x \leq y$

EXAMPLE   Evaluate the wff $\forall z Lcz$ in each structure.
In S1, this becomes $\forall z(0 \leq z)$, or "Every natural number is greater than or equal to 0." This is true.
In S2, this becomes $\forall z(0 \geq z)$, or "Every natural number is less than or equal to 0." This is false.
In S3, this becomes $\forall z(-1 \geq z)$, or "Every negative number is less than or equal to -1." This is true.
In S4, this becomes $\forall z(0 \leq z)$, or "Every integer is greater than or equal to 0." This is false.

Notice how the range of the quantifier $\forall$ varies from domain to domain.

CHALLENGE 3
1. Evaluate the wff $\exists x(Lxc \,\&\, x \neq c)$ in each structure (we provide the answer for S1).

> In S1, this becomes $\exists x(x \leq 0 \,\&\, x \neq 0)$, or "Some natural number is less than or equal to 0 and not equal to 0." This is false.

2. Evaluate the wff $\forall yLyc \lor \forall yLcy$ in each structure.
3. Evaluate the wff $\forall y(Lyc \lor \neg Lyc)$ in each structure.
4. Evaluate the wff $\exists z\forall xLzx$ in each structure (we provide the answer for S3).

> In S3, this becomes $\exists z\forall x(z \geq x)$, or "There is some negative number that is greater than or equal to every negative number." This is true; -1 is the number.

Checking for Validity

It is much easier to show that a wff is *not* valid using the notion of structures than to show that it is valid. To show that a wff is not valid, all we have to do is to find one structure in which the wff is false.

EXAMPLE $(\exists xFx \,\&\, \exists xGx) \Rightarrow \exists x(Fx \,\&\, Gx)$

Let's see if we can interpret this to come out false. To make the conditional false, we need to make the premise true and the conclusion false. So we need an interpretation that makes $\exists xFx$ and $\exists xGx$ true but $\exists x(Fx \,\&\, Gx)$ false. Consider the following structure:

> Domain: human beings
> Fx is "x is male"
> Gx is "x is female"

Then $\exists xFx$ is true since there are males, and $\exists xGx$ is true since there are females. Therefore $\exists xFx \,\&\, \exists xGx$ is true. But $\exists x(Fx \,\&\, Gx)$ is not true since nothing is both male and female. Thus $(\exists xFx \,\&\, \exists xGx) \Rightarrow \exists x(Fx \,\&\, Gx)$ is false in a structure and so is not valid.

It is much trickier to show that a wff or argument form is valid since this means showing, in effect, that it is true in *all* structures. But it can be done if we attend to the meanings of the quantifiers.

EXAMPLE $\exists x(Fx \,\&\, Gx) \Rightarrow (\exists xFx \,\&\, \exists xGx)$

If a structure makes the left side false, it makes the whole conditional true. So let's consider any structure S that makes $\exists x(Fx \,\&\, Gx)$ true. Now, if S makes the conclusion true, S makes the conditional true, and so every structure will make the conditional true.

Since S makes $\exists x(Fx \,\&\, Gx)$ true, there is some object, say β, in the domain of S that satisfies $Fx \,\&\, Gx$; that is, $Fx \,\&\, Gx$ is true of β.

CHALLENGE 4   See if you can find another structure that makes $(\exists xFx \,\&\, \exists xGx) \Rightarrow \exists x(Fx \,\&\, Gx)$ false. Find a structure in which it is true. (Finding a structure that shows a wff *A* false is *exactly* like finding a structure that shows a wff $\neg A$ true. So you can show any wff is consistent by finding a structure that makes it true.)

Hence Fx is true of β and so is Gx. But if Fx is true of β, then we have $\exists xFx$ (i.e., if β has the property Fx, then *something* has the property). Similarly, Gx is true of β, and so $\exists xGx$. Thus if S makes $\exists x(Fx\ \&\ Gx)$ true, it makes $\exists xFx\ \&\ \exists xGx$ true.

Hence every structure satisfies $\exists x(Fx\ \&\ Gx) \Rightarrow (\exists xFx\ \&\ \exists xGx)$, and so it is valid.

So it is possible to reason about structures, but only in a rough-and-ready sort of way. If you know that $\forall xAx$ is true in a structure, then you know that Ax is true of each object in the domain of the structure (in particular, Ac is true for every name c). If Ax is true of each object in the domain, then $\forall xAx$ is true in that structure. Analogously, if $\exists xAx$ is true in a structure, then Ax is true of at least one object in the domain, whether or not that object has a name. And if some object in the domain has property Ax, then of course $\exists xAx$ (hence $At \Rightarrow \exists xAx$ must be valid for any term t).

If you want more precise formulations of the method for dealing with quantifiers, then you should look forward to the introduction and elimination rules in part 6. The precise rules are a bit complicated to state because we have to consider more than what's true or false in a structure; we also have to pay attention to how the *symbols* like free variables and temporary names interact with each other. But the rules are exact—no more rough-and-ready!

SUMMARY: We have defined structures and briefly explained how any structure for a wff makes the wff true or false if the wff is closed and makes the wff true of or false of any object in the structure if the wff is open.

LOGICAL THEORY FOR PREDICATE LOGIC

> Good too, Logic, of course, in itself, but not in fine weather.
> —ARTHUR HUGH CLOUGH

Structures are so defined that every structure that assigns an interpretation to the predicate symbols and names of a closed wff assigns a unique truth value to that wff (if the wff is open, the structure interprets it as a complex property). Thus the collection of structures determines the interesting logical properties of any wff. This enables us to give precise definitions for the logical properties we talked about in

• Notice, by the way, that these definitions aren't stated in any predicate language. That is, they aren't expressed by wffs. Instead, the definitions are expressed in English and say something about wffs. For this reason, we call English a "metalanguage" for predicate languages; it's the language we use to talk about predicate languages. If valid formulas express the laws of logic, the following definitions and remarks express the laws of metalogic.

"Logical Form" in part 2 (it would be advisable to reread that subsection now). Following are some of the most important definitions.

Let A be any closed wff. Then
A is **valid** iff every structure makes A true.
A is **consistent** iff at least one structure makes A true.
A is **inconsistent** (or **contradictory**) iff no structure makes A true.

Let Ax be any open wff. Then
A is **valid** iff every structure makes A true of every object in that structure.
A is **consistent** iff at least one structure makes A true of at least one object.
A is **inconsistent** (or **contradictory**) iff no structure makes A true of any object.

These categories divide up wffs the following way:

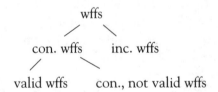

The valid wffs are like laws of logic. They can always be relied on, but they don't tell us much about the real world. Propositions whose forms are contradictions should be avoided—they can never be true. Most of our communication consists of wffs that are consistent but not valid. They can be true, and when they are, they give us information about the real world.

These definitions, and those following, should be memorized. You can get a better feel for the concepts involved and their interrelations by responding to Challenge 1. Answering the questions show what is often the case in studying logic—that we sharpen our reason by reasoning about logic as well as by reasoning in logic.

For example, we know that $B \vee A$ is valid whenever A is. The reason is that if A is valid, A is T in every structure. Since $B \vee A$ is T whenever A is T, $B \vee A$ is T in every structure. Thus $B \vee A$ is valid.)

CHALLENGE 1

1. If *A* is consistent, is *A* also valid?
2. If *A* is valid, is *A* also consistent?
3. If *A* is valid, what kind of wff is ¬*A*?
4. If *A* is not valid, can you say what kind of wf ¬*A* is?
5. If *A* is consistent, what can you say about ¬*A*?
6. If *A* is valid, explain why *B* ⇒ *A* is also valid.
7. If *A* is a contradiction, explain why *A* ⇒ *B* is valid.
8. If *A* is a tautology (valid according to the truth tables), then is *A* valid (true in all structures)? Can you explain?

More definitions:

Let A and B be any wffs. Then
A **implies** B iff whenever A is true in a structure, B is true in that structure
(or, if A and B are open, whenever A is true of an object in a structure, B is true of the object in that structure).
A is **equivalent** to B iff A and B are true in exactly the same structures
(or, if A and B are open, they are true of exactly the same objects in the same structures).

Implication is a crucial logical concept. A implies B when there is some logical connection between A and B. If you know A and know that A implies B, then you know B. We use implication to deduce far-flung conclusions of a premise or premises.

It is easy to see that equivalence is just two-way implication. If A is equivalent to B, then A and B are true in exactly the same structures. So if A is true in a structure, B is (hence A implies B) and if B is true in a structure, A is (hence B implies A).

Last definitions:

Let A, B, C, and D be any wffs. Then
A, B, and C **imply** D iff any structure that makes A, B, and C each true also makes D true.
A set of wffs is **mutually consistent** iff there is at least one structure that makes them all come out true.

CHALLENGE 2

1. Show that if *A* implies *B* and *B* implies *A*, then *A* is equivalent to *B*.
2. Show that *A* implies *B* iff the wff *A* ⇒ *B* is valid.
3. Show that *A* is equivalent to *B* iff the wff *A* ⇔ *B* is valid.

CHALLENGE 3

1. Show that the three wffs *A*, *B*, and *C* imply *D* iff the single wff (*A* & *B* & *C*) implies *D*.
2. Show that if *A*, *B*, and *C* imply a contradiction, they are not mutually consistent.

Valid wffs are the basic laws of predicate logic. They reveal the essential connections between the basic operations (negation, conjunction, etc.) and the quantifiers and identity. When a statement has the form of a valid wff, the statement will be true; indeed, it can't be false.

Valid wffs are also important because they include the implications and equivalences. Implications capture the valid principles of reasoning with the basic operations. *A* & *B* implies *A*. The wffs *A* and *A* ⇒ *B* together imply *B*. Equivalences are important not only because they are two-way implications but also because whenever *A* and *B* are equivalent, then one can be replaced by the other in any truth-functional context. For example, ¬¬*A* and *A* are equivalent, and one can replace the other. In general, if *A* and *B* are equivalent, then they both are true in exactly the same structures, and so both contribute the same thing to any wff in which they occur as parts.

Finally, consistency is important because when we make statements about the world, we intend to speak the truth. If we contradict ourselves, then regardless of what is really true, we must have told a falsehood. Inconsistent descriptions or theories cannot be true of anything.

SUMMARY: We have defined, for wffs of predicate languages, the concepts of validity, consistency, and inconsistency. We have defined two relations among wffs, implication and equivalence. All the definitions are given in terms of structures.

LOGICAL LAWS: BASIC VALID WFFS AND IMPLICATIONS

Logical consequences are the scarecrows of fools and the beacons of wise men.

—T. H. Huxley

In this section, we present a list of some of the more important valid formulas of predicate logic with identity. You should try to see the formulas as (almost) obvious, formulas whose validity is clear from the *intended meaning* of such words as "for all" ($\forall$), "there is" ($\exists$) "and" ($\&$), and so on. When in doubt, you can try to convince yourself of the validity of any wff by showing that it is true in every structure. We don't give such demonstrations now; instead we wait until "Deduction" in part 6.

Remember the Replacement Principle!

The replacement principle holds for predicate logic as well as statement logic. If A and B are equivalent wffs, W_A is a wff that contains A as a part, and W_B is like W_A except that one or more occurrences of A in W_A are replaced by B, then W_A is equivalent to W_B.

EXAMPLE $Fx \& Gx$ is equivalent to $Gx \& Fx$, and therefore $\exists x(Fx \& Gx)$ is equivalent to $\exists x(Gx \& Fx)$.

It should be intuitively clear that the replacement principle holds in predicate logic. Compare the procedures for determining whether W_A and W_B are true or false in a given structure. Now W_A and W_B are exactly alike except where A is replaced by B. But by assumption A and B are equivalent; that is, they are both true in exactly the same structures (or true of the same objects in the same structures). So determining the truth value for W_A using A will give exactly the same result as determining the truth value for W_B using B.

Elementary Principles

Where Wx is any formula and t is any term (similarly for any variable besides x):

> $\forall x Wx \Rightarrow Wt$ or what comes to the same thing $\forall x Wx \therefore Wt$
> "If everything W's, then t W's" or "If all are W, t is W"
> $Wt \Rightarrow \exists x Wx$ or what comes to the same thing $Wt \therefore \exists x Wx$
> "If t is W, then something is W"
> $Wt \Rightarrow \forall x Wx$ is *not* valid and generally false.

To understand the last principle, note that "If Madonna is a woman, then everybody is a woman" is false. Indeed, the predicate expression "If x is a woman, then everybody is a woman" has many false instances, for example, Madonna. (Curiously, the predicate expression has true instances, e.g., George Washington.) Similarly, $\exists x W x \Rightarrow W t$ is *not* valid and generally false.

Hence $\forall x W x \Rightarrow \exists x W x$ but not vice versa.

Quantifiers and Connectives

Let Wy and Sy be any wfs (we use y only for variety). Then

(Quantifier Exchange 1) $\neg\forall y W y \Leftrightarrow \exists y \neg W y$
"Not everything is W iff something is not W."

CHALLENGE 1
What does the latter conditional say in English? Find a structure in which $\neg\forall y W y \Rightarrow \forall y \neg W y$ is F.

By the way, $\forall y \neg W y \Rightarrow \neg\forall y \, W y$, but not vice versa.

Similarly (we'll now abbreviate "Quantifier Exchange" as QE)

(QE2) $\neg\exists y W y \Leftrightarrow \forall y \neg W y$
"Nothing is W iff everything is not W."

Moreover, $\neg\exists y W y \Rightarrow \exists y \neg W y$, but not vice versa. Hence,

$$\forall y W y \Leftrightarrow \neg\exists y \neg W y \quad \text{and} \quad \exists y W y \Leftrightarrow \neg\forall y \neg W y$$

To understand this last equivalence, note that $\neg\forall y W y \Leftrightarrow \exists y \neg W y$ by QE1, so by the inference that $A \Leftrightarrow B$ implies $\neg A \Leftrightarrow \neg B$, we have

$$\neg\neg\forall y W y \Leftrightarrow \neg\exists y \neg W y.$$

CHALLENGE 2
Show that $\exists y W y \Leftrightarrow \neg\forall y \neg W y$ follows from the law $\neg\exists y W y \Leftrightarrow \forall y \neg W y$.

But since $\neg\neg\forall y W y$ is equivalent to $\forall y W y$ by the replacement principle, the last statement is equivalent to

$$\forall y W y \Leftrightarrow \neg\exists y \neg W y$$

Observe that we have just seen how to define either of the quantifiers in terms of the other and negation.

The quantifiers interact with the other connectives as follows:

$(\forall y W y \,\&\, \forall y S y) \Leftrightarrow \forall y (W y \,\&\, S y)$
"Both everything is W and everything is S iff everything is both W and S"

$$\exists y(Wy \ \& \ Sy) \Rightarrow (\exists yWy \ \& \ \exists ySy) \qquad \text{but not}$$
$$(\exists yWy \ \& \ \exists ySy) \Rightarrow \exists y(Wy \ \& \ Sy)$$
$$(\forall yWy \lor \forall ySy) \Rightarrow \forall y(Wy \lor Sy) \qquad \text{but not}$$
$$\forall y(Wy \lor Sy) \Rightarrow (\forall yWy \lor \forall ySy)$$
$$(\exists yWy \lor \exists ySy) \Leftrightarrow \exists y(Wy \lor Sy)$$

$\forall y(Wy \Rightarrow Sy) \Rightarrow (\forall yWy \Rightarrow \forall ySy)$ but not vice versa.
"If everything is such that if it's W, then it's S, then if everything is W, then everything is S"

An example of this last wff is "If all whales are mammals, then if everything's a whale, everything's a mammal."

$$\forall y(Wy \Rightarrow Sy) \Rightarrow (\exists yWy \Rightarrow \exists ySy)$$

However, $\exists y(Wy \Rightarrow Sy) \Rightarrow (\exists yWy \Rightarrow \exists ySy)$ is not valid.

Suppose Wz is a substitution instance of Wy and Wy is a substitution instance of Wz (check "Predicate Languages" for definitions). This means that Wz is exactly like Wy except that Wz has a free z in all and only those places that Wy has a free y. Then it really doesn't matter which variable we use:

$$\forall yWy \Leftrightarrow \forall zWz \qquad \text{and} \qquad \exists yWy \Leftrightarrow \exists zWz$$

CHALLENGE 3 Find a structure in which $\forall y(Wy \lor Sy) \Rightarrow (\forall yWy \lor \forall ySy)$ is F.

CHALLENGE 4 What does $\forall y(Wy \Rightarrow Sy) \Rightarrow (\exists yWy \Rightarrow \exists ySy)$ say? Can you argue that every structure makes it true?

CHALLENGE 5 Find a structure in which $\exists y(Wy \Rightarrow Sy) \Rightarrow (\exists yWy \Rightarrow \exists ySy)$ is false. (*Hint:* Remember a peculiarity of $\Rightarrow$, namely, F $\Rightarrow$ F is T.)

Several Quantifiers

We can exchange adjacent $\forall$'s because of the following:

$\forall x\forall yRxy \Leftrightarrow \forall y\forall xRxy$
"Everything R's everything iff everything is R'd by everything"

Notice, by the way, that $\forall x\forall yRxy \Leftrightarrow \forall y\forall xRyx$, while valid, is not a quantifier exchange. The two sides are basically the same formula with x substituted for y and vice versa. They exhibit the common pattern $\forall\square\forall\bigcirc R\square\bigcirc$. The biconditional says that everything R's everything iff everything R's everything! More generally, in any string of $\forall$'s, we can exchange them:

$$\forall x\forall y\forall zRxyz \Leftrightarrow \forall z\forall x\forall yRxyz$$

and so on.

207

EXAMPLE   Suppose $\forall x\forall y Rxy$ is true in a structure S. Then $\forall y Rxy$ expresses a property that must be true of each object in (the domain of) S. But if $\forall y Rxy$ is true of β in S, then Rxy must be true of all pairs $\langle \beta, \alpha \rangle$ for every α in S. In other words, Rxy is true of every pair of objects in S, so $\forall x Rxy$ is true of every object α in S. Thus $\forall y\forall x Rxy$ is true in S.

Laws similar to $\forall$ hold for $\exists$. We can exchange adjacent $\exists$'s because of the following:

$$\exists x\exists y Rxy \Leftrightarrow \exists y\exists x Rxy$$

Notice, by the way that $\exists x\exists y Rxy \Leftrightarrow \exists y\exists x Ryx$, while valid, is not a quantifier exchange. The two sides are basically the same formula with x substituted for y and vice versa. More generally, in any string of $\exists$'s, we can exchange them; for example,

$$\exists x\exists y\exists z Rxyz \Leftrightarrow \exists z\exists x\exists y Rxyz$$

and so on.

The tricky part is with mixed quantifiers. $\forall x\exists y Rxy$ is *not* the same as $\exists y\forall x Rxy$:

$$\exists y\forall x Rxy \Rightarrow \forall x\exists y Rxy \qquad \text{but not vice versa.}$$

Of course, it's the order of the quantifiers that matters, not which variable comes first. So $\exists x\forall y Rxy \Rightarrow \forall y\exists x Rxy$ but not vice versa.

Identity

The valid wffs involving identity are obvious if you remember that $x = y$ is T iff x and y are the same object.

$\forall x(x = x) \qquad \forall x\forall y(x = y \Rightarrow y = x)$
$\forall x\forall y\forall z((x = y \ \& \ y = z) \Rightarrow x = z)$
$\forall x\forall y(x = y \Rightarrow (Wx \Leftrightarrow Wy))$
$\forall x\exists y(x = y)$
$Wc \Leftrightarrow \exists x(Wx \ \& \ x = c)$

SUMMARY: We have seen the basic laws of predicate logic. If you memorize them and use the replacement principle, you'll be in a good position to prove validity for any valid wff you'll encounter. But for the moment it suffices for you to use these wffs as a handy reference. In the chapter on deduction, we'll return to the matter of proving them.

SYMBOLIZATION IN PREDICATE LOGIC

I dislike arguments of any kind. They are always vulgar, and often convincing.

—Oscar Wilde, *The Importance of Being Ernest*

In part 1 you formalized English statements in terms of predicate logic. Now that you've learned some serious logic, we want to discuss the process more systematically. We won't talk about formalizing argument forms yet, but only about simple statement formulations that make use of what you've learned.

Basics

Using Sentential, we could formalize "Tom is a wise, old man" only as P (or perhaps as P_1 & P_2 & P_3). With predicate logic, we can express the subject–predicate nature of the assertion as Wc & Oc & Mc, a modest improvement. We can now see that the three conjuncts have something in common. Each is a one-place predicate with a common subject.

Things get even better. In predicate logic, we can distinguish between

"Murray and Jean are Nigerian"	Nc & Nd
"Murray and Jean are married"	Mcd

(where c is Murray and d is Jean; Nz is "z is Nigerian" and Mwx is "w is married to x." Often we will omit the explicit interpretation of the symbols when they can be easily guessed.)

In general, relative clauses of natural languages are handled by conjoining formulas of predicate logic, as in

"Murray, who is Nigerian, is
married to Jean" Mcd & Nc

(and *not*, as one might expect, $M(Nc)d$. This isn't a wff according to our rules.) Although relative clauses can be very complex, the process just reiterates:

"Murray, who is Nigerian, is
married to Jean, the daughter
of Olga and Bill" Mcd & Nc & $Robd$ & Fd

However, this increase in symbolic sophistication is without much logical power. No new argument forms are revealed to be valid. It doesn't much matter if we write the units as P or as Fc when the only logical laws we have (such as A & B ∴ A) ignore the internal structure of the units. Symbolic sophistication matters only when it goes along with sophistication involving logical inferences.

Things change once we introduce identity, for we do have valid inferences involving identity.

"Murray and Jean are married" Mcd
"Murray is the Saskatchewan
Stud" $c = e$
∴ "The Saskatchewan Stud and
Jean are married"   ∴ Med

The argument form is valid (it will be called identity elimination E), but no plausible translation of the English into Sentential is valid.

CHALLENGE 1   Formalize (can you guess at the validity of the forms using structures?).

1. Superman flies.
   Clark Kent is Superman.
   ∴ Clark Kent flies.

2. Marilyn Monroe is Norma Jean Baker.
   Norma Jean Baker is unknown.
   ∴ Marilyn Monroe is unknown.

"is"

Mention of identity brings up the important issue of "is." This word serves several different logical functions, and you should be careful not to confuse them.

The "is" of Predication

"Cheryl is black and Denise is
white."   *Bc & Wd*

Here the "is" does nothing but convert an adjective ("black" or "white") into a verb phrase ("is black" and "is white"). We could imagine English performing this conversion another way, for example, by making the adjectives into verbs, as in "Cheryl blacks and Denise whites" (compare to "Cheryl jogs and Denise runs"). Similarly, "Murray is Nigerian" might have been expressed as "Murray Nigerians."

In summary, the "is" of predication is merely a grammatical device that adds nothing to the logical structure of a sentence.

The "is" of Identity It's altogether different when "is" is used to express identity.

"Murray is the Saskatchewan
Stud" $c = e$
"Mark Twain is Samuel Cle-
mens" $a = b$
"Two plus two is four" $2 + 2 = 4$

In these cases "is" actually represents the two-place relation of identity or equality (recall that we would write this as *Ixy* if $x = y$ weren't so common).

In identity statements we are saying that the thing on the left is the very same object as the thing on the right (though we might be wrong, as when we say that $2 + 2 = 5$). With the "is" of predication, no such identity is suggested. When we say "Cheryl is black," we don't mean $c = b$ ("Cheryl is identical to black or blackness"). We mean she has a certain property—being black (Bx).

Bertrand Russell, whom we referred to in part 4 ("Bertrand the First"), once said that it was a scandal that English used the same word for such different logical purposes. However, it's hopeless to try to change things now, so we simply have to make the best of it. While we're on the subject, though, let's mention two *other* logically distinct uses of "is."

The "is" of Existence When we say things like "There is a God" or "There is an even prime number," we're using "is" (or more accurately, "there is") to express existence. The correct formalizations, of course, are

$$\exists x Gx \qquad \text{and} \qquad \exists z(Ez \ \& \ Pz)$$

"Is" could be eliminated from these statements if we paraphrased them as "God exists" or "Even prime numbers exist."

The "is" of Tense "Cheryl jogs" is easily symbolized by Jc, but what about "Cheryl is jogging"? To say that "Cheryl is jogging" is to say she's jogging now (even though she probably wasn't jogging earlier and probably will stop jogging later). In analogous fashion, "Tom is bald" might contrast with "Tom wasn't bald" before.

By and large we simply ignore the issue of tense in this book. In general, we try to pretend that nothing changes in the world that we're talking or arguing about in logic, at least not while we're talking or arguing about it. Thus, if necessary, we imagine Cheryl as jogging ceaselessly or Tom as being bald eternally.

On the other hand, if it really mattered, we could incorporate tense by adding the tensed operators N, P, F (from "Formal Languages: Variations of Sentential" in part 3). Alternatively we could add another variable to tensed predicates to indicate time. So "is jogging" becomes not Jx but "is jogging at time t" or Jxt. The phrase "is bald" (Bx) gives way to "is bald at time t" or Bxt. Thus "Cheryl is jogging now" might be Jct_0; "Cheryl was jogging" might be $\exists y$("y is before t_0" $\&\ Jcy$). In the end, the question of tense is a difficult one and how best to formalize tensed sentences is an open question of symbolic logic.

We have spent some time on the many meanings of "is" not only to alert you to potential difficulties in formalizing but, more importantly, to let you see one of the great advantages of logical formalization. It's not that logic always succeeds in capturing the meaning of English. Rather, it is that in the attempt to capture these meanings in the very strict vocabulary of predicate logic, we often discover a host of subtleties and ambiguities of which we were not explicitly aware. *Logic can teach us as much when we are unable to formalize as it can when we can formalize easily.*

EXERCISE 1 **Explain the uses of "is" in each of the following and formalize where possible.**

1. Batman is Bruce Wayne.
2. Batman is atrocious.
3. Batman is changing clothes.
4. There is a bat.

Quantifiers

Of course, the whole point behind predicate logic is quantification—that's what lifts us to a new level of valid argument forms and makes formalizing in predicate logic worthwhile.

Unrestricted Quantification The expression $\forall xAx$, where Ax is any predicate, can symbolize such statements as

Everything is A	Everything is an A
Everything is such that it A's	All are A
All things A	All are such that they A
Each thing A's	Each thing is an A
Anything A's	Anything is an A

In general, the difference between the readings on any line depends on the grammar of the English. For example, "Everything jogs," "Everything is red," "Everything is such that it's a yellow submarine"— all are just $\forall x\forall x$ for different Ax. The reading "Every x is A" (or "every x A's") is both barbarous—we don't say that in English—and misleading. The barbarity we can forgive, but it is misleading to think that $\forall xAx$ is referring to anything, least of all referring to x's. The wff $\forall xAx$ simply says that the property Ax is universally true. Having chastised anyone who reads that as "Every x is A," we confess that we will sometimes use that barbarous and misleading locution. Do as we say, not as we do.

Another problem is that there are very few properties that everything has! In fact, the only such properties are logical properties. Everything is red or is not red. Everything is identical to itself. And so on. The situation is improved somewhat when we specify a domain, such as the set of natural numbers or the collection of all people. In the former case, we get such truths as "Everything (i.e., every natural number) is even or odd" or "Everything (i.e., all natural numbers) is greater than or equal to zero." But there is a better way of handling restricted quantification than by restricting domains. We'll turn to it in a moment, but first let's mention some other quantifiers.

The wff $\exists xAx$, where Ax is any predicate, can symbolize such statements as

Something is A	Something is an A
Something is such that it A's	There are A's
There is an A	There are things that A
A thing A's	

Often "a" denotes existential quantification as in

$$\text{"Tom owns a dog"} \qquad \exists x(Dx \ \& \ Otx)$$

CHALLENGE 2

Could "Fido is a dog" mean "Fido is identical to some dog," that is, $\exists x(Dx \& f = x)$? This is surely convoluted but can you explain why Df is logically equivalent to $\exists x(Dx \& f = x)$? Thus both formalizations serve our purposes equally well. (So choose the simplest!)

However, "a" is often a grammatical part of the predicate with no hint of quantification at all; for example, "Fido is a dog" is just Df where f is Fido and Dx is "x is a dog."

Finally, "Nothing A's" or "Nothing is an A" can be formalized in either of two ways,

$$\neg \exists x Ax \qquad \text{and} \qquad \forall x \neg Ax$$

CHALLENGE 3   Formalize (and, if you can, test for validity using structures).

1. Everything is such that if it's a man, then it's mortal.
   Socrates is a man.
   ∴ Socrates is mortal.
2. All are such that if they're vampires, then they're supernatural.
   Nothing is supernatural.
   ∴ There are no vampires.
3. Everything that is a snark is a boojum.
   Something is not a snark.
   ∴ Something is not a boojum.
4. Formalize argument 7 from the Introduction.
5. Formalize argument 8 from the Introduction.

Restricted Quantification An English construction that is much more common than unrestricted quantification is the restricted variety, or categoricals. These are expressions such as "All A are B," "Some A are B," and "No A are B." Thus we have

$$\text{"All A are B"} \qquad \forall x(Ax \Rightarrow Bx)$$

EXAMPLES

"All whales are mammals"   "Every woman is mortal"
"Every Sophist student is female"   "All professors are wise"
"Any square is a rectangle"   "A poet is an artist"

Notice that the English "a," which usually indicates ∃ or simple predicate, can sometimes stand for ∀. This ∀ use is called the "generic use," where "a G" can mean any old G or an arbitrary G. So, "A whale is a mammal" means all whales are mammals.

What we are saying in "All A are B" is that "Everything is such that if it is A, then it is B." The A's are included among the B's.

Hence, the restricted quantification comes out as an unrestricted quantification of a conditional. Thus "All women are mortal" means the same as "Everything in the universe is such that *if* it is a woman, *then* it is mortal" or "Everything in the universe is such that *either* it's *not* a woman or it's mortal." In terms of wffs, we have

$$\forall x(Wx \Rightarrow Mx) \qquad \text{or} \qquad \forall x(\neg Wx \lor Mx)$$

EXERCISE 2 Show that the two wffs at the left are equivalent. (What's the relevant principle to use?)

Why not translate "All A are B" by $\forall x(Ax \ \& \ Bx)$? The reason is that this formula asserts of each thing in the universe that it is both A and B, and "All A are B" does not assert that.

Because of the peculiarity of $\Rightarrow$ (F $\Rightarrow$ T is T and so is F $\Rightarrow$ F), we get some surprising truth values for "All A are B" statements. For example, "All unicorns are male" is true (for the same reason that "If Jim is a unicorn, then Jim is a male" is true—namely, there are no unicorns, so the antecedent is always false!). By the same token, "All unicorns are female" is equally true (just as "If Jim is a unicorn, then Jim is female" is true).

Now let us turn to the existential quantifier.

$$\text{"Some A are B"} \qquad \exists x(Ax \ \& \ Bx)$$

EXAMPLES
  "Some cows are Holsteins"   "There is an even prime"
  "Some Sophist student is a
      jogger"   "There exists a wise professor"
  "A white crow exists"   "Some people sing"

What are we saying by "Some A is B" is that something is such that it is both an A and a B or that A's and B's have an object(s) in common. Hence the restricted quantification "Some woman is winsome" means the same as the unrestricted quantification "Something is such that it is both a woman and winsome."

Why not translate "Some A are B" by $\exists x(Ax \Rightarrow Bx)$ in parallel to the $\forall$ case? Because this formula doesn't say that there is some A that is B. It says there is something such that either it's not an A or it's a B. Thus $\exists x$("x is a woman" $\Rightarrow$ "x is over 100 feet tall") is T (although "Some woman is over 100 feet tall" is F). Why? Because, Jim Henle (and any other nonwoman) satisfies the conditional "x is a woman" $\Rightarrow$ "x is over 100 feet tall" (remember, F $\Rightarrow$ anything is T).

Because "Some A are B" implies that there exist things that are A and B, we get some weird results. "Some vampires are male" is false because there are no vampires (those movies you see are make-believe). Similarly (get ready for this) "Some unicorns are male" and "Some unicorns are female" are both false even though "All unicorns are male" and "All unicorns are female" are both true! The explanation is simple: $\forall x(Ux \Rightarrow Fx)$ is T and $\exists x(Ux \& Fx)$ is F whenever Ux is true of nothing ($\neg\exists xUx$).

The above techniques can be reiterated indefinitely:

"Every Swede who is married to a Norwegian kicked some silly Pole who loves himself"

(which is basically of the form "Every A is B") becomes

$\forall x$("x is a Swede who is married to a Norwegian" $\Rightarrow$ "x kicked some silly Pole who loves himself")

becomes

$\forall x$(Sx & "x is married to a Norwegian" $\Rightarrow$ $\exists y$("x kicked y" & "y is a silly Pole who loves himself")

becomes

$\forall x([Sx \& \exists y(Mxy \& Ny)] \Rightarrow \exists y(Kxy \& Py \& Ty \&$ "y loves himself"))

becomes

$\forall x([Sx \& \exists y(Mxy \& Ny)] \Rightarrow \exists y(Kxy \& Py \& Ty \& Lyy))$

Briefly, we present a few other quantifiers.
"No A are B" ("No Sophist College students are men") can be represented as

$$\neg\exists x(Ax \& Bx) \quad \text{or} \quad \forall x(Ax \Rightarrow \neg Bx)$$

"Only A are B." Interestingly enough, this is just $\forall x(Bx \Rightarrow Ax)$, or "all B are A." Thus "all and only A are B" is either

$$\forall x(Ax \Rightarrow Bx) \& \forall x(Bx \Rightarrow Ax) \qquad \text{or} \qquad \forall x(Ax \Leftrightarrow Bx)$$

CHALLENGE 4

1. Show the equivalence of the wffs $\neg\exists x(Ax \& Bx)$ and $\forall x(Ax \Rightarrow \neg Bx)$.

2. Show the wffs of problem 1 are not equivalent to $\neg\forall x(Ax \Rightarrow Bx)$.

216

EXAMPLES

"All bachelors are unmarried men" $\forall z(Bz \Rightarrow (Uz \ \& \ Mz))$
"Only bachelors are unmarried men" $\forall z((Uz \ \& \ Mz)) \Rightarrow Bz)$
"All and only bachelors are unmarried
   men" $\forall z(Bz \Leftrightarrow (Uz \ \& \ Mz))$

Of course, Uz ("z is unmarried") is short for $\neg\exists y(M^2 zy)$, where $M^2 zy$ is "z is married to y."

EXERCISE 3 **Formalize (can you check for validity in terms of structures?).**

1. All women are strong.
   Some professor is a woman.
   ∴ Some professor is strong.

2. All women are strong.
   Some professor is strong.
   ∴ Some professor is a woman.

3. Every bachelor is unmarried.
   Jim has a wife.
   ∴ Jim is not a bachelor.

4. Every child is a human.
   ∴ All teachers of children are teachers of humans.

CHALLENGE 5 Taking the domain to be people, formalize and analyze "There is someone who shaves all those and only those who don't shave themselves." (*Hint:* Use the predicate *Sxy* for "*x* shaves *y.*" This logical form is a quite important.)

"any"

Sometimes "any" is easily symbolized by ∀: "Any Sophist student is female" is just $\forall x(Sx \Rightarrow Fx)$. But we invite you to formalize the following in an effort to understand how you use "any."

CHALLENGE 6 Symbolize the following, paying close attention to the meaning.

1. Everyone barks.
   Anyone barks.
   Someone barks.

2. Not everyone barks.
   Not anyone barks.
   Not even one barks.

3. If everyone barks, Fido does.
   If anyone barks, Fido does.
   If someone barks, Fido does.

4. If Fido barks, everyone barks.
   If Fido barks, anyone barks.
   If Fido barks, someone barks.

Your research might have showed you that sometimes "any" is best represented by a universal quantifier (problem 1) and sometimes by an existential quantifier (problem 2). One rule of thumb is simple:

When "any" and "every" seem like they can be interchanged ("everyone agrees" and "anyone agrees"), the universal quantifier works for both. But when you can hear a difference between the two cases ("not everyone agrees" and "not anyone agrees"), then "any" should be represented by an existential quantifier.

But there's a more elegant way of expressing the point. We can say that "any," like "every," is represented by a universal quantifier but *when you hear a difference between "any" and "every," you're hearing a difference in the scope of the two universal quantifiers*. This explanation predicts that English speakers will hear a difference between "any" and "every" only where scope is an issue. So, for example, the difference between "not everyone agrees" and "not anyone agrees" can be expressed as $\neg\forall x Ax$ and $\forall x\neg Ax$, respectively. (Notice that this coheres with the previous rule of thumb, because $\forall x\neg Ax$ is equivalent to $\neg\exists x Ax$). On the other hand, "everyone agrees" and "anyone agrees" must both be $\forall x Ax$, because there is no room for scope ambiguity.

By the same token, "If everyone barks, Fido does" is $\forall x Bx \Rightarrow Bf$, while "If anyone barks, Fido does" is $\forall x(Bx \Rightarrow Bf)$ or, equivalently, $\exists x Bx \Rightarrow Bf$.

In conclusion we note that it is difficult to do very serious formalization without a firm command of logical principles. It would be sad, indeed, for students to come to blows over whether $\forall x(Bx \Rightarrow Bf)$ or $\exists x Bx \Rightarrow Bf$ is the correct formalization of "If anyone barks, Fido does." Eventually we'll see that these wffs are equivalent.

Unfortunately, it is practically impossible to proceed far in logic without being able to interpret the symbols to some extent. So we'll try to teach you some formalization, then some logical principles, then more formalization, then more principles, and so on.

SUMMARY: There are some standard rules (and common pitfalls) for finding the logical form of English statements. Formalization, like translation, is an art, not a science, and is best learned by practice. With this in mind, we invite you to continue on to the next section, where we do some simple but extended practice.

POLES AND NORWEGIANS

The particular reveals the universal.
—OLE WROBLEWSKI

Remember that expressions like "all A are B" and "Every A is B" are naturally symbolized as $\forall x(Ax \Rightarrow Bx)$, while "Some A is B" and "There is an A which is B" are naturally symbolized as $\exists x(Ax \mathbin{\&} Bx)$.

Now suppose you have a formal language interpreted over the domain of people where:

Nx	is	"x is Norwegian"	Hyw	is	"y hates w"
Pz	is	"z is Polish"	b	denotes	"Lenny"
Su	is	"u is silly"			

(Recall that the choice of variables is arbitrary, eg., we use x only to convey that N[ ] is [ ] is Norwegian.)

EXERCISE   **Formalize the following sentences.**

1. All Norwegians are silly.

2. Every Pole is Norwegian.

3. Someone hates Lenny.

4. Some Pole hates Lenny.

5. All Norwegians hate Lenny.

6. All Norwegians hate someone.

7. All silly Norwegians hate a Pole.

8. Some silly Pole hates all silly Norwegians.

9. Some silly Pole hates all silly Norwegians who hate Lenny.

10. Not every Norwegian is silly.

11. Not any Norwegian is silly.

12. If everyone hates Lenny, Lenny does.

13. If anyone hates Lenny, Lenny does.

14. Everyone hates someone but no one is hated by all.

15. Someone hates everyone and some are hated by all.

with & about logic

games

Games mean many things to many people; to me they are an art form of great potential beauty.

—Sid Sackson

In this section we consider games of the following sort: There are two players, player 1 and player 2, who alternate making moves in the game (player 1 goes first). The game ends after a fixed number of moves. At the end of the game one player wins; there are no ties. We will say that one player has a **winning strategy** if she can always win the game by playing appropriately (no matter how her opponent plays). We might think of a winning strategy as a set of instructions that, if followed, guarantees a win.

We begin with the simplest possible situation, a game in which there is only one move by player 1 and then the game ends (a little silly but we have to start somewhere). We will call this a "one-game."

Proposition: For any one-game, one of the two players has a winning strategy.

Proof: There are just two possibilities here. Either there is a move that player 1 can make that will win the game for her, or there isn't. In the first case she has a winning strategy (namely, make such a move). In the second case, player 2 has a winning strategy (namely, don't do anything).

We can illustrate this with predicate logic. Let Wx be the one-place predicate "Player 1 makes move x and wins." Then the first case is

$\exists x\, Wx$ "Player 1 has a winning strategy"

and the second is

$\neg \exists x Wx$

which is equivalent to

$\forall x \neg Wx$ "Player 2 has a winning strategy"

Now let us consider two-games, games where there are a total of two moves.

> *Proposition:* For any two-game, one of the two players has a winning strategy.
> *Proof:* This time we will use predicate logic at the start. Let Wxy now be a two-place predicate meaning "Player 1 makes move x and then player 2 makes move y and then player 1 wins."

Certainly, then, we have

$$\exists x \forall y Wxy \lor \neg \exists x \forall y Wxy$$

This is just the form $P \lor \neg P$. The first case, $\exists x \forall y Wxy$, states simply that player 1 has a winning strategy. It says that there is a move she can make ($\exists x$) such that no matter what player 2 does ($\forall y$), player 1 will win (Wxy).

What about the second case, $\neg \exists x \forall y Wxy$? By our earlier work, this is equivalent to

$$\forall x \neg \forall y Wxy$$

and this in turn is equivalent to

$$\forall x \exists y \neg Wxy$$

which simply states that player 2 has a winning strategy. It says that no matter what player 1 does ($\forall x$), there is an appropriate response that player 2 can make ($\exists y$) such that player 2 wins ($\neg Wxy$).

> *Proposition:* For any three-game, one of the two players has a winning strategy.
> *Proof:* I think you can see how this goes. Let $Wxyz$ be the three-place predicate "Player 1 makes move x then player 2 makes move y and then player 1 makes move z and then player 1 wins."

Then again,

$$\exists x \forall y \exists z Wxyz \lor \neg \exists x \forall y \exists z Wxyz$$

is true ($P \vee \neg P$). The first says that player 1 has a winning strategy and the second is equivalent to

$$\forall x \exists y \forall z \neg Wxyz$$

which says that player 2 has a winning strategy.

Without proving it, you can probably see that the following is true:

> *Proposition:* For any n and for any n-game, one of the two players has a winning strategy.

It can be fun to apply this to a particular game, the game of queens. In this game, a chess queen is placed at the lower right corner of a rectangular board.

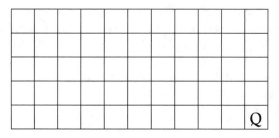

Players take turns moving the queen. Only three kinds of moves are allowed: moving straight up (as far as you like), moving left (as far as you like), and moving diagonally up and left (again, as far as you like). The first player who cannot move (because the queen is at the top left) loses.

In queens, the size of the board at the start of the game is important. If we start with an n-by-m board, we will call the game "n–m queens."

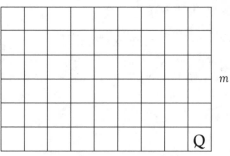

Proposition: Player 1 has a winning strategy for 2–1 queens.

Proof: This is pretty simple: All player 1 has to do is move left one square.

Proposition: Player 1 has a winning strategy for 2–2 queens.

Proof: Again, all player 1 has to do is move diagonally one square.

Proposition: Player 2 has a winning strategy for 3–2 queens.
Proof: This is trickier. We have to show that no matter what move player 1 makes, player 2 can respond and win. From the chart

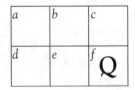

there are four squares that player 1 can legally move to — *b*, *c*, *d*, and *e*. Examining each case separately, we see that in each one player 2 can move to square *a* and win.

EXERCISE Discover who has the winning strategies for these games, and prove your answer. How many boards can you find where player 2 has a winning strategy?
1. 2–3 queens
2. 3–3 queens
3. 3–1 queens
4. 4–1 queens
5. 4–2 queens
6. 4–3 queens
7. 5–2 queens
8. 5–3 queens
9. 5–4 queens
10. 6–3 queens
11. 6–4 queens
12. 7–5 queens

BASIC

One cannot escape the feeling that these mathematical formulae have an independent existence and an intelligence of their own, that they are wiser than we are, wiser even than their discoverers, that we get more out of them than was originally put into them.

—Heinrich Hertz

BASIC is perhaps the simplest and most natural computer language. Certainly it is the most widespread. It was invented over twenty-five years ago by John Kemeny and Thomas Kurtz. Professional programmers and academicians tend to sneer at BASIC. It is wordy and encourages bad habits, but it is easy to use and it gets the job done.

A Brief Introduction to BASIC Computer Language

1. To use BASIC, find a computer, turn it on, and type "BASIC" (and press return). For most "PC-compatible" machines, this will put you into BASIC and you will be able to write programs. For more recent models, "QBASIC" or "GWBASIC" does it.

2. *Variables* are letters.

3. *Expressions* are combinations of letters, numbers, and mathematical symbols: $+$, $-$, $*$ (multiplication), $/$ (division), and so on.

4. *Statements* are mathematical, of the form:

$$\underline{\hspace{2cm}} \qquad \underline{\hspace{2cm}} \qquad \underline{\hspace{2cm}}$$
$$\text{expression} \qquad <, =, \text{ or } > \qquad \text{expression}$$

5. All commands are numbered. The computer executes them in order (except as described in 6b). (Modern versions of BASIC do not need line numbers, but they tolerate them.)

6. Some available commands:
   a. LET $\underline{\hspace{1.5cm}}$ = $\underline{\hspace{1.5cm}}$
      variable   expression
      This command changes the value of the variable.

      EXAMPLE   LET X=10

   b. GOTO $\underline{\hspace{1.5cm}}$
            line number
      This command sends the computer to a different line of the program.

      EXAMPLE   GOTO 40

   c. IF $\underline{\hspace{1.5cm}}$ THEN $\underline{\hspace{1.5cm}}$
         statement   command
      This command checks to see if the statement is true. If it is,

then the computer executes the command and moves on. Otherwise it just moves on.

EXAMPLE   IF X>0 THEN Y=1/X

d. PRINT _____
           variable
This command prints the current value of the variable.

EXAMPLE   PRINT X

There are many more commands, different types of variables, and so on. This is enough, however, to get started.

Some Sample Programs

A simple program to add two numbers:

```
10 LET A = 345 +7654
20 PRINT A
```

A simple, absolutely pointless, never-ending program:

```
10 GOTO 10
```

A program that multiplies A times B by adding A to itself B times:

```
10 LET A = 7
20 LET B = 5
30 LET C = C + A
40 LET B = B − 1
50 IF B > 0 THEN GOTO 30
60 PRINT C
```

To see what this does, make a chart and keep track of the value of the variables as the program is executed. Initially, all variables are 0.

A	B	C
0	0	0

The first commands assign new values to A and B:

A	B	C
0	0	0
7	5	

The next lines look a little peculiar. They are not statements, however; they are commands. "LET C = C + A" means "Take the old values of C and A, add them, then let this be the new value of C." After the next two lines are executed, our chart looks like this:

A	B	C
0	0	0
7	5	7
	4	

Now we check to see if B is greater than 0. It is, so we go to line 30. After two more lines, the chart looks like this:

A	B	C
0	0	0
7	5	7
	4	14
	3	

Again, B is greater than 0, so we continue, until at last we have

A	B	C
0	0	0
7	5	7
	4	14
	3	21
	2	28
	1	35
	0	

B is no longer greater than 0, so we go on to statement 60, print "35," and stop.

EXERCISES

1. What does the following program do?

   ```
   10 LET A = 1
   20 LET B = 5
   30 LET A = A * 2
   40 LET B = B − 1
   50 IF B > 0 THEN GOTO 30
   60 PRINT A
   ```

   What happens if we change the "5" in line 20 to "3"? What if we change it to "7"? Can you say how the output depends on the number we put here?

2. What does the following program do?

   ```
   10 LET B = 5
   20 LET A = A + B
   30 LET B = B − 1
   40 IF B > 0 THEN GOTO 20
   50 PRINT A
   ```

   What happens if we change the "5" in line 10 to "3"? What if we change it to "7"? Can you say how the output depends on the number we put here?

3. What does the following program do?

   ```
   10 LET A = 1
   20 LET B = 5
   30 LET A = A * B
   40 LET B = B − 1
   50 IF B > 0 THEN GOTO 30
   60 PRINT A
   ```

   What happens if we change the "5" in line 20 to "3"? What if we change it to "7"? Can you say how the output depends on the number we put here?

4. What does the following program do?

```
10 LET A = 7
20 LET B = 5
30 LET C = 1
40 LET C = C * A
50 LET B = B − 1
60 IF B > 0 THEN GOTO 40
70 PRINT C
```

How does the output of this program depend on the initial values of A and B (in this case 7 and 5)?

binary

I will not go so far as to say that to construct a history of thought without profound study of the mathematical ideas of successive epochs is like omitting Hamlet from the play which is named after him. That would be claiming too much. But it is certainly analogous to cutting out the part of Ophelia. The simile is singularly exact. For Ophelia is quite essential to the play, she is charming—and a little mad.

—ALFRED NORTH WHITEHEAD

As we have described earlier, computers communicate internally with streams of pulses of two sorts, which we are calling 0s and 1s. How does a computer use the pulses to represent numbers?

The answer is a number system based on 2, instead of our usual number system, which is based on 10. In our decimal system, digits range from 0 to 9, and each digit in a number stands for a power of 10. For example, 34,725 means:

$$5 \text{ times } 1 \ (=10^0)$$
$$\text{plus} \quad 2 \text{ times } 10$$
$$\text{plus} \quad 7 \text{ times } 10 \cdot 10$$
$$\text{plus} \quad 4 \text{ times } 10 \cdot 10 \cdot 10$$
$$\text{plus} \quad 3 \text{ times } 10 \cdot 10 \cdot 10 \cdot 10$$
$$\text{or} \quad 3 \cdot 10^4 + 4 \cdot 10^3 + 7 \cdot 10^2 + 2 \cdot 10^1 + 5 \cdot 10^0$$

In base 2, or the **binary system,** we use only the digits 0 and 1. The number 110101, then, means

```
          1 times 1
plus   0 times 2
plus   1 times 2 · 2
plus   0 times 2 · 2 · 2
plus   1 times 2 · 2 · 2 · 2
plus   1 times 2 · 2 · 2 · 2 · 2
or     1 · 2^5 + 1 · 2^4 + 0 · 2^3 + 1 · 2^2 + 0 · 2^1 + 1 · 2^0
```

$$1 \cdot 2^5 + 1 \cdot 2^4 + 0 \cdot 2^3 + 1 \cdot 2^2 + 0 \cdot 2^1 + 1 \cdot 2^0$$

which is 32 + 16 + 0 + 4 + 0 + 1 = 53 in base 10.

Any number can be represented in base 2. The system was invented by Gottfried Leibniz in the seventeenth century, but it was only a curiosity until the twentieth. Leibniz suggested that missionaries in China use it as evidence of the power of God, that everything (all numbers) could come from just two symbols.

We can see this number system at work in personal computers by using a little BASIC. Go to a computer and give the appropriate command to start up BASIC. Next, type in

PRINT (11 and 26)

Now press return and watch what happens. The computer will respond with the number 10. Why?

Here is what is happening. The computer is looking at these two numbers in binary. The decimal 11 is binary 1011 (8 + 0 + 2 + 1), and 26 is 11010 (16 + 8 + 0 + 2 + 0). The computer compares the two sequences and performs the "and" operation (as in "Logic Circuits"), that is, it looks at the rightmost digit of each:

```
    1  0  1  1   =   11
 1  1  0  1  0   =   26
             0
```

It now thinks, 1 and 0 is 0 (or T & F is F). Then it looks at the next rightmost pair of digits and does the same comparison:

```
    1  0  1  1   =   11
 1  1  0  1  0   =   26
          1  0
```

This process is repeated until we have

229

$$1 \quad 0 \quad 1 \quad 1 \quad = \quad 11$$
$$1 \quad 1 \quad 0 \quad 1 \quad 0 \quad = \quad 26$$
$$0 \quad 1 \quad 0 \quad 1 \quad 0 \quad = \quad 10 \quad (0 + 8 + 0 + 2 + 0)$$

Now type

PRINT (11 or 26)

and press return. This time you will get 27, because the computer is performing the "or," or ∨, operation:

$$1 \quad 0 \quad 1 \quad 1 \quad = \quad 11$$
$$1 \quad 1 \quad 0 \quad 1 \quad 0 \quad = \quad 26$$
$$1 \quad 1 \quad 0 \quad 1 \quad 1 \quad = \quad 27 \quad (16 + 8 + 0 + 2 + 1)$$

There is one more logical operation that BASIC understands: the exclusive "or," or "xor." Type

PRINT (11 xor 26)

and press return, and you will get 17:

$$1 \quad 0 \quad 1 \quad 1 \quad = \quad 11$$
$$1 \quad 1 \quad 0 \quad 1 \quad 0 \quad = \quad 26$$
$$1 \quad 0 \quad 0 \quad 0 \quad 1 \quad = \quad 17 \quad (16 + 0 + 0 + 0 + 1)$$

The exclusive "or" (see "Formalizing English" in part 4) sometimes written $\veebar$, has the following truth table:

P	Q	$P \veebar Q$
T	T	F
T	F	T
F	T	T
F	F	F

Think of it as saying "either P or Q is true, but not both."

EXERCISES   **Translate the following numbers from binary to decimal.**

　　1. 101　　　2. 1101　　　3. 101101　　　4. 111001101

Translate the following numbers from decimal to binary.

    5. 3   6. 6   7. 9   8. 12   9. 13

   10. 23   11. 35   12. 47   13. 75   14. 123

Compute the following using BASIC or by hand as in the text.

   15. (12 and 23)   16. (9 and 13)   17. (35 and 47)

   18. (9 or 23)   19. (13 or 47)   20. (35 or 75)

   21. (12 xor 13)   22. (23 xor 35)   23. (75 xor 123)

Note: In BASIC, if you try using "not," you get something peculiar and not very meaningful. If you try "implies" or "iff," you get an error message.

TRIVIAL

> But he knew little out of his way, and was not a pleasing companion, as like most great mathematicians i have met with, he expected universal precision in everything said, or was forever distinguishing upon trifles, to the disturbance of all conversation.
>
> — BENJAMIN FRANKLIN

For various reasons, computer scientists are interested in languages that are even more primitive than BASIC. One such stripped-down language is TRIVIAL. It is actually a small, restricted part of BASIC.

Allowable Commands of TRIVIAL

INPUT X

At this command, the computer pauses and waits for the operator to type in a number. The number then becomes the value of X. Other variables may be used as well.

GOTO _____
          line number

LET X = X + 1

Other variables may be used as well.

IF X > 0 THEN LET X = X − 1

Other variables may be used as well.

IF X = 0 THEN GOTO _____
                    line number

Other variables may be used as well.

STOP

Some Sample Programs

There is no command for adding 2 to a number. This program accomplishes the same thing, however.

```
10 INPUT X
20 LET X = X + 1
30 LET X = X + 1
40 STOP
```

Here is a program that transfers the value of X to Y.

```
10 INPUT X
20 IF X = 0 THEN GOTO 60
30 IF X > 0 THEN LET X = X − 1
40 LET Y = Y + 1
50 GOTO 20
60 STOP
```

Make a chart to see how this program goes. Note that in TRIVIAL, as in BASIC, all variables start out as 0.

This program does something trickier—it adds two numbers.

```
10 INPUT X
20 INPUT Y
30 IF Y = 0 THEN GOTO 70
40 X = X + 1
50 IF Y > 0 THEN LET Y = Y − 1
60 GOTO 30
70 STOP
```

EXERCISES

1. What does this program do? Can you describe the output as a function of the input?

```
10 INPUT X
20 IF X = 0 THEN GOTO 70
30 IF X > 0 THEN LET X = X − 1
40 LET Y = Y + 1
50 LET Y = Y + 1
60 GOTO 20
70 STOP
```

2. What does this program do?
```
10 INPUT X
20 INPUT Y
30 IF X = 0 THEN GOTO 70
40 IF X > 0 THEN LET X = X − 1
50 IF Y > 0 THEN LET Y = Y − 1
60 GOTO 30
70 STOP
```

3. What does this program do?
```
10 INPUT X
20 INPUT Y
30 IF Y = 0 THEN GOTO 150
40 IF X = 0 THEN GOTO 90
50 W = W + 1
60 W = W + 1
70 IF X > 0 THEN LET X = X − 1
80 GOTO 40
90 IF W = 0 THEN GOTO 130
100 IF W > 0 THEN LET W = W − 1
110 LET X = X + 1
120 GOTO 90
130 IF Y > 0 THEN LET Y = Y − 1
140 GOTO 30
150 STOP
```

algorithm

> "Begin at the beginning," the King said gravely, "and go till you come to the end: then stop."
>
> —Lewis Carroll, *Alice's Adventures in Wonderland*

Historians care about truth. Scientists care about truth. Poets, judges, sports fans, investors, and lovers—all care about truth. Probably the most unsettling aspect of logic is that logicians *don't* care about truth. Truth is incidental. Logicians care about the logical relationships between statements, such as implication, equivalence, and validity.

Logicians in turn are unsettled by computer scientists. In computer science the most important element is neither truth nor validity but **procedure.**

233

Computer scientists call their procedures **algorithms.** They invent, study, and test algorithms. An algorithm is a well-defined, step-by-step procedure. Its chief characteristics:

1. At every stage there is no ambiguity about what is to be done.
2. The procedure eventually ends.

Sentential Validity

There is an algorithm for deciding whether an argument in Sentential is valid:

1. Construct a truth table for the conclusion and all the premises.
2. Examine each line in turn to see if the conclusion is false and every premise is true. If such a line is found, the argument is invalid; otherwise, the argument is valid.

Assuming that we understand algorithms for constructing truth tables, the instructions are clear. The procedure will end after a finite number of steps, since there will be only a finite number of lines in the truth table.

Note that there is no similar algorithm for arguments in English. Natural languages are difficult, perhaps impossible, to reduce to mechanics. It is a goal of linguistics, however, to find better and better approximations of English for which algorithms do exist. In fact, some extremely good approximations have been created. There are hand-held computers on the market, for example, that can translate simple sentences from English to French.

Primality

There is an algorithm for deciding if a given number n is prime.

1. Examine every number k from 2 up to but not including n. If k divides n evenly, then n is not prime; otherwise it is.

We can provide greater detail.

1. Set $k = 2$.
2. If k divides n evenly, then print "NOT PRIME" and stop.

3. Add 1 to k.

4. If $k = n$ then print "PRIME" and stop.

5. Go to step 2.

The concept of algorithm is similar to that of computability — with a difference. Something is **computable** if there is a well-defined procedure for computing it. Unlike algorithms, the procedure need not always terminate. As this definition is somewhat vague, mathematicians and philosophers have tried to define it more precisely. Kleene, Church, Turing, Post, Markov, and many others proposed definitions, all of which were discovered to be equivalent.

Essentially, "computable" means that a computer program can be written to compute the desired object. The program can be written in languages as simple as BASIC or even TRIVIAL.

We can talk of **decidable sets.** A set is decidable if we can write a program that will tell us, on input n, if n is in the set.

The Set of Numbers Greater than 17

Following is a very simple program in Basic to decide whether a number is in the set of numbers greater than 17:

```
10 INPUT N
20 IF N > 17 THEN PRINT "YES": STOP
30 PRINT "NO": STOP
```

The Set of Even Numbers

Following is a very simple program in BASIC to compute whether a number is in the set of even numbers (we assume that the input is a natural number).

```
10 INPUT N
20 IF N = 1 THEN PRINT "NO": STOP
30 IF N = 0 THEN PRINT "YES": STOP
40 N = N − 2
50 GOTO 20
```

It is a most astonishing fact that there are sets that are not decidable. This is a very deep logical result. We sketch a proof of it in "Notes, References, Hints, and Some Answers."

the busy beaver

Reason is not come to repeat the universe but to fulfil it.
—GEORGE SANTAYANA

Suppose we write a program in TRIVIAL such that

1. we do not use the INPUT statement.
2. the last line of the program is STOP, and the program does eventually stop.
3. the program has exactly 20 steps.

How large can the variable X be when the program finally halts?

This is an example of a busy beaver problem. Specifically, it is the 20-busy-beaver problem. At first sight, the problem seems a little silly. Isn't this the obvious program?

```
10 LET X = X + 1
20 LET X = X + 1
30 LET X = X + 1
40 LET X = X + 1
50 LET X = X + 1
60 LET X = X + 1
70 LET X = X + 1
80 LET X = X + 1
90 LET X = X + 1
100 LET X = X + 1
110 LET X = X + 1
120 LET X = X + 1
130 LET X = X + 1
140 LET X = X + 1
150 LET X = X + 1
160 LET X = X + 1
170 LET X = X + 1
180 LET X = X + 1
190 LET X = X + 1
200 STOP
```

When the program is run, the value of X ends up as 19. Is this the best we can do?

Not at all. Consider this program:

```
10 LET Y = Y + 1
20 LET Y = Y + 1
30 LET Y = Y + 1
40 LET Y = Y + 1
50 IF Y > 0 THEN LET Y = Y − 1
60 IF Y = 0 THEN GOTO 200
70 LET X = X + 1
80 LET X = X + 1
90 LET X = X + 1
100 LET X = X + 1
110 LET X = X + 1
120 LET X = X + 1
130 LET X = X + 1
140 LET X = X + 1
150 LET X = X + 1
160 LET X = X + 1
170 LET X = X + 1
180 LET X = X + 1
190 GOTO 50
200 STOP
```

Make a chart to see what happens here. You should finish with X at 36. Can you do better?

We have found that it is a little easier working with these programs if you use a little shorthand. We write the program above as

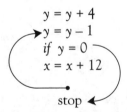

$$y = y + 4$$
$$y = y - 1$$
$$if\ y = 0$$
$$x = x + 12$$

stop

By the way, this is probably called the busy beaver problem because the computer works like a busy beaver.

We get a different problem by varying the number of steps permitted in the program.

Good luck!

informal logic

syllogisms

> When your little boys, or little girls, can solve *Syllogisms*, I fancy they
> will be much more eager to have fresh *Pairs of Premisses* supplied them,
> than any *riddles* you can offer.
>
> —LEWIS CARROLL, SYMBOLIC LOGIC

Aristotle is responsible for the earliest work in formal logic. He analyzed arguments, called syllogisms, constructed using a very restricted
part of Greek. The only statements permitted were the following
forms:

> All . . . are . . .
> No . . . are . . .
> Some . . . are . . .
> Some . . . are not . . .
> . . . is a . . .
> . . . is not a . . .

A typical syllogistic argument was

> All men are mortal.
> Socrates is a man.
> ∴ Socrates is mortal.

All possible arguments consisting of two premises and a conclusion
were analyzed (there are not that many *different* ones).

Since that time, much of the available logical energy was ex-
pended in the search for clever ways to remember which of the arguments were valid. The great eighteenth-century mathematician
Leonhard Euler developed one method. It was later improved by the
nineteenth-century logician John Venn. Charles Lutwidge Dodgson
(as Lewis Carroll, the author of *Alice's Adventures in Wonderland*)
wrote about another method in a book called *The Game of Logic*. The
method we present here is a mixture of Euler's and Venn's.

As an example, consider the Socrates syllogism. We represent
men and mortals as circles (recall Venn diagrams).

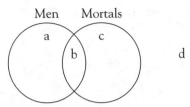

The first premise states that region a is empty. We represent that by shading it in.

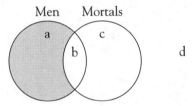

The second states that Socrates lies inside the circle of men, in our diagram region b.

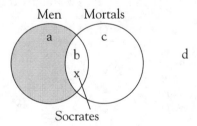

Clearly from the picture, Socrates lies inside the circle of mortals, and so the conclusion is justified.

Another example:

Some students do not favor Herrell's ice cream.
All fans of Herrell's ice cream are overweight.
∴ Some students are not overweight.

We will need three circles.

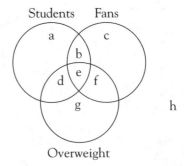

The first premise says that there are students outside the fans circle. That means something in either a or d.

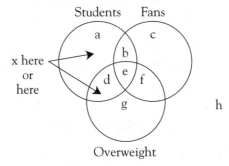

The second premise says that regions b and c are empty.

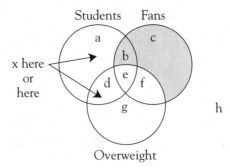

The conclusion, that there are students outside the overweight circle, is not justified, since the students mentioned are not compelled to be in region a.

EXERCISE
a. **Translate each syllogism using predicates and quantifiers.**
b. **Using Venn diagrams, decide whether or not each syllogism is valid.**

c **If the syllogism is invalid, find a structure in which the premises are true and the conclusion false.**

1. All roads lead to Rome.
   Some interstate highways are roads.
   ∴ Some interstate highways lead to Rome.

2. No decent person collects ham sandwiches.
   Some collectors of ham sandwiches are emotionally immature.
   ∴ No decent person is emotionally immature.

3. All logicians glow in the dark.
   Some logicians are not consulted by the president on a daily basis.
   ∴ Some people who are consulted by the president on a daily basis do not glow in the dark.

4. All hyperglutenous maloids experience snifterhood.
   Some of those who do not experience snifterhood also fail to practice oggentrophy.
   ∴ Some objects that fail to practice oggentrophy are in fact hyperglutenous maloids.

5. Some texts are tedious.
   Some tedious books are full of obnoxious exercises.
   ∴ Some texts are full of obnoxious exercises.

6. All important political figures have skeletons in their closets.
   Some important political figures do not appear on late-night television.
   ∴ Some persons with skeletons in their closets do not appear on late-night television.

7. All movie sequels are box office bonanzas.
   All box office bonanzas do not receive critical acclaim.
   ∴ Some movie sequels do not receive critical acclaim.

fallacies

When you have no basis for argument, abuse the plaintiff.
—Cicero

This is an old-fashioned section. Much of the rationale for discussing fallacies disappears with proper symbolization. Logic books of fifty years ago (and some today too), however, devote much time and space to the analysis of fallacies of arguments. The approach we have taken is to examine the relevance of statements and their degree of support and to use common sense. The ancients were systematic and academic. They categorized errors of reasoning and gave many of these categories Latin names.

A **fallacy** is a pattern of reasoning that can lead from true premises to false conclusions. To early logicians, there were three types of fallacies: material, verbal, and formal. The first is the most general category. The second deals with errors involving the improper use of words. The third category is concerned with common mistakes in syllogistic logic. We will not discuss this group.

Material Fallacies

Fallacy of Accident This is described as the fallacy of arguing a specific instance from a general law. An example is: "Everyone should see Niagara Falls some time in their life. Therefore, murderers in prison for life should be taken to see the falls." Now in fact, this appears to be an instance of

$$\forall x Bx$$
$$\therefore Bc$$

a perfectly valid argument in predicate logic. Where is the fallacy?

Looking at this with the benefit of predicate logic, we can see that what is happening is that a statement is made that appears universal but in fact is not. One might say, "All robins go south for the winter," without meaning to include robins in captivity (if there are any). Thus, the fallacy of accident consists of interpreting a statement that is generally true (most x's are B) as universally true (all x's are B).

Converse Fallacy of Accident This is the fallacy of concluding a general law from a specific case. An example is: "Malcolm served us the most ghastly potato salad. I guess beauticians are lousy cooks." In form, this looks like

$$Bm\ \&\ \neg Cm$$
$$\therefore \forall x(Bx \Rightarrow \neg Cx)$$

the converse of the fallacy of accident. In a sense, however, it is similar, in that again, a universal statement is erroneously made. Actually, it is a more grievous error. In the fallacy of accident, we might observe thousands of birds and decide that all birds can fly; we would then conclude that penguins can fly. In the converse fallacy of accident, we might generalize on the basis of a single case.

Ignoratio Elenchi or Irrelevant Conclusion This is the fallacy (or tactic) of appearing to argue one point while concentrating on another. This category has subcategories:

Ad hominem This is the fallacy of attacking not the argument of another person but the person himself. An example is "Of course the tax is a bad idea. The Democrats are supporting it, and they are tax-and-spend fanatics." This is one of the most common fallacies. It is particularly insidious as it closely resembles a very reasonable argument, the appeal to authority.

An argument of the form "So-and-so says blah blah; therefore we should believe blah blah" is forceful if so-and-so is a respected authority. (If so-and-so is not an authority, the argument is not good, for example, when sports heroes endorse beer.) An argument of the form "So-and-so says blah blah; therefore we should *reject* blah blah" is never good.

Ad Populum This is the fallacy of appealing to popular sentiment. An example is naming a breakfast cereal introduced in February 1991 *Desert Stormies*: "Buy this cereal and show everyone your support for our troops!" This is a fallacy because there is no connection between patriotism and breakfast cereals.

On the other hand, not every appeal to sentiment is fallacious. Is the argument "Congress should pass a universal health care plan because that is what the public overwhelmingly favors" fallacious? Well, you can say yes—this is the fallacy *ad populum*, because whether a universal health care plan is good or bad does not depend on whether it is popular. But you can also say no, since this is a democracy, and Congress has a responsibility to defer to public opinion.

Ad Baculum This is the fallacy of appealing to fear. An example is "Of course it's terrible that the Japanese bought Rockefeller Center. Do you want the Japanese owning Manhattan?"

The problem is always whether the fear is justified. Witch hunts, for example, are appeals to fear. Some of the citizens of Salem, Massachusetts, were raised to believe in witches; the extraordinary steps they took to protect themselves may seem unjustified to us today, but were the citizens really behaving fallaciously?

A current problem is the fear of child molestation. In recent years there have been scores of teachers and day-care workers accused of improper behavior to children in their care. People are so fearful of this crime that extreme steps have been taken to ensure that teachers and day-care workers can't touch our children. Are these steps justified or are we behaving fallaciously?

Ad Vercundiam   Appealing to conventional propriety. An example is: "I wouldn't vote for him. He knits sweaters." The fallacy is applying conventional wisdom—men shouldn't knit —where it has no relevance.

Once again, the appeal to convention is not always fallacious. If you are designing the interior of a bank, you can reject a row of toilets (in decorator colors) opposite the tellers' windows as unconventional, to say the least. Convention can be relevant.

Petitio Principii, Circulus in Probando, or Begging the Question
This is the fallacy of circular reasoning. *Petitio principii* consists of using the conclusion as a premise, usually in a disguised form. For example, in 1992, a referendum was held in South Africa. The issue was whether the white minority should surrender its monopoly on power. Only whites were allowed to vote. In fact, over 60 percent supported majority rule, but had the vote gone the other way, it would have been a classic case of circular reasoning. The justification for white rule would be that whites had ruled it so.

Fallacy of the Consequent   This fallacy is really just general lack of support for an argument. An example is the answer "Because" to the question "Why is the sky blue?"

Fallacy of False Cause   An example here will clearly illustrate what this fallacy is: "Every year you plant zinnias, the Red Sox win the division. You should plant zinnias this year so the Sox will win again."

Pluriam Interrogationem, or Fallacy of Many Questions This is the tactic of asking a question that presumes what you are trying to prove. The classic example is "Have you stopped beating your wife?" The question is "loaded."

This fallacy is a common problem in polling. Often the questions that are asked make subtle or overt presumptions that bias the answers. A recent mailing from the League of Conservation Voters contains a "ballot." One of the questions is "Would you be willing to spend as little as 3 cents a day to help educate voters and hold politicians accountable?" A yes vote favors government spending on an education campaign, but a no appears to favor it as well: It just suggests that three cents a day may not be enough.

Verbal Fallacies

Verbal fallacies all employ the ambiguity that abounds in natural languages. Here the word "fallacy" takes on a slightly different meaning, a sort of error. A word, a sentence will have two meanings. The ambiguity is then exploited. Often the fallacy does not occur in a formal argument but in simple discourse.

Equivocation Equivocation is using a word in two different ways in the same argument. The word "mean," for example, can indicate either nastiness or stinginess. Instances of equivocation can be very subtle. Two sides in an international dispute may both favor a just peace, but that does not mean they agree, since each understands something different by the phrase "a just peace."

In a more subtle example, we might argue that legalizing armed assault will result in less crime by noting that there would be fewer (i.e., no) persons guilty of armed assault. Reducing crime sounds good, but "crime" includes armed assault. On the other hand, in this argument, "crime" changes its meaning. In the first instance, it includes armed assault, and in the second, it doesn't.

A comic example of equivocation is the following:

Fido is my dog.
Fido is a father.
∴ Fido is my father.

The word with two "meanings" is "my."

Amphibology This fallacy is the purposeful use of grammatical ambiguity. For example, a shop called "The Little Used Book Store" could sell used books that are small, or it could be a small store that sells used books, or it could sell books that have been used only a little and so on.

Composition and Division In this fallacy, collective phrases are used to confuse. Classically these are two different fallacies. Composition refers to using a noun collectively in the minor premise of a syllogism and distributively in the major; division is the reverse. (It is not necessary to define these terms to understand this fallacy.) Here is an example: At the beginning of World War II, American citizens of Japanese ancestry were incarcerated in camps. Officially this policy was to protect them from their fellow citizens. In reality, the government feared that because Japan was now our enemy, every Japanese individual was a potential enemy. Thus the government committed the fallacy of division. (There is also equivocation in "Japanese," between ancestry and citizenship.)

Accent This fallacy exploits the difference in meaning resulting from accenting different words in a sentence. Examples are "I had a *wonderful* meal" versus "*I* had a wonderful meal" versus "I *had* a wonderful meal" versus "I had a wonderful *meal*" or even "I had *a* wonderful meal."

Figure of Speech This is the fallacy of interpreting literally a figure of speech, such as "I nearly died." This fallacy is seldom a serious problem; it is more often the subject of jokes.

EXERCISES Characterizing fallacies is like using terms of art: The fallacy being committed is sometimes unclear. That said, try these:

1. What is the fallacy suggested by the quotation at the opening of this section?
2. What is the fallacy committed by the quotation at the opening of "Law Boards: Reading Comprehension" in part 2?
3. What is the fallacy committed by the quotation at the opening of "Supporting Statements" in part 3?

4. What is the fallacy committed by the quotation at the opening of "Premises" in part 6?

5. What is the fallacy committed by the quotation at the opening of "Loofah Loofah Loofah" in part 3?

6. What fallacy is committed by *The Digestor's Digest*, page 6, in part 7?

7. The sentence "Buffalo buffalo buffalo buffalo buffalo" is ambiguous. Which verbal fallacy does it illustrate?

8. The fallacy of *petitio principii* seems to be the argument $B \therefore B$, which seems perfectly valid. Why are we saying here that it is a fallacy?

9. Write your own examples of each of the fallacies listed in this section.

rabbinic logic

GOD: Thou shalt not boil the kid in its mother's milk. (Exodus 23:19)
MOSES: Oh, you mean we shouldn't serve meat and dairy products at the same meal?
GOD: No no, I said: Thou shalt not boil the kid in its mother's milk.
MOSES: Ah, you mean we should have one set of dishes for serving meat and another for serving dairy.
GOD: No no no! Thou shalt not boil the kid in its mother's milk!
MOSES: Oh, I know! You mean we have to wait four hours after eating meat before we can eat dairy!
GOD: Oh, do what you want. You will anyway.

—ANONYMOUS

In Judaism, the Old Testament, which is the Hebrew scriptures and is regarded by Jews as the revealed word of God, contains the core of Jewish law. From this core, a succession of scholars has constructed a massive and detailed religious code, the rabbinic law, which includes the Talmud and many other texts. The extensive clarifications and additions are a monumental work that has taken thousands of years and continues to be debated and amended.

The original biblical injunctions specifically detailed later in the Talmud, Midrash, and other rabbinic texts, are not extensive. They are incomplete and occasionally contradictory. Rabbis justify their conclusions on the basis of logical rules, or hermeneutical principles.

There are at least three systems of rabbinic logic. Rabbi Ishmael's thirteen rules is perhaps the most useful. We will examine four of them.

Consider the following problem. In Leviticus 18:6, it is stated that you may not marry anyone who is related to you. The following twelve verses then explicitly list relatives you may not marry—father, mother, sister, and so on. Nowhere in the list is cousin. May you marry a cousin? On the one hand, cousins are not specifically prohibited. On the other, Leviticus 18:6 states that you may not marry a relative. Rabbinic law applies Ishmael's rule IV to resolve this, allowing marriage to a cousin.

Rule IV: .כלל ופרט אין בכלל אלא מה שבפרט
Kelal ufrat ein bikhlal ela ma shebifrat.
The general includes nothing but the particular.

This rule is applied to passages where a general statement is followed by a particular. In applying rule IV, rabbinic law concludes from the statements in Leviticus (taken in the order given) that the first statement is not necessarily true!

This rule essentially takes two premises and removes one of them. The idea might be that the first statement is sort of rhetorical and the second explains the meaning of the first.

EXAMPLE
A parent says to a child, "Don't you ever cross that street again!" and then later, "If I'm not there and you want to cross, you just wait until Bobby can take you." Of course, it is the second statement that really expresses the law; the first is to get the child's attention.

The essential feature of Ishmael's rule IV is that the second statement represents a more specific law.

Some of Ishmael's rules, like rule IV, can be formalized roughly in predicate language and some cannot. It is not clear that formalization helps. We will examine a few more. As you can see from the Leviticus example, these rules are not necessarily valid in predicate logic.

Rule V: פרט וכלל נעשה הכלל מוסיף על הפרט
ומרבינן הכלל.

> *Perat ukhlal naaseh hakelal mosif al haperat umarvinan hakelal.*

The general adds to the particular.

This rule is applied to two premises as before, a general statement and a particular statement, but this time the particular statement comes first. This time the conclusion is that both statements remain true.

EXAMPLE

A parent says to a child, "No, you can't watch television now. No television before 5:00 o'clock on weekdays." The parent certainly intends the more general statement.

Contrast this with rule IV. The difference is the order of the premises, something that matters not at all in predicate logic.

Rule VI: כלל ופרט וכלל אי אתה דן אלא כעין
הפרט.

> *Kelal ufrat ukhlal i attah dan ela ke-ein haperat.*

You deal only with that which is similar to the particular.

EXAMPLE

You ask your brother what he wants for his birthday and he says, "Oh, you can get me anything not too expensive." Then he adds, "I like hats; I need running shorts; and I always like T-shirts." He says "anything" but clearly what he would like is clothing.

The rule is not specific about what is "similar."

Rule VIII: כל דבר שהיה בכלל ויצא מן הכלל ללמד
לא ללמד על עצמו יצא אלא ללמד על
הכלל כלו יצא.

> *Kol davar shehayah bikhlal veyatza min hakelal lelammed lo lelammed al atzmo yatza ela lelammed al hakelal kullo yatza.*

Any item that is included in a general and is expressly singled out is meant to show something not about itself but about the general in which it is included.

EXAMPLE

A teacher says to a class, "If you just write 'true,' then it's wrong," and after the quiz says, "Look at Johnny's paper. For every question he has a whole sentence explaining his answer." The teacher is saying that he expects every answer to be justified.

This is a powerful rule, one that enables an extension from particular to general.

• The examples are all taken from expositions of Ishmael's rules. Some examples appear in several expositions. The chapter and verse references are to the King James version of the Bible; capitals and italics are per the original. As we indicated before, this is not ordinary logic. It does, however, exercise the logical skills of comprehending, recognizing patterns, and determining relevance. If you have difficulty, you might consult the chapter and verse to see the context.

Good luck!

CHALLENGE   In each of the following situations, a biblical passage is given and a hypothetical question is asked. Decide which of Ishmael's rules applies and then use it to decide the question.

1. If any man of you bring an offering unto the LORD, ye shall bring your offering of the cattle, *even* of the herd, and of the flock. (Leviticus 1:2)
   Are nondomesticated cows (i.e., cattle not of the herd) acceptable as offerings?

2. And thou shalt bestow that money for whatsoever thy soul lusteth after, for oxen, or for sheep, or for wine, or for strong drink, or for whatsoever thy soul desireth: and thou shalt eat there before the LORD thy God, and thou shalt rejoice, thou and thine household (Deuteronomy 14:26)
   Can you use the money for new clothes, if that is what you desire?

3. For all manner of trespass, *whether it be* for ox, for ass, for sheep, for raiment, *or* for any manner of lost thing, which *another* challengeth to be his, the cause of both parties shall come before the judges; *and* whom the judges shall condemn, he shall pay double unto his neighbor. (Exodus 22:9)
   If the judges condemn a man for a lost jug of oil, should he pay double?

4. Thou shalt not suffer a witch to live. (Exodus 22:18)
   A man also or woman that hath a familiar spirit, or that is a wizard, shall surely be put to death: they shall stone them with stones: their blood *shall be* upon them. (Leviticus 20:27)
   If a man is guilty of witchcraft but is not a wizard and does not have a familiar spirit, is that person to die, and if so, should it be by stoning?

5. Thou shalt not see thy brother's ox or his sheep go astray, and hide thyself from them: thou shalt in any case bring them again unto thy brother (Deuteronomy 22:1)
   In like manner shalt thou do with his ass: and so shalt thou do with his raiment: and with all lost thing of thy brother's, which he hath lost, and

which thou hast found, shalt thou do likewise: thou mayest not hide thyself." (Deuteronomy 22:3)

If you see a melon, which, it turns out, belongs to someone else, are you obliged to bring it to him?

6. Thou shalt not wear a garment of divers sorts, *as* of woollen and linen together. (Deuteronomy 22:11)

Are we allowed to wear corduroy pants made of 75% cotton and 25% polyester?

7. If a man deliver unto his neighbor an ass, or an ox, or a sheep, or any beast, to keep; and it die, or be hurt, or driven away, no man seeing it: *Then* shall an oath of the LORD be between them both, that he hath not put his hand unto his neighbor's goods; and the owner of it shall accept *thereof*, and he shall not make *it* good. (Exodus 22:10)

If I borrow your lamb and it runs away, and I swear I have not taken it, do I have to make restitution?

Cathy meets God

I have spent a lot of time searching through the Bible for loopholes.
—W. C. Fields

Cathy, the obnoxious junior, is at it again. In last night's bull session, Cathy attacked Wanda, the bright but vulnerable first-year student who's your best friend. You all had been discussing the religious symbolism in Madonna videos. Wanda said that everyone should worship God in her own way and that Madonna was simply responding to the Inner Light God had instilled in her. Cathy exploded.

"God? Don't tell me you still believe in that patriarchal bull. The idea of a long-haired white male father figure making all the decisions is just a chauvinist myth!"

"Well, no . . . ." Wanda was a feminist.

"How could there be a God when there's all this evil in the world? Children die, wars are fought, diseases rage, but God is supposed to be perfectly good, anti-evil, and at the same time perfectly powerful, able to do anything. So why does He allow all this unhappiness?"

Wanda certainly looked unhappy.

"And another thing. The idea of a God doesn't even make sense logically. How can anything be all-powerful? If God could do anything, God could make any size stone. But could God make a stone so big God couldn't lift it? Either way, you have to admit there is something God can't do."

EXERCISES

1. In her last two paragraphs, Cathy gives arguments that can be formalized. Formalize the first argument. Is it valid?

2. Formalize the second argument. Is it valid?

3. Compose a rebuttal to the argument you formalized in problem 1.

4. Compose a rebuttal to the argument you formalized in problem 2.

curiosities & puzzles

the digestor's digest

The Digestor's Digest also features a "fun page." On the fun page, all articles are completely false and all ads are completely true. Unfortunately, in the rush to get out the first issue of the *Digest,* the banner reading "FUN PAGE" was left out, so it is not clear which page is the fun page. There is only one fun page. Actually, it is possible to figure out that page 1 is not the fun page. (How?) You may not be able to tell at this point which page *is* the fun page, but nonetheless there are conclusions you can draw about pages 2, 3, and now 4.

The Digestor's Digest

Vol. I No. 1	Page 4

Fast Food News

The breakfast menu at Burger Mad now features the delicious new "Crois-sausage," with the least cholesterol of all fast food sandwiches.

Fast Food News

The breakfast menu at O'Donnell's now features the delicious new "Egg O'Muffin," with the least cholesterol of all fast food sandwiches. There is an ad on this page.

exam warning IV

Well, well, well! The letters continue to roll in! Among the less hostile, and certainly the most interesting, is the following:

Hey, you guys—

> *Quit fooling around! Teresa's argument can be carried all the way. You can show that the exam can't be on the next-to-next-to-last page and that it can't be on the next-to-next-to-next-to-last page, and so on. This means that you can't have the exam anywhere in the book, so you jokers lied in "Exam Warning I."*
>
> *Look, I know I'm right about this, unless you bums try to find some cheap way to weasel out of it.*
>
> *And another thing . . . money back, or else.*

Disrespectfully,

Peter Predicate

Well! We don't know exactly what to say to this. We won't say, however, that we aren't worried. If Peter is right, a *surprise* exam may be logically impossible. This would be a disappointment for us, as we're sure it would be for our readers.

But we've been in tight spots before! We remain confident in our Surprise Examination. When we've had a chance to think about the problem, we'll respond.

the game of logic

Logic is the art of going wrong with confidence.
—W. H. Auden

The immortal author of the Alice books was in private life Charles Lutwidge Dodgson, mathematician and logician of Christ Church at Oxford University. He made no really important contributions to these fields, but he wrote extensively and engagingly. Perhaps his most interesting work was the creation of a method for solving syllogisms. In some ways, it is superior to Euler's and Venn's.

Carroll devised a two-part board to analyze syllogisms:

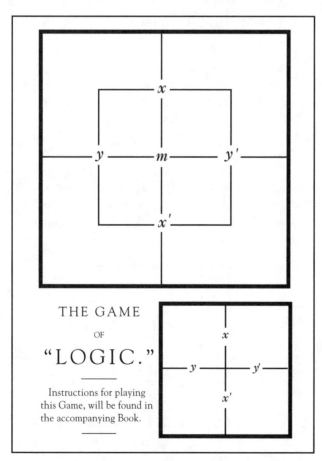

• Carroll uses the notation x' for the negation of x (or, if we are thinking of sets, the complement of x).

It looks odd, but it is really a form of a three-circle Venn diagram, where the circles become

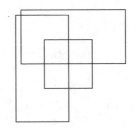

The advantage to Carroll's diagram was that the outside region was now enclosed.

Carroll's second innovation was to use colored disks as markers to record statements. Let us use nickels and pennies. Pennies will represent empty sections, and nickels nonempty ones.

EXAMPLE   (from Carroll's *Symbolic Logic*)
Some candles give very little light;
Candles are *meant* to give light.
∴ Some things, that are meant to give light, give very little.

Carroll used the middle square, marked "*m*," to represent the middle term, the predicate that appears in both of the premises. In this case, that is "is a candle." Let *x* be "gives very little light." Let *y* be "is meant to give light." Then we represent the first premise as follows:

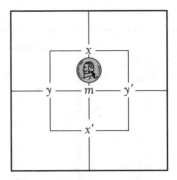

The nickel is on the border to indicate that it could be in either of the two regions. We add the second premise:

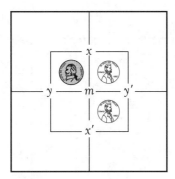

The pennies indicate empty regions, so notice that the nickel has been pushed over. Carroll uses the smaller board to record the information gained:

Now we see that the conclusion is indicated by the diagram, so the argument is valid.

EXAMPLE
    No professors are ignorant.
    All ignorant people are vain.
    ∴ No professors are vain.

The middle term is "is ignorant." Let x be "is a professor" and y be "is vain." We first have

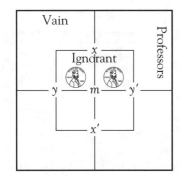

Then we have

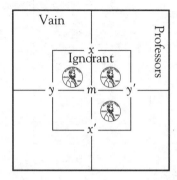

There is really nothing to record on the smaller diagram, and so the conclusion is not justified (there *could* be something in the upper left corner, in the *xy* square), so the argument is invalid.

EXERCISE   Analyze these syllogisms from *Symbolic Logic*.

1. All wise men walk on their feet.
   All unwise men walk on their hands.
   ∴ No man walks on both.

2. Some unauthorized reports are false.
   All authorized reports are trustworthy.
   ∴ Some false reports are not trustworthy.

3. A prudent man shuns hyaenas.
   No banker is imprudent.
   ∴ No banker fails to shun hyaenas.

4. No frogs are poetical.
   Some ducks are unpoetical.
   ∴ Some ducks are not frogs.

the sorites of Lewis Carroll

> Mathematics does not exercise the judgement and if too exclusively pursued, may leave the student very ill qualified for moral reasoning.
> —R. Whately

The word **sorites** (pronounced "sor-EYE-teez") has two logical connections. In this chapter, it is a puzzle resembling a syllogism with many premises. The task is to discover the conclusion, which is not given. Lewis Carroll invented many sorites to amuse and to demonstrate his method for solving them. All the sorites given here are his.

In Greek, the literal meaning of *sorites* is "heaped up" (connoting here a heap of premises). It has come to refer also to the paradox of the heap (see "The Paradox of the Heap" in part 9). Don't get them confused—they are different.

EXAMPLE
1. Babies are illogical.
2. Nobody is despised who can manage a crocodile.
3. Illogical persons are despised.

One way to solve these is to draw Venn diagrams with more circles, since there are more predicates (four in this case). Carroll's system easily allows more predicates, as you can see:

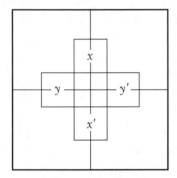

Four predicates

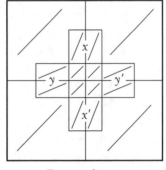

Five predicates

When you encounter a sorites with many more premises, however, Carroll's system becomes problematic.

The other method is to find pairs of premises with a common term and use them to deduce a statement. We could take example statements 2 and 3 and conclude

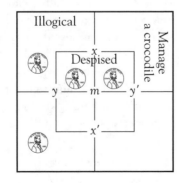

4. Persons who can manage a crocodile are not illogical.
   Now with a new diagram, we combine statements 4 and 1:

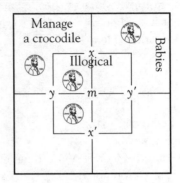

5. Babies cannot manage crocodiles.

We have used all the premises, so this is the conclusion.

EXERCISE   Find conclusions for these sorites of Carroll.

1. No terriers wander among the signs of the zodiac;
   Nothing that does not wander among the signs of the zodiac, is a comet;
   Nothing but a terrier has a curly tail.

2. Things sold in the street are of no great value;
   Nothing but rubbish can be had for a song;
   Eggs of the Great Auk are very valuable;
   It is only what is sold in the street that is really *rubbish*.

3. I despise anything that cannot be used as a bridge;
   Everything, that is worth writing an ode to, would be a welcome gift to me;
   A rainbow will not bear the weight of a wheel-barrow;
   Whatever can be used as a bridge will bear the weight of a wheel-barrow;
   I would not take, as a gift, a thing that I despise.

4. Animals are always mortally offended if I fail to notice them;
   The only animals that belong to *me* are in that field;
   No animal can guess a conundrum, unless it has been properly trained in a Board-School;
   None of the animals in that field are badgers;
   When an animal is mortally offended, it always rushes about wildly and howls;
   I never notice any animal, unless it belongs to me;
   No animal, that has been properly trained in a Board-School, ever rushes about wildly and howls.

5. For enthusiasts only!

260

I don't like walking with any London-friend of mine, unless he wears a tall hat;

The Colonel is ready to play billiards with any man who is not the subject of general conversation, unless he happens to be fat;

A man, who knows what o'clock it is and who never yields to me in argument, is unattractive;

No old tight-rope-dancer ever rouses me to enthusiasm;

Any novelist, whom I take pleasure in cutting, always cuts me dead;

A man, who goes about in kid-gloves, but without his coat, is a humbug;

All my intimate friends in London are young men;

No man, who is the subject of general conversation, ever rouses me to enthusiasm, unless he is a horsey man;

A man, who has his wits about him and does not choose his own wines, is always "at home" when I call;

A man, who is a good shot and never tells pointless anecdotes, is sure to have a good temper;

All humbugs, who write novels, are intimate friends of mine;

I like to walk with a good-tempered man, unless he goes about in his shirt-sleeves;

A man, who never loses his umbrella, and is not easily taken in, is sure to be an early riser;

Fat men, who do not dance on the tight-rope, are universally respected;

I regard with contemptuous pity a man who fails in life, and who runs across the street;

A man, who does not stick to business, is not likely to be elected Mayor, unless he has bushy whiskers;

An elephant hunter always rouses me to enthusiasm, unless he happens to be a farmer;

Any London friend of mine, who tells pointless anecdotes, is a humbug;

I never invite an old man to dinner, unless he has lent me money;

A man, who does not stick to business, does not run across the street, and has bushy hair, is in no danger of getting a bad fall;

A man, who gets up late and sometimes loses his umbrella, has little chance of marrying an heiress;

An old man, who cares for appearances, always wears kid-gloves;

A good-tempered man never cuts me dead, unless he is a humbug;

A man, who never tells pointless anecdotes and has never lent me money, has his wits about him;

A man, who chooses his own wines and always yields to me in argument, is the sort that I invite to dine with me;

I always try to be civil to a man who fails in life, unless he has bushy whiskers;

All farmers are horsey men;

A novelist is a dull companion, unless he rouses me to enthusiasm;

All men, who get up early, and stick to business and win universal respect, are rich;

Any London friend of mine, to whom I try to be civil, will probably be elected Mayor;

Any good-tempered man, who has lent me money and does not care for appearances, is willing to shake hands with me when I am in rags;

The only men, with whom the Colonel will play billiards, are either horsey men or farmers;

I always invite an attractive man to dine with me, provided he is rich;

A man, who is apt to walk to tip-toe and whom I regard with contemptuous pity, is sure to be one who sticks to business;

The only men, who are always "at home" to me, but whom I never invite to dinner, are magistrates;

I always make an intimate friend of a man who will shake hands with me when I am in rags and will give up his umbrella to me when it is raining;

Any London friend of mine, who understands horses, is universally respected;

An unattractive man, who chooses his own wines, is easily taken in;

I have sufficient courage to insult any novelist, unless he happens to be a good shot;

An old man, who is apt to walk on tip-toe, will probably get a bad fall;

A man, who never knows what o'clock it is, and who has never lent me money, will probably marry an heiress;

No London-friend of mine, who has his wits about him, is easily taken in;

I never forget any old man who is willing to shake hands with me when I am in rags;

A novelist, who does not stick to business, is sure to fail in life;

I do not dare to insult an ill-tempered man, unless he happens to be an intimate friend of mine;

Those magistrates, who will not shake hands with me when I am in rags, always choose their own wine;

All dull companions are either horsey men or elephant-hunters;

Men, who wear tall hats and kid-gloves, always cut me dead;

A man, who has bushy whiskers and is universally respected, is apt to walk on tip-toe;

I delight in cutting a man, whom I perfectly remember, but who will not give up his umbrella to me when it is raining.

DEDUCTION, INFINITY, AND A HAIRCUT

contents

263

GOAL: To develop a clear approach to validity. The method of structures is wonderful for showing consistency— and nonvalidity. If ¬A is true in a structure, A is not valid. But the method of structures does not show validity clearly. The method of deduction does. We specify a few rules for manipulating logical symbols. And we say things like A implies B if it is possible to start from A and reach B eventually by applying only those explicit rules. The specific rules we give are especially useful because they're so closely tied to the meaning of the logical symbols. Learn the rules and you will understand the symbols. Understand the symbols and the rules will seem obvious.

FORMAL LOGIC: DEDUCTIONS

MAIN CONNECTIVES

He who will not reason is a bigot; he who cannot is a fool; and he who does not, is a slave.

—WILLIAM DRUMMOND

Any wff of predicate logic has only one of eight possible forms:

Negation:	$\neg A$
Conjunction:	$A \ \& \ B$
Alternation:	$A \vee B$
Conditional:	$A \Rightarrow B$
Biconditional:	$A \Leftrightarrow B$
Universal quantification:	$\forall x A x$
Existential quantification:	$\exists x A x$
Atomic wff:	$F^n t_1 \ . \ . \ . \ t_n$ (The most important atomic wff is $t_1 = t_2$.)

Any subwffs of a wff (such as A, B, and Ax above) in turn have one of these eight forms. Thus any wff of predicate logic is associated with a unique syntactic tree with that wff at the top of the tree, the subwffs of the main connective of the wff in the next line, and so on down to the atomic wffs.

EXAMPLE

$$((\exists x A x \ \& \ \exists x B x) \Leftrightarrow \exists x (A x \& \ B x)) \text{ (Main connective; } \Leftrightarrow)$$

$((\exists x A x \ \& \ \exists x B x) \text{ (Main connective: \&)} \qquad \exists x (A x \ \& \ B x)) \text{ (Main connective: } \exists)$

$\exists x A x \text{ (Main connective } \exists) \qquad \exists x B x \qquad (A x \ \& \ B x) \text{ (Main connective: \&)}$

$A x \quad \text{(Atomic)} \qquad\qquad\qquad B x \qquad\quad A x \quad B x \quad \text{(Atomic)}$

264

You read about syntactic trees in parts 3 and 5, where we discussed the formal languages Sentential and predicate. You should reread the relevant sections before going on.

The deduction rules apply to the main connective of a wff. *They do not apply to subwffs.* Only one set of rules can apply to a given wff at a given stage of deduction depending on what the main connective is. Remember this! It is the *Key* to deductions.

We will present you with a rule of $\exists$-elimination, which says, roughly, that if you have a wff of the form $\exists x W x$, you may infer a wff of the form $W c^*$, where c^* is a temporary name. We will express this rule as $\exists x W x \therefore W c^*$. It applies iff $\exists$ is the main connective of the wff; *otherwise not.*

EXAMPLE

    1. $\exists x(Ax \,\&\, Bx)$ 2. $\exists x Ax \,\&\, \exists x Bx$
       $\therefore Ac^* \,\&\, Bc^*$ $\therefore Ac^* \,\&\, Bc^*$ (Wrong! Wrong!)

The rule can be applied in case 1, but *not* in case 2.

We will present you with a rule of $\&$-introduction which says, roughly, that if you have two wffs of forms W and V, you may infer a wff of the form $W \,\&\, V$. We will express this rule as $W, V \therefore W \,\&\, V$. It can only be applied to create a wff with a main connective $\&$; *otherwise not.*

EXAMPLE

    1. $\exists x Ax, \exists x Bx$ 2. $\exists x Ax, \exists x Bx$
       $\therefore \exists x Ax \,\&\, \exists x Bx$ $\therefore \exists x(Ax \,\&\, Bx)$ (Wrong! Wrong!)

The rule can be applied in case 1 but *not* in case 2.

This discussion might seem trivial, but 93 percent of the mistakes students make when doing deductions can be traced to misreading (sometimes willfully) the main connective. Read this again after you've studied deductions.

EXERCISE Explain why in the examples both cases 1 are correct and both cases 2 are incorrect. The explanation turns on what the main connective of the complex wff is.

SUMMARY: The definition of well-formed formula ensures that every wff of a formal language has a main connective. The deduction rules to follow are keyed to the main connective.

265

DEDUCTION

Sir, I have found you an argument; but I am not obliged to find you an understanding.

—SAMUEL JOHNSON

In "Interpreting Predicate Logic by Structures" in part 5, and in "Logical Form" in part 2 we defined logical validity as being "true in all structures." This concept "true in all structures" was left rather vague, or, as we prefer to say, "intuitive." (WARNING: Remember the ambiguity of the word "validity." A wff is valid iff it is true in all structures; an argument is valid [or its premises imply its conclusion] iff in any structure in which the premises are true, the conclusion is. The connecting idea is that the wff $A \Rightarrow B$ is valid iff the argument $A \therefore B$ is valid.)

The problem was, you'll recall, that we presented no clear method for showing whether a wff was true in all structures. To be sure, it was often easy to find a particular structure in which some wff A was true (and hence $\neg A$ was false, and hence $\neg A$ was *not* valid). The problem was showing that a wff was true in all structures.

So we're going to switch gears for a while to present a new technique for showing validity. We'll start off with the truth functions of Sentential and then turn to quantifiers and identity symbols.

The technique is called "deduction" or "natural deduction" because it is very close to how humans actually reason, progressing step by step from the premises of an argument to a conclusion.

The basic idea is this: We begin with a list of **simple inference rules,** rules for inferring a conclusion from a premise (or premises). An argument form will be deductively valid if we can deduce the conclusion by successively applying these basic inferences rules to the premises.

Moreover, there is an added bonus to our listing of the inference rules: They will sum up the meanings of the logical symbols. Even if you know no other logic, if you know and understand the inference rules, you will understand the logical symbols! Intuitively, the rules capture the meaning of the logical symbols completely.

For each logical symbol ($\neg$, &, $\vee$, $\Rightarrow$, $\Leftrightarrow$, $\exists$, $\forall$, and =) we'll list two types of rules, an **introduction** or **entry rule** and an **exit** or **elimination rule.** For example, the &-elimination (&E for short) rules tell you how to eliminate a conjunction, if you have one. In other words, they tell you what you may conclude if you know something of the form A & B. Similarly, the $\forall$-elimination ($\forall$E) rule tells you how to eliminate a universal quantification, if you have one. In other words, it tells you what you may conclude if you know something of the form $\forall x Ax$.

In a similar vein, the &-introduction (&I) rules tell you how to add a conjunction, if you want one. In other words, they tell you what you need to conclude something of the form A & B. Similarly, the $\forall$-introduction ($\forall$I) rule tells you how to add a universal quantifier, if you want one. In other words, it tells you what you need to conclude something of the form $\forall x Ax$.

In the following discussion, A, B, and C can be any wffs in a predicate language. You might review "Predicate Languages" in part 5 before proceeding.

Here are the basic inference rules:

Logical Symbol	Introduction Rule	Elimination Rule
$\neg$	$A \Rightarrow (B \,\&\, \neg B)$ $\therefore \neg A$	$\neg\neg A$ $\therefore A$

The standard way of establishing that a negation ($\neg A$) is T is to show that the unnegated statement (A) leads to a contradiction or absurdity. If $A \Rightarrow (B \,\&\, \neg B)$ is T, then since $B \,\&\, \neg B$ is F, so is A. Hence we know $\neg A$ is T. On the other hand, we can't just eliminate $\neg$ from a statement; this can be done only under special circumstances, such as double negation. (NOTE: The comments to the right of the wff give the justification for listing the wff, for example, whether it is a premise or is the result of applying a rule to the wff on the line with the number specified.)

EXAMPLE $\quad \neg\neg\neg\neg A \therefore A$

1. $\neg\neg\neg\neg A$ premise
2. $\neg\neg A$ $\neg$E, 1
3. A $\neg$E, 2

Logical Symbol	Introduction Rule	Elimination Rules	
&	A, B $\therefore A \,\&\, B$	$A \,\&\, B$ $\therefore A$	$A \,\&\, B$ $\therefore B$

267

Notice that &-introduction requires two premises, one for each conjunct (and hence two line numbers in the justification). On the other hand, we have two rules of &-elimination, since given A & B, we may conclude either conjunct.

EXAMPLE A & $B \therefore B$ & A

    1. A & B premise
    2. A &E, 1
    3. B &E, 1
    4. B & A &I, 3, 2

Logical Symbol	Introduction Rules		Elimination Rule
$\vee$	A $\therefore A \vee B$	B $\therefore A \vee B$	$A \vee B, A \Rightarrow C, B \Rightarrow C$ $\therefore C$

We have two rules of $\vee$-introduction since we can conclude $A \vee B$ given either component alone (compare this to &I). $\vee$-elimination is called "argument by cases." If you know that either $A \vee B$ is true, and you know each yields C separately, then you may conclude C. (It's called "argument by cases" because people often say: Suppose $A \vee B$. In case 1, A is true, but $A \Rightarrow C$, so C; in case 2, B is true, but $B \Rightarrow C$, so C. Hence in either case, C is true, $\therefore C$.)

EXAMPLE A & $B \therefore A \vee B$

    1. A & B premise
    2. A &E, 1
    3. $A \vee B$ $\vee$I, 2

Logical Symbol	Introduction Rule	Elimination Rule
$\Rightarrow$	(to be presented later)	$A, A \Rightarrow B$ $\therefore B$

These rules are probably the most important in logic. $\Rightarrow$-introduction is a bit complicated to state, so we'll save it for last. $\Rightarrow$-elimination is often known by its Latin name, *modus ponens*. When you have a conditional $(A \Rightarrow B)$ and the antecedent of the conditional (A), then you have the consequent (B). Acceptance of this law distinguishes human beings as rational animals.

EXAMPLE $(A \& (A \Rightarrow B)) \therefore B$
1. $(A \& (A \Rightarrow B))$ premise
2. A & E, 1
3. $A \Rightarrow B$ &E, 1
4. B $\Rightarrow$ E, 2, 3

Logical Symbol	Introduction Rule	Elimination Rules	
$\Leftrightarrow$	$A \Rightarrow B, B \Rightarrow A$ $\therefore A \Leftrightarrow B$	$A \Leftrightarrow B$ $\therefore A \Rightarrow B$	$A \Leftrightarrow B$ $\therefore B \Rightarrow A$

In effect, these laws define $A \Leftrightarrow B$ as $(A \Rightarrow B) \& (B \Rightarrow A)$. Compare them to the rules for &.

The nice thing about deduction rules is that they extend naturally to the quantifiers and the identity symbol. Before giving you any extended examples of deductions, we'd like to list these other rules. As before, A, B, and C can be any wffs; x is any variable; s and t are any terms; Ax is an arbitrary wff A where the x draws attention to a *possible* free variable. If Ax is a wff, At is a substitution instance of Ax. That means that each free x in Ax is replaced by t *as long as* no variable in t gets bound in the replacement. (See "Predicate Languages" in part 5 for a review of the definitions.) Remember: At and Ac^* are substitution instances of Ax (not vice versa; Ax need not be a substitution instance of At).

• WARNING: Calling these rules by the names "introduction" and "elimination" rules is a mnemonic device—it makes them easy to remember. *The rules do not allow you to introduce or eliminate connectives at will!* Every year there are some readers, who, when stuck on a problem, reason thus: $A \therefore \neg A$ ($\neg$-introduction) or $\neg A \therefore A$ ($\neg$-elimination). Such readers inevitably become discouraged and fail to understand logic, and some even succumb to the lure of hard drugs. Don't be one of them. *Think what a rule means before you apply it.* END WARNING

Logical Symbol	Introduction Rule	Elimination Rule
$\exists$	At (t any term) $\therefore \exists x Ax$ (or $\exists y Ay$, etc.)	$\exists x Ax$ $\therefore Ac^*$ The c^* is a temporary name. It does not appear before in the deduction and is not in the conclusion.

$\exists$-introduction is an easy rule: You can always existentially quantify a position in a wff. Indeed, you can pass from Rzz to $\exists y Rzy$ (Rzz is a substitution instance for Rzy (where z is substituted for y), but not vice versa) and from that to $\exists x \exists y Rxy$ (after all, if Rzz is ever true, there really is something that bears R to something!). $\exists$-elimination corresponds to a form natural reasoning. "We know someone committed the murders; let's call him or her 'Jack the Ripper' ($=c^*$)." So now we can pretend that Jack the Ripper (or c^*) is the killer's name and continue to reason. Of course, it would be silly to use the same name twice in a single deduction. "We know someone is the Queen, let's call her 'Jack the Ripper' ($=c^*$). My God, the Queen is a serial murderer!" No, that's faulty logic. The second time around, we should use d^* or e^* or d'^* and not assume any of these are equal to c^*. (The * reminds us that the name is not real but only temporary.)

EXAMPLE $\exists x(Fx \ \& \ Gx) \ \therefore \exists x Gx$

1.	$\exists x(Fx \ \& \ Gx)$	premise
2.	$Fc^* \ \& \ Gc^*$	$\exists$E, 1
3.	Gc^*	&E, 2
4.	$\exists x Gx$	$\exists$I, 3

Logical Symbol	Introduction Rule	Elimination Rule
$\forall$	Ax $\therefore \forall x Ax$ $\forall$-introduction rule applies provided that the variable x is not free in any premise of the deduction (hence Ax is not such a premise) and Ax does not include any temporary name like c^*.	$\forall x Ax$ $\therefore At$ (t any term)

• WARNING: We must distinguish between the *premise(s) of a rule* and the *premise(s) of a deduction*. The premises of a rule are just the wffs we apply the rule to, so of course x is free in the premise of the rule for $\forall$-introduction. The premises of a deduction are wffs that we assume for the deduction: Our only goal is to show that the conclusion follows from those wffs. If x is free in any of those premises, then $\forall$-introduction can't be applied to it.

$\forall$-elimination, like $\exists$-introduction, is straightforward. Just drop the $\forall x$ (or $\forall y$, etc.) and replace every resulting free occurrence of x by the term t. $\forall$-introduction, like $\exists$-elimination, is trickier. The basic idea is that you may conclude $\forall x Ax$ if Ax is true of each object. So given $Fx \lor \neg Fx$, it follows by $\forall$-introduction that $\forall x(Fx \lor \neg Fx)$. But just because a wff Ax occurs in your deduction, you don't necessarily know that Ax is true of everything. Maybe your Ax was just a given or a premise (Ax might be "x is an even number" or "x is a serial murderer" or "x lives in Boca Raton"). In such cases, it would be most unwise to conclude $\forall x Ax$. Finally, temporary names also present a problem and must be eliminated before using ∀-introduction. (Here's one reason. Given ∃yAxy, for example, x has a spouse," you might conclude Axc*, where we call x's spouse c*, by ∃-elimination. But c* depends on x [different people have different spouses]. It is unwise to conclude ∀xAxc*; that is, everyone is married to c*!)

Logical Symbol	Introduction Rule	Elimination Rules	
$=$	$\therefore \forall x(x = x)$	$s = t, As$ $\therefore At$	$s = t, At$ $\therefore As$

=-introduction says that you can introduce $\forall x(x = x)$ whenever you wish and so, given ∀-elimination, this means you can introduce $t = t$ for any term t. = -elimination is also known as "Leibniz's law," the indiscernibility of identicals. If s *is* t, then any property of s is a property of t. We need a second version of the law to ensure that = is symmetric; that is, order doesn't matter in $s = t$. We could dispense with the second version if we added the principle $s = t \therefore t = s$.

A deduction from premises is a finite sequence of wffs (or statements of natural language) such that each is either a premise or follows from previous wffs (statements) by a rule of inference. We say that wffs A, B, C, and D deductively imply W iff there is a deduction of W from A, B, C, and D. We say that W is deductively valid iff there is a deduction of W without premises. Such deductions are sometimes called proofs. After we examine the rule for ⟹-introduction, you will understand how there can be deductions from no premises.

EXAMPLE   ∃y∀xRxy ∴ ∀x∃yRxy
1. ∃y∀xRxy   premise
2. ∀xRxc*   ∃E, 1
3. Rxc*   ∀E, 2
4. ∃yRxy   ∃I, 3
5. ∀x∃yRxy   ∀I, 4

EXERCISE   Try to supply the justifications in the following deductions. WARNING: We have included some phony deductions
that contain a mistaken step. Can you spot them?

271

1. $(P \lor Q) \Rightarrow R, P \quad \therefore R$
   1. $(P \lor Q) \Rightarrow R$
   2. P
   3. $(P \lor Q)$
   4. R

2. $\exists xFx \quad \therefore \exists yFy$
   1. $\exists xFx$
   2. $Fc*$
   3. $\exists yFy$

3. $\exists zGz \ \& \ \exists zHz \quad \therefore \exists z(Gz \ \& \ Hz)$
   1. $\exists zGz \ \& \ \exists zHz$
   2. $\exists zGz$
   3. $Gc*$
   4. $\exists zHz$
   5. $Hc*$
   6. $Gc* \ \& \ Hc*$
   7. $\exists z(Gz \ \& \ Hz)$

4. $Fd \quad \therefore \exists y(Fy \ \& \ y = d)$
   1. Fd
   2. $\forall x(x = x)$
   3. $d = d$
   4. $Fd \ \& \ d = d$
   5. $\exists y(Fy \ \& \ y = d)$

5. $\forall x\exists yRxy \quad \therefore \exists y\forall xRxy$
   1. $\forall x\exists yRxy$
   2. $\exists yRxy$
   3. $Rxc*$
   4. $\forall xRxc*$
   5. $\exists y\forall xRxy$

6. $\exists zFz, \forall y(Fy \Leftrightarrow Gy) \quad \therefore \exists xGx$
   1. $\exists zFz$
   2. $Fc*$
   3. $\forall y(Fy \Leftrightarrow Gy)$
   4. $Fc* \Leftrightarrow Gc*$
   5. $Fc* \Rightarrow Gc*$
   6. $Gc*$
   7. $\exists xGx$

CHALLENGE Try to deduce the conclusions from the premises in the following argument forms.

1. $P \Rightarrow Q, \quad Q \Rightarrow R, \quad P \quad \therefore R$
2. $\forall xFx, \forall x(Fx \Rightarrow \neg\neg Gx)$
   $\quad \therefore \forall xGx$
3. $\forall yFy \quad \therefore \forall zFz$

SUMMARY: The method of natural deduction provides a powerful technique for showing that wffs or argument forms are valid.

HYPOTHETICAL REASONING: DEDUCTION FROM ASSUMPTIONS

Pity the Unicorn
Pity the Hippogriff,
Souls that were never born
Out of the land of If!
—MARTHA OSTENSO

The rule of $\Rightarrow$-introduction is significantly different from the other rules, but it is also one of the most familiar, since we use it all the time in ordinary life. For example, a detective like Sherlock Hemlock might say in the course of reasoning about a crime, "*Assume* the butler killed the cow. He would have had to move the body from the bedroom down to the kitchen and grind it into hamburger before the police arrived. But he could not possibly have done this alone. *Therefore* the butler must have had help—if he did it."

Now what has Hemlock established by this reasoning? Not that the butler did it; that was an assumption. Not that the butler had help; that is true only if the assumption is true. What the reasoning proves is the conditional: If the butler did it, then he had help. In logical terms:

"The butler killed the cow" $\Rightarrow$ "The butler had help"

In general, in order to establish a statement of the form

$$A \Rightarrow B$$

we *assume* A and then (using premises or other assumptions) *deduce* B. If we can deduce B from A, we count that as a deduction of $A \Rightarrow B$. *This is the rule of $\Rightarrow$-introduction.*

Let's look at some examples and then formulate the $\Rightarrow$I rule a bit more precisely.

EXAMPLE 1 $P \Rightarrow Q, Q \Rightarrow R \therefore P \Rightarrow R$
  1. $P \Rightarrow Q$ premise
  2. $Q \Rightarrow R$ premise
  3. P assumption

4.		Q	$\Rightarrow$E, 1, 3
5.		R	$\Rightarrow$E, 2, 4
6. $P \Rightarrow R$			$\Rightarrow$I, 3–5 (the assumption, P, is now said to be "discharged")

Notice that we indent (or push to the right) that assumption and all wffs that depend on it. We unindent (or pop to the left) when we introduce the conditional, since the truth of the conditional does not depend on any assumption. (When we introduce the conditional, we are said to "discharge" the assumption. We discharge it because it is no longer needed.) *Finally, notice that the discharged assumption appears as the* antecedent *(left side) of the* $\Rightarrow$, *while the conclusion appears as the* consequent *(right side) of the* $\Rightarrow$. (Please commit this comment to memory; it will save you many embarrassing misapplications of $\Rightarrow$-introduction. Thank you.)

EXAMPLE 2 $P \Rightarrow Q \therefore \neg Q \Rightarrow \neg P$

1. $P \Rightarrow Q$			premise
2.	$\neg Q$		assumption
3.		P	assumption
4.		Q	$\Rightarrow$ E, 1, 3
5.		$Q \& \neg Q$	&I, 2, 4
6.	$P \Rightarrow (Q \& \neg Q)$		$\Rightarrow$ I, 3–5 (thus, P is discharged or "unassumed")
7.	$\neg P$		$\neg$I, 6
8. $\neg Q \Rightarrow \neg P \Rightarrow$ I, 2–7			(thus $\neg Q$ is discharged or "unassumed")

Notice that in this proof, we have a deduction from an assumption *inside* a deduction from an assumption. These *nested* subdeductions are rather like nested parentheses. As with parentheses, we can repeat the pattern as often as we like—([{()}])—but like parentheses, we can never close the outer deduction before we close the inner one; that is, the pattern ({)} is not allowed.

By the way, the pattern of the proof in example 2 is quite common. $\neg$I is often called "proof by contradiction." You assume the negation of what you want to show, next show that this opposite leads to a contradiction, then apply the rule of $\neg$I to get what you want. (For more on this technique read "Proof by Contradiction" later in this part.) In fact, you can often reason backward to set up a deduction. Suppose you want to show $P \Rightarrow Q \therefore \neg Q \Rightarrow \neg P$. Since you want to show a conditional statement, $\neg Q \Rightarrow \neg P$, your last step will be $\Rightarrow$I. So begin by assuming $\neg Q$ and deducing $\neg P$.

274

Now what do you want to show? You want to show a negation, $\neg P$. Therefore your last step will be $\neg$I. You need to get $P \Rightarrow (A \& \neg A)$ (where A is any old formula; you just want to get a contradiction).

Now you want to show a conditional, $P \Rightarrow (A \& \neg A)$. Therefore your last step will be $\Rightarrow$I. Begin by assuming P and then deduce a contradiction.

Notice that by this backward reasoning, you figure out that you need the assumptions $\neg Q$ and P to get a contradiction and your premise is $P \Rightarrow Q$. One application of $\Rightarrow$E gives you your contradiction. (For more techniques on constructing deductions, read on!)

Some important things to remember are the following:

1. Always indent when you make an assumption.
2. Every assumption must be discharged by an application of $\Rightarrow$ I (i.e., the deduction must be unindented).
3. If you assume A and show B, then $\Rightarrow$ I will give $A \Rightarrow B$.
4. After you unindent, you may not use any indented line later in the proof (of course, a statement that can be justified without the assumption can be reused even if it first appears indented). More precisely, you may not use anything that *follows only from* the assumption, since such statements are not necessarily true without the assumption.

Finally, we must modify the rule ∀I slightly because of $\Rightarrow$I:

Logical Symbol	Introduction Rule
∀	Ax $\therefore \forall x Ax$ provided that the variable x is not free in any premise of the deduction (and so Ax must not be a premise of the deduction) or in any undischarged assumption, and provided that Ax does not include any temporary name like c^*.

Thus it is incorrect to assume, say, "x is young" and then apply ∀I to the assumption to conclude $\forall x$("x is young").

A Labor-Saving Device

Deduction works as a rigorous logical method because there is a specific set of rules allowed. In principle, no other rules are needed to show any valid wff or argument form valid. *In practice*, as we go along deducing valid wffs and derived rules, each result can be used in later deductions. Instead of repeating the proof of a result each time we use it, we can just state the result and where it came from. Deduction, in other words, is cumulative. The more we prove, the more tools we have to prove things with. This is why mathematicians number their theorems in the order in which they are proved.

EXAMPLE 3 $(P \Rightarrow Q) \Rightarrow (\neg Q \Rightarrow \neg P)$

1.	$P \Rightarrow Q$	assumption
2.	$\neg Q \Rightarrow \neg P$	from 1 by previous example.
3.	$(P \Rightarrow Q) \Rightarrow (\neg Q \Rightarrow \neg P)$	$\Rightarrow$I, 1–2

(Note that if you do not like to refer to previous work, you could replace lines 1 and 2 above with the eight lines of the previous deduction.)

EXERCISE 1   **Provide the justification for each step in the following proofs.**

1. $(P \& Q) \Rightarrow R$ $\therefore P \Rightarrow (Q \Rightarrow R)$

   1. $(P \& Q) \Rightarrow R$
   2. P
   3. Q
   4. $P \& Q$
   5. R
   6. $Q \Rightarrow R$
   7. $P \Rightarrow (Q \Rightarrow R)$

2. $\forall x(Ax \Rightarrow B)$ $\therefore \exists x Ax \Rightarrow B$ (as long as x is not free in B)

   1. $\forall x(Ax \Rightarrow B)$
   2. $\exists x Ax$
   3. $Ac*$
   4. $Ac* \Rightarrow B$
   5. B
   6. $\exists x Ax \Rightarrow B$

   (Step 4 would not be legitimate if x were free in B; can you see why?)

One More Rule (for experts only)

As we just said, we don't need any more rules. Anything we want can be deduced from the introduction and elimination rules (indeed, any wff that is true in all interpretations can be deduced from those rules). But sometimes the deductions are a bit roundabout and require some ingenuity.

So what is the real point of deductions? If we view them only as part of a formal game played with symbols, then we should develop all the important valid wffs from just these basic ones. For example, we should deduce $A \vee \neg A$ without using any premises! (This can be done. Assume $\neg(A \vee \neg A)$ and deduce a contradiction. We challenge you!) Sometimes we will ask you to do just this. On the other hand, an ingenious deduction of $A \vee \neg A$ is not necessary to establish its validity. A two-line truth table tells us that $A \vee \neg A$ is valid. Recall that we introduced deductions to deal with quantifiers and identity because those concepts were beyond truth tables. But the truth tables are very accessible and sufficient for tautologies. Why should we give up the ease and simplicity of that approach merely to work with identity and quantifiers? We don't have to. Instead we can adopt a new rule of convenience.

> *Tautology:* If A implies B according to truth tables, then in a deduction you can always list B after A and give as the justification "Taut." Obviously, if B itself is a tautology, you may list B and give the justification "Taut."

In other words, we can use truth tables to augment our deductions!

Here is an example of the use of the rule of tautology.

• ATTENTION: The rule of tautology is a rule of "art." Theoretically it could replace all the introduction and elimination rules for truth functions! It should be used only when you are thoroughly comfortable with the ordinary rules. *You should not use it here or in any of the sections in this part.* Taut. will make our work much easier in later parts where we will be doing some serious deductions.

EXAMPLE 4 $\exists x\, Ax \Rightarrow B$ $\therefore \forall x(Ax \Rightarrow B)$ (as long as x is not free in B)

1.	$\exists x\, Ax \Rightarrow B$	premise	7.	B	
2.	$\neg(Ax \Rightarrow B)$	assumption	8.	$B \,\&\, \neg B$	
3.	$Ax \,\&\, \neg B$	taut., 2	9.	$\neg(Ax \Rightarrow B) \Rightarrow (B \,\&\, \neg B)$	
4.	Ax		10.	$\neg\neg(Ax \Rightarrow B)$	
5.	$\neg B$		11.	$Ax \Rightarrow B$	
6.	$\exists x\, Ax$		12.	$\forall x(Ax \Rightarrow B)$	

EXERCISE 2   Fill in the justifications in the deduction in example 4.

CHALLENGE

Show each of the following.

1. $\exists z \neg Az$
   $\therefore \neg \forall z Az$

   Hint: Apply $\exists E$, then assume $\forall z Az$ and deduce a contradiction.

2. $\forall w \neg Aw$
   $\therefore \neg \exists w Aw$

   Hint: Assume $\exists w Aw$ and deduce a contradiction.

3. $\neg \exists x Ax$
   $\therefore \forall x \neg Ax$

   Hint: Assume Ax and use $\exists$-introduction to contradict the premise.

4. $\neg \forall u Au$
   $\therefore \exists u \neg Au$

   Hint: Assume $\neg \exists u \neg Au$ and then apply what you just proved in problem 3.

Observe that the Challenge problems show the validity of what we earlier called the quantifier exchange rules, QE1 and QE2:

$$\neg \forall y By \Leftrightarrow \exists y \neg By \qquad \text{and} \qquad \neg \exists y By \Leftrightarrow \forall y \neg By$$

and hence the validity of

$$\forall y By \Leftrightarrow \neg \exists y \neg By \qquad \text{and} \qquad \exists y By \Leftrightarrow \neg \forall y \neg By$$

SUMMARY: See Table 6.1.

TABLE 6.1 Summary of "Deduction" and "Hypothetical Reasoning: Deduction from Assumptions"

Logical Symbol	Introduction Rule	Elimination Rule
&	P Q $\therefore P\&Q$	$P\&Q \quad P\&Q$ $\therefore P \quad \therefore Q$
$\vee$	P $\therefore P \vee Q$	$P \vee Q$ $P \rightarrow R$ $Q \rightarrow R$ $\therefore R$
$\rightarrow$	Assume P. Conclude Q. $\therefore P \rightarrow Q$	P $P \rightarrow Q$ $\therefore Q$
$\neg$	$P \rightarrow (Q \,\&\, \neg Q)$ $\therefore \neg P$	$\neg\neg P$ $\therefore P$
$\leftrightarrow$	$P \rightarrow Q$ $Q \rightarrow P$ $\therefore Q \leftrightarrow P$	$P \leftrightarrow Q \qquad P \leftrightarrow Q$ $\therefore P \rightarrow Q \quad \therefore Q \rightarrow P$
$\forall$	Px[1] $\therefore \forall x Px$	$\forall x Px$ $\therefore Pt$
$\exists$	Pt $\therefore \exists x Px$	$\exists x Px$[2] $\therefore Pc*$

[1] Provided that the variable x is not free in any premise (hence Px is not a premise) or in any undischarged assumption and Px does not include any temporary name like $c*$.
[2] Where $c*$ is a temporary name that has not appeared earlier in the proof and does not appear in the conclusion.

PROVING VALIDITY

The man who makes no mistakes does not usually make anything.
—Edward Jon Phelps

One Crucial Ingredient in Composing Proofs

Make mistakes.

Composing a proof is one of the most difficult of tasks. In this section we present some strategies, but the most important advice we can give you is to feel free to make mistakes. A good mistake is a treasure. An instructive failure will tell you more about proof, about logic, than a lucky success.

If you haven't a clue, the *worst* thing you can do is nothing. The *best* thing you can do is guess. Of course, it might not work, but when you find out why it doesn't work, your next guess will be better and the guess after that better still.

Some great discoveries have been made by leaps of intellect. Most were made by persistent and informed guessing. The ability to err is the true mark of genius.

Two Starting Principles

1. Start at the beginning. Examine your premises, the statements you are given. Look at what you can do with each of them.
2. Start at the end. Examine the desired conclusion, the statement that is at the end of your proof. See what you must do to produce it.

A Detailed Strategy

Our strategy in constructing proofs is nothing more than the two principles above fleshed out. We merely take each possible statement form (&, ¬, ⇒, ∀x, and so on). We imagine what we could do with such a statement as a premise, and we imagine what we would have to do if such a statement were the conclusion. Each form leads to two detailed suggestions.

Table 6.2 summarizes the method. In the left column is a list of wff forms. The middle column provides a strategy for using each form if it appears as a premise. If the form appears as the conclusion, the right column provides a strategy for reaching it.

Using Table 6.2 is simple, almost mechanical, in fact. Suppose, for example, $P \& Q$ is a premise. The table tells us to conclude P and conclude Q. We could call this the "&-premise strategy." We are really just using the &-elimination rule. It hardly requires any thought.

Now suppose $P \Rightarrow Q$ is the conclusion. The table tells us to assume P and prove Q. This is because the ⇒-introduction rule yields $P \Rightarrow Q$. To use this, we must assume P and then prove Q. We could call this is the "⇒-conclusion strategy."

Note that the strategies in the first column all correspond to the elimination rules of inference. Similarly, the strategies in the second column correspond to the introduction rules.

Note that some strategies are a little vague. The ∀-premise strategy tells you to conclude P____, but it does not tell you what goes in the blank. This is for you to fill in. Not right away, perhaps. It may not be clear for some time what should be in the blank.

Finally, note that we do not guarantee anything. In the course of our deductions, there will be gaps that the table will not tell you how to fill. There will be false starts and dead ends. You may have to start over or retrace your steps.

TABLE **6.2** Methodological Summary

wff	As Premise	As Conclusion
$P \& Q$	Conclude P and Q.	Prove P and Q separately.
$P \lor Q$	Prove $P \rightarrow$ ____, $Q \rightarrow$ ____, then conclude ____.	Prove either P or Q.
$P \rightarrow Q$	Prove P, then conclude Q.	Assume P and prove Q.
$\neg P$	If $\neg P$ is $\neg\neg Q$, conclude Q.	Assume P *and prove* ____ $\& \neg$____.
$P \leftrightarrow Q$	Conclude $P \rightarrow Q$ and $Q \rightarrow P$.	Prove $P \rightarrow Q$ and $Q \rightarrow P$.
$\forall x Px$	Conclude P____.	Prove Px for variable x.
$\exists x Px$	Conclude Pc^* for some new temporary name.	Prove P____.

EXAMPLE 1
$$\forall x(Px \Rightarrow Qx)$$
$$\therefore \forall y Py \Rightarrow \forall z Qz$$

Begin by looking at the outline of a proof:

$$\forall x(Px \Rightarrow Qx)$$
.
.
.
$$\forall y Py \Rightarrow \forall z Qz$$

We can apply the ∀-premise strategy or the ⇒-conclusion strategy, since the premise is a universal statement and the conclusion is an implication. The ∀-premise strategy tells us to conclude $P\_\_\_ \Rightarrow Q\_\_\_$. We don't know what term, variable, or constant goes in the blank. It can be anything we like, variable or constant. We can decide later.

$$\forall x(Px \Rightarrow Qx)$$
$$P\_\_\_ \Rightarrow Q\_\_\_$$
$$\cdot$$
$$\cdot$$
$$\cdot$$
$$\forall y Py \Rightarrow \forall z Qz$$

Next we use the ⇒-conclusion rule. We will assume $\forall y Py$ and try to prove $\forall z Qz$.

$$\forall x(Px \Rightarrow Qx)$$
$$P\_\_\_ \Rightarrow Q\_\_\_$$
$$\forall y Py$$
$$\cdot$$
$$\cdot$$
$$\cdot$$
$$\forall z Qz$$
$$\forall y Py \Rightarrow \forall z Qz$$

Our givens now include $\forall y Py$, and our intermediate conclusion is now $\forall z Qz$. We can use the ∀-premise strategy again and conclude $P\_\_\__1$. As before, we can put anything we like in $\_\_\__1$. We use "$\_\_\__1$" instead of "$\_\_\_$" because we don't know yet if we want the two to be the same. They *can* be the same, of course.

$$\forall x(Px \Rightarrow Qx)$$
$$P\_\_\_ \Rightarrow Q\_\_\_$$
$$\forall y Py$$
$$P\_\_\__1$$
$$\cdot$$
$$\cdot$$
$$\cdot$$
$$\forall z Qz$$
$$\forall y Py \Rightarrow \forall z Qz$$

Now there are two strategies to choose from. We could try the ⇒-premise strategy on $P\_\_\_ \Rightarrow Q\_\_\_$ or the ∀-conclusion strategy on

$\forall z Q z$. The first says that we should prove P___ sometime so that we can conclude Q___. Does that seem helpful? Remembering that ___ and ___₁ can be whatever we like, we see that if we choose ___₁ to be the same as ___, this will work. (*Note:* We can't be sure at this point that this is a good idea. Well, then, shouldn't we hold off? No! Nothing ventured, nothing gained! If it doesn't succeed, we can always go back.)

$\forall x(Px \Rightarrow Qx)$
$\quad P$___ $\Rightarrow Q$___
$\qquad \forall y Py$
$\qquad P$___
$\qquad Q$___
$\qquad\quad .$
$\qquad\quad .$
$\qquad\quad .$
$\qquad \forall z Q z$
$\quad \forall y Py \Rightarrow \forall z Q z$

It's still not clear how to bridge the gap. Let's try the $\forall$-conclusion strategy. This says we need to prove Qz.

$\forall x(Px \Rightarrow Qx)$
$\quad P$___ $\Rightarrow Q$___
$\qquad \forall y Py$
$\qquad P$___
$\qquad Q$___
$\qquad\quad .$
$\qquad\quad .$
$\qquad\quad .$
$\qquad Qz$
$\qquad \forall z Q z$
$\quad \forall y Py \Rightarrow \forall z Q z$

Aha! All we have to do is put z in the blank and we are done!

1.	$\forall x(Px \Rightarrow Qx)$	premise		5.	Qz	$\Rightarrow$E, 2, 4
2.	$Pz \Rightarrow Qz$	$\forall$E, 1		6.	$\forall z Q z$	$\forall$I, 5
3.	$\forall y Py$	assumption		7.	$\forall y Py \Rightarrow \forall z Q z$	$\Rightarrow$I, 3–6
4.	Pz	$\forall$E, 3				

EXAMPLE 2
    (no premise)
    $P \Leftrightarrow \neg\neg P$

    The only strategy we can apply is the $\Leftrightarrow$-conclusion strategy. This tells us to prove $P \Rightarrow \neg\neg P$ and $\neg\neg P \Rightarrow P$. We will be using the $\Leftrightarrow$-introduction rule, so our proof will look like this:

$$\cdot$$
$$\cdot$$
$$\cdot$$

$$P \Rightarrow \neg\neg P$$
$$\cdot$$
$$\cdot$$
$$\cdot$$

$$\neg\neg P \Rightarrow P$$
$$(P \Rightarrow \neg\neg P) \,\&\, (\neg\neg P \Rightarrow P)$$
$$P \Leftrightarrow \neg\neg P$$

    Again, there is only one applicable strategy to get the required conditionals, $\Rightarrow$-conclusion. To end up with those implications we will have to assume statements:

$$P$$
$$\cdot$$
$$\cdot$$
$$\cdot$$

$$\neg\neg P$$
$$P \Rightarrow \neg\neg P$$
$$\neg\neg P$$
$$\cdot$$
$$\cdot$$
$$\cdot$$

$$P$$
$$\neg\neg P \Rightarrow P$$
$$(P \Rightarrow \neg\neg P) \,\&\, (\neg\neg P \Rightarrow P)$$
$$P \Leftrightarrow \neg\neg P$$

    Now, how can we fill in the gaps?

For the first gap, we use the ¬-conclusion strategy and prove $\neg P \Rightarrow (\underline{\quad} \ \& \ \neg\underline{\quad})$. We don't yet know what should go into the blank.

$$P$$
.
.
.

$$\neg P \Rightarrow (\underline{\quad} \ \& \ \neg\underline{\quad})$$
$$\neg\neg P$$
$$P \Rightarrow \neg\neg P$$
$$\neg\neg P$$
.
.
.

$$P$$
$$\neg\neg P \Rightarrow P$$
$$(P \Rightarrow \neg\neg P) \ \& \ (\neg\neg P \Rightarrow P)$$
$$P \Leftrightarrow \neg\neg P$$

Working backward again, we know we will assume $\neg P$ and try to prove $\underline{\quad} \ \& \ \neg\underline{\quad}$ (we still don't know what goes in the blank).

$$P$$
$$\neg P$$
.
.
.

$$\underline{\quad} \ \& \ \neg\underline{\quad}$$
$$\neg P \Rightarrow (\underline{\quad} \ \& \ \neg\underline{\quad})$$
$$\neg\neg P$$
$$P \Rightarrow \neg\neg P$$
$$\neg\neg P$$
.
.
.

$$P$$
$$\neg\neg P \Rightarrow P$$
$$(P \Rightarrow \neg\neg P) \ \& \ (\neg\neg P \Rightarrow P)$$
$$P \Leftrightarrow \neg\neg P$$

285

But now we see what we can put in the blank. We can use P, since we have P and $\neg P$ already.

$$P$$
$$\neg P$$
$$P \And \neg P$$
$$\neg P \Rightarrow (P \And \neg P)$$
$$\neg\neg P$$
$$P \Rightarrow \neg\neg P$$
$$\neg\neg P$$
$$\cdot$$
$$\cdot$$
$$\cdot$$
$$P$$
$$\neg\neg P \Rightarrow P$$
$$(P \Rightarrow \neg\neg P) \And (\neg\neg P \Rightarrow P)$$
$$P \Leftrightarrow \neg\neg P$$

Now for the second gap: This time we use the $\neg$-premise strategy on $\neg\neg P$. It instructs us to use the $\neg$-elimination rule and conclude P. This shows us that there really is no gap at all; the proof is complete.

1.	P	assumption
2.	$\neg P$	assumption
3.	$P \And \neg P$	&I, 1, 2
4.	$\neg P \Rightarrow (P \And \neg P)$	$\Rightarrow$I, 2–3
5.	$\neg\neg P$	$\neg$I, 4
6.	$P \Rightarrow \neg\neg P$	$\Rightarrow$I, 1–5
7.	$\neg\neg P$	assumption
8.	P	$\neg$E, 7
9.	$\neg\neg P \Rightarrow P$	$\Rightarrow$I, 7–8
10.	$(P \Rightarrow \neg\neg P) \And (\neg\neg P \Rightarrow P)$	&I, 6, 9
11.	$P \Leftrightarrow \neg\neg P$	$\Leftrightarrow$I, 10

One More Trick

When you seem to have exhausted all avenues, there is one more strategy that often does the trick: contradiction. We will discuss this method in "Proof by Contradiction" later in this part. In practice the use of contradiction is quite simple. To prove P, assume $\neg P$ and try to prove ____ & $\neg$____. We have included at the end of the exercises some proofs where this last resort is both necessary and sufficient.

EXERCISE   Prove the following.

1. $\forall x(P \Rightarrow Qx)$
   $\therefore P \Rightarrow \forall x Qx$

2. $\exists x(P \Rightarrow Qx)$
   $P \Rightarrow \exists x Qx$

3. $P \Rightarrow \neg P$
   $\therefore \neg P$

4. $P \Rightarrow \forall x Qx$
   $\therefore \forall x(P \Rightarrow Qx)$

5. $P \Rightarrow \exists x Qx$
   $\therefore \exists x(P \Rightarrow Qx)$

6. $\neg P$
   $\therefore P \Rightarrow \neg P$

7. $\neg(P \vee Q)$
   $\therefore \neg P \; \& \; \neg Q$

8. $\neg P \vee \neg Q$
   $\therefore \neg(P \; \& \; Q)$

9. $\exists x Px \vee \exists x Qx$
   $\therefore \exists x(Px \vee Qx)$

10. $P \vee Q$
    $\neg P$
    $\therefore Q$

11. (no premise)
    $\therefore P \vee \neg P$

PROVING INVALIDITY

> Prediction is difficult, especially of the future.
> —Niels Bohr

Not every argument is valid. In sentential logic, we can check the validity of an argument using truth tables. The process is mechanical, routine. For checking either validity or invalidity, truth tables do the job.

In predicate logic, the situation is considerably more difficult. There are no truth tables. In their absence, we use a system of deduction to establish validity. As you have seen, this is far from routine.

To establish **invalidity,** recall "A Shortcut for Checking Arguments" in part 4. This shortcut provided an alternative to truth tables. Essentially, the method involved attempting to find a situation (a line in the truth table) where the premises were true but the conclusion was false. This method can also be applied to arguments in predicate logic, but it is not simple or sure. It is sometimes called the "method of counterexamples," because it involves finding an example that counters the argument.

EXAMPLE
   $\forall x Px \Rightarrow Qd$
   $\therefore \forall x(Px \Rightarrow Qd)$

Can the premise be true and the conclusion false? Let's examine them. The premise is a conditional. There are two ways for an implication to be true: if $\forall x Px$ is false or if Qd is true. The conclusion is a universal statement. If this is false, then for some x, $Px \Rightarrow Qd$ must be false. Now this tells us something, because for *this* to be false, Px must be true and Qd must be false.

If Qd is false, that doesn't help make the premise true. We then need that $\forall x Px$ is false. At the same time, we want Px to be true for some x. Is this possible?

We can use Venn diagrams (see "Sets" in part 4) as we did in "Syllogisms" in part 5 to help picture the situation. Let one circle contain the things that are P and another circle contain things that are Q.

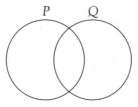

We want Qd to be false. This is not difficult.

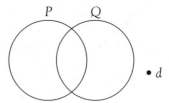

We want something to have property P, but not everything. Actually, since we put d outside P as well as Q, we already know not everything has property P. All we need is something in P as well.

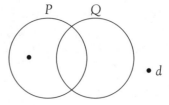

Now the premise is true and the conclusion false.

To be especially careful, let's construct a concrete example. Our universe will be all people. *Px* will mean "*x* is president of the United States." Then ∀*xPx* is false, but for some *x*, *Px* is true. Now we can choose *Q* and *d* so that *Qd* will be false. We could have *Qx* mean "*x* is a Supreme Court justice" and let *d* be "Tom Cruise." With these choices, the premise is true, but the conclusion is false; thus the argument is invalid.

EXAMPLE

∀*x*(*Px* ⇒ *Fx*)

∀*xFx*

∴∃*xPx*

Hmmm . . . if the premises are true, then everything has property *F*, and whenever anything has property *P*, then it has property *F*. Well, if the second premise is true, then the first follows automatically, doesn't it? It doesn't matter whether *P* is true of an object or not—since *F* is true of every object, *Px* ⇒ *Fx* has to be true.

What about the conclusion? It says something has property *P*. Can that be false? Presumably so, since all we have to do is make everything *F* and we get both premises.

So, we pick a universe, say, all cold cereals. Now choose *F* so that everything *F*s: say, *Fx* means "*x* is usually served with milk." Now choose *P* so that nothing has property *P*: say, *Px* means "*x* has a cousin living in Terre Haute." Are the premises true? Certainly. The first premise states that any cold cereal with a cousin living in Terre Haute is usually served with milk. The second premise says that all cold cereals are usually served with milk. The conclusion states that there is a cold cereal with a cousin living in Terre Haute. This is false; thus the argument is invalid.

If we use pictures, the first premise is

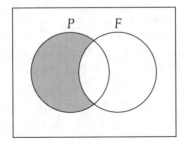

and the second is

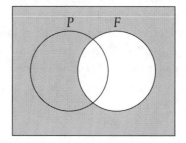

and the conclusion is

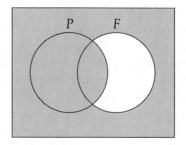

We can easily create a situation where the first two are true and the last false:

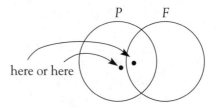

EXAMPLE

$\exists x Px \Rightarrow Q$

$\therefore \exists x(Px \Rightarrow Q)$

If the premise is true, we need that either $\exists x Px$ is false or Q is true. If the conclusion is false, we need that, for every x, $Px \Rightarrow Q$ is false, a pretty strong statement: it means that for every x, Px is true and Q is false. But that means that the premise can't be true. That means that the argument is valid.

Do you believe this reasoning? If not, you should try to prove it. In fact, we will prove it here, using the techniques from "Proving Validity." Here is the premise and conclusion.

$\exists x Px \Rightarrow Q$
.
.
.
$\exists x (Px \Rightarrow Q)$

Moving backward and using the ∃-conclusion strategy, we get

$\exists x Px \Rightarrow Q$
.
.
.
$P\underline{\quad} \Rightarrow Q$
$\exists x (Px \Rightarrow Q)$

Then we use the ⇒-conclusion strategy:

$\exists x Px \Rightarrow Q$
$\qquad P\underline{\quad}$
.
.
.
$\qquad Q$
$P\underline{\quad} \Rightarrow Q$
$\exists x (Px \Rightarrow Q)$

Now, to use the ⇒-premise strategy, we want to prove $\exists x Px$ somehow so that we can use the premise. Aha! If we have Px, then we have $\exists x Px$:

1. $\exists x Px \Rightarrow Q$ premise
2. $\qquad Px$ assumption
3. $\qquad \exists x Px$ ∃I, 2
4. $\qquad Q$ ⇒E, 1, 3
5. $Px \Rightarrow Q$ ⇒I, 2–4
6. $\exists x (Px \Rightarrow Q)$ ∃I, 5

One question remains: Will our methods always succeed? Suppose we must determine whether an argument is valid or invalid. We attempt to prove it. Perhaps we fail. Then we attempt to disprove it by finding an appropriate universe. Suppose we fail here as well. We are becoming familiar, in logic, with impossibility. Is this another case? Can it be that we are attempting something that cannot be done? By definition, if an argument is invalid, there is a universe where the premises are true and the conclusion false. But if it is valid, is there necessarily a proof? We answer this question later, in the section on completeness.

EXERCISES   Using the method of counterexamples, determine whether each of the arguments is valid or invalid. If invalid, construct a universe to demonstrate that fact. If valid, prove it.

1. $\forall x \neg Fx$
   $\therefore \neg \forall x Fx$

2. $\neg \forall x Fx$
   $\therefore \forall x \neg Fx$

3. $Fq \lor \exists x Px$
   $\therefore Fq \lor Pq$

4. $\exists x(Px \Rightarrow Fx)$
   $\therefore \exists x Px \Rightarrow \exists x Fx$

5. $\forall x Px \lor \forall x Fx$
   $\forall x(Px \lor Fx)$

6. $\exists x Px \Rightarrow \exists x Fx$
   $\therefore \exists x Px \Rightarrow \exists x Fx$

7. $\forall x Px \Rightarrow \forall x Fx$
   $\therefore \forall x(Px \Rightarrow Fx)$

8. $\forall x(Px \Rightarrow Fx)$
   $\exists x Px$
   $\therefore \exists x Fx$

9. $\exists x(Px \Rightarrow Fx)$
   $\forall x Px$
   $\therefore \forall x Fx$

10. $\forall x(Px \Leftrightarrow Fx)$
    $\exists x \neg Fx$
    $\therefore \forall x \neg Px$

11. The following argument is due to the philosopher Jaakko Hintikka: Suppose we accept the following principle: If a deed r is such that doing it forces you to do a second deed s, which is morally wrong, then the first deed is morally wrong. Then *failing* to do any deed x implies that x is morally wrong. Is this a valid argument?

FORMALIZING FOR VALIDITY IN PREDICATE LOGIC

> "What the hell are you getting so upset about?" he asked her bewilderedly in a tone of contrite amusement. "I thought you didn't believe in God."
>
> "I don't," she sobbed, bursting violently into tears. "But the God I don't believe in is a good God, a just God, a merciful God. He's not the mean stupid God you make Him out to be."
>
> —JOSEPH HELLER, *CATCH 22*

In this section we ask you to join your new-found expertise in deduction with your old skills of formalization to decide the validity of certain arguments presented in English. Some of the following examples have important lessons to teach, but most are somewhat tongue in cheek. In fact, the most important applications of predicate logic to natural language and to ordinary life are not isolated applications of formalization and deduction, such as the following. The following are just for practice and entertainment.

In fact, the most important applications of logic are more global —cases where we attempt to formalize an entire theory or several interconnected concepts or a subvocabulary of English. You'll see many examples of these serious applications in the rest of the book. But it will be useful for you to attempt to integrate your skills of formalization, deduction, and working with structures.

CHALLENGE Formalize each of the following arguments in predicate language. If the predicate form is valid, find a deduction of the conclusion from the premises. If it is not valid, find a structure in which the premises are all true but the conclusion is false. (WARNING: There is no such thing as the unique correct formalization for an argument in English. Be sure to ask yourself whether the argument seems valid, and don't be afraid to use your intuition to check your formalization.)

1. All men are mortal.
   Socrates is a man.
   Socrates is Plato's-teacher.
   ∴Plato's-teacher is mortal.
   Hint: Treat "Plato's-teacher" as a single name.

2. Something is the mother of all battles.
   ∴Every battle has a mother.

3. Socrates is mortal.
   ∴There is something that is both identical to Socrates and is mortal.

4. Someone broke the Ming vase.
   Someone tied the dog's ears together.
   Anyone who both broke the Ming vase and tied the dog's ears together is dastardly.
   ∴Someone is dastardly.

5. ∴Every cute Pole is Polish.

6. Every battle has a mother.
   ∴Something is the mother of all battles.

7. If anyone has a friend, she or he wishes the best for that friend.
   No bad person wishes the best for anyone.
   ∴No bad person is his own friend.
   Hint: Use Fxy for "y is x's friend" and Wxy for "x wishes the best for y."

8. All buffalo are timid.
   ∴Any friend of a buffalo is a friend of a timid thing.
   Hint: This requires a two-place predicate, *Fxy.*

9. Every Pole who hates a Norwegian is silly.
   Anyone is silly who hates himself.
   No Pole hates himself.
   ∴No Pole hates a Norwegian.

10. I love Madonna.
    Everyone loves a lover.
    ∴Madonna loves me!

11. Peter Piper paints portraits of all and only those portrait painters from Peoria
    who do not paint their own portrait.
    ∴Peter Piper is not a portrait painter from Peoria.

12. Every number is divisible by a prime number.
    For any number *n*, there is a larger number not divisible by any prime number
    less than or equal to *n*.
    Given any two numbers, either one is less than or equal to the other or it is
    larger than the other.
    ∴For any number, there is a prime number larger than it.

---

with & about logic
in Hell with Raymond Smullyan

When we've been there ten thousand years,
Bright shining as the sun,
We've no less days to sing God's praise
Than when we first begun.
                    —JOHN NEWTON, "AMAZING GRACE"

Do I contradict myself?
Very well then I contradict myself,
I am large, I contain multitudes.
                    —WALT WHITMAN, LEAVES OF GRASS

Raymond Smullyan is a very creative man. A logician and philosopher, Smullyan is also a marvelous teacher who is responsible for
some of the most enjoyable books on logic ever written. Some of the
Digestor's Digest pages are based on puzzles from his books, such as
What Is the Name of This Book? and *To Mock a Mockingbird*.

A few years ago, Smullyan invented a thought experiment that
beautifully illustrates some important ideas about infinite sets. He
imagines a somewhat playful devil who likes to give his victims a
chance of escaping Hell.

1. To some people arriving in Hell, the devil makes the following
promise: "I will choose a number from 1 to 100. Once I choose this
number, I won't change my choice. Each day, you may try to guess the
number I have chosen. If you guess correctly, then you may leave
Hell. If not, you stay, but you can always guess again the next day."

What happens?

It really depends on the person. If he is not very smart, he might
spend a long time in Hell, but with a proper strategy, he is out in
at most 100 days. If he guesses 1 on the first day, 2 on the second,
3 on the third, and so on, he is guaranteed to escape by day 100.
On the other hand, if 7 is his lucky number, he might decide to guess
it each day, in which case he will stay in Hell until it freezes over
(unless 7 is the devil's number!). The devil, after all, chose one number and doesn't change it, so there is no point in guessing 7 more than
once.

2. When the devil is in a mean mood, he makes the same promise, except that instead of a number, he chooses a word from *Webster's
Third International Dictionary*.

What happens now?

Once again, a smart person will escape. If, for example, she goes
through the dictionary page by page, guessing every word, she will
eventually hit upon the word the devil chose. Furthermore, she can
count the number of words and know the limit of her stay in Hell.

3. When the devil wants to present a greater intellectual challenge, he makes the same proposition but chooses from an infinite set,
the set of numbers 1, 2, 3, . . .

What can happen?

There are an infinite number of numbers, but with a good strategy, escape is certain. If you guess 1 on the first day, 2 on the second, 3
on the third, and so on, you will eventually guess the devil's number
and so be free. As before, you could follow a poor strategy and never
escape (you could guess only odd numbers, but if the devil picked 24,

you would never leave Hell). The important point is that there *is* a strategy that will guarantee escape in a *finite* number of days.

4. Another challenge: This time the devil picks an integer (the integers are the positive and negative whole numbers and zero):

$$\ldots, -3, -2, -1, 0, 1, 2, 3, \ldots$$

Is there a strategy for escaping? Guessing, for example 0, 1, 2, 3 and so on won't work, for the devil might have chosen a negative number. Nevertheless there is a strategy. Suppose you guess the numbers in this order:

$$0, -1, 1, -2, 2, -3, 3, \ldots$$

Then eventually you will escape!

If you think about it, this strategy sort of handles two infinities at once,

$$0, 1, 2, \ldots \qquad \text{and} \qquad -1, -2, -3, \ldots$$

The strategy works by taking turns, first guessing from one infinite set, then guessing from the other.

5. Finally, for particularly vile sinners, the devil chooses a pair of natural numbers, with the first one less than the second (such as 3 and 7, or 541,545 and 2,030,045, or 847,384,932,716 and 2,729,494,822,727,121,319). This is like handling an infinite number of infinities at once:

$$
\begin{array}{ccccc}
1,2 & 1,3 & 1,4 & 1,5 & 1,6 \quad \ldots \\
2,3 & 2,4 & 2,5 & 2,6 & 2,7 \quad \ldots \\
3,4 & 3,5 & 3,6 & 3,7 & 3,8 \quad \ldots \\
\cdot & \cdot & \cdot & \cdot & \cdot \\
\cdot & \cdot & \cdot & \cdot & \cdot \\
\cdot & \cdot & \cdot & \cdot & \cdot
\end{array}
$$

Can we do this? Is there a strategy for guessing that will get us out of Hell in a finite number of days?

Yes there is! We must get tricky, however. What we do is list all the possible pairs in an infinite triangle:

	1,2	1,3	1,4	1,5	1,6	1,7	1,8	. . .

```
1,2      1,3      1,4      1,5      1,6      1,7      1,8      . . .

         2,3      2,4      2,5      2,6      2,7      2,8      . . .

                  3,4      3,5      3,6      3,7      3,8      . . .

                           4,5      4,6      4,7      4,8      . . .

                                    5,6      5,7      5,8      . . .

                                             6,7      6,8      . . .

                                                      7,8      . . .
                                                           .
                                                         .
```

Now we guess these pairs in this order:

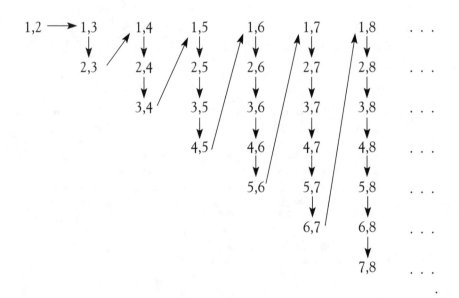

With a little thought, you can see that eventually we will escape from Hell. Thus, no matter what pair of numbers the devil chooses, we will guess that pair in a finite number of days.

You see, we hope, the difference here between an infinite set and a finite one. With the finite set, you can actually find a limit to your stay, since you know the size of the finite set. With an infinite set, you can't be sure *how soon* you will escape, but at least in the cases we've looked at you know it will be in a finite number of days. If you live forever, this means your time in Hell will be relatively insignificant!

Is this true of *all* infinite sets?

EXERCISE   Can you find strategies for escaping Hell under the following circumstances?

1. The devil chooses a Massachusetts license plate (three letters followed by three digits).

2. The devil chooses a perfect square (1, 4, 9, etc.).

3. The devil chooses a pair of natural numbers, but the first number doesn't have to be smaller than the second.

4. The devil chooses a fraction.

5. The devil chooses a nonsense word (any string of letters, meaningful or not) ten letters long (like "dksadflsdy" or "ooopsiboov").

6. The devil chooses a nonsense word that may be of any length.

7. What difference would it make if the devil allowed guesses only on Sundays?

8. What difference would it make if the devil allowed guesses only on March 17?

9. What difference would it make if the devil allowed guesses only on March 17 in years that are perfect squares? The last perfect square year was 1936 ($= 44^2$) and the next is 2025 ($= 45^2$).

no (certain) escape

You may complete as many generations as you please, nor the less, however, will that everlasting death await you; and for no less long a time will he be no more in being, who beginning with today has ended his life, than the man who has died many months and years ago!

—LUCRETIUS

My bounty is as boundless as the sea,
My love as deep; the more I give to thee
The more I have, for both are infinite.

—WILLIAM SHAKESPEARE

In "In Hell with Raymond Smullyan," the devil chooses from different sets, but each time a clever method is discovered that enables the poor soul to escape from Hell. More than enables, it *guarantees* escape in a *finite number of days*.

Actually, what we are doing is showing that these sets are "countable." If we think of the numbers 1, 2, 3, and so on, as the counting numbers, then each of our methods counts the sets. For example, the set of pairs of numbers with the first number less than the second is counted thus:

1. 1,2
2. 1,3
3. 2,3
4. 1,4
5. 2,4
   .
   .
   .

This method shows that the two sets, the counting numbers and the number pairs, are in some sense the same size. After all, we have matched them up. If we are in a room with hundreds of people and hundreds of chairs, how can we tell if there are more chairs than people or vice versa? We ask everyone to take a seat (that is, we match up the people and the chairs).

Looking at it this way, we seem to be saying that all the infinite sets mentioned in "In Hell with Raymond Smullyan" are the same size. Does that seem surprising? *Are* all infinite sets the same size? Are all infinite sets countable? Or is there some set so large that if the devil selects from it, there is no strategy that will assure escape from Hell?

There *is* such a set. It's the set of decimal numbers. In fact, just the set of decimal numbers between 0 and 1 is large enough.

The proof of this fact is nothing short of amazing. After all, to show that a set is countable, you need only find a pairing. To show that a set is uncountable, you must show that no pairing exists, a much more difficult task. You must demonstrate *impossibility*.

When one of the authors of this book saw this proof for the first time, he knew he wanted to be a mathematician. Making a fortune, sending a rocket to the moon, writing a rock opera, or leading a nation to war or peace—these paled beside the deed he had just witnessed. He understood that in a certain sense mathematicians were the most powerful beings on earth.

The discovery of an uncountable infinite set was made by Georg Cantor in 1873. We will present his proof to you in terms of the devil.

We are back in Hell. This time the devil decides to choose a decimal number between 0 and 1. Such numbers begin like 0.5204765365 . . . ,   0.023819574593 . . . ,   .50000 . . . , 0.2222222333333 . . . , and so on. Each one goes on forever.

We will show that there is no strategy for escaping Hell. This doesn't mean that you can't get lucky and guess the number. What this does mean is that there is no guarantee that you will guess it, as there is with countable sets. With countable sets, if you use the right strategy, you will escape in a finite number of days, no matter what your luck is.

Suppose, for example, this is your guessing strategy. Note that each number goes on forever. Don't worry about how one can "guess" such a number. In Hell, they have ways of doing this!

1. 0.2168432 . . .
2. 0.1909643 . . .
3. 0.4481963 . . .
4. 0.2304177 . . .
5. 0.6160302 . . .

.
.
.

These numbers may appear random, but this is just an example. We are making no assumptions about the strategy. Now we will find a real number that is not guessed by your strategy. We do this by examining the digits shown in boldface in your guesses:

1. 0.**2**168432 . . .
2. 0.1**9**09643 . . .
3. 0.44**8**1963 . . .
4. 0.230**4**177 . . .
5. 0.6160**3**02 . . .

.
.
.

We choose for the first digit of our number a digit different from **2**– say, 3; for the second digit, we choose a number different from **9**– say 4; for the third, a number different from **8**– say 3; and so on. Each time we pick a digit *different* from the one in the list. For simplicity, if the digit is even, we replace it with 3, and if the digit is odd, we replace it with 4. The number we get,

$$0.34334 \ldots$$

cannot be in the list that you guess! It can't be the first number because the first number has a different first digit. It can't be the second number, because that number has a different second digit. It can't be the 16,825th number, because that has a different 16,825th digit, and so on.

Remember, your list must work no matter what number the devil chooses. If this is the number that the devil chose, then you will stay in Hell forever.

You may wonder if the number we constructed,

$$r = 0.34334 \ldots$$

could be somewhere farther down the list. It couldn't, because r was carefully constructed to prevent that possibility. The 1,000,000th digit of r, for example, was chosen specifically so that r would not be the 1,000,000th number in the list.

"Well," you say, "perhaps this was just a lousy strategy. Sure, this list missed a few numbers, and r is one of them, but maybe with cleverness a complete list could be constructed."

But it can't. We can do this to *any* list. Given any list, there are numbers that are not on the list. *No* list is complete!

Well, how many numbers are missing from the list?

Too many to count! Recall that as we produce a guess, we have many choices. The first digit, for example, could have been 0, 1, 3, 4, 5, 6, 7, 8, or 9. Every step of the way, we had choices. There are very many numbers that are not on the list. Intuitively, if we could count the numbers *off* the list, then we could count *all* numbers, since we can count the numbers *on* the list. But we can't count all decimal numbers. Cantor's proof shows us that there are limits to what we can count, even with infinity.

Galileo noticed that we can pair up the set of numbers {1, 2, 3, 4, . . . } and the set of perfect squares: {1, 4, 9, 16, . . . } in the most natural way: 1 pairs up with 1, 2 pairs up with 4, 3 pairs up with 9, and so on, each number pairing up with its square. He took this as an argument that the two sets are the same size. On the other hand, he argued, the set of squares is properly contained in the set of natural numbers:

$$\{\mathbf{1}, 2, 3, \mathbf{4}, 5, 6, 7, 8, \mathbf{9}, 10, . . . \}$$

so it should be a distinctly smaller set. He regarded this as a paradox and drew the lesson that infinite sets cannot be treated as finite ones. In particular, it is useless to compare the sizes of infinite sets.

Nearly 300 years later, Cantor drew a different conclusion. He accepted the first argument that sets can be compared by pairing and rejected the second. He determined that it was meaningful to compare infinite sets. The natural numbers and the squares really are the same size. Indeed, many other infinite sets are also that same size.

CHALLENGE   Comment on the mathematical content of the following quotations.
1. The quotations at the beginning of "In Hell with Raymond Smullyan"
2. The quotations at the beginning of "No (Certain) Escape"

infinite tasks

. . . affection beholdeth merely the present; reason beholdeth the future and sum of time.

—F. Bacon

Mathematicians, philosophers, and recreational thinkers often like to contemplate performing an infinite number of tasks. The key is to imagine the infinite number of tasks as consuming only a finite amount of time, if we think of time at all.

Crossing the Street

You do not ordinarily think of crossing the street as involving an infinite number of tasks, but consider: To cross the street, you must first reach the halfway point. You must then reach the point three-fourths of the way across. You must then reach the point seven-eighths of the way across. You must then reach the point fifteen-sixteenths of the way across. . . . Thus, in order to cross the street, you must reach infinitely many points.

The Greek philosopher Zeno proposed a version of this as a paradox. He argued that because it is impossible to accomplish an infinite number of tasks, you cannot cross the street, and more generally, motion is impossible. We hope, on the contrary, that this example will convince you that it *is* possible to do an infinite number of things. In reality, you are doing them faster and faster, and so they take up only a finite length of time.

Part of the problem with infinity is that it has many interpretations. For some, it is by definition "that which can never be attained." With this definition, crossing the street, even if it involves all those points mentioned above, is not infinite, since it can be done.

The notion of infinity we are using here, however, is "not finite." In that sense, crossing the street involves (in theory) passing an infinite number of points.

Hilbert's Hotel

Imagine a hotel with an infinite number of rooms. The rooms are numbered 1, 2, 3, and so on. The hotel is also full of an infinite number of guests, one in each room. (This section is not for the squeamish. If you have a problem with infinite hotels or an infinite number of people, we suggest that you move on.)

Now a traveler arrives and needs a room. Does the manager turn him away? Certainly not. She asks the person in room 1 to move to room 2, the person in room 2 to move to room 3, the person in room 3 to move to room 4, and so on. The movement is done all at once. Everyone has a room to move into, and when they have finished, room 1 is vacant and the traveler has a place to stay.

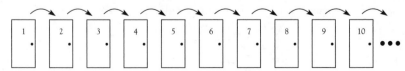

If a second traveler arrives, this same maneuver can be done again. In fact, it can be done any finite number of times.

Now suppose an *infinite* number of travelers arrive. Assume that we can count the guests, and we call them traveler 1, traveler 2, traveler 3, and so on. We can't ask our guests to move up an infinite number of rooms, because, for example, where would the person in room 1 go? There is no room "infinity." Every person must have a room with a finite room number. Is there any way all the new arrivals can be accommodated?

Certainly! The manager asks the occupant of room 1 to move to room 2, the occupant of room 2 to move to room 4, the occupant of room 3 to move to room 6, and so on. The occupant of room r moves to room $2r$.

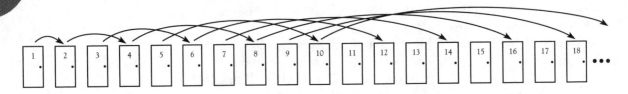

When all this is done, all the new arrivals can occupy a room because all the odd-numbered rooms are vacant!

The Tennis Ball Problem

Tom is in a large box, empty except for himself. Jim is standing outside the box with an infinite number of tennis balls (numbered 1, 2, 3, . . .). Jim throws balls 1 and 2 into the box. Tom picks up a tennis ball and throws it out. Next Jim throws in balls 3 and 4. Tom picks up a ball and throws it out. Next Jim throws in balls 5 and 6. Tom picks up a ball and throws it out. This process goes on an infinite number of times until Jim has thrown all the balls in. Once again, we ask you to accept accomplishing an infinite number of tasks in a finite period of time.

Here is the question: How many balls are in the box with Tom when the action is over?

The answer is somewhat disturbing: It depends. Not enough information has been given to answer the question. There might be an infinite number of balls left, or there might be none!

Suppose, for example, we add the information that when Jim throws in 1 and 2, Tom throws out 1, when Jim throws in 3 and 4, Tom throws out 3, and when Jim throws in 5 and 6, Tom throws out 5, ... You can easily see that Tom will never throw out an even-numbered ball, so when all is done, Tom will be sharing the box with balls 2, 4, 6, 8, ...

This makes a lot of sense, because after one stage, there is one ball in the box (two balls in, one ball out, $2 - 1 = 1$); after two stages, there are two balls in the box (four balls in, two balls out, $4 - 2 = 2$); after three stages, there are three balls in the box ($6 - 3 = 3$). The number of balls in the box keeps growing. It seems that there ought to be an infinite number there at the end.

But now consider this scenario: When Jim throws in 1 and 2, Tom throws out 1. When Jim throws in 3 and 4, Tom throws out 2. When Jim throws in 5 and 6, Tom throws out 3. At every opportunity, Tom throws out the lowest-numbered ball still in the box. When the action is over, *there are no balls in the box!*

This may seem difficult to believe, but ask yourself: If there is a ball in the box, what is its number? It can't be number 563, because that was the 563rd ball that Tom threw out. All balls have a finite number, and every ball with a finite number was thrown out. There are no balls in the box.

The Traffic Light

A man starts to cross the street. When he is halfway across, a policeman turns the traffic light red. When he is three-quarters of the way across, the policeman turns the light green. When he is seven-eighths of the way across, the policeman turns the light red again. When he is fifteen-sixteenths of the way across, the policeman turns the light green again, and so on. When the man finally reaches the other side of the street, is the light green or red?

EXERCISES

1. Go home and do an infinite number of things.
2. Suppose an infinite number of families came to Hilbert's

Hotel. Family 1 has one person in it; family 2 has two persons in it; family 3 has three persons in it; and so on. Each room at the hotel can contain only one person. Are there enough rooms for the new guests?

3. In the tennis ball problem, is it possible to have exactly one tennis ball in the box with Tom at the end?

4. The United States government is in debt. The debt is supported by borrowing. The government borrows money when it needs it by selling bonds, which the government pays off after a fixed number of years (this number varies, but for all practical purposes, it is never more than 25). We have the following facts:

   a. Every dollar borrowed is eventually paid back, at most 25 years later.

   b. The debt grows larger each year (this is not inevitable, but it is a very reasonable expectation).

   After an infinite number of years, does the government owe money, and if so, how much?

5. The paradox of the traffic light is sometimes used to argue that we can't accomplish infinite tasks. Do you agree?

6. Each example in this section involves doing an infinite number of tasks. In each case, is there a last task done?

7. Some of these examples have a grain of sense in them. Some do not. What do you think?

infinity: potential and actual

To see the infinite is to be seen by the infinite.
—Giordano Bruno

We've been discussing infinity, but now we want to step back and discuss the *idea* of infinity. Everyone agrees that we have an idea of infinity, but there is a deep controversy about that idea and what it represents. The controversy extends beyond mathematics to philosophy and even to theology.

The ancient Greeks, at least those who thought about it, believed that there was no *actually* infinite thing, mathematical or otherwise. They thought one could invoke the idea of infinity only when there was a *potential* for going on or repeating a process. To say that the natural numbers are infinite was to say that they were potentially infinite, that is, one could always add one more natural number (there was no last). Aristotle resolved Zeno's paradoxes about motion (see "Paradox" in part 1) by claiming that physical distance is not actually infinitely divisible, but only potentially so. So you don't actually have to perform an infinite number of steps to cross a given distance, first getting halfway, then three-fourths of the way, and so on. Instead, this distance is only potentially infinitely divisible. You *can* divide it in half; then, *if you choose*, you can divide the second half in half; then, *if you choose*, you can divide the remainder in half, and so on. To say that the distance is potentially infinitely divisible is simply to say that however many times you have divided it, you can divide it another time.

It is sometimes said that the Greeks had a "horror" of the actual infinite and because of their fear, Greek mathematical development was seriously stunted. Now let's leap ahead to the Middle Ages and theology. Theologians were inclined to say that God was infinitely powerful, and by "infinitely powerful" they did not mean mere potential infinity. They did not mean that God could just do a more difficult task today than God did yesterday. They meant that God was actually, at any given moment, *infinitely* powerful. Indeed, God was an *actually infinite being,* not just a potentially infinite being.

In the early seventeenth century, Descartes used the idea of actual infinity to argue for God's existence. Descartes thought that humans could come up with the idea of potential infinity on their own. We could think of a potentially infinitely powerful creature who, for example, just kept lifting bigger and bigger weights. But Descartes insisted along with the medievals that our idea of God is not that of a potentially infinite being but of an actually infinite being. Now how can we finite human beings arrive at the idea of an actual infinity? Nothing in the world gives it to us; the world gives us only the idea of potential infinity. So, Descartes concluded, the idea of actual infinity must have been implanted in us by an actually infinite being. If there were no such being, we'd have no such idea. We have the idea; therefore there is such a being.

Despite Descartes and the medieval philosophers (or perhaps because of them), mathematicians remained suspicious of the actual infinite. They thought that only the idea of potential infinity should be allowed in mathematics. However, a great mathematical revolution occurred in the second half of the nineteenth century, brought about chiefly by Georg Cantor. Cantor argued that there were actually infinite objects in mathematics, and he developed a precise mathematical theory of the infinite.

Of course, it's easy to point (with a metaphysical finger) to infinite objects in mathematics—the set of natural numbers, for example. To be sure, Aristotle could argue that you're not pointing at an actually infinite object—there is no actual set or object consisting of all the natural numbers. All there is is a rule for going on: "Add 1 to a number and the result is a number." The "set of numbers" exists only potentially.

But Cantor and other mathematicians had a powerful counterargument. Mathematicians, and even the rest of us, accept things like π (the ratio of the circumference of a circle to its diameter) as "real numbers," on a par with 3 and 22/7. Cantor and others showed that numbers like π could be expressed only by infinite sequences—in the case of π, the sequence begins 3.14159 . . .—that go on forever without repetitions. If π is actual, then infinite sets are actual.

Curiously, Cantor relied less on this argument than he did on the philosophical arguments used by Descartes and medieval theologians. Cantor wrote several papers arguing that these philosophers accepted the idea of actual infinity and used the theological ideas of infinity to defend his mathematical theory!

Many mathematicians of his time ignored Cantor's arguments; in fact, they thought he was a bit looney, and, at least according to mathematical folklore, Cantor had several nervous breakdowns because of the antagonism his work aroused. But his theory of the infinite captivated younger mathematicians, and today the dominant idea of infinity in mathematics is of actual infinity—objects like sets of numbers that are actually infinite.

Nevertheless, there is still considerable controversy in philosophy, mathematics, and theology about the idea of infinity.

proof by contradiction

The proof is by *reductio ad absurdum*, and *reductio ad absurdum*, which Euclid loved so much, is one of a mathematician's finest weapons. It is a far finer gambit than any chess gambit: a chess player may offer the sacrifice of a pawn or even a piece, but a mathematician offers *the game*.
　　　　　　　　　　　　—G. H. HARDY, *A MATHEMATICIAN'S APOLOGY*

Of all the proof techniques of mathematicians and philosophers, the one that appears most daring is "proof by contradiction," or *reductio ad absurdum*. Mysterious, dramatic, confusing, and controversial, it illustrates issues of logic that are partly ethical and partly aesthetic. The idea is that to prove a proposition P, one assumes its negation $\neg P$ and then proves from this a contradiction.

In everyday conversation, proof by contradiction is used frequently. For example, we argue that because the ground is dry, it did not rain last night. We reason that if it had rained, then the ground would be wet. This would contradict the fact that the ground is dry. Thus, it did not rain last night.

In our deduction rules, proof by contradiction is embodied in the $\neg I$ rule:

$$A \Rightarrow (B \ \& \ \neg B)$$
$$\therefore \neg A$$

The method is effective in part because it gives us an additional hypothesis. If we are trying to prove P, then we add $\neg P$ to our givens. Furthermore, instead of having to prove the single proposition P, we may finish the proof by proving any contradiction at all. We give a few examples.

EXAMPLE
Our first example is one of the loveliest. It is Euclid's proof that the number of primes is infinite. Recall from high school that a prime number is a natural number greater than 1 that has no divisors other than itself and 1. (The first few primes are 2, 3, 5, 7, 11, 13, 17.)

Euclid supposes to the contrary that there is a largest prime. Let us suppose this largest prime is n. Now multiply together all the numbers from 1 to n and add 1:

$$k = 1 \times 2 \times 3 \times 4 \times 5 \times \cdots \times n + 1$$

This new number can't be prime since it is larger than n. Since it is not prime, it must have prime divisors. But according to our assumption, all the primes are less than or equal to n, and none of these can divide k, since they all divide $k - 1$. This is a contradiction.

Notice that the (false) assumption that there is a greatest prime was a powerful tool in the proof, since it gave us an extra assumption that we could use.

A major objection is that occasionally this method will tell us that something exists but will not tell us how to get it. Such proofs are called *nonconstructive*. The following is an example:

EXAMPLE
There is a real number that is not rational (i.e., there is a decimal number that cannot be represented as a fraction).

Suppose there are no such numbers. Then the real numbers and the rational numbers are one and the same. But we learned in "In Hell with Raymond Smullyan" that the rationals are countable, and we learned in "No (Certain) Escape" that the decimal numbers are not countable. This is a contradiction. Thus, we know there are real numbers that are not rational, although we have not seen a single one.

Many mathematicians would be unsatisfied with this proof, for while it does prove there are irrational numbers, it gives us no idea what they are. This would be considered a blemish by some and a sin by others. This is what we mean by an aesthetic issue. The following proof is more specific. It, too, is a proof by contradiction, but it yields a specific rational number.

EXAMPLE
The square root of 2 is an irrational number.

We suppose that $\sqrt{2}$ is rational; that is, it is equal to a fraction p/q . Of course, it will be equal to many fractions (just as 0.5 is equal to $\frac{1}{2}$, $\frac{3}{6}$, $\frac{419}{838}$, etc.), so let p/q be the fraction with the *smallest positive numerator* p that equals $\sqrt{2}$. We write this as $\sqrt{2} = p/q$. If we multiply both sides of this equation by q, then we get

$$q\sqrt{2} = p$$

Now, if we square both sides, we get

$$2q^2 = p^2$$

This tells us that p^2 is an even number. It is easy to see that this further means that p is even (exercise: prove this by contradiction!). Hence, for some k,

$$p = 2k$$

Now we square this

$$p^2 = 4k^2$$

and so

$$2q^2 = p^2 = 4k^2$$

and

$$q^2 = 2k^2$$

But this tells us that q^2 is even, and then of course q must be even too. Altogether, we conclude that the fraction p/q can be simplified by dividing both the numerator and denominator by 2. But then p is *not* the smallest numerator of a fraction equaling $\sqrt{2}$. This is a contradiction.

Our final example demonstrates the nonconstructive nature of proof by contradiction in a unique way.

EXAMPLE

A seven-year-old boy was eating dinner with his parents (true story!) and discussing what he called "remainders." According to his definition, if everybody but one were alike in some respect, then the one who was different would be called a "remainder." He proceeded something like this: "All of us are remainders. Daddy, you are a remainder because you are drinking cranberry juice and Mama and I are drinking milk. I am a remainder because I am having a hamburger and you and Mama are having cheeseburgers. And Mama, you are a remainder, because you are the only one who is not a remainder."

What is most intriguing about this proof is that while Mama must clearly be a remainder, there is nothing in the proof that tells us in what respect she is actually a remainder!

EXERCISES

1. How is the last example a proof by contradiction?
2. Prove that if p^2 is even, then p is even.
3. The following is from W. S. Gilbert's operetta *Yeoman of the Guard*.

Now observe. She said "Hands off!" Whose hands? Thine. Off whom? Off *her*. Why? Because she is a woman. Now, had she *not* been a woman, thine hands had not been set upon her at all. So the reason for the laying on of hands is the reason for the taking off of hands, and herein is contradiction contradicted!

This suggests an interesting proof by contradiction. The passage seems to provide two premises: $W \Rightarrow H$ (because she is a woman, you put your hands on her) and $W \Rightarrow \neg H$ (because she is a woman, you should take your hands off her). Use these to prove by contradiction that she (whoever she is) is not a woman!

4. Something must be wrong with the reasoning in 3 above. What is it?

informal logic
Anita Hill and Arlen Specter

Myself when young did eagerly frequent
Doctor and Saint, and heard great argument
  About it about; but evermore
Came out by the same Door as I went.
—OMAR KHAYYAM (EDWARD FITZGERALD)

The following is taken from the transcript of the hearings conducted by the Senate Judiciary Committee on the nomination of Clarence Thomas to the Supreme Court. The excerpt comes from the questioning of Clarence Thomas by Senator Arlen Specter.

SPECTER: The issue of the article in *USA Today*, I think, is a very compelling one, because I believe, and I'm going to ask you about this, that Professor Hill testified in the morning and demolished her testimony in the afternoon. And what I want to examine with you for the next few minutes is an extremely serious question as to whether Professor Hill's testimony in the morning was or was not perjury. And I do not make that statement lightly. But we are searching here for what happened. And nobody was present with a man and a woman when this tragedy arose. And the quality of her testimony and the inferences are very significant on the underlying question as to credibility. And I'm going to read you extensive extracts from the testimony, which I reread this morning. And I think it ought to be noted that we proceed here on a very short timetable. Senator Thurmond asked me to undertake this job on Wednesday, and I started on in Thursday, and we're in hearings on Friday, and we're reading overnight text this morning.

And the start of it was my question to Professor Hill about the *USA* article on Oct. 9, where Anita Hill was told by Senate staffers her signed affidavit alleging sexual harassment by Clarence Thomas would be the instrument that would quietly and behind the scenes would force him to withdraw her [sic] name.

Now, I'm about to go through the transcript where I asked Professor Hill about this repeatedly. And at one point she consulted her attorney. And throughout an extensive series of questions yesterday morning, flatly denied that any Senate staffer had told her that her coming forward would lead to your withdrawal. And in the afternoon, she flatly changed that by identifying a Senate staffer, who she finally said told her that she was told that if she came forward you would withdraw or might withdraw your nomination.

The transcript, which is prepared overnight, does not reveal the part where she consulted with her attorney. But I asked my staffers to review the tape, because I recollected that. And they did find the spot which I referred to. But I want to make that plain that it is not in the written transcript.

I start, Judge Thomas, on page 79 of the record, where I questioned Professor Hill. The *USA Today* reported on Oct.

9, quote, Anita Hill was told by Senate staffers her signed affidavit alleging sexual harassment by Clarence Thomas would be the instrument that would quietly and behind the scenes would force him to withdraw his name.

Now, I'm not reading all of it, because I can't in the time we have here, but if anybody disagrees with anything I read, they're at liberty to add whatever they choose.

On page 80, question: Did anybody ever tell you that, by providing the statement, that there would be a move to request Judge Thomas to withdraw his nomination?

Ms. Hill: I don't recall any story about pressing—using this to press anyone.

Later on page 80, Ms. Hill: Quote, I don't recall anything being said about him being pressed to resign.

Page 81, Senator Specter: Well, aside from, quote, quietly and behind the scenes pressing him to withdraw, any suggestion that just the charges themselves in writing would result in Judge Thomas withdrawing, going away?

Ms. Hill: I don't recall that at all, no.

Skipping ahead to page 82, this is the middle of one of my questions: You have testified with some specificity about what happened 10 years ago. I would ask you to press your recollection as to what happened within the last month.

Ms. Hill: And I have done that, Senator, and I don't recall that comment. I do recall there might have been some suggestion that if the F.B.I. did the investigation that the Senate might get involved, that there may be, that a number of things might occur. But I really, I have to be honest with you, I cannot verify the statement that you are asking me to verify. There is not really more that I can tell you on that.

Then skipping ahead to page 84, Senator Specter: Would you not consider it a matter of real importance if someone said to you: Professor, you won't have to go public, you won't have to—your name won't have to be disclosed, you won't have to do anything, just sign the affidavit, and this, as *USA Today* reports, would be the instrument that quietly and behind the scenes would force him to withdraw his name. Now, I'm asking you whether it happened. I'm asking you now only if it did happen whether that would be the kind of statement to you which would be important and impressed upon you that you could remember in the course of four or five weeks.

Now it's at this time that she consulted with her attorney according to my recollection and according to my staff's looking at the tape. And then she says: I don't recall a specific statement, and I cannot say whether that comment would have stuck in my mind. I really cannot say.

Then in the afternoon session, I asked Professor Hill, at page 203, to begin if you could proceed from there to recount who called you and what those conversations consisted of as it led to your coming forward to the committee. And then, on a long answer, inserted at the end, not responsively, because I wasn't asking about the *USA* article anymore, she says, and this appears at the bottom of 203: It even included something to the effect that the information might be presented to the candidate and to the White House. There was some indication that the candidate, or excuse me, the nominee, might not wish to continue the process.

On the following page, 204, continuing in the middle of the page, Senator Specter: So Mr. Brudney did tell you Judge Thomas might not wish to go forward with his nomination if you came forward? Ms. Hill: Yes.

Now Judge Thomas, what do you make of that change of testimony?

THOMAS: Senator, I think that the individuals such as Jim Brudney, Senator Metzenbaum's staff, who are on the ed and labor committee, should be brought to hearings like this to confront the people in this country for this kind of effort.

And I think that they should at some point have to confront my family.

SPECTER: Judge Thomas, I went through that in some detail because it is my legal judgment, having had some experience in perjury prosecutions, that the testimony of Professor Hill in the morning was flat-out perjury, and that she specifically changed it in the afternoon, when confronted with the possibility of being contradicted. And if you recant during the course of the proceeding, it's not perjury. So I state that very carefully as to what she had said in the morning.

But in the context of those continual denials and consulting the attorney and repeatedly asking the question, with negative responses, that simply stated, was false and perjurious, in my legal opinion. And the change in the afternoon was a concession, flatly, to that effect.

EXERCISES

1. State clearly Senator Specter's argument and conclusion.
2. Which parts of the extract are relevant to his arguments and which are not?
3. Compose a rebuttal to his argument.
4. Compose a rebuttal to your argument.

Bush, Clinton, and Perot

Here comes the orator, with his flood of words and his drop of reason.
— BENJAMIN FRANKLIN

In October 1992 the presidential candidates George Bush, Bill Clinton, and H. Ross Perot met for a series of televised debates. In the first of these, the candidates were asked questions by the press in turn. The candidate who was asked the question had two minutes to answer and his opponents had a minute each to respond. We are going to analyze a part of this debate from a logical point of view. The questions we will ask are "Is the candidate answering the question?", "Is the response relevant?", and if the candidate makes an argument, "Is the argument sound?"

Here is how it began:

Q: The first topic tonight is what separates each of you from the other. Mr. Perot, what do you believe tonight is the single most important separating issue of this campaign?

PEROT: I think the principal issue that separates me is that five-and-a-half million people came together on their own and put me on the ballot. I was not put on the ballot by any PAC money, by any foreign lobbyist money, by any special interest money. This is a movement that came from the people. This is the way the framers of the Constitution intended our government to be, a government that comes from the people.

Over time we have developed a government that comes at the people, that comes from the top down, where the people are more or less treated as objects to be programmed during the campaign with commercials and media events and fear messages and personal attack and things of that nature. The thing that separates my candidacy and makes it unique is that this came from millions of people in 50 states all over this country who wanted a candidate that worked and belonged to nobody but them. I go into this race as their servant. And I belong to them. So this comes from the people.

Before going further, what can we say about Mr. Perot's response? To be absolutely strict, he does not answer the question. The question is what issue separates the candidates—presumably an attempt to find some point where the three candidates have a distinct and important disagreement. Instead, Perot discusses how his *candidacy* is different.

This is a rather small point; Perot's answer is still pretty relevant. Logically however, it has some irony. To Perot, his candidacy is different because it is supported primarily by people who support him for his own sake, not for any position ("interest") he has. In other words, when asked what issue separates the candidates, Perot replies that it is exactly his own issuelessness!

Perot also implies that the other candidates are supported by lobbies and special interests, though he does not say what these are, and that such support is wrong, though he does not say why.

Now we continue:

MODERATOR: Governor Clinton, one-minute response.

CLINTON: The most important distinction in this campaign is that I represent real hope for change, a departure from trickle-down economics, a departure from tax-and-spend economics to invest in growth. But before I can do that, I must challenge the American people to change and they must decide. Tonight I have to say to the President: Mr. Bush, for 12 years you've had it your way: You've had your chance and it didn't work. It's time to change. I want to bring that change to the American people. But we must all decide first: Do we have the courage to change for hope in a better tomorrow?

Clinton follows Perot's lead, not answering with an issue but with how he sees the difference in the candidates. He goes on to imply that things are in bad shape, that change is needed, and that he is more likely to effect change than the others.

He provides no support for these statements, and the rest of his response is what we might call rhetoric. It is stirring but contains nothing of content. He manages to suggest subtly that those who vote for him are somehow courageous.

MODERATOR: President Bush, one-minute response.
BUSH: Well, I think one thing that distinguishes is experience—I think we've dramatically changed the world. I'll talk about that a little bit later, but the changes are mind-boggling for world peace. Kids go to bed at night without the same fear of nuclear war.

And change for change sake isn't enough. We saw that message in the late 70's. We heard a lot about change and what happened, that misery index went right through the roof. But I've—my economic program, I think is the kind of change we want.

And the way we're going to get it done is we're going to have a brand new Congress. A lot of them were thrown because of all the scandals. I'll sit down with them, Democrats and Republicans alike, and work for my agenda for American renewal, which represents real change.

But I'd say if you had to separate out, I think it's experience at this level.

Bush follows the pattern of his opponents, ignoring issues and stating instead that he is the one candidate with experience.

In his second paragraph, he comments on Governor Clinton's response. His comment that change for change sake is not enough is not relevant, since Clinton clearly intends change because of bad but unstated conditions. Bush then implies that we do need change and that he will deliver it. He suggests that Congress, not himself, is responsible for the lack of change.

Again, no support is given for this statement. Note that while "change" is clearly already important in this debate, no one has said what change is needed.

It is important to note that we must be tempered in our criticism. The candidates are responding on the spot. They don't have time to compose clear, compelling oratory. Furthermore, logic may not be their most important consideration. Their audience may be better reached by emotional or humorous appeals. We also note that the paragraphs were set up not by the candidates but by *The New York Times*, which printed the transcript of the debate.

CHALLENGE   Analyze each of the following responses by the candidates:

1. Q: Governor Clinton, how do you respond to the President on the—you have two minutes—on the question of experience. He says that is what distinguishes him from the other two of you.

   CLINTON: I believe experience counts but it's not everything. Values, judgment and the record that I have amassed in my state also should count for something. I've worked hard to create good jobs and to educate people. My state now ranks first in the country in job growth this year, fourth in the reduction of poverty, first in overall economic performance, according to a major news magazine. That's because we believe in investing in education and in jobs.

   And we have to change in this country. You know, my wife, Hillary, gave me a book about a year ago in which the author defined insanity as just doing the same old thing over and over again and expecting a different result. We have got to have the courage to change. Experience is important, yes. I've gotten a lot of good experience in dealing with ordinary people over the last year, month. I've touched more people's lives and seen more promise than anybody else who's run for President this year. And I think the American people deserve better than they're getting.

   We have gone from first to 13th in the world in wages in the last 12 years, since Mr. Bush and Mr. Reagan have been in. Personal income has dropped while people have worked harder. In the last four years there have been twice as many bankruptcies as new jobs created. We need a new approach. This same old experience is not relevant. We're living in a new world after the cold war and what works in this new world is not trickle-down, not government for the benefit of the privileged few, not tax and spend, but a commitment to invest in American jobs and American education, controlling American health-care costs and bringing the American people together.

   That is what works, and you can have the right kind of experience and the wrong kind of experience. Mine is rooted in the real lives of real people, and it will bring real results if we have the courage to change.

2. MODERATOR: President Bush, one minute to respond.

   BUSH: I just thought of another, another big difference here between me—I don't believe Mr. Perot feels this way, but I know Governor Clinton did. I want to accurately quote him. He thinks, I think he said that the country is coming apart at the seams. Now, I know the only way he can win is to make everybody believe the economy is worse than it is. But this country's not coming apart at the seams, for heaven's sakes. We're the United States of America. We—in spite of the economic problems—we are the most respected economy around the world. Many would trade for it. We've been caught up in a global slowdown. We can do much much better, but we ought not try to convince the American people that America is a country that's coming apart at the seams. I would hate to be running for President and think that the only way I could win would be to convince everybody how horrible things are. Yes there are big problems. And yes people are hurting. But I believe that this agenda for American renewal I have is the answer to do it and I believe we can get it done now whereas we didn't in the past, because you're going to have a whole brand new bunch of people in the Congress that are going to have to listen to the same American people I'm listening to.

3. MODERATOR: Mr. Perot, a minute response, sir.

PEROT: Well, they got a point. I don't have any experience in running up a $4 trillion debt. I don't have any experience in gridlock government, where nobody takes responsibility for anything and everybody blames everybody else. I don't have any experience in creating the worst public school system in the industrialized world, the most violent crime-ridden society in the industrialized world. But I do have a lot of experience in getting things done. So if we're at a point in history where we want to stop talking about it and do it, I've got a lot of experience in figuring out how to solve problems, making the solutions work and then moving on to the next. I've got a lot of experience in not taking 10 years to solve a 10-minute problem. So if it's time for action, I think I have experience that counts. If there's more time for gridlock and talk and finger-pointing, I'm the wrong man.

4. Q: President Bush, the question goes to you. You have two minutes. And the question is this: Are there important issues of character separating you from these other two men?

BUSH: I think the American people should be the judge of that. I think character is a very important question.

I said something the other day where I was accused of being like Joe McCarthy, because I questioned—I put it this way: I think it's wrong to demonstrate against your own country or organize demonstrations against your own country in foreign soil. I just think it's wrong.

I—maybe they say, well, it's a youthful indiscretion. I was 19 or 20 flying off an aircraft carrier, and that shaped me to be Commander in Chief of the armed forces.

And I'm sorry, but demonstrating—it's not a question of patriotism. It's a question of character and judgment. They get on me—Bill's gotten on me about "Read my lips" some. When I make a mistake I'll admit it.

But he has made—made—not admitted a mistake. And I just find it impossible to understand how an American can demonstrate against his own country in a foreign land, organizing demonstrations against it, when young men are held prisoner in Hanoi or kids out of the ghetto were drafted.

Some say, well, you're a little old-fashioned. Maybe I am, but I just don't think that's right.

Now whether it's character or judgment, whatever it is, I have a big difference here on this issue. And so we'll just have to see how it plays out, but I—I couldn't do that. And I don't think most Americans could do that.

And they all say, well, it was a long time ago. Well, let's admit it then. Say I made a terrible mistake. How could you be Commander in Chief of the armed forces and have some kid say when you have to make a rough decision as I did in Panama or in, in Kuwait, and then have some kid jump up and say, "Well, I'm not going to go. The Commander in Chief was organizing demonstrations halfway around the world during another era."

So there are differences. But that's about the main area where I think we have a difference. I don't know about—we'll talk about that a little with Ross here in a bit.

5. MODERATOR: Mr. Perot, you have one minute.

PEROT: I think the American people will make their own decisions on character, and at a time when we have work to do and we need action. I think they need to clearly understand the backgrounds of each person. And I think the press can play a huge role in making sure that the backgrounds are clearly presented in an objective way. Then, make a decision. Certainly anyone in the White House should have the character to be there. But, I think it's very important to measure when and where things occurred. Did they occur when you were a young person in your formative years? Or did they occur while you were a senior official in the Federal Government? When you're a senior official in the Federal Government spending billions of dollars of taxpayers' money and you're a mature individual and you make a mistake, then that was on our ticket. If you make it as a young man, time passes. So I would say, just, you know, look at all three of us. Decide who you think will do the job, pick that person in November because believe me, as I've said before, the party's over and it's time for the cleanup crew. And we do have to have change and people who never take responsibility for anything when it happens on their watch and people who are in charge. . . .

MODERATOR: Your time is up.

PEROT: Your time is up.

MODERATOR: Time is up.

PEROT: Time is up.

6. MODERATOR: Governor Clinton, you have one minute.

CLINTON: Ross gave a good answer, but I've got to respond directly to Mr. Bush. You have questioned my patriotism. You even brought some right-wing Congressmen into the White House to plot how to attack me for going to Russia in 1969–1970 when over 50,000 other Americans did. Now I honor your service in World War II. I honor Mr. Perot's service in uniform and the service of every man and woman who ever served, including Admiral Crowe who was your Chairman of the Joint Chiefs and who is supporting me. But when Joe McCarthy went around this country attacking people's patriotism, he was wrong. He was wrong. And a Senator from Connecticut stood up to him named Prescott Bush. Your father was right to stand up to Joe McCarthy. You were wrong to attack my patriotism. I was opposed to the war but I love my country and we need a President who will bring this country together, not divide it. We've got enough division. I want to lead a unified country.

the adventure of the dancing men

How often have I said to you that when you have eliminated the impossible, whatever remains, however improbable, must be the truth?
— ARTHUR CONAN DOYLE

"The Adventure of the Dancing Men" is one of Sir Arthur Conan Doyle's stories about Sherlock Holmes, the greatest fictional detective of all time. What follows is the start of that story.

Holmes had been seated for some hours in silence with his long, thin back curved over a chemical vessel in which he was brewing a particularly malodorous product. His head was sunk upon his breast, and he looked from my point of view like a strange, lank bird, with dull gray plumage and a black topknot.

"So, Watson," said he, suddenly, "you do not propose to invest in South African securities?"

I gave a start of astonishment. Accustomed as I was to Holmes's curious faculties, this sudden intrusion into my most intimate thoughts was utterly inexplicable.

"How on earth do you know that?" I asked.

He wheeled round upon his stool, with a steaming test-tube in his hand, and a gleam of amusement in his deep-set eyes.

"Now, Watson, confess yourself utterly taken aback," said he.

"I am."

"I ought to make you sign a paper to that effect."

"Why?"

"Because in five minutes you will say that it is all so absurdly simple."

"I am sure that I shall say nothing of the kind."

"You see, my dear Watson"—he propped his test-tube in the rack, and began to lecture with the air of a professor addressing his class—"it is not really difficult to construct a series of inferences, each dependent upon its predecessor and each simple in itself. If, after doing so, one simply knocks out all the central inferences and presents one's audience with the starting-point and the conclusion, one may produce a startling, though possibly a meretricious effect. Now, it was not really difficult, by an inspection of the groove between your left forefinger and thumb, to feel sure that you did *not* propose to invest your small capital in the gold fields."

"I see no connection."

"Very likely not; but I can quickly show you a close connection. Here are the missing links of the very simple chain: 1. You had chalk between your left finger and thumb when you returned from the club last night. 2. You put chalk there when you play billiards, to steady the cue. 3. You never play billiards except with Thurston. 4. You told me, four weeks ago, that Thurston had an option on some South African property which would expire in a month, and which he desired you to share with him. 5. Your check book is locked in my drawer, and you have not asked for the key. 6. You do not propose to invest your money in this manner."

"How absurdly simple!" I cried.

"Quite so!" said he, a little nettled. "Every problem becomes very childish when once it is explained to you."

commercial logic I

R.S.V.P.

I ACCEPT

Please enter my Introductory Subscription beginning with three free issues of *World Monitor Magazine*. After receiving my free issues I may cancel if I choose, and keep the three free issues. Otherwise, I will honor your invoice for $14.97 and receive 9 more issues (a total of 12). That's a 50% savings off the basic subscription price.

I'M NOT SURE

I'm not sure, but I'd like to give *World Monitor Magazine* a try. So send me my three free issues with no strings attached. If I choose to subscribe, I'll honor your invoice for $14.97 and receive 9 more issues (a total of 12). If I'm not satisfied, I will write "cancel" on the invoice, return it, and owe nothing. The first three issues will be mine to keep, free.

curiosities & puzzles

The Digestor's Digest

Vol. I, No. 1   Page 5

Don't Read!

After testing numerous dietary journals and newsletters, researchers have concluded that none are completely reliable. In particular, we note that this page of this publication is completely false.

Don't Eat!

After testing numerous breakfast foods, both homemade and commercial, researchers have concluded that none are completely safe. In particular, we note with regret that this page of this publication is inedible.

exam warning V

Well! Never before have we received so much mail! It is a delight to hear from so many readers! However, the theme running through most of the letters—that we have been somehow dishonest—is most distressing.

We regret that space

does not permit us

to print any of your letters.

The attack on our veracity, however, is totally without foundation. The argument that we cannot put the exam on any page *seems* sound, we admit. In our hearts, however, we believe in our Surprise Examination! And we would not lie to you! You have our word! We hope to present a full explanation soon.

Our attorneys have asked us not to comment further.

the barbershop problem

What is it that's greater than God, the dead eat it, and if the living eat it, they die?

— RAYMOND SMULLYAN, *What Is the Name of This Book?*

This puzzle was invented by Lewis Carroll. It precipitated a fight with another Oxford logician, John Cook Wilson, that lasted almost two years. It further raised philosophical issues about the meaning of implication that attracted Bertrand Russell and initiated a discussion that continued for over fifty years.

There are many versions of the puzzle. The following one appeared in the *Lewis Carroll Picture Book* (1899), a collection of previously unpublished writings.

"What, *nothing* to do?" said Uncle Jim. "Then come along with me down to Allen's. And you can just take a turn while I get myself shaved."

"All right," said Uncle Joe. "And the Cub had better come too, I suppose?"

The "Cub" was *me*, as the reader will perhaps have guessed for himself. I'm turned *fifteen*—more than three months ago; but there's no sort of use in mentioning *that* to Uncle Joe: he'd only say "Go to your cubbicle, little boy!" or "Then I suppose you can do cubbic equations?" or some equally vile pun. He asked me yesterday to give him an instance of a Proposition in A. And I said "All uncles make vile puns." And I don't think he liked it. However, that's neither here nor there. I was glad enough to go. I *do* love hearing those uncles of mine "chop logic," as they call it; and they're desperate hands at it, *I* can tell you!

"That is not a logical inference from my remark," said Uncle Jim.

"Never said it was," said Uncle Joe; "it's a *Reductio ad Absurdum*" [Latin for "reduced to an absurdity," or proof by contradiction].

"*An Illicit Process of the Minor!*" [syllogistic fallacy] chuckled Uncle Jim.

That's the sort of way they always go on, whenever *I'm* with them. As if there was any fun in calling me a minor!

After a bit, Uncle Jim began again, just as we came in sight of the barber's. "I only hope *Carr* will be at home," he said. "Brown's so clumsy. And Allen's hand has been shaky ever since he had that fever."

"Carr's *certain* to be in," said Uncle Joe.

"I'll bet you sixpence he *isn't!*" said I.

"Keep your bets for your betters," said Uncle Joe. "I mean" — he hurried on, seeing by the grin on my face what a slip he'd made — "I mean that I can *prove* it logically. It isn't a matter of *chance*."

"Prove it *logically!*" sneered Uncle Jim. "Fire away, then! I defy you to do it!"

"For the sake of argument," Uncle Joe began, "let us assume Carr to be *out*. And let us see what that assumption would lead to. I'm going to do this by *Reductio ad Absurdum*."

"Of course you are!" growled Uncle Jim. "Never knew any argument of *yours* that didn't end in some absurdity or other!"

"Unprovoked by your unmanly taunts," said Uncle Joe in a lofty tone, "I proceed. Carr being out, you will grant that if Allen is *also* out, *Brown* must be at home?"

"What is the good of *his* being at home?" said Uncle Jim. "I don't want *Brown* to shave me! He's too clumsy."

"Patience is one of those inestimable qualities —" Uncle Joe was beginning; but Uncle Jim cut him off short.

"*Argue!*" he said. "Don't *moralize!*"

"Well, but *do* you grant it?" Uncle Joe persisted. "Do you grant me that, if Carr is out, it follows that if Allen is out Brown *must* be in?"

"Of course he must," said Uncle Jim; "or there'd be nobody to mind the shop."

"We see, then, that the absence of Carr brings into play a certain Hypothetical [conditional], whose *protasis* [antecedent, the "if" part of the conditional] is "Allen is out," and whose *apodosis* [consequent, the "then" part] is 'Brown is in.' And we see that, so long as Carr remains out, the Hypothetical remains in force?"

"Well, suppose it does. What then?" said Uncle Jim.

"You will also grant me that the truth of a Hypothetical—

I mean is *validity* as a logical *sequence* [in our definitions, he really means *truth* not validity]—does not in the least depend on its *protasis* being actually *true*, nor even on its being *possible*. The Hypothetical 'if you were to run from here to London in five minutes you would surprise people' remains true as a sequence, whether you can do it or not."

"I can't do *it*," said Uncle Jim.

"We have now to consider *another* Hypothetical. What was that you told me yesterday about Allen?"

"I told you," said Uncle Jim, "that ever since he had that fever he's been so nervous about going out alone, he always takes Brown with him."

"Just so," said Uncle Joe. "Then the Hypothetical "if Allen is out Brown is out" is *always* in force, isn't it?"

"I suppose so," said Uncle Jim. (He seemed to be getting a little nervous himself now.)

"Then, if Carr is out, we have *two* Hypotheticals, "if Allen is out Brown is *in*," and "if Allen is out Brown is *out*," in force at once. And two *incompatible* Hypotheticals, mark you! They can't *possibly* be true together!"

"*Can't* they?" said Uncle Jim.

"How *can* they?" said Uncle Joe. "How *can* one and the same *protasis* prove two contradictory *apodoses*? You grant that the two *apodoses* 'Brown is *in*' and 'Brown is *out*' are contradictory, I suppose?"

"Yes, I grant you *that*," said Uncle Jim.

"Then I may sum up," said Uncle Joe. "If Carr is out, these two Hypotheticals are true together. And we know that they *cannot* be true together. Which is absurd. Therefore Carr *cannot* be out. There's a nice *Reductio ad Absurdum* for you!"

Uncle Jim looked thoroughly puzzled; but after a bit he plucked up courage, and began again. "I don't feel at all clear about that *incompatibility*. Why shouldn't those two Hypotheticals be true together? It would seem to me that would simply prove '*Allen* is in.' Of course, it's clear that the *apodoses* of those two Hypotheticals are incompatible—'Brown is in' and 'Brown is out.' But why shouldn't we put it like this? If Allen is out, Brown is *out*. If Carr and Allen are *both* out, Brown is *in*. Which is absurd. Therefore Carr and Allen can't be *both* of them out. But so long as Allen is *in*, I don't see what's to hinder Carr from going *out*."

"My dear, but most illogical, brother!" said Uncle Joe. (Whenever Uncle Joe begins to "dear" you, you may make pretty sure he's got you in a cleft stick!) "Don't you see that you are wrong by dividing the *protasis* and the *apodosis* of that Hypothetical? Its *protasis* is simply 'Carr is out'; and its *apodosis* is sort of a sub-Hypothetical, 'If Allen is out, Brown is *in*.' And a most absurd *apodosis* it is, being hopelessly incompatible with that other Hypothetical, that we know is *always* true, 'If Allen is out, Brown is *out*.' And it's simply the assumption 'Carr is out' that has caused this absurdity. So there's only *one* possible conclusion. *Carr is in!*"

How long this argument *might* have lasted, I haven't the least idea. I believe *either* of them could argue for six hours at a stretch. But, just at this moment, we arrived at the barber's shop; and, on going inside, we found—

The quarrel between Carroll and Wilson was not philosophical. It appears that Wilson simply did not understand material implication. He took the part of one of the uncles, and Carroll took the other.

EXERCISE **Who is right, Uncle Jim or Uncle Joe?**

English 254

Myrtle Hamwich slept through most of her 8:00 A.M. classes of English 254, "Obscure British Novels of 1873." She is now in trouble. She is ten minutes into the final and stumped on the only question, which reads:

> For each of the novels below, list the major theme, the principal character, and the month of publication:
> *Colonel Boddicker's Mistake*
> *The Secret of Sutcliffe Manor*
> *Inspector Palmer Decides*
> *At the Sign of the Blue Goose*
> *Lady Quisenberry's Whim*

Myrtle studied all night on decaf, and while the facts are in her head, they are hard to extract. She knows, for example, that these five

English 254 Worksheet

	Reverend Stengel	Dame Dahlia	Nottingham Billy	Julia Williams	Morgan McGraw	January	February	March	April	May	depravity	romance	mystery	explorer	libraries
Colonel's Mistake															
Sutcliffe Manor															
Inspector Palmer															
Blue Goose															
Lady's Whim															
depravity															
romance															
mystery															
explorer															
libraries															
January															
February															
March															
April															
May															

books were published in the first five months of the year. She further recalls that one book, focusing on the depravity of the British upper classes, was published a month after the book featuring the Reverend Tobias Stengel, and that if some book preceded them, it was not the turgid romance.

She knows that one of the books concerns the adventures of an infant Arctic explorer. She is pretty sure that *The Secret of Sutcliffe Manor* was published last. The novel with Dame Dahlia Warren came right after the one with the racehorse, Nottingham Billy. Neither of these two was *Colonel Boddicker's Mistake*.

A few more details float to the surface of Myrtle's tortured brain: Julia Williams stars in *Inspector Palmer Decides*, which was not about the depravity of the British upper classes. Morgan McGraw was the chief character in the social commentary that exposed the conditions then prevailing in Victorian lending libraries. Finally, *Lady Quisenberry's Whim* was a mystery story that did not feature Reverend Stengel.

In this precarious state, can Myrtle Hamwich ace the test?

Title	Theme	Character	Month
Colonel's Mistake			
Sutcliffe Manor			
Inspector Palmer			
Blue Goose			
Lady's Whim			

7

SYMBOLIC SOPHISTICATION, INDUCTION, AND BUSINESS LOGIC

GOAL: To see how predicate logic can provide powerful logical techniques involving counting, descriptions, and functions, and to get more practice understanding and working with predicate logic.

FORMAL LOGIC: SOME SYMBOLIC SOPHISTICATION

QUANTIFIERS AND ARITHMETIC

> Numbers are free creations of the human mind.
> —RICHARD DEDEKIND

It's easy to say there is at least *one* thing that F's. That's simply $\exists x Fx$. How do we say there are at least *two* things that F?

One suggestion is $\exists x \exists y (Fx \ \& \ Fy)$, but this doesn't work. Just because the variables are different, it doesn't mean that the things asserted to exist are different. In fact, it's quite easy to get this formula from the mere assumption of Fa:

Fa	assumption
$Fa \ \& \ Fa$	taut., 1
$\exists y (Fa \ \& \ Fy)$	$\exists I$

If $Fa \ \& \ Fa$, then surely there is some y such that $Fa \ \& \ Fy$. But then

$$\exists x \exists y (Fx \ \& \ Fy) \quad \exists I$$

Well, then, how do we say that at least two things F? Simply as

$$\exists x \exists y (Fx \ \& \ Fy \ \& \ x \neq y)$$

That is, we specify that x and y are different. (Notice that we couldn't derive this wff from Fa or $Fa \ \& \ Fa$.)

CHALLENGE 1   How do we say that at least three things F? (Be sure to specify that the three things are all different.)

In general, we can say that at least n things have property F for any number n.

334

Is it possible to say that at most one thing F's? This would not imply that anything actually F's, but only that *no more* than one thing F's. Suppose it's true that at most one thing F's, and suppose that Fx and Fy. Then what must be the relation between x and y? Obviously, $x = y$. So we can say "at most one thing F's" by saying

$$\forall x \forall y ((Fx \,\&\, Fy) \Rightarrow x = y)$$

(According to Alfred North Whitehead, this expresses the creed of Unitarians: There is one God—at most!)

CHALLENGE 2 Another way of saying that at most one thing F's would be to deny that at least two things F, that is, $\neg \exists x \exists y (Fx \,\&\, Fy \,\&\, x \neq y)$. Show that this is equivalent to the preceding.

In a similar fashion we can go on to say "at most two things F," "at most three things F," and so on. "At most two things F" would be

$$\forall x \forall y \forall z ((Fx \,\&\, Fy \,\&\, Fz) \Rightarrow (x = y \lor x = z \lor y = z))$$

CHALLENGE 3 What would "at most three things F" be?

Since we can say that at least one thing F's and at most one thing F's, we can say that exactly one thing F's:

$$\exists x Fx \,\&\, \forall x \forall y ((Fx \,\&\, Fy) \Rightarrow x = y)$$

Similarly, exactly two things F is

$$\exists x \exists y (Fx \,\&\, Fy \,\&\, x \neq y) \,\&\, \forall x \forall y \forall z ((Fx \,\&\, Fy \,\&\, Fz)$$
$$\Rightarrow (x = y \lor x = z \lor y = z))$$

CHALLENGE 4 What would "exactly three things F" be?

It's possible to express the "exactly" locution much more efficiently. To say that exactly one thing F's, we can say

$$\exists x (Fx \,\&\, \forall y (Fy \Rightarrow x = y))$$

CHALLENGE 5   Show this expression is equivalent to the other way of saying exactly one thing F's.

CHALLENGE 6   Give an analogous way of saying exactly two things F.

If I have two apples and two oranges, then I have four pieces of fruit. We are inclined to think of this as a result of elementary arithmetic. The great philosophers Frege and Russell realized that we could derive this result in logic alone. They went on to suggest that perhaps all of mathematics could be derived from logic. Let us see how the simple result of the four pieces of fruit might be obtained.

Let Ax be "x is an apple" and Ox be "x is an orange." We now know how to say that there are exactly two apples;

$$\exists x \exists y (Ax \,\&\, Ay \,\&\, x \neq y \,\&\, \forall z(Az \Rightarrow (z = x \lor z = y)))$$

and similarly for oranges,

$$\exists x \exists y (Ox \,\&\, Oy \,\&\, x \neq y \,\&\, \forall z(Oz \Rightarrow (z = x \lor z = y)))$$

To say there are exactly four apples or oranges is "just"

$$\exists x \exists x' \exists x'' \exists x''' \,[(Ax \lor Ox) \,\&\, (Ax' \lor Ox') \,\&\, (Ax'' \lor Ox'') \,\&\,$$
$$(Ax''' \lor Ox''') \,\&\, x \neq x' \,\&\, x \neq x'' \,\&\, x \neq x''' \,\&\, x' \neq x'' \,\&\,$$
$$x' \neq x''' \,\&\, x'' \neq x''' \,\&\, \forall z((Az \lor Oz)$$
$$\Rightarrow (z = x \lor z = x' \lor z = x'' \lor z = x'''))]$$

Now from the first premise, it follows by applying $\exists E$ (we have omitted the asterisks) twice that

$$Aa \,\&\, Ab \,\&\, a \neq b \,\&\, \forall z(Az \Rightarrow (z = a \lor z = b))$$

and from the second premise it follows that

$$Oc \,\&\, Od \,\&\, c \neq d \,\&\, \forall z(Oz \Rightarrow (z = c \lor z = d))$$

Since $Ax \Rightarrow Ax \lor Ox$ and $Ox \Rightarrow Ax \lor Ox$, we have

$$Aa \lor Oa, \; Ab \lor Ob, \; Ac \lor Oc, \; Ad \lor Od$$

We also have $a \neq b$ and $c \neq d$. How do we know $a \neq c$ and $a \neq d$? For this we need another premise that is implicit in English. Nothing is both an apple and an orange, $\neg\exists x(Ax \,\&\, Ox)$. Other ways of saying this are

$$\forall x(Ax \Rightarrow \neg Ox) \quad \text{and} \quad \forall x(Ox \Rightarrow \neg Ax)$$

Now we can show $a \neq c$. Suppose $a = c$. Then since Oc, we have Oa by the identity rule. But we have Aa, and so by our new premise we have $\neg Oa$. Thus we get $Oa \,\&\, \neg Oa$, which is impossible. Hence $a \neq c$. Similarly, $a \neq d$, $b \neq c$, and $b \neq d$. All that remains is to show that if $Az \vee Oz$, then z is a, b, c, or d. But if Az, then z is a or b; and if Oz, then z is c or d and that does it.

That two apples and two oranges make four pieces of fruit is not a matter of mathematics or horticulture—it is a law of logic.

SUMMARY: Predicate logic enables us to express such locutions as "there are exactly n F's" and to deduce particular arithmetical relations holding between such locutions.

FUNCTIONS

The form remains, the function never dies.
—William Wordsworth

It is not too much of an exaggeration to say that functions are at the heart of symbolic logic. This might seem a bit surprising at first, since we've not discussed functions very much, but by the end of this section, we'll have explained how properties, connectives, and quantifiers can all be viewed as special cases of functions. However, let's begin our discussion of functions with some familiar examples.

We were all introduced to functions in elementary school during arithmetic lessons. Functions are operations that "transform" one number into another, or, more accurately, functions are operations that when applied to one number—the "argument"—yield another number—the "value." The successor function $x + 1$ transforms any number into its successor. Applied to 7, the successor function yields the value $8(=7 + 1)$; when 29 is the argument, $30(=29 + 1)$ is the value. Another example of a function is x^2. We might think of the

337

argument of a function as an input to the function and its value as an output. In that case, the function itself would be analogous to a computer.

Both $x + 1$ and x^2 are one-place functions; that is, they apply to one argument at a time. Addition, $x + y$, and multiplication, $x * y$, are two-place functions. When applied to two arguments, they yield a value: $7 + 5 = 12$ and $7 * 5 = 35$.

We represent functions by (what else?) function symbols. Function symbols, like names, are linguistic expressions, while functions, like objects, are entities in the world. One-place function symbols include fx, gy, and hz (the choice of variables doesn't matter here); two-place functions can be written as fxy, gyz, or hyz (again, the choice of variables doesn't generally matter, but identical variables, as in fxx, changes f into a one-place function, for example, $x + x = 2x$). When details matter, we indicate an n-place function symbol by $f^n x_1 x_2 \ldots x_n$. Although we generally write the function symbol before the variables it applies to, we sometimes bow to ordinary practice and write it between the variables, such as $x + y$ instead of $+xy$. Notice that function symbols are very much like predicate symbols. In general, our convention is to represent function symbols by lowercase letters and predicate symbols by uppercase letters.

What's the difference between function symbols and predicate symbols? The grammatical difference is that predicate symbols when applied to terms make wffs—either statements or complex properties. Function symbols when applied to terms make more terms, namely complex names. Recall the definition of "terms" and "wffs" from "Predicate Languages" in part 5:

Term
1. Any variable, name, or temporary name is a term.
2. If f^n is an n-place function symbol and $t_1, t_2, \ldots, t_n$ are any n terms, then $f^n(t_1 t_2 \ldots t_n)$ is also a term.

The semantic difference between predicate symbols and function symbols is that predicate symbols stand for properties or relations, things that are true or false of actual individuals. Function symbols stand for functions, operations, or transformations of individuals that yield more individuals.

Before looking at the logic of functions, let's look at a few more concrete examples. In physics, we have distance traveled is a function of time and average speed. In our notation, this becomes $dxy = x * y$,

• WARNING: Although the official definition of "term" includes surrounding parentheses, we often omit the parentheses if doing so causes no confusion.

where x is the time and y the average speed. Degrees Celsius is a function of degrees Fahrenheit. In our notation, this function is $cx = \frac{5}{9} * (x - 32)$, where x is the degrees in Fahrenheit.

In daily life, we have a person's body temperature is a function of the person and the time the temperature is taken: $\text{temp}(p, t) = z$. (Normally, $\forall p \forall t (\text{temp}(p, t) = 98.6° \text{ F})$.) The phrase "mother of" can be construed as a function (almost) yielding, for the argument x, the value of the mother of x. (We'll explain the "almost" shortly, but for now, ask yourself who is the value of "mother of Adam.")

The Logic of Functions

Functions and identity go hand in hand. A major use of the identity symbol is to simplify functional expressions, as in $4 * 5 = 20$ or $\text{temp}(\text{Tom}, 6/6/94) = 98.6°$. The logic of functions can be expressed using identity. It is essentially this:

> Every function has a unique value for every argument.

First, let's show that every function has a value for every argument, that is,

$\forall x \exists y (fx = y)$
1. $\forall z (z = z)$
2. $fx = fx$
3. $\exists y (fx = y)$
4. $\forall x \exists y (fx = y)$

EXERCISE Fill in the justification for each step in this deduction.

Thus a function must always have a value for every object in the domain (and so "mother of Adam" must have a value if "mother of" picks out a function for the domain of human beings). This means that while $x + y$ and $x * y$ are functions over the natural numbers (the sum or product of any two natural numbers is a natural number), subtraction, $x - y$, is not strictly a function over the natural numbers. No natural number is the value of $3 - 8$. Of course, if we consider the integers, subtraction is a function, since $3 - 8 = -5$. On the other hand, division is not a function over the integers, since $\frac{2}{3}$ is not defined.

As you might guess, the demand that functions be everywhere defined (or total) has led mathematicians to invent new numbers, such as negative numbers and fractions to serve as values. (Recently logicians have relaxed this demand somewhat and have begun to consider partial functions, which need not be defined for every possible argument.)

We saw that the laws of logic require that functions have a value for every argument. Now let's see why this value is unique. One way of expressing this is that a function can't have two values for a given argument, which we can prove as follows:

$\forall x \forall y \forall z((fx = y \,\&\, fx = z) \Rightarrow y = z)$

1.	$(fx = y \,\&\, fx = z)$	assumption
2.	$fx = y$	&E, 1
3.	$fx = z$	&E, 1
4.	$y = z$	=E, 2, 3 (To see how =E applies, regard $fx = z$ as Afx. Then since $fx = y$ we get Ay by =E, i.e., $y = z$.)

5. $(fx = y \,\&\, fx = z) \Rightarrow y = z$ $\quad\quad$ ⇒I, 1–4
6. $\forall x \forall y \forall z((fx = y \,\&\, fx = z) \Rightarrow y = z)$ $\quad$ ∀I, 5(3 times)

Notice once again the connection between the logic of functions and the logic of identity.

The requirement that functions have a unique value for each argument means that, technically, "square root of x" is not a function, since both 2 and -2 are square roots of 4. For this reason, mathematicians interpret the symbol $\sqrt{}$ as the "positive square root of," thus making it into a function symbol.

CHALLENGE 1

Show that $\forall x \forall y(x = y \Rightarrow fx = fy)$ is a valid law of logic. Show that $\forall x \forall y(fx = fy \Rightarrow x = y)$ is *not* valid by finding a universe and an interpretation of f that makes it false.

Functions and Relations

In many disciplines, from economics to physics, one hears of "functional relationships." The idea behind this is that functions are intimately related to a certain kind of relation. If we think about it, it is clear that functions give rise to relations. The expression $fx = y$ expresses a two-place relation between x and y, which we could easily write as Rxy. (In general, an n-place function $f^n x_1 \ldots x_n$ gives rise to an $(n + 1)$–place relation $Rx_1 \ldots x_n y$. There must be an extra place for the function's value.)

If Rxy is the relation determined by $fx = y$, then the logical facts about the function carry over to the relation

$$\forall x \exists y Rxy \qquad \text{and} \qquad \forall x \forall y \forall z((Rxy \,\&\, Rxz) \Rightarrow y = z)$$

These propositions are not generally true of relations. Both are false when Rxy is the relation "x is a parent of y." However, when they are true of a relation, then that relation is called a "functional relation"; it determines a function which assigns to every x a unique value y. Indeed, it is possible to get by without ever introducing function symbols at all. Whenever we wanted to deal with a function, we could deal with the corresponding functional relation instead.

Composition of Functions

One great advantage of functional notation is its flexibility. Functions compose with one another quite naturally. That is, you can take the value of one function fx as the argument of another gy. The result is $g(fx)$. In fact, $g(fx)$ is a new function. For any input x, it yields a unique output z. The value z is obtained by first obtaining the intermediary value, $fx = y$, and then obtaining $gy = z$.

For example, by composing the "father of" function with itself, we obtain father of (father of x), which is just the paternal grandfather of x. If $fx = 2 * x$ and $gx = x^2$, then $g(fx) = (2 * x)^2$, or $4 * x^2$.

Without functional notation, composition of functions could not be expressed so easily. If the function $fx = y$ were represented by the relation Rxy and the function $gx = y$ by the relation Sxy, then in order to express the composite function $g(fx) = y$, we would have to write $\exists z(Rxz\ \&\ Szy)$.

Frege and Functions

Gottlob Frege, whom we have mentioned several times, was the founder of modern logic. Frege's goal was to apply logic to mathematics. But he thought that the essence of mathematics was its concept of function, and he recognized that classical Aristotelean logic could not handle functions. Consequently, he invented a new kind of logic, predicate logic, that was especially adapted to functions.

Recall that predicates express properties and relations. One-place predicates like Fx express properties, and many-place predicates like Rxy or $Sxyz$ express many-place relations. For Frege, a property (or n-place relation) was just a one-place function (or n-place function) whose arguments were drawn from the universe of discourse and whose values were the truth values T or F.

• Frege thought there was only one universe of discourse—the universe of all things.

The property of humans "is female" is just a function from the universe of humans to the set {T, F} such that "x is female" = T of all

341

and only the female humans. The numerical relation $x < y$ is a two-place function from the universe of numbers to the set {T, F}. "$x < y$" = T of all and only those pairs such that the first element is less than the second. So "3 < 4" = T and "4 < 3" = F. Indeed, we might say that the whole point of talking about truth values, the objects T and F, is just to make properties and relations a kind of function.

Moreover, the connectives ¬, &, ∨, ⇒, and ⇔ can also be interpreted as functions, as truth functions whose arguments and values are T or F. Thus ¬ is a one-place truth function, and the others are two-place. The truth tables tell us explicitly what value a truth function has for each possible argument. Notice how nicely truth functions compose with each other: ¬¬A is just the identity function ¬¬T = T, ¬¬F = F. The equivalences of propositional logic are nothing but truth-functional identities. To say that

$$\neg(A \,\&\, B) \Leftrightarrow (\neg A \vee \neg B)$$

is a tautology or is valid is just to say that the composed functions yield identical values:

$$\neg((x) \,\&\, (y)) = (\neg(x) \vee \neg(y))$$

no matter what truth values, T or F, are substituted for x and y.

Furthermore—and this was a key point for Frege—the truth functions compose with properties and relations. Recall that "x is female" was interpreted as a function from the universe of humans to the truth values. Then the composition ¬"x is female" will also be a function from the universe of humans to the truth values except that it will have the opposite value to "x is female." Similarly, the composite function "x is female" & "x is strong" will be a property, that is a function from the universe of humans to the truth values. Notice how smoothly everything works out!

Finally, the quantifiers ∀x and ∃x can themselves be interpreted as functions if we allow higher-level (or "second-order") functions. Their arguments are not individuals but properties and relations. Their values, like those of the truth functions, are the truth values T and F. Thus ∀xFx can be construed as a function that takes properties like Fx as arguments. If Fx applies universally (to everything in the universe of discourse), then ∀xFx = T. Otherwise, ∀xFx = F. Similarly, if Fx applies at least once, then ∃xFx = T; otherwise ∃xFx = F.

Once again we find that, under Frege's functional view, there is elegant composition. In the functional interpretation, $\neg\forall xFx$ is a function from properties to truth values, as are $\forall x\neg Fx$ and $\exists x\neg Fx$. As functions, it works out that the first and third functions give the same values for the same arguments: $\neg\forall xFx = \exists x\neg Fx$ for every choice of F, but the first and second do not: $\neg\forall xFx \neq \forall x\neg Fx$.

In conclusion, let's try to work out the semantics of quantifiers applied to relations. We want to see $\forall xRxy$ as a case of functional composition, so we should be able to figure out what function it represents. Rxy is a two-place function from the universe of discourse to the truth values $\{T, F\}$. $\forall xAx$ is a higher-order function from properties to the truth values $\{T, F\}$. Now consider any object c from the universe of discourse. Rxc will express a property, that is, a one-place function from the universe to truth values. Consequently, $\forall x$, as a function, will apply to Rxc, yielding a truth value T if Rxc is always true and F otherwise. But this works out for each object c in the universe. Thus $\forall xRxy$ must be a one-place function from the universe of discourse to the truth values. In other words, $\forall xRxy$ is just a complex one-place property—which was just what we wanted it to be!

On the one hand this might seem a bit trivial—everything works out like it's supposed to. But remember that no human before Frege knew this triviality, and Frege was only able to see it because he looked at everything in terms of functions. As we said earlier, it is not too much of an exaggeration to say that functions are at the heart of symbolic logic.

CHALLENGE 2 Explain how, according to Frege, $\exists x\neg Rxy$ can be seen as a one-place function that takes arguments from the universe of discourse and has values in $\{T, F\}$.

SUMMARY: The language of logic becomes far more flexible when function symbols are added. Predicate languages with function symbols conveniently describe mathematics and science. For Frege, at least, the fundamental ideas of symbolic logic were based on the idea of functions.

''THE'': RUSSELL'S THEORY OF DEFINITE DESCRIPTIONS

It may be thought excessive to devote two chapters to one word ["the"], but to the philosophical mathematician it is a word of very great importance: like Browning's Grammarian with the enclitic $\delta\varepsilon$, I would give the doctrine of this word if I were "dead from the waist down" and not merely in prison.

— BERTRAND RUSSELL

Russell's essay "On Denoting" was published in *Mind* in 1905. In it Russell propounded his theory of definite descriptions and in so doing introduced modern logic to philosophers. F. P. Ramsey called Russell's theory "a paradigm of analysis," and T. S. Eliot said that "On Denoting" was one of the few times that philosophy reached the status of art.

Logical Background—A Refresher Course

"Cindy is female" has the logical form Fc. "Cindy" is a name that denotes Cindy; "is female" is a predicate (or verb phrase) that picks out, depending on one's philosophical theories, either (1) the *property* of being female, or, as Russell said, (2) the *propositional function* of being female (Fx) (for different values of x, Fx yields different propositions) or, as Frege said, (3) the *concept* of being female (Fx) (for different values of x, Fx yields either the true or the false). These different explanations all amount to pretty much the same thing.

Now consider sentences like "Someone is female," "Everyone is female", and "No one is female." It is not very promising to view them as being of the forms Fs and Fe and Fn. What do the s, e, and n stand for? Russell, like Frege, realized that such sentences are very different from the traditional subject–predicate form (Ps; that is, "s is P"). Such sentences do not express propositions about particular things—there is no one named "someone," nor are there general things like the "average person." In fact, such sentences don't say anything about things at all. They express propositions about properties (or about propositional functions or about concepts).

"Someone is female," symbolized $\exists x Fx$, says that the property Fx has at least one instance. "Everyone is female," symbolized $\forall x Fx$, says that Fx applies to everything in the universe; any object is an instance of an F. "No one is female" says that Fx has no instances. It can be symbolized as $\neg \exists x Fx$ or as $\forall x \neg Fx$. Indeed, one quantifier is sufficient for logic, since both $\forall$ and $\exists$ can be defined in terms of the other:

$$\exists x Fx \Leftrightarrow \neg \forall x \neg Fx \quad \text{and} \quad \forall x Fx \Leftrightarrow \neg \exists x \neg Fx$$

Descriptions

Russell called certain English phrases "descriptions." Indefinite descriptions were phrases like "a man" or "some apple." We have just seen that indefinite descriptions are not to be treated as names but by existential quantification, $\exists$. Definite descriptions were phrases beginning with "the," for example, "the woman," "the president of Sophist College," and "the (present) king of France." The problem with definite descriptions is that they really do look like names, at least like complex names. If "Tom is bald" has the form Bt, then "The president of Sophist is bald" seems to have the form Bp (where p is a complex name of the actual president of Sophist College) and "The king of France is bald" seems to have the form Bk (where k is . . . wait, what does k denote? There is no king of France!).

Let's be clear about the source of the difficulty. The problem is with nondenoting subject terms. There is no problem with predicates that don't have instances, like square circles or 20-foot-tall college students. In general, take your favorite predicate Fx. Then $\neg Fx$ is also a predicate, and so is $Fx \,\&\, \neg Fx$. But we know nothing satisfies this predicate, and we can express our knowledge as $\neg \exists x(Fx \,\&\, \neg Fx)$. A predicate is meaningful even if there is nothing that has the property that the predicate expresses. The problem with subject terms, like "Mary Lincoln," "Paris," and ostensibly "the king of France," is that they seem to get their very meaning from what they denote: therefore no denotation, no meaning. So "The king of France is bald" should be like "XXLGRPH is bald"—perfectly meaningless. But it doesn't seem meaningless. In summary, this is the predicament Russell found himself in.

1. "The king of France is bald" is a meaningful sentence.
2. It seems to have the form Bk.
3. But if it has the form Bk, then it is meaningful only if k denotes something.

A philosopher named Meinong accepted all these assumptions and concluded that "the king of France" does denote something only what it denotes is nonexistent, something that merely "subsisted." Russell thought this conclusion was ridiculous. Whatever was, existed. There could be nothing that didn't exist. Since he was sure of clauses 1 and 3, he thought the trouble must be with 2.

By the way, there are other problems related to nondenoting definite descriptions. According to the law of the excluded middle, that is, $P \vee \neg P$, either the present king of France is bald or the present king of France is not bald. Yet both alternatives seem to imply that there is a king of France. However, as Russell noted, if you look through all the hairy things in the universe and then through all the nonhairy things, you still won't find the king of France!

Definite Descriptions

Consider an arbitrary sentence of the form "The F is G." (Russell wrote this as $G(\imath xFx)$.) What do we mean when we utter this? We mean three things, according to Russell:

1. There is an F.
2. There is no more than one F.
3. That F is G (or given points 1 and 2, that any F is G).

There are two crucial facts about this analysis. The first is that the phrase "the F" has disappeared from the analysis. True, the phrase "F" still occurs, but it occurs as a predicate, not a subject, and we have seen that empty predicates are not a difficulty. So we can explain "The F is G" without actually using the subject term "the F." The second crucial fact is that all the clauses in the analysis can be explained in logic.

1. There is an F. $\qquad\qquad\qquad$ $\exists xFx$
2. There is no more than one F. $\qquad$ $\forall x\forall y(Fx \,\&\, Fy \Rightarrow x = y)$
3. That F is G (really, every F is G). $\quad$ $\forall x(Fx \Rightarrow Gx)$

Thus on Russell's analysis, English sentences of the form "The F is G" really have the logical form

$$\exists xFx \,\&\, \forall x\forall y(Fx \,\&\, Fy \Rightarrow x = y) \,\&\, \forall x(Fx \Rightarrow Gx)$$

This is a far cry from the apparently simple Gf that we began with. Russell said that "the F," as in "the king of France," was an incomplete symbol. He meant that one could not explain its meaning in isolation, that one could not explain its meaning by stating what it stood for if it stood for anything. Instead, the meaning of "the" was to be explained by showing how the presence of "the" contributed to the logical structure of sentences containing it, that is, by showing how the sentences could be paraphrased without using the word "the." In effect, Russell turned definite descriptions into complex quantifiers.

Note that on Russell's analysis, sentences with definite descriptions could be false in three ways. For example, "The king of France is bald" comes out meaningful but false—there is no such king. "The student in college is human" is also meaningful but false—there is more than one student. "The president of the United States is female" is meaningful but false—he's male.

Logical Equivalents

Our original analysis of "The F is G" was

$$\exists xFx \ \& \ \forall x \forall y(Fx \ \& \ Fy) \Rightarrow x = y) \ \& \ \forall x(Fx \Rightarrow Gx)$$

Two equivalent analyses are

$$\exists x(Fx \ \& \ \forall y(Fy \Rightarrow x = y) \ \& \ Gx) \tag{1}$$
$$\exists x \forall y((Fy \Leftrightarrow x = y) \ \& \ Gx) \tag{2}$$

Let us review some logic and see if we can deduce the original from analysis (1). If that expression holds, it must hold of something; let's call that thing c^* (this is the rule of $\exists$E). So we get

1. $Fc^* \ \& \ \forall y(Fy \Rightarrow c^* = y) \ \& \ Gc^*$

From 1 it obviously follows that Fc^* (by &E), and from Fc^*, it follows that something is F, that is, $\exists xFx$ (by $\exists$I).

Now let's show that $\forall x \forall y((Fx \ \& \ Fy) \Rightarrow x = y)$. To do this we assume

2. $Fx \ \& \ Fy$ for any x, y

and try to show that $x = y$. Now, from 1 we have that $\forall y(Fy \Rightarrow c^* = y)$ by &E. This just says that anything that F's is c^*. So it follows (by using $\forall$E twice) that $Fx \Rightarrow c^* = x$ and $Fy \Rightarrow c^* = y$. But since 2 tells us that both Fx and Fy, we have $c^* = x$ and $c^* = y$ and so $x = y$ by the identity rule (=E). Thus by assuming $Fx \ \& \ Fy$, we can show $x = y$; hence by the rule for introducing $\Rightarrow$,

$$((Fx \ \& \ Fy) \Rightarrow x = y)$$

Since this holds for arbitrary x and y, we are entitled to introduce $\forall x$ and $\forall y$:

$$\forall x \forall y((Fx \ \& \ Fy) \Rightarrow x = y)$$

Finally, let's show that $\forall x(Fx \Rightarrow Gx)$. As above, we begin with an assumption:

3. Fx

Now, we know from 1 that $\forall y(Fy \Rightarrow c^* = y)$, "Anything that F's is c^*." Since this holds for everything, it holds for x, so $Fx \Rightarrow c^* = x$. By 3 we have Fx, so $x = c^*$. But we also have Gc^* from 1.

Since $x = c^*$ and since Gc^*, we have Gx by $=$E. Thus $Fx \Rightarrow Gx$ (by $\Rightarrow$I) and so by $\forall$I we have $\forall x(Fx \Rightarrow Gx)$, which was the last thing to prove.

In a similar way, we can show that the original analysis implies (1) and that (1) and (2) are equivalent.

CHALLENGE 1   Using the sections on deduction in part 6 as a guide, write out a formal version of the foregoing deduction, putting in all the steps.

CHALLENGE 2   Show by deduction that

$$\exists x Fx \ \& \ \forall x \forall y((Fx \ \& \ Fy) \Rightarrow x = y) \ \& \ \forall x(Fx \Rightarrow Gx)$$

implies

$$\exists x(Fx \ \& \ \forall y(Fy \Rightarrow x = y) \ \& \ Gx)$$

Scope

Russell's theory has interesting consequences. For example, it predicts a certain ambiguity in "the" sentences, for instance, in "The F is not G." In the latter sentence, are we denying that "The F is G," or are we asserting of the F that it is a non-G? In the first case, we say that "not" has a greater scope than the definite description. Hence it is called an external negation. Expressing "The F is G" as

$$\exists x(Fx \ \& \ \forall y(Fy \Rightarrow x = y) \ \& \ Gx)$$

external negation is just

$$\neg\exists x(Fx \ \& \ \forall y(Fy \Rightarrow x = y) \ \& \ Gx)$$

In the second case, we say that the definite description has larger scope than negation. Hence the negation is called internal negation and is represented

$$\exists x(Fx \ \& \ \forall y(Fy \Rightarrow x = y) \ \& \ \neg Gx)$$

Notice that for the external negation to be true, "The F is G" must be false in any of the three ways it can be; but for the internal negation to be true, there must be a unique F that is not G. With this distinction, we can solve the earlier puzzle of the law of the excluded middle. Consider again "The king of France is bald or the king of France is not bald." For this to be of the form $A \vee \neg A$, the negated clause must be an external negation. But for A and $\neg A$ to each imply there is a king of France, the negated clause must be read as an internal negation.

CHALLENGE 3   How would Russell analyze the following reasoning?
Either the Massachusetts vampire is male or it is not male.
If it's male then there is a Massachusetts vampire.
If the Massachusetts vampire is not male, then there is a Massachusetts vampire.
∴There is a Massachusetts vampire.

It is easy to find other cases of scope ambiguity involving definite descriptions. We think they are impressive evidence for Russell's theory. For example, consider "Tom believes that the Queen of England dances polkas." Can you hear two distinct readings?

If "believes" has wider scope than "the," Tom believes the *proposition* that the Queen of England dances polkas. Perhaps he doesn't even know Elizabeth II, but he thinks this is a requirement for all English royalty, perhaps because Tom mistakenly thinks the English royal family originated in Poland. When "believes" has wider scope than "the," this is called the "*de dicto*" sense of belief.

On the other hand, if "the" has wider scope than "believes," then the Queen of England is such that Tom believes *of her* that she dances polkas. He might have seen Elizabeth II dancing polkas at a London pub and not even have guessed that she was the queen of England! This is the "*de re*" sense of belief.

Disguised Descriptions

If that were all that could be said about Russell's account of definite descriptions, his theory would still have enormous significance for philosophy, logic, and linguistics. But, in addition, Russell (and other philosophers such as those from the school of logical positivism) felt that the theory of definite descriptions could be used to lay the groundwork for philosophical analysis. Philosophy was to be seen as the clarification of our concepts by means of logic. Although he began by explaining definite descriptions in contrast to names, Russell then switched gears and argued that most names, proper and common, were really disguised descriptions! A name like "Moses," for example, was short for "the man who led the Israelites out of Egypt and who was raised by the Pharaoh's daughter." "Moses" could not be a true name, Russell argued, for if it were, then we could not sensibly ask "Did Moses really exist?" Our mere understanding of the name would guarantee that Moses existed, but surely that is not true.

Thus the business of philosophy was to find the real logical analysis of propositions. Statements of science like "Hydrogen is a gas" would become "The lightest element is a gas." In the end, we could purify our language, at least in theory, so that the only things that remained were observation properties (red, hard), general concepts of logic, and logically proper names. The only logically proper or true names, according to Russell, were "this" and "that," as in "This seems red to me" (but sometimes he suggested that "I," "here," and "now" might be true names). Talk of everything else would be built up from this basis by logical constructions, such as those provided by the theory of definite descriptions.

Thus began the grand program of logical analysis, which dominated Anglo–American–Germanic philosophy for many decades. We might add that there is an enormous philosophical literature on the topic of "the." Many philosophers have disputed Russell's account, and many have defended it. It is rather surprising to think that the investigation of such a little word has proven to be so productive in philosophy and logic.

with & about logic

measuring uncertainty

> As far as the laws of mathematics refer to reality, they are not certain;
> and as far as they are certain, they do not refer to reality.
>
> —ALBERT EINSTEIN

Our logic is a two-valued logic. Either statements are true or they are false. We will later (in "The Excluded Middle" in part 8) introduce a three-valued logic, but here we go all the way to consider a logic where there are infinitely many truth values. We will assign as truth values the numbers from 0 to 1, inclusive. A truth value of 1 means absolutely true; a truth value of 0 means absolutely false.

This logic is actually the mathematical theory of probability. We normally consider probabilities not as truth values but as measures of likelihood. To say that a statement has truth value x is better described by saying that it has *probability x*.

The theory and its companion, the science of statistics, are well developed, sophisticated, and subtle. Here, however, we will give you just three general principles.

Principle 1   If a situation can be divided into n equally likely, mutually exclusive possibilities, then each of these has probability $\frac{1}{n}$.

EXAMPLE 1   In flipping a coin, we generally resolve the situation into two possibilities: heads and tails. Since we conceive of these as being equally likely, and since they are mutually exclusive (they can't both happen at once), they each have probability $\frac{1}{2}$.

Think of the universe of possibilities (probability = 1)

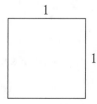

as being divided into *n* equal pieces with each piece being assigned probability $\frac{1}{n}$:

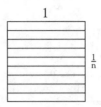

In both pictures the probability matches the area of the rectangle.

EXAMPLE 2   In rolling a fair die, the probability that a particular number comes up is $\frac{1}{6}$, because there are six possible numbers and each is equally likely.

EXAMPLE 3   In rolling two dice, we cannot apply principle 1 to the sum, since the possible sums (2, 3, . . . , 11, 12) are *not* equally likely.

> *Principle 2*   If *P* and *Q* are two mutually independent events, then the probability of *P* & *Q* is the product of the probabilities of *P* and *Q*.

It will help us to introduce some notation that is frequently used. To represent the probability of a statement *P*, we write "Pr[*P*]." Principle 2 then says that if *P* and *Q* are independent, then Pr[*P* & *Q*] = Pr[*P*]Pr[*Q*].

Think of the universe of possibilities as being divided up in two ways:

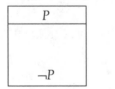

If we look at the two together, principle 2 is merely that area is length times width:

Pr [P] {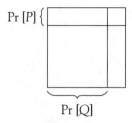

Pr [Q]

"Independent" means that neither event affects the other. If the events are not independent, we couldn't represent them as slicing up the square at right angles.

EXAMPLE 4   When rolling two dice, the roll of the first die and the roll of the second die are independent events. What is the probability that we roll two 4s? The answer is $(\frac{1}{6})(\frac{1}{6}) = \frac{1}{36}$.

Principle 3 If P and Q are mutually exclusive events, then $Pr[P \vee Q] = Pr[P] + Pr[Q]$.

If the events are mutually exclusive, then in our picture they are represented by sets that do not intersect:

The probability of the union of the sets is the sum of the two probabilities.

EXAMPLE 5   What is the probability that the sum rolled on two dice is 8? This can happen in five different ways, a 2 on the first die and a 6 on the second, a 6 on the first and a 2 on the second, a 3 on the first and a 5 on the second, a 5 on the first and a 3 on the second, and finally a 4 on both dice. These are mutually exclusive events, each with a probability of $\frac{1}{36}$, so the probability of the disjunction is $\frac{5}{36}$. To illustrate:

353

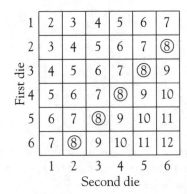

Second die

EXERCISES

1. If we roll one die, what is the probability that the number that comes up is odd?

2. If we roll one die, what is the probability that the number that comes up is greater than 2?

3. If we roll two dice consecutively, what is the probability that the first number is odd and the second is a 4?

4. If we roll two dice, what is the probability that the sum is 4?

5. If we roll two dice, what is the probability that the sum is 7?

6. If we roll two dice, what is the probability that the first number is larger than the second?

Bayes' law and Sherlock Holmes

But is it probable that probability gives assurance?
—BLAISE PASCAL

The logic of probability differs from that of Sentential in that knowing the truth values of P and of Q does not always tell us the truth values of $P \vee Q$, $P \Rightarrow Q$, and so on. That is, we can say for sure that $T \vee F$ is T and $T \& F$ is F. But, for example, we can say nothing about 0.5 & 0.5 unless we know what the propositions P and Q are.

Let P be "I roll a number less than 4 on the die," let Q be "I roll an even number on the die," and let R be "I roll an odd number on the die." Then the probabilities of P, Q, and R are all 0.5, but the probability of P & Q is $\frac{1}{6}$, while the probability of P & R is $\frac{1}{3}$. This situation does not violate principle 2 from the last section because the statements are not independent. Information about Q and R affects the probability of P. That is, knowing Q is true makes P less likely and knowing R is true makes P more likely.

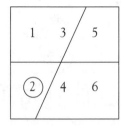 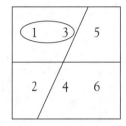

There is a rule that gives us something concrete to say about this, however. We begin by defining a new symbol, $|$. $P \mid Q$ reads "P given Q" and the probability of this event is the probability that P is true assuming that Q is. This kind of probability is called **conditional probability.**

Principle 4 (Bayes' Law)

$$\Pr[P \& Q] = \Pr[P \mid Q]\Pr[Q] = \Pr[Q \mid P]\Pr[P]$$

A picture will help.

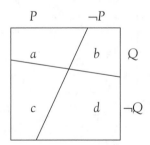

If we assume that Q is true, then we are in either region a or b in the diagram above. The probability of $P \mid Q$ is the ratio of region a to regions a and b combined. The probability of $P \mid Q$, then, is the fraction of $a \cup b$ taken up by a. In other words,

$$\Pr[P \mid Q] = \frac{\Pr[P \& Q]}{\Pr[Q]}$$

This is just Bayes' law again.

EXAMPLE 1   What is the probability that I roll a 3, given that I rolled an odd number? One solution: There are three odd numbers, one of which is a 3, so there is one chance in three, or $\frac{1}{3}$. Another solution: Bayes' law says that the probability of both happening is $\frac{1}{6}$, and then we must divide that by the probability that the number is odd ($\frac{1}{2}$). The result is $\frac{2}{6}$, or $\frac{1}{3}$.

EXAMPLE 2   Recall the argument in "The Adventure of the Dancing Men" in part 6. We presented it as a deductive argument, and as such it has a flaw (see Notes, References, Hints, and Some Answers). But let's look at it inductively. Let P be "Watson has chalk on his hand," and let Q be "Watson played billiards." Essentially, the argument is that because we have $Q \Rightarrow P$ and P, then we have Q: invalid. On the other hand, Holmes's reasoning seems tempting. The reason for this is that there is a missing premise, namely that the probability that Watson had chalk on his hand but *didn't* play billiards is extremely small. If we analyze this using conditional probability, then what we are interested in is the probability that Watson played billiards (Q) given that he had chalk on his hand (P), that is, the probability of $Q \mid P$.

We start by filling in the probabilities in the following figure:

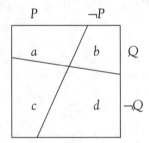

We said that the probability of P & $\neg Q$ is extremely small. Let us put it at 0.001; this, then, is the probability of being in region c.

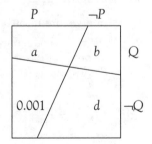

The probability of P is $\frac{1}{7}$ (let's say that Watson plays once a week).

This is the measure of region *a* plus region *c*, so we now have the following:

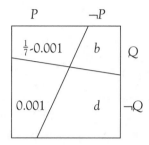

Finally, the conditional probability we are looking for is the measure of *a* divided by the sum of the measures of *a* and *c*, or

$$\frac{\frac{1}{7} - 0.001}{\frac{1}{7} - 0.001 + 0.001} = 0.993$$

This is very close to 1, and so Holmes's reasoning is inductively well justified.

EXERCISES

1. What is the probability of rolling an even number on a die given that you rolled a number less than 5?

2. What is the probability of rolling a 4 or 5 on a die given that you rolled an odd number?

3. What is the probability of rolling a 7 on two dice given that the first die was a 2?

4. What is the probability when rolling two dice that the sum is odd, given that the sum is less than 5?

5. Suppose you flip a coin and then roll a die. What is the probability that you roll a 6 given that you flip a tails?

Consider a disease so rare that it strikes only 3 out of a 1000 people. Let us say that there is a test to determine whether you have the disease and that this test is 95% accurate. Let P be the statement "I have the disease," and let Q be "I have tested positive for the disease."

6. What is $\Pr[P]$?

7. What is $\Pr[P \ \& \ Q]$?

8. What is Pr[¬P & Q]?

9. What is Pr[P & ¬Q]?

10. What is Pr[¬P & ¬Q]?

11. What is Pr[Q]?

12. What is Pr[P | Q]?

13. What is Pr[Q | P]?

14. Suppose Q is true; that is, the test tells me that I have the disease. Which of the probabilities from 6 through 13 is most meaningful to me? Assuming this is a nasty disease, should I panic?

inductive logic

Back off, man, I'm a scientist!

—DAN ACKROYD AND HAROLD RAMIS, *GHOSTBUSTERS*

Inductive logic is the logic of science. It deals with doubt. It is the scientist's tool for measuring the worth of evidence, for managing and controlling uncertainty.

What Is Inductive Logic?

The basic principle behind induction is that if an experiment is *frequently* performed and a certain result occurs *most* of the time, then we can say with *some degree* of confidence that the result will continue to occur if the experiment is repeated *often* under circumstances *essentially* the same.

You will notice the many qualifiers in this principle! The mathematical theory of probability and statistics (introduced in "Measuring Uncertainty" and "Bayes' Law and Sherlock Holmes") was developed to give us a better idea of what is meant by "frequently," "most," and so on. In 400 years, there has been much progress, but there are tremendous mathematical, logical, and even philosophical difficulties.

Does Inductive Logic Work?

Yes! It has been enormously successful. From measuring the efficacy of medical treatment, to predicting weather, to assessing economic health, to sampling opinion, induction has proved its worth again and again.

"Proved its worth"? What does that mean? Why, we trust induction because, as we said, we've used it thousands of times and it's given us meaningful, often spectacular results! Naturally, we expect such success to continue.

Do you see the problem with the defense of induction? Our justification for the principle of inductive logic is based on inductive logic itself! Compare this to another logic, which we will call "Mom" logic. Here is what we do: Whenever we wish to know if our results are correct, we ask our Mom. This is great, because no matter what it is, she always says, "Of course you're right, dear." No matter! Now let's evaluate Mom logic. How do we do that? We ask Mom! She says, "Of course you're right, dear!"

What Is the Supporting Evidence?

Fundamental to induction is the gathering of data. Suppose we have a theory. To evaluate the theory, we search for events that tend to confirm or deny it. The problem is that the very notion of a "confirming instance" is not well understood. It *should* be simple, but even a statement as direct as "All _____ are _____" causes difficulties.

Consider the statement "All ravens are black." Clearly, observing a raven and noticing that it is black should count as a confirming instance. On the other hand, the statement "All ravens are black" is logically equivalent to the statement "All things that are not black fail to be ravens" (compare the truth table of $C \Rightarrow B$ with that of $\neg B \Rightarrow \neg C$). Is a green Volkswagen, then, a confirming instance? Well, it fails to be a raven! Does this mean I can gather evidence for the statement just by watching cars go by?

This paradox, suggested by the philosopher Carl Hempel, is only the beginning of the problems posed by the idea of a confirming instance. There are examples where the obvious confirming instance actually disproves the theory! Martin Gardner (see "Notes, References, Hints, and Some Answers") suggests the following example: Take ten cards numbered from 1 to 10. Shuffle them and place them face down in a row. Our hypothesis is that no card with value n is in the nth position from the left. Suppose now that you turn over the first eight cards. Each card confirms our hypothesis: The first card is not the 1, the second card is not the 2, and so on. Suppose that none of the cards face up is the 10. Now you turn over the ninth card. It is

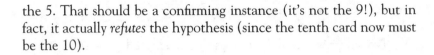

the 5. That should be a confirming instance (it's not the 9!), but in fact, it actually *refutes* the hypothesis (since the tenth card now must be the 10).

When Do We Have Enough Evidence?

Never, really. In life, there is no certainty. Even in mathematics, where there *is* certainty, there are also surprises. Consider the following: Take a natural number. If it is even, divide by 2. If it is odd, multiply by 3 and add 1. Do this again: If it is even divide by 2, otherwise multiply by 3 and add 1. Do it again. Do it again and again and again. What happens? Let's look at an example: If we start with 17, we must multiply by 3 and add 1, getting 52. Now we can divide by 2, getting 26. Again we can divide by 2, getting 13. Now we must multiply by 3 and add 1, getting 40. Continuing, we obtain the following sequence:

$$17, 52, 26, 13, 40, 20, 10, 5, 16, 8, 4, 2, 1$$

Thus we reach the number 1. Now try another number, say 23.

$$23, 70, 35, 106, 53, 160, 80, 40, 20, \ldots$$

We see we again reach 1. Will this always happen?

This is known as the Collatz "3n + 1" problem. The evidence that it will always happen is very strong. Using computers, mathematicians have checked that every number below 1,000,000,000,000 reaches 1. Is that enough?

As we said, strange things can happen in mathematics. There is a notorious statement of mathematics that is *also* true for all numbers below 1,000,000,000,000 (the exact statement is not important or attractive). Unfortunately, it has been proven that this statement is *not* true for all numbers. All that is known, however, is that it is false for some number below 1,650,000,000,000,000,000,000,000,000, 000,000,000,000,000,000,000,000,000,000,000,000,000,000, 000,000,000,000,000,000,000,000,000,000,000,000,000,000, 000,000,000,000,000,000,000,000,000,000,000,000,000,000, 000,000,000,000,000,000,000,000,000,000,000,000,000,000, 000,000,000,000,000,000,000,000,000,000,000,000,000,000, 000,000,000,000,000,000,000,000,000,000,000,000,000,000, 000,000,000,000,000,000,000,000,000,000,000,000,000,000,

000,000,000,000,000,000,000,000,000,000,000,000,000,000,000,000,
000,000,000,000,000,000,000,000,000,000,000,000,000,000,000,000,
000,000,000,000,000,000,000,000,000,000,000,000,000,000,000,000,
000,000,000,000,000,000,000,000,000,000,000,000,000,000,000,000,
000,000,000,000,000,000,000,000,000,000,000,000,000,000,000,000,
000,000,000,000,000,000,000,000,000,000,000,000,000,000,000,000,
000,000,000,000,000,000,000,000,000,000,000,000,000,000,000,000,
000,000,000,000,000,000,000,000,000,000,000,000,000,000,000,000,
000,000,000,000,000,000,000,000,000,000,000,000,000,000,000,000,
000,000,000,000,000,000,000,000,000,000,000,000,000,000,000,000,
000,000,000,000,000,000,000,000,000,000,000,000,000,000,000,000,
000,000,000,000,000,000,000,000,000,000,000,000,000,000,000,000,
000,000,000,000,000,000,000,000,000,000,000,000,000,000,000,000,
000,000,000,000,000,000,000,000,000,000,000,000,000,000,000,000,
000,000,000,000,000,000,000,000,000,000,000,000,000,000,000,000,
000,000,000,000,000,000,000,000,000,000,000,000,000,000,000,000,
000,000,000,000,000,000,000,000,000,000,000,000,000,000,000,000,
000,000,000. Clearly, in the case of the Collatz conjecture and others, no finite amount of data will be sufficient to confirm.

Are There Always Answers to Scientific Questions?

The facts of the universe are certainly elusive. Unfortunately, we do not even have the assurance that they exist! Quantum theory says, for example, that it is not possible to say that a certain particle will be in a certain place at a certain time. The most that can be said is that the particle will be here with some probability or there with some probability. We are not talking about what we can *know*, but what is *true!*

A logic has been devised by mathematicians and physicists to deal with this. Called "quantum logic," it is founded on an understanding of the experimental nature of physics.

Any Other Problems?

We have only touched on the difficulties. The problem remains of formalizing modes of reasoning beyond deductive logic. It is an important area of research and the subject of hundreds of books and articles. Quantum logic is just one example. More recently Keith Devlin has developed a logic to understand the concept of information and to model the spread of information.

Finally, we should emphasize that despite all this, inductive logic is probably the most widely practiced and most widely successful logic today. Even the masters of deductive logic, the mathematicians, rely on it heavily to discover, if not to prove, their theorems.

EXERCISE **We have prepared two special inductive logic puzzles for readers of *Sweet Reason*.** The puzzles are in the form of computer programs that run on all PC-compatible machines. The software can be obtained by anyone with access to Internet. Use ftp to connect to emmy @ smith.edu and sign on as "anonymous." You will be asked to type in your e-mail address for identification. Following this, you should change to binary mode, move to the directory "dist," and then get the programs puzzle1.exe and puzzle2.exe. Versions of ftp vary. The following sequence of commands is typical:

```
binary
cd dist
cd logic
get puzzle1.exe
get puzzle2.exe
bye
```

Once you have these programs, you can run them by typing the name (without the ".exe") on any PC-compatible computer.

Each puzzle consists of nine universes for you to explore. When you enter them, you face a blank screen on the computer. You type something and press the Enter key, and the computer responds. Type something else and the computer may respond differently. In each universe, you are to discover how the computer is programmed to answer you. The universes become progressively more difficult.

logic programming

I feel that controversies can never be finished, nor silence imposed upon the Sects, unless we give up complicated reasoning in favor of simple calculation, words of vague and uncertain meaning in favor of fixed symbols . . . . When controversies arise, there will be no more necessity of disputation between two philosophers than between two accountants. Nothing will be needed but that they should take pen in hand, sit down with their counting tables and (having summoned a friend, if they like) say to one another: Let us calculate.

—G. W. Leibniz

In this remarkable passage, Leibniz envisioned a time when formal language would advance to such a state that it could routinely transcribe philosophical arguments. In the middle of the seventeenth century, this profound philosopher and one of the greatest mathematicians in history forecast the future of linguistics, logic, and computer science. If the philosopher Wittgenstein had been right and all complex propositions were truth-functional combinations of elementary propositions, then Leibniz would have been right: The method of truth tables would be the method of calculation! But Wittgenstein was wrong. So perhaps "forecast" is not apt, since the dream is not yet realized, and many argue that it never can be. Nonetheless, a major goal of computer science is to formalize human thought. We have seen BASIC accomplish a very limited part of that. A much more sophisticated computer language, Prolog, achieves far more.

Developed as a tool for artificial intelligence projects, Prolog is a realization of a subset of predicate logic. Its name, in fact, is derived from the phrase *programmation en logique*. We'll describe it briefly here and then show how neatly it can reflect various aspects of logic.

There are two modes in Prolog: one in which facts and rules are introduced and another in which queries can be made about these facts and rules.

Facts

Facts look like

```
male(george).
eats(marvin, salad).
p.
bowl(soup).
```

Each fact ends with a period. Constants and predicates begin with lowercase letters or "_". A word like "ham" can be a constant, as in "polish(ham).", or a one-place predicate, "ham(sandwich).", or a two-place predicate, "ham(heston, tencommandments).", or simply "ham." It can actually be all four of these at once, so some care must be taken!

Queries

In the query mode, one can inquire about statements. If you stated "bowl(soup)." in the first mode, and then you ask bowl(soup)?

the computer will respond

yes

We say in this case that the query "succeeds." [*Note:* The computer in query mode types "?−" and we type "bowl(soup)", so the query would actually be "?−bowl(soup)" but we write it in the more natural order here.)

Rules

A rule looks a bit like an implication:

a:-b.

It consists of a head (in this case *a*) and a body (in this case *b*). The head is like a fact, and the body is like a query. Together they are an instruction to the computer that if *b* succeeds, then *a* succeeds. We could think of this as $a \Leftarrow b$. Indeed, in some implementations of Prolog, one writes "$<-$" instead of ":−". Example: mammal :− cat

Connectives

To extend the language, there are three connectives: "not" for ¬, "," for &, and ";" for ∨. For example,

icy(day):−
    wet(day),
    freezing(day).

means: (wet(day) & freezing(day)) $\Rightarrow$ icy(day). Connectives may be used in queries and in the body of a rule, but *not* in facts and *not* in the head of a rule. This limitation is severe and means some parts of predicate language can't be handled by Prolog.

Variables and Quantification

Variables are words beginning with a capital letter. They are automatically quantified universally in facts and rules and automatically quantified existentially in queries. For example, as a fact,

friend(X).

says $\forall X[\text{friend}(X)]$. If you later query

friend(tinkerbell)?

the computer will respond

yes

If, on the other hand, you state as a fact

yucky(eggplant).

and later query

yucky(X)?

the computer interprets this as asking "$\exists X[\text{yucky}(X)]$?" and so answers

X = eggplant

There are public domain (free) implementations of Prolog available for PC-compatible computers. We have tested one produced by Expert Systems Limited (ESL), which also produces commercial versions. It can be obtained by anyone with Internet access using ftp as described in "Inductive Logic." The node is ai.uga.edu. The program is called "Prolog2," and it can be found "zipped" as eslpdpro.zip in directory ai.prolog.

Example 1   Kinship Relations

Kinship relations are just the sort of logical structure Prolog can express easily. Following is a portion of a genealogical table.

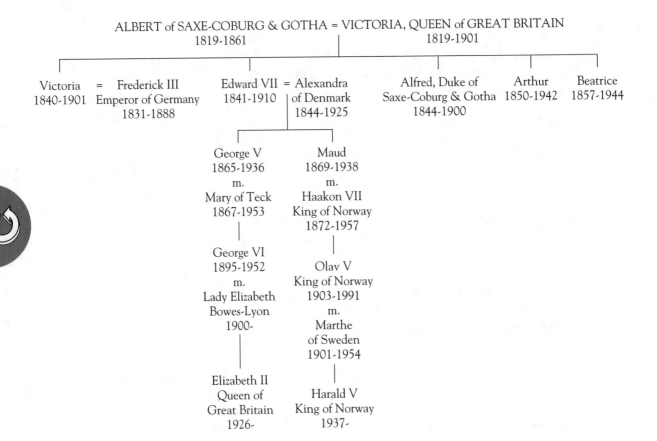

ALBERT of SAXE-COBURG & GOTHA = VICTORIA, QUEEN of GREAT BRITAIN
1819-1861   1819-1901

Victoria   =   Frederick III   Edward VII = Alexandra   Alfred, Duke of   Arthur   Beatrice
1840-1901   Emperor of Germany   1841-1910 | of Denmark   Saxe-Coburg & Gotha 1850-1942   1857-1944
              1831-1888   1844-1925   1844-1900

George V   Maud
1865-1936   1869-1938
m.   m.
Mary of Teck   Haakon VII
1867-1953   King of Norway
              1872-1957

George VI
1895-1952   Olav V
m.   King of Norway
Lady Elizabeth   1903-1991
Bowes-Lyon   m.
1900-   Marthe
                of Sweden
                1901-1954

Elizabeth II
Queen of   Harald V
Great Britain King of Norway
1926-   1937-

Source: Burke's Peerage

There is quite a lot of information in this family tree. We can capture it using just two predicates, "wife" and "parent". We type into Prolog all instances of wifehood and parenthood, for example, wife(alexandra, edward) and parent(victoria, arthur). We then can define additional predicates using rules. For example,

husband(X, Y):−wife(Y, X).

neatly defines "husband" and

married(X, Y):−wife(X, Y);
              husband(X, Y).

defines "married".

366

We can save some effort stating all the parenting relationships. Instead of listing all parents, just list one for each and include the rule:

parent(X, Y):−married(X, Z),
              parent(Z, Y).

Suppose, for example, that we stated

parent(alexandra, maud).
wife(alexandra, edward).

and then queried

parent(edward, maud)?

The computer will use the rules above and answer

yes

The possibilities go on and on. We can define "grandparent", "uncle", "cousin", and so on.

Example 2   Arithmetic

An important event in the history of both logic and mathematics was the construction of a set of axioms for arithmetic by the Italian Giuseppe Peano. He began with a single constant, "zero," and a function s standing for "successor". When you see $s(a)$, think of this as "$a + 1$". The whole numbers, then, are zero, $s(\text{zero})$, $s(s(\text{zero}))$, $s(s(s(\text{zero})))$, and so on.

Now Peano defines addition with just two rules:

$$n + \text{zero} = n$$
$$n + s(m) = s(n + m)$$

The first is surely true. The second translates to $n + (m + 1) = (n + m) + 1$, also true. You must wonder, however, is this enough to define addition for all numbers?

Since Prolog will accept functions, we can enter these two rules. We use "add" as a predicate and write "add(p, q, r)" to mean "$p + q = r$".

```
add(X, zero, X).
add(X,s(Y),Z):−
   add(X, Y, W),
   s(W)=Z.
```

Prolog is amazing. This is all it takes. If we query, for example,

add(s(s(zero)), s(s(zero)), X)?

we get

X = s(s(s(s(zero))))

—in other words, two plus two equals four!

Prolog and Puzzles

Prolog does not solve puzzles well. It can do some of the sorites of Lewis Carroll but with so much effort that it isn't worth it. The difficulty lies in the restrictions on what can go into facts and the heads of rules (e.g., there are no connectives and no negation). Because of these limitations, Prolog's responses to some queries seem very odd. Take, for example, its answer to questions about which it has been told nothing. Suppose we have no facts and no rules and then query

grump?

The computer will say:

no

Well, it has to say something. It has to decide if "grump" is true or false. It simply decides on false. If we ask

not grump?

the computer will say

yes

Does Prolog simply deny anything it's never heard of? Maybe, but suppose you state as a rule

smedley :- not fizzle

Then it can't say no to both smedley and fizzle. How will it choose? So we query

smedley?

and Prolog replies

yes

There is an answer to this. What Prolog is doing is telling us what it can *prove*. If it has never heard of grump, then it can't prove grump, so it says no.

But what about "not grump"? Prolog can't prove that either, can it? Shouldn't it say no to this too? Of course, if it did, its logic would be very different from ours, since it would be saying "grump" and "¬grump" are both false.

The key is that "not" is *not* interpreted as "it is not true that . . ." but rather as "I can't prove that . . . ." Thus when we ask "not grump?" Prolog responds with yes because it has tried to prove "grump" and failed! Now we see why it says yes to "smedley". It sees that "smedley" follows from "not fizzle", so it checks out "not fizzle". It does this by trying to prove "fizzle". It proceeds exhaustively, attempting to prove "fizzle". It fails and declares "not fizzle" true, then it concludes "smedley".

As you have surely realized, evaluating arguments in predicate logic can be extremely difficult. We try to find a deduction of the argument's conclusion from its premises. If we fail, it might be because the argument is invalid, but perhaps it is just because we weren't smart enough to find the deduction. Then we try to disprove the argument —to find a universe where the premises are true and the conclusion false. We might fail here, too. Then we're in trouble. How does Prolog evaluate arguments?

The key is that for a restricted part of Predicate, there is a decision procedure that can say in a finite period of time whether or not a proof exists. This is not true of full predicate languages. This explains how a language such as Prolog is possible, and it explains why we're not allowed certain things such as "not" in a fact.

As we stated in "Algorithm" in part 5, the focus of computer science is neither truth nor validity but procedure. Prolog is not built so that ⇒ or any other symbol has a certain *meaning*. Prolog is not built so that any fact will have a certain *consequence*. Rather, Prolog is built to follow a certain *procedure*.

EXERCISES **Consider Queen Victoria's descendents (use the family tree at the beginning of this section).**

1. Write a rule to define "father".

2. Write a rule to define "grandfather".

3. Write a rule to define "cousin" (first cousin).

4. Write a rule to define "ancestor".

In the example of Peano's arithmetic, multiplication is also defined by two rules, $n \times 0 = 0$ and $n \times s(m) = n \times m + n$.

    5. Write these rules in Prolog.

One way to write a list in Prolog is with brackets, for example, [orange, lemon] and [new_york, chicago, chocolate, vanilla]. It is fairly easy to define a predicate "append" which can glue two lists together, that is, append(a, b, c) is true if c is the list you get when you take the lists a and b and string them together. For example, append([u, v], [k], [u, v, k]) is true. Using this predicate, we can define a new predicate "wff", which will state accurately whether a given list is a grammatically correct wff in Sentential with Polish notation (see "Formal Languages: Variations of Sentential" in part 3).

Here is a start. First we list three atomic wffs:

wff([p]).
wff([q]).
wff([r]).

So far, our only wffs are [p], [q], and [r]. Next, we state a rule that if one list is a wff, then we can add a negation sign (in this case $-$) to it to get another wff:

wff(X):$-$append([$-$],Y,X),
      wff(Y).

Now our wffs include [$-, p$], [$-, -, q$], and so on.

EXERCISES

    6. Write a rule that says we can take any wff and put "Ax" in front of it to form a new wff. (Think of this as $\forall x$. Prolog does not have the proper symbols.) Now our wffs will include [Ax, p], [$-$, A$x, -, q$], and so on.

    7. Write a rule that says we can take any two wffs and put "&" in front of them to form a new wff. New wffs will include lists like [&, Ax, p, q] and [$-$, &, &, p, Ax, r, A$x, -, p$].

informal logic

the W-4

When all clock radios are outlawed, only outlaws will have clock radios!!

—BILL GRIFFITH, *PINHEAD'S PROGRESS*

You are Fanny P. Osgood. It's Labor Day and time for you to fill out your W-4 form, the Employee's Withholding Allowance Certificate. It is important that you do this properly so that enough taxes are withheld. If enough are not withheld, you will have to pay interest on the taxes you owe.

EXERCISE

1. Fill out the W-4 form that follows. To help you, your 1992 tax return is included. In addition, the information below may (or may not) be useful:

    You are an electrical engineer; your husband, Matthew, is a teacher.

    Of your wage income recorded on line 7 of form 1040, $25,588.51 was Matthew's.

    For purposes of filling out the W-4, you estimate that your 1993 figures will look roughly the same as your 1992 figures, but increased by 5 percent.

    You are paid on the first of the month.

    Last year, too little was withheld from your paycheck and the government charged you interest and a small penalty. You want to avoid that this year at all costs.

    Your mother-in-law came in second in a bridge tournament seven years ago in Boise, winning a handsome mug which you accidentally broke when you left it on the burner of her stove last April.

2. Repeat the exercise, but this time try to minimize the amount withheld.

1993 Form W-4

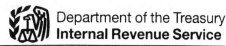

**Department of the Treasury
Internal Revenue Service**

Purpose. Complete Form W-4 so that your employer can withhold the correct amount of Federal income tax from your pay.

Exemption From Withholding. Read line 7 of the certificate below to see if you can claim exempt status. *If exempt, complete line 7; but do not complete lines 5 and 6.* No Federal income tax will be withheld from your pay. Your exemption is good for one year only. It expires February 15, 1994.

Basic Instructions. Employees who are not exempt should complete the Personal Allowances Worksheet. Additional worksheets are provided on page 2 for employees to adjust their withholding allowances based on itemized deductions, adjustments to income, or two-earner/two-job situations. Complete all the worksheets that apply to your situation. The worksheets will help you figure the number of withholding allowances you are entitled to claim. However, you may claim fewer allowances than this.

Head of Household. Generally, you may claim head of household filing status on your tax return only if you are unmarried and pay more than 50% of the costs of keeping up a home for yourself and your dependent(s) or other qualifying individuals.

Nonwage Income. If you have a large amount of nonwage income, such as interest or dividends, you should consider making estimated tax payments using Form 1040-ES. Otherwise, you may find that you owe additional tax at the end of the year.

Two-Earner/Two-Jobs. If you have a working spouse or more than one job, figure the total number of allowances you are entitled to claim on all jobs using worksheets from only one Form W-4. This total should be divided among all jobs. Your withholding will usually be most accurate when all allowances are claimed on the W-4 filed for the highest paying job and zero allowances are claimed for the others.

Advance Earned Income Credit. If you are eligible for this credit, you can receive it added to your paycheck throughout the year. For details, get Form W-5 from your employer.

Check Your Withholding. After your W-4 takes effect, you can use Pub. 919, Is My Withholding Correct for 1993?, to see how the dollar amount you are having withheld compares to your estimated total annual tax. Call 1-800-829-3676 to order this publication. Check your local telephone directory for the IRS assistance number if you need further help.

Personal Allowances Worksheet

For 1993, the value of your personal exemption(s) is reduced if your income is over $108,450 ($162,700 if married filing jointly, $135,600 if head of household, or $81,350 if married filing separately). Get Pub. 919 for details.

A Enter "1" for **yourself** if no one else can claim you as a dependent . . . . **A** _____

B Enter "1" if: {
- You are single and have only one job; or
- You are married, have only one job, and your spouse does not work; or
- Your wages from a second job or your spouse's wages (or the total of both) are $1,000 or less.
} . . **B** _____

C Enter "1" for your **spouse**. But, you may choose to enter -0- if you are married and have either a working spouse or more than one job (this may help you avoid having too little tax withheld) . . . . **C** _____

D Enter number of **dependents** (other than your spouse or yourself) whom you will claim on your tax return . . . . . **D** _____

E Enter "1" if you will file as **head of household** on your tax return (see conditions under **Head of Household,** above) . **E** _____

F Enter "1" if you have at least $1,500 of **child or dependent care expenses** for which you plan to claim a credit . . **F** _____

G Add lines A through F and enter total here. **Note:** *This amount may be different from the number of exemptions you claim on your return* ▶ **G** _____

For accuracy, do all worksheets that apply.
- If you plan to **itemize or claim adjustments to income** and want to reduce your withholding, see the Deductions and Adjustments Worksheet on page 2.
- If you are **single** and have **more than one job** and your combined earnings from all jobs exceed $30,000 OR if you are **married** and have a **working spouse or more than one job,** and the combined earnings from all jobs exceed $50,000, see the Two-Earner/Two-Job Worksheet on page 2 if you want to avoid having too little tax withheld.
- If **neither** of the above situations applies, **stop here** and enter the number from line G on line 5 of Form W-4 below.

----------------------- **Cut here and give the certificate to your employer. Keep the top portion for your records.** -----------------------

Form **W-4**	**Employee's Withholding Allowance Certificate**	OMB No. 1545-0010
Department of the Treasury Internal Revenue Service	▶ **For Privacy Act and Paperwork Reduction Act Notice, see reverse.**	**1993**

1 Type or print your first name and middle initial   Last name

2 Your social security number

Home address (number and street or rural route)

3 ☐ Single ☐ Married ☐ Married, but withhold at higher Single rate.
Note: *If married, but legally separated, or spouse is a nonresident alien, check the Single box.*

City or town, state, and ZIP code

4 If your last name differs from that on your social security card, check here and call 1-800-772-1213 for more information . . . . ▶ ☐

5 Total number of allowances you are claiming (from line G above or from the worksheets on page 2 if they apply) . **5** _____

6 Additional amount, if any, you want withheld from each paycheck . . . . **6** $ _____

7 I claim exemption from withholding for 1993 and I certify that I meet **ALL** of the following conditions for exemption:
- Last year I had a right to a refund of **ALL** Federal income tax withheld because I had **NO** tax liability; **AND**
- This year I expect a refund of **ALL** Federal income tax withheld because I expect to have **NO** tax liability; **AND**
- This year if my income exceeds $600 and includes nonwage income, another person cannot claim me as a dependent.

If you meet all of the above conditions, enter "EXEMPT" here . . . . ▶ **7** _____

Under penalties of perjury, I certify that I am entitled to the number of withholding allowances claimed on this certificate or entitled to claim exempt status.

Employee's signature ▶ _____   Date ▶ _____ , 19 ___

8 Employer's name and address (Employer: Complete 8 and 10 only if sending to the IRS)

9 Office code (optional)

10 Employer identification number

Cat. No. 10220Q

Deductions and Adjustments Worksheet

Note: *Use this worksheet only if you plan to itemize deductions or claim adjustments to income on your 1993 tax return.*

1 Enter an estimate of your 1993 itemized deductions. These include: qualifying home mortgage interest, charitable contributions, state and local taxes (but not sales taxes), medical expenses in excess of 7.5% of your income, and miscellaneous deductions. (For 1993, you may have to reduce your itemized deductions if your income is over $108,450 ($54,225 if married filing separately). Get Pub. 919 for details.) **1** $ _____

2 Enter: { $6,200 if married filing jointly or qualifying widow(er)
$5,450 if head of household
$3,700 if single
$3,100 if married filing separately } . . . . . . **2** $ _____

3 **Subtract** line 2 from line 1. If line 2 is greater than line 1, enter -0- . . . . . . **3** $ _____

4 Enter an estimate of your 1993 adjustments to income. These include alimony paid and deductible IRA contributions **4** $ _____

5 **Add** lines 3 and 4 and enter the total . . . . **5** $ _____

6 Enter an estimate of your 1993 nonwage income (such as dividends or interest income) . . . . . **6** $ _____

7 **Subtract** line 6 from line 5. Enter the result, but not less than -0- . . . . **7** $ _____

8 **Divide** the amount on line 7 by $2,500 and enter the result here. Drop any fraction . . . . **8** _____

9 Enter the number from Personal Allowances Worksheet, line G, on page 1 . . . . **9** _____

10 **Add** lines 8 and 9 and enter the total here. If you plan to use the Two-Earner/Two-Job Worksheet, also enter the total on line 1, below. Otherwise, **stop here** and enter this total on Form W-4, line 5, on page 1 . . . . **10** _____

Two-Earner/Two-Job Worksheet

Note: *Use this worksheet only if the instructions for line G on page 1 direct you here.*

1 Enter the number from line G on page 1 (or from line 10 above if you used the Deductions and Adjustments Worksheet) **1** _____

2 Find the number in **Table 1** below that applies to the **LOWEST** paying job and enter it here . . . . **2** _____

3 If line 1 is **GREATER THAN OR EQUAL TO** line 2, subtract line 2 from line 1. Enter the result here (if zero, enter -0-) and on Form W-4, line 5, on page 1. **DO NOT** use the rest of this worksheet . . . **3** _____

Note: *If line 1 is **LESS THAN** line 2, enter -0- on Form W-4, line 5, on page 1. Complete lines 4–9 to calculate the additional withholding amount necessary to avoid a year-end tax bill.*

4 Enter the number from line 2 of this worksheet . . . . **4** _____

5 Enter the number from line 1 of this worksheet . . . . **5** _____

6 **Subtract** line 5 from line 4 . . . . **6** _____

7 Find the amount in **Table 2** below that applies to the **HIGHEST** paying job and enter it here . . . . **7** $ _____

8 **Multiply** line 7 by line 6 and enter the result here. This is the additional annual withholding amount needed **8** $ _____

9 Divide line 8 by the number of pay periods remaining in 1993. (For example, divide by 26 if you are paid every other week and you complete this form in December 1992.) Enter the result here and on Form W-4, line 6, page 1. This is the additional amount to be withheld from each paycheck . . . . **9** $ _____

Table 1: Two-Earner/Two-Job Worksheet

Married Filing Jointly		All Others	
If wages from **LOWEST** paying job are—	Enter on line 2 above	If wages from **LOWEST** paying job are—	Enter on line 2 above
0 - $3,000	0	0 - $6,000	0
3,001 - 8,000	1	6,001 - 11,000	1
8,001 - 13,000	2	11,001 - 15,000	2
13,001 - 18,000	3	15,001 - 19,000	3
18,001 - 22,000	4	19,001 - 24,000	4
22,001 - 27,000	5	24,001 - 50,000	5
27,001 - 31,000	6	50,001 and over	6
31,001 - 35,000	7		
35,001 - 40,000	8		
40,001 - 60,000	9		
60,001 - 85,000	10		
85,001 and over	11		

Table 2: Two-Earner/Two-Job Worksheet

Married Filing Jointly		All Others	
If wages from **HIGHEST** paying job are—	Enter on line 7 above	If wages from **HIGHEST** paying job are—	Enter on line 7 above
0 - $ 50,000	$350	0 - $30,000	$350
50,001 - 100,000	660	30,001 - 60,000	660
100,001 and over	730	60,001 and over	730

Form **1040**

Department of the Treasury—Internal Revenue Service
U.S. Individual Income Tax Return (M) **1992**

IRS Use Only—Do not write or staple in this space.

For the year Jan. 1–Dec. 31, 1992, or other tax year beginning , 1992, ending , 19

OMB No. 1545-0074

Label

(See instructions on page 10.)

Use the IRS label. Otherwise, please print or type.

Your first name and initial: **Fanny P.**   Last name: **Osgood**

Your social security number: **123 : 45 : 6789**

If a joint return, spouse's first name and initial: **Matthew**   Last name: **Simon - Osgood**

Spouse's social security number: **987 : 65 : 4321**

Home address (number and street). If you have a P.O. box, see page 10.   **132 College Lane**   Apt. no.

City, town or post office, state, and ZIP code. If you have a foreign address, see page 10.   **Northampton MA 01060**

For Privacy Act and Paperwork Reduction Act Notice, see page 4.

Presidential Election Campaign

(See page 10.)

Do you want $1 to go to this fund? **✓ Yes** / No

If a joint return, does your spouse want $1 to go to this fund? **✓ Yes** / No

Note: Checking "Yes" will not change your tax or reduce your refund.

Filing Status

(See page 10.)

Check only one box.

1. Single
2. **✓** Married filing joint return (even if only one had income)
3. Married filing separate return. Enter spouse's social security no. above and full name here. ▶
4. Head of household (with qualifying person). (See page 11.) If the qualifying person is a child but not your dependent, enter this child's name here. ▶
5. Qualifying widow(er) with dependent child (year spouse died ▶ 19). (See page 11.)

Exemptions

(See page 11.)

6a **✓** Yourself. If your parent (or someone else) can claim you as a dependent on his or her tax return, **do not** check box 6a. But be sure to check the box on line 33b on page 2

b **✓** Spouse

No. of boxes checked on 6a and 6b: **2**

c Dependents:

(1) Name (first, initial, and last name)	(2) Check if under age 1	(3) If age 1 or older, dependent's social security number	(4) Dependent's relationship to you	(5) No. of months lived in your home in 1992
Geraldine S. Osgood	✓		daughter	8
Bella T. Osgood		246 : 810 : 121	daughter	12

If more than six dependents, see page 12.

No. of your children on 6c who:
- lived with you **2**
- didn't live with you due to divorce or separation (see page 13)

No. of other dependents on 6c

d If your child didn't live with you but is claimed as your dependent under a pre-1985 agreement, check here ▶ ☐

e Total number of exemptions claimed

Add numbers entered on lines above ▶ **4**

Income

Attach Copy B of your Forms W-2, W-2G, and 1099-R here.

If you did not get a W-2, see page 9.

Attach check or money order on top of any Forms W-2, W-2G, or 1099-R.

7	Wages, salaries, tips, etc. Attach Form(s) W-2	7	**87,981 62**
8a	**Taxable** interest income. Attach Schedule B if over $400	8a	**2,213 17**
b	**Tax-exempt** interest income (see page 15). DON'T include on line 8a 8b		
9	Dividend income. Attach Schedule B if over $400	9	
10	Taxable refunds, credits, or offsets of state and local income taxes from worksheet on page 16	10	
11	Alimony received	11	
12	Business income or (loss). Attach Schedule C or C-EZ	12	**365 44**
13	Capital gain or (loss). Attach Schedule D	13	
14	Capital gain distributions not reported on line 13 (see page 15)	14	
15	Other gains or (losses). Attach Form 4797	15	
16a	Total IRA distributions 16a b Taxable amount (see page 16)	16b	
17a	Total pensions and annuities 17a b Taxable amount (see page 16)	17b	
18	Rents, royalties, partnerships, estates, trusts, etc. Attach Schedule E	18	
19	Farm income or (loss). Attach Schedule F	19	
20	Unemployment compensation (see page 17)	20	
21a	Social security benefits 21a b Taxable amount (see page 17)	21b	
22	Other income. List type and amount—see page 18	22	
23	Add the amounts in the far right column for lines 7 through 22. This is your **total income** ▶	23	**90,560 23**

Adjustments to Income

(See page 18.)

24a	Your IRA deduction from applicable worksheet on page 19 or 20 24a		
b	Spouse's IRA deduction from applicable worksheet on page 19 or 20 24b		
25	One-half of self-employment tax (see page 20) 25		
26	Self-employed health insurance deduction (see page 20) 26		
27	Keogh retirement plan and self-employed SEP deduction 27		
28	Penalty on early withdrawal of savings 28		
29	Alimony paid. Recipient's SSN ▶ 29		
30	Add lines 24a through 29. These are your **total adjustments** ▶	30	

Adjusted Gross Income

31	Subtract line 30 from line 23. This is your **adjusted gross income.** If this amount is less than $22,370 and a child lived with you, see page EIC-1 to find out if you can claim the "Earned Income Credit" on line 56 ▶	31	**90,560 23**

Cat. No. 11320B   Form **1040** (1992)

15

Tax Compu-tation (See page 22.)	32	Amount from line 31 (adjusted gross income)	**32** 90,560 23
	33a	Check if: ☐ **You** were 65 or older, ☐ Blind; ☐ **Spouse** was 65 or older, ☐ Blind. Add the number of boxes checked above and enter the total here . . . . ▶ 33a	
	b	If your parent (or someone else) can claim you as a dependent, check here . . ▶ 33b ☐	
	c	If you are married filing separately and your spouse itemizes deductions or you are a dual-status alien, see page 22 and check here . . . . ▶ 33c ☐	
	34	Enter the larger of your: { **Itemized deductions** from Schedule A, line 26, **OR Standard deduction** shown below for your filing status. **But if you checked any box on line 33a or b,** go to page 22 to find your standard deduction. **If you checked box 33c,** your standard deduction is zero. • Single—$3,600 • Head of household—$5,250 • Married filing jointly or Qualifying widow(er)—$6,000 • Married filing separately—$3,000 }	**34** 13,809 85
	35	Subtract line 34 from line 32	**35** 76,750 38
	36	If line 32 is $78,950 or less, multiply $2,300 by the total number of exemptions claimed on line 6e. If line 32 is over $78,950, see the worksheet on page 23 for the amount to enter .	**36** 9,200 00
If you want the IRS to figure your tax, see page 23.	37	**Taxable income.** Subtract line 36 from line 35. If line 36 is more than line 35, enter -0-	**37** 67,550 38
	38	Enter tax. Check if from **a** ☑ Tax Table, **b** ☐ Tax Rate Schedules, **c** ☐ Schedule D, or **d** ☐ Form 8615 (see page 23). Amount, if any, from Form(s) 8814 ▶ **e**	**38** 14,267 00
	39	Additional taxes (see page 23). Check if from **a** ☐ Form 4970 **b** ☐ Form 4972 . .	**39**
	40	Add lines 38 and 39 . . . . ▶	**40** 14,267 00
Credits (See page 23.)	41	Credit for child and dependent care expenses. Attach Form 2441	**41**
	42	Credit for the elderly or the disabled. Attach Schedule R .	**42**
	43	Foreign tax credit. Attach Form 1116	**43**
	44	Other credits (see page 24). Check if from **a** ☐ Form 3800 **b** ☐ Form 8396 **c** ☐ Form 8801 **d** ☐ Form (specify)___	**44**
	45	Add lines 41 through 44	**45**
	46	Subtract line 45 from line 40. If line 45 is more than line 40, enter -0- . . . . . ▶	**46** 14,267 00
Other Taxes	47	Self-employment tax. Attach Schedule SE. Also, see line 25	**47**
	48	Alternative minimum tax. Attach Form 6251	**48**
	49	Recapture taxes (see page 25). Check if from **a** ☐ Form 4255 **b** ☐ Form 8611 **c** ☐ Form 8828	**49**
	50	Social security and Medicare tax on tip income not reported to employer. Attach Form 4137 .	**50**
	51	Tax on qualified retirement plans, including IRAs. Attach Form 5329	**51**
	52	Advance earned income credit payments from Form W-2	**52**
	53	Add lines 46 through 52. This is your **total tax** . . . . ▶	**53** 14,267 00
Payments Attach Forms W-2, W-2G, and 1099-R on the front.	54	Federal income tax withheld. If any is from Form(s) 1099, check ▶ ☐	**54** 11,631 77
	55	1992 estimated tax payments and amount applied from 1991 return .	**55**
	56	**Earned income credit.** Attach Schedule EIC	**56**
	57	Amount paid with Form 4868 (extension request)	**57**
	58	Excess social security, Medicare, and RRTA tax withheld (see page 26) .	**58**
	59	Other payments (see page 26). Check if from **a** ☐ Form 2439 **b** ☐ Form 4136	**59**
	60	Add lines 54 through 59. These are your **total payments** . . . . ▶	**60** 11,631 77
Refund or Amount You Owe Attach check or money order on top of Form(s) W-2, etc., on the front.	61	If line 60 is more than line 53, subtract line 53 from line 60. This is the amount you **OVERPAID.** ▶	**61**
	62	Amount of line 61 you want **REFUNDED TO YOU** . . . . ▶	**62**
	63	Amount of line 61 you want **APPLIED TO YOUR 1993 ESTIMATED TAX** ▶ **63**	
	64	If line 53 is more than line 60, subtract line 60 from line 53. This is the **AMOUNT YOU OWE.** Attach check or money order for full amount payable to "Internal Revenue Service." Write your name, address, social security number, daytime phone number, and "1992 Form 1040" on it	**64** 2,635 23
	65	Estimated tax penalty (see page 27). Also include on line 64 **65** 58 57	

Sign Here Keep a copy of this return for your records.	Under penalties of perjury, I declare that I have examined this return and accompanying schedules and statements, and to the best of my knowledge and belief, they are true, correct, and complete. Declaration of preparer (other than taxpayer) is based on all information of which preparer has any knowledge.		
	▶ Your signature *Fanny P. Osgood*	Date 4/15/93	Your occupation *electrical engineer*
	▶ Spouse's signature. If a joint return, BOTH must sign. *Matthew Sim-Osgood*	Date 4/15/93	Spouse's occupation *teacher*
Paid Preparer's Use Only	Preparer's signature ▶	Date	Check if self-employed ☐	Preparer's social security no.
	Firm's name (or yours if self-employed) and address ▶		E.I. No. ___ ZIP code ___

16

Canadian customs

> Let us consider the reason of the case. For nothing is law that is not reason.

> —SIR JOHN POWELL

This is a true story. Jim was visiting Canada in the summer of 1990. He flew to Toronto and took with him a $75 silver bowl. Also flying to Toronto was his sister-in-law from the Philippines. He was to give her the bowl to take back to the Philippines as a wedding present for his brother-in-law. Did Jim have to declare the bowl on the Canadian customs form? The instructions for the form follow.

PERSONAL EXEMPTIONS FOR RESIDENTS OF CANADA

Residents of Canada may claim goods duty and tax free if the following conditions are met:

EXEMPTIONS	CDN. FUNDS	MINIMUM ABSENCE FROM CANADA
Yearly	$300.00	7 Days (Must be a full 7 days)
Any Time	$100.00	2 Days (48 hours)
Any Time	$ 20.00	24 Hours

— Only one of the above exemptions can be claimed on one trip and you cannot pool your exemption with other travellers;

— You cannot claim a duty free 24 hours exemption if the value of the goods exceeds $20 Cdn. funds and alcohol and tobacco products cannot be included in this exemption;

— Alcohol and tobacco products (see limits below) are only allowed as part of your 48 hour and yearly exemptions;

— Goods to follow can only be claimed under the $300.00 yearly exemption and must have been acquired outside continental North America to qualify;

— Goods not eligible for a personal exemption may be imported on payment of the applicable duty and taxes;

NOTE: ALL GOODS PURCHASED, RECEIVED AS GIFTS OR ACQUIRED IN ANY MANNER WHILE OUTSIDE OF CANADA MUST BE DECLARED WHETHER OR NOT THEY ARE CLAIMED AS PART OF YOUR PERSONAL EXEMPTION.

PERSONAL EXEMPTIONS FOR VISITORS TO CANADA

Visitors to Canada may bring in duty and tax free:

— Personal effects needed for the visit, provided no articles will be left in Canada. Alcohol and tobacco products are allowed (see limits below);

— Gifts to residents of Canada for their personal use, not exceeding $40 Cdn. per gift.

ALCOHOLIC BEVERAGES — TOBACCO PRODUCTS — QUANTITIES — AGE LIMITS

— 40 oz. (1.1 litres) of liquor or wine or 24 × 12 oz. bottles or cans (8.2 litres) of beer or ale

A Traveller must be 18 years of age or older to import alcoholic beverages into the provinces of Alberta, Manitoba, Quebec and Prince Edward Island. A traveller must be 19 years of age or older to import alcoholic beverages into all other provinces or territories.

— 200 cigarettes and 50 cigars or cigarillos and 2 lbs. (0.91 kg.) of tobacco

A traveller must be 16 years of age or older to import tobacco products into Canada.

Restricted or Controlled Goods

Goods such as firearms, other weapons, drugs or articles made or derived from endangered species may be restricted or controlled, or may require a special admission permit.

If you are bringing such goods or other doubtful items, please inform the Customs Inspector of that fact during your personal interview.

ALL GOODS MUST BE DECLARED, INCLUDING GOODS PURCHASED AT DUTY FREE STORES IN CANADA OR ABROAD.

GOODS NOT DECLARED — OR FALSELY DECLARED — MAY BE SEIZED OR FORFEITED AND YOU MAY FACE PROSECUTION.

the logic tea

If this is coffee, please bring me some tea; but if this is tea, please bring me some coffee.

—ABRAHAM LINCOLN

It is the custom for the logic majors to have a modest tea with milk and cookies each Thursday afternoon before the colloquium talk. The student with the highest GPA has the honor of pouring hot water over the tea bags and serving his or her admiring fellow students. The tea is held in the logic lounge, which is equipped with an electric hot water pot and a sink. To save the environment, styrofoam cups are no longer used; the department last year bought a dozen mugs from the Salvation Army store. Usually Oreos, Double Oreos, Chocolate-covered Mint Oreos, tea bags, sugar, and a quart of milk are purchased for the gathering. This week, LaTina Chu Flynn, winner of last year's Tarski Prize, will have the honor of pouring, and runner-up Butch Mirsky will serve.

Out of curiosity, the majors looked at a copy of 105 CMR 590.000: State (Massachusetts) Sanitary Code Chapter X, "Minimum Sanitation Standards for Food Establishments." Some of this document is reproduced here. Do any of the regulation's provisions apply to the logic tea.

EXERCISE
1. Do the students need a permit?
2. Do they need any additional equipment?
3. Are the facilities adequate?
4. Is their shopping list appropriate?
5. Do they need to wash their fingernails?
6. What else should the students be aware of?

590.001: continued

590.001: continued

(B) Definitions.

(1) <u>Adulterated Food</u> means the definition in M.G.L. c. 94, s. 186.

(2) <u>Board of Health</u> means the appropriate and legally designated health authority of the city, town, or other legally constituted governmental unit within the Commonwealth having the usual powers and duties of the board of health of a city or town.

(3) <u>Bulk Food</u> means unpackaged or unwrapped, processed or unprocessed food provided in a retail food store in aggregate containers from which quantities desired by the consumer are withdrawn. The term does not include fresh fruits, fresh vegetables, nuts in the shell, wrapped candies, or food displayed in a salad bar.

(4) <u>Business Days</u> means Monday through Friday excluding legal holidays.

(5) <u>Caterer</u> means any person who prepares food intended for individual portion service and transports it to another location, or who prepares and serves food at a food service establishment other than one for which he holds a permit, for service at a single meal, party or similar gathering.

(6) <u>Commissioner</u> means the Commissioner of Public Health.

(7) <u>Corrosion-resistant materials</u> means those materials that are capable of maintaining their original surface characteristics under prolonged influence of the use environment, including the expected food contact and the normal use of cleaning compounds and sanitizing (bactericidal) solutions.

(8) <u>Critical violation</u> means the following:

(a) Food from an unapproved or unknown source or food which is or may be adulterated, contaminated or otherwise unfit for human consumption is found in a food establishment;

(b) Potentially hazardous food that is held longer than necessary for preparation or service at a temperature which is greater than 45°F (7°C) (in the case of cold food) or less than 140°F (60°C) (in the case of hot food);

(c) Insufficient facilities to maintain product temperature;

(d) Re-service of potentially hazardous food or unwrapped food that has been served to customers unless such re-service is pursuant to 105 CMR 590.006(G);

(e) A person infected with a communicable disease that can be transmitted by food is working as a food handler in a food establishment;

(f) A person not practicing strict standards of cleanliness and personal hygiene which may result in the potential transmission of illness through food is employed in a food establishment;

(g) Equipment, utensils and food-contact surfaces are not cleaned and sanitized effectively and may contaminate food during preparation, storage or service;

(h) Sewage or liquid waste is not disposed of in an approved and sanitary manner, or the sewage or liquid waste contaminates or may contaminate any food, areas used to store or prepare food, or any areas frequented by customers or employees;

(i) Toilets and facilities for washing hands are not provided, properly installed or designed, accessible or convenient;

(j) The supply of water is not from an approved source or is not under pressure and the food establishment does not use single service articles and/or bottled water from an approved source;

(k) A defect exists in the system supplying potable water that may result in the contamination of the water;

(l) Insects, rodents or other animals are present on the premises (unless allowed by 105 CMR 590.027(F)(3)];

(m) Toxic items are improperly labeled, stored or used; or

(n) Any other violation of these regulations so designated by the board of health after written notice to the permit holder that the violation has the potential to seriously affect the public health.

(B) Definitions.

(1) <u>Adulterated Food</u> means the definition in M.G.L. c. 94, s. 186.

(2) <u>Board of Health</u> means the appropriate and legally designated health authority of the city, town, or other legally constituted governmental unit within the Commonwealth having the usual powers and duties of the board of health of a city or town.

(3) <u>Bulk Food</u> means unpackaged or unwrapped, processed or unprocessed food provided in a retail food store in aggregate containers from which quantities desired by the consumer are withdrawn. The term does not include fresh fruits, fresh vegetables, nuts in the shell, wrapped candies, or food displayed in a salad bar.

(4) <u>Business Days</u> means Monday through Friday excluding legal holidays.

(5) <u>Caterer</u> means any person who prepares food intended for individual portion service and transports it to another location, or who prepares and serves food at a food service establishment other than one for which he holds a permit, for service at a single meal, party or similar gathering.

(6) <u>Commissioner</u> means the Commissioner of Public Health.

(7) <u>Corrosion-resistant materials</u> means those materials that are capable of maintaining their original surface characteristics under prolonged influence of the use environment, including the expected food contact and the normal use of cleaning compounds and sanitizing (bactericidal) solutions.

(8) <u>Critical violation</u> means the following:

(a) Food from an unapproved or unknown source or food which is or may be adulterated, contaminated or otherwise unfit for human consumption is found in a food establishment;

(b) Potentially hazardous food that is held longer than necessary for preparation or service at a temperature which is greater than 45°F (7°C) (in the case of cold food) or less than 140°F (60°C) (in the case of hot food);

(c) Insufficient facilities to maintain product temperature;

(d) Re-service of potentially hazardous food or unwrapped food that has been served to customers unless such re-service is pursuant to 105 CMR 590.006(G);

(e) A person infected with a communicable disease that can be transmitted by food is working as a food handler in a food establishment;

(f) A person not practicing strict standards of cleanliness and personal hygiene which may result in the potential transmission of illness through food is employed in a food establishment;

(g) Equipment, utensils and food-contact surfaces are not cleaned and sanitized effectively and may contaminate food during preparation, storage or service;

(h) Sewage or liquid waste is not disposed of in an approved and sanitary manner, or the sewage or liquid waste contaminates or may contaminate any food, areas used to store or prepare food, or any areas frequented by customers or employees;

(i) Toilets and facilities for washing hands are not provided, properly installed or designed, accessible or convenient;

(j) The supply of water is not from an approved source or is not under pressure and the food establishment does not use single service articles and/or bottled water from an approved source;

(k) A defect exists in the system supplying potable water that may result in the contamination of the water;

(l) Insects, rodents or other animals are present on the premises (unless allowed by 105 CMR 590.027(F)(3)];

(m) Toxic items are improperly labeled, stored or used; or

(n) Any other violation of these regulations so designated by the board of health after written notice to the permit holder that the violation has the potential to seriously affect the public health.

590.001: continued

(28) Potable water means water from any source or supplier approved by the Department of Environmental Quality Engineering or the Department for human consumption.

(29) Potentially hazardous food means any food that consists in whole or in part of milk or milk products, eggs, meat, poultry, fish, shellfish, edible crustacea, or other ingredients, including synthetic ingredients, and which is in a form capable of supporting rapid and progressive growth of infectious or toxigenic microorganisms. The term does not include: raw, clean, whole, uncracked, odor-free shell eggs; foods that have a pH level of 4.6 or below or a water activity (a_w) value of 0.85 or less under standard conditions; food products in hermetically sealed containers processed to prevent spoilage, and dehydrated, dry or powdered products so low in moisture content as to preclude development of microorganisms.

(30) Pushcart means a non-self-propelled vehicle limited to serving non-potentially hazardous foods or wrapped food prepared at a food processing or food service establishment and maintained at proper temperatures, or limited to the preparation and service of frankfurters.

(31) Reconstituted means dehydrated food products recombined with water or other liquids.

(32) Residential kitchen means a kitchen in a private home where food is prepared for consumption by the family.

(33) Retail food store means any establishment or section of an establishment where food and food products are offered to the consumer and intended for off-premises consumption. The term includes delicatessens that offer prepared food in bulk quantities only. The term does not include roadside markets that offer only fresh fruits and fresh vegetables for sale; food service establishments; bakeries; or food and beverage vending machines.

(34) Safe material means articles manufactured from or composed of materials that may not reasonably be expected to result, directly or indirectly, in their becoming a component or otherwise affecting the characteristics of any food. If materials used are food additives or color additives as defined in the Federal Food, Drug, and Cosmetic Act (21 USC ss. 301 et seq.), they are "safe" only if they are used in conformity with regulations established pursuant to that Act. Other materials are "safe" only if, as used, they are not food additives or color additives as so defined, and are used in conformity with all applicable regulations of the Food and Drug Administration.

(35) Safe temperatures as applied to potentially hazardous food, means temperatures of 45°F ($\neq$ 7°C) or below and 140°F (60°C) or above unless otherwise specified in these regulations, and 0°F ($\neq$ -18°C) or below for frozen foods.

(36) Sanitization means effective bactericidal treatment by a process that provides enough accumulative heat or concentration of chemicals for enough time to reduce the bacterial count, including pathogens, to a safe level on cleaned food contact surfaces of utensils and equipment.

(37) Sealed means free of cracks or other openings that permit the entry or passage of moisture.

(38) Single-service articles means items used by the retailer or consumer such as cups, containers, lids, plates, knives, forks, spoons, stirrers, straws, napkins, toothpicks, packaging materials, including bags, closures and similar articles intended for contact with food and designed for one-time use. The term does not include "single use" articles such as number 10 cans, aluminum pie pans, bread wrappers and similar articles into which food has been packaged by the manufacturer.

(39) Tableware means reusable eating and drinking utensils.

(40) Temporary food establishment means a food establishment that operates at a fixed location for a period of time of not more than 14 consecutive days in conjunction with a single event or celebration.

590.005: continued

(I) Food Product Thermometers. Metal stem-type numerically scaled indicating thermometers, accurate to ±2°F ($\neq$ ±1°C) shall be provided and used to assure attainment and maintenance of proper temperatures during preparation of all potentially hazardous foods.

(J) Thawing Potentially Hazardous Foods. Potentially hazardous foods shall be thawed:

(1) In refrigerated units at a temperature not to exceed 45°F ($\neq$ 7°C); or

(2) Under potable running water at a temperature of 70°F ($\neq$ 21°C) or below, with sufficient water velocity to agitate and float off loose food particles into the overflow and for a period not to exceed that reasonably required to thaw the food; or

(3) In a microwave oven only when the food will be immediately transferred to conventional cooking units as part of a continuous cooking process or when the entire, uninterrupted cooking process takes place in the microwave oven; or

(4) As part of the conventional cooking process.

590.006: Food Display and Service

(A) Potentially Hazardous Foods. Potentially hazardous foods shall be held at an internal temperature of 45°F ($\neq$ 7°C) or below or at an internal temperature of 140°F (60°C) or higher during display, except that rare roast beef that is offered for sale hot shall be held at a temperature of at least 130°F ($\neq$ 55°C).

(B) Frozen Foods. Foods intended for sale or service in a frozen state shall be displayed or held at an air temperature of 0°F ($\neq$ -18°C) or below, except for frozen desserts being held for immediate service to consumers or during defrost cycles and brief periods of loading or unloading. Frozen foods shall be displayed below or behind product fill lines according to cabinet manufacturer's specifications.

(C) Food Display. Food on display, other than whole, unprocessed raw fruits and unprocessed raw vegetables, shall be protected from contamination by the use of packaging, or by the use of easily cleanable display cases, serving line or salad bar protector devices, covered containers for self-service, or by other effective means. All food shall be displayed above the floor in a manner that will protect the food from contamination. Hot or cold food units shall be provided to assure the maintenance of potentially hazardous food at the required temperature during display. Unpackaged potentially hazardous food shall not be provided for consumer self-service in retail food stores except as part of a salad bar operation governed by 105 CMR 590.032.

(D) Food Dispensing for Immediate Consumption.

(1) Milk and milk products for drinking purposes shall be provided to the consumer in an unopened, commercially filled package not exceeding 1 pint in capacity, or drawn from a commercially filled bulk milk container stored in a mechanically refrigerated bulk milk dispenser. Where a bulk dispenser for milk and milk products is not available and portions of less than 1/2 pint are required for mixed drinks, cereal, or dessert service, milk and milk products may be poured from a commercially filled container of not more than 1/2 gallon capacity.

(2) Cream, half and half, or nondairy creaming or whitening agents shall be provided in a single service package, an individual service container, or drawn from a refrigerated dispenser designed for such service. Individual service containers shall not be re-served and shall be cleaned and sanitized after each use.

(3) Condiments, seasonings and dressings for self-service use shall be provided in individual packages, or in dispensers or con-

590.009:   Employee Cleanliness

Employees engaged in food preparation, service and warewashing operations shall thoroughly wash their hands and the exposed portions of their arms with soap or detergent and warm water before starting work, after smoking, eating, or using the toilet, before and after handling raw meat, raw poultry, or raw seafood, and as often as is necessary during work to keep them clean. Employees shall keep their fingernails trimmed and clean.

590.010:   Employee Clothing

(A) Employees shall wear clean outer clothing.

(B) Employees shall use effective hair restraints when working in food preparation areas and where necessary to prevent the contamination of food or food-contact surfaces.

590.011:   Employee Practices

(A) Employees shall maintain a high degree of personal cleanliness and shall conform to good hygienic practices during all working periods.

(B) Employees shall consume food or use tobacco only in designated areas. Such designated areas shall not be located in food preparation areas or in areas where the eating or tobacco use of an employee may result in contamination of food, equipment, or utensils.

(C) All employees shall wash their hands thoroughly with soap and warm water in an adequate hand-washing facility before starting work, between any changes in processing or operations, and as often as necessary to remove soil and contamination. The hands of all employees shall be kept clean while engaged in handling of food and food contact surfaces.

590.012:   Equipment and Utensils: Design, Fabrication and Location

(A) __Materials.__
(1) __General__. Multi-use equipment and utensils shall be constructed and repaired with safe materials, including finishing materials; shall be corrosion-resistant and nonabsorbent; and shall be smooth, easily cleanable, and durable under conditions of normal use. Single-service articles shall be made from clean, sanitary, safe materials. Equipment, utensils, and single-service articles shall not impart odors, color, taste, nor contribute to the contamination of food.
(2) __Solder__. If solder is used, it shall be composed of safe materials and be corrosion-resistant.
(3) __Wood__. Hard maple or equivalent nonabsorbent wood that meets the general requirements set forth in 105 CMR 590.012(A)(1) may be used for cutting blocks, cutting boards, and bakers' tables. Wood may be used for single-service articles such as chopsticks, stirrers, or ice cream spoons. Wood shall not be used as a food-contact surface under other circumstances, except for contact with raw fruits, raw vegetables, and nuts in the shell.
(4) __Plastics and rubber materials__. Safe plastic or safe rubber or safe rubber-like materials that are resistant under normal conditions of use to scratching, scoring, decomposition, grazing, chipping, and distortion, that are of sufficient weight and thickness to permit cleaning and sanitizing by normal warewashing methods, and that meet the general requirements set forth in 105 CMR 590.012(A)(1), are permitted for repeated use.
(5) __Mollusk and crustacea shells__. Mollusk and crustacea shells may be used only once as a serving container. Further re-use of such shells for food service is prohibited.

590.012:   continued

space between it and adjoining equipment units and adjacent walls or ceilings shall be not more than 1/32 inch (0.8 mm) and, if exposed to seepage, the space shall be sealed.
(4) __Aisles and working spaces__. Aisles and working spaces between units of equipment and between equipment and walls, shall be unobstructed and of sufficient width to permit employees to perform their duties readily without contamination of food or food-contact surfaces by clothing or personal contact. All easily movable storage equipment such as dollies, skids, racks, and open-ended pallets shall be positioned to provide accessibility to working areas.

590.013:   Equipment and Utensils: Cleaning and Sanitization

(A) __Cleaning Frequency__.
(1) Utensils and food-contact surfaces of equipment shall be cleaned and sanitized:
(a) Each time there is a change in processing between raw beef, raw pork, raw poultry or raw seafood, or a change in processing from raw to ready-to-eat foods;
(b) After any interruption of operations during which time contamination may have occurred; and
(c) After final use each working day.
(2) Tableware shall be washed, rinsed, and sanitized after each use.
(3) Where equipment and utensils are used for the preparation of potentially hazardous foods on a continuous or production-line basis, utensils and the food-contact surfaces of equipment shall be cleaned and sanitized at intervals throughout the day on a schedule based on food temperature, type of food, and amount of food particle accumulation.
(4) The food-contact surfaces of cooking devices and the cavities and door seals of microwave ovens shall be cleaned at least once each day of use, except that this shall not apply to hot oil cooking equipment and hot oil filtering systems. The food-contact surfaces of all baking equipment and pans shall be kept free of encrusted grease deposits and other accumulated soil.
(5) Non-food-contact surfaces of equipment, including transport vehicles, shall be cleaned as often as is necessary to keep the equipment free of accumulation of dust, dirt, food particles, and other debris.

(B) __Wiping Cloths__.
(1) Cloths used for wiping food spills on food-contact surfaces of equipment shall be cleaned and rinsed frequently in one of the sanitizing solutions permitted in 105 CMR 590.013(C)(8) and used for no other purpose. These cloths shall be stored in the sanitizing solution between uses.
(2) Cloths used for cleaning non-food-contact surfaces of equipment shall be cleaned and rinsed as specified in 105 CMR 590.013(B)(1) and used for no other purpose. These cloths shall be stored in the sanitizing solution between uses.
(3) Single-service disposable towels are permitted in lieu of wiping cloths or sponges if they are discarded after each use.

(C) __Manual Cleaning and Sanitizing__.
(1) For manual cleaning and sanitizing of equipment and utensils, except tableware, a sink with two or three compartments shall be provided and used. For manual cleaning of tableware, a sink with three compartments shall be provided and used. Sink compartments shall be large enough to accomodate the immersion of most equipment and utensils, and each compartment of the sink shall be supplied with hot and cold running potable water. Where immersion in sinks is impracticable (e.g., because equipment is too large),

590.029: continued

(E) Toilets. Operators of mobile food units and pushcarts shall obtain the use of adequate and suitable toilet facilities where handwashing facilities are available. No such operator shall return to his work, after using the toilet, without first thoroughly washing his hands.

(F) Sanitary Operation. The truck, wagon, or other vehicle, mobile stand or pushcart shall be clean and in a sanitary condition. It shall be so constructed and arranged that food, drink, and utensils will not be exposed to insects, rodents, dust, or other contamination. Only food free from adulteration shall be sold or served. All articles of food and all food shall be served in clean single-service containers. All sandwiches, pastries, and other such items of food shall be wrapped in a clean sanitary outer wrapping and shall be protected from contamination until served. Soda straws and spoons shall be individually wrapped. Sugar shall be served only from a sanitary sugar dispenser or in individually wrapped servings. Adequate refrigerated compartments shall be provided on each mobile food unit in which to store such articles as meat sandwiches, salad sandwiches, and extra supplies of soups and other readily perishable foods. Cream, half and half, and non-dairy creaming and whitening agents shall be provided in single-service containers. Mobile food units designed to dispense hot foods shall be provided with suitable units to rapidly heat such foods and to keep such food hot until served. Kitchens or other food preparation areas where food is prepared for service in mobile food units and pushcarts shall comply with all the applicable requirements for food establishments.

(G) Exemption for Certain Units. Mobile food units and pushcarts serving or offering for sale only frankfurters or food prepared, packaged in individual servings, transported and stored under conditions meeting the requirements of these regulations, or beverages that are not potentially hazardous and are dispensed from covered urns or other protected equipment, need not comply with requirements of these regulations pertaining to the necessity of water and sewage systems nor with those requirements pertaining to the cleaning and sanitization of equipment and utensils if the required equipment for cleaning and sanitization exists at the base of operations.

(H) Base of Operations.
(1) Mobile food units or pushcarts shall operate from a fixed food establishment and shall report at least daily to such location for all food and supplies and for all cleaning and servicing operations.
(2) The food establishment used as a base of operations for mobile food units or pushcarts shall be constructed and operated in compliance with the requirements of these regulations.

(I) Mobile Food Unit Servicing Area.
(1) A mobile food unit servicing area shall be provided at the food establishment and shall include at least overhead protection for any supplying, cleaning, or servicing operation. Within this servicing area, there shall be a location provided for the flushing and drainage of liquid wastes separate from the location provided for water servicing and for the loading and unloading of food and related supplies. This servicing area will not be required where only packaged food is placed on the mobile food unit or pushcart or where mobile food units do not contain waste retention tanks.
(a) The surface of the servicing area shall be constructed of a smooth nonabsorbent material, such as concrete or machine-laid asphalt and shall be maintained in good repair, kept clean, and be graded to drain.
(b) The construction of the walls and ceilings of the servicing area is exempted from the provisions of 105 CMR 590.022.

590.029: continued

(2) Potable water servicing equipment shall be installed according to law and shall be stored and handled in a way that protects the water and equipment from contamination.
(3) The mobile food unit liquid waste retention tank, where used, shall be thoroughly flushed and drained during the servicing operation. All liquid waste shall be discharged to a sanitary sewage disposal system in accordance with 105 CMR 590.016.

590.030: Temporary Food Establishments

(A) General. A temporary food establishment shall comply with the requirements of these regulations, except as otherwise provided in 105 CMR 590.030. The board of health may impose additional requirements to protect against health hazards related to the conduct of the temporary food establishment, may prohibit the sale of some or all potentially hazardous foods, and when no health hazard will result, may waive or modify requirements of these regulations pursuant to the provisions of 105 CMR 590.061.

(B) Restricted Operations. Whenever a temporary food establishment is permitted to operate without complying with all the requirements of these regulations, the following requirements are applicable. Only those potentially hazardous foods requiring limited preparation, such as hamburgers and frankfurters that only require seasoning and cooking, shall be prepared or served. The preparation or service of other potentially hazardous foods including pastries filled with cream or synthethic cream, custards, and similar products, and salads or sandwiches containing meat, poultry, eggs or fish is prohibited. This prohibition does not apply to any potentially hazardous food that has been prepared and packaged under conditions meeting the requirements of these regulations, is packaged in individual servings, is stored at a temperature of 45°F ($\stackrel{>}{=}$ 7°C) or below or at a temperature of 140°F (60°C) or above in facilities meeting the requirements of 105 CMR 590.004, 590.006 and 590.007, and is served directly in the unopened container in which it was packaged.

(C) Ice. Ice that is consumed or that contacts food shall be made under conditions meeting the requirements of 105 CMR 590.015(F). The ice shall be in chipped, crushed, or cubed form and in single-use safe plastic or wet-strength paper bags filled and sealed at the point of manufacture. The ice shall be held in these bags until it is dispensed in a way that protects it from contamination.

(D) Equipment.
(1) Equipment shall be located and installed in a way that prevents food contamination and that also facilitates cleaning the equipment and establishment.
(2) Food-contact surfaces of equipment shall be protected from contamination by consumers and other contaminating agents. Effective shields for such equipment shall be provided, as necessary, to prevent contamination.

(E) Single-Service Articles. All temporary food establishments without effective facilities for cleaning and sanitizing tableware shall provide only single-service articles for use by the consumer.

(F) Water. Enough potable water shall be available in the establishment for food preparation, for cleaning and sanitizing utensils and equipment, and for handwashing. A heating facility capable of producing enough hot water for these purposes shall be provided on the premises.

(G) Wet Storage. Storage of packaged food in contact with water or

590.051: continued

Department, the Commissioner or his authorized representative determines that compliance with these regulations has not been effected, he shall, in writing, notify the appropriate board of health of such determination, allotting a reasonable time in which compliance shall be effected, and requesting that the board of health, in writing, notify the Commissioner of what action will be and has been taken, to effect compliance with these regulations.

(2) If the Commissioner is not so notified, or if after notification he determines that action sufficient to effect compliance with the provisions of these regulations has not been taken, the board of health shall be deemed to have failed to effect compliance with these regulations.

(3) Whenever any board of health has failed after a reasonable length of time to enforce these regulations, the Department may enforce these regulations in any way that a local board of health is authorized to act to effect compliance.

(4) Notwithstanding any other provision of these regulations, if the Department determines that an imminent health hazard exists resulting from the operation of a food establishment it may without prior notice to the board of health take whatever action is necessary to effect compliance with these regulations.

(D) **Interpretation of Regulations.** The Director may from time to time issue written interpretations and guidelines as necessary to promote uniform application of these regulations. Upon the written request of a board of health or permit holder, the Director may investigate and/or advise on particular questions regarding interpretations of these regulations.

590.052:   Permit: Issuance

(A) **Permit Required to Operate.**
(1) No person shall operate a food establishment unless he is the holder of a valid permit granted to him by the board of health. In addition, the operator of each mobile food unit or pushcart shall obtain a permit to operate from the board of health in whose jurisdiction he sells his product.
(2) Only a person who complies with the requirements of these regulations shall be entitled to receive and retain a permit.
(3) The permit shall be posted on the premises of the food establishment.
(4) A permit shall not be transferable from a person or a place.

(B) **Application for Permit.**
(1) Any person desiring to operate a food establishment shall make written application for a permit on a form provided by the board of health and approved by the Department. The application shall include:
    (a) The applicant's name; the owner's name if different from the applicant; the applicant's post office address; whether such applicant is an individual, partnership, or corporation, and, if a partnership or corporation, the names of the partners or corporate officers together with their home addresses, state of incorporation, and name and address of local agent;
    (b) The name and location of the proposed food establishment;
    (c) The type of food establishment (i.e. food service establishment or retail food store)
    (d) The type of permit (i.e. annual, seasonal or temporary);
    (e) The signature of the applicant or applicants; and
    (f) Any other information required by applicable law.
(2) Applications for mobile food unit or pushcart permits shall include a list of the handwash and toilet facilities available on each route.

590.052:   continued

(3) Payment of any fees required by law shall accompany the application.

(C) **Permit.**
(1) There shall be one food establishment permit form. The permit shall indicate:
    (a) Whether the permit is annual, seasonal or temporary; and
    (b) Each of the following food establishment operations permitted:
        1. Food service establishment
        2. Retail food store
        3. Residential kitchen
        4. Mobile food unit
        5. Pushcart
(2) The permit shall state:
    (a) The name and address of the food establishment;
    (b) The name of the permit holder;
    (c) The date of expiration;
    (d) Any restrictions on the type of operations allowed.

(D) **Expiration and Renewal of Permit.**
(1) A permit shall expire no later than one (1) year from the date issued.
(2) An annual food establishment permit may be renewed by applying at least thirty (30) days prior to the expiration of the permit. Application for a permit shall be made in writing on a form provided by the board of health and approved by the Department.

(E) **Conditions for Issuance.** After receipt of an application for an original or renewal permit, the board of health shall make an inspection of the food establishment. When inspection reveals that the applicable requirements of these regulations have been met, a permit shall be issued to the applicant by the board of health.

(F) **Copies of Permit.** The permit shall be made out in duplicate. One copy shall be given to the applicant, and one shall be placed on file with the board of health.

(G) **Notification of Changes.**
(1) Change in ownership, name or location. A permit holder shall notify the board of health within 48 hours after any change in ownership, and at least 30 days prior to any change of the name or location of the food establishment and shall promptly submit to the board of health an application for a new or amended permit, together with written documentation reflecting such change.
(2) Remodeling or change in operations. A permit holder shall submit plans in accordance with 105 CMR 590.058 any time an establishment is being remodeled or a new operation added and shall promptly submit to the board of health an application if a new or amended permit is required.

(H) **Temporary Food Establishment Permits.** A permit for a temporary food establishment may be issued for a period of time which shall not exceed 14 days, and the permit shall state the inclusive dates, location, and any restrictions in the operations allowed.

(I) **Mobile Food Units or Pushcarts.** A permit for a mobile food unit or pushcart may be issued for a period of time which shall be determined by the board of health, and the permit shall state the inclusive dates, location(s), and any restrictions in the operations allowed.

(J) **List of Food Establishments.** The board of health shall submit to the Department by July 31st each year a list of all food establishments granted permits. The list shall include the name, address and

commercial logic II

TO: James M Hence

curiosities & puzzles

The Digestor's Digest

Vol. 1, No. 1	Page 6

For Dieters:

Burger Mad has invented the most amazing treat, the "Choco-Butter Toffee-Waffle." Although it is composed entirely of butter, honey, milk chocolate, marshmallows, and chicken fat, laboratory tests show that it has fewer calories than all other breakfast foods combined!

For Dieters:

O'Donnell's old favorite, the "Bowl O'Mush" with high-fructose corn flakes, is now available in a special artificially soured version. This is not the fun page.

exam warning VI

By now, you have had sufficient warning, and so it is time for our

Surprise Examination!

1. Before I turned to this page I
   a. had no idea it would be the exam.
   b. guessed that it would be the exam.
   c. knew it would be the exam.
   d. thought it would be another *Digestor's Digest*.
   e. thought this was my French book.

2. In Exam Warning I, Jim and Tom
   a. told the truth and I believed them.
   b. told the truth but I doubted them.
   c. lied but I believed them.
   d. lied and I doubted them.
   e. said a number of things and I still don't know whether they are
      true or false.

3. The argument that Laura Logic gives
   a. is absolutely correct and I believe it.
   b. seems OK, but I don't believe it.
   c. has a flaw, but I believed it at the time.
   d. has a flaw, and I spotted it right away.
   e. was good then but has a flaw now.

4. The argument that Teresa Truthtable gives
   a. is absolutely correct and I believe it.
   b. seems OK, but I don't believe it.
   c. has a flaw, but I believed it at the time.
   d. has a flaw, and I spotted it right away.
   e. was good then but has a flaw now.

5. The reasoning of Peter Predicate
   a. is absolutely correct and I believe it.
   b. seems OK, but I don't believe it.
   c. has a flaw, but I believed it at the time.
   d. has a flaw, and I spotted it right away.
   e. was good then but has a flaw now.

Extra Credit: Since you were surprised, what is going on? Can there be
surprise exams?

Lewis Carroll's "what the tortoise said to Achilles"

. . . you ought to start with Logic.
For thus your mind is trained and braced,
In Spanish boots it will be laced,
That on the road of Thought may be,
It henceforth creep more thoughtfully,
And will not crisscross here and there,
Will-o'-the-wisping through the air.
Days will be spent to let you know
That what you once did at one blow,
Like eating and drinking so easy and free,
Can only be done with One, Two, Three.
—GOETHE, *Faust*

Achilles had overtaken the Tortoise, and had seated himself comfortably on its back.

"So you've got to the end of our race-course?" said the Tortoise. "Even though it *does* consist of an infinite series of distances? [See "*Paradox*" in part 1.] I thought some wiseacre or other had proved that the thing couldn't be done?"

"It *can* be done," said Achilles. "It *has* been done! *Solvitur ambulando* [It has been solved by walking]. You see the distances were constantly *diminishing*; and so—"

"But if they had been constantly *increasing*?" the Tortoise interrupted.

"Then I shouldn't be *here*," Achilles modestly replied; "and *you* would have got several times round the world, by this time!"

"You flatter me—*flatten*, I mean," said the Tortoise; "for you are a heavy weight, and *no* mistake! Well now, would you like to hear of a race-course, that most people fancy they can get to the end of in two or three steps, while it *really* consists of an infinite number of distances, each one longer than the previous one?"

"Very much indeed!" said the Grecian warrior, as he drew from his helmet (few Grecian warriors possessed *pockets* in those days) an enormous note-book and a pencil. "Proceed! And speak *slowly*, please! *Short-hand* isn't invented yet!"

"That beautiful First Proposition of Euclid!" the Tortoise murmured dreamily. "You admire Euclid?"

"Passionately! So far, at least, as one *can* admire a treatise that wo'n't [*sic*] be published for some centuries to come!"

"Well now, let's take a little bit of the argument in that First Proposition—just *two* steps, and the conclusion drawn from them. Kindly enter them in your note-book. And, in order to refer to them conveniently, let's call them A, B, and Z:

"(A) Things that are equal to the same are equal to each other.

"(B) The two sides of this Triangle are things that are equal to the same.

"(Z) The two sides of this Triangle are equal to each other.

"Readers of Euclid will grant, I suppose, that Z follows logically from A and B, so that any one who accepts A and B as true, *must* accept Z as true?"

"Undoubtedly! The youngest child in a High School—as soon as High Schools are invented, which will not be till some two thousand years later—will grant *that*."

"And if some reader had *not* yet accepted A and B as true, he might still accept the *Sequence* as a *valid* one, I suppose?"

"No doubt such a reader might exist. He might say 'I accept as true the Hypothetical Proposition [i.e., implication] that, *if* A and B be true, Z must be true; but I *don't* accept A and B as true.' Such a reader would do wisely in abandoning Euclid, and taking to football."

"And might there not *also* be some reader who would say 'I accept A and B as true, but I *don't* accept the Hypothetical?'"

"Certainly there might. *He*, also, had better take to football."

"And *neither* of these readers," the Tortoise continued, "is *as yet* under any logical necessity to accept Z as true?"

"Quite so," Achilles assented.

"Well, now, I want you to consider *me* as a reader of the *second* kind, and to force me, logically, to accept Z as true."

"A Tortoise playing football would be—" Achilles was beginning.

"—an anomaly, of course," the Tortoise hastily interrupted. "Don't wander from the point. Let's have Z first, and football afterwards!"

"I'm to force you to accept Z, am I?" Achilles said musingly. "And your present position is that you accept A and B, but you *don't* accept the Hypothetical—"

"Let's call it C," said the Tortoise.

"—but you *don't* accept."

"(C) If A and B are true, Z must be true."

"That is my present position," said the Tortoise.

"Then I must ask you to accept C."

"I'll do so," said the Tortoise, "as soon as you've entered it in that note-book of yours. What else have you got in it?"

"Only a few memoranda," said Achilles, nervously fluttering the leaves; "a few memoranda of—of the battles in which I have distinguished myself!"

"Plenty of blank leaves, I see!" the Tortoise cheerily remarked. "We shall need them *all*!" (Achilles shuddered.) "Now write as I dictate:

"(A) Things that are equal to the same are equal to each other.

"(B) The two sides of this Triangle are things that are equal to the same.

"(C) If A and B are true, Z must be true.

"(Z) The two sides of this Triangle are equal to each other.

"You should call it D, not Z," said Achilles. "It comes *next* to the other three. If you accept A and B and C, you *must* accept Z."

"And why *must* I?"

"Because if follows *logically* from them. If A and B and C are true, Z *must* be true. You don't dispute *that*, I imagine?"

"If A and B and C are true, Z must be true," the Tortoise thoughtfully repeated. "That's *another* Hypothetical, isn't it? And, if I failed to see its truth, I might accept A and B and C, and *still* not accept Z, mightn't I?"

"You might," the candid hero admitted; "though such obtuseness would certainly be phenomenal." Still, the event is *possible*. So I might ask you to grant one more Hypothetical!"

"Very good. I'm quite willing to grant it, as soon as you've written it down. We will call it

"(D) If A and B and C are true, Z must be true.

"Have you entered that in your note-book?"

"I *have*!" Achilles joyfully exclaimed, as he ran the pencil into its sheath. "And at last we've got to the end of this ideal race-course! Now that you accept A and B and C and D, *of course* you accept Z."

"Do I?" said the Tortoise innocently. "Let's make that quite clear. I accept A and B and C and D. Suppose I *still* refused to accept Z?"

"Then Logic would take you by the throat, and *force* you to do it!" Achilles triumphantly replied. "Logic would tell you 'You ca'n't [*sic*] help yourself. Now that you've accepted A and B and C and D, you *must* accept Z!' So you've no choice, you see."

"Whatever *Logic* is good enough to tell me is worth *writing down*," said the Tortoise. "So enter it in your book, please. We will call it

"(E) If A and B and C and D are true, Z must be true.

"Until I've granted *that*, of course, I needn't grant Z. So it's quite a *necessary* step, you see?"

"I see," said Achilles; and there was a touch of sadness in his tone.

Here the narrator, having pressing business at the Bank, was obliged to leave the happy pair, and did not again pass the spot until some months afterwards. When he did so, Achilles was still seated on the back of the much-enduring Tortoise, and was writing in his note-book, which appeared to be nearly full. The Tortoise was saying "Have you go that last step written down? Unless I've lost count, that makes a thousand and one. There are several millions more to come. And *would* you mind, as a personal favour—considering what a lot of instruction this colloquy of ours will provide for the Logicians of the Nineteenth century—would you mind adopting a pun that my cousin the Mock-Turtle will then make, and allowing yourself to be re-named *Taught-Us*?"

"As you please!" replied the weary warrior, in the hollow tones of despair, as he buried his face in his hands. "Provided that *you*, for *your* part, will adopt a pun the Mock-Turtle never made, and allow yourself to be re-named *A Kill-Ease*!"

CHALLENGE   Has the tortoise shown that it is impossible to get to the conclusion of this or any other logical argument? If not, where is there an error?

the far side

COMPLETENESS, DISBELIEF, DEBATES, AND DINNER

contents

FORMAL LOGIC: COMPLETENESS

with & about logic

informal logic

curiosities & puzzles

GOAL: To explore the connection between deductions and structures. The completeness theorem shows that the two approaches to logic are equivalent. Mathematicians have exploited this idea in geometry and the axiomatic method.

FORMAL LOGIC: COMPLETENESS

GEOMETRY

[Thomas Hobbes] was 40 years old before he looked on Geometry; which happened accidentally. Being in a Gentleman's Library, Euclid's *Elements* lay open and 'twas the 47 El. libri 1 [the Pythagorean Theorem]. He read the Proposition. By G---, sayd he (he would now and then sweare an emphaticall Oath by way of emphasis) this is impossible! So he reads the Demonstration of it, which referred him back to such a Proposition; which proposition he read. That referred him back to another, which he also read. Et sic deinceps [and so forth] that at last he was demonstratively convinced of that trueth. This made him in love with Geometry.

—John Aubrey, *Brief Lives*

We have tackled proof and have experienced some of its difficulties. In this chapter we present a profound example from geometry that illustrates many of the issues we have wrestled with.

The story begins with Euclid, the Greek mathematician whose *Elements* (circa 300 B.C.) was the starting point for all geometric theory. Euclid based his geometry on five postulates, statements about lines and points that he asserted without proof. That all of geometry could follow from just five statements is, when you think of it, staggering, but within a few hundred years, mathematicians were attempting to reduce these five to four.

The feeling was that the fifth postulate actually was a logical consequence of the first four; that is, the argument

first postulate
second postulate
third postulate
fourth postulate
∴ fifth postulate

was valid.

Beginning as early as Ptolemy (second century B.C.), mathematicians struggled to find a proof. Many (Ptolemy, Proclus, Saccheri) thought they had found one; others (Poseidonius, Clavius, Kepler,

Desargues, al-Din, Wallis, Lorenz, Cataldi, Thibault, Playfair, Lambert, Legendre) could prove only statements such as "*If* we can prove ——, *then* we will be able to prove the fifth postulate."

Here is Playfair's version of the postulate: Given a line and a point not on the line,

there is a unique line through the point parallel to the given line.

The great breakthrough occurred in the early nineteenth century when three mathematicians, Karl Friedrich Gauss, János Bolyai, and Nikolai Ivanovich Lobachevski, all independently came to the conclusion that *no proof exists*—that for over two thousand years, some of the greatest minds in the world had been searching for something that wasn't there.

How can we ever know that no proof exists? As in "Proving Invalidity" in part 6, we can show this by finding a universe where the first four postulates are true and the fifth is false.

What does it mean for the fifth postulate to be false? There are really two ways. The fifth states that there is exactly one line through the point parallel to the given line. One way to contradict this is to say that there are no lines through the point parallel to the given line.

A second way is to say that there are many lines through the point parallel to the given line.

Both of these propositions may seem absurd to you. You may feel that the fifth postulate is intuitively obvious, that in the *real* world, it is *true*. We will discuss reality later, but for the moment, consider this argument:

All United States senators are members of Congress.
George Bush is not a United States senator.
∴ George Bush is not a member of Congress.

Is this reasoning valid or invalid? It is tempting (even after you have read much logic) to say it is valid because George Bush is not a member of Congress, but the argument is invalid. We see this by formalizing it:

$\forall x(Sx \Rightarrow Cx)$
$\neg Sb$
$\therefore \neg Cb$

Now we can draw a Venn diagram to show that we can make both premises true and the conclusion false:

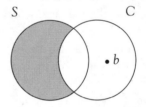

Additionally, we can describe a universe where this is the case. Let Sx mean "x is a grocery," let Cx mean "x is a store," and let b be K-mart. Then since all groceries are stores and K-mart is not a grocery, the two premises are true but the conclusion "K-mart is not a store" is false.

What have we done? We have taken the original argument and reinterpreted "United States senator" as "grocery" and "member of Congress" as "store." Our point is that if the original argument is valid, then *it is valid no matter how we interpret the predicates*.

Back to geometry: Our predicates are "is a point" and "is a line." Euclid's geometry can also be formalized, though not as easily. We can, for example, use predicates Px for "x is a point," Lx for "x is a line," and Oxy, for "x is on y." We will use the notation introduced in "Quantifiers and Arithmetic" in part 7, $\exists!z$, meaning, "there is a unique z such that." Then the fifth postulate is

$\forall x \forall y ((Px \ \& \ Ly \ \& \ \neg Oxy) \Rightarrow \ \cdots$ (For every x and y, if x is any point not on line y . . .)

$\cdots \exists! z \cdots$ (. . . then there is a unique z, such that . . .)

$\cdots (Lz \ \& \ Oxz \cdots$ (. . . z is a line passing through x . . .)

$\cdots \ \& \ \forall t \neg (Otz \ \& \ Oty)))$ (. . . and z is parallel to y.)

Now instead of thinking of Px as "x is a point in the plane," think of it as "x is a point on a perfect sphere." Instead of interpreting Lx as "x is a straight line in the plane," think of it as "x is a great circle on the perfect sphere." A **great circle** is a circle whose center is also the center of the sphere. On the earth, the equator is a great circle but the other latitude lines are not.

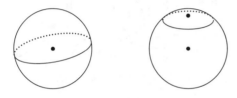

All longitude lines, however, are great circles.

With this interpretation, the first four postulates are true, but the fifth postulate is false. There are no lines parallel; in fact, in this geometry, called **spherical geometry,** every pair of lines intersects somewhere.

There is also a universe in which there are many parallel lines. Interpret "points" as points inside a particular circle, and interpret "lines" as portions of circles that intersect the particular circle at right angles.

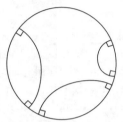

We also include as "lines" all diameters. In this geometry, called **hyperbolic geometry,** given a point and a line,

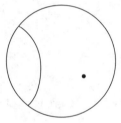

there are many lines through the point that do not intersect the given line.

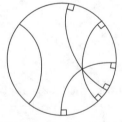

Back to reality: Is the fifth postulate true or false in the universe in which we live? As logicians, we don't care, of course; truth is merely detail. As philosophers, we are quite interested. Kant, for example, took the position that the fifth postulate had to be true *a priori*, as a matter of necessity. Gauss was the first (1830) to realize the importance of the question. He suggested that the angles of large triangles could be measured to find out. (In Euclidean geometry, the sum of the angles of any triangle is exactly 180 degrees. In hyperbolic geometry, the sum is always less than 180 degrees, and in spherical geometry, it is always more.)

If a geometry is not Euclidean, it is usually described as "curved." The truth is that real space is not Euclidean. This was first suggested by Einstein's theory of relativity and later verified experimentally. Space is indeed curved, and the curvature is due to the presence of mass in the universe.

THE COMPLETENESS THEOREM

Logic can be patient for it is eternal.
—OLIVER HEAVISIDE

There are two fundamentally different definitions of implication, and the discussion of the last section dramatizes that difference. One definition is that A implies B iff there is a deduction of B from A using the introduction and elimination rules. This definition is often called **syntactic** because only the syntax or grammar of the language is needed to formulate the definition. The other definition of implication is that A implies B iff in every structure which makes A true, B is true. This kind of definition is often called **semantic** because it appeals to meanings or interpretations of wffs, specifically, to structures and concepts like "true."

Similarly, we have two definitions of a valid wff, one syntactic and one semantic. A wff is syntactically valid iff there is a deduction of it without premises. A wff is semantically valid iff it is true in all structures. We can focus our attention on either implication or valid wffs because the implication $A, B, C \therefore D$ is the same as the validity of the wff $(A \mathbin{\&} B \mathbin{\&} C) \Rightarrow D$ in both cases. Thus the two definitions agree on the wffs that each declares valid iff they agree on the implications or valid arguments they accept.

As we saw in the last section for thousands of years a major goal of mathematics was to find a deduction of Euclid's fifth postulate from the first four—in other words, to show that postulates 1 through 4 imply postulate 5 syntactically. In fact, this goal is impossible. The discovery of this impossibility, however, did not come syntactically. Instead, it was shown that the first four postulates do *not* imply the fifth semantically. But why should the discovery that the first four

399

postulates could be true in a structure even though the fifth was false discourage the search for a formal deduction of the fifth from the other four?

The brief answer is the "completeness theorem," which itself was not proven until the twentieth century. The completeness theorem states that syntactic implication is equivalent to semantic implication: Both the method of deductions and the method of structures yield the same answer to every question of the form "does A imply B?" Sometimes the claim that syntactic implication is contained in semantic implication is called the consistency theorem. It assures us that the precise formulation of our introduction and elimination rules is correct; those rules can never lead us from truth to falsity. The inverse claim that semantic implication is contained in syntactic implication is occasionally also called the completeness theorem. It assures us that our rules are complete; thus they enable us to prove all purely logical truths.

The completeness theorem is important for a number of reasons. One is convenience. Syntactic implication is much easier to show than semantic implication (especially when the premises and conclusions are somewhat complex). It is generally easier to come up with one deduction than to survey all structures and realize that a given conclusion is true in every structure in which given premises are. Furthermore, semantic implication is much easier to refute than syntactic implication. It is generally easier to come up with one structure that refutes an implication than to survey all possible deductions and realize that none show a given conclusion follows from given premises.

It's interesting to note that such logical giants as Frege and Russell never even contemplated the completeness theorem. They had such concepts as the distinction between logical symbols ($\neg$, & $\forall$) and nonlogical symbols (Fx for "x is male," c for Rev. Gary Davis) and of logical rule ($\Rightarrow$-elimination). But they had no concept of formal language or of structure. Indeed, they focused on the idea of logical truth rather than the idea of a formula's being valid. They didn't have concepts or the terminology to express the completeness theorem.

A precise proof of the completeness theorem would take more time than is appropriate for an introductory text. But we can appreciate the outline of the proof if we restrict our attention to statement logic and the introduction and elimination rules for the truth functions. With the exception of $\Rightarrow$ I, the rules of statement logic are straightforward and the concept of truth tables is crystal clear compared to that of structures.

>**Little Completeness Theorem.** Suppose A and B are any wffs of statement logic. Then A implies B semantically; that is, every line in the truth table for $A \Rightarrow B$ yields true iff A implies B syntactically (i.e., there is a deduction of B from A).

We first show the easy part: If there is a deduction of B from A, then in the joint truth table of A and B, B is true in every line that A is (i.e., $A \Rightarrow B$ is a tautology).

>**Lemma.** All the introduction and elimination rules of statement logic are *truth preserving*; that is, if any assignment of truth values to statement letters makes the premise(s) of a rule true, it makes the conclusion of the rule true.

EXAMPLE   Suppose A and $A \Rightarrow B$ are both made true by an assignment of truth values to their sentence letters. Then B must be made true (since $T \Rightarrow F$ is F), and so the rule $\Rightarrow$E is truth preserving.

In fact, $\Rightarrow$I also preserves truth, hence the lemma is proven. The remaining difficulty is simply explaining what it means for $\Rightarrow$I to be truth preserving. Some logic texts don't include $\Rightarrow$I as a basic rule, in part because of this difficulty.

The $\Rightarrow$I rule is that if by assuming (and indenting) C, we can then derive D by the other rules, then we can conclude (unindented) $C \Rightarrow D$. In a deduction without premises, we can make the remarkable claim that fully unindented formulas like $C \Rightarrow D$ must be tautologies, but in a deduction using premises such as A, all that follows is that A implies $C \Rightarrow D$.

The reason that $\Rightarrow$I is truth preserving is that the other rules are all truth preserving as you showed: Hence they ensure us that if C is true, then D must be true, and so $C \Rightarrow D$ cannot be false, given the truth of any premise such as A. Consequently, $C \Rightarrow D$ and so the final conclusion, B, is true if A is. (This argument should be modified slightly if there are further assumptions inside the subdeduction in question.)

In summary, if in statement logic A syntactically implies B, then A semantically implies B.

What about the other direction? Is every case of semantic implication validated by a deduction? Yes, and you have already seen a hint

EXERCISE Verify that all the other rules except $\Rightarrow$I are truth preserving.

of how the proof goes in "A Shortcut for Checking Arguments" in part 4. The strategy is to try to make the premise(s) of a purported implication true and the conclusion false. If we succeed, fine, but if we fail, we want to be able to turn our effort into a deduction of the conclusion from the premises.

Essentially, what we do is describe a method that accomplishes systematically what we did somewhat loosely in "Proving Validity" and "Proving Invalidity" in part 6. That is, given an argument, the method either finds a deduction or else discovers a line in the truth table that shows that the argument is invalid.

Given the argument A ∴ B, we start by supposing that there is no deduction, and we search for the elusive line in the truth table that makes A true and B false, that is,

$$A \quad \text{and} \quad \neg B$$

Our procedure is to simplify these statements using the elimination rules. We hope to simplify to the point where everything is either a statement letter or the negation of a statement letter. That will make it easy to assign truth values to the letters (and so locate a line in the truth table). If we assign T to each unnegated letter and F to each negated letter, this will make our original statements A and ¬B true.

EXAMPLE   Does P imply $(\neg(P \,\&\, Q) \vee R)$?
We begin with

$$P$$

and

$$\neg(\neg(P \,\&\, Q) \vee R)$$

The second statement is equivalent to

$$\neg\neg(P \,\&\, Q) \,\&\, \neg R$$

Using &-elimination, we get

$$\neg\neg(P \,\&\, Q)$$

and

$$\neg R$$

Using ¬-elimination and &-elimination again,

$$P$$
$$Q$$

Now we're down to statement letters P, Q, and $\neg R$. We assign P and Q the truth value T and R the value F. This indeed makes the premise (P) true and the conclusion $(\neg(P \& Q) \lor R)$ false. Observe that we could replace the appeal to equivalence by adopting a ¬∨-elimination rule:

$$\frac{\neg(A \lor B)}{\neg A \& \neg B}$$

EXAMPLE Does P imply $(\neg(\neg P \& Q) \lor R)$?

We begin with

$$P$$

and

$$\neg(\neg(\neg P \& Q) \lor R)$$

The second statement is equivalent to

$$\neg\neg(\neg P \& Q) \& \neg R$$

(¬∨-elimination.) Using &-elimination, we get

$$\neg\neg(\neg P \& Q)$$

and

$$\neg R$$

and using ¬-elimination, we get

$$(\neg P \& Q)$$

Using &-elimination again,

$$\neg P$$

and

$$Q$$

Again we are down to statement letters and their negations, but this time the list has a contradiction. We have, from the top, P, $\neg R$,

CHALLENGE   Write a deduction for this argument, following the blueprint given.

$\neg P$, and Q. There is no way to assign truth values that will make them all true. This means that the argument is actually valid. Moreover, we have the blueprint of a deduction!

We start with P as premise. We assume the negation of what we wish to prove (this will be a proof by contradiction), then proceed by the steps above to deduce $\neg P$. From the contradiction $P \& \neg P$, we conclude the negation of the assumption (the double negation of the conclusion), giving us the conclusion.

Unfortunately, the formal proof of the completeness theorem is more complicated. The thoughtful reader might have wondered about wffs such as $B \vee C$. Neither B nor C follows from $B \vee C$. What do we do?

We proceed by allowing the list of statements to branch. Whenever formulas like $B \vee C$ or $\neg (B \& C)$ or $B \Rightarrow C$ appear in the list, we branch:

$$
\begin{array}{ccc}
B \vee C & \neg (B \& C) & B \Rightarrow C \\
\diagup \diagdown & \diagup \diagdown & \diagup \diagdown \\
B \qquad C & \neg B \quad \neg C & \neg B \quad C
\end{array}
$$

If any branch has a consistent set of letters and negated letters, that branch will yield a line of the truth table making true the wffs on top of the list. If, on the other hand, each branch contains contradictions, then, as before, the wffs on top of the list deductively imply a contradiction.

The case of predicate languages is more complicated, but in outline is much the same.

SUMMARY: The completeness theorem shows that the two definitions of implication (and hence the two definitions of a valid wff) are equivalent. Consequently, we can use whichever is more efficient for our purposes.

AXIOMATIZATION AND BOOLEAN ALGEBRA

Pure mathematics was discovered by Boole, in a work which he called the Laws of Thought (1854).

— BERTRAND RUSSELL

In "Sets" in part 4, we noticed the close relationship between the algebra of sets and the algebra of sentential logic. We saw that $\cap$

behaves remarkably like &, that $\cup$ behaves remarkably like $\vee$, and that the complement A^c of a set A bears a striking resemblance to the negation of a statement. Indeed, it is easy to see that an equivalence such as

$$p \vee (q \,\&\, r) \Leftrightarrow (p \vee q) \,\&\, (p \vee r)$$

corresponds neatly to the set equality

$$(P \cup (Q \cap R) = (P \cup Q) \cap (P \cup R)$$

When mathematicians see things like this, they wonder if they have been working too hard. They wonder if they could save time by abstracting the elements common to both situations.

Here is a simpler example: A storekeeper is asked for nine cans of cola. She picks up a six-pack and three loose cans. She learned many years ago that if she puts six cans together with three more cans, she will have nine cans. Later, she sells a canned ham at six dollars and a melon at three dollars for a total of nine dollars. She knows that six dollars and three dollars together make nine dollars.

In fact, the storekeeper is basing both facts on an abstract idea: the idea of number. She understands the equation $6 + 3 = 9$. The number 6 is an abstraction; it is not cans on a shelf or bills in a cash-register. It represents what is common among all collections of six objects (see "Where Do Numbers Come From?" in part 9). She understands how this abstraction can be realized in different contexts.

In a similar way, the nineteenth-century mathematician George Boole abstracted the common ideas from sets and propositions to arrive at the idea of an "algebra." The algebra he constructed now bears his name.

A **Boolean algebra** is a set B of things, together with two operations ♠ and ♣ on B, satisfying the following axioms:

1. Both operations are commutative: $x\,♣\,y = y\,♣\,x$ and $x\,♠\,y = y\,♠\,x$, for all x and y.

2. Each operation is distributive over the other: $x\,♣\,(y\,♠\,z) = (x\,♣\,y)\,♠\,(x\,♣\,z)$ and $x\,♠\,(y\,♣\,z) = (x\,♠\,y)\,♣\,(x\,♠\,z)$ for all x, y, and z.

3. There is an identity for ♠, an element **0** such that $x\,♠\,0 = 0\,♠\,x = x$ for all x.

4. There is an identity for ♣, an element **1** such that $x\,♣\,1 = 1\,♣\,x = x$ for all x.

Note: The symbols ♠ and ♣ are not standard. We have used them because they are generally free of other mathematical connotations. Classically, $+$ and $\cdot$ are used.

405

5. For every x in B, there is a unique element x' such that both $x ♠ x' = \mathbf{1}$ and $x ♣ x' = \mathbf{0}$.

EXAMPLE TRUTH TABLES   Let us suppose that we have just two atomic wffs in Sentential, P and Q. Then there are exactly sixteen possible truth tables:

P Q	1	2	3	4	5	6	7	8	9	10	11	12	13	14	15	16
T T	T	T	T	T	T	T	T	T	F	F	F	F	F	F	F	F
T F	T	T	T	T	F	F	F	F	T	T	T	T	F	F	F	F
F T	T	T	F	F	T	T	F	F	T	T	F	F	T	T	F	F
F F	T	F	T	F	T	F	T	F	T	F	T	F	T	F	T	F

We can form a Boolean algebra using the columns. We will use & for ♣, ∨ for ♠, and ¬ for '. For example,

$$\text{(column 7)} \ ♣ \ \text{(column 13)} = \text{(column 15)}$$

since

T & F	is	F
F & F	is	F
F & T	is	F
T & T	is	T

Similarly, we have

$$\text{(column 3)}' = \text{(column 14)}$$
$$\text{(column 9)} \ ♠ \ \text{(column 2)} = \text{(column 1)}$$

Is this a Boolean algebra? All we have to do is check the five axioms. This is mostly routine work. What is $\mathbf{1}$? It's the truth table with all T's. What is $\mathbf{0}$? It's the truth table with all F's.

EXAMPLE SETS   Let us take the set of all students at Sophist College. Our Boolean algebra consists of all subsets of this set. This is a huge algebra. Even with only 723 students, the algebra has more than

1,000,000,000,000,000,000,000,000,000,000,000,000,000,000,000,
000, 000, 000, 000, 000, 000, 000, 000, 000, 000, 000, 000, 000, 000, 000,
000, 000, 000, 000, 000, 000, 000, 000, 000, 000, 000, 000, 000, 000, 000,
000, 000, 000, 000, 000, 000, 000, 000, 000, 000, 000, 000, 000, 000,
000, 000, 000, 000, 000, 000, 000, 000, 000, 000, 000, 000, 000, elements! We will use $\cap$ for ♣ $\cup$ for ♠. Instead of $'$, we will use ^{c}.
Again, this results in a Boolean algebra. What is **1**? It's the set of all
students at Sophist. What is **0**? It's the set of no students (the empty
set). What is {all sophomores at Sophist}$'$? It's {all freshmen, juniors,
and seniors at Sophist}.

Both examples can be modified to be infinite. In the truth table
example, we can have an infinite number of atomic wffs; in the sets
example, we can take the set of all natural numbers and then look at
its subsets.

But why bother? Doesn't this merely make everything more difficult to understand? Neither sets nor propositions are easy in the first
place. After considerable effort, you get used to them, but Boolean
algebras . . . ?

To answer this, let's return to the storekeeper. She knows, for
example, that 5 percent of 28 is 1.4. This is a fact about abstract
numbers. Now she rings up a purchase of $28 and figures that the 5
percent sales tax amounts to $1.40. She later picks up a package of
laundry soap and reads that it now contains (for the same price) 5
percent more soap. The old package contained 28 ounces, and she
realizes that the new one contains 29.4 ounces. The point is that
knowledge of the abstract object transfers to the concrete. Any work
we do in the abstract pays out benefits in all applications.

Here is an example: We can prove that in every Boolean algebra

$$(a ♣ b)' = a' ♠ b'$$

If we translate this to truth tables, we get

$$\neg(t_1 \,\&\, t_2) = \neg t_1 \vee \neg t_2$$

This is true for all truth tables; in fact, it is a tautology that we can
prove by deduction. We can also apply this to sets to get

$$(A \cap B)^c = A^c \cup B^c$$

This is true for all sets. In fact, it is an equation that we can prove with
Venn diagrams. The point is, however, that we do not need deduction or Venn diagrams, since we have already proven the statement
for Boolean algebras. We have already done the work.

EXAMPLE: A VERY SMALL BOOLEAN ALGEBRA   At the very least, a Boolean algebra must have **0** and **1**. Actually, this is all it needs. There is a Boolean algebra consisting only of **0** and **1**.

EXAMPLE NUMBERS   Consider all the numbers that divide 210 evenly. There are 16 of them: 1, 2, 3, 5, 6, 7, 10, 14, 15, 21, 30, 35, 42, 70, 105, and 210. This, too, is a Boolean algebra. The operation ♣ is "greatest common divisor" and ♠ is "least common multiple." For example, 15 ♣ 6 = 3, and 10 ♠ 35 = 70. The **0** is 1 (we hope this isn't confusing) and the **1** is 210.

Finding the ′ is a bit tricky. Take 10. 10′ should be a number such that the least common multiple of 10 and 10′ is 210 and the greatest common divisor of 10 and 10′ is 1. Well, in the second case, that means that 10 and 10′ have no common factors, so 10′ could be 1, 3, 7, or 21. Since we want the least common multiple of 10 and 10′ to be 210, that means the answer is 21.

The process of collecting the necessary assumptions is called **axiomatization**. The most famous example is Euclid's *Elements*. It is only within the last hundred years, however, that the practice has become widespread.

EXERCISES

1. In a Boolean algebra, what is **0**′ and what is **1**′?
2. In the numbers example, find 2′, 3′, 5′, and 7′. Can you find a formula for n'?
3. In the diagram below, the vertices form a Boolean algebra.

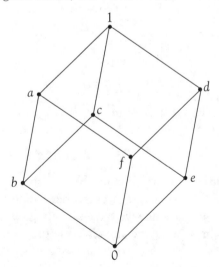

In the figure, **0** is the bottom point, and **1** is the top point. For any two points s and t, s ♣ t is the highest point that is directly below both s and t:

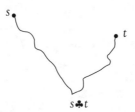

Similarly, s ♠ t is the lowest point that is directly above s and t:

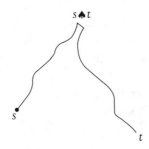

For each point x, find x'.

4. Not every diagram leads to a Boolean algebra. Each of the diagrams below fails but for different reasons. In each case, which axiom fails?

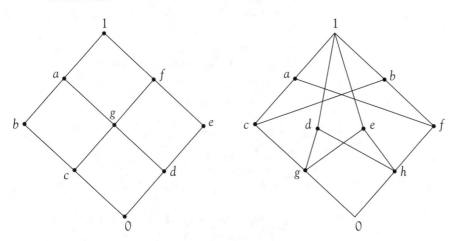

5. Find a deduction for $\neg(t_1 \& t_2) \Leftrightarrow (\neg t_1 \vee \neg t_2)$. (This is not easy.)

6. Show by Venn diagrams that $(A \cap B)^c = A^c \cup B^c$.

We're going to prove $(a \clubsuit b)' = a' \spadesuit b'$ for all Boolean algebras. To do so, we need some lemmas (propositions whose only purpose is to help us prove more propositions).

7. Fill in the reasons for each step (each reason should be one of the axioms).

Lemma 1 : $1 \spadesuit a = 1$.

$$1 = a \spadesuit a'$$
$$= a \spadesuit (a' \clubsuit 1)$$
$$= (a \spadesuit a') \clubsuit (a \spadesuit 1)$$
$$= 1 \clubsuit (a \spadesuit 1)$$
$$= a \spadesuit 1$$
$$= 1 \spadesuit a$$

For each of the following, fill in the reasons (you may use previous lemmas as well as axioms).

8. Lemma 2: $0 \clubsuit a = 0$

$$0 = a \clubsuit a'$$
$$= a \clubsuit (a' \spadesuit 0)$$
$$= (a \clubsuit a') \spadesuit (a \clubsuit 0)$$
$$= 1 \spadesuit (a \clubsuit 0)$$
$$= a \clubsuit 0$$
$$= 0 \clubsuit a$$

9. Lemma 3: $(a \clubsuit b) \clubsuit a' = 0$

$$(a \clubsuit b) \clubsuit a' = a' \clubsuit (a \clubsuit b)$$
$$= 0 \spadesuit (a' \clubsuit (a \clubsuit b))$$
$$= (a \clubsuit a') \spadesuit (a' \clubsuit (a \clubsuit b))$$
$$= (a' \clubsuit a) \spadesuit (a' \clubsuit (a \clubsuit b))$$
$$= a' \clubsuit (a \spadesuit (a \clubsuit b))$$
$$= a' \clubsuit ((a \clubsuit 1) \spadesuit (a \clubsuit b))$$
$$= a' \clubsuit (a \clubsuit (1 \spadesuit b))$$
$$= a' \clubsuit (a \clubsuit 1)$$
$$= a' \clubsuit a$$
$$= 0$$

10. Lemma 4: $a \spadesuit (a' \spadesuit b) = 1$

$$a \spadesuit (a' \spadesuit b') = 1 \clubsuit (a \spadesuit (a' \spadesuit b))$$
$$= (a \spadesuit a') \clubsuit (a \spadesuit (a' \spadesuit b))$$
$$= a \spadesuit (a' \clubsuit (a' \spadesuit b))$$
$$= a \spadesuit ((a' \spadesuit 0) \clubsuit (a' \spadesuit b))$$
$$= a \spadesuit (a' \spadesuit (0 \clubsuit b))$$
$$= a \spadesuit (a' \spadesuit 0)$$
$$= a \spadesuit a'$$
$$= 1$$

Now we are ready to prove $(a \clubsuit b)' = a' \spadesuit b'$. We will use the last axiom. It says that $(a \clubsuit b)'$ is the *unique* element z such that $(a \clubsuit b) \spadesuit z = 1$ and $(a \clubsuit b) \clubsuit z = 0$. What we will do is show that $a' \spadesuit b'$ *also* has these properties, and since $(a \clubsuit b)'$ is unique, then the two must be the same. Thus, we must prove $(a \clubsuit b) \spadesuit (a' \spadesuit b') = 1$ and $(a \clubsuit b) \clubsuit (a' \spadesuit b') = 0$. Fill in the reasons.

11. Lemma 5: $(a \clubsuit b) \spadesuit (a' \spadesuit b') = 1$

$$(a \clubsuit b) \spadesuit (a' \spadesuit b') = (a' \spadesuit b') \spadesuit (a \clubsuit b)$$
$$= ((a' \spadesuit b') \spadesuit a) \clubsuit ((a' \spadesuit b') \spadesuit b)$$
$$= (a \spadesuit (a' \spadesuit b')) \clubsuit (b \spadesuit (a' \spadesuit b'))$$
$$= (a \spadesuit (a' \spadesuit b')) \clubsuit (b \spadesuit (b' \spadesuit a'))$$
$$= 1 \clubsuit 1$$
$$= 1$$

12. Lemma 6: $(a \clubsuit b) \clubsuit (a' \spadesuit b') = 0$

$$(a \clubsuit b) \clubsuit (a' \spadesuit b') = ((a \clubsuit b) \clubsuit a') \spadesuit ((a \clubsuit b) \clubsuit b')$$
$$= ((a \clubsuit b) \clubsuit a') \spadesuit ((b \clubsuit a) \clubsuit b')$$
$$= 0 \clubsuit 0$$
$$= 0$$

with & about logic
believing and knowing

> Lord, I believe; help thou my unbelief.
> —Augustine

Knowledge and belief are both central concepts of philosophy, psychology, and common sense. To form beliefs and to act on them is the hallmark of a rational being. The lower animals, on the other hand, seem only to respond to stimuli. Some philosophers have suggested that having beliefs is the essential property of a mind, that no merely physical thing could have beliefs. Others have argued that eventually even computers will be able to have beliefs.

Knowledge is traditionally defined as belief plus other things. To know something, you must believe it—it must be true, and you must have good reason to believe it (no lucky guesses). Gaining knowledge is often considered a primary human good and is the primary rationale for establishing schools. The study of knowledge is itself a major branch of philosophy (called epistemology). One of the central questions of epistemology is that of skepticism—do we really know anything? Perhaps life is just a dream, full of sound and fury, signifying nothing. In this section, we're going to bypass the major questions and try to get some handle on the details of belief and knowledge. We hope to get some practice reading predicate symbolism and to make some headway on the Surprise Exam arguments of Laura Logic and company.

Knowledge and belief are best construed as relations, Bxp and Kxp, between intelligent beings on the one hand—you, me, Alexei, Julianna—and propositions or statements on the other—$2 + 2 = 4$, Paris is the capital of France, Henle's middle name is Juan. (There is a second sense of "knowing" according to which it's a relation between people and things, like "I know Jim," "Jim knows French," "Bo knows baseball." That sense is not relevant here.)

Thus, if a is Alexei and b is Julianna and p is the proposition "God exists," then "Alexei knows that God exists" can be represented as Kap and "Julianna believes that God doesn't exist" can be represented as $Bb'\neg p'$. (Strictly speaking, our usage is somewhat lax. In the wffs representing knowledge and belief, a name for the statement appears in the second place, just like a name for the subject appears in the first place. Hence our writing "'$\neg p$'" is slightly illicit. We should write instead "the negation of p." However, no harm will come from the looser, but more suggestive usage. So occasionally we enclose the believed proposition in single quotation marks, as '$\neg p$' or 'A & B.') Perhaps we should treat these propositions as three-place relations $Kxyt$ and $Bxyt$ to allow a place for time. Then we could express change of mind as in "I used to believe that Santa Claus brought me toys, but I don't believe it now." We ignore this complication in what follows.

All the laws of logic apply to belief and knowledge. By the law of the excluded middle, either x believes y or x doesn't believe y—$Bxy \lor \neg Bxy$. But this is not to say that for any statement y either x believes y or x believes its negation—$Bxy \lor Bx\neg y$. There might be many things that x has no opinion about. Indeed, it seems quite reasonable that for any person there will be some statement that the person has no opinion about—$\forall x \exists y (\neg Bxy$ & $\neg Bx\neg y)$.

Are there any general statements that hold true for belief and knowledge? We're interested in what can be expressed using the symbols of logic. Any general truth can be seen as a law or principle governing the concepts of knowledge and belief. So we might say our project is to sketch the logic of these concepts. Let's begin with belief.

An inconsistent believer would have inconsistent or contradictory beliefs: x is inconsistent iff $\exists p(Bxp \,\&\, Bx\neg p)$. This would be true if x believed that God exists and x believed that God doesn't exist, or if x believed that the world was round and x believed that the world was not round. Note that this is not the same as having a false belief —$Bxp \,\&\, \neg p$—all humans are fallible. But are we actually inconsistent? There is at least some reason to idealize the situation and assume that all believers are consistent—$\forall x\neg\exists p(Bxp \,\&\, Bx\neg p)$—or what amounts to the same thing, $\forall x\,\forall p(Bxp \Rightarrow \neg Bx\neg p)$.

One good reason for supposing that believers are consistent is so that we can suppose that they are rational. Let's say that a believer x is rational if she applies *modus ponens* ($\Rightarrow$E) when she can; that is, if Bxp and $Bx\,'p \Rightarrow q\,'$, then, Bxq.

CHALLENGE 1
Show that these formulas are equivalent.

EXAMPLES

    If x believes "it rains" and x believes "it rains" $\Rightarrow$ "ground's wet," then x believes "ground's wet."

    If x believes "Gorbachev's in danger" and x believes that "Gorbachev's in danger" $\Rightarrow$ "the United States is in danger," then x believes "the United States is in danger."

Let's call the claim that believers are rational the "principle of *modus ponens* for belief," or MPB for short, and formalize it as

$$\forall x\,\forall p\,\forall q((Bxp \,\&\, Bx\,'p \Rightarrow q\,') \Rightarrow Bxq)$$

CHALLENGE 2
Show that MPB is equivalent to the wff

$\forall x\,\forall p\,\forall q(Bx\,'p \Rightarrow q\,'$
$\qquad\qquad \Rightarrow (Bxp \Rightarrow Bxq))$

Next, we say a believer is logical is she believes any truth of logic; that is, if p is valid, then Bxp. The claim that all believers are logical can be called the "principle of logical belief," or LB, and represented informally as

    for any p, if p is valid, then Bxp

CHALLENGE 3

Show that, given LB and MPB, if x believes p & q, then x believes q— Bx'p & q' $\Rightarrow Bxq$.

CHALLENGE 4

Suppose x is inconsistent, logical, and rational. Show that x believes anything, that is, Bxq for any statement q. Thus, in the presence of inconsistent belief, MPB and LB lead to a trivial concept of belief.

PUZZLE Human beings are fallible and so believe false statements. You are reasonable and probably believe you are fallible. O.K., give one example of a false belief you have.

CHALLENGE 5

Knowers are consistent. Show that TC implies that $\forall x\forall p(Kxp \Rightarrow \neg Kx$'$\neg p$').

EXAMPLES

A & $B \Rightarrow B$ is valid $\therefore Bx$'A & $B \Rightarrow B$'
$\forall xFx \Leftrightarrow \neg\exists x\neg Fx$ is valid $\therefore Bx$'$\forall xFx \Leftrightarrow \neg\exists x\neg Fx$'

We mention a few more putative principles of belief. A very famous one is known as "double B," or BB. It says that if you believe something, you believe that you believe it —$\forall x\forall p(Bxp \Rightarrow Bx$'$Bxp$'). Does this seem plausible to you? An example: If x believes x loves y, x believes that x believes x loves y.

How about the converse law, $\forall x\forall p(Bx$'Bxp' $\Rightarrow Bxp)$? It would be rash to assume that all of x's beliefs were true, but could x be wrong in his beliefs about his beliefs?

Let us now turn to knowledge and see whether any of these alleged principles of belief carry over or whether new principles arise. The traditional analysis of knowledge is "justified true belief." In effect, it defines Kxp by

$$Kxp \text{ iff } p \text{ \& } Bxp \text{ \& "}x \text{ is justified in believing } p\text{"}$$

The most prominent contrast between knowledge and belief is the truth condition for knowledge, TC, which we can express (with a grain of salt) as

$$\forall x\forall p(Kxp \Rightarrow p)$$

EXAMPLES OF TC

If you know the earth is round, then the earth is round.
If you know the earth is flat, then the earth is flat.

We are infallible as knowers. This does not mean that we can't be wrong when we claim knowledge. All it means is that if x claims to know p but $\neg p$ is the case, then x doesn't really know p. In other words, $\forall x\forall p(\neg p \Rightarrow \neg Kxp)$. On the other hand, x can still believe a falsehood, even though it is false.

The second important difference between knowledge and belief concerns justification. Belief is a brute mental fact. You can happen to believe p just because your parents told you, or you were brainwashed, or you're slightly batty. What you believe is independent of how you came to believe it. Not so with knowledge. Lucky guesses don't count as knowledge; you must actually have acceptable reasons for your beliefs to count as knowledge. We won't go into the matter of acceptable reasons here. That is one of the primary issues of epistemology. But we will say that a logical demonstration certainly counts as an acceptable reason. Thus an analogous principle to LB, logical knowledge (LK), holds for knowledge:

$$\text{If } p \text{ is valid, then } Kxp$$

Similarly, MPK should hold for knowledge—we can extend knowledge by logical reasoning:

$$Kx'p \Rightarrow q' \Rightarrow (Kxp \Rightarrow Kxq) \qquad \text{for any } x, p, q$$

(You should write down some instances of LK and MPK to be sure you know what they mean.)

Finally, philosophers have seriously debated the "if you know something, you know that you know it" (KK) principle:

$$Kxp \Rightarrow Kx'Kxp' \qquad \text{for any } x, p, q$$

In the past, philosophers were more inclined to accept this principle, but it has come under some serious criticism recently. On the other hand, the principles LK, MPK, and TC seem very plausible, at least as idealizations. Can you think of any objections to them?

We've traced out a minimal logic of belief and knowledge. Later we shall see how some of these principles are relevant to the surprise exam argument.

the law of the excluded middle

> There are three kinds of logicians in the world, those who accept the law of the excluded middle and those who don't.
>
> —ANONYMOUS

What can be more certain than a law of logic? And what law of logic is simpler or more certain than the law of the excluded middle, for any statement A, either A is T or A is F ($\neg A$ is T). There is no middle ground between truth and falsity, hence the name "excluded middle."

And what can be more convincing than the truth table demonstration of this fact?

A	A ∨ ¬A
T	T
F	T

In this section, we'll mention three reasons logicians have given for thinking that the law of the excluded middle should not be a law of logic. Of course, if it's not a law of logic, then there is something wrong with the truth table explanation that suggests that it is.

The Problem of Future Contingents

Beginning with Aristotle, philosophers have worried that if the law of the excluded middle were valid, this might force an unwanted fatalism upon us. The argument for fatalism goes something like this.

Suppose that there is to be an election tomorrow and that your favored candidate is David Bar-Hillel. By the law A ∨ ¬A, either David Bar-Hillel will win the election tomorrow or David Bar-Hillel will not win the election tomorrow. This alternation is logically true, so it is true now, and so one of its alternants must be true now. Suppose it's the first. Then Bar-Hillel will win, and if he will win, there's no need for you to vote for him. Suppose it's the second that's true. Then Bar-Hillel won't win, and if he won't win, there's no point in your voting for him. Either way, your vote is wasted.

This fatalistic conclusion is not very attractive to most people, but it is clear that similar arguments could be given for any statement about the future.

If we're unhappy with the conclusion, and we believe the only way to avoid it is to give up the law of the excluded middle, then we have a motive for altering logic. The Polish logician Lukasiewicz took just this tack. He suggested modifying logic by adding a third value, "neither true nor false," which he represented by I. We give a few of Lukasiewicz's revised truth tables below.

CHALLENGE 1 Give a fatalistic argument explaining why you don't need to be careful when you're crossing the street. Be sure to highlight the presence of the law of the excluded middle in your argument.

416

A	¬A		A	B	A ∨ B		A	B	A & B
T	F		T	T	T		T	T	T
I	I		T	I	T		T	I	I
F	T		T	F	T		T	F	F
			I	T	T		I	T	I
			I	I	I		I	I	I
			I	F	I		I	F	F
			F	T	T		F	T	F
			F	I	I		F	I	F
			F	F	F		F	F	F

Notice that according to the tables, A ∨ ¬A does not always get the value T; sometimes it gets the value I (when A is I). He suggested that statements about the future that are contingent or dependent on circumstances should not be regarded as true or as false but only as indeterminate, or I. Hence the law of the excluded middle does not apply to such statements and our argument for fatalism does not go through.

Vague Predicates

Another alleged difficulty for the law of the excluded middle concerns vague predicates, such as "is tall," "is heavy," and "is bright." In traditional logic, we like to think of predicates as being perfectly precise — "is six feet tall" or "is a U.S. citizen." For a precise predicate Fx, it makes sense to suppose of any object c that either Fc or ¬Fc. But what of vague predicates? Either Tom is overweight or he is not. Must that be true? Some philosophers suggest that there is a middle ground; Tom might *fail to* be overweight, but we shouldn't go far as to say that he's not overweight. Vague predicates carry some of the same potential for argumentative fallacy that future contingents did: If Tom's not overweight, then drinking one more milkshake won't hurt him. And if he's already, one more milkshake won't make that much difference. Down the hatch!

But what if Tom's on the borderline between obesity and happy poundage? Hasn't this natural middle alternative been unfairly excluded? The ancients recognized the difficulty of applying precise logic to vague predicates and gave a special name to a paradigm case: the "paradox of the heap," or the sorites paradox. Suppose someone

CHALLENGE 2

Can you find an objection to your argument for fatalism that does not involve the excluded middle? If there was another flaw in the argument, then we might not have to abandon the law of the excluded middle.

CHALLENGE 3

Can you explain why Lukasiewicz included the following lines in his tables: T ∨ I is T, F ∨ I is I, T & I is I, and F & I is F?

417

were to dump a heap of sand in your yard. If you removed just one grain from the heap, you'd still have a heap of sand left. (Otherwise, you might have to specify an exact number that differentiates heaps —say 18,000 grains of sand—from nonheaps—say 17,999 grains of sand or less. This seems ludicrous.) Then if you removed just one grain from the slightly smaller heap, you'd still have a heap of sand left. And so on.

Now, if you continued this argument through 18,000 or so steps, you'd come to the conclusion that even one grain of sand constitutes a heap! But that is ridiculous. Something has gone wrong somewhere. A few logicians, among them the great Frege, concluded that logic simply doesn't apply to vague predicates. More exactly, Frege suggested that vague predicates don't designate concepts. This position is tenable as long as we can get by without using vague predicates. But if the rational person must appeal to vagueness, then we should look for an alternative logic that takes vagueness into account.

The computer scientist Zadeh has proposed a new kind of logic to deal with vague predicates, which is called fuzzy logic, or sometimes degrees-of-truth logic. Zadeh claims that the true–false dichotomy is misleading, just as the black–white dichotomy is. In reality we find many shades of gray and many degrees of truth. A statement like "Robins are birds" is very, very true. A statement like "Chickens are birds" is pretty true, and a statement like "Ostriches are birds" is only somewhat true according to our usual ways of thinking. For Zadeh and his followers, truth comes in degrees. Precise predicates (being exactly six feet tall) have only two degrees, total truth or total falsity. Vague predicates are fuzzy–they may come in many degrees.

According to Zadeh, the usual laws of logic do not apply to fuzzy predicates. Here is how he solves the paradox of the heap. That someone dumped a heap of sand in your yard, he admits, is very certainly true (say 0.9999% true). And each conditional — if you take one grain of sand from a heap, the result is still a heap — is also very true. But when you chain these conditionals together, you lose some truth value. $A \Rightarrow B$ might be 0.99% true and $B \Rightarrow C$ might be 0.99% true, but their conjunction (and hence the conditional $A \Rightarrow C$) might be only 0.98% true. The more conditionals you chain, the more truth you lose. Eventually you can even pass from a virtual truth (there is a heap of sand in my yard) to a virtual falsehood (this one grain of sand is a heap).

Zadeh's logic is difficult to describe on an elementary level. But it agrees with a certain intuition we have (one step in the sorites paradox does not cause problems; it is the sheer number of steps that causes the difficulty). And fuzzy logic is generating excitement among many engineers and computer scientists.

Infinity and Intuitionism

The last objection to the law of excluded middle is perhaps the most serious one. According to a group of logicians known (misleadingly) as "intuitionists," classical logic rests on a fundamental mistake. The fundamental mistake is to regard the concepts of true and false as if they indicated some match between our statements and the world. So we say either P matches the world (T) or it doesn't (F). Instead, say the intuitionists, the fundamental modes of speech are "justified assertion" and "justified denial." We are justified in asserting P (saying P is T") only when we have some kind of convincing demonstration of P. Similarly, we are justified in asserting $\neg P$ (saying P is F) only when we have some kind of convincing demonstration that P is impossible. Quite obviously, under this interpretation, $P \vee \neg P$ is not generally valid. For we may be in no position to assert P and in no position to deny P. We may just be ignorant.

At first glance, intuitionists seem to confuse the subjective grounds for our assertions with the objective grounds of their being true or false. Even though we are ignorant of whether P or $\neg P$, says the classical logician, exactly one of these propositions is true in objective reality. But the deep intuitionist criticism is that classical logic misdraws the subjective–objective distinction. There is really no subject-independent, objective reality! This controversy has excited much discussion in recent philosophy with defenders of classical logic calling themselves "realists" and defenders of intuitionism, "anti-realists."

One exciting outcome of the debate is the thought that there is a deep connection between logic and metaphysics. We can bring this idea out by considering the intuitionists' concept of infinity. For intuitionists, infinity is not a big number or a big set—it is simply a rule for going on. (Hence intuitionists' concept of infinity is very like the ancient concept of potential infinity.) A universal statement about numbers, $\forall x F x$, holds only if we establish that each number x has property F. An existential statement about numbers, $\exists x F x$, holds only if we construct a number that has property F. However, for many statements about natural numbers, it will neither be that $\forall x F x$ nor

EXERCISE   Show that $\exists x \neg Fx$ is classically equivalent to $\neg\forall xFx$ and hence that $\forall xFx \vee \exists x \neg Fx$ is classically equivalent to the law of the excluded middle.

that $\exists x \neg Fx$, so that $\forall xFx \vee \exists x \neg Fx$ is not intuitionistically valid. But it *is* classically valid.

The classical logician insists that either $\forall xFx$ holds, that is, Fx holds for each of the infinitely many natural numbers, or that $\exists x \neg Fx$ holds, regardless of whether we know it. The intuitionist replies that this is a superstitious view of numbers, that it presupposes that the numbers are already there without any input from human beings. This is just not so according to intuitionists; numbers are human creations, like paintings or symphonies.

Intuitionist logic is the most developed and the most interesting of alternative logics. Its crucial feature is the denial of $\neg$E: $\neg\neg A \Rightarrow A$ is not intuitionistically valid (even though we can refute any refutation of A, it does not follow that we can demonstrate A). Because many classical laws of logic rest on the law of $\neg$E, they must be given up. These include the law of the excluded middle, the definitions of the truth functions in terms of each other, and the definitions of each quantifier in terms of the other.

Intuitionistic logic can be derived if we keep all the deduction rules from the sections on deduction except $\neg$E. Thus $\neg\neg A \therefore A$ must be given up. If in its place, we put $C \,\&\, \neg C \therefore B$, we get intuitionistic logic.

Intuitionistic logic and the philosophy and mathematics behind it were developed by the Dutch logician L. E. J. Brouwer. It was the Dutch who kept this school alive for the first half of the century until it took hold among logicians at large.

from puzzle to paradox

To expect the unexpected shows a thoroughly modern intellect.
—Oscar Wilde

Many forms of the surprise exam puzzle have been discussed in the last fifty years. Sometimes a teacher announces that there will be an exam on one day of the next week and the students will not know even on the morning of the exam that there will be an exam that day. Sometimes a judge decrees that a criminal will be hanged on a certain day of the next week, but the criminal will not know on the morning of his hanging that he will be hanged that day (the surprise hanging puzzle). Or there might be a series of eggs, one of them rotten, and it is said that you won't know which one is the rotten one until after you break it open.

In each case the scenario seems perfectly plausible, but in each case there is an argument that the scenario is actually impossible. The arguments are basically the same. Here is a rough version for the egg case.

It can't be the last egg we open that is rotten, for otherwise we'd know it to be rotten before we broke it open (since we've already opened all the other eggs). But if we got to the next-to-last egg without any surprise, then since we've eliminated the last egg as a surprise egg, any surprise rotten egg must be the next-to-last egg. Hence we'd know the next-to-last egg is rotten but then we wouldn't be surprised. We continue to reason in this manner, eliminating all possibilities and conclude that we can't be surprised by a rotten egg in any position. Of course, when we open the first, or fifth, or last egg and find it rotten, we are surprised! We just proved it couldn't happen!

The gist of the surprise puzzle in terms of exams is this. Initially a surprise exam seems possible. But then the student seems to have a perfectly good argument that a surprise exam can't be given. Not only does this conflict with our intuition that the teacher *could* give a surprise exam, but the very fact that the student is convinced that there cannot be a surprise exam makes it *easier* for the teacher to surprise him! ("Hey! I thought you couldn't do that," the student complains.)

The puzzle, then, is to resolve the conflict. We should either find a flaw in the student's reasoning or explain why the teacher can't really give a surprise exam after all. Not too many people opt for the latter alternative, since it seems so obvious that the teacher can surprise her students (but we've known a few people who think the puzzle shows that surprise exams are logically impossible). Most people feel there's something wrong with the argument.

Many people say the fault of the argument is that the student "reasons backwards," eliminating first the last day, then the next to the last day, and so on. It is true that the student proceeds this way, but the reasoning is unobjectionable. The student doesn't have to get to the last day in order to eliminate it. He can know today that if he gets to the last day without an exam, then he will know the exam will be on the last day. This would conflict with the teacher's announcement, and the student can know this on the first day.

In our opinion, the student gives a valid argument—at least a valid argument if we assume some commonly accepted principles of

CHALLENGE 1

Write out a version of the surprise hanging puzzle. Try to be careful and convincing. Exactly what does the judge say to the prisoner? What is the prisoner's argument? Where is the puzzle?

421

knowledge. (One of the interesting things about puzzles and paradoxes is that they focus our attention on principles that are commonly accepted without much thought.) But the crucial fact of the student's argument is that he does not merely assume that what the teacher said is true, he assumes that *he knows* that what the teacher said is true. To appreciate this point, consider what happens when the student survives the next-to-last day without an exam. Given that an exam will come that week, it is true that the exam will be on the last day ("tomorrow" from his point of view). Although the teacher has said that the student won't know the exam will be "tomorrow," so far there is no contradiction. The exam is tomorrow, the last day, and the student does not know the exam is tomorrow. These are consistent statements. (Compare: "Frege was the greatest logician the world has ever seen but Madonna doesn't know that Frege was the greatest logician the world has ever seen." Perfectly reasonable.) To get a contradiction, the student needs to know the exam will be tomorrow (this is what contradicts the surprise element). Even if he knows that the exam hasn't been on any other day this week, he still can't conclude that he knows the exam is tomorrow unless he knows the exam is on one day this week. So it is not enough that the student assumes that what the teacher said is true; he must assume that he knows that what the teacher said is true.

Perhaps you can now see the outline of a solution to the surprise exam puzzle. We can accept that the student's *argument* is correct! Then, since he derives a contradiction from his assumption, this means his *assumption* is wrong. His assumption is that he knows that what the teacher said is true; it is not simply that what the teacher said is true. (If the latter were his assumption, then the teacher *couldn't* give a surprise exam.) But the student's assumption is that he knows what the teacher said is true, and it is this assumption that the student's argument refutes. Consequently, it is false that the student knows that there will be a surprise exam next week, even though an honest teacher told him. And because he doesn't know, it is relatively easy for the teacher to surprise him.

Let's try to give a version of the argument in symbolic form. This particular version is useful, because it eliminates time from the puzzle. We imagine a teacher telling her students that they will have an exam the very day of her announcement only they don't know they have an exam that day (today)! A major advantage of symbolization is that it forces us to recognize certain general principles about knowledge that the student uses in his argument — even if the student's use is not explicit. You should keep in mind the possibility that one or more of the "principles" of knowledge are really just false beliefs on the part of the student! That would be another way to resolve the puzzle.

In general, we'll let S stand for any statement and let $K(S)$ stand for the statement that the student knows statement S before the relevant time, or in this case, before the last day. This notation glosses over some crucial points. We really should consider a knowledge relation Kxy—"person x knows statement y." And we should distinguish between a statement S and a name of the statement "S"—it's the name that fits with the knowledge predicate, as we saw in "Believing and Knowing." But the present choice is simpler and accurate enough for starters.

Now let T be the statement "The students will have an exam today." Hence $K(T)$ is the statement that the student knows he will have an exam today and $\neg K(T)$ is the statement that the student doesn't know he will have an exam today. The teacher begins by announcing

$$T \ \& \ \neg K(T) \tag{1}$$

The student begins by assuming that he knows that what the teacher said is true. (She, the teacher, is honest, intelligent, never wrong, and so on.) So the student assumes

$$K(T \ \& \ \neg K(T)) \tag{2}$$

Let's see how the student can derive a contradiction from wff (2).

Because of the logical facts that

$$(A \ \& \ B) \Rightarrow A \qquad \text{and} \qquad (A \ \& \ B) \Rightarrow B$$

it is a matter of logic that

$$(T \ \& \ \neg K(T)) \Rightarrow T \qquad \text{and} \qquad (T \ \& \ \neg K(T)) \Rightarrow \neg K(T) \tag{3}$$

Now, let's assume that the student knows logic! In particular, we assume the principle of logical knowledge, LK—"If A is valid, $K(A)$." We can apply LK as in the following examples:

Since $\neg\neg T \Leftrightarrow T$ is valid, the student knows it: $K(\neg\neg T \Leftrightarrow T)$.
Since $(A \ \& \ B) \Rightarrow B$ is valid, $K((A \ \& \ B) \Rightarrow B)$.

Given LK and line (3), it follows that the student knows line (3). Thus

$$K[(T \ \& \ \neg K(T)) \Rightarrow T] \qquad \text{and} \qquad K[(T \ \& \ \neg K(T)) \Rightarrow \neg K(T)] \tag{4}$$

Because of (2), we know that the student knows the antecedent of each conditional (because (2) is just $K(T \& \neg K(T))$). Unfortunately, that's not enough to conclude that the student knows the consequent of the conditional. For that we need another principle of knowledge — you know what follows from what you know:

$$(K(A \Rightarrow B) \& K(A)) \Rightarrow K(B)$$

or equivalently

$$K(A \Rightarrow B) \Rightarrow (K(A) \Rightarrow K(B))$$

Recall that this is the principle of *modus ponens* knowledge, or MPK. Notice it is different both from $\Rightarrow$E and from LK. By MPK we have

$$K[(T \& \neg K(T)) \Rightarrow T] \Rightarrow (K[T \& \neg K(T)] \Rightarrow K(T)) \qquad (5)$$

and so by (2), (4), and $\Rightarrow$E (twice), we have

$$K(T) \qquad (6)$$

Perhaps it would be useful to see the steps arranged as a logical deduction.

1. $K(T \& \neg K(T))$ premise
2. $(T \& \neg K(T)) \Rightarrow T$ Taut., $(A \& B) \Rightarrow A$
3. $(T \& \neg K(T)) \Rightarrow \neg K(T)$ Taut., $(A \& B) \Rightarrow B$
4. $K[(T \& \neg K(T)) \Rightarrow T]$ LK, 2
5. $K[(T \& \neg K(T)) \Rightarrow \neg K(T)]$ LK, 3
6. $K[(T \& \neg K(T)) \Rightarrow T] \Rightarrow$
       $K[T \& \neg K(T)] \Rightarrow K(T)$ MPK
7. $K[T \& \neg K(T)] \Rightarrow K(T)$ $\Rightarrow$E, 4, 6
8. $K(T)$ $\Rightarrow$E, 1, 7

CHALLENGE 2

Derive statement (7) $K(\neg K(T))$ in a similar fashion.

If you met the challenge, you have now proven that $K(T)$ (the student knows there will be an exam tomorrow) and $K(\neg K(T))$ (the student knows that he does not know there is an exam tomorrow), but this is still not quite a contradiction — although it sure is strange, given the meaning of K ("knows").

However, we get a contradiction by invoking one more principle of knowledge. This is the truth condition, which states that you can know only true things. In words, what you know is true. Recall that in symbols the truth condition (TC) is $K(S) \Rightarrow S$ for any statement S. (More exactly, $K(\text{"}S\text{"}) \Rightarrow S$.) Hence

$$K(\neg K(T)) \Rightarrow \neg K(T) \qquad (8)$$

This is just TC applied with (7) as S.

Now by (7), (8), and standard logic ($\Rightarrow$E), we have

$$\neg K(T) \tag{9}$$

Since we already have $K(T)$ (this is just (6), which we proved above), we have derived a contradiction $K(T)\ \&\ \neg K(T)$ from the premise or from assumption (2). Consequently, the student's argument establishes that, given the principles of knowledge LK, MPK, and TC, he doesn't know what the teacher said is true

$$\neg(2) \qquad \text{or} \qquad \neg K[T\ \&\ \neg K(T)]$$

This argument is important for a number of reasons. First, since it concerns only a single day, it dispels the idea that time is a crucial ingredient of the puzzle. Second, it shows that the student really needs the assumption that he knows what the teacher said and not merely the weaker assumption that what the teacher said is true. This helps to explain our conflicting intuitions: The student gives a good argument (from assumption (2)), but the argument doesn't prove that what the teacher said (1) is false.

Finally, our version highlights some of the epistemic principles involved in the argument. Most people pass over these without explicitly mentioning them, but in dealing with a paradox, it is important to get all your assumptions on the board, even such commonsensical ones as LK, MPK, and TC.

Have we really resolved the puzzle? Perhaps to some extent, but we're left with a residual puzzle. The student cannot know that what the teacher said is true even if he has very good evidence for it. In fact, he can't know it even if he has the best possible evidence for that kind of statement! Indeed, he can't know it even if God told him the teacher was telling the truth! (Just suppose God told him and the student claimed to know that what God said was true. That's assumption (2), and the argument shows that this assumption is contradictory.) In fact, the student can't know if what the teacher said is true even if the teacher herself is God! This is very surprising if not actually paradoxical.

Well, it's pretty close to paradoxical (not being able to trust God, that is). What would make it really paradoxical for a logician? Suppose we had an argument just as good as the student's argument that he can't know what the teacher said was true, only this argument showed that he *did know* what the teacher said was true. That would be a paradox!

CHALLENGE 3

Can you find another derivation of a contradiction using (1) and (2) but not using TC?

Among the many essays written on the surprise exam and its variants, by far the greatest is by two philosophical logicians, Montague and Kaplan. They did something better than solve the surprise exam puzzle. They found a genuine paradox lying at its foundation. Their paper is called "A Paradox Regained," and the paradox they found they called the "paradox of the knower."

Suppose the teacher said to you students not that you will have a surprise exam but instead a statement G, where

G:= "You do not, and will not, know that this very statement is true."

Well, suppose the statement is false. Then you *do* or *will know* it is true, and so by the truth condition for knowledge (TC), the statement is true. So if it is false, it's true. Therefore it must be true—the teacher is telling the truth.

Did you follow that argument? We hope so—after all, it is a pretty simple logical argument. Hence by the principle of logical knowledge (LK), you ought to know the conclusion of the argument. So you know statement G. But since G says you don't know G, then G is false.

Hence G is both true and false, and this is impossible. But this argument uses no extra assumptions. It is a valid argument that utilizes the epistemic principles mentioned plus one other. Let us finish up by formalizing the paradox of the knower.

Consider the statement

"You don't know that statement G is true"   or $\neg K(G)$ (a)

Since G is that very statement, we can write this information as

$$G \Leftrightarrow \neg K(G) \qquad (b)$$

(In fact, we can prove in more advanced logic that there are statements like G that refer to themselves in just this fashion.)

Could G be false? Suppose so. Since G says you don't know it, if G is false, then you *do know* G. But if you know G, then it is true (because of TC, the principle that you know only truths). Thus if G is false, it is true. This must mean that G is true. Hence, if we assume TC, then G is true.

Thus $K(G) \Rightarrow G$ implies G. In English, the truth condition— you only know truths—implies that you don't know G.

This result is quite curious but not in itself disastrous. It shows that there are some truths that you don't know. But you probably never thought of yourself as omniscient. G is an example of a truth you don't know.

The paradox sets in when you reflect on your relation to G. It's not that you irrationally believe G or that you took a lucky guess. It is that you seem to have given a very good proof of G! But if you've proven G, then surely you know what you've proven; you know G (that's the principle LK). And if you know G, then G is false and this is a contradiction. A contradiction is never true, so there is something wrong with your reasoning. What?

Before answering that, let's try to prove that you know G. What we do is go back over the above argument that TC implies G and use it to show that someone who follows the argument knows G. We saw above that the following is a logical principle:

$$[K(G) \Rightarrow G] \Rightarrow G \quad \text{or, more generally,} \quad TC \Rightarrow G$$

That is, you can deduce this from the principles of logic. Recall that what you can deduce from the principles of logic (LK), you know.

$$TC \Rightarrow G \text{ is valid} \therefore K(TC \Rightarrow G)$$

So we have that you know that if the truth condition (only truths are known) is true, then you don't know G.

By the principle MPK,

$$K(TC \Rightarrow G) \Rightarrow [K(TC) \Rightarrow K(G)]$$

(If you know that the truth condition implies G, then if you know the truth condition, you know G.) But you do know the antecedent, therefore, by $\Rightarrow$E,

$$K(TC) \Rightarrow K(G)$$

Now, do you know that the truth condition obtains (is $K(TC)$ true)? That is, do you know that you don't know falsehoods? Most people would say yes. They would say that truth is part of the meaning of "knowledge" just as male is part of the meaning of "bachelor." You know the truth condition obtains because you know what the word "know" means. Perhaps more critically, if you don't know that the truth condition obtains, perhaps you shouldn't be so willing to agree to it. But we're all inclined to agree to TC. Thus we should claim knowledge of the truth condition:

$$K(TC)$$

CHALLENGE 4

Fill in the remaining reasons for the following deduction:

1. $\neg G$ assumption
2. $\neg\neg K(G)$ (b)
3. $K(G)$
4. $K(G) \Rightarrow G$
5. G
6. $G \,\&\, \neg G$
7. $\neg G \Rightarrow (G \,\&\, \neg G)$
8. $\neg\neg G$
9. G

Hence it follows by $\Rightarrow$E that

$$K(G)$$

But if you go back and look at the definition of G, that is, $G \Leftrightarrow \neg K(G)$, you'll see that $K(G) \Leftrightarrow \neg G$. Thus we have $\neg G$, and so we have derived both G and $\neg G$.

This, then, is the paradox of the knower. It is a valid argument from certain premises about knowledge that seems to be exceedingly plausible. It is this paradox that is hiding behind the puzzle of the surprise exam. No wonder we have a hard time figuring out what is wrong with students' arguments that a surprise exam is impossible, even though we are quite sure that a surprise exam is possible. In one sense, there is nothing wrong with the students' arguments. It follows logically from certain commonplace assumptions about knowledge. Let us recapitulate.

We know that we can construct a self-referential statement that says "You don't know this statement." More formally, we can find a wff G with the property that we can logically prove that

$$G \Leftrightarrow \neg K(G)$$

Now, if we assume TC, $K(A) \Rightarrow A$ for any statement A, then with A replaced by G, we can show G is true, that is, TC implies G.

However, if we add the assumptions that what we prove in logic, we know (LK), that we can extend knowledge by applying logic, especially $\Rightarrow$E (MPK), and that we know the truth condition obtains (KTC), then we can prove that we know G, which is equivalent to $\neg G$. That is

$$LK, MPK, KTC \text{ imply } \neg G$$

Putting this all together, we have

$$TC, LK, MPK, KTC \text{ imply } G \ \& \ \neg G$$

From elementary logic, you know that the principles on the left can't all be true; they're inconsistent. But which one should you give up?

CHALLENGE 5   Assuming that the argument of the knower's paradox is correct, just which of the above principles would you give up? Can you think of any way to hold to all four principles and still avoid contradicting yourself via the paradox of the knower? WARNING: This issue is still being debated by logicians and philosophers, so don't worry if you can't figure out the "right answer"!

• The logician who showed this was Kurt Gödel. In fact, the knower's paradox can be viewed as an English version of Gödel's first theorem, which is that "this statement can't be proven in arithmetic" can't be proven in arithmetic.

informal logic

more Bush, Clinton, and Perot

> Elinor agreed with it all, for she did not think he deserved the compliment of rational opposition.

> —JANE AUSTEN

CHALLENGE   The following excerpts are taken from the second 1992 presidential debate. Unlike the first debate, questions came from the audience, not reporters. As before, you are challenged to critique the performances.

1. Q: I'd like to ask Governor Clinton: Do you attribute the rising cost of health care to the medical profession itself? Or do you think the problem lies elsewhere, and what specific proposals do you have to tackle this problem?

    CLINTON: I've had more people talk to me about their health care problems, I guess, than anything else. All across America, you know, people that lost their jobs, lost their businesses, had to give up their jobs because of their children.

    So let me try to answer you in this way. Let's start with a premise. We spend 30 percent more of our income than any nation on earth on health care. And yet we insure fewer people. We have 35 million people without any insurance at all. I see them all the time. A hundred thousand Americans a month have lost their health insurance just in the last four years. So if you analyze where we're out of line with other countries you come up with the following conclusions: No. 1, we spend at least $60 billion a year on insurance, administrative costs, bureaucracy and government regulation that wouldn't be spent in any other nation. So we have to have, in my judgment, a drastic simplification of the basic health insurance policies of this country. Be very comprehensive for everybody.

    Employers would cover their employed. Government would cover the unemployed. No. 2, I think you have to take on specifically the insurance companies and require them to make some significant change in the way they rate people into big community pools. I think you have to tell the pharmaceutical companies they can't keep raising drug prices at three times the rate of inflation. I think you have to take on medical fraud. I think you have to help doctors stop practicing defensive medicine. I've recommended that our doctors be given a set of national practice guidelines and that if they follow those guidelines, that raises the presumption that they didn't do anything wrong. I think you have to have a system of primary and preventive clinics in our inner cities and our rural areas so people can have access to health care.

The key is to control the cost and maintain the quality. To do that you need a system of managed competition where all of us are covered in big groups and we can choose our doctors and our hospitals across a wide range, but there is an incentive to control costs and I think there has to be—I think Mr. Perot and I agree on this, there has to be a national commission of health care providers and health care consumers that set ceilings to keep health costs in line with inflation plus population growth.

Now let me say, some people say we can't do this but Hawaii does it. They cover 98 percent of their people and their insurance premiums are much cheaper than the rest of America. And so does Rochester, N.Y. They now have a plan to cover everybody and their premiums are two-thirds of the rest of the country. This is very important. It's a big human problem and a devastating economic problem for America. And I'm going to send a plan to do this within the first hundred days of my Presidency. It's terribly important.

Q: Thank you. Sorry to cut you short, but President Bush, health care reform.

2. BUSH: [Comment on a previous exchange.] She asked the question, I think, is whether the health care profession was to blame.

No. One thing to blame is these malpractice lawsuits. They are breaking the system. It costs 20 to 25 billion dollars a year and I want to see those outrageous claims capped. Doctors don't dare to deliver babies sometimes because they're afraid that somebody's going to sue them. People don't dare—medical practitioners—to help somebody along the highway that are hurt, because they're afraid that some lawyer's going to come along and get a big lawsuit. So you can't blame the practitioners for the health problem.

And my program is this. Keep the government as far out of it as possible. Make insurance available to the poorest of the poor through vouchers, next range in the income bracket through—tax credits. And get on about the business of pooling insurance. A great big company can buy—Ross got a good-size company, been very successful. He can buy insurance cheaper than mom and pop store on the corner. But if those mom and pop stores all get together and pool, they too can bring the cost of insurance down. So, I want to keep the quality of health care—that means keep government out of it. I want to do—I don't like this idea of these boards. It all sounds to me like you're going to have some government setting price. I want competition and I want to pool the insurance and take care of it that way.

And have—here's another point. I think medical care should go with the person. If you leave a business, I think your insurance should go with you to some other business. You shouldn't be worrying if you get a new job as to whether that's going to—and part of our plan is to make it what they call portable. A big word, but that means, if you're working for the Jones company, you go to the Smith company, your insurance goes with you. And I think it's a good program. I'm really excited about getting it done too.

Q: Mr. Perot.

3. PEROT: We have the most expensive health care system in the world; 12 percent of our gross national product goes to health care. Our industrial competitors who are beating us in competition spend less and have better health care. Japan spends a little over 6 percent of its gross national product, Germany spends 8 percent. It's fascinating. You bought a front-row box seat and you're not happy with your health care, and you're saying we've got bad health care but very expensive health care. Folks, here's why. Go home and look in the mirror. You won this country but you have no voice in it the way it's organized now. And if you want to have a high-risk experience comparable to bungee jumping, go in to Congress some time when they're working on this kind of legislation, when the lobbyists are running up and down the halls. Wear your safety-toed shoes when you go.

And as a private citizen, believe me, you are looked on as a major nuisance. The facts are, you now have a government that comes at you and you're supposed to have a government that comes from you. Now there are all kinds of good ideas, brilliant ideas, terrific ideas on health care. None of them ever get implemented because—let me give you an example. A senator runs every six years, he's got to raise 20,000 bucks a week to have enough money to run. Who's he going to listen to, us? Or the folks running up and down the aisles with money—the lobbyists, the PAC money. He listens to them. Who do they represent? The health care industry.

Now you've got to have a government that comes from you again, you've got to reassert your ownership in this country and you've got to completely reform our government. And at that point they'll just be like apples falling out of a tree—the programs will be good because the elected officials will be listening to—I said the other night I was all ears? I would listen to any good idea? I think we ought to do plastic surgery on all of these guys so that they are all ears too, and listen to you. Then you get what you want, and shouldn't you? You pay for it, why shouldn't you get what you want as opposed to what some lobbyist who cuts a deal, writes the little piece in the law and it goes through. That's the way the game's played now.

4. Q: My name is Vin Smith. I work in the financial field counseling retirees, and I'm particularly concerned about three major areas. One is the Social Security Administration where the trust fund is projected to be insolvent by the year 2036, and we funded the trust fund with IOU's in the form of Treasury bonds. The pension guarantee fund, which backs up our private retirement plans for retirees, is projected to be bankrupt by the year 2026, not to mention the cutbacks by private companies and Medicare is projected to be bankrupt, maybe as soon as 1997. And I would like from each of you a specific response as to what you intend to do for retirees relative to these issues. Not generalities but specifics, because I think they're very disturbing issues.

Q: President Bush, may we start with you?

BUSH: Well, the Social Security—you're an expert, and I can, I'm sure, learn from you the details of the pension guarantee fund and the Social Security fund. The Social Security system was fixed about five years and I think it's projected out to be sound beyond that. So at least we have time to work with it.

But on all these things, a sound economy is the only way to get it going. Growth in the economy is going to add to these—add to the overall prosperity and wealth. I can't give you a specific answer on pension guarantee funds; all I know is that we have firm government credit to guarantee the pensions and that is very important. But it's—it's the full faith and credit of the United States in space—in spite of our difficulties is still pretty good. It's still the most respected credit. So I would simply say as these dates get close you're going to have to reorganize and refix as we did with the social security fund. And I think that's the only answer.

The most—more immediate answer is to do what this lady was suggesting we do, and that is to get this deficit down and get on without adding to the woes and the restructure. One thing I've called for has been stymied and I'll keep on working for it is a whole financial reform legislation. It is absolutely essential in terms of bringing our banking system and credit system into the new age instead of having it living back in the dark ages. And it's a big fight and I don't want to give my friend Ross another shot at me here, but I am fighting with the Congress to get this through. And you can't just go up and say, "I'm going to fix it." You've got some pretty strong-willed guys up there that argue with you. But that's what the election's about. I agree with the Governor. That's what the election is about. And sound fiscal policy is the best answer I think to the—all the three problems you mentioned.

5. Q: Thank you. Mr. Perot.

PEROT: Yes, on the broad issue here. When you're trying to solve a problem, you get the best plans. You have a raging debate about those plans. Then, out of that debate with leadership comes consensus. Then, if the plans are huge and complex like health care, I would urge you to implement pilot programs. Like the old carpenter who says measure twice and cut once. Let's make sure this thing's as good as we all think it is at the end of the meeting. Then finally our Government passes laws and freezes the plan in concrete. Anybody that's ever built a successful business will tell you, you optimize, optimize, optimize after you put something into effect. The reason Medicare and Medicaid are a mess is we froze them. Everybody knows how to fix them. There are people all over the Federal Government, if they could just touch it with a screwdriver could fix it.

Now back over here. See, we've got a $4 trillion debt and only in America would you have $2.8 trillion of it or 70 percent of it, financed five years or less. Now that's another thing for you to think about when you go home tonight. You don't finance long-term debt with short-term money. Why did our Government do it? To get the interest rates down. A 1 percent increase in the interest rates and that $2.8 trillion is $28 billion a year. Now when you look at what Germany pays for money and what we don't pay for money, you realize it's quite a spread, right. And you realize this is a temporary thing and there's going to be another sucking sound that runs our deficit through the roof. You know, and everybody's ducking it so I'm going to say it. That we are not letting that surplus stay in the bank. We are not investing that surplus like a pension fund. We are spending that surplus to make the deficit look smaller to you than it really is.

Now that's put you in jail in corporate America if you kept books that way, but in government it's just kind of the way things are. That's because it comes at you not from you. Now then, that money needs to be—they don't even pay interest on it, they just write a note for the interest.

Q: Mr. Perot, can you wrap it up?

PEROT: So now then, that's important. See, do you want to fix the problem or sound bite it? I understand the importance of time but— see here's how we get to this mess we're in. This is just 1 of 1,000 . . . .

433

Q: But we've got to be fair.

PEROT: Now then, to nail it, there's one way out. A growing expanding job base, a growing expanding job base to generate the funds and the tax revenues to pay off the mess and rebuild America. We got a double hit. If we're $4 trillion down, we should have everything perfect, but we don't. We've got to pay it off and build money to renew it— spend money to renew it and that's going to take a growing expanding job base. That is Priority 1 in this country. Put everybody that's breathing to work. And I'd love to be out of workers and have to import them like some of our international competitors.

Q: Mr. Perot, I'm sorry I'm going to . . .

PEROT: Sorry.

Q: And I don't want to sound bite you, but we are trying to be fair to everyone.

PEROT: O.K. No, absolutely. I apologize.

6. Q: All right, Governor Clinton.

CLINTON: I think I remember the question. And let me say first of all—I want to answer your specific question but first of all we all agree that there should be a growing economy. What you have to decide is who's got the best economic plan. And we all have ideas out there, and Mr. Bush has a record. So I don't want you to read my lips, and I sure don't want you to read his. I just—I do hope you will read our plans. Now specifically . . .

BUSH: That's the first rule.

CLINTON: Specifically, one: on Medicare, it is not true that everyone knows how to fix it; there are different ideas. The Bush plan, the Perot plan, the Clinton—we have different ideas. I am convinced, having studied health care for a year, hard, and talking to hundreds and hundreds of people all across America, that you cannot control the costs of Medicare until you control the costs of private health care and public health care, with managed competition, a ceiling on costs and radical reorganization of the insurance markets. You've got to do that, we've got to get those costs down.

Six increases in the payroll tax—that means people with incomes of $51,000 a year or less pay a disproportionately high share of the Federal tax burden which is why I want some middle-class tax relief. What do we have to do? By the time the century turns, we have got to have our deficit under control. We have to work out of so that surplus is building up so when the baby boomers like me retire, we're O.K. No. 3, on the pension funds, I don't know as much about it but I will say this. What I would do is to bring in the pension experts of the country, take a look at it and strengthen the pension requirements further because it's not just enough to have a guarantee. We had a guarantee on the S&L's right? We had a guarantee and what happened? You picked up a $500 billion bill because of the dumb way the Federal Government deregulated. So I think we are going to have to change and strengthen the pension requirements on private retirement plans.

presidential debates

It is not necessary to understand things in order to argue about them.
—BEAUMARCHAIS

We can have debates just like presidential candidates. We're not experts in foreign affairs or tax policy, but this is not a problem. We are interested in logic, not issues, so our ignorance is perfectly acceptable. The following rules allow us to debate without knowing much at all.

Rules

1. There are three entities, the two candidates and the press. Each is represented by a group of two or three students.

2. Each candidate is described loosely (some sample descriptions follow these rules).

3. The press first asks one candidate a question. The group representing the candidate has a minute to confer, then two minutes to answer the question. The group representing the other candidate has a minute to confer and then a minute to reply. In response, the group representing the first candidate may, with no conference, present a one-minute rebuttal.

4. The press then asks the second candidate a question and the procedure continues.

5. At any time, candidates and the press *may invent any "facts" they like, so long as the "facts" do not contradict previously introduced "facts."* For example, the press could ask, "Congressman Tweet, can you tell us why you voted against the Fair Employment Bill last year, which would have prevented employers from discriminating against workers with bad breath?" The group representing Tweet may never have heard of this bill before, since the press

435

made it up, but they could still respond: "The bill was a badly flawed piece of legislation that also required that every employer supply breath mints to all employees. It would have cost small businessmen thousands of dollars." Tweet would *not* be allowed to say, "Actually, I didn't vote against the bill, in fact, I was the chief sponsor," because that would contradict a previously introduced fact.

Here is another example of creative fact production from a real class debate. A governor was challenged about his opposition to a federal water pollution bill that would have supplied his state with all the funds necessary to clean up all the rivers in his state. The governor replied (after much thought and consultation) that there were no rivers in his state!

6. The class will judge the debaters on the basis of
   a. how relevant the answers are to the questions.
   b. how logically correct the reasoning is.
   c. how persuasive the answers are.

Each debate team should be given a score between 1 and 5 by every member of the class.

The candidates should be interesting as individuals and should have very different positions and outlooks. Here are two such:

Senator Violet Snort From an Eastern state, activist in foreign policy affairs. Favors U.S. intervention to preserve democracies. Wants to reintroduce the draft. Is liberal on domestic issues, wants to tax the rich, give to the poor.

Governor Barbara Grumble From a Western state, isolationist foreign policy: wants to cut defense spending in half and stay out of other countries. Conservative on domestic issues, wants to privatize the Postal Service and public schools (i.e., let these be run by private businesses).

EXERCISES
1. Write a question for Senator Snort.
2. Write a reply by Senator Snort to your question.
3. Write a rebuttal by Governor Grumble to your reply.
4. Write a question for Governor Grumble, one that puts the Governor in an awkward position.

5. Write a reply by Governor Grumble to your question; if possible, make the reply one that helps her to escape from an awkward position and puts her opponent in an awkward position.

6. Write a rebuttal by Senator Snort to your reply, one that extricates her from her awkward position.

It is useful, for class debates, to have a store of candidates. Here are two more:

Madeleine Kim Chief Executive Officer of Swindex Electronics, an enormously successful multinational corporation, mostly U.S.-owned. Kim has been highly visible as a manager, and the company's position as a supplier of rocket guidance systems has made her rich and influential. Her autobiography, *Kim!*, was a best seller and she used it to popularize her philosophy of self-help. She consequently opposes government programs to help the unemployed, handicapped, and other disadvantaged people. Her company's international success has also convinced her of the importance of global cooperation. She believes we have nothing to fear from any country that drinks Pepsi and watches TV on Swindex Infinitron sets.

General Samantha Allen "General Sam," as her staff sometimes call her, worked her way up through the air force ranks until she was picked for a succession of cabinet posts. She is tough: tough on drugs, tough on Cuba, tough on polluters, tough on dictators, tough on reporters. She believes in making people, corporations, government agencies, and countries do what's good for them.

EXERCISES   Prepare appropriate, in-character answers to the following reporters' questions.

7. For CEO Kim: You are on record as opposing a law requiring that all children under the age of 5 wear seat belts with shoulder straps in automobiles. I understand you are generally in favor of letting people fend for themselves, but don't our children deserve some care?

8. For General Sam: When reports appeared in the papers detailing the miserable performance of high school students on standardized tests, you called for "boot camps" for C, D, and E students. Could you explain how military discipline might help someone learn algebra?

9. For CEO Kim: You oppose government "give-away" programs to businesses and individuals, yet your own company,
Swindex, has profited handsomely from a number of tax
breaks that look a lot like give-aways. Why should the government help a rich corporation and not a poor mother?

10. For General Sam: Recent reports say that Cuba is supporting
the drug trade. Would you support a military strike there to
change the government?

You can never have too many candidates. Here are two more:

Dr. Jane Plane A former astronaut and physicist, Dr. Plane made
several shuttle flights, carrying out experiments in particle physics.
Currently a professor and author, Dr. Plane holds very conservative
views. She favors traditional values and traditional roles. She is a
libertarian, one who believes that except for defense, highways, and
police, government should not interfere with the rights of citizens.
She opposes, for example, public education. She has few known views
on foreign policy. She favors free trade.

Senator Melba Drinkwater Senator Drinkwater was appointed to fill
the term of her late husband, Senator Harry Drinkwater, one of the
South's great conservative leaders. Melba, however, surprised her
supporters by being quite liberal. She had not been in office more
than a week when she voted for doubling the minimum wage. Since
then she has shocked her state by opposing tobacco subsidies and
favoring higher taxes for the rich. What will she do next?

**EXERCISES   Prepare answers to the following reporters' ques-
tions.**

11. For Dr. Plane: How do you explain your opposition to public
education?

12. For Senator Drinkwater: You oppose the demolition of a
slum district in Chicago because it is the only remaining
habitat of the rare cockroach, *Stilopyga gigantea*. Isn't this
carrying ecology too far?

13. For Dr. Plane: You oppose the drafting of women and emphasize traditional roles, but you yourself have hardly had a
traditional career. Aren't you being inconsistent?

14. For Senator Drinkwater: The Senate is debating cutting off
funding for "art" that is pornographic. What is your position?

parliamentary debates

In our civilization, and under our republican form of government, brain is so highly honored that it is rewarded by exemption from the cares of office.

—AMBROSE BIERCE, *THE DEVIL'S DICTIONARY*

The debating format set up in "Presidential Debates" may seem to you rather artificial. You may be more familiar with a different style of debating that used to be popular on college campuses and even now is widely practiced in high schools. In these debates, real issues are discussed by debaters who have studied them very thoroughly. From our point of view, these debates are less interesting because truth is at least as important as logic.

In recent years, yet another form of debate has started to catch on, called "parliamentary-style" debating, or "off-topic" debating. It is modeled after debates in the British parliament. The debates are lively, almost raucous. Logic is all-important. Currently there are competitive teams at hundreds of colleges and universities.

The rules are somewhat elaborate. We present here a simplified version more appropriate for classroom (and party) use.

There are two teams, the government and the opposition. The government team consists of the prime minister and a member of the government. The opposition team consists of the leader of the opposition and a member of the opposition. A judge is also needed.

At the start, a resolution is given to the government team by the judge. It can be serious ("We should close all nuclear power plants" or "College education should be free for all citizens") or frivolous ("*Calvin and Hobbes* is better than *Doonesbury*" or "The food they give us here is delicious"). The topic should be debatable without requiring special knowledge.

The government team argues in favor of the resolution, while the opposition opposes it. All speeches are limited to *two minutes* (this is drastically shorter than in real collegiate debates). The teams are allowed a few minutes before the debate to plot strategy, then the debate begins as follows:

1. The prime minister speaks.
2. The leader of the opposition speaks.
3. The member of the government speaks.
4. The member of the opposition speaks.

5. The leader of the opposition speaks.
6. The prime minister speaks.

In all the speeches, the speaker may attack previous arguments. In all but the last speech, new arguments may be introduced (no new arguments are permitted in the prime minister's last speech because there is no opportunity for the opposition to rebut them).

The opposition may introduce a counterproposal. If, for example, the government is arguing that the national deficit should be reduced by holding bake sales, the opposition can argue for garage sales instead.

The audience is expected to choose the winner. Members of the audience should take notes on the points made in each speech. They should rate the arguments and counterarguments.

Speakers should always be referred to by title, such as the "honorable member," the "honorable leader," and so on.

Rules

You may consider each of these rules as optional. Together they bring the debate closer to the version now played at intercollegiate tournaments.

1. The debate topic given is vague rather than specific, such as "No man is an island," "Marriages are made in heaven," or "Freedent's the one that took the stick out of gum." It is then the government's task to form the proposition, based loosely on the topic, and to define its terms. For example, from "Marriages are made in heaven," it could choose the proposition "Charles and Diana are happily married," "Congress should pass laws outlawing divorce," or even "Reese's Peanut Butter Cups are the greatest candy bar." (For the last one, the government would explain, "Reese's Peanut Butter Cups are a marriage of peanut butter and chocolate. It is thus heavenly.")

   The government is responsible for defining its terms. For example, if the proposition is "Congress should pass laws outlawing divorce," it should explain what they mean by "divorce." If they don't define the term, then the opposition is free to say "It seems to us that 'divorce' can mean the dissolution of any long-standing association or alliance. The dissolution, for example, of East Germany from the Warsaw Pact amounts to a divorce. Not only was that divorce beneficial ultimately for the peace of Europe, but it is also something that no law passed by Congress can affect." You can see that the government would be in trouble!

Finally, the proposition must be "debatable," that is, something that the opposition has a chance of arguing against. The government can't oppose divorce and define divorce as the involuntary dismemberment of human beings. That would not be fair play.

2. Allow longer speeches. In real debates, the first four are 8 minutes long and the last two are 4 minutes.

3. Allow heckling. Heckling is when the speaker is interrupted by shouts from the opposing side. The rules are generally that such interruptions must be brief and clever. To roar "Nonsense!" is not clever. To interject even two sentences is not brief. The idea is to add fun to the debate. Don't adopt this rule if it makes participants nervous or hostile.

4. Allow "points of order." If a member of the nonspeaking team believes a rule has been violated, he or she may rise and say "Point of order" and then explain the breach. The judge will then rule on it. Without this rule, the judge is responsible for spotting illegal behavior. With the rule, it is the responsibility of the other team to point illegal behavior out.

5. Allow "points of privilege." A point of privilege is called if a member feels her or his remarks have been misrepresented or her or his character has been assaulted. Again, the judge should rule.

EXERCISE Find some people and debate something!

commercial logic III

On the back of a bottle of Aussie Moist Shampoo, we find the following:

Salon Directions
Wet hair, apply shampoo, work into full lather, rinse thoroughly, repeat.

Question: Why couldn't the computer scientist get out of the shower?

curiosities & puzzles

The Digestor's Digest

Vol. I, No. 1	Page 7

Breakfast Review

We recently visited an aspiring new eatery, the upscale International House of Oat Bran. We were pleasantly surprised by the service and decor. Most impressive was the menu featuring scores of mouth-parching oaty delights.

Breakfast Review

We recently visited an aspiring new eatery, the downscale Sunken Donuts. The waiter was surly and the food was vile. After one taste we were ready to sue. If they hadn't thrown us out, we would have left. While this may read like a review, it isn't. Believe it or not, this is an ad.

exam warning VII

Have you seen the exam yet?

If not, we have nothing to say. It's not here. Go away.

If you have, and were indeed surprised, read "From Puzzle to Paradox."

Peano's dots

> I never could make out what those damned dots meant.
> —Lord Randolph Churchill

Logical notation has gone through many changes. It used to be common to write $\Rightarrow$ as $\supset$, and $\equiv$ has frequently been used in place of $\Leftrightarrow$. In place of &, older books use a period. Even today, $\sim$ is often used for $\neg$.

These differences are easy enough to master; it simply means substituting one symbol for another. Much stranger is the use of dots, pioneered by Guiseppe Peano. These replace (in some cases) parentheses. Rules vary from author to author, but the general idea is that if you see a pile of dots on one side of a connective, as in

$$\langle \text{stuff} \rangle \supset:. \langle \text{more stuff} \rangle$$

it means that you should include on that side of the connective everything you see until you get to a larger pile of dots (or to the end, if there is no larger pile of dots). For example,

$$a \supset b .\supset: c \supset. d \supset e$$

means

$$(a \Rightarrow b) \Rightarrow (c \Rightarrow (d \Rightarrow e))$$

whereas

$$a \supset b .\supset. c \supset d :\supset e$$

means

$$((a \Rightarrow b) \Rightarrow (c \Rightarrow d)) \Rightarrow e$$

What do you do if the connective is already a dot (some authors use a dot instead of & for conjunction)? Well, you just pile all the dots together and figure it out. But if you see a pile, how do you know if one of the dots is a conjunction? And if one is, how do you know how many dots are on one side and how many are on the other?

To confuse you further, sometimes parentheses are mixed in as well. When that happens, treat everything inside a pair of parentheses separately.

To top it off, ancient practice did not include the $\forall$ sign. Instead of writing "$\forall x P x$," one wrote "$(x)Px$." Also, it was customary to enclose the existential quantifier in parentheses: "$\exists x P x$" was written "$(\exists x) P x$."

CHALLENGE   Translate these wffs from antique to modern. To add to the flavor, we use Greek letters.

1. $\sigma \supset \varphi .\equiv: \chi . \psi . \supset \sim \theta$
2. $\gamma \equiv :\psi \vee \varphi . \supset : \theta . \sigma . \equiv \chi$
3. $\varphi :. (x)\psi \supset \gamma . \vee \sigma$
4. $\sim ((x)\varphi \supset . (z)\sigma .(\exists y)\psi)$
5. $(\sigma \supset \varphi .\supset: \chi \supset .\psi \supset \theta) . \sim (\gamma \supset \varphi .\supset. \varphi \supset \sigma: \supset \theta)$
6. $\gamma \vee. \theta .\psi: \supset \chi :: \varphi \supset \sigma .\equiv. \alpha . \sigma$

Translate these wffs from modern to antique.

7. $(\sigma \Rightarrow \chi) \Leftrightarrow \theta$
8. $(\varphi \mathbin{\&} \gamma) \Rightarrow \neg(\chi \vee \psi)$
9. $\forall x \neg \forall y \neg \forall z((\sigma \Leftrightarrow ((\varphi \Rightarrow \chi) \mathbin{\&} \psi)) \vee \theta)$
10. $((\gamma \vee \sigma) \Rightarrow (\theta \mathbin{\&} (\varphi \Rightarrow \chi))) \mathbin{\&} (((\chi \Rightarrow \psi) \mathbin{\&} (\varphi \Leftrightarrow \theta)) \Rightarrow \sigma)$

Charles Dana Gibson

CHALLENGE   Formalize: "It is not true that if Charlie is a fool then he and his money are soon parted." Prove from this that Charlie is a fool.

A RESOLVE.

Cousin Kate: "Now that you are well off, Charlie, you mustn't let them say of you, 'A fool and his money are soon parted.'"

Cousin Charles: "No, you bet I won't. I'll show them that I am an exception to the rule."

the family reunion II: the women

Recall "The Family Reunion" in part 4; you will need it.

Your mother assigned you the task of hosting a luncheon for the wives and girlfriends of Edwin, Edgar, Eduardo, Edsel, and Crazy Eddie. This was no fun at all, since (1) they all have irritating dietary demands, (2) they don't like each other much, (3) you don't like them any better than the Eds, and consequently (4) you haven't ever figured out their names or associations.

One of these, for example, is Madeleine. You've never forgiven her for not inviting you to her wedding, but whom did she marry? In any case, you decided to snub her slightly, not putting her at the end of the table or on your immediate left or right. Your table, by the way, looks like this:

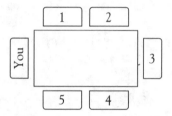

Then there's Madge. She also hates Madeleine. And there's this woman whose name you don't know at all. The family always refers to her as "Madame." You don't know why. She's left-handed and insists (as such people often do) on not sitting to anyone's right. She doesn't eat beef.

The eating habits of your guests are nothing short of bizarre. Madeleine claims allergies to foods beginning with the letter "g." Edgar's wife refuses to eat anything costing less than $15. She got the lobster. One woman lives on anchovy crepes. Another restricts her organic intake to one-celled creatures. You fixed her a yeast omelet. Salt, but no pepper.

In the end, you coped. Fortunately, you remembered about Madge and Madeleine and didn't put them opposite or next to each other. Nothing awful happened, except you were one dinner short and had to send out for a Big Mac.

Who else was there? A very odd woman: a former nun who now calls herself Madonna. She claimed she was allergic to shellfish, but when her neighbor wasn't looking, she got a whole lobster claw. Next to her was Madeira, perpetually frowning, some of her hair dyed a dangerous purple. She's attached to somebody—not Edwin or Edgar, though. Oh, yes, she's the one with the omelet.

You were smart enough to seat the anchovy crepes away from you, but they ended up next to Madame, who complained to you about it afterwards. You were less intelligent about the roasted garlic.

How did you do it? Where did they sit? What did they eat?

PARADOX, IMPOSSIBILITY, AND THE LAW

9

contents

GOAL: To explore new logical worlds and to boldly go where few introductory students have gone before—and at the same time to practice basic logical techniques. We review Frege's attempt to derive numbers from logic, consider some radical alternatives to the logic presented so far, and reveal the paradox that lies at the heart of modern logic.

FORMAL LOGIC: DEEPER INTO LOGIC

WHERE DO NUMBERS COME FROM?

The mathematics and the metaphysics,
Fall to them as you find your stomach serves you.
—WILLIAM SHAKESPEARE

Suppose you wanted to check that you have as many fingers on your left hand as you do on your right (including thumbs). One way to do this would be to count the fingers on your left hand, presumably getting 5, then count the fingers on your right hand, presumably getting 5 again. Since $5 = 5$, you conclude that the number of fingers on your left hand is the same as the number on your right.

If we let Fx be the property "x is a finger on your left hand" and Gx be the property "x is a finger on your right hand," and we abbreviate "the number of F's" by $[\![Fx]\!]$, then your reasoning is something like this—

• Think of the notation $[\![Fx]\!]$ as expressing a function from properties to numbers. That is, $[\![Fx]\!]$ assigns to each property Fx, the number of things that F.

$$\begin{aligned}
[\![Fx]\!] &= 5 \\
[\![Gx]\!] &= 5 \\
\therefore\, [\![Fx]\!] &= [\![Gx]\!]
\end{aligned}$$

—because of the law that $a = c, b = c \therefore a = b$.

This reasoning is perfectly correct, but it does presuppose that you know about numbers. There is another way of proceeding that is both simpler and more profound. Just touch your hands together and notice that your fingers match up perfectly. That is,

Every finger on your left touches one on your right.
Every finger on your left touches only one on your right.
Every finger on your right is touched by one on your left.

Technically, we say there is a **one-to-one** (or 1–1) **correspondence** between the fingers on your left and the fingers on your right hands.
Now your reasoning is something like this—

$[\![Fx]\!] = [\![Gx]\!] \Leftrightarrow$ There is a 1–1 correspondence between Fx and Gx.

There is a 1–1 correspondence between Fx and Gx.

$\therefore [\![Fx]\!] = [\![Gx]\!]$

—because of the law $P \Leftrightarrow Q, Q \therefore P$. Notice that in the second case, you have not mentioned specific numbers at all! Indeed, the deep fact about numbers is this: The number of F's equals the number of G's if and only if there's a 1–1 correspondence between F and G. You needn't even mention the idea of numbers, for you can conclude that there are just as many F's *as* G's from the fact that there is a 1–1 correspondence (or perfect match) between the F's and the G's.

The essence of numbers lies in 1–1 correspondences, or perfect matches. The essence of 1–1 correspondences, in turn, lies in logic. In a moment, we'll write out a definition of 1–1 correspondence in logical notation. But first let's further develop our intuition with a more realistic problem.

Imagine that you live in a community of primitive people, say ten or twenty thousand years ago. You are a shepherd. Every morning you let the sheep out of their pen, and every evening you let them back in again. Here's the hard part: Your chief tells you to be sure that you don't lose any sheep, that just as many return as leave. Unfortunately, your tribe hasn't learned about numbers yet. (The best minds are only able to count to three before getting stuck!) But you are smart, and so you use the idea of 1–1 correspondence to do your job.

This time let Fx be "x is a sheep that went in the morning" and Gx be "x is a sheep that returned at night." You can be sure that $[\![Fx]\!] = [\![Gx]\!]$ by establishing a 1–1 correspondence between the F's and G's.

Here's what you do. You take an empty basket and a pile of pebbles and you stand by the gate. You put one pebble in the basket for each sheep that leaves the pen. This establishes a 1–1 correspondence between F and H, where Hx is "x is a pebble in the basket." Thus we have $[\![Fx]\!] = [\![Hx]\!]$ because of the 1–1 correspondence.

At night you stand by the gate with your basket and remove one pebble as each sheep enters. In the happy case that you take out the last pebble as the last sheep is going into the pen, you have found that there is a 1–1 correspondence between Hx (pebbles) and Gx (sheep at night). Thus $[\![Hx]\!] = [\![Gx]\!]$, and so you can conclude that $[\![Fx]\!] = [\![Gx]\!]$. In other (than number) words, as many sheep returned as left the pen. Notice that you accomplished the whole thing without any

451

mention of numbers. Strictly speaking, you appealed to the following reasoning:

> There is a 1–1 correspondence between F and H.
> There is a 1–1 correspondence between H and G.
> Therefore, there is a 1–1 correspondence between F and G.

CHALLENGE 1

a. Suppose as the last sheep returned at night, you still had pebbles in your basket. What would you conclude?

b. Suppose as you remove the last pebble from the basket, several more sheep file by. What would you conclude?

c. Suppose that you remove the last pebble as the last sheep goes by. Can you conclude that the very same sheep returned as left that morning?

CHALLENGE 2   Suppose a large number of students are standing around a classroom. How can you find out if there are just as many students as chairs without counting either?

CHALLENGE 3   Suppose there are a lot of boys and girls at a party. How can you find out if there are as many boys as girls without counting?

The concept of 1–1 correspondence is at the root of our dealings with numbers and infinity. In other chapters of this book, we encounter these correspondences in a more intuitive fashion. Here we want to define this notion precisely in order to give you practice in reading logical symbols.

We get at the idea of 1–1 correspondence via the concept of function. Recall that functions are a basic part of the logician's toolkit, on par with objects and properties of objects. Functions are "operations" or "assignments." A function assigns to each object in the given universe exactly one object. So in the universe of people, "the father of" function assigns to each individual c a single object d, the father of c. We express functions, like properties, using variables: the father of $x = y$, or more abstractly, $fx = y$. If h assigns to a the object b, we write $ha = b$, calling a an **argument** of h and b the **value** of h for argument a.

By logical convention, every function has a value for every argument:

$$\forall x \exists y (hx = y)$$

In fact, this value is unique, for if $hx = y$ and $hx = z$ then, by the laws of identity, $y = z$.

Functions are important to the idea of a 1–1 correspondence. There is a 1–1 correspondence between F and G only if ($\Rightarrow$) there is a function h that assigns an object that G's to each thing that F's:

$$\forall x(Fx \Rightarrow \exists y(Gy \ \& \ hx = y))$$

or more simply

$$\forall x(Fx \Rightarrow G(hx))$$

However, the existence of such a function does not guarantee a 1–1 correspondence between F and G. This is because a function might assign the *same* value to several arguments. For example, the father of Julia may also be the father of Victor; more generally, $h(a) = c$ and $h(b) = c$ even though $a \neq c$.

The accompanying figure shows a function hx that assigns the same value to two arguments (b and c).

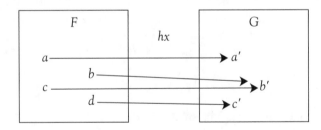

A function itself is 1–1 if no two arguments ever get the same value. In symbols

$$\forall x \forall y(x \neq y \Rightarrow hx \neq hy)$$

or, what amounts to the same thing,

$$\forall x \forall y(hx = hy \Rightarrow x = y)$$

(Notice that both of these are very different from

$$\forall x \forall y(x = y \Rightarrow hx = hy)$$

which is just an instance of a law of identity.)

However, not even the existence of a 1–1 function from F to G guarantees a 1–1 correspondence between F and G, for some things in G might not be assigned to anything in F.

CHALLENGE 4 Can you prove that $\forall x \exists y(hx = y)$ and that $\forall x \forall y \forall z((hx = y \ \& \ hx = z) \Rightarrow y = z)$? Recall "Functions" in part 7.

453

The accompanying figure is an example of a 1–1 function jx that fails to be a perfect match between F and G.

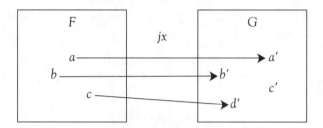

So we need one final clause insuring that everything in G is assigned to some F. The technical term is that the function h takes F **onto** G. In symbols, this becomes

$$\forall x(Gx \Rightarrow \exists y(Fy \,\&\, hy = x))$$

Now we can define 1–1 correspondence in terms of logic. There is a 1–1 correspondence between F and G if there is a function h such that

1. h assigns a G to each object that F's:

$$\forall x(Fx \Rightarrow G(hx))$$

2. h is 1–1 (it assigns different G's to different F's):

$$\forall x\forall y(x \neq y \Rightarrow hx \neq hy)$$

3. h is onto (every G is assigned to some F):

$$\forall x(Gx \Rightarrow \exists y(Fy \,\&\, hy = x))$$

Putting it all together in symbols, we have

There is a 1–1 correspondence between F and G
if and only if ($\Leftrightarrow$)
$$\exists h\,[\forall x(Fx \Rightarrow G(hx)) \,\&\, \forall x\forall y(x \neq y \Rightarrow hx \neq hy)$$
$$\&\, \forall x(Gx \Rightarrow \exists y(Fy \,\&\, hy = x))]$$

The accompanying figure shows a 1–1 correspondence fx between F and G.

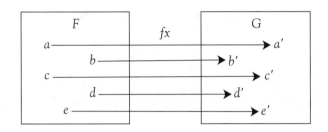

CHALLENGE 5

a. Write out what it means to say "There is a 1–1 correspondence between F and F (i.e., between F and itself). This should be true; there are just as many F's as F's.

b. The identity function i is the rather trivial function defined by

$$ix = x \qquad \text{for all } x$$

Show that the identity function is a 1–1 correspondence between F and F.

CHALLENGE 6

a. Write out what it means to say "There is a 1–1 correspondence between G and F." (If there is a 1–1 correspondence between F and G, then there is a 1–1 correspondence between G and F. The crucial step in proving this is to notice that if hx is a 1–1 function, then the inverse of h, $h^{-1}y$, defined as $h^{-1}y = x \Leftrightarrow hx = y$, is also a 1–1 function. This is technically messy but conceptually easy. Intuitively, h^{-1} assigns to an object y precisely the object x that h assigned y to.)

b. Assuming that h^{-1} is a function, show that it is a 1–1 correspondence between G and F if h is a 1–1 correspondence between F and G.

CHALLENGE 7

Suppose h is a 1–1 match between F and G and j is a 1–1 match between G and H. Show there is a 1–1 match between F and H. (To show this, consider the compound function jhx: $jhx = z$ iff $\exists y(hx = y \ \& \ jy = z)$. In words, to find the value of jh on x, first find the value of h for x, then find the value of j when hx is its argument.)

One-to-one correspondences or perfect matches divide up the properties in the universe (fingers on Tom's left hand, male dogs in Hadley, or more generally, Fx, Gx, or Hx) into classes such that every property in a class is 1–1 equivalent to every other property in that class (such classes are called **equivalence classes**). Each such class determines a unique number 0, 1, 2, and so on. The great logicians Frege and Russell proposed that numbers simply be defined as equivalence classes.

For example, the number 0 would just be the class of empty properties:

$$0 = \{F \mid \neg \exists x Fx\}$$

The number 1 would be the class of properties with one member. This is not circular, because we can define "property with one member" without mentioning 1:

$$1 = \{F \mid \exists x(Fx \ \& \ \forall y(y \neq x \Rightarrow \neg Fy))\}$$

Similarly,

$$2 = \{F \mid \exists x \exists y(Fx \ \& \ Fy \ \& \ x \neq y \ \& \ \forall z((z \neq x \ \& \ z \neq y) \Rightarrow \neg Fz))\}$$

and so on for the other numbers.

It was the genius of Frege and Russell to realize that the particular nature of numbers was less important than their connection to 1–1 matches. What really matters is that numbers satisfy the principle

$$[\![Fx]\!] = [\![Gx]\!] \Leftrightarrow \exists h \ (h \text{ is a 1–1 function from } F \text{ onto } G)$$

In other words, what matters is that the same number be assigned to properties in a 1–1 correspondence with each other.

Frege drew the following analogy with direction. In order to understand the idea of the direction of a line, you don't need some mystical grasp of a queer entity called "direction." All you have to do is recognize whether the direction of two lines is the same or not, and to do that all you have to do is grasp the fact that

> the direction of L = the direction of K
> if and only if L is parallel to K.

Similarly, to understand numbers, all you need to do is recognize whether two properties have the same number of things satisfying them or not, and to do that all you have to do is check if there is a 1–1 correspondence between them. It matters very little what we take the numbers to be. (But Frege insisted that we must take them to be some specific things. He wanted us to be able to tell that Julius Caesar wasn't a number!) We can define the ordinary arithmetical operations of addition and multiplication in terms of the underlying 1–1 correspondences.

We make one final but crucial point about 1–1 correspondences. When it comes to checking on the number of F's, does it matter which 1–1 function you use? Could you get different answers with different choices? For example, might *h* be a 1–1 function from *F* onto *G* and *j* be a 1–1 function from *F* to *G* but not onto *G*?

Consider a practical question. We want to check if there are exactly as many students as chairs in a room, so we ask each student to take a seat. Suppose every student is seated and there are three empty chairs. Is it sensible to worry that this was just an accident? Should we ask the students to shuffle around and sit in other chairs to see if this time every chair gets taken?

That seems absurd. Intuitively it seems that if there is a 1–1 function from *F* onto *G*, then every 1–1 function from *F* to *G* is onto. Conversely, if there is a 1–1 function from *F* not onto *G*, then every 1–1 function from *F* to *G* is not onto.

Now if *F* and *G* are properties with only a finite number of instances, then if one 1–1 function from *F* to *G* is onto, any 1–1 function is. This fact gives rise to a very nice feature of numbers: Either there is no 1–1 function that goes from *F* to *G* (so *F* has more instances than does *G* and so *F* is larger than *G*), or there is a 1–1 function from *F* to *G*. And either every 1–1 function from *F* to *G* is onto (so *F* and *G* have the same number of instances) or every 1–1 function from *F* to *G* is not onto (so *G* has more instances than does *F* and so *G* is larger than *F*).

Next we notice another attractive feature of our approach to numbers. It applies equally well to finite and infinite. When we defined 1–1 correspondence and defined $[\![Fx]\!] = [\![Gx]\!] \Leftrightarrow$ "There is a 1–1 correspondence between *F* and *G*," we never specified that *F* be finite (like "finger on my left hand") or infinite (like "natural number"). In other words, our basic definition of number applies equally well in principle to infinite cases and finite cases!

Finally, we notice a paradox concerning infinite numbers. Let *Gx* be the property "*x* is a natural number," that is, *x* is 1 or 2 or 3 and so on. Let *Fx* be "*x* is the square of a natural number," that is, *x* is 0 or 1 or 4 or 9, and so on. Are there as many *F*'s as *G*'s or are there more *G*'s than *F*'s? Galileo found that both facts were true, as we shall show.

There are more *G*'s than *F*'s. Consider the identity function *ix* = *x*. This is a 1–1 function from *F* to *G* but not onto *G*. Every square is matched up with a natural number (the square itself):

```
F: 0 1    4       9                    16      . . .
   | |    |       |                    |
G: 0 1 2 3 4 5 6 7 8 9 10 11 12 13 14 15 16 17 . . .
```

but many natural numbers are left out of the matching.

On the other hand, there are as many G's as F's. For consider the (positive) square root function $\sqrt{x} = y$ (where $y^2 = x$). This is a 1–1 function from G to F that is onto. Every square is matched up with a natural number, and every natural number is matched up with a square:

$$F: 0 \quad 1 \quad 4 \quad 9 \quad 16 \quad 25 \quad 36 \quad 49 \quad 64 \quad 81 \quad 100 \ \ldots$$
$$| \quad | \quad | \quad | \quad | \quad | \quad | \quad | \quad | \quad | \quad |$$
$$G: 0 \quad 1 \quad 2 \quad 3 \quad 4 \quad 5 \quad 6 \quad 7 \quad 8 \quad 9 \quad 10 \ \ldots$$

When Galileo first noticed this seeming paradox, he claimed that it showed that the concept of infinity was incoherent. The first argument seems to show conclusively that there are fewer squares than numbers; the second argument seems to show conclusively that there are exactly as many squares as numbers. Galileo concluded that the idea of size did not apply to infinite sets.

Several centuries later the great logical genius Cantor found a flaw in Galileo's reasoning. We've seen Cantor's position in "No (Certain) Escape" in part 6. But for the moment we rest content with a fundamental insight of early logicians such as Frege and Russell. Numbers, as measures of quantity, can be (virtually) logically defined as "equivalence classes" of properties, that is, as collections of all properties such that there is a 1–1 correspondence among the objects having those properties.

THE PARADOX OF THE HEAP

And Mountainous error be too highly heap'd
For truth to o'erpeer.
           —WILLIAM SHAKESPEARE

The paradox of the heap, also known as the sorites paradox, was propounded in ancient Greece. It has many variations; here are a few. The first one is close to the original version.

Suppose this huge mound of sand is a heap.
If one removes one grain from a heap of sand, one is left with a heap of sand.

By applying the second principle repeatedly to the first, one is eventually forced to conclude that one grain of sand constitutes a heap of sand.

Here is a variation about rich people:

Anyone with $1,000,000 is rich.
If anyone with $n is rich, then anyone with $(n − 1) is rich.
∴ Anyone with $0 is rich (by repeatedly applying the second principle to the first).

Here is the sorites paradox in the other direction:

Anyone with $0 is not rich.
If anyone with $n is not rich, then anyone with $(n + 1) is not rich.
∴ Anyone with $1,000,000 is not rich (by repeatedly applying the second principle to the first).

Here is a scandalous version due to Sextus Empiricus:

It is not immoral to touch your mother's big toe with your little finger.
Little differences don't matter.
∴ Incest is not immoral.

A predicate that might be susceptible to the paradox is often called a "vague predicate." Indeed, vague predicates are sometimes defined as predicates that are susceptible to the sorites paradox. A partial list of vague predicates includes "rich," "poor," "fat," "thin," "tall," "short," "red," "green," "hairy," "bald," "child," "adult," "is a heap," "is not a heap," "is a mountain," and "is not a mountain."

Now let's try to formalize some version of the paradox using the techniques of predicate logic and explain exactly why it is a paradox. Consider this version:

Anyone with $1,000,000 is rich.
If anyone with $n is rich, then anyone with $(n − 1) is rich.
∴ Anyone with $0 is rich.

Let the formal predicate "Rich(x)" represent the property of numbers that anyone with $x is rich and let the constants "1,000,000" and "0" stand for their usual referents, the numbers

CHALLENGE 1 List five more vague predicates. Construct variants of the paradox of the heap for two of your predicates.

459

1,000,000 and 0. Then we can formalize the sorites paradox in classical logic as follows:

"Anyone with $1,000,000 is rich." is Rich(1,000,000)
"If anyone with n is rich, then anyone with $(n-1)$ is rich." is
$\quad \forall x(\text{Rich}(x) \Rightarrow \text{Rich}(x-1))$
"Anyone with $0 is rich." is Rich(0)

In brief:

Rich(1,000,000)
$\forall x(\text{Rich}(x) \Rightarrow \text{Rich}(x-1))$
$\therefore \text{Rich}(0)$

The conclusion appears to follow from the premises using two rules of classical logic repeatedly, $\forall$-elimination and *modus ponens*, or $\Rightarrow$-elimination:

$$\forall E \quad \forall x Ax \qquad\qquad\qquad \Rightarrow E \quad A, \quad A \Rightarrow B$$
$$\therefore At \text{ (for any term } t) \qquad\qquad \therefore B$$

Thus we argue:

1.	Rich(1,000,000)	premise
2.	$\forall x(\text{Rich}(x) \Rightarrow \text{Rich}(x-1))$	premise
3.	Rich(1,000,000) $\Rightarrow$ Rich(999,999)	$\forall$E, 2
4.	Rich(999,999)	$\Rightarrow$E, 1, 3
5.	Rich(999,999) $\Rightarrow$ Rich(999,998)	$\forall$E, 2
6.	Rich(999,998)	$\Rightarrow$E, 4, 5
7.	Rich(999,998) $\Rightarrow$ Rich(999,997)	$\forall$E, 2
8.	Rich(999,997)	$\Rightarrow$E, 6, 7

$$\cdot$$
$$\cdot$$
$$\cdot$$

2,000,000.	Rich(1)	$\Rightarrow$E, 1,999,998, 1,999,999
2,000,001.	Rich(1) $\Rightarrow$ Rich(0)	$\forall$E, 2
2,000,002.	Rich(0)	$\Rightarrow$E, 2,000,000, 2,000,001

The argument certainly appears to be logically valid; that is, the premises seem to imply the conclusion because only (two) logical rules are used to derive the conclusion.

The preceding remarks generate a puzzle. It is commonly held that sorites arguments are valid derivations of the conclusion from two premises. Yet the following argument form is *not* valid.

Fc where Fx is a predicate like $\mathrm{Rich}(x)$
$\forall x(Fx \Rightarrow Ffx)$ where fx is a function like $x - 1$
$\therefore Fd$

CHALLENGE 2

Show that this form is not valid by finding a structure that makes the premises true and the conclusion false. (*Hint:* reinterpret *fx* as another function.) Explain why this implies that there cannot be a deduction of the conclusion from the premises.

If you've met Challenge 2, then you realize there is something suspicious about the standard claim that the sorites paradox is based on a logically valid argument from only two premises. At the very least, the version

$\mathrm{Rich}(1{,}000{,}000)$
$\forall x(\mathrm{Rich}(x) \Rightarrow \mathrm{Rich}(x - 1))$
$\therefore \mathrm{Rich}(0)$

must hide some implicit assumptions (since the pure logical form is not valid).

In the following we'll ignore this interesting problem (see "Notes, References, Hints, and Some Answers"), for if we grant that the sorites paradox or paradox of the heap is based on a valid argument of classical logic from true premises to a false conclusion, then we have some motivation to modify classical logic. This interpretation is perhaps the most common interpretation of professional philosophers today, so it is worth exploring.

Even if we assume that the argument is valid, we should concede that the conclusion is false; in reality, $\neg\mathrm{Rich}(0)$—having \$0 does not make anyone rich. Yet if the conclusion is false and if the argument is valid, one of the premises must be false. Which one?

$\mathrm{Rich}(1{,}000{,}000)$
$\forall x(\mathrm{Rich}(x) \Rightarrow \mathrm{Rich}(x - 1))$

Surely the first premise must be true if the word "rich" is to have any meaning. If there are any quibbles about millionaires being rich, we could start the argument with billionaires or even trillionaires! That seems to leave the second premise as the guilty party.

But if the second premise is false, then its negation must be true. After all, we learned early in the book that any statement A has a negation, $\neg A$, which differs in truth values so that

A	$\neg A$
T	F
F	T

What is the negation of the second premise? Of course, it's just $\neg\forall x(\text{Rich}(x) \Rightarrow \text{Rich}(x-1))$, but we'd like to have a better understanding of what that means. That's why we spent so much time on negation in this book.

Recall the general logical principles

$$\neg\forall xAx \Leftrightarrow \exists x\neg Ax \quad (not \;\neg\forall xAx \Leftrightarrow \forall x\neg Ax)$$

In English "Not everything is an A" is equivalent to "Something is not an A." (We also have $\neg\exists xAx \Leftrightarrow \forall x\neg Ax$: "Nothing is an A" is equivalent to "Each (every) thing is not an A.") Thus

$$\neg\forall x(\text{Rich}(x) \Rightarrow \text{Rich}(x-1))$$

is equivalent to

$$\exists x\neg(\text{Rich}(x) \Rightarrow \text{Rich}(x-1))$$

Now we need a simple equivalent of negated conditionals $\neg(B \Rightarrow C)$. Recall that the truth table for $\Rightarrow$ is

B	C	$B \Rightarrow C$
T	T	T
T	F	F
F	T	T
F	F	T

and so that for $\neg(B \Rightarrow C)$ is just

B	C	$\neg(B \Rightarrow C)$
T	T	F
T	F	T
F	T	F
F	F	F

so $\neg(B \Rightarrow C)$ is logically equivalent to $B \;\&\; \neg C$. Thus

$$\neg\forall x(\text{Rich}(x) \Rightarrow \text{Rich}(x-1))$$

is equivalent to

$$\exists x \neg (\text{Rich}(x) \Rightarrow \text{Rich}(x - 1))$$

which in turn is equivalent to

$$\exists x (\text{Rich}(x) \ \& \ \neg \text{Rich}(x - 1))$$

CHALLENGE 3 Deduce $\exists x (\text{Rich}\,x) \ \& \ \neg \text{Rich}(x - 1))$ from $\neg \forall x (\text{Rich}(x) \Rightarrow \text{Rich}(x - 1))$ using just the introduction and elimination rules!

So if $\forall x (\text{Rich}(x) \Rightarrow \text{Rich}(x - 1))$ is false, there is some number x such that anyone with \$$x$ is rich but those with \$$(x - 1)$ are not rich. But what number could that possibly be? The essence of vague predicates seems to be that there is no sharp dividing line (notice the difference between "there is no sharp dividing line" and "we don't know the sharp dividing line").

This is very different from precise predicates like "having more than \$100." For such predicates it is perfectly true that $\exists x (\text{Have}(x) \ \& \ \neg \text{Have}\,(x - 1))$, for example, when $x = \$101$.

So it looks like $\forall x (\text{Rich}(x) \Rightarrow \text{Rich}(x - 1))$ is as solid as $\text{Rich}(1,000,000)$. And since the argument from the premises to the conclusion is valid, the conclusion must be true. But it's false. Something has gone radically wrong. That's why the situation is a paradox.

Before we proceed with technical logic, let us suggest a philosophical resolution of the paradox. One way to look at things is to blame the vague predicates themselves—such predicates are essentially incoherent and are therefore bound to lead to contradiction. They do not really represent concepts—like the predicates of mathematics or science. On this stark view, the bottom line is that rationality is incompatible with vagueness. Rationality (and logic) is intimately tied to precision. Vagueness doesn't make sense, and the sorites paradoxes are taken to show that vagueness doesn't make sense.

This is an intriguing philosophical position, and of course we're tempted to discuss its philosophical merits. (If vague predicates are incoherent, why do we get along so well with them? Or *do* we get along so well? Consider "One more cigarette can't hurt me!" Maybe vague predicates are a barrier to humanity's progress.) But here we want to suggest another possibility.

Vague predicates are not irrational. They are merely unsuited to classical logic. Vague predicates are rational because there is another kind of logic that reveals the rationality behind them! What a strange thought! The logic you spent so much time learning is not an outline of universal truth; at best, it's an outline of universal precise truths. Perhaps there are alternatives to classical logic that can resolve the sorites paradox without eliminating vague predicates from our rational lives.

Let's briefly explore three such logics. Obviously, you can't expect to understand these systems of logic in their entirety. But the crude sketches here might whet your appetite for further investigation and deepen your understanding of classical logic by explaining how there can be alternatives.

These three alternative logics, some of which we've already mentioned, are

1. three-valued logics (T, F, and something else)
2. supervaluations and truth value gaps
3. intuitionistic logic

Three-Valued Logic

Classical logic insists that there are only two truth values, true and false. Every proposition or meaningful declarative sentence is either true or false (not true); if it's false, then its negation is true. The ancients said there was no middle ground, no third way. Quite naturally, this leads to the law of the excluded middle.

According to three-valued logic—as you've already seen in our discussion of the law of the excluded middle—there is an alternative to T and F, which we've called I, although it doesn't matter how we label it. Classical logicians claimed that every meaningful predicate "Px" denoted a property Px that divided the universe into two classes —the extension of the property, that is, the collection of things that had the property, $\{x \mid Px\}$, and the antiextension of the property, that is, the collection of things that lacked the property, $\{x \mid \neg Px\}$. Thus for any individual thing a, you knew that $Pa \vee \neg Pa$.

Three-valued logicians accept the claims of the classical logicians for precise predicates, but they interpret vague predicates differently. For these logicians, vague predicates don't divide the universe of things in half. Instead, vague predicates, such as "Vx," divide the universe into (1) the extension of the property, $\{x \mid Vx\}$, the collection of things that have the property; (2) the antiextension of the property, $\{x \mid \neg Vx\}$, the collection of things that actually lack the property; and (3) a penumbra or middle ground, a collection of things that neither have nor lack the property. Instead of espousing two-valued truth tables containing only T's and F's, the three-valued logicians espouse three-valued truth tables containing T's, F's, and I's.

Here is their first problem: What is the correct account of the logical operations $\neg$, &, $\vee$, $\Rightarrow$, $\Leftrightarrow$, $\forall$, and $\exists$ according to three-valued logic? Should F & I count as I because an indeterminate value is present, or should F & I count as F because a conjunction is F if each item is? We discussed this problem in "The Law of the Excluded Middle" in part 8.

Here is the second problem: How do we relate this intuitively appealing account to the sorites paradox? A natural suggestion is that the statement $\forall x(\text{Rich}(x) \Rightarrow \text{Rich}(x - 1))$ is neither T nor F but I, and so it cannot be used as a premise in an argument. Unfortunately, it seems to follow that all the laws of logic are unavailable for vague predicates. The statement $\text{Rich}(c) \vee \neg\text{Rich}(c)$ will be I for any c in the penumbra or middle ground, and so $\forall x(\text{Rich}(x) \vee \neg\text{Rich}(x))$ will be I. So how does the third truth value account differ from the simple claim that vague predicates are simply irrational?

Finally, even if the three-valued logicians could account for logical operators and the sorites paradox, they would have to deal with the objection that their solution to the question has merely transferred the problem of drawing a line between rich and not rich to the problem of drawing a line between rich on the one hand and neither rich nor not rich on the other.

Supervaluations and Truth Value Gaps

A more sophisticated variant of the three-valued logics is supervaluation. According to this theory, there are only two truth values, T and F, but some propositions do not get a truth value in some situations (or, what comes to the same thing, some property neither applies nor fails to apply to a given object). Like three-valued logicians, supervaluationists allow for the possibility of gaps in truth value. But they put an interesting twist in how they assign truth values to complex statements.

In a nutshell their idea is this: As before, every vague predicate "Vx" divides the universe of objects into three classes, the extension of V, the antiextension of V, and the penumbra of V. In this they agree with the three-valued logicians. Where the supervaluationists differ is in how they assess the truth or falsity of complex statements. In particular, they introduce the notion of a "sharpening" of a vague predicate V. Roughly speaking, a sharpening of V is a precise predicate P such that the (positive) extension of V is included in the extension of P and antiextension of V is included in the antiextension of P. Notice that a vague predicate V will have many sharpenings.

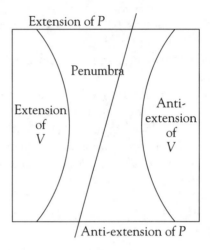

EXAMPLE Suppose that the extension of the vague predicate "Rich" includes all those dollar amounts above or equal to $1,000,000, and the antiextension includes all those dollar amounts less than or equal to $100,000. Then any precise predicate of the form "x is greater than or equal to n" for n between 100,000 and 1,000,000 will be a sharpening of "Rich." So "having more than $523,659" would be one sharpening of "Rich." The positive extension of having more than $523,659 includes all rich people, and the negative extension includes all those who are definitely not rich.

CHALLENGE 4 Explain why $Va \vee \neg Va$ is true in the supervaluationist account for objects in the penumbra although Va and $\neg Va$ are both not true. (*Hint:* Consider the multiplicity of sharpenings.)

The twist of the supervaluationist is that if $A(V)$ is a complex statement involving the vague predicate V, $A(V)$ will be true (false) iff it is true (false) for all sharpenings of V. This has many curious consequences. Among them is that for any object a in the penumbra of V, $Va \vee \neg Va$ will be true, because every sharpening obeys the law of the excluded middle, $P \vee \neg P$. On the other hand, although $Va \vee \neg Va$ is true for any object a in the penumbra, neither Va nor $\neg Va$ is true.

Supervaluationists are thus able to provide a solution to the sorites paradox. According to their theory

$\neg \forall x (\text{Rich}(x) \Rightarrow \text{Rich}(x - 1))$ or equivalently

$$\exists x (\text{Rich}(x) \,\&\, \neg \text{Rich}(x - 1))$$

is true although Rich(n) & $\neg$Rich($n - 1$) isn't true for any particular n! This all makes perfect logical sense (for supervaluationists!) but whether it resolves the paradox is another question.

Intuitionism

As we saw in a previous chapter, intuitionists reject the law of the excluded middle and so reject the thought that any meaningful predicate divides the universe of discourse into an extension and antiextension. But intuitionists are very different from the proponents of truth gaps or supervaluations. For intuitionists there are only two truth values, true and false. However, they recognize that we cannot always judge which truth value holds for a given statement (everyone acknowledges this as a practical limitation on human beings). In addition, intuitionists maintain that this limitation is intrinsic to logic. Human beings will never be able to overcome it.

In "The Law of the Excluded Middle" in part 8, we saw that intuitionists do not accept the law of the excluded middle (as even supervaluationists do), primarily because they reject the law of $\neg$-elimination. They don't believe that $\neg\neg A$ implies A. Recall that for intuitionists, the symbols of logic are not explained by any truth tables but by rules. To assert $\neg A$ is to assert that you know there is a demonstration that the hypothesis A yields a contradiction. To assert $\neg\neg A$ is to assert that you know there is a demonstration that the hypothesis $\neg A$ yields a contradiction. But the latter might be true without your knowing any demonstration that A is true.

Now if the principle of $\neg$-elimination is given up, then a crucial step in the development of the sorites paradox fails. Remember that a naive view of the paradox of the heap is to see it as a refutation of the second premise, namely, $\forall x(\text{Rich}(x) \Rightarrow \text{Rich}(x - 1))$. The problem with this interpretation is that in classical logic $\neg\forall x(\text{Rich}(x) \Rightarrow \text{Rich}(x - 1))$ is equivalent to $\exists x(\text{Rich}(x)$ & $\neg\text{Rich}(x - 1))$, but we're not able to specify any number n such that Rich(n) & $\neg$Rich($n - 1$). Here is the critical point: The logical law that $\neg\forall x Ax$ is equivalent to $\exists x \neg Ax$ is not valid in intuitionistic logic.

So the intuitionists can accept $\neg\forall x(\text{Rich}(x) \Rightarrow \text{Rich}(x - 1))$; indeed, the sorites paradox can be construed as a proof of this. But they are not compelled to accept $\exists x(\text{Rich}(x)$ & $\neg\text{Rich}(x - 1))$. Consequently, the sorites paradox cannot be constructed in intuitionistic logic, at least not directly. So if we accepted intuitionistic

CHALLENGE 5

Show that $\neg\forall x Ax$ implies $\exists x \neg Ax$ in standard logic, and note where you use $\neg$-elimination in your deduction!

logic, instead of the logic we have learned, we might not have to deal with the sorites paradox.

Actually the situation is somewhat more complicated. Some philosophers argue that the sorites paradox can be constructed in intuitionistic logic, while others argue that it can't be constructed in classical logic. In any case, everyone would like to see an explanation of why vague predicates should be treated like the (potentially infinite) predicates of intuitionist logic. Nevertheless, despite all these unanswered questions, if you've read this far and understood at least half of what you've read, you're better off than some professional philosophers and logicians!

SUMMARY: The paradox of the heap challenges our logical acumen and the correctness of classical two-valued predicate logic. Alternative approaches to classical logic have been propounded to resolve the paradox, including three-valued logic, supervaluations, and intuitionism.

RUSSELL'S PARADOX AND FREGE'S MISTAKE

People usually serve the choice wine first. . . .
What you have done is keep the choice wine until now.
— JOHN THE APOSTLE

Why are logicians interested in paradoxes? Partly because they are challenges to our reason. A paradox unresolved is an affront to our understanding of the concepts involved. Paradoxes almost always teach us something about those concepts. The existence of a paradox shows that we have not grasped all there is to grasp about certain concepts and the logic that deals with them. Furthermore, paradoxes are, like puzzles, fun. Finally, the discipline of modern logic arose from a paradox called Russell's paradox. The story behind Russell's paradox is the guiding myth or folktale of modern logic, and we want to share it with you.

Let's begin by reviewing the simple barber paradox. As you'll recall, it concerns a village with a barber who cuts the hair of all those and only those who don't cut their own hair. The complexity of the description leads us to believe that there really could be such a place

—until we wonder who cuts the barber's hair. Does she cut her own hair? Then she violates the requirement to cut the hair of only those who don't cut their own hair. Does she not cut her own hair? Then she violates the command to cut the hair of all those who don't cut their own hair. Our conclusion is that there can be no such barber. The statement that there is is logically contradictory.

It will be useful to formalize this, not only for the practice it provides but because it will help set up the story of Frege's magnificent discovery, his critical mistake, and his heroic response. For convenience, we'll drop talk of barbers and villages and formalize the simpler

> There is someone who shaves all those and only those
> who don't shave themselves.

Of course, we represent the locution "there is someone" by the existential quantifier $\exists$, so the statement becomes

$\exists y$ ("y shaves all those and only those who don't shave themselves")

The key step in the formalization is recognizing the two-place relation "—— shaves ——," or "w shaves v." ("Shaves" is a two-place relation, like "loves.") Although it is a two-place relation, one person can do it all by himself ("I shave myself." I also love myself, and sometimes I could kick myself).

If we consider an arbitrary person x, how do we say "x shaves himself"?

$$\text{"}x \text{ shaves } x\text{"}$$

How do we say "x doesn't shave himself"?

$$\neg(\text{"}x \text{ shaves } x\text{"})$$

There are two conditions on our imaginary barber y. First, y shaves all those who don't shave themselves. In other words, for any arbitrary x, if x doesn't shave himself, then y shaves x:

$$\forall x(\neg(\text{"}x \text{ shaves } x\text{"}) \Rightarrow \text{"}y \text{ shaves } x\text{"})$$

The second condition is that y shaves only those who don't shave themselves. In other words, for any arbitrary x, if y shaves x, then x doesn't shave himself:

$$\forall x(\text{"}y \text{ shaves } x\text{"} \Rightarrow \neg(\text{"}x \text{ shaves } x\text{"}))$$

Putting these together we get

$$\forall x(\text{``}y \text{ shaves } x\text{''} \Leftrightarrow \neg(\text{``}x \text{ shaves } x\text{''}))$$

Recall that the story of the barber posits that there is some y satisfying this:

$$\exists y \forall x(\text{``}y \text{ shaves } x\text{''} \Leftrightarrow \neg(\text{``}x \text{ shaves } x\text{''}))$$

This statement is contradictory, as can be seen as follows. Suppose it were true. Then there would have to be someone b^* (for "barber") who was the mysterious shaver:

$$\forall x(\text{``}b^* \text{ shaves } x\text{''} \Leftrightarrow \neg(\text{``}x \text{ shaves } x\text{''}))$$

But if the statement holds for all things ($\forall x$), it holds for b^* herself

$$\text{``}b^* \text{ shaves } b^*\text{''} \Leftrightarrow \neg(\text{``}b^* \text{ shaves } b^*\text{''})$$

Obviously this is impossible.

Modern logic was discovered by Gottlob Frege, a German mathematician and philosopher (1848–1925). It was he who discovered how to manipulate the quantifiers ($\forall$ and $\exists$), the truth functions ($\neg$, &, and $\Rightarrow$), variables, and predicates. It was Frege who taught us how to formalize using the logical symbols, and it was he who taught us the essential rules for drawing conclusions, such as those used to derive the contradiction implicit in the barber's paradox. It is not unreasonable to say that Frege was the greatest logician who ever lived. He took a subject that had been essentially unchanged since its codification by Aristotle over 2000 years ago and completely revolutionized it, just as Einstein revolutionized physics and Darwin revolutionized biology.

Unfortunately, Frege's genius was largely unrecognized in his lifetime. His standards were so high, his ideas so novel, his symbolization so extraordinary for the time that few understood him. It did not help his cause that he scheduled his lectures for 7:00 A.M. and mumbled them while facing the blackboard (the lectures were not well attended). Nevertheless, among his few students and correspondents were the titans of early twentieth-century logic, philosophy, and mathematics.

Still, Frege had a plan. He was not interested in logic simply for its own sake but had in mind resolving some ancient philosophical problems. What is mathematics? How is knowledge of mathematics possible? The standard answers to these questions did not satisfy Frege. Some people say that mathematics deals with ideas, but Frege wondered how it is that my idea of 4 agrees with your idea of 4. Some people say that mathematics is a game played with formal symbols, but Frege wondered why a game should be so useful and why we should feel so bound by mathematical results if mathematics is indeed a game. Finally, some people believe that there is a mysterious realm of mathematical objects for which human beings have a special mental faculty, a sort of ESP, for intuiting those objects. Frege thought this belief was a superstition.

Frege had his own answer to these questions; in essence, mathematics is nothing but logic, he said. If one takes the symbols and rules of modern logic (the logic Frege created) and adds just one subtle touch, the concept of set, then all of mathematics follows. That is, according to Frege, every concept of mathematics can be explicitly defined in terms of logic, and every statement of mathematics can be translated by a wff of logic. The rules of mathematics are just the logical rules described in "Deduction" in part 6. Finally, all of the basic principles (axioms) of mathematics can be derived from the fundamental laws of logic.

These were amazing assertions. The Western philosophical tradition had rarely seen such surprising claims expressed so precisely. Yet Frege set about demonstrating these claims. He did not argue about them the way philosophers usually do (with plenty of logical leaps) but attempted to prove them line by line, the way mathematicians do! Frege might not have been popular, but he was surely supported by the rightness of his cause. When he deduced mathematics from logic, he figured, then his procedures would be vindicated. After writing an initial book outlining his project, *The Foundations of Arithmetic*, he began work on a two-volume set in which the project was developed in detail, *The Fundamental Laws of Arithmetic*.

The one concept of Frege's not mentioned in "Predicate Logic" in part 5 (but see "Sets" in part 4) is the concept of **set** (or **class** or **collection**). We often talk about sets of things, generally representing them using curly brackets. For example,

{Jim, Tom} is a set of two things, namely Jim and Tom.
{0, 2, 4, 6, 8} is the set of even numbers less than 10.
{a, e, i, o, u} is the set of standard vowels of English.

Often we specify a set in terms of a common property of its members:

{$x \mid x$ is a tiger} is the set consisting of all tigers
{$y \mid y$ is a female} is the set of all females

471

$\{x \mid Fx\}$ is the set of all things that have property Fx, whatever Fx is.

The wff $x \in y$ expresses the thought that x is a member of set y. Thus $x \in \{$Jim, Tom$\}$ iff x is Jim or x is Tom; $x \in \{y \mid y \text{ is a female}\}$ iff x is a female; more generally, $x \in \{x \mid Fx\}$ iff Fx. To say that x is a member of the set of things that F says precisely that x F's, or Fx.

Finally, Frege added only two new principles to basic logic. One simply said that sets with the same members were the same sets (e.g., $\{$Jim, Tom$\}$ = $\{$Tom, Jim$\}$). More generally

$$x = y \Leftrightarrow \forall z (z \in x \Leftrightarrow z \in y)$$

The other principle asserted that every property determined a set: Given any property F, there was a set consisting of all those things that had F. In symbols,

$$\text{For each } F, \exists y (y = \{x \mid Fx\})$$

Another way of writing this is just

$$\text{For each } F, \exists y \forall x (x \in y \Leftrightarrow Fx)$$

With those two properties in place, Frege began his detailed derivation of mathematics from the basic principles of logic.

Just as the second volume of *Fundamental Laws of Arithmetic* was going to press, however, Frege received a letter from the young British philosopher and logician Bertrand Russell. Russell's letter called Frege's attention to the axiom of set existence:

$$\text{For each } F, \exists y \forall x (x \in y \Leftrightarrow Fx)$$

Russell asked what happens when we consider F to be the property "does not belong to itself," or $\neg(x \in x)$. Some sets seem to belong to themselves, like the set of all sets and the set of all abstract objects. But many sets don't belong to themselves; for example, the set of all women is not a woman, and the set $\{$Tom, Jim$\}$ is neither Tom nor Jim. According to Frege's principle, there should be a set consisting of all and only those sets that don't belong to themselves:

$$\exists y \forall x (x \in y \Leftrightarrow \neg(x \in x))$$

CHALLENGE 1

Show that the formula at the bottom of this page is inconsistent.

CHALLENGE 2

Compare this formula to the statement of the barber paradox. What do they have in common?

Thus, Russell showed that Frege's "basic principle of logic" was not a principle of logic. In fact, it was not even true; it was contradictory. When Frege realized the gap in his foundation for arithmetic, he said, "Arithmetic totters." But his life's work lay in ruins. Years later, Russell wrote about Frege's response to this situation.

As I think about acts of integrity and grace, I realise there is nothing in my knowledge to compare with Frege's dedication to truth. His entire life's work was on the verge of completion, much of his work had been ignored to the benefit of men infinitely less capable, his second volume was about to be published, and upon finding that his fundamental assumption was in error, he responded with intellectual pleasure clearly submerging any feelings of personal disappointment. It was almost superhuman and a telling indication of that of which men are capable if their dedication is to creative work and knowledge instead of cruder efforts to dominate and be known.

Such is Frege's tragic story, and it reveals both the early promise of modern logic—one might discover the secret of mathematics and human thought—and the pitfalls—one might get caught in contradiction. Indeed, many mathematicians and philosophers hesitated to pursue this new field precisely because of their fears that their work might turn out to be contradictory.

But the more adventurous went on. Because of the many brilliant aspects of Frege's achievement, the fact that a basic premise was inconsistent came to be seen as a *challenge*, not a handicap. Repair the contradiction! Succeed where Frege failed! Modern logic did, indeed, overcome Frege's mistake. It has become the language of mathematics and an essential tool of philosophy; it forms the foundation for computer science and has inspired the development of modern linguistics. For this reason, Frege's achievements are honored by logicians and the story of his one, tragic mistake is memorialized under the title "Russell's paradox."

Would that you or I would make such a mistake as Frege's!

473

with & about logic

life

> The world is everything that is the case.
> —WITTGENSTEIN

Imagine a rectangular grid stretching to infinity in all directions. Most squares in the grid are empty, but some contain a single cell.

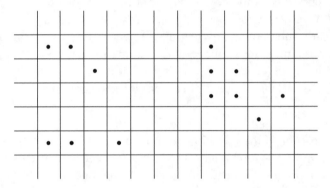

Imagine that time is divided into "generations." In each new generation some cells die, some survive, and some are born. In Life, however, life is not capricious. There are two exact rules determining what happens in each square of the grid. These rules are simple and unalterable.

Rule 1 A cell dies if it is adjacent to more than three or fewer than two other cells (orthogonally or diagonally). In the following example, the cells marked with an × are cells that will die.

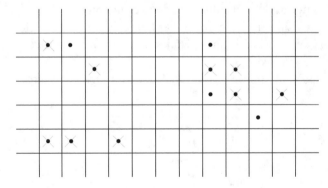

Rule 2 A cell is born in a square if that square is adjacent to exactly three living cells. In the following example, cells are born in the squares marked with an ○.

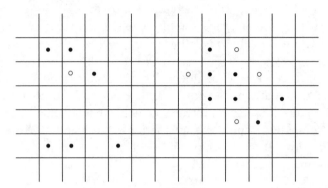

The births and deaths take place simultaneously to create the next generation:

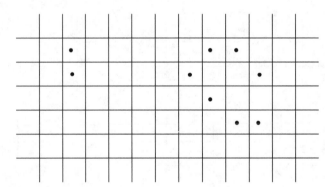

This process continues. The next few generations look like this:

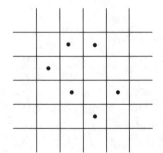 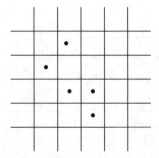 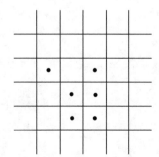

Why are we looking at this? What does it mean? How is it related to anything else in this book?

1. On one level, this is a logical exercise. The cells (called "cellular automata" obey strict rules. We can hope that with some effort we will be able to determine the behavior of the cells over time.
2. On another level, Life is connected to infinity, impossibility, computers, geometry, and the ultimate meaning of the universe.
3. Finally, this is going to be a lot of fun.

The first step is to experiment. This is easiest to do if you have access to a computer model of Life. One model is available on Internet. To obtain the program Life.exe, which will work on all PC-compatible computers, follow the instructions at the end of "Inductive Logic" in part 7. If this is not possible, you can use pencil and paper or checkers and a checkerboard.

EXERCISES Explore the following configurations. What becomes of them?

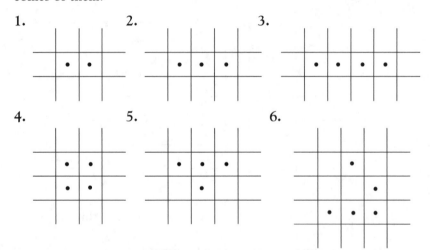

The example in exercise 6 is called a "glider." It is one reason the study of Life has attracted so much attention in so few years. It is hard to watch the glider in action without wanting to know more about the variety of forms Life can take.

There are actually many forms of cellular automata—that is, there are many possible rules for the birth and death of cells, many possible kinds of grids, and many different dimensions. Among the forms of cellular automata used, Life is a particularly attractive one. It was invented by John Horton Conway, one of world's most creative mathematicians.

Early in the history of Life (around 1970), it was noticed that some life patterns die out and some reach a sort of steady state. The question was asked, Are there any patterns that grow without stopping? Are there any patterns where the total number of living cells continues to increase without bound?

The answer was discovered in 1971 by William Gosper, who found a "glider gun," a configuration that launches gliders at regular intervals. By producing a steady stream of gliders, the gun adds unbounded quantities of matter to the universe.

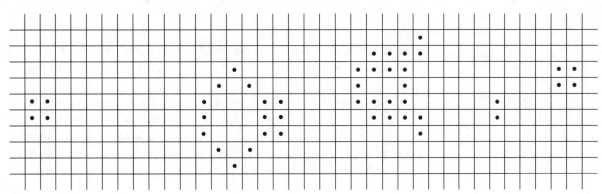

The engineer in us is charmed by the glider gun and wants to know what else we can build. The mathematician in us is challenged and wants to know if it is possible to predict what will happen to a given configuration. The philosopher in us is freaked out and wants to know if Life has any connection to *real* life.

First, the engineer: What can we build? There's a lot that we can build. We can, in fact, build a computer! Streams of data (the 0s and 1s we have discussed before) can be formed from streams of gliders at regular intervals. The presence of a glider is a 1; the absence is a 0. We can build *and-*, *or-*, and *not-*gates (see "Logic Circuits" in part 4). We can construct memory storage. In short, we can build the entire apparatus of a genuine computer.

There is a lot of work involved in this. The glider streams must be thinned out so that our streams can cross each other without confusion. The gates are not easy to construct. We need other specially designed objects to carry out certain tasks. The "eater" is particularly useful for gobbling up unwanted gliders and other garbage:

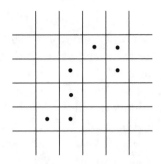

Second, the mathematician: Can we predict what will happen to configurations? In a word, no. In general, predicting the ultimate fate of a Life configuration is very hard. How hard? In fact, it is the hardest conceivable problem! This is an astonishing statement. Everyone who has taken mathematics knows there are lots of hard problems. How can one say with such assurance that this is the *hardest*?

The reason is the computer we can build. Take, for example, the Goldbach conjecture. This is a famous problem of mathematics that has been unsolved for 250 years. It is simple to state: Is it true that every even number greater than 2 is the sum of two primes? It is easy to start checking:

$$4 = 2 + 2$$
$$6 = 3 + 3$$
$$8 = 3 + 5$$
$$10 = 3 + 7 \text{ (or } 5 + 5)$$
$$12 = 5 + 7$$
$$14 = 3 + 11 \text{ (or } 7 + 7)$$
$$16 = 3 + 13 \text{ (or } 5 + 11)$$
$$18 = 5 + 13 \text{ (or } 7 + 11)$$

Simple to state, but it must be considered one of the most difficult to resolve, for it has defeated the best minds in mathematics.

We can construct a computer to work on Goldbach's problem. That computer can be set up to check every even number, one after the other. It can be programmed to self-destruct if it finds a counter-example (that is, an even number that is not the sum of two primes). Otherwise it just keeps on working. This computer begins as a configuration, an enormous array of cells scattered over a huge area. As generations pass, cells are born and cells die. Gliders glide, eaters eat, logical gates process data in the form of streams of gliders, in short, the computer computes. Now if we could predict what will happen to this configuration, then that prediction would answer Goldbach's problem. If we knew that the configuration would end in total destruction, then Goldbach's conjecture is false. If we knew that the activity would never cease, then Goldbach's conjecture is true.

This is the case for other mathematical problems. In fact, for every problem, there is a corresponding computer we can build such that the solution to the problem is connected to the fate of the computer. Thus, no problem can be harder than the problem of predicting the Life history of configurations!

Finally, the philosopher: Does Life have anything to do with the real world? Maybe! The engineer can build computers. In fact, she can build a computer that can *reproduce*. The computer can also be programmed to build an exact copy of itself some distance away and then destroy the original copy (effectively moving itself). Sounds like real life, doesn't it?

Now imagine an infinite grid, and imagine that cells are scattered over it randomly and endlessly. The probability (see "Measuring Uncertainty" in part 7) that somewhere in the grid one of these self-reproducing machines will be found is 1. Actually, there will be many. Some will be hardier than others. Some will have defenses, patrols that cruise the periphery looking for enemies, squadrons of warships that attack and destroy alien life forms. Thus we can suppose that some sort of natural selection will take place, that the best machines will survive, wiping out the more fragile ones. Really does sound like life, doesn't it?

To one man, Ed Fredkin, the father of "digital physics," it doesn't just *sound* like life, it *is* life. Fredkin suspects (believes?) that the universe is a cellular automaton (not necessarily the Life version but some version). He believes that the fundamental unit of the universe is not the molecule, not the atom, not the electron, proton, neutron, or any other subatomic particle. The building block of the universe is not matter or energy but information—1s and 0s, yeses and noes, ons and offs. If this is the case, real life is completely determined, that is, since life must follow the rules of the automaton, the future is fixed. It is written. On the other hand, since prediction is hard (very hard), we will never know for sure what will happen!

Finally, if we are merely a cellular automaton, who set us in motion? How did all this come to be?

hypergame

The man who listens to Reason is lost; Reason enslaves all whose minds are not strong enough to master her.
—George Bernard Shaw, *Man and Superman*

This is a special paradox. It was discovered by a friend of ours, Bill Zwicker, around 1980. It has elegance, charm, wit, beauty, and depth.

Bill starts by defining the idea of a finite game. A two-person game is finite, he declares, if it always ends after a finite number of moves. Tic-tac-toe is a finite game. Queens is a finite game. Chess is a finite game, because there are little-known rules that prevent it from going on indefinitely.

The game of "dealer's choice," in which the dealer at a table of card players chooses which version of poker to play, inspired Bill to invent Hypergame. In Hypergame, the first player chooses a finite game. The players then play that game until it ends. Thus, the first move of Hypergame is the choice of a game. The second move of Hypergame is the first move of the chosen game. The third move of Hypergame is the second move of the chosen game, and so on.

Theorem 1 Hypergame is a finite game.

Proof: The proof is very simple. When Hypergame is played, a game is chosen and then played. The chosen game is finite, so it takes only a finite number of moves to end. Hypergame takes the same number of moves plus one, so Hypergame also takes only a finite number of moves.

Theorem 2 Hypergame is not a finite game.

Proof: The proof of this theorem is also simple. To show that Hypergame is not finite, we have to give only one example of a play of Hypergame that is infinite. Here it is: Player 1 must first choose a finite game. Suppose player 1 chooses Hypergame (it is, after all, a finite game by theorem 1). Now player 2 makes the first move in the game chosen by player 1. The game chosen is Hypergame, so player 2 must choose a finite game. Player 2 chooses Hypergame! Now player 1 must make a third move in Hypergame, that is, the second move of the game she chose earlier, that is, the first move of the game player 2 just chose. This means she must choose a finite game, and again she chooses Hypergame. The play looks like this:

Player 1: "Hypergame!"
Player 2: "Hypergame!"
Player 1: "Hypergame!"
Player 2: "Hypergame!"
Player 1: "Hypergame!"
Player 2: "Hypergame!"
Player 1: "Hypergame!"
Player 2: "Hypergame!"

.
.
.

This will go on forever, and so Hypergame is not a finite game.

the busy beaver is not computable

> One of the merits of a proof is that it instills a certain doubt as to the
> result proved.
>
> — BERTRAND RUSSELL

In "The Busy Beaver" in part 5, we introduced a pleasant problem:
How large can a 20-step TRIVIAL program make the variable X
when it stops? This problem is actually a special case of a general one:
Given a number k, how large can a k-step program make X?

Of course, there is an answer for each k. Theoretically, this defines a function (see "Functions" in part 7). We could call it $BB(k)$, or
the "busy beaver number of k." How could you go about finding it?

We could look at all the k-step programs. Given $k = 20$, for example, we could examine each 20-step program, looking for the one
that left X largest. That is a lot of programs (easily more than a
trillion). But how do you look at a program?

If the program is simple, we might be able to tell, just by examination, what X will be when it stops. Or we might be able to tell that
it won't stop, in which case we discard it. On the other hand, if it is
not clear what a program does, then we might have to run the program and see what happens.

This is just the problem. If the program doesn't stop soon, we
can't conclude that it will never stop. It might stop after a long, long,
long time.

481

The natural question is, Can we compute BB(k)? The answer is no, and the proof is a classic of logic. It combines computer science, philosophy, and mathematics.

What do we mean by "compute"? To a computer scientist, a function is computable if there is a computer program that computes it. That is, there is a program that, given input k, responds with BB(k). This working definition is really a philosophical position, known as "Church's thesis" after the logician Alonzo Church. It has stood the test of time in the sense that no one has yet found a function that is intuitively "computable" that cannot be computed by a program.

Church actually formulated his thesis in terms of a specific language somewhat like TRIVIAL. Surprisingly, the choice of language (among programming languages currently in use) is not critical. This is an important, early result of computer science. In fact, TRIVIAL will do. TRIVIAL is not actually trivial. Everything you can do in higher languages (BASIC, FORTRAN, PROLOG, Pascal, C, ADA, etc.) you can do in TRIVIAL (it just takes longer and requires more steps).

Now we proceed by contradiction. We suppose that there is a TRIVIAL program that will compute BB. The first step of this program will be "INPUT X", and the last will be "STOP". In between, the program will increase and decrease and increase X until at the end, X will equal the value of BB(X). This program has a certain number of steps; let us say it has n steps. We'll use the program to get a contradiction. We will add to the beginning to create a large X, and then let the program compute BB(X).

In the Notes, References, Hints, and Some Answers for "The Busy Beaver," we introduced a nine-line program segment that doubles a number. We abbreviated this as

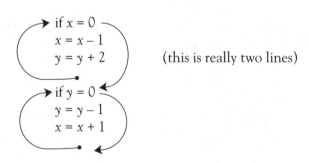

(this is really two lines)

We first remove "INPUT X". Then we attach to the start of the program "LET X = X + 1", followed by J copies of the doubling machine:

LET X = X + 1
⟨our 9-line doubling machine⟩
⟨our 9-line doubling machine⟩
.
.   } J of these
.
⟨our 9-line doubling machine⟩
⟨our BB program without INPUT X⟩

The total program will be $1 + 9J + (n - 1)$ lines long. What will it do? It will first make X equal to 1, then double it J times, increasing it to 2^J; then it will compute BB of this number, that is, $BB(2^J)$, and stop.

On the other hand, since the program is exactly $1 + 9J + (n - 1) = n + 9J$ lines long and is written in TRIVIAL, it must be that it cannot make X greater than $BB(n + 9J)$. By definition, $BB(n + 9J)$ is the largest X can get in a program of length $n + 9J$.

Note the obvious fact that if a is greater than b, then $BB(a)$ is greater than $BB(b)$, that is, $a > b \Rightarrow BB(a) > BB(b)$.

Now we get a contradiction. It is a mathematical fact that no matter how large n is, we can find a J such that $n + 9J$ is less than 2^J. We then have that our program produces $BB(2^J)$ and that this is less than $BB(n + 9J)$, even though 2^J is greater than $n + 9J$. That is, $2^J > n + 9J$, but $\neg BB(2^J) > BB(n + 9J)$. This contradicts our obvious fact! This is impossible!

impossibility

Alice laughed. "There's no use trying," she said: "one can't believe impossible things."

"I daresay you haven't had much practice," said the Queen. "When I was your age, I always did it for half-an-hour a day. Why, sometimes I've believed as many as six impossible things before breakfast."

—LEWIS CARROLL, *THROUGH THE LOOKING GLASS*

Socrates said that the greatest of all knowledge is to know that you do not know. Logic has achieved this in a way matched by no other discipline. Impossibility does not merely happen. It is part of the fiber, the soul of logic. Furthermore, we do not merely suspect this, we know it.

We have already met impossibility. It is impossible to prove or disprove Euclid's fifth postulate from the first four (see "Geometry" in part 8). It is impossible to compute the busy beaver function (see the preceding section). Mathematicians of the nineteenth century proved many such results, including the impossibility of trisecting an angle with a straight edge and compass and the impossibility of solving all fifth-degree equations by radicals. These are only incidents, however. The organic nature, the ubiquity of impossibility, is a leap beyond.

The leap was made by Kurt Gödel. In 1931, he proved what is surely one of the most remarkable theorems of the twentieth century: the "incompleteness theorem." Loosely speaking, it states that any logical system satisfying certain conditions will be incomplete; that is, there will be questions it is unable to resolve. Take, for example, arithmetic. We discuss a system of axioms for arithmetic in "Logic Programming" in part 7. This system is incomplete. There are statements about numbers that can be neither proven nor disproven.

Specifically, the incompleteness theorem says that for any collection of axioms that is (1) consistent, (2) strong enough to define arithmetic, and (3) "easily describable," there exists a statement that can be neither proven nor disproven. Such statements are called "undecidable."

Consistency is necessary, of course. If a system is inconsistent, then it can prove anything (see "Bertrand the First" in part 4).

By "easily describable," we mean, roughly, that one could write a computer program to list the axioms. The axioms can even be infinite in number, so long as a program running for an infinite length of time could list each eventually.

Note that there are many such undecidable statements. If, for example, p is undecidable, then we could add it to our list of axioms. We could then apply the theorem to this new axiom system and find yet another undecidable statement.

Another example: In "No (Certain) Escape" in part 6, we showed that the set N of natural numbers is strictly smaller in size than the set R of real numbers. Is there a set of intermediate size

$$N < ? < R$$

Cantor thought there was not, that is, that every set strictly larger than N was at least as large as R. Cantor couldn't prove this, and his guess became known as Cantor's continuum hypothesis, or CH. In 1939 Gödel himself showed that if the standard axioms for set theory are consistent, then it is impossible to disprove CH. In other words, if those axioms are consistent, then adding on CH does not create an inconsistency. In 1963 Paul Cohen showed that it is impossible to prove CH from those other axioms.

Another example: We have provided you with a system of deduction for Sentential. That system is complete in the sense that given any valid argument, that argument can be deduced within the system. Our system for predicate logic is also complete (see "The Completeness Theorem" in part 8). Any formula that is valid or true in every model can be derived as a theorem. Nevertheless, there is an important difference between Sentential and predicate logic. For Sentential, there is a procedure for deciding, given any wff, whether it is valid or not, namely, the use of truth tables. There is no such procedure in predicate logic. In fact, Gödel's theorem establishes the impossibility of such a procedure.

Gödel proved a second incompleteness theorem, which is really a corollary to the first. It states that no system with the properties listed can ever demonstrate its own consistency. Actually, the statement "This system is consistent" is one of those theorems that cannot be proven or disproven (assuming the system *is* consistent)!

This is *very* disturbing. If our system is inconsistent, all our results, all our work is in jeopardy. This is essentially what happened to Frege (see "Russell's Paradox and Frege's Mistake"). The best we can do is prove *relative* consistency. The work of Gödel shows that assuming set theory is consistent, then set theory plus CH is also consistent. Thus, adding CH does not increase the danger of inconsistency. In other words, set theory plus CH is relatively consistent to set theory.

This is not true of all new axioms. MC (an axiom asserting the existence of a monstrously large set called a "measurable cardinal") is an axiom that does increase the danger; that is, set theory plus MC is not relatively consistent to set theory. In fact, while we cannot prove MC (so ¬MC is safe), it is nonetheless true that we cannot prove that we cannot disprove MC! Most astonishing of all, we can prove this.

Well, then, do we play it safe? Shall we stick to arithmetic? Forget set theory and these exotic, intoxicating, cosmic axioms?

Of course, arithmetic isn't really safe either. We will never *know* that arithmetic is consistent. It seems inconceivable that it's not, but . . . Frege once thought that arithmetic tottered . . . .

---

informal logic

Quayle, Gore, and Stockdale

GORE: That's just not true.
QUAYLE: Foreign aid.
GORE: It's not true.
QUAYLE: Senator, it's in your book, on page 304.
GORE: No, it's not. No, it's not. No, it's not.

CHALLENGE   The following excerpts are taken from the vice-presidential debate among Danforth Quayle, Albert Gore, and James B. Stockdale. Once again, you are challenged to critique the performances.

1. Q: I thought since you're running for vice president that we ought to start off by talking about the vice presidency itself. The vice president presides over the Senate, he casts the deciding vote in case of a tie, but his role really depends on the assignments that are given to him by the president.

   However, if a president should die in office or is unable to serve for any other reason, the vice president automatically becomes president. And that has happened five times this century.

   So the proposition I put on the table for you to discuss is this: What role would each of you like to play as vice president, what areas interest you, and what are your qualifications to serve as president if necessary?

   In the case of Vice President Quayle, who we're starting with, suppose you tell us the role that you did play in the first term and what you would like to do in the second term. Go ahead, sir.

   QUAYLE: Well, then, I won't give you that answer. Qualifications: I've been there, Hal. I've done the job. I've been tested; I've been vice president for four years. Senator Gore referred to us being elected to the Congress together in 1976. I've done the job. I've done many things for the president.

But even as vice president, you never know exactly what your role is going to be from time to time. And let me just give you an example of where I was tested under fire and in a crisis.

President Bush was flying to Malta in 1989 to meet with President Gorbachev; they had known each other before.

A coup broke out in the Philippines. I had to go to the Situation Room. I had to assemble the President's advisers. I talked to President Aquino. I made the recommendation to the president. The president made the decision. The coup was suppressed; democracy continued in the Philippines; the situation was ended.

I've been there. And I'll tell you one other thing that qualifies you for being president. And it's this, Hal: You've got to stand up for what you believe in. And nobody's ever criticized me for not having strong beliefs.

Q: Admiral Stockdale.

2. STOCKDALE: My association with Mr. Perot is a very personal one and as I have stood in and finally taken his running-mate position, he has granted me total autonomy. I don't take advantage of it but I am sure that he would make me a partner in decisions, in health care, the way to get this economy back on its feet again in every way. I have not had the experience of these gentlemen but, to be any more specific—but, I know I have his trust and I intend to act in a way to keep that situation alive. Thank you.

Q: Senator Gore.

3. GORE: Bill Clinton understands the meaning of the words teamwork and partnership. If we're successful in our efforts to gain your trust and lead this nation, we will work together to put our country back on the right track again. The experience that George Bush and Dan Quayle have been talking about includes the worst economic performance since the Great Depression. Unemployment is up, personal income is down, bankruptcies are up, housing starts are down. How long can we continue with trickle-down economics when the record of failure is so abundantly clear? Discussions of the vice presidency tend sometimes to focus on the crisis during which a vice president is thrust into the Oval Office and, indeed, one third of the vice presidents who have served have been moved into the White House, but the teamwork and partnership beforehand—and hopefully that situation never happens—how you work together is critically important. The way we've

worked together in this campaign is one sample. Now I'd like to say in response to Vice President Quayle—he talked about Malta and the Philippines—George Bush has concentrated on every other country in the world. When are you guys going to start worrying about our people here, in the United States of America, and get our country moving again?

Q: Again I will ask the audience please do not applaud. It takes time from the candidates. All right. Now we have five minutes for discussion and go ahead Vice President Quayle.

4. QUAYLE: The answer to that is very simple that we are not going to raise taxes to create new jobs. We have a plan to create jobs. But that wasn't the question. The question dealt with qualifications. Teamwork and partnership may be fine in the Congress, Senator Gore. That's what Congress is all about, compromise, teamwork, working things out. But when you're president of the United States, or when you're vice president and you have to fill in like I did the night of the crisis in the Philippines, you've got to make a decision. You've got to make up your mind. Bill Clinton, running for president of the United States, said this about the Persian Gulf war. He said, "Had I been in the Senate, I would have voted with the majority. It was a close vote, but I agreed with the arguments of the minority." You can't have it both ways. You have to make a decision. You cannot sit there in an international crisis and sit there and say well, on one hand it's—this is O.K., and on the other hand this is O.K. You've got to make the decision. President Bush has made the decisions. He's been tested. He's got the experience. He's got the qualification. He's got the integrity to be our president for the next four years.

Q: Mr. Vice President. Admiral Stockdale, it's your turn to respond.

STOCKDALE: O.K., I thought this was just an open session, this five-minute thing, and I didn't have anything to add to his, but I will—.

GORE: Well, I'll jump in if—if you don't want it.

QUAYLE: I thought anyone could jump in whenever they wanted to.

Q: O.K., whatever pleases you gentlemen is fine with me, you're the candidates.

QUAYLE: But I want Admiral Stockdale's time!

Q: This is not the Senate—this is not the Senate where you can trade off time. Go ahead, Senator Gore.

GORE: I'll let you all figure out the rules. I've got some points that I want to make here, and I still haven't gotten an answer to my question on when you guys are going to start worrying about this country. But I want to elaborate on it before—.

QUAYLE: Why doesn't—why doesn't the Democratic Congress—

Q: Let him talk, sir.

QUAYLE: —pass the jobs bill?

Q: Let him say his thoughts.

GORE: I was very patient in letting you get off that string of attacks. We've been listening to—

QUAYLE: They're good points.

5. GORE: —to trickle-down economics for twelve years now and you all still support trickle-down to the very last drop. And you, talking about this point of concentrating on every other country in the world, as opposed to the people of our country right here at home, when George Bush took former Secretary of State Baker out of the State Department and put him in charge of the campaign and made him chief of staff in the White House, Mr. Baker, who's quite a capable man, said that for these last four years George Bush was working on the problems of the rest of the world and in the next four years he would target America. Well, I want you to know we really appreciate that, but Bill Clinton and I will target America from day 1. We won't wait four years before we concentrate on the problems in this country.

He went on to say that it's really amazing what George Bush can do when he concentrates. Well it's time that we had a president like Bill Clinton who can concentrate, and will concentrate, and work on the problems of real people in this country. You know, our country is in trouble. We simply cannot continue with this philosophy of giving huge tax cuts to the very wealthy, raising taxes on middle-income families the way Bush and Quayle have done, and then waiting for it to work.

How much longer will it take, Dan, for trickle-down economics to work, in your theory?

QUAYLE: Well, we're going to have plenty of time to talk about trickle-down government which you're for—

GORE: Well, I'd like to hear the answer.

QUAYLE: But the question is, the question is, which you have failed to address, and that is: Why is Bill Clinton qualified to be president of the United States? You've talked about Jim—

GORE: Oh, I'll be happy to answer that.

QUAYLE: You've talked about Jim Baker. You've talked about trickle-down economics.

Q: Now wait a minute. The question was about—

QUAYLE: You've talked about the worst economy in 50 years.

GORE: I'll be happy to answer.

QUAYLE: You haven't told us one reason why Bill Clinton—

GORE: May I answer?

QUAYLE: —is qualified to be president of the United States—

GORE: I'll be happy to answer.

QUAYLE: —and how—I want to go back and make a point.

GORE: Well, you've asked me a question, let—if want an answer—

QUAYLE: I have not asked you a question. I've made a statement.

GORE: And I will answer yours.

QUAYLE: I have not asked a question, I've made a statement that you have not told us why Bill Clinton is qualified to be president of the United States. I pointed out what he said about the Persian Gulf war. But let me repeat it for you. Here's what he said, Senator, you know full well what he said.

GORE: May I answer your question?

QUAYLE: I'm making a statement, then you can answer it.

Q: Can, can we give Admiral Stockdale a chance to come in here please, and again, audience—

QUAYLE: But he said, Hal, here's what he said. If the—I mean this is the Persian Gulf war, the most important event in his political life, and here's what Bill Clinton said: "If it's a close vote, I'd vote with the majority—"

Q: Let's give Admiral Stockdale a chance to come in.

QUAYLE: "—but I agreed with the minority." That qualifies you for being president of the United States? I hope America is listening very closely to this debate.

6. STOCKDALE: And I think America is seeing right now the reason for this nation is in gridlock. The trickle-downs and the tax-and-spends, or whatever you want to call them, are at swords' points; you can't get this economy going. Over here we've got Dan, whose president is going to take eight years to balance the budget, and on my left, the senator, whose boss is going to get halfway balanced in four years. Ross Perot has got a plan to balance the budget five years in length from start to finish. And we're people of the nonprofessional category who are just sick of this terrible thing that happened to the country, and we've got a man who knows how to fix it. And I'm working for him.

law boards: logical reasoning

> All thieves who could my fees afford
> Relied on my orations,
> And many a burglar I've restored
> To his friends and his relations.
> —W. S. GILBERT

This is another section of the LSATs. The questions all deal with what we have been calling informal arguments.

1. Before the administration of Ronald Reagan (1981–1989), the federal bureaucracy grew each year more than 5 percent.

   Which of the following statements below is inconsistent with this statement?
   (A) In 1989, the federal bureaucracy grew 3 percent.
   (B) In 1976, the federal bureaucracy grew 7 percent.
   (C) In 1978, the federal bureaucracy grew 4 percent.
   (D) In 1990, the federal bureaucracy grew 7 percent.
   (E) In 1984, the federal bureaucracy grew 6 percent.

2. The fire truck never goes out unless the fire alarm is pulled.

   Which of the following statements can be logically inferred from this statement?
   (A) If there is a fire, then the fire truck goes out.
   (B) If the fire alarm is pulled, then the fire truck will go out.
   (C) If the fire truck goes out, then there is a fire.
   (D) If the alarm is not pulled, then the fire truck will not go out.
   (E) If the fire truck doesn't go out, then the fire alarm was not pulled.

3. SALESMAN: That tire you bought was a 48-month tire. You bought it four-and-a-half years ago. You shouldn't expect it to last any longer.

   CUSTOMER: But you said it had a lifetime guarantee. I want you to replace it.

   Which of the following could reasonably explain the dispute?

   I. The customer thinks the tire is ruined but the salesman thinks it is not.

   II. The customer thinks "lifetime" refers to his life but the salesman thinks it refers to the tire's life.

III. The customer thinks the tire is less than 48 months old, but the salesman thinks it is older.

(A) I only
(B) II only
(C) III only
(D) I and II
(E) II and III

4. First-year students taking a course in introductory writing may choose to use word processors on either JCN computers or on KDO computers. It was noticed that the students using JCN computers wrote better papers. The instructors concluded that JCN was a better computer on which to learn to write.

   The argument for this conclusion would be weakened if
   (A) some of the students chose to use typewriters.
   (B) JCN went bankrupt.
   (C) the weakest students taking the course generally chose KDO computers.
   (D) the students themselves preferred KDO computers.
   (E) it was discovered that JCN computers are cheaper.

5. From recent studies, it now seems probable that a high-fiber diet will reduce the chance of heart disease and colon cancer. Eggs are virtually free of fiber. It follows that eating eggs for breakfast is probably not a healthy practice.

   Which of the following are NOT relevant objections to this argument?

   I. A more important reason that eggs are unhealthy is that they contain large amounts of cholesterol.

   II. It is not certain that a high-fiber diet reduces health risk, only probable.

   III. A diet may contain many low-fiber items and still be high in fiber.

   (A) I only
   (B) II only
   (C) III only
   (D) I and II
   (E) II and III

Questions 6, 7, and 8 all refer to the following five arguments.

(A) Governor Smirnov used campaign funds for personal expenses. This is a clear violation of the election laws. He should be indicted and stand trial.

(B) Governor Smirnov has been in office now for nearly twelve years. No one can be in power that long without yielding to temptation. He must be guilty of something.

(C) Governor Smirnov stands accused of malfeasance by Senator Fong. The Senator herself has been involved in so many shady deals that her accusation alone convinces me of the governor's innocence.

(D) "You have my word that I have not abused the trust. I am and always have been a gentleman, and gentlemen do not lie. I have never used public funds for private purposes."—Governor Armistead Smirnov

(E) The alleged indiscretion of Governor Smirnov is in reality only an accounting error. Such errors are not criminal; on the contrary, they are innocent and quite common. Prosecution is totally unwarranted.

6. Which of the arguments commits the fallacy of attacking the source of the argument rather than the argument itself?

7. Which of the arguments commits the fallacy of circular reasoning?

8. Which of the arguments proceeds from a dubious generalization?

9. The liberals are all supporting the national health care bill now before Congress. The vote is scheduled for next week. De la Cruz is opposing the bill, so I don't think she is a liberal after all.

   Which of the following arguments has the same structure as this argument?

(A) All cats see well in the dark. Consequently, my cat Martha should be able to find her supper dish at night even with the light out.

(B) If one works hard at it, one can make excellent bread. Every time I have bread at the Dolphin, I am impressed by how poor it is. They must not put much effort into it.

(C) Every good year for suspender sales is followed by a good year for leather belts. Last year was a lousy year for suspenders, so I expect this year to be lousy for belts.

(D) All our students visit the Career Development Office some-time during their senior year. You are a junior and of course you may visit any time, but you will certainly do so next year.

(E) Anyone who really loves barbecue finds their way to Zazu's Pit, which is way out on Route 31 near the rendering plant. Judge Beulah eats there twice a week, so I think he is a true barbecue lover.

10. Nearly every veteran of the Korean War still living is now re-ceiving social security benefits.

     Which of the following can be deduced from this sentence?

     I. Nancy is not receiving social security benefits, so she is not a Korean War veteran.

     II. George was not a veteran of the Korean War, so he is probably not receiving social security benefits.

     III. Max fought in the Korean War, so he is probably receiving social security benefits.

(A) I only
(B) II only
(C) III only
(D) I and II
(E) I and III

11. Every really talented writer writes at least one book that is a commercial success.

     Which of the following is a logical consequence of this sen-tence?

(A) Lawrence Yellowstocking, who can't even write a decent shopping list, will never write a successful novel.

(B) Mabel Thorndike, who has written one hit after another, must be one of the great talents of the age.

(C) Sybil Strawberry, whose books have never sold more than a few copies, will someday write a best seller.

(D) Luthor Labandera, who died without even publishing a book and who is known only to a few experts on Persian limericks, cannot be regarded as a very good writer.

(E) Romeo Rubberbiscuit, who writes poor (though immensely popular) books, will eventually write a masterpiece.

12. Senator Shortcake's bill would deregulate the postal service. It would permit the service to set its own rates, salaries, schedules, and rules. It would also allow private companies to deliver mail in competition with the postal service. Free competition in this way would guarantee that the public would receive the best possible service. A company that charged too much, for example, would lose business because another company would charge less. Likewise, a company that lost mail or was slow in delivering it would not stay in business long.

Which of the following statements, even if true, does NOT weaken this argument?

(A) The tremendous cost of starting a mail delivery company makes it unlikely that a competitor will ever arise.

(B) Some out-of-the-way towns may lose service if it is unprofitable for any company to serve them.

(C) There will be a great deal of confusion with different companies selling different stamps.

(D) The streets will be cluttered with dozens of different mailboxes.

(E) We have already deregulated the package delivery service, taking away a great deal of business from the postal service.

13. Only fishermen with valid licenses are permitted to fish for trout, and they are limited to a maximum of three fish and a maximum of five total pounds of fish per day.

Which of the following does NOT logically follow from this statement?

(A) If Mabel brought home four trout, then she is in violation of the law.

(B) If Diego did not violate the law but did not have a license, then he didn't fish for trout.

(C) If Hiro had a valid license but broke the law, then he caught more than three trout and they weighed more than five pounds.

(D) If Trudy caught two trout weighing two pounds each and violated the law, then she doesn't have a license.

(E) If Max fished for trout without a license, he violated the law even if he caught no trout.

14. The Bible says, "Thou shalt not kill." What could be clearer? And yet in dozens of ways this society of ours kills and kills. What

disturbs me most is our abundant use of capital punishment. Most of us, whatever our religious beliefs, like to think that we respect the Ten Commandments, of which that is one. Why, then, do we violate it so thoroughly by putting to death fellow human beings?

Which of the following (if true) is NOT a reasonable objection to this argument?

(A) In the original Hebrew, the word translated as "kill" really meant "murder," and execution is not murder.

(B) The Bible also says, "An eye for an eye, a tooth for a tooth," indicating that a murderer should be deprived of his life.

(C) If we take the Bible literally, then we can't kill mosquitoes, chickens, or even onions and carrots. It is clearly ridiculous to take the Bible literally.

(D) For criminals, the fear of death is sometimes the only deterrent. Without the death penalty, there would be more murders, just as without traffic fines drivers would speed.

(E) Actually, very few of us take our moral code from the Bible.

15. "The company would like to raise wages more than the 2.1 percent we are offering, but the economic situation prevents us from doing so. To raise wages 5 percent, as the union demands, would raise our total costs by more than 4 percent, which could put us out of business."

Which of the following is LEAST relevant to the company's argument?

(A) The cost of labor is the largest factor in the cost of production.

(B) If the price of the product were raised 4 percent, fewer would be sold.

(C) In the last year, labor costs have actually fallen, since the workers have become more efficient.

(D) The workers have not had a raise in over three years.

(E) In the last year, profits fell by 8 percent.

Questions 16 and 17 refer to the following argument.

STUDENT: Professor Ramsbottom, I think I should be given some credit for problem 13 on the test. The correct answer is B, and that is one of the answers I gave.

16. The student's argument is weakened by which of the following?

   I. The student wrote down all the possible answers on his answer sheet.
   II. The test was a take-home.
   III. It was clearly stated that only one answer should be given.

   (A) I only   (D) I and II
   (B) II only   (E) I and III
   (C) III only

17. The student's argument is strengthened by which of the following?

   I. The student wrote "B, D," and most of the class did the same.
   II. The instructions for this section said to write all correct answers.
   III. This test was the only grade for the course.

   (A) I only   (D) I and III
   (B) I and II   (E) I, II, and III
   (C) II only

18. It is a shame that students no longer say the Pledge of Allegiance each morning. It was a serious mistake to abandon the practice, which is the most effective way to teach children to love their country. How are we to nurture patriotism now?

   Which of the following is NOT a reasonable way to attack this argument?
   (A) It is a violation of freedom of speech to require students to recite a required set of words.
   (B) If the argument were sound, then we should teach multiplication tables by requiring students to recite them each morning.
   (C) It makes no sense to require students to swear allegiance to a flag, which is merely a colored piece of cloth.
   (D) Requiring the oath violates the religious freedom of groups for which such demonstrations are forbidden.
   (E) If the argument were sound, then we should teach our children to love us by requiring each morning that they swear their allegiance to us.

19. Of course, mean people do mean things, but who is responsible for the greatest suffering? Is it the greedy bank executive who embezzles millions, or is it the well-meaning economist whose policies cause a recession? Is it the corrupt monarch who pillages his neighbors, or the godly zealot who starts a holy war? We can count on sinners to commit our everyday, small-time, penny-ante nastiness, but real evil _____.

   Which of the following is a logical conclusion to the paragraph?
   (A) needs a professional
   (B) must be committed by an intellectual
   (C) requires a thoroughly depraved individual
   (D) can only be effected by someone who believes he is doing good
   (E) is the result of bad luck

20. A recent survey found that men who were college graduates scored higher on the Case–Rameau IQ test than men who did not go to college.

   It is reasonable to conclude from this that
   (A) intelligence, as measured by the Case–Rameau IQ test, and higher education are linked in some way.
   (B) a college education is likely to increase your intelligence, as measured by the Case–Rameau IQ test.
   (C) those who have a high intelligence quotient, as measured by the Case–Rameau IQ test, are more likely to go to college.
   (D) there is a quality in some people that makes them more likely to go to college and to score high on the Case–Rameau IQ test.
   (E) men who have gone to college are more likely to take the Case–Rameau IQ test.

21. "If we vote for Montgomery, he will reduce spending on the environment in order to save money. If we vote for the other one, taxes will be lowered and there will be no money for the environment. No matter what, the environment will lose."

   Which of the following arguments most resembles in form this argument?
   (A) If we go to the movie tonight, we can work tomorrow night, and if we go to the movie tomorrow, we can work tonight. No matter what, we can go to a movie.

(B) If I take introductory logic in the fall, I can take intermediate logic in the spring. If I don't take introductory logic in the fall, I can still take it in the spring. No matter what, I will be able to take introductory logic this year.

(C) I won't be able to sleep tonight if I don't finish the paper. If I don't sleep tonight, I'll flunk the test tomorrow. No matter what, I'm going to get a bad grade.

(D) I'm sunk if she asks for reports today. I'm sunk if she asks for reports tomorrow. No matter what, she will ask for reports either today or tomorrow.

(E) If I go right on King Street, I'll have a traffic light at Summer Street. I'll have a traffic light at State Street, though, if I don't turn. No matter what, I'll face a traffic light.

law boards: analytical reasoning

"Just what the hell did you mean, you bastard, when you said we couldn't punish you?" . . .

"I didn't say that you couldn't punish me, sir."

"When?" asked the colonel.

"When what, sir?"

"Now you're asking me questions again."

"I'm sorry, sir. I'm afraid I don't understand your question."

"When didn't you say we couldn't punish you? Don't you understand my question?"

"No sir. I don't understand."

"You've just told us that. Now suppose you answer my question."

"But how can I answer it?"

"That's another question you're asking me."

"I'm sorry sir. But I don't know how to answer it. I never said you couldn't punish me."

"Now you're telling us when you did say it. I'm asking you to tell us when you didn't say it."

Clevinger took a deep breath. "I always didn't say you couldn't punish me, sir."

—JOSEPH HELLER, CATCH 22

The problems in this section are a bit like logical puzzles. It is usually a good idea to draw a diagram (almost any diagram) of the situation to help your analysis.

Questions 1–6 pertain to the following paragraph.

There are eight people, M, N, O, P, Q, R, S, and T, on the debate team of Sophist College. The coach must arrange them in four pairs for competition. She is obliged to place T, who is best, in the first pair. N and O, who are the next best, must be placed in either of the first two pairs. Q and S are very antagonistic and cannot work together. M can work only with either P or T. R is the worst and definitely goes to pair 4.

1. If N is placed in pair 2, then which of the following must be true?
    (A) O is not placed in pair 1.
    (B) M is not placed in pair 1.
    (C) P is not placed in pair 1.
    (D) Q is not placed in pair 1.
    (E) S is not placed in pair 1.

2. If M is placed with T, then which of the following must be true?

    I.   N is placed in pair 2.
    II. P is placed in pair 3.
    III. Q is placed in pair 4.

    (A) I only
    (B) II only
    (C) III only
    (D) I and II only
    (E) I and III only

3. If S is placed with T, then which of the following must be false?
    (A) Q is placed in pair 4.
    (B) N is placed in pair 2.
    (C) M is placed in pair 3.
    (D) P is placed in pair 4.
    (E) O is placed in pair 2.

4. If Q is placed in pair 4, then which of the following must be true?
    I.   S is placed in pair 3.
    II. P is placed in pair 3.
    III. N and O are placed in pair 2.

(A) I only
(B) II only
(C) III only
(D) I and II only
(E) I and III only

5. If M is placed before S, then which of the following must be true?
    (A) If Q is in pair 2, then S is in pair 4.
    (B) If Q is in pair 4, then Q is in pair 2.
    (C) If Q is in pair 2, then N is in pair 1.
    (D) If Q is before M, then N is in pair 2.
    (E) If N is in pair 2, then O is in pair 2.

6. If N is placed with Q, then which of the following must be false?
    (A) O is placed in pair 1.
    (B) P is placed in pair 4.
    (C) S is placed in pair 4.
    (D) Q is placed in pair 2.
    (E) N is placed in pair 2.

Questions 7–12 pertain to the following paragraph.

The city of New Schmutz collects garbage seven days a week. Garbage is collected in each area of the city, A, B, C, D, E, F, and G, on a different day. A's garbage is collected the day after C's. D's and F's garbage is collected on consecutive days (though not necessarily in that order). E's and B's garbage is not collected on consecutive days, nor is E's and G's garbage.

7. If D's garbage is collected three days after A's, then which of the following must be true?
    (A) A's and B's garbage is collected on consecutive days.
    (B) B's and C's garbage is collected on consecutive days.
    (C) C's and D's garbage is collected on consecutive days.
    (D) D's and E's garbage is collected on consecutive days.
    (E) E's and F's garbage is collected on consecutive days.

8. If C's garbage is collected on Wednesday and F's on Monday, then which of the following must be true?

    I. E's garbage is collected on Tuesday.
    II. G's garbage is collected on Saturday.

III. B's garbage is collected on Sunday.

(A) I only
(B) II only
(C) III only
(D) I and II only
(E) I and III only

9. If G's garbage is collected the day after A's, then which of the following must be true?

I. D's garbage is collected the day after F's.
II. C's garbage is collected the day after E's.
III. F's garbage is collected the day after B's.

(A) I only
(B) II only
(C) III only
(D) I and II only
(E) I and III only

10. If D's garbage is collected on Friday, then which of the following must be true?
(A) If C's garbage is collected on Tuesday, then E's garbage is collected on Thursday.
(B) If A's garbage is collected on Tuesday, then F's garbage is collected on Thursday.
(C) If B's garbage is collected on Tuesday, then F's garbage is collected on Saturday.
(D) If F's garbage is collected on Thursday, then A's garbage is collected on Tuesday.
(E) If F's garbage is collected on Saturday, then B's garbage is collected on Tuesday.

11. If G's garbage is collected three days after D's, then which of the following must be true?
(A) B's garbage is collected the day after A's.
(B) C's garbage is collected the day after E's.
(C) F's garbage is collected the day after G's.
(D) D's garbage is collected the day after F's.
(E) G's garbage is collected the day after B's.

12. If A's garbage is collected on Tuesday, then which of the following must be true?
    (A) A's and B's garbage is not collected on consecutive days.
    (B) B's and C's garbage is not collected on consecutive days.
    (C) C's and D's garbage is not collected on consecutive days.
    (D) D's and E's garbage is not collected on consecutive days.
    (E) E's and F's garbage is not collected on consecutive days.

Questions 13–18 pertain to the following paragraph.

A garden is planned with flowering shrubs—rhododendron, azalea, honeysuckle, viburnum, laurel, and rose—planted in four quadrants, north, south, east, and west, around a central fountain. Because of shade, only laurel or rhododendron can be planted in the north quadrant, and honeysuckle can be planted only in the south. Because of clashing colors, the roses and azaleas cannot be planted together; on the other hand, there are too few rose bushes to fill one quadrant. Two quadrants will have one variety each, and two will have two varieties. For symmetry, the quadrants with two varieties must face each other.

13. If the viburnum is planted alone, then which of the following must be false?
    (A) The honeysuckle is opposite the rhododendron.
    (B) The roses are opposite the laurel.
    (C) The azaleas are opposite the viburnum.
    (D) The roses are opposite the rhododendron.
    (E) The roses are opposite the azaleas.

14. If laurel is planted with the azaleas, then which of the following must be false?
    (A) The laurel is opposite the viburnum.
    (B) The azaleas are opposite the roses.
    (C) The honeysuckle is opposite the rhododendron.
    (D) The roses are opposite the honeysuckle.
    (E) The viburnum is opposite the azaleas.

15. If the rhododendron is planted in the west quadrant, then which of the following must be true?
    (A) The roses are planted in the east quadrant.
    (B) The viburnum is planted in the east quadrant.
    (C) The laurel is planted in the east quadrant.

(D) The azaleas are planted in the east quadrant.

(E) The honeysuckle is planted in the east quadrant.

16. If the honeysuckle is not planted alone, then which of the following must be true?

   I. The viburnum is planted alone.
   II. The laurel is planted alone.
   III. The azaleas are planted alone.

   (A) I only
   (B) II only
   (C) III only
   (D) I and II only
   (E) I and III only

17. If the rhododendron is planted in the north quadrant, then which of the following must be false?
   (A) The azaleas and viburnum are planted in neighboring quadrants.
   (B) The roses and azaleas are planted in neighboring quadrants.
   (C) The viburnum and laurel are planted in neighboring quadrants.
   (D) The laurel and honeysuckle are planted in neighboring quadrants.
   (E) The rhododendron and laurel are planted in neighboring quadrants.

18. If the rhododendron is planted in the north quadrant, then which of the following must be true?
   (A) The laurel is not planted with the roses.
   (B) The laurel is not planted with the rhododendron.
   (C) The laurel is not planted with the viburnum.
   (D) The laurel is not planted with the azaleas.
   (E) The laurel is not planted alone.

Questions 19–24 pertain to the following paragraph.

Sophist College must schedule six freshman seminars during fifty-minute time slots beginning at 8:00 A.M., 9:00 A.M., 10:00 A.M., 11:00 A.M., 2:00 P.M., 3:00 P.M., and 4:00 P.M. The chemistry seminar ("Organic Compounds in Sugarless Gum") is a laboratory and requires two consecutive slots. The mathematics seminar ("Theory of Lotteries") must be in the morning. The history seminar ("Street Gangs of the Enlightenment") must be held in either the last morning slot or the last afternoon slot. The philosophy seminar ("Situational Ethics in Professional Hockey") must precede the Western civilization seminar ("Subcultures of California"), which in turn must precede the history seminar. The English seminar ("Imagery and Symbolism in Automobile Advertising") can be at any hour.

19. If history is in the morning, then which of the following must be true?
    (A) Chemistry is being taught at 9:00.
    (B) Western civilization is being taught at 8:00.
    (C) Philosophy is being taught at 10:00.
    (D) English is being taught after Western civilization.
    (E) Philosophy is being taught after mathematics.

20. If Western civilization is the next course after chemistry, then which of the following must be true?

    I. Mathematics is being taught at 8:00
    II. English is being taught at 2:00
    III. Western civilization is being taught at 11:00

    (A) I only
    (B) II only
    (C) III only
    (D) I and II only
    (E) I and III only

21. If chemistry is the next course after history, then which of the following must be true?

    I. Philosophy is being taught in the morning.
    II. English is being taught in the afternoon.
    III. Mathematics is being taught after Western civilization.

    (A) I only
    (B) II only
    (C) III only
    (D) I and II only
    (E) I and III only

22. If mathematics is being taught at 9:00, then which of the following must be true?
    (A) If philosophy is at 10:00, then English is at 4:00.
    (B) If English is at 4:00, then philosophy is at 10:00.
    (C) If English is at 2:00, then philosophy is at 8:00.
    (D) If philosophy is at 8:00, then English is at 2:00.
    (E) If history is at 4:00, then chemistry is at 10:00.

23. If Western civilization is being taught at 9:00, then which of the following must be true?
    (A) Mathematics and Western civilization are being taught consecutively (though not necessarily in that order).
    (B) Philosophy and Western civilization are being taught consecutively (though not necessarily in that order).
    (C) Chemistry and English are being taught consecutively (though not necessarily in that order).
    (D) Chemistry and history are being taught consecutively (though not necessarily in that order).
    (E) English and Western civilization are being taught consecutively (though not necessarily in that order).

24. If Western civilization is being taught at 10:00, then which of the following must be true?
    (A) Chemistry is being taught in the morning.
    (B) Philosophy is being taught in the afternoon.
    (C) English is being taught in the afternoon.
    (D) History is being taught in the afternoon.
    (E) Chemistry is being taught in the afternoon.

law boards: rules and disputes

Rule Forty-two. All persons more than a mile high to leave the court.
—Lewis Carroll, *Alice's Adventures in Wonderland*

For many years, one section of the LSAT was devoted to questions with a definite legal flavor. Problems such as the ones in this chapter are no longer a part of the test, but they pose interesting challenges for logic students, so we have included them.

No legal knowledge is required. Each series centers on a dispute. All the facts of the dispute are given, along with all the legal or quasilegal principles involved. Each set of problems is preceded by a collection of facts, a dispute, and exactly two rules. The rules usually contain a potential conflict. Here is an example:

Example

Facts At 4:13 P.M. on November 13, Maury approached the intersection of Pine and Rivera streets in his cerise Chevette. He was moving north on Pine, when he realized that he had forgotten his notes on Dante. At the intersection, which was marked "No Left Turn," Maury stopped at the red light. When the light turned green, Maury executed a U-turn. Officer Singh, watching from a cruiser on Rivera, gave chase and pulled him over.

• *Note*: Everything in these scenarios is fictitious: The Facts, the Disputes, and the Rules.

Dispute Maury is charged with making an illegal U-turn.

Rules

1. State law permits U-turns whenever the maneuver can be done in safety.
2. U-turns are illegal wherever left turns are prohibited.

The problems consist of questions, but *you are not expected to answer them*. Instead you must decide each question is *relevant* to the problem; if it is, you must decide if the rules are in *conflict*; if they are not, you must decide if there are *sufficient facts to answer the question*. Specifically, you choose one of the following:

(A) The question is relevant and sets up a conflict between the rules.
(B) The question is relevant and causes no conflict in the rules, but more information is needed to answer it.
(C) The question is relevant, causes no conflict in the rules, and can be answered with the information provided.
(D) The question is not relevant to the dispute.

Questions

1. If the turn was made in complete safety, is Maury guilty?
2. Was the turn made in complete safety?

3. At the completion of the turn, was Maury facing west?

4. If the turn was dangerous because of oncoming traffic, is Maury guilty?

This is a fairly simple set of questions. The answers:

1. A. First, the statement is relevant, since the question asked is the dispute itself. Rule (1) says that the turn was legal. Rule (2) says that it was not.

2. B. Again, this is relevant, since the information is needed to know if rule (1) applies. There is not sufficient information to know this, so the answer is B.

3. D. This is not relevant to whether or not a U-turn is legal. This statement is clearly irrelevant, but often relevance can trick you. Suppose, for example, one of the rules stated that drivers must wear a seat belt when driving. Suppose the question was Was Maury wearing a seat belt at the time? What would the correct answer be? It would be D, not relevant. Why? Because the dispute is the charge that Maury had illegally made a U-turn, not that he had failed to wear a seat belt.

4. C. Rule (2) says the turn is illegal, and Rule (1) does not apply.

Now, some for you.

Questions 1–6

Facts Professor Montague prefers to give take-home tests in his course, "The Pre-Romantic English Novel." In his test on *Pride and Prejudice* by Jane Austen, the instructions read, "All work must be done individually. Do not consult with anyone other than myself or look at any book or notes relevant to the material on the test." Boris Nelson, a student in the class, was seen reading *Sense and Sensibility*, also by Jane Austen, during the period of the examination.

Dispute The honor board was asked to consider whether a failing grade should be recorded for Mr. Nelson for cheating on his English exam.

Rules

1. The academic honor code states that a student who cheats on a proper examination should be given a failing grade. Cheating is

defined as a violation of the rules for the assignment established by the instructor.

2. The faculty code states that all take-home examinations given by the faculty must be "open book" and that no student can be penalized for consulting written material during the period of the exam.

Questions

1. Is *Sense and Sensibility* relevant to the test?
2. If Professor Montague's test was proper and *Sense and Sensibility* is relevant, should Mr. Nelson be given a failing grade for cheating on it?
3. If the test violates the Faculty Code, can it be proper?
4. If the test violates the Faculty Code, should Prof. Montague be reprimanded?
5. Did Mr. Nelson do any work on the test after reading *Sense and Sensibility?*
6. If the exam is not proper, should Mr. Nelson be given a failing grade for cheating on it?

Questions 7–12

Facts Malcolm Pedante was an assistant professor of history at Sophist College for six years when he was denied tenure. At that time he was given one more year of teaching before he had to leave. The tenure fight had been a difficult one, in which Pedante had expected support from his colleagues and had been disappointed. His unhappiness led him to plan revenge on the college.

Pedante resolved to get even with Sophist by deliberately teaching his students a falsehood. He decided that it should be something that was not central so that the error would not be detected easily. On the other hand, he felt it should be significant enough to call attention to itself eventually. In the end, he taught his students of modern European history that France had won the Franco-Prussian war. He supplied them with battles, dates, heroes, and a treaty. At the end of the year, he left Sophist College and took a job at an advertising agency.

Herman Ferrier was a student of Professor Pedante in the tainted course. In his last year, Ferrier applied to graduate schools in history. He was a promising student, had excellent recommendations, scored

509

well on the standardized tests, and had very good prospects of acceptance at the best schools. He particularly wished to go to Harvard. Harvard was seriously interested in him and invited him for an interview. The interview was a disaster, chiefly because Ferrier insisted over frequent objections that France had won the Franco-Prussian War. Ferrier discovered his error shortly afterwards, and when he was rejected by Harvard, he sued Sophist College.

Dispute Should Sophist College be held liable for Ferrier's rejection by Harvard?

Rules

1. State law says that any organization performing a service for hire is liable for any injury suffered as a result of that service.
2. The state constitution guarantees the right of free speech to all citizens.

Questions

7. Is the rejection of Ferrier by Harvard a consequence of Pedante's teaching?
8. Does free speech include the right to lie?
9. Did France win the Franco-Prussian War?
10. If Pendante had announced at the start of class that he intended to give one lecture during the semester that was totally untrue, is Sophist College liable for Ferrier's rejection?
11. If Pedante gave no warning of his intentions, and if his teaching resulted in Ferrier's rejection, is he liable?
12. If the state's interpretation of free speech protects the right of Professor Pedante to say whatever he likes, is Sophist College liable?

Questions 13–19

Facts Dawn Franklin entered Sophist College with a strong interest in psychology. She declared her major in psychology in her first year, during which she took "Psychological Statistics" as part of the requirements. In her second year, she took the more advanced statistics course, "Regression Analysis," which had as a prerequisite "Introduction to Statistics," "Psychological Statistics," or "Statistics for Social Scientists." After successfully completing "Psychological Statistics" and "Regression Analysis," she discovered that she was more interested in statistics than psychology. In her third year, she switched her major to statistics. It is now January of her fourth year and she is one semester short of her B.A. She has not taken "Introduction to Statistics," which the catalog states is required for the major. The department is refusing to allow her to take it.

Dispute Ms. Franklin is petitioning the academic council for permission to take "Introduction to Statistics" for credit in the spring.

Rules

1. "Introduction to Statistics" may not be taken for credit after taking "Regression Analysis."
2. Students must be allowed access to all courses required for their major.

Questions

13. Is "Psychological Statistics" acceptable in place of "Introduction to Statistics" for the statistics major?
14. If "Psychological Statistics" is acceptable in place of "Introduction to Statistics" for the statistics minor, can Ms. Franklin minor in statistics?
15. Does auditing constitute access to a course?
16. If there is no alternative to taking "Introduction to Statistics" for credit, can Ms. Franklin take "Introduction to Statistics" in the spring?
17. If Ms. Franklin received a grade of B or higher in "Regression Analysis," will auditing "Introduction to Statistics" satisfy the requirement for the major?
18. Did Ms. Franklin receive a grade of B or higher in "Regression Analysis"?
19. If auditing constitutes access, and if the department allows Ms. Franklin to audit "Introduction to Statistics" but will not consider this as satisfying the requirement, will it be possible for her to graduate with a major in statistics?

Questions 20–25

Facts Each year at Sophist College, Film 101, "The History of Motion Pictures, 1900–1930," is one of the most popular courses on campus. This year, it was taught by a visiting professor, Dr. Hovic. During the third week, the class saw *Birth of a Nation*, D. W. Griffith's epic made from the novel *The Clansman*. There were several African-American students in the class, and one of them, Yolanda Lewis, protested on the grounds that the film was racist. Dr. Hovic replied that whatever its content, the film was a great work of art and that the class had to deal with it. "Regardless of your own feelings, we must judge the film on its own terms. We must accept for the moment the Ku Klux Klan as a band of heroes." Ms. Lewis asked the academic council to consider the case.

Dispute Dr. Hovic was brought before the academic council for possible censure for his remarks in class.

Rules

1. The academic code at Sophist College requires the censure of any student or teacher using language that is threatening to any member of the community or that in any way abridges his or her rights.
2. The constitution of the faculty board guarantees complete academic freedom to all members of the community, including the right of free speech.

Questions

20. If the words of Dr. Hovic were threatening to Ms. Lewis, should he be censured?
21. Can Dr. Hovic's remarks be considered threatening if no other African-American students protested?
22. Did the syllabus also include any films by African-American filmmakers?
23. If a student in the class supported the professor in words that threatened Ms. Lewis, should that student be censured?
24. If the teacher's remarks were not threatening and did not abridge anyone's freedom, should he be censured?
25. If Ms. Lewis's complaint abridges Dr. Hovic's freedom of speech, should she be censured?

curiosities & puzzles

The Digestor's Digest

Sorry! This page got torn and crumpled! You may not be able to figure out the articles and ads here. But you might be able to discover what words are missing.

This is the last page of the *Digest*. It is now possible to deduce which page is the fun page.

exam warning VIII

Hey! Not Fair!

You just turned to the last exam warning hoping to catch the exam by surprise!

Well, it won't work. Tom and Jim have hidden the exam in this book so cleverly that you cannot *possibly* know before you see it what page it is on.

We are shocked and saddened by your lust for instant gratification, your obvious lack of self-control, and—let's be frank—your intellectual dishonesty!

Would you treat Stephen King this way?

quiz on Polish notation

Each question has only one correct answer. (*Wskazówka: Nie trzeba znać polskiego by odpowiedzieć na te pytania.*)

• *Hint:* You do not need to understand this remark to answer the questions.

1. Ach czemuż ciebie tacąc siły nie mam tyle! Jakże was zapomnieć, szczęścia drogie chwile?
   The correct answer to this question is
   a. e   b. d   c. c   d. b   e. a

2. Tu mnie miłość pociąga, tam ojczyzna woła; lecz na jej głos, kto Polak, któż się oprzeć zdoła?
   a. dla
   b. all of the above
   c. none of the above
   d. none of the above
   e. dla

3. Na cóż jęków tyle?
   The correct answer to question 5 is
   a. c   b. b   c. e   d. a   e. d

4. Pierwszam miał myśl, że ciebie godniejszym się stanę. Mogłażeś ty zapomnieć?
   a. all of the above
   b. none of the above
   c. all of the above
   d. miłość
   e. szczęście

5. Czyż ci nawet niemiłe i samo wspomnienie?
   The correct answer to question 3 is
   a. e   b. a   c. b   d. d   e. c

Tom and Jim's excellent adventure

It is a mere accident that we have no memory of the future.
— BERTRAND RUSSELL

Well, what if there is no tomorrow? There wasn't one today!
— HAROLD RAMIS AND DANNY RUBIN, *GROUNDHOG DAY*

November 14

Engineers at Sophist College's Chronosynclastic Institute have just succeeded in building a time machine. They haven't tested it yet, and they aren't really sure how it works. It might move the whole world forward or backward, or it may transport only its contents. They call it the "Infundibula," and the honor of its first voyage has been awarded to Tom and Jim for the purpose of testing a number of logical, mathematical, and philosophical principles.

First of all, there is the question of causation. The *principle of causality* states that if an event of type A causes an event of type B, then a type A event will always cause a type B event. The *principle of causal determinism* states that everything has a cause. Together, these imply that time is a line that doesn't branch, that is, from each present only one future can follow. Tom and Jim want to know if this principle is correct.

Another question concerns the flow of time. Does it have a direction — does it always go forward? Most physical laws are bidirectional — they work the same whether time goes forward or backward. Can time ever be reversed? What would that mean? Would we notice?

In addition to these questions, there are others concerning free will, the law of the excluded middle, and counterfactual conditionals, as well as various problems about the paradoxes of time travel that have attracted science fiction authors.

The machine is striking in appearance. It looks remarkably like a 1976 Volare station wagon, with pillars instead of wheels. The controls are on the dashboard. It can be set for the past or the future, and a dial indicates the time jump in years, months, days, and minutes. There is an AM-FM radio.

You (the reader) are going to accompany Tom and Jim on their adventures! Occasionally you will have to make decisions for them. Their first adventure begins now. To find out what happens, turn to page 525.

LAST WORDS

Die, my dear doctor? That's the last thing I shall do!
— Last words of Lord Palmerston

This book had several goals. We wished, first of all, to present logic in all its variety. As a means of expression, as an analytic tool, as a blunt instrument, and as a source of amusement, logic is everywhere. We hope the reader understands now its ubiquity. We hope further that the reader can recognize logic, such as it is, in political speech, in the legal code, in advertising jingles, in philosophical speculation, and in virtually every human utterance.

Our other goal was to spread the appreciation of logic. Logical arguments are powerful. There is no denying their force: They are inescapable, incontrovertible, insistent, inexorable. But logic has many other appearances.

Logic is light. Logic is ephemeral, elusive, will-o'-the-wisp. Logic is everywhere and nowhere in particular. It is comedy. It is wherever you are not. It is within you. It is without.

Logic is deep. In many respects, the most profound discoveries of the human race are logical. Science tells us the truth about our world. Literature tells us the truth about ourselves. But logic — logic gives us the laws of truth.

Most of all, logic is beautiful. Logic is a feast of color, harmony, and wit. The best logical arguments are works of art. They inspire the same feelings of joy, revelation, and peace as great works of poetry and music. They fill us with awe for the men and women who gave them birth.

But in the end, what sort of entity is logic? How can it be so common and so special? What is the nature of a thing that is at once a monument and a joke, a reality and a dream, a weapon and a charm?

Is logic eternal? Has it always existed and are we only the discoverers? Is it fundamental to our universe? Will we learn more? Is there more we can never learn?

Or is logic our work? Is logic the fruit of the human mind — our weakness and our strength? Is it our nature?

Is logic our triumph? Or is it our fate?

NOTES, REFERENCES, HINTS, AND SOME ANSWERS

GERTRUDE STEIN: The Answer! The Answer!
INTERLOCUTER: What is the answer?
GERTRUDE STEIN *(smiling)*: Ah, what is the question?
— LAST WORDS OF GERTRUDE STEIN

1 A TASTE OF LOGIC

FORMAL LOGIC

INTRODUCING THE LANGUAGE OF LOGIC   *page 8*

The opening quotation is from Littlewood's *Miscellany* (Cambridge University Press, 1986), a collection of mathematical anecdotes and recollections. Littlewood and G. H. Hardy formed one of the most fruitful mathematical collaborations of all time. We quote Hardy later from his own, rather darker reminiscences.

The general concept of relations (between things in general, not just kinship relations) was quite puzzling to both philosophers and logicians prior to the twentieth century. Hume distinguished between "natural" or "common sensible" relations and "philosophical" relations. Ernest Harrison stands in the natural relation to Oxford University "*x* was educated at *y*," but he stands in no natural relation to Madonna. However, Ernest Harrison stands in many philosophical (or artificial) relations to Madonna, such as "*x* lived in the same century as *y*."

An especially perplexing matter was whether an object could stand in a relation to itself. Several eminent logicians, such as the Englishman F. H. Bradley, denied that it was possible ("The whole point of a relation," they might say "is to relate *one* thing to *another*.") It is this view that Ernest Harrison was adopting when he denied that he was related to himself. This view is bound to cause problems. Identity ($x = x$) cannot be regarded as a relation, nor can suicide be regarded as a special case of killing ("*x* kills *x*").

Bertrand Russell, the greatest logician England ever produced, repudiated this view of relations and reformulated logic to allow for relations—in the general form *Rxy*—to include the special case *Rxx*.

Question 1   I am that man's father.

In Formal Logic in part 1, we restate each challenge and answer every one. In the balance of the book, we don't restate the challenge and we provide the answers only to every other item.

CHALLENGE 1 Interpretations and Examples   Write English sentences or phrases that express the meanings of these formulas.

1. *Fc*   Tom Tymoczko is female.
2. *Mea*   Adrienne Rich is married to Jim Henle
3. *d = c*   Aristotle is Adrienne Rich
4. *Racb*   Jim Henle and Tom Tymoczko beget Madonna.
5. *Rcab*   Tom Tymoczko and Jim Henle beget Madonna (Logic does not know that the order of the begetors doesn't matter).
6. *Rabc*   Jim Henle and Madonna beget Tom Tymoczko.
7. *y = b*   *y* is (identical to) Madonna.
8. *Fa & Ga*   Jim Henle is female and Jim Henle is male.
9. *Mxb*   *x* is married to Madonna.
10. ¬*Fx*   *x* is not female.
11. *Fx & Gx*   *x* is female and *x* is male.

CHALLENGE 2 Translation and Logical Analysis   Using only the symbols that have been introduced, write the formulas that express the meanings of these sentences.

1. Madonna is married to Aristotle.   *Mbd*
2. Aristotle is male.   *Gd*
3. Aristotle is married to Madonna.   *Mdb*
4. *x* is a child of Aristotle and Tom Tymoczko.   *Rdcx*
5. Jim Henle is Madonna.   *a = b*
6. Madonna is herself.   *b = b* (!)
7. Adrienne Rich is not herself.   ¬(*e = e*) or, as we sometimes write, *e ≠ e*
8. Aristotle and Jim Henle beget Adrienne Rich.   *Rdae*
9. Jim Henle is male and Tom Tymoczko is female.   *Ga & Fc*
10. Tom Tymoczko is not married to Jim Henle.   ¬*Mca*

Question 2 "Jim Henle" is a name in English that refers to the human being, Jim Henle. Jim Henle is a human being in Massachusetts who does not, intrinsically, refer to anything.

Question 3 The English expression "Santa Claus" looks like a name and functions like a name according to the rules of English syntax. This is one good reason for representing it by a name in logic. On the other hand, "Santa Claus" does not refer to anything! There is no Santa Claus. If you search throughout the universe, you won't find anything named "Santa Claus" (although you might find plenty of "Santa Claus pictures" and "Santa Claus stories" and "department store Santa Clauses"). This is one good reason for denying that "Santa Claus" should be represented in logic by a name or constant.

CHALLENGE 3 Write the formulas that are *read* or pronounced as follows.

1. Both *Fx* and *Bx*. *Fx* & *Bx*
2. Something is *G*. $\exists z Gz$ (or $\exists x Gx$ or $\exists y Gy$ and so on)
3. It's not the case that either *Fd* or *Fe*. $\neg(Fd \lor Fe)$
4. Either not *F* of *d* or *F* of *d*. $(\neg Fd \lor Fd)$
5. *F* of *x* and that *x* bears the relation *M* to *a*. *Fx* & *Mxa*
6. There is something such that both *b* bears *M* to it and it is *G*. $\exists y(Mby \& Gy)$ or $\exists x(Mbx \& Gx)$ and so on
7. Everything is either *F* or not *F*. $\forall x(Fx \lor \neg Fx)$ or $\forall w(Fw \lor \neg Fw)$ and so on
8. Either everything is *F* or everything is not *F*. $\forall x Fx \lor \forall x \neg Fx$ or $\forall w Fw \lor \forall w \neg Fw$ and so on
9. If not *F* of *a*, then *G* of *a*. $\neg Fa \Rightarrow Ga$
10. It's not the case that if *F* of *a*, then *G* of *a*. $\neg(Fa \Rightarrow Ga)$
11. Both *R* of *x*, *y*, *z* and either *M* of *x*, *y* or not *M* of *x*, *y*. $Rxyz \& (Mxy \lor \neg Mxy)$

Note: At present we have not established rules for the use of parentheses. The challenges are meant to suggest to you that such rules would be important.

CHALLENGE 4 Write the formulas that express the meanings of these sentences (regardless of how they are pronounced).

1. Jim Henle is married to Aristotle and Aristotle is male. *Mad* & *Gd*
2. There is someone Jim Henle is married to who is male. $\exists x(Max \& Gx)$
3. There is someone Jim Henle is married to and someone is male. $\exists x Max \& \exists x Gx$
4. Madonna has a husband. $\exists z(Mbz \& Gz)$ or other variables, *x*, *y* replacing *z*.
5. Tom Tymoczko is a husband. $\exists x(Mcx \& Gc)$ or $\exists x Mcx \& Gc$

6. *y* has a husband. ∃*z*(*Myz* & *Gz*) or other variables, *x, w* replacing *z* (but not *y*!).
7. There is someone Adrienne Rich is married to. ∃*xMex*
8. Adrienne Rich and Madonna beget Jim Henle. *Reba*
9. There is some *y* such that Adrienne Rich and *y* beget Jim Henle. ∃*yReya*
10. Adrienne Rich is a parent of Jim Henle. ∃*yReya*
11. Adrienne Rich is a father of Jim Henle. ∃*y*(*Reya* & *Ge*)

CHALLENGE 5   Write English sentences that express the meaning of these formulas.

1. ∃*xMcx*   Tom Tymoczko is married. (Someone is such that Tom Tymoczko is married to her/him.)
2. ∃*yMcy*   Same as 1.
3. ¬∀*zMza*   Not everyone is married to Jim Henle. (Not all are married to Jim Henle.)
4. ∀*x*(*Fx* ∨ ¬*Fx*)   Everyone is either female or not female.
5. ∀*xFx* ∨ ¬∀*xFx*   (Either) everyone is female or not everyone is female.
6. ∀*z*(*Fz* ⇔ ¬*Gz*)   Everyone is female iff not male.
7. ∃*y*(*Rayc* & *Gc*)   Tom Tymoczko is a son of Jim Henle. There is someone who together with Jim Henle begets Tom Tymoczko and Tom T. is male.
8. ∃*y*(*Rayc* & *Ga*)   Jim Henle is Tom Tymoczko's father. There is someone who together with Jim Henle begets Tom Tymoczko and Jim H. is male.
9. ∀*x*(*Mxa* ⇒ *Max*)   Anyone married to Jim Henle is such that Jim Henle is married to them. For any person, if that person is married to Jim Henle, then Jim Henle is married to that person. This is trivial for marriage, but absolutely false for parents and other relations.
10. ¬∃*z*(*Mza* & ¬*Maz*)   There is no one who is married to Jim but (and) Jim is not married to him/her.
11. ∃*z*¬*Mza*   Someone is not married to Jim Henle.
12. ∃*x*∃*y*¬*Mxy*   Someone is not married to someone. There are persons, call them *x* and *y*, such that *x* is not married to *y*.
13. ∀*x*∀*y*(*Mxy* ⇒ ¬(*x* = *y*))   No one is married to themselves. For any married couple, each is not identical to the other. For any persons *x* and *y*, if *x* is married to *y*, then *x* is not identical to *y*.

CHALLENGE 6   A considerable portion of the kinship terms of English are definable in our minimal vocabulary. Some exceptions involve time, such as "stepson" or "ex-wife," but perhaps these are not kinship terms. More interesting are terms that classify relations by order of birth. The Chinese of Fukien Provence, for example, have in place of the generic "sister" terms like *a-tze* (pronounced "ah-tze") meaning "eldest (or first) sister." In order to express the relation "*x* is a-tze to *y*" we would need an additional predicate *Oxy* to express "*x* is older than *y*" (and some fancy logical manipulation to express that no other sister of *y* is older than *x*!). With this addition, we could define eldest sister, second sister, and so on.

Another difficulty for our vocabulary is provided by some Native American languages, such as Sioux. These languages have kinship terms that vary not only according to the gender of the person referred to (as do "sister" and "brother") but also according to the gender of the speaker! So a Sioux boy, but not a Sioux girl, could call his older brother *tibola*.

with & about logic

paradox   *page 17*

The paradox of Achilles and the Tortoise is one of four paradoxes of motion propounded by Zeno of Elea, who lived in the fifth century B.C. There is a great deal of mystery surrounding Zeno and his paradoxes. Our sources for Zeno himself are meager. It is believed that he composed the paradoxes to support Parmenides in his claim that all things are one and unmoving.

Regardless of their purpose, the questions he raised have kept philosophers and mathematicians busy ever since. At times in the last 2000 years, they have seemed trivial and easy to explain. At other times, they have seemed baffling. Early in the twentieth century, for example, Bertrand Russell felt they were completely demystified. Today, however, we are again baffled. For a good introduction and a number of provocative essays, see *Zeno's Paradoxes*, edited by Wesley C. Salmon (Bobbs-Merrill, 1970).

The Barber Paradox is due to Russell.

The paradox of the Cretan is due to Epimenides. Curiously, it is alluded to in the Bible (Titus 1:12). In a letter to Titus, Paul is speaking of the Cretans when he says, "One of themselves, even a prophet of their own, said, The Cretans are always liars, evil beasts, slow bellies." Apparently Paul did not realize that Epimenides was formulating a logical paradox and not confessing to a general depravity among Cretans!

In most of these paradoxes, self-reference is a suspiciously recurring theme (see "The Title of the Section on Self-Reference" in part 2). We recommend a splendid little volume, *Vicious Circles and*

Infinity, An Anthology of Paradoxes, edited by Patrick Hughes and George Brecht (Doubleday, 1975).

Another possible solution to the liar paradoxes is that "is true" is not completely defined or definable. That is, there are sentences for which truth cannot be determined. What is truth, anyhow?

informal logic

page 21 *negation*

Richard Wilbur, former poet laureate of the United States, wrote a book called *Opposites* (Harcourt Brace Jovanovich, 1973), exploring the concept of opposites. Our favorite stanza is from poem 14:

> What is the opposite of *penny?*
> I'm sorry, but there isn't any—
> Unless you count the change, I guess,
> Of someone who is *penniless*.

EXERCISE

1. Jim Henle is not bald.

3. Either Tom is not bald or Jim is not bald.

5. Tom and Jim are not rock stars *or* Neither Tom nor Jim is a rock star.

7. Either Dick is not married or Jane is not married.

9. At least one mollusk is not female.

11. At least one geology major is amphibious.

13. There is someone Jean can't outrun.

15. There is some student at the university of whom Sue is not a friend.

17. No student is friends with everyone at the university. *Or,* Every student is not friends with someone at the university.

curiosities & puzzles

page 24 quiz

1. T or F   2. F   3. T

The questions are rigged in such a way that you must answer T on the third question to get question 2 correct. If you answer T to 2 and F to

3, then your answer to 2 is wrong, since 2 says that the answers to 2 and 3 are the same, you said T, but in fact you answered them differently (T and F). If you answer F to 2 and 3, then your answer to 2 is again wrong, since 2 says that the answers to 2 and 3 are the same, you said F, but in fact you did answer them the same (F and F).

Thus you must answer T to 3. Having done this, an answer of either T or F will do for 2. On the other hand, if you answer T for 2, then nothing works for 1. If you answer F for 2, then either T or F is a correct answer for 1.

Tom and Jim's Excellent Adventure

(continued from page 516)

November 14

Before tackling philosophical problems, Jim has a mathematical one. Today the weatherperson said, "There is a 50% chance of rain tomorrow." Jim has always wondered what this means. He wants to test it by traveling a day into the future to see if it does rain, returning, then going back to the future, returning, and so on, and so on. He wants to see if about 50 percent of the time it does rain and about 50 percent of the time it doesn't.

Tom thinks this is a waste of the Infundibula. If you agree with Tom, turn to page 638. If you agree with Jim, turn to page 589.

2 EVERYTHING ALL AT ONCE AND A WARNING

FORMAL LOGIC: OVERVIEW

page 26 **TRUTH AND FALSITY**

Question 1 a. True c. False

CHALLENGE 1

1.

A B	¬A ∨ B		yes
T T	F	T	
T F	F	F	
F T	T	T	
F F	T	T	

3.

A B	¬(A & ¬B)		A ⇒ B
T T	T	F F	
T F	F	T T	
F T	T	F F	
F F	T	F T	

CHALLENGE 2 1. F 3. F 5. T 7. T 9. F 11. T ($\forall x Sx$ is false, and F ⇒ F is true.) 13. T 15. F 17. T 19. F (The teachers may not have teachers.)

CHALLENGE 3 1. F 3. T 5. T 7. T 9. T because *Sc* is *F.* 11. T 13. T 15. F 17. T 19. F (What if *x* is 0?)

page 31 **LOGICAL FORM: THE KEY TO LOGIC**

CHALLENGE 1

2. One example each:
   a. Either I don't bring the umbrella or it's a sunny day.
   b. I'm going to the track and if I'm lucky, we can eat steak tonight.
   c. There is a God.

CHALLENGE 2 Possible answers: $A \Rightarrow A$, $A \Leftrightarrow A$, $(A \Rightarrow B) \vee (B \Rightarrow A)$, $\exists x A x \Leftrightarrow \exists y A y$

CHALLENGE 4 Possible answers: $A \,\&\, \neg A$, $A \,\&\, (A \Rightarrow \neg A)$, $\exists x A x \,\&\, \forall x \neg A x$

CHALLENGE 5 Possible answers: $A \,\&\, B$ and $B \,\&\, A$, $A \vee B$ and $B \vee A$, $A \Rightarrow B$ and $\neg A \vee B$, A and A

CHALLENGE 6 Possible answers: A implies $A \vee B$, $A \Leftrightarrow B$ implies $A \Rightarrow B$, B implies $\neg A \Rightarrow B$, $A \Leftrightarrow B$ implies $\neg A \vee B$

The Frege quotation is from his *Foundations of Arithmetic*, translated by J. L. Austin (Blackwell, 1950).

ARGUMENT FORM: THE KEY TO REASONING

page 35

CHALLENGE 1

All presidents of the United States are men.
Tom Tymoczko is a man.
∴ Tom is a president of the United States.

All women are nonpresidents of the United States.
Jim Henle is a nonpresident of the United States.
∴ Jim Henle is a woman.

CHALLENGE 2 1. valid 3. valid 5. valid 7. invalid (Think of Fx, "x is all white," and "Gx, "x is all black.

with & about logic

paradox and W. S. Gilbert

page 39

See *The Complete Plays of Gilbert and Sullivan* by W. S. Gilbert (Norton, 1976). Gilbert's other work of interest is the *Bab Ballads*, on which he based some of the plots and songs in the operettas. This work is out of print, but copies can be found in used book stores.

page 41 ## The Orb and Post

Readers may remember that at the 1988 Olympics in Seoul, a Canadian sprinter, Ben Johnson, won the 100-meter run but then lost the gold medal when he failed a test for steroids.

We would like to give credit for this lovely satire, but we do not know its author. It came to our attention through colleagues who attended a mathematics conference in Maine a few years ago. We have made only minor changes.

page 42 ## paradoxes and psychology

For more on this subject, we recommend *Pragmatics of Human Communication* by Watzlawick, Beavin, and Jackson (Norton, 1967), from which the quotations were taken. The paradoxical injunctions come from p. 200, the self-refuting father is mentioned on p. 190, and the inconsistent mother appears in a footnote on page 214.

For one account of the connection between logic and Zen, see *Gödel, Escher, Bach* by Douglas Hofstadter (Basic Books, 1979).

page 44 ## the title of the section on self-reference

Gödel, Escher, Bach is by Douglas Hofstadter (Basic Books, 1979).

"This Article Should Not Be Rejected by *Mind*" appeared in *Mind,* vol. 99 (October 1990).

EXERCISES

1. We think so. It reminds us of a village in England in which one hobbyist has constructed a scale model of the town that is very large (it takes up an entire yard). The scale model is so large, in fact, that it is represented, in miniature, in the scale model, and so on, and so on. An example similar to the genetic code will be seen in the section "Life" in part 9.

3. How about the title of this section? How about the title of Raymond Smullyan's book *This Book Needs No Title?* How about the title of Abbie Hoffman's book *Steal This Book!?* How about the following, from an advertisement for the *Boston Globe* appearing in the *Boston Globe* on April 5, 1990?

Have you seen the *Globe* today?

informal logic

how to argue

page 53

A few additional comments:

It is not always clear in Cathy's discussion what "democracy" is. One can often gain control of an argument by setting its parameters. In this case, you might improve your position by providing a convenient definition of "democracy."

Is Mencken an expert? It's not clear what an expert is here. Political science, despite the name, is not precisely a science. There are vigorous arguments about almost any issue.

One can also argue that the Mencken quote supports democracy, or is at least neutral. After all, he is saying that under a democratic system we get what we deserve. Perhaps the remark displays more cynicism about us than about our government.

rebuttal

page 59

Hints for Cathy's reply:

Since your opponent has not defined "democracy," you could do so, and do so in a way that might be to your advantage. Even more important than defining democracy is defining "good." When is a government good? If it gives peace? Prosperity? You might offer the examples of Korea and Taiwan or even Spain.

You might harp on the lack of participation in government in this country, especially among the poor. You might attack schools more vigorously. You can find plenty of ammunition if you know where to look.

Note: There is more to making and defending arguments than logic. It helps to know things. It helps to have thought about the issues. The reader who would like to argue successfully is urged to acquire knowledge and seasoning simply by reading newspapers. Read a paper everyday and discuss what you read.

law boards: reading comprehension

page 64

1. E 3. C 5. C 7. C 9. B 11. C 13. E 15. A

If you are interested in more practice problems, there are many large, reasonably priced books on the LSAT in most bookstores. Also, you may write to Publications, Law Services, Box 40, 661 Penn Street, Newtown, PA 18940. They will send you their Information Book, which contains sample problems.

curiosities & puzzles

page 72 *The Digestor's Digest*, page 1

It's a puzzle. What can we find out—are they ads or articles? You can work from several angles. You might notice that the two pieces are contradictory (they both claim their product has the most protein). This tells you that at least one is an advertisement.

What about the first one? It claims that it is not an ad. Can an article claim that? Certainly, it would be the truth. Can an ad claim that? Certainly, it would be false! This doesn't help. So far, the first could be either an ad or an article.

What about the second? It claims that it is the only ad. An article certainly can't claim that—it would be false. Can an ad claim that? Only if the first piece is also an ad. This then is our answer. Both are ads. The cereal with the most protein is neither Grittibits nor Wheezies. Probably Tofutsies.

page 74 talking heads

1. "Ask not what your country can do for you, ask what you can do for your country." (*Portrait of J. F. Kennedy by David Lee Iwerks, National Portrait Gallery, Smithsonian Institution/Art Resource, NY*)

2. "I am not a crook." (*Portrait photograph of Richard M. Nixon by Philippe Halsman, National Portrait Gallery, Smithsonian Institution/Art Resource, NY*)

3. "I have a dream." (*Portrait photograph of Martin Luther King, Jr., by Benedict J. Fernandez, National Portrait Gallery, Smithsonian Institution/Art Resource, NY*)

4. "All men are created equal." (*Stipple engraving of Thomas Jefferson attributed to John Norman after Rembrandt Peale, National Portrait Gallery, Smithsonian Institution/Art Resource, NY*)

5. "You can fool all of the people some of the time, and some of the people all of the time, but you can't fool all of the people all of the time." (*Photograph of Abraham Lincoln by Anthony Berger, National Portrait Gallery, Smithsonian Institution/Art Resource, NY*)

Note that cartoon 6 is not written with proper logical grammar! (*Wayne's World photograph of Dana Carvey by Suzanne Tenner copyright © 1992 by Paramount Pictures/The Kobal Collection, NY*)

Tom and Jim's Excellent Adventure

November 17

The time machine seems to be useless. Time is a line. If Jim travels back one day, he becomes Jim Henle-of-November-16, not Jim Henle-of-November-17-who-is-visiting-November-16. The problem is pointed out to the engineers, who make some adjustments so that when the button is pushed the contents of the machine do not change, just the world around it. In this way, no memory is lost.

Now Jim wants to investigate the paradox of time travel. The standard question is, What if you went back in time and killed your grandfather before your father was conceived? Jim doesn't plan anything so hostile or drastic. He decides to go back one day and give himself a haircut. What will happen? Will his own hair be affected? It should, because he is altering his own past. On the other hand, it shouldn't, because that would seem to violate the laws of physics. Either way, something very interesting will happen!

Tom thinks this is a bad idea, but he doesn't know why. If you agree with Tom, go to page 613. If you want to see Jim cut Jim's hair, go to page 636.

3 STATEMENT LOGIC, FORMAL LANGUAGES, AND INFORMAL ARGUMENTS

FORMAL LOGIC: STATEMENT LOGIC

FORMAL LANGUAGES: SENTENTIAL   *page 76*

The symbols ¬, &, ∨, ⇒ and ⇔ are called *connectives*; although the one-place connective ¬ does not actually connect wffs, it is called a connective by tradition. The important point is that all of these symbols of Sentential are linguistic. They are not really the logical operations of negation, conjunction, and so on, but only a particular symbolization of the operations. For example, the symbol & could denote the operation conditional (if we wanted), and ⇒ could denote conjunction.

It is absolutely crucial to keep in mind the distinction between arbitrarily chosen symbols and the operations or concepts those symbols are chosen to symbolize.

EXERCISE 1   a, i, j

CHALLENGE 1   Tom's mother and father are ancestors. If *x* is an ancestor of Tom, then so are *x*'s parents, or any parent of an ancestor of Tom is also an ancestor of Tom.

CHALLENGE 2

P Q R	P & (Q ∨ R)		(P & Q) ∨ **R**	
T T T	T	T	T	T
T T F	T	T	T	T
T F T	F	T	F	T
T F F	F	F	F	F
F T T	F	T	F	T
F T F	F	T	F	F
F F T	F	T	F	T
F F F	F	F	F	F

We see that the tables are not the same and thus the placement of parentheses matters.

EXERCISE 2

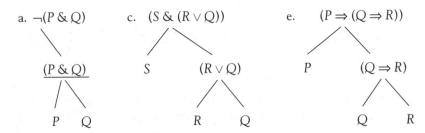

a. ¬(P & Q)   c. (S & (R ∨ Q))   e.   (P ⇒ (Q ⇒ R))

532

g. $\neg((S \,\&\, (P \vee \neg Q)) \Leftrightarrow (\neg S \vee (\neg P \,\&\, \neg\neg Q)))$

$\underline{((S \,\&\, (P \vee \neg Q)) \Leftrightarrow (\neg S \vee (\neg P \,\&\, \neg\neg Q)))}$

$(S \,\&\, (P \vee \neg Q))$ $(\neg S \vee (\neg P \,\&\, \neg\neg Q))$

S $(P \vee \neg Q)$ $\neg S$ $(\neg P \,\&\, \neg\neg Q)$

P $\neg Q$ $\underline{S}$ $\neg P$ $\neg\neg Q$

$\underline{Q}$ $\underline{P}$ $\neg Q$

$\underline{Q}$

FORMAL LANGUAGES: VARIATIONS ON SENTENTIAL

page 80

EXERCISE 1   a. $\neg(P \,\&\, Q)$ c. $\neg(\neg P \,\&\, \neg Q)$ e. $S \vee (P \Leftrightarrow Q)$

EXERCISE 2   a. $\Rightarrow P \Rightarrow QR$ c. $\neg\&P \vee Q\neg P_1$
e. $\Leftrightarrow \vee \neg P \neg Q \neg\&PQ$

EXERCISE 3

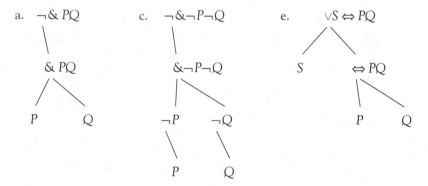

a. $\neg\&\,PQ$

$\&\,PQ$

P Q

c. $\neg\&\neg P\neg Q$

$\&\neg P\neg Q$

$\neg P$ $\neg Q$

P Q

e. $\vee S \Leftrightarrow PQ$

S $\Leftrightarrow PQ$

P Q

CHALLENGE 1 Naturally, every wff of Weak Sentential is a wff of Sentential. The reverse is not true, but in fact, the expressive power of Weak Sentential is just as great as Sentential. This is because every wff of Sentential can be paraphrased in Weak Sentential. In technical terms, any wff of Sentential is

533

equivalent to a wff of Weak Sentential. Here is an example: The wff $P \Rightarrow Q$ can be written as $\neg P \vee Q$. Compare the truth tables of these two expressions: They are identical. How would you paraphrase $P \Leftrightarrow Q$? Further challenge: Can we weaken Weak Sentential still further without loss of expressive power? We answer this question in "Logic Circuits" in part 4.

EXERCISE 4 $\Diamond \Diamond p,\ \neg \Box q,\ \Box(p \Rightarrow \Diamond q)$, and infinitely many others

EXERCISE 5

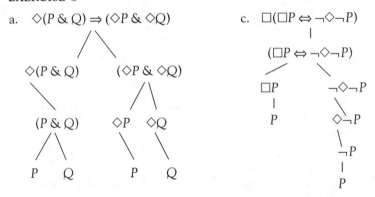

a. $\Diamond(P \& Q) \Rightarrow (\Diamond P \& \Diamond Q)$

c. $\Box(\Box P \Leftrightarrow \neg \Diamond \neg P)$

CHALLENGE 2   *Hint:* Take the definition of, say, the grammar of Modal Sentential. Make the appropriate changes for Tensed Sentential. (The only change involves showing how the one-place connectives N, F, and F generate new wffs.)

CHALLENGE 3

1. It is a little difficult to write an answer to this now (April 16, 1994) that will remain reasonable throughout the life of this edition of *Sweet Reason.* We should specify whether the duration of "now" is this instant, this minute, this week, and so on. To make our answers last, we'll let "now" be this century.

   An R such that $\neg PR$ & NR: "This is the twentieth century."
   An R such that NR & $\neg FR$: "This is the twentieth century."
   A Q such that $\neg NQ$ & FQ: "This is the twenty-first century."

2. a. It states that if at some time ago it was true that previously A had been true, then today it is the case that A was previously. This is valid in Tensed Sentential.

   b. This does not seem valid, but it hinges upon how we segment time here. Consider A, "There is only one day left to file your 1993 tax forms." I wrote this on April 16, 1994. The statement was true the day before, but it was not true on any day before that. If we are going by days, then PA but not PPA. On

534

the other hand, if we go by hours, then we might argue that PPA is true, since the day before at noon, PA was true (in that it was true three hours before). More generally, PA ⇒ PPA will be valid as long as time does not have a first moment (perhaps time goes back forever) that is followed by a second moment (perhaps time is continuous). If A is true at the first moment, PA will be true at the second moment, but PPA will then be false.

TRUTH TABLES

page 84

EXERCISE

1. a and d have the same truth tables. b and c have the same truth tables and so are equivalent. Otherwise, no wff implies another.

		a	b
3. **P Q R**		$P \Rightarrow (Q \Rightarrow R)$	$(P \Rightarrow Q) \Rightarrow R$
T T T		T **T** T T T	T T T **T** T
T T F		T **F** T F F	T T T **F** F
T F T		T **T** F T T	T F F **T** T
T F F		T **T** F T F	T F F **T** F
F T T		F **T** T T T	F T T **T** T
F T F		F **T** T F F	F T T **F** F
F F T		F **T** F T T	F T F **T** T
F F F		F **T** F T F	F T F **F** F

The truth tables are not the same. There are rows where $(P \Rightarrow Q) \Rightarrow R$ is false but $P \Rightarrow (Q \Rightarrow R)$ is not, so the wffs are not equivalent. Since there are no rows where the reverse is true, $(P \Rightarrow Q) \Rightarrow R$ implies $P \Rightarrow (Q \Rightarrow R)$.

5. The truth table consists of all T's, so $P \Rightarrow Q$ is logically equivalent to $\neg P \lor Q$.

	a	b	c	d
7. **P**	$P \& \neg P$	**P**	$\neg P$	$P \Rightarrow \neg P$
T	T **F** F	T	F	T **F** F
F	F **F** T	F	T	F **T** T

c and d are equivalent, and b, c, and d are each implied by a. Notice that d ($P \Rightarrow \neg P$) is not contradictory but is logically equivalent to $\neg P$!

535

CHALLENGE 1

1. Not necessarily. *P* is consistent, that is, sometimes true, but not a tautology.
3. Inconsistent. If *A* is always true, then ¬*A* is always false.
5. It is not valid. If *A* is not always false, then ¬*A* is not always true.
7. The only F in the truth table for *P* ⇒ *Q* is on the line where *P* is true and *Q* is false. If *P* is a contradiction, then *P* is never true, and under these circumstances *P* ⇒ *Q* is true.

CHALLENGE 2

1. If *A* is true, then since *A* implies *B*, *B* must be true. If *A* is false, then *B* cannot be true (or else *A* would be true since *B* implies *A*) and therefore *B* is false. So *A* and *B* are both true or both false. This shows that they are equivalent.
3. In any line of the truth table for *A*, *B*, and *A* ⇔ *B*, either both *A* and *B* are true or both are false (since *A* is equivalent to *B*). In both cases, *A* ⇔ *B* is true. Thus *A* ⇔ *B* is a tautology. On the other hand, if *A* ⇔ *B* is a tautology, there is no case where *A* and *B* take opposite truth values. Hence *A* is equivalent to *B*.

CHALLENGE 3

1. Suppose *A*, *B*, and *C* imply *D*. Then if (*A* & (*B* & *C*)) is true, then each of *A*, *B*, and *C* must be true individually, and so *D* is true. Thus (*A* & (*B* & *C*)) implies *D*. Now suppose that (*A* & (*B* & *C*)) implies *D*. Then if each of *A*, *B*, and *C* are true, then (*A* & (*B* & *C*)) is true, and so *D* is true. Thus *A*, *B*, and *C* imply *D*.

SOME BASIC TAUTOLOGIES AND IMPLICATIONS

page 93

EXERCISES

1. For example 1:

X Y Z W	$X \Rightarrow (Y \Rightarrow (Z \Rightarrow W))$			$X \Rightarrow ((Y \& Z) \Rightarrow W)$		
T T T T	**T**	T	T	**T**	T	T
T T T F	**F**	F	F	**F**	T	F
T T F T	**T**	T	T	**T**	F	T
T T F F	**T**	T	T	**T**	F	T
T F T T	**T**	T	T	**T**	F	T
T F T F	**T**	T	F	**T**	F	T
T F F T	**T**	T	T	**T**	F	T
T F F F	**T**	T	T	**T**	F	T
F T T T	**T**	T	T	**T**	T	T
F T T F	**T**	F	F	**T**	T	F
F T F T	**T**	T	T	**T**	F	T
F T F F	**T**	T	T	**T**	F	T
F F T T	**T**	T	T	**T**	F	T
F F T F	**T**	T	F	**T**	F	T
F F F T	**T**	T	T	**T**	F	T
F F F F	**T**	T	T	**T**	F	T

2. a. Since $\neg\neg B$ is equivalent to B, $A \& \neg\neg B$ is equivalent to $A \& B$ by the replacement principle.

   c. We use the equivalence stated earlier in the section, $(A \& (B \& C)) \Leftrightarrow ((A \& B) \& C)$, which for convenience we will call (&). (&) gives us the equivalence of $(Y \& (Z \& W))$ and $((Y \& Z) \& W)$, and then using the replacement principle, $(X \& (Y \& (Z \& W))) \Leftrightarrow (X \& ((Y \& Z) \& W))$. (&) also gives us the equivalence of $(X \& (Y \& Z))$ and $((X \& Y) \& Z)$, and the replacement principle then gives us $((X \& (Y \& Z)) \& W) \Leftrightarrow (((X \& Y) \& Z) \& W)$. Now (&) gives us $(X \& ((Y \& Z) \& W)) \Leftrightarrow ((X \& (Y \& Z)) \& W)$, and putting these together, we have $(X \& (Y \& (Z \& W))) \Leftrightarrow (((X \& Y) \& Z) \& W)$.

Tom and Jim's Excellent Adventure

November 17

Tom points out that no experiments are needed to show that the counterfactual conditional is different. The system of sentential logic is one way of interpreting English sentences, but logicians recognize that English is far more complicated. Sentential fails to capture all the shades and nuances of English: irony, sarcasm, invective, and so on. The point is that the English meaning of "If Dukakis had won in 1988, then Dan Quayle would have been vice president" is not the meaning in Sentential, and logicians knew that before the time machine was invented. Turn to page 587.

with & about logic

page 99   buffalo buffalo buffalo

EXERCISE   Bison intimidate bison.

CHALLENGES

1. a. There are two ways: "Bison (that) bison intimidate, intimidate bison" and "Bison intimidate bison (that) bison intimidate."
   c. Here is one way: "Bison [that] bison intimidate intimidate bison [that] bison intimidate."
2. From three *buffalo*'s we can get five simply by replacing a noun (bison) with a noun phrase (bison [that] bison intimidate). From five we can get seven, and so on. This takes care of all odd numbers of *buffalo*'s. Starting with two *buffalo*'s, we can take care of the even numbers.

artificial and natural languages

page 100

EXERCISES

1. a. S

NP + VP	Rule 1
Det + N + VP	Rule 2
a + N + VP	Rule 4
a + girl + VP	Rule 5
a + girl + V + NP	Rule 3
a + girl + fed + NP	Rule 6
a + girl + fed + Det + N	Rule 2
a + girl + fed + the + N	Rule 4
a + girl + fed + the + woman	Rule 5

2. a. *Hint:* How will you ever get a verb in front? The only rule that achieves this is 3, but for that you need a verb phrase already in front.

rewrite rules and finite automata

page 104

Regular languages can be described in yet another way, through the use of *regular expressions*. These generally use the star (*), which we mentioned in "Buffalo Buffalo Buffalo." For example, Buffalo is represented by the expression

$$buffalo^*$$

(meaning any number of *buffalo*'s). The other regular language mentioned in the chapter is represented by

$$(ba)^*(a \mid bb)$$

(any number of *ba*'s, followed by either *a* or *bb*).

If we restrict our rewrite rules to rules of the form

⟨a single capital letter⟩
        → ⟨a string of capital letters and lowercase letters⟩

we get what are called *context-free languages*. These languages *can* be tested for emptiness; that is, there is an algorithm that will decide if any legitimate sentences exist. There are still drawbacks, however. There is no algorithm that will decide, for two sets of rules, whether the two languages are actually the same.

If we restrict our rewrite rules to rules of the form

⟨a single capital letter⟩
    → ⟨one capital letter, possibly followed by lowercase letters⟩

or

⟨a capital letter⟩ → ⟨lowercase letters⟩

then we get a regular language. This corresponds to rules that merely add to the front end of sentences.

To learn more about this, pick up any text on formal language theory, a field at the intersection of linguistics and computer science. A very reasonable book is *A First Course in Formal Language Theory* by V. J. Rayward-Smith (Blackwell Scientific Publications, 1983).

EXERCISES

1.

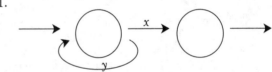

2. S → X
   X → Xy
   X → Zx
   Z → ε

5.

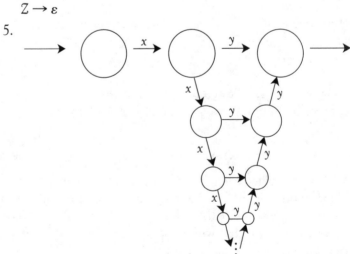

6.

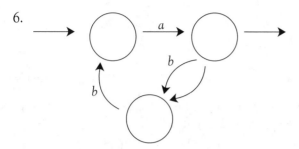

8. a.

8. c. Impossible.

EXTRA CHALLENGE Find regular expressions for the languages in exercises 1, 3, and 6. Answers: *y★x, ab★c, a(bba|ba)★* (There are other ways as well.)

loofah loofah loofah

page 109

We don't know when the *buffalo* craze began. We first learned of it at a mathematics conference in Boulder, Colorado, in 1981. "Loofah" means both a kind of sponge and the act of sponging something with that kind of sponge. So in theory, loofah could loofah loofah. Some of these words might be contested.

informal logic

page 109 *conclusions*

EXERCISE

1. Mr. Pipes is wrong when he says that the Turks are the second-largest ethnic group in Islam.

3. The air show should not have been held.

5. Nuclear power should not be considered as an energy source.

7. The continued high price of gasoline is justified.

9. This is not literally an argument but an entreaty. Not everything is an argument.

page 115 *supporting statements*

EXERCISE

1. The support here is pretty good. The only statement we might need is one that clarifies the meaning of "compete," to make sure that what we mean is to score competitively on mathematics exams.

3. Not bad, but an additional statement is needed—that a being that is all-loving would wish to prevent the suffering of an innocent child. This statement could be attacked, for example, on the grounds that temporary suffering of the child would ensure it eternal happiness.

5. A statement is needed that execution is murder. The argument is debatable.

7. Terrible. We need a statement that eating (not *what* he ate) caused stomach cancer. In addition, we need a statement that not eating would have saved him.

9. Pretty good. One also needs, however, a statement that there are no benefits from smoking that outweigh the risk of lung cancer.

11. Not bad, but an additional statement is needed that says that taxation would be effective in discouraging smoking.

relevance *page 119*

EXERCISE

1. All statements are relevant.

3. Statement [e] is not actually needed, but it does not detract from the argument as an irrelevant statement would.

5. All statements are relevant.

7. Statement [a] is not relevant. It is there to assuage the patriotism of the reader. Statement [h] is actually relevant, when you acknowledge its real meaning. The conclusion of the argument is that we should not go to war in the Gulf. The writer sets up two possible reasons for going to war and attacks both. The second reason is to keep the price of energy low. He attacks this by suggesting that conservation could be used instead of war. The administration says that it is working on conservation. The suspicious statement [h] says that the administration's word is not to be trusted. Statement [j] is rhetorical; it is added for emphasis.

premises *page 124*

EXERCISES

1. a, c, d, e

3. a, c, d + e (states that it would be a waste)

5. a, b, c, d, f, g, h

7. c, d, f, g, h, i, and possibly b

Cathy has breakfast *page 128*

It should be clear by now that the views of Cathy do not necessarily reflect those of the authors (or the publisher). We recognize that we are touching on controversial subjects. We were surprised, however, at the storm of protest that greeted us when our own class read this argument. We repeat here what we told them: To argue effectively, one must separate logical and emotional issues. Whether the subject is peace, patriotism, or toasted oat cereals, you must put aside sentiment to deal objectively with the relevant facts.

EXERCISES

1. The conclusion is clearly that eating Cheerios is bad. The relevant statements are "It's got sugar in it," "Sugar is bad for you," "You pump sugar into your blood. Your body has to counterattack with insulin. That drives down your blood sugar and so you get hungry before your eleven-o'clock class," "Cheerios has more salt per ounce than potato chips," "Salt is bad for you. It gives you high blood pressure. Would you pour milk on a bowl of potato chips and eat it for breakfast?" "The U.S. uses sugar to oppress third-world nations. It buys sugar at inflated prices from giant plantations. It's a bribe. It guarantees the power and wealth of the ruling class while discouraging industrialization. Those countries then sell us their raw materials cheap and buy our products. They might as well be colonies," "That's why they hate us. Even after the revolution. They seize our embassies, they support terrorists, and they call us the great Satan," "They also have this real dumb shape."

2. *Hints for rebuttal:* Check the total sugar (sucrose) content of Cheerios—it's actually lower than that of Grape Nuts. The fallacy in the sentence about pouring milk on a bowl of potato chips can be rebutted easily. You can argue that foreign policy should not be made at the breakfast table. You can praise the shape!

curiosities & puzzles

page 130 *The Digestor's Digest, page 2*

Again, the two pieces disagree, so at least one is an ad. Could the first be an ad? It claims that the other is an ad. If the first is an ad, that claim is not true, so the second is an article. Is this possible? The second claims that the two pieces are equally correct. This is not true if the first is an ad and the second is an article. We have reached a dead end, so the first cannot be an ad.

We know now that the first is an article. This tells us that the second is an ad. Checking this, we see that everything fits.

a nonlogical puzzle

page 132

- a. 26 letters of the alphabet
- c. 1001 Arabian Nights
- e. 54 cards in a deck (with the jokers)
- g. 88 piano keys
- i. 18 holes on a golf course
- k. 90 degrees in a right angle
- m. 8 sides on a stop sign
- o. 4 quarts in a gallon
- q. 5 digits in a zip code
- s. 11 people on a football team
- u. 29 days in February in a leap year
- w. 40 days and nights of the Great Flood

self-referential puzzles

page 132

1.
¹9

2.
¹1	²1
³6	4

3.
¹9	²8	³1
⁴8	3	0
⁵2	7	9

4.

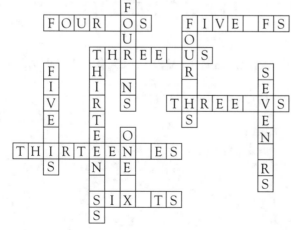

545

An article by Lee Sallows on the construction of reflexicons appeared in *Word Ways*, August 1992 (vol. 25, no. 3).

Tom and Jim's Excellent Adventure

November 17

Tom and Jim arrive a little early, before their own selves leave for the past. It seems an embarrassing situation, although no one knows why. Appropriately, the Jim they find has hair four inches long.

Putting their (four) heads together, they realize there is no paradox. The original Jim and Tom have been visiting not their past but the past of an alternative universe. After all, in their own past, they were never visited! Are they back now in their old universe? Difficult to say. There are two Jims, two Toms, and two Infundibulae.

Jim 1 (our Jim) suggests that they now have a good opportunity to investigate counterfactual conditionals. Go to page 562.

4 VALID ARGUMENTS, CONVINCING ARGUMENTS, AND PUNK LOGIC

FORMAL LOGIC: VALID ARGUMENTS

page 136 VALID ARGUMENT FORMS

CHALLENGE 1

1. a. Invalid

P Q	P ⇒ Q
T T	T
T F	F
F T	**T**
F F	T

c. Valid

Q R T	Q ⇒ R	R ⇒ T	Q ⇒ T
T T T	T	T	T
T T F	T	F	F
T F T	F	T	T
T F F	F	T	F
F T T	T	T	T
F T F	T	F	T
F F T	T	T	T
F F F	T	T	T

e. Valid

P Q	Q ⇒ P
T T	T
T F	T
F T	F
F F	T

g. Valid

P Q	Q ∨ ¬Q
T T	T
T F	T
F T	T
F F	T

i. Invalid

Q P R	Q ∨ P	¬R ∨ ¬P	R ⇒ ¬Q
T T T	T	F	F
T T F	T	T	T
T F T	T	T	F
T F F	T	T	T
F T T	T	F	T
F T F	T	T	T
F F T	F	T	T
F F F	F	T	T

3. See Challenge 13 in "Formalizing for Validity."

FORMALIZING FOR VALIDITY

page 138

CHALLENGE

1. $L ⇒ S$, S ∴ L (L = "You learn logic," S = "You study."). Invalid. In the truth table, consider the line:

L S	L ⇒ S
F T	T

Both premises are true, but the conclusion is false.

3. $G \Rightarrow L$ (or $\neg G \vee L$), $L \Rightarrow R$, $\neg G \Rightarrow \neg S \therefore S \Rightarrow L$ (L = "You learn logic," G = "You graduate," R = "You read this book," S = "You get into law school.") Valid.

G L R S	G ⇒ L	L ⇒ R	¬G ⇒ ¬S	S ⇒ L
T T T T	**T**	**T**	**T**	**T**
T T T F	**T**	**T**	**T**	**T**
T T F T	T	F	T	T
T T F F	T	F	T	T
T F T T	F	T	T	F
T F T F	F	T	T	T
T F F T	F	T	T	F
T F F F	F	T	T	T
F T T T	T	T	F	T
F T T F	**T**	**T**	**T**	**T**
F T F T	T	F	F	T
F T F F	T	F	T	T
F F T T	T	T	F	F
F F T F	**T**	**T**	**T**	**T**
F F F T	T	T	F	F
F F F F	**T**	**T**	**T**	**T**

5. $D \Rightarrow M$, $D \therefore M$ (D = "You advocate the legalization of drugs," M = "You send a message . . . ." Valid.

D ⇒ M	D M
T	**T T**
F	T F
T	F T
T	F F

7. $L \Rightarrow (M \& C \& I)$, $I \Rightarrow W$, $\neg W \therefore \neg L$ (L = "Drugs are legalized," M = "There will be money to treat addicts," C = "There will be less drug-related crime," I = "The mob will lose its main source of income," W = "The mob will wither away and die." Valid.

548

L	M & C	I W	L ⇒ (M & C & I)	I ⇒ W	¬W	¬L
T	T	T T	T	T	F	F
T	T	T F	T	F	T	F
T	T	F T	F	T	F	F
T	T	F F	F	T	T	F
T	F	T T	F	T	F	F
T	F	T F	F	F	T	F
T	F	F T	F	T	F	F
T	F	F F	F	T	T	F
F	T	T T	T	T	F	T
F	T	T F	T	F	T	T
F	T	F T	T	T	F	T
F	**T**	**F F**	**T**	**T**	**T**	**T**
F	F	T T	T	T	F	T
F	F	T F	T	F	T	T
F	F	F T	T	T	F	T
F	**F**	**F F**	**T**	**T**	**T**	**T**

9. $\neg I \Rightarrow (F \& \neg S)$ or $(I \lor (F \& \neg S))$, $I \Rightarrow J \therefore S \Rightarrow J$ (I = "Interest rates will rise," F = "The Fed intervenes," S = "The stock market falls," J = "Many will lose their jobs." Valid.

I F S J	¬I ⇒ (F & ¬S)	I ⇒ J	S ⇒ J
T T T T	**T**	**T**	**T**
T T T F	T	F	F
T T F T	**T**	**T**	**T**
T T F F	T	F	T
T F T T	**T**	**T**	**T**
T F T F	T	F	F
T F F T	**T**	**T**	**T**
T F F F	T	F	T
F T T T	F	T	T
F T T F	F	T	F
F T F T	**T**	**T**	**T**
F T F F	**T**	**T**	**T**
F F T T	F	T	T
F F T F	F	T	F
F F F T	F	T	T
F F F F	F	T	T

11. $L \Rightarrow R$, $L \vee \neg L$, $\neg L \Rightarrow P$, $(R \vee P) \Rightarrow S$ ∴ S (L = "The next president's policy is to legalize drugs," R = "The next president's policy reduces addiction," P = "The next president's policy proclaims the danger of drugs," S = "The next president's policy is a success." Valid. But is opposing legalization the negation of legalization? If not, then $\neg L$ should be replaced by O, but the argument is still valid.

L R P S	$L \Rightarrow R$	$L \vee \neg L$	$\neg L \Rightarrow P$	$(R \vee P) \Rightarrow S$
T T T T	**T**	**T**	**T**	**T**
T T T F	T	T	T	F
T T F T	**T**	**T**	**T**	**T**
T T F F	T	T	T	F
T F T T	F	T	T	T
T F T F	F	T	T	F
T F F T	F	T	T	T
T F F F	F	T	T	T
F T T T	**T**	**T**	**T**	**T**
F T T F	T	T	T	F
F T F T	T	T	F	T
F T F F	T	T	F	F
F F T T	T	T	F	T
F F T F	T	T	T	F
F F F T	T	T	F	T
F F F F	T	T	F	T

13. This argument has many words in it, but the argument boils down to just this: $T \Rightarrow R$, R ∴ T (T = "Raising taxes was the right thing to do," R = "The country recovered." Invalid. It is possible for both premises to be true yet the conclusion false. This happens if T is false and R is true. *Note:* This is actually an answer to Challenge 3 in "Valid Argument Forms."

15. C, S ∴ G (C = "Clark Kent wears glasses," S = "Superman is Clark Kent," G = "Superman wears glasses." Invalid. Of course, there is some validity to this argument, but Sentential is unable to express it.

page 142 A SHORTCUT FOR CHECKING ARGUMENTS

EXERCISE

1. The only way for the conclusion to be false is if R is false and P is true. Now if P is true, Q must be true or else the first premise is false. With these assignments, which were forced upon us,

the second premise is false. Hence it is impossible to make both premises true and the conclusion false, hence the argument is valid.

3. To make the conclusion false, we need only that either U or R is false. Let's try R first. If R is false, then we need S true for the first premise to be true. Now we need T true to save the second premise. With S and T true, the fourth premise is automatically true. To make the third premise true, we need only that U is false. This is possible, and so we have found a line of the truth table that demonstrates that the argument is invalid: S and T true, U and R false.

FORMALIZING ENGLISH   *page 144*

& and "and"

For more on Grice's theory, see his "Logic and Conversation" in *The Logic of Grammar*, edited by Donald Davidson and Gilbert Harman (Dickinson, 1975).

EXERCISES

1. There is certainly a conversational implicature that I do not approve of Jim, since it appears I have pointedly not addressed his mathematical qualifications. On the other hand, there is no *logical* implication, since I could cancel the implicature by subsequently praising Jim's research and teaching.

∨ and "or"

EXERCISE Homer spoke falsely if the logical form of the sentence was (clean ⇔ go out) (exclusive or). In fact, the logical form is only (clean ∨ ¬go out), that is, (¬clean ⇒ ¬go out). Homer can cancel the conversational implicature (clean ⇒ go out) by adding, for example, " . . . and the cleaning better be done before it rains."

⇒ and if . . . then

Another justification for the truth table of ⇒ derives from a legal analogy. It is the law that if a car is parked on State Street in Northampton, Massachusetts, between the hours of 10:00 A.M. and 6:00 P.M. (Sundays and holidays excepted), then "Violation" must not be showing on the parking meter. This is a legal if . . . then. Clearly, if you are parked on State Street and have put money in the meter (T, T), then you are obeying the law (T $\Rightarrow$ T is T). Just as clearly, if you are parked on State Street during the critical hours and have not put money in the meter (and no one else has) (T, F), then you are not obeying the law (T $\Rightarrow$ F is F). On the other hand, if you did not park on State Street but for some obscure reason put money in the meter (F, T), are you disobeying the law? Of course not (F $\Rightarrow$ T is T). And finally, if you have never driven a car and have never left Vladivostok in your life (F, F), are you violating the city ordinances of Northampton, Massachusetts? No (F $\Rightarrow$ F is T).

with & about logic

page 153 Miniac

EXERCISE

1 and 2. If the answer to question 2 is correct, then the truth value of Miniac's answer to question 1 is the same as the truth value of the answer to question 2. Question 2's answer is correct, and so question 1's answer is correct, and so it will rain tomorrow.

3. We don't know!

4. For a hint, see "Paradox" in part 1 and "The Title of the Section on Self-Reference" in part 2. What happens to the argument when the first answer is incorrect but the second flip comes up "heads"?

page 156 flipism

Copies of the original comic, *Walt Disney's Comics and Stories* #149, are hard to find. In 1984–1985, the latest price guide that we have, it cost $3 in good condition, $9 in fine condition, and $18 in mint condition. It has been reprinted twice, however, once in 1970 by Gold Key (*Walt Disney's Comics and Stories* #365, $.70, $2, $4) and most recently in 1991 by Walt Disney publications (*Walt Disney's Comics and Stories* #561, $1.50 in 1991).

Here is the rest of *Flipism*, story and art by Carl Barks. Even at this reduced scale, one can appreciate his work: Every panel develops the plot and every line enhances characterization. His plots are often striking.

CHALLENGE   What paradox from ''Paradox'' in part 7 does this story most resemble?

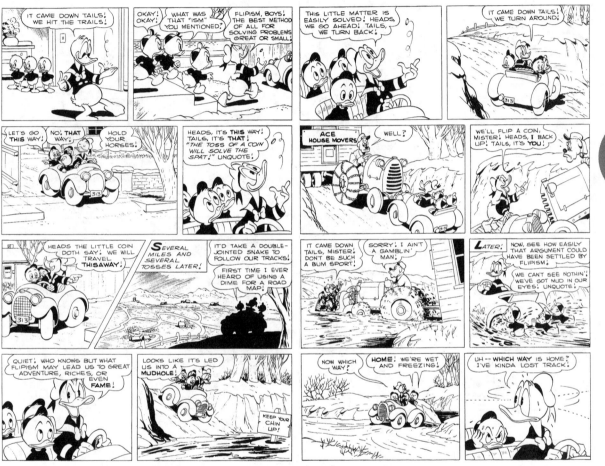

3   4

From *Walt Disney's Comics and Stories* #149, 1952. Reprinted by permission.

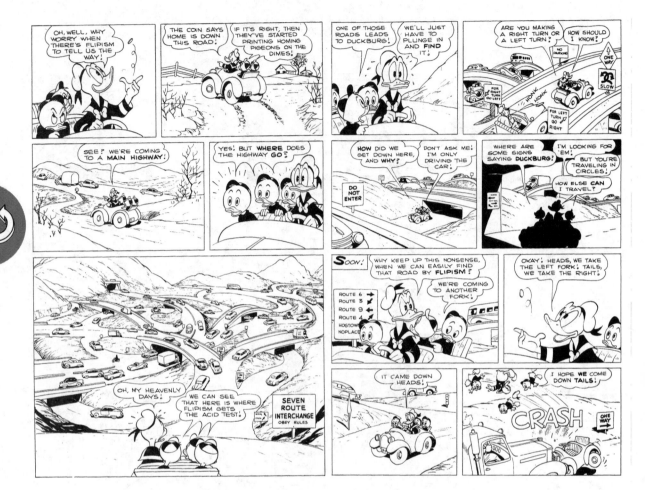

5

6

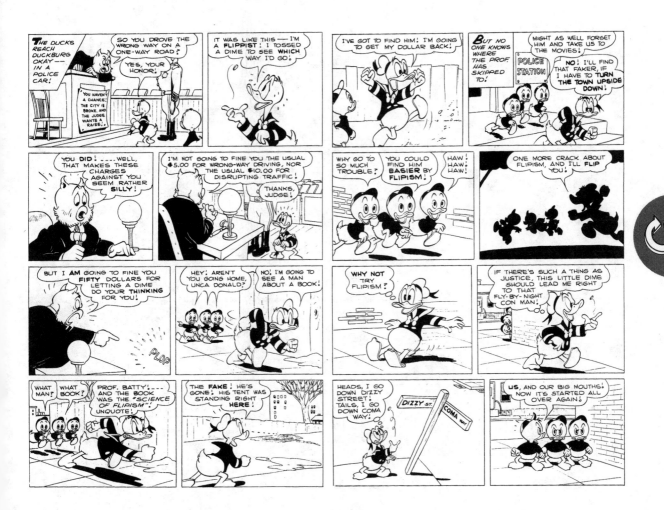

7

8

9   10

The story by Barks most resembles the paradox of Euathus, law student of Protagoras. If Donald finds Professor Batty, then Flipism is no joke, it works! On the other hand, if he doesn't, then he should get his money back. Consequently,

Donald finds Batty ⇔ he has nothing to demand of him.

page 157   sets

CHALLENGE
1. a. $p \cup q^c$ c. $(p \cap q)^c$ e. $p^c \cup q^c$

2. a.
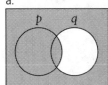
c.
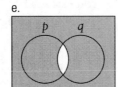
e.

3. Among these three, (c) and (e) are the same, so ¬(*P* & *Q*) and ¬*P* ∨ ¬*Q* are equivalent. If we include (b), (d) and (f), then there are additional equivalences.

EXERCISES

1. 45

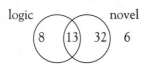

logic   novel
8 (13) 32) 6

2. a. 4, 6, 7, 8
   b. 1, 3, 4, 7
   c. 8 combinations:

(1)	(2)	(3)
for	for	for
for	for	opp.
for	opp.	for
for	opp.	opp.
opp.	for	for
opp.	for	opp.
opp.	opp.	for
opp.	opp.	opp.

   Does this remind you of something?
   d. 3%, 1%, 21%, 20%, 23%, 1%, 12%, 19%
   e. Either support (3) and oppose (1) and (2) or support all three. Each gives you 57% of the vote.

3.

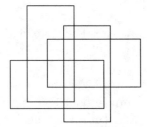

5. You can see how Lewis Carroll handled this in "The Game of Logic" in part 4.

Tom and Jim's Excellent Adventure

November 15

It is raining cats and dogs. Quickly Jim sets the dial for 24 hours in the past and pushes the button. Turn to page 589.

---

page 162 logic circuits

EXERCISES

1. a. The result is 110111. The effect is that of $\neg P \lor Q$.
   c. *Hint:* This contraption behaves the same as a much simpler mechanism.
3. *Hint:* This is $\neg P \lor \neg Q$. It will look a little like the figure in exercise 1c.

page 164 Bertrand the First

The opening quotation was called to our attention while reading *The Annotated Alice* by Lewis Carroll, notes and introduction by Martin Gardner (Forum Books, 1960). This is a fascinating edition of the *Alice* books with much insight into their creator.

informal logic

page 165 *criticizing arguments*

EXERCISES

1. The following answers are not complete. There are many ways to attack most arguments. (1) At first glance, the argument looks very tight. There is, however, a possible flaw. The argument assumes that all the Muslims of Pakistan, India, and Bangladesh belong to the same ethnic group. This may not be so, depending on what we mean by "ethnic group." Almost

certainly they speak different languages. It might be argued that even the Muslims of Pakistan alone belong to several ethnic groups. (3) One can argue that the shows are not a "great threat." One can also argue that they are not a waste, citing benefits such as entertainment, help in recruiting for the Air Force, and so on. (5) One could argue the Victorian position that suggestive behavior does matter, but if this position is repugnant, there is an alternative. It is not clear from the letter whether Souter had any choice but to rule as he did. We can note the argument begs the question. Once the conviction is overturned, it's misleading to call the defendant a rapist. We do not have the Constitution of the State of New Hampshire before us, but justices of the State Supreme Court must respect it. Possibly it forced Souter in this case. (7) One can argue that the evidence presented does not mean that the war is solely about oil; there could be many contributing factors. The cruelty of the invasion certainly played a role in convincing many people in government of the necessity for action. Other factors, such as our leadership role or fear of a possible new nuclear power, could also be pertinent. As for the economic motive, one can argue that unless faced down, Saddam Hussein could control not just Kuwaiti oil, but Saudi as well, and eventually all the oil in the gulf. The economic dislocation this could cause in the United States alone would be very great.

3. One can argue that some attempts to restrict drug use have been successful. One can argue that legalization will increase drug use. One can argue that despite the lure of profits, the government should not prey upon the weaknesses and sins of some of its citizens. Of course, evidence would be required to support such claims. Has the establishment of state lotteries done anything for those addicted to betting? Finally, one can argue that it is the government's responsibility to protect citizens from harming themselves. Many states require that seatbelts be worn, for example.

5. There may be two "arguments." (1) Clearly [Knave wrote it] ⇒ [Knave imitated somebody else's hand], but this does not imply [Knave wrote it] (check the truth table). (2) Again, ([Knave wrote it] & [Knave didn't sign it]) ⇒ [Knave meant some mischief] is true, and [Knave didn't sign it] is also true,

but these do not imply [Knave wrote it] (check the truth table).

page 169 *writing arguments*

It is helpful to work in pairs on this assignment. Each writes arguments for both sides. Next, each criticizes the other's arguments as in "Criticizing Arguments," noting the weak premises and weak links. Finally, the arguments are rewritten by the original authors.

page 173 *a good paragraph*

Of course, what we mean in exercise 3 and exercise 4 is to choose a *different* column or letter to examine. Logically, however, a lazy and/ or calculating student could simply copy his/her answer from exercise 2. The honest and conscientious teacher would then give full credit for this while silently cursing the authors for permitting such a pointless response.

page 176 *Cathy goes to war*

The quotation at the beginning of this section comes from the classic film *The Third Man*. The screenplay was by Graham Greene, but this line was written by Orson Welles who played Harry Lime, the character who speaks it.

EXERCISES

1. Some hints: (1) Argue that the economic benefits of war can be duplicated in peacetime. (2) Argue that the loss of life and productive capacity caused by war is an economic minus. (3) Argue that killing people is bad.

This is just a start. Whatever else you do, however, you must point out the logical fallacy in Cathy's last two sentences. In Sentential, we would formalize this as:

Mon $\Rightarrow$ Hero, $\neg$Mon, $\therefore$ Bum. This is clearly invalid. If we add the unspoken but implied premise that $\neg$Hero $\Rightarrow$ Bum, this is *still* invalid. How do you point this out in an English debate? It is a little difficult to bring out Sentential if your opponent does not know his truth tables. The best method is to use an analogy. Show that the argument form is invalid by making an analogous argument where the absurdity is clearer. For example, you could say, "If your reasoning were truly correct, then I could argue that the sun won't set tonight! Here: You agree that if I buy you a hot fudge sundae, then surely the sun will set tonight. Well, I'm not going to buy you a hot fudge sundae, so by your reasoning, the sun won't set!"

curiosities & puzzles

The Digestor's Digest, page 3

page 177

If you enjoy these puzzles, you should look at some books by Raymond Smullyan, whose puzzles about knights (who always tell the truth) and knaves (who always lie) inspired them. His first book, *What Is the Name of This Book?* (Prentice-Hall, 1978), is a classic.

the family reunion

page 179

The diagram in this chapter is very useful in organizing the information you are given. For example, you are told that your nephrew is the one who did not invite you to his wedding. Find the cell that corresponds to "nephew" and "wedding" and put an X in it. Similarly, enter as many of the clues as you can into the chart. Use the fact that for each item and category there must be exactly one match. For example, "Harvard" has exactly one match with {nephew, uncle, cousin, step-cousin, ?}, that is, exactly four of the boxes below "Harvard" opposite this category will be X-ed and one will be checked.

ANSWER

Edgar tried to borrow money. His relationship is unknown.
Edwin goes to Harvard. He is your cousin.
Eduardo lives with an ex-nun. He is your nephew.
Edsel is mad at you for mixing him up with Edwin. He is your stepcousin.
Crazy Eddie didn't invite you to his wedding. He is your uncle.

punk logic

page 181

Laura Logic was the stage name of punk rock saxophonist Susan Whitby of the band X-Ray Specs. Photograph by Erica Echenberg/ Redferns.

Tom and Jim's Excellent Adventure

November 17

An example of a counterfactual conditional is the following: "If Dukakis had won in 1988, then Dan Quayle would have been vice president." Normally, we would look upon this as an if–then sentence, $P \Rightarrow Q$. The P here is false and the Q is true, so by convention, we would say that the sentence is true. On the other hand, this doesn't seem to capture the real meaning of the sentence. To one who has not been handicapped by a semester of logic, this sentence has something fundamentally wrong with it. Common sense would tell us that if Dukakis had won, Lloyd Bentsen would be vice president, not Quayle.

The sentence cannot be adequately understood without considering alternative universes: worlds in which the P ("Dukakis wins") is true. Jim 1 asks Jim 2 who won in 1988 in this universe. Jim 2 says Bush. Jim 1 suggests using the time machine to search for more alternative universes, hoping to find one where Dukakis won. Toms 1 and 2 think this is dangerously stupid. If you agree with Jim 1, turn to page 574. If you are a stick-in-the-mud, turn to page 538.

5 PREDICATES, PROGRAMS, AND ANTIQUE LOGIC

FORMAL LOGIC: PREDICATE LOGIC

page 184 PREDICATE LANGUAGES

EXERCISE 1 a, c, g (y does not need to appear inside), h. Not e, since *a* is not a variable.

EXERCISE 2 a. $(\exists w\underline{Fw} \vee \exists w\underline{Fw})$ c. Rya & $\forall y\underline{Gy}$
e. $\forall x\forall y \,((Rxy \,\&\, Fz) \Rightarrow \exists z\underline{Rxz})$

EXERCISE 3 a. open, y in Gy free b. closed c. open, x free
d. open, z free

EXERCISE 4
1. (a) Rty (b) $(\forall xRxy \Rightarrow Ft)$ (c) $t = t$
2. (a) Rtz (b) $\exists yRxy$ (c) Can't substitute z for free y here.

VARIATIONS ON THE THEME OF PREDICATE LANGUAGES

page 189

EXERCISE b, c, d, e

FROM STATEMENT LOGIC TO PREDICATE LOGIC

page 193

CHALLENGE

1. $(Fa \vee Ga)$ & $(Fb \vee Gb)$ & $(Fc \vee Gc)$ versus $(Fa \,\&\, Fb \,\&\, Fc) \vee (Ga \,\&\, Gb \,\&\, Gc)$. The second implies the first, but not the reverse. Suppose, for example, F is true only of a, and G is true only of b and c. Then the first is true, but the second is false.

3. The first says nothing F's: $\neg Fa \,\&\, \neg Fb \,\&\, \neg Fc$. The second says it is not true that everything F's: $\neg(Fa \,\&\, Fb \,\&\, Fc)$. The first implies the second, but not the reverse. Suppose, for example, that Fa and Fb but $\neg Fc$. Then the second is true but not the first.

5. The first says everything has both property H and J: $(Ha \,\&\, Ja)$ & $(Hb \,\&\, Jb)$ & $(Hc \,\&\, Jc)$. The second says everything has property H and everything has property J: $(Ha \,\&\, Hb \,\&\, Hc)$ & $(Ja \,\&\, Jb \,\&\, Jc)$. They are equivalent.

7. The first says P implies that everything F's: $P \Rightarrow (Fa \,\&\, Fb \,\&\, Fc)$. The second says that for every object in the universe, P implies that object has property F: $(P \Rightarrow Fa)$ & $(P \Rightarrow Fb)$ & $(P \Rightarrow Fc)$. They are equivalent.

9. The first says that for every object, that object bears the relation R to all objects: $(Raa \,\&\, Rab \,\&\, Rac)$ & $(Rba \,\&\, Rbb \,\&\, Rbc)$ & $(Rca \,\&\, Rcb \,\&\, Rcc)$. The second says that for every object, all objects bear the relation R to it: $(Raa \,\&\, Rba \,\&\, Rca)$ & $(Rab \,\&\, Rbb \,\&\, Rcb)$ & $(Rac \,\&\, Rbc \,\&\, Rcc)$. They are equivalent.

11. The first says that for every object, that object bears the relation R to some object: $(Raa \vee Rab \vee Rac)$ & $(Rba \vee Rbb \vee Rbc)$ & $(Rca \vee Rcb \vee Rcc)$. The second says that there is some object such that all objects bear the relation R to it: $(Raa \,\&\, Rba \,\&\, Rca) \vee (Rab \,\&\, Rbb \,\&\, Rcb) \vee (Rac \,\&\, Rbc \,\&\, Rcc)$. The second implies the first, but not the reverse. Suppose, for example, that the relation Rxy is

interpreted "*x* is not the same as *y*." Then the first is true and the second is false in a universe with more than one object.

page 196   INTERPRETING PREDICATE LOGIC

CHALLENGE 1   *S* makes $A \lor B$ true iff either *S* makes *A* true or *S* makes *B* true. *S* makes $A \Leftrightarrow B$ true iff either *S* makes both *A* and *B* true or else *S* makes both *A* and *B* false.

CHALLENGE 2   *S* makes $\forall x A x$ true iff *S* makes *Ax* true of every object *x* in the universe of discourse.

CHALLENGE 3

1. In S2, this becomes $\exists x (x \geq 0 \,\&\, x \neq 0)$ or "Some natural number is greater than or equal to 0 and not equal to 0." This is true. In S3, this becomes $\exists x (x \geq -1 \,\&\, x \neq -1)$ or "Some negative integer is greater than or equal to -1 and not equal to -1." This is false. In S4, this becomes $\exists x (x \leq 0 \,\&\, x \neq 0)$ or "Some integer is less than or equal to 0 and not equal to 0." This is true.

3. In S1, this becomes $\forall y (y \leq 0 \lor \neg y \leq 0)$ or "Every natural number is either less than or equal to 0 or else not less than or equal to 0." This is true. In S2, this becomes $\forall y (y \geq 0 \lor \neg y \geq 0)$ or "Every natural number is either greater than or equal to 0 or else not greater than or equal to 0." This is true. In S3, this becomes $\forall y (y \geq -1 \lor \neg y \geq -1)$ or "Every negative number is either greater than or equal to -1 or else not greater than or equal to -1." This is true. In S4, this becomes $\forall y (y \leq 0 \lor \neg y \leq 0)$ or "Every integer is either less than or equal to 0 or else not less than or equal to 0." This is true.

CHALLENGE 4   A structure in which this statement is false: Domain of human beings *Fx* mean *x* was born before 1990, *Gx* means *x* was born after 1991. A structure in which the statement is true: Domain of human beings, *Fx* means "*x* was born before 1990," *Gx* means "*x* is male."

page 201   LOGICAL THEORY FOR PREDICATE LOGIC

Compare this section with "Logical Theory for Statement Logic" in part 3. Compare also the answers to the challenges.

CHALLENGE 1 (*Note:* These answers would be the same in statement logic.)
1. not necessarily
3. inconsistent

5. only that it's not valid
7. because a false statement implies any statement

CHALLENGE 2

1. If A is true, then since A implies B, B must be true. If A is false, then B cannot be true (or else A would be true since B implies A) and therefore B is false.

3. In any structure, either both A and B are true or both are false (since A is equivalent to B). In both these cases, $A \Leftrightarrow B$ is true. Thus $A \Leftrightarrow B$ is valid. Conversely, if $A \Leftrightarrow B$ is valid, then A and B must have the same truth values in any structure, so A and B are equivalent.

CHALLENGE 3

1. Suppose A, B, and C imply D. Then if $(A \& B \& C)$ is true in a structure, then each of A, B, and C must be true in that structure, and so D is true in the structure. Thus $(A \& B \& C)$ implies D. Now suppose that $(A \& B \& C)$ implies D. Then if each of A, B, and C are true in a structure, then $(A \& B \& C)$ is true in the structure and so D is true in the structure. Thus A, B, and C imply D.

LOGICAL LAWS: BASIC VALID WFFS AND IMPLICATIONS
page 204

CHALLENGE 1   If everything doesn't W, then not all things W. Consider the domain of all human beings, and let Wy be "y was born in Wisconsin."

CHALLENGE 2   This follows from the observation that $A \Leftrightarrow \neg B$ and $\neg A \Leftrightarrow B$ have the same truth tables. There are other ways to show this.

CHALLENGE 3   If either everything W's or everything S's, then everything either W's or S's.
If everything either W's or S's, then either everything W's or everything S's. Consider the domain of all human beings, and let Wx be "x is female" and Sx be "x is male."

CHALLENGE 4   If everything that W's S's, then if something W's, something S's. In any structure in which everything that W's S's, then if something W's, then that object S's too, hence some object S's.

CHALLENGE 5   Consider the domain of all human beings, where Wx means "x wrote under the pseudonym 'Saki'" and Sy means "y flowers in early April and produces small bright red berries by August." Note that $\exists y Wy \Rightarrow \exists y Sy$ is false (H. H. Munro wrote under the pseudonym "Saki," no human being flowers and produces berries), but that $\exists y(Wy \Rightarrow Sy)$ is true (let y be "Madonna").

page 209   SYMBOLIZATION IN PREDICATE LOGIC

CHALLENGE 1

1. *Fs, c = s ∴ Fc*; valid
2. The most obvious formalization; *m = n, Un ∴ Um*; valid. This is somewhat unsatisfying, however. While the argument is logically valid, the premises are true and the conclusion is arguably false. Perhaps "is unknown" isn't really a property of a person but is a relation between a person and a name. Then one and the same person could be well known under one name but not well known under another (Jesse James, Mr. Howard).

EXERCISE 1

    1. identity   2. predication   3. tense   4. existence

CHALLENGE 2   If *Df* is true in a structure, then there must be some object in the domain identical to *f*, and so this object has property *D*, hence ∃x(*Dx* & *f = x*). Similarly, if ∃x(*Dx* & *f = x*) is true is a structure, then there must be some object in the domain with property *D* that is identical with the object named by *f*, so *f* has property *D*.

CHALLENGE 3

1. ∀x(*Mx* ⇒ *Dx*), *Ms* ∴ *Ds*; valid
3. ∀x(*Sx* ⇒ *Bx*), ∃x¬*Sx* ∴ ∃x¬*Bx*; invalid. Consider the domain of all human beings, with *Sx* being "*x* is a certified public accountant" and *Bx* being "*x* is a human being."
5. ∀x¬(*c > x*), ∀x¬(*x > p*) ∴ *c > p* where *c* is cold spaghetti and *p* is peace and freedom.

EXERCISE 2   Replacement principle. The truth tables of A ⇒ B and ¬A ∨ B are the same.

CHALLENGE 4

1. By (QE2), ¬∃x(*Ax* & *Bx*) is equivalent to ∀x¬(*Ax* & *Bx*). Then note that ¬(*A* & *B*) has the same truth table as *A* ⇒ ¬*B*. So by the replacement principle, ∀x¬(*Ax* & *Bx*) is equivalent to ∀x(*Ax* ⇒ ¬*Bx*).

CHALLENGE 5   ∃x∀y(*Sxy* ⇔ ¬*Syy*)   This is contradictory.

EXERCISE 3

    1. ∀x(*Wx* ⇒ *Sx*), ∃x(*Px* & *Wx*) ∴ ∃x(*Px* & *Sx*); valid
    3. ∀x(*Bx* ⇒ ∀y¬*Mxy*), ∃x(*Mjx* & *Fx*) ∴ ¬*Bj*; valid

4. This is tricky. The argument is intuitively valid but not with the form $\forall x(Cx \Rightarrow Hx) \therefore \forall x(Tx \Rightarrow Sx)$. The correct formalization is $\forall x(Cx \Rightarrow Hx) \therefore \forall x(\exists y(Txy \ \& \ Cy) \Rightarrow \exists y(Txy \ \& \ Hy))$.

CHALLENGE 6

1. $\forall xBx$, $\forall xBx$, $\exists xBx$
2. $\neg \forall xBx$, $\neg \exists xBx$ (or $\forall x \neg Bx$), $\neg \exists xBx$
3. $\forall xBx \Rightarrow Bf$, $\exists xBx \Rightarrow Bf$ (or $\forall x(Bx \Rightarrow Bf)$), $\exists xBx \Rightarrow Bf$

POLES AND NORWEGIANS

page 218

EXERCISE

1. $\forall x(Nx \Rightarrow Sx)$
3. $\exists xHxb$
5. $\forall x(Nx \Rightarrow Hxb)$
7. $\forall x((Nx \ \& \ Sx) \Rightarrow \exists y(Hxy \ \& \ Py))$
9. $\exists x((Sx \ \& \ Px) \ \& \ \forall y((Sy \ \& \ Ny \ \& \ Hyb) \Rightarrow Hxy))$
11. $\neg \exists x(Nx \ \& \ Sx)$
13. $\exists xHxb \Rightarrow Hbb$
15. $\exists x \forall yHxy \ \& \ \exists x \forall yHyx$

There are, of course, several ways of doing these.

with & about logic

games

page 220

The game of Queens was invented independently by W. A. Wythoff (1907) and Rufus P. Isaacs (1960). A thorough analysis leads to the Fibonacci numbers and the golden mean. See Martin Gardner's *Penrose Tiles to Trapdoor Ciphers*, W. H. Freeman, 1989.

EXERCISE

1. Player 2. This is the mirror-image of the example in the text.

3. Player 1. She can move directly to the upper-left corner.

5. Player 1. She can move to square g, and then it is just like the example in the text.

a	b	c	d
e	f	g	h

7. Player 1. This is like problem 5.

9. Player 1. This is again like problem 5. The first player can move to the square that is in the third column, second row.

11. Well, now we are getting a little tricky. There is a nice way to answer all these questions at once. Draw a giant rectangle. Then beginning at the upper left, fill in squares with either a '1' or '2,' depending on which player has a winning strategy starting from that square. We start like this:

2	1	1	1	1	1
1	1	2			
1	2				
1					
1					
1					

At each new square, ask yourself, "Can I reach a 2-square from here?" If you can, label it "1." If you can't, label it "2." For example, all these are 1s:

2	1	1	1	1	1
1	1	2	1	1	1
1	2	1	1	1	1
1	1	1	1	1	
1	1	1	1	1	1
1	1	1		1	1

The figure makes sense, because if you are at one of those squares, you can move to a 2-square, where your opponent will not be able to win. Now we find two 2s:

2	1	1	1	1	1	1	1
1	1	2	1	1	1	1	1
1	2	1	1	1	1	1	1
1	1	1	1	1	2		
1	1	1	1	1	1		
1	1	1	2	1	1	1	
1	1	1				1	1	1
1	1	1				1	1

and so on:

2	1	1	1	1	1	1	1
1	1	2	1	1	1	1	1
1	2	1	1	1	1	1	1
1	1	1	1	1	2	1	1
1	1	1	1	1	1	1	2
1	1	1	2	1	1	1	1
1	1	1	1	1	1	1	1
1	1	1	1	2	1	1	1

BASIC

page 223

EXERCISES

1. Prints 32. Prints 8. Prints 128. If we put in any number n, it will print 2^n.

3. Prints 120. Prints 6. Prints 5040. If we put in any number n, it will print the product of the whole numbers from 1 to n (also called "n factorial," or $n!$).

binary

page 228

EXERCISES

1. 5   3. 45   5. 11   7. 1001   9. 1101   11. 100011
13. 1001011   15. 4   17. 35   19. 47   21. 1   23. 48

TRIVIAL

page 231

EXERCISES

1. This program takes whatever X is, doubles it, and puts it in Y. It does this by repeatedly subtracting 1 from X and adding 2 to Y.

3. This program computes X times 2^Y. There is a giant loop that the program goes through exactly Y times:

```
30 IF Y = 0 THEN GOTO 150
.
.
.
130 IF Y > 0 THEN LET Y = Y − 1
140 GOTO 30
150 STOP
```

Inside this loop, the program first doubles X and puts the result in W:

```
40 IF X = 0 THEN GOTO 90
50 W = W + 1
60 W = W + 1
70 IF X > 0 THEN LET X = X − 1
80 GOTO 40
```

It then puts the result back into X:

```
90 IF W = 0 THEN GOTO 130
100 IF W > 0 THEN LET W = W − 1
110 LET X = X + 1
120 GOTO 90
```

The result is that of taking X and then multiplying it by 2 a total of Y times, or $X2^Y$.

page 233   algorithm

A proof that there is a nondecidable set of natural numbers is as follows.

Take all BASIC programs and number them in alphabetical order. This gives each program a sort of ID number. We'll define a noncomputable set, which we'll call L. Given a natural number n, here is how we decide whether or not n is in L: We take the nth program and run it. If it asks us to input a number, then we feed in n itself. If the program stops and says no, then we declare n to be in L, otherwise (if the program says yes or fails to stop), we declare n to be not in L.

Note that while every algorithm will have a program to implement it (many, actually), the reverse is not true, since a large number of programs fail to end (have an infinite loop)—and by our definition, algorithms must terminate. An example in BASIC is

```
10 GOTO 10
```

Anyhow, our set L is definitely strange. Is it computable? If it is, then some program computes it, and that program has an ID number. Say it's program #34,788,254. But then we ask, is 34,788,254 in L? Well, how do we find out? We run program #34,788,254. What does it say? If it says no, then #34,788,254 is in L—but then program #34,788,254 fails to compute L, because it said no! Okay, perhaps it says yes. Then #34,788,254 is not in L—but then again, program #34,788,254 fails to compute L because it said yes!

This shows that program #34,788,254 doesn't compute L. A similar argument shows that program #6,420,495,872,333 also doesn't compute L, and so on. No program computes L, and so L is not computable!

You may be wondering: We say L is not computable, but it seems that we have actually given an algorithm for deciding whether or not a number is in L. All we do is run the nth program, input n, and wait for the result. Doesn't this compute L?

It doesn't and here is why: The nth program may not end. It may have an infinite loop. In that case, n is not in L, but how will we know? We're waiting for the program to halt. It doesn't halt. When do we stop waiting for it? The procedure is not an algorithm because it doesn't include any way for deciding in a finite number of steps whether or not n is in L.

But our program would be an algorithm if there were an algorithm for deciding when a program has an infinite loop. This is called the "halting problem," and it is of great importance historically, mathematically, and philosophically. Essentially, we have just proven that the halting problem has no algorithm, since if it did, L would be computable, but L is not computable.

Tom and Jim's Excellent Adventure

November 17

Jim enters the machine. Tom sets the dial for one day in the future and pushes the button. He opens the door and Jim walks out.

"What day is it?" Tom asks.

"November 18, Jim replies. He then describes his memories of the past twenty-four hours. He says they tried the Infundibula, but it didn't work. He remembers swapping syllogisms with Tom for a few hours, then going to see *Back to the Future, Part XVII*. They realize that his memories are of his past but not necessarily Tom's future.

This makes sense to Tom—it *had* to be this way. "You're from a different universe!" he says. "If there were only one universe and only one Jim, you would now be a day older than yourself! You still haven't seen your future."

Go to page 600.

page 236 the busy beaver

Indeed, you can do better. First of all, you can improve the last program by increasing the number of lines that are "LET Y = Y + 1" and decreasing the number of lines that are "LET X = X + 1." The program essentially multiplies 3 times 12. By changing the proportions, we can multiply 7 times 8 to get 56:

$$y = y + 8$$
$$y = y - 1$$
$$\text{if } y = 0$$
$$x = x + 8$$

stop

Another simple change is to move the line "$y = y - 1$." This increases our total to 8 times 8, or 64:

$$y = y + 8$$
$$\text{if } y = 0$$
$$x = x + 8$$
$$y = y - 1$$

stop

And another simple change boosts us to 9 times 8:

$$y = y + 8$$
$$x = x + 8$$
$$\text{if } y = 0$$
$$y = y - 1$$

stop

Actually, this just scratches the surface. We can go astronomically higher with a simple device that doubles the size of X:

$$\text{if } x = 0$$
$$x = x - 1$$
$$y = y + 2$$

$$\text{if } y = 0$$
$$y = y - 1$$
$$x = x + 1$$

Compare this with exercise 3 in "TRIVIAL."
We can incorporate this into a program by

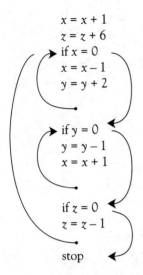

$$x = x + 1$$
$$z = z + 6$$
if $x = 0$
$$x = x - 1$$
$$y = y + 2$$

if $y = 0$
$$y = y - 1$$
$$x = x + 1$$

if $z = 0$
$$z = z - 1$$

stop

This gives us 128! You can get much, much more. Try it yourself!

Note: There is an interesting problem here. Clearly, there is a best answer to this question, but that answer is not known. If we limit the number of program steps to some very small number, like 3, then we can find the best answer without too much trouble. Well, then, is there any systematic method for finding out the best answer for programs with more steps? For "systematic method," read "method that a computer can carry out."

Tom and Jim's Excellent Adventure

November ??

The two pairs get in their time machines, rev the engines, and peel off. Our original Tom and Jim, going backward and forward, visit universe after universe. They never travel more than a day at a time in either direction. Sometimes they find no Tom or Jim, sometimes they find many.

They finally land in a universe where Dukakis won the presidency in 1988. To their surprise, Quayle was his vice president! It turns out that in this world Quayle is a Democrat. Apart from this he seems no different.

Tom is now fed up. The time machine is out of gas. Lately the universes they visit are full of Toms and Jims. There is no room in his house, and more Toms are arriving every hour. The neighbors are asking questions.

CHALLENGE   Write a satisfying, logically consistent end to this adventure!

informal logic

page 238   *syllogisms*

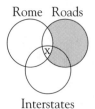

Rome   Roads

Interstates

1. a. Valid
    b. $\forall x(RDx \Rightarrow RMx)$
        $\exists x(Ix \,\&\, RDx)$
        $\therefore \exists x(Ix \,\&\, RMx)$

3. a. Invalid.

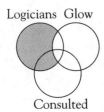

Logicians Glow

Consulted

b. $\forall x(Lx \Rightarrow Gx)$
$\exists x(Lx \ \& \ \neg Cx)$
$\therefore \exists x(Cx \ \& \ \neg Gx)$

d. Suppose there are no things x such that Cx, say, for example, that our universe is students at Sophist College and Cx means "x is 4 years old." Suppose that Lx means "x is a first-year student," and Gx means "x eats at the dining hall." Then the premises could be true, but the conclusion is false (in our universe).

5. a. Invalid.

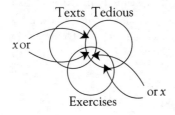

Texts Tedious

x or

or x

Exercises

b. $\exists x(Tx \ \& \ TDx)$
$\exists x(TDx \ \& \ Ex)$
$\therefore \exists x(Tx \ \& \ Ex)$

d. Suppose our universe is the collection of all books. Let Tx mean "x was written before 1700." Let TDx mean "x has appeared in hardcover," and let Ex mean "x was written after 1950."

7. a. Invalid.

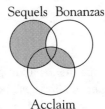

Sequels Bonanzas

Acclaim

575

b. $\forall x(Mx \Rightarrow Bx)$
$\forall x(Bx \Rightarrow \neg Cx)$
$\therefore \exists x(Mx \ \& \ \neg Cx)$

d. Suppose our universe consists of all months of the year. Let Mx mean "x begins with the letter 'Z'" (we know, there aren't any), let Bx mean "x ends with the letter 't'", and let Cx mean "x is a winter month."

--------- **Tom and Jim's Excellent Adventure** ---------

November 15

Jim plans to go back a day into the past. To make sure that he doesn't do this over and over again forever, he writes a note to himself saying, "On November 15, I, James Henle, sent myself back into the past. If you, James Henle, read this and have no memory of this event, then *don't go back to the past again!*" He seals the note in an envelope addressed to himself and leaves the envelope on his desk.

Jim tells Tom what he is doing. Tom again thinks this is dumb, but he is not sure why. If you agree with Tom, go to page 580. If you want to try the experiment, go to page 633.

page 241 *fallacies*

The taxonomy of fallacies presented in this chapter is taken from the eleventh edition of the *Encyclopaedia Britannica*. This edition is often considered the most erudite and sells for hundreds of dollars at used book sales. Many of the individual articles were written by distinguished academics. However, the article on fallacy was not signed.

EXERCISES
1. *Ad Hominem*
3. Fallacy of the Consequent
5. *Petitio Principii*
7. Amphibology
8. *Petitio principii* is *not*: B, $\therefore$ B. *Petitio principii* means adding the conclusion, B, to the list of premises. In *petitio principii* you are actually changing the argument.

rabbinic logic

page 247

The study of rabbinic law is extremely rich, with connections to Christian and Islamic thought, legal theory, rhetoric, and even literary criticism. A proper discussion would range over thousands of years of intellectual history.

A warm topic of debate seems to be the extent to which rabbinic rules were influenced by Hellenistic rhetoric (e.g., syllogistic logic; see "Syllogisms" in part 5). In view of the dissimilarity to our logic, one might see no connection, but the issue is not simple to resolve.

In the line from Exodus at the beginning of this section, we substituted "boil" for "seethe" in the King James Version.

The verses in Leviticus get more colorful than those described in this section. Here, for example, is 18:17:

> Thou shalt not uncover the nakedness of a woman and her daughter, neither shalt thou take her son's daughter, or her daughter's daughter, to uncover her nakedness; *for* they *are* her near kinswomen: it *is* wickedness.

We have heard another Jewish logic joke. It should be told with the proper inflection, pause, and shrug; it may not read well. It may be that only the authors—or only one of the authors—finds it funny:

P.

So why not Q?

Sources consulted include Louis Jacobs, "Hermeneutics," *The Encyclopedia Judaica*, vol. 8 (Macmillan, 1972), pp. 366–372; Moses Mielziner, *Introduction to the Talmud* (Bloch, 1968 [original edition 1894]); David Daube, "Rabbinic Methods of Interpretation and Hellenistic Rhetoric," *Hebrew College Annual* 22 (1949):239–264; Herman L. Strack, *Introduction to the Talmud and Midrash* (Harper & Row, 1965, pp. 93–98.

CHALLENGE

1. No; not justified by the passage. Rule IV applies. The particular statement, which states that cattle of the herd or flock are acceptable, takes precedence over the general.

2. No. Apply rule VI. New clothes are not similar to the items mentioned.

3. No. Apply rule VI again. The listed examples are ox, sheep, ass, and raiment. A jug of oil is not in these classes.

4. Yes and yes. Apply rule VIII. The general rule that witches are to be put to death has been added to by the statement that a certain sort of witch is to be stoned. From this, all witches must be stoned.

5. No. We find this one especially difficult. According to Moses Mielziner, the rule to apply is VIII. According to Mielziner, the second passage singles out certain items that must be returned and somehow implies they are items whose ownership can be readily established. Rule VIII is then used to conclude that anything which is to be returned is something whose ownership can be readily established. We think the opposite conclusion is more easily obtained from rule V.

6. Yes. Apply rule IV.

7. Yes. Apply rule V.

page 251 *Cathy meets God*

EXERCISES

1. Let G be "God exists," GP be "God is good and all-powerful," and E be "there is evil in the world." Then the argument is

$$G \Rightarrow GP$$
$$(G \ \& \ GP) \Rightarrow \neg E$$
$$E$$
$$\therefore \neg G$$

It is valid.

Note: This is not the only way to do this.

3. An argument can be valid and yet unsound if one or more of the premises is untrue. One could attack virtually any of these premises. The first: You could argue that God is not all-powerful. Some religions hold that God created the world but cannot interfere in it. The second: You could easily argue that a perfectly good and powerful God might still choose not to intervene. This could be for reasons we don't understand or because intervention might result in greater evils or because it is necessary for the souls of men that they suffer and choose freely good over evil. Finally, you could argue that the third is false, that the calamities listed are not evil.

curiosities & puzzles

page 253 *The Digestor's Digest, page 4*

The problem of the fun page adds a new feature. Refer to *Digest* page 1. What if this were the fun page? The first piece states that it is not an advertisement. Could this be an article? If so, then since articles must be false on the fun page, the statement that it is not an advertisement must be false, but of course it isn't. Could this be an ad? If so, then since ads tell the truth on the fun page, the statement that it is not an ad must be true, but of course it isn't. Thus, the first piece can't be either an ad or an article, so this is not the fun page.

Letting the reader tackle *Digest* page 2, we now consider page 3. Could it be the fun page? Suppose it is. The second piece is contradictory. Thus it must be lying, and so it is an article. Since it lies, Chem-treats *is* the best-tasting cereal, thus the first piece is also lying and is an article. The reader should have figured out earlier that if it is not the fun page, then both pieces are ads. What can we conclude? At this point, we don't know if page 3 is the fun page. We don't know if either piece is an ad or an article. We *do* know, however, that both are lying, and we know that Chem-treats is the best-tasting cereal!

the game of logic
page 255

The diagram in this chapter is Carroll's, from his book *The Game of Logic*, as reprinted in *Symbolic Logic*, a book of Carroll's logic writings edited with annotations and an introduction by William Warren Bartley III (Charles N. Potter, 1977).

EXERCISE   1. invalid   3. valid

the sorites of Lewis Carroll
page 258

Another interesting book of Carrolliana is the *Lewis Carroll Picture Book*, edited by Stuart Dodgson Collingwood (Unwin, 1899).

EXERCISE
1. Comets don't have curly tails.
3. Rainbows are not worth writing odes to.
5. No London novelist is old.

—————— **Tom and Jim's Excellent Adventure** ——————

November 15

Tom says that before you go back into the past, you should check to see if there is a note! Startled, Jim looks on his desk. Sure enough, there is an envelope addressed to him! Eagerly he tears it open and reads, "On November 15, I, James Henle, sent myself back into the past. If you, James Henle, read this and have no memory of this event, then *don't go back to the past again!*"

"You see! You did go back, and you have no memory of it!" says Tom.

Jim concentrates hard.

CHALLENGE   This is one time travel experiment you can try at home! Write yourself a note just like the one Jim wrote to himself (but of course put *your* name on it). Seal it in an envelope, address it to yourself, and put it on your desk. Wait 10 minutes, and then look to see if there is a note for you on your desk. If there is, read it!

Go to page 609.

6 DEDUCTION, INFINITY, AND A HAIRCUT

FORMAL LOGIC: DEDUCTIONS

page 264 MAIN CONNECTIVES

EXERCISE

Cases 1: In the first, we are applying $\exists E$ to $\exists x W x$ where Wx is $(Ax \ \& \ Bx)$. In the second, we are applying $\&I$ to W, V where W is $\exists x A x$ and V is $\exists x B x$.

Cases 2: In the first, there is no Wx that will serve because the form of the premise is not existential; it is conjunctive. This means $\exists xAx$ & $\exists xBx$ cannot be expressed as $\exists x$(something). In the second, the conclusion is not a conjunction; it is existential. That is, $\exists x(Ax$ & $Bx)$ cannot be expressed as (something) & (something else).

DEDUCTION   *page 266*

EXERCISE
1. 1. premise
    2. premise
    3. $\vee$I, 2
    4. $\Rightarrow$E, 1,3

3. 1. premise
    2. &E, 1
    3. $\exists$E, 2
    4. &E, 1
    5. Whoops! An attempt to use $\exists$E, but a *different* temporary name must be used! Phony deduction!
    6. &I, 5,3
    7. $\exists$I, 6 (but the entire proof is invalidated by step 5)

5. 1. premise
    2. $\forall$E, 1
    3. $\exists$E, 2
    4. Whoops! An attempt to use $\forall$I, but this is not legal if the wff contains a temporary name. Phony deduction.
    5. $\exists$I, 4 (but the entire proof is invalidated by step 4)

CHALLENGE
1. 1. $P \Rightarrow Q$ premise
    2. $Q \Rightarrow R$ premise
    3. P premise
    4. Q $\Rightarrow$E, 1, 3
    5. R $\Rightarrow$E, 2, 4
3. 1. $\forall yFy$ premise
    2. Fz $\forall$E, 1
    3. $\forall zFz$ $\forall$I, 2

581

page 273 **HYPOTHETICAL REASONING: DEDUCTION FROM ASSUMPTIONS**

EXERCISE 1 1. premise 2. assumption 3. assumption 4. &I, 2, 3 5. ⇒E, 4, 1 6. ⇒I, 3–5 7. ⇒I, 2–6

EXERCISE 2 4. &E, 3 5. &E, 3 6. ∃I, 4
7. ⇒E, 1, 6 8. &I, 5, 7 9. ⇒I, 2–9 10. ¬I, 9
11. ¬E, 10 12. ∀I, 11

CHALLENGE

1.
1.	∃z¬Az	premise
2.	¬Ac*	∃E, 1
3.	∀zAz	assumption
4.	Ac*	∀E, 3
5.	Ac* & ¬Ac*	&I, 2, 4
6. ∀zAz ⇒ (Ac* & ¬Ac*)		⇒I, 3–5
7. ¬∀zAz		¬I, 6

2.
1.	∀w ¬Aw	premise
2.	∃wAw	assumption
3.	Ac*	∃E, 2
4.	¬Ac*	∀E, 1
5.	Ac* & ¬Ac*	&I, 3, 4
6. ∃wAw ⇒ (Ac* & ¬Ac*)		⇒ I, 2–5
7. ¬∃wAw		¬I, 6

3.
1.	¬∃xAx	premise
2.	Ax	assumption
3.	∃xAx	∃I, 2
4.	∃xAx & ¬∃xAx	&I, 1, 3
5. Ax ⇒ (∃xAx & ¬∃xAx)		⇒I, 2–4
6. ¬Ax		¬I, 5
7. ∀x¬Ax		∀I, 6

4.
1.	¬∀uAu	premise
2.	¬∃u¬Au	assumption
3.	∀u¬¬Au	(by 3., above)
4.	¬¬Au	∀E, 3
5.	Au	¬E, 4
6.	∀uAu	∀I, 5
7.	∀uAu & ¬∀uAu	&I, 1, 6
8. ¬∃u¬Au ⇒ (∀uAu & ¬∀uAu)		⇒ I, 2–7

9. ¬¬∃u¬Au   ¬I, 8
10. ∃u¬Au   ¬E, 9

PROVING VALIDITY   *page 279*

This section owes much to Dan Velleman's excellent book *How to Prove It* (Cambridge University Press, 1994). Dan is a set theorist. The interested reader is urged to see his careful and complete exposition of the mathematician's art of proof.

EXERCISE

1. 1. $\forall x(P \Rightarrow Qx)$ premise
    2. P assumption
    3. $P \Rightarrow Qx$ $\forall$E, 1
    4. Qx $\Rightarrow$E, 2, 3
    5. $\forall x Qx$ $\forall$I, 4
    6. $P \Rightarrow \forall x Qx$ $\Rightarrow$I, 2–5

3. 1. $P \Rightarrow \neg P$ premise
    2. P assumption
    3. $\neg P$ $\Rightarrow$E, 1, 2
    4. $P \,\&\, \neg P$ &I, 2, 3
    5. $P \Rightarrow (P \,\&\, \neg P)$ $\Rightarrow$I, 2–4
    6. $\neg P$ ¬I, 5

5. 1. $P \Rightarrow \exists x Qx$ premise
    2. P assumption
    3. $\exists x Qx$ $\Rightarrow$E, 1, 2
    4. Qc^* $\exists$E, 3
    5. $P \Rightarrow Qc^*$ $\Rightarrow$I, 2–4
    6. $\exists x(P \Rightarrow Qx)$ $\exists$I, 5

7. 1. $\neg(P \vee Q)$ premise
    2. P assumption
    3. $P \vee Q$ $\vee$I, 2
    4. $(P \vee Q) \,\&\, \neg(P \vee Q)$ &I, 1, 3
    5. $P \Rightarrow (P \vee Q) \,\&\, \neg(P \vee Q)$ $\Rightarrow$I, 2–4
    6. $\neg P$ ¬I, 5
    7. Q assumption
    8. $P \vee Q$ $\vee$I, 7
    9. $(P \vee Q) \,\&\, \neg(P \vee Q)$ &I, 1, 8
    10. $Q \Rightarrow (P \vee Q) \,\&\, \neg(P \vee Q)$ $\Rightarrow$I, 7–9
    11. $\neg Q$ ¬I, 10
    12. $\neg P \,\&\, \neg Q$ &I, 6, 11

9. We will do this problem in detail. The ∨-premise strategy suggests proving $\exists x Px \Rightarrow$ ___ and $\exists x Qx \Rightarrow$ ___, but we don't know what goes in the blank:

$\exists x Px \lor \exists x Qx$

.

.

.

$\exists x Px \Rightarrow$ ___

.

.

.

$\exists x Qx \Rightarrow$ ___

.

.

.

$\exists x (Px \lor Qx)$

It would certainly help things if the conclusion, $\exists x (Px \lor Qx)$, could go in the blank. We could try this. Of course, this might not work. But so what? If it doesn't, we just go back and try something else.

$\exists x Px \lor \exists x Qx$

.

.

.

$\exists x Px \Rightarrow \exists x (Px \lor Qx)$

.

.

.

$\exists x Qx \Rightarrow \exists x (Px \lor Qx)$
$\exists x (Px \lor Qx)$

Applying the ⇒-conclusion strategy to the two conclusions yields

584

$$\exists x Px \lor \exists x Qx$$
$$\exists x Px$$
$$\cdot$$
$$\cdot$$
$$\cdot$$
$$\exists x(Px \lor Qx)$$
$$\exists x Px \Rightarrow \exists x(Px \lor Qx)$$
$$\exists x Qx$$
$$\cdot$$
$$\cdot$$
$$\cdot$$
$$\exists x(Px \lor Qx)$$
$$\exists x Qx \Rightarrow \exists x(Px \lor Qx)$$
$$\exists x(Px \lor Qx)$$

Now applying the ∃-premise strategy gives us

$$\exists x Px \lor \exists x Qx$$
$$\exists x Px$$
$$Pc*$$
$$\cdot$$
$$\cdot$$
$$\cdot$$
$$\exists x(Px \lor Qx)$$
$$\exists x Px \Rightarrow \exists x(Px \lor Qx)$$
$$\exists x Qx$$
$$Qd*$$
$$\cdot$$
$$\cdot$$
$$\cdot$$
$$\exists x(Px \lor Qx)$$
$$\exists x Qx \Rightarrow \exists x(Px \lor Qx)$$
$$\exists x(Px \lor Qx)$$

Note the use of two different temporary names. We cannot assume that they are the same. Now we apply the ∃-conclusion strategy:

$$\exists x Px \lor \exists x Qx$$
$$\exists x Px$$
$$Pc*$$

.
.
.

$$P\underline{\quad} \lor Q\underline{\quad}$$
$$\exists x(Px \lor Qx)$$
$$\exists x Px \Rightarrow \exists x(Px \lor Qx)$$
$$\exists x Qx$$
$$Qd*$$

.
.
.

$$P\underline{\quad}_1 \lor Q\underline{\quad}_1$$
$$\exists x(Px \lor Qx)$$
$$\exists x Qx \Rightarrow \exists x(Px \lor Qx)$$
$$\exists x(Px \lor Qx)$$

We don't know what goes in _____ and _____₁, but we'll forge ahead anyway. We use the only strategy left, ∨-conclusion; we should try to prove P _____ or Q _____ . *Now* we see what _____ should be. It should be c*, and _____₁ should be d*.

1. $\exists x Px \lor \exists x Qx$	premise
2. $\quad\exists x Px$	assumption
3. $\quad\quad Pc*$	∃E, 2
4. $\quad\quad Pc* \lor Qc*$	∨I, 3
5. $\quad\quad \exists x(Px \lor Qx)$	∃I, 4
6. $\quad\exists x Px \Rightarrow \exists x(Px \lor Qx)$	⇒I, 2–5
7. $\quad\exists x Qx$	assumption
8. $\quad\quad Qd*$	∃E, 7
9. $\quad\quad Pd* \lor Qd*$	∨I, 8
10. $\quad\quad \exists x(Px \lor Qx)$	∃I, 9
11. $\quad\exists x Qx \Rightarrow \exists x(Px \lor Qx)$	⇒I, 7–10
12. $\exists x(Px \lor Qx)$	∨E, 1, 6, 11

Now we are done.

11.　1.　　　　　　$\neg(P \lor \neg P)$　　　　　　　　assumption
　　　2.　　　　　　　　P　　　　　　　　　　　assumption
　　　3.　　　　　　　$P \lor \neg P$　　　　　　　　　$\lor$I, 2
　　　4.　　　　　　$(P \lor \neg P) \mathbin{\&} \neg(P \lor \neg P)$　　　　$\&$I, 1, 3
　　　5.　　　$P \Rightarrow (P \lor \neg P) \mathbin{\&} \neg(P \lor \neg P)$　　　$\Rightarrow$I, 2–4
　　　6.　　　　　　　$\neg P$　　　　　　　　　　　$\neg$I, 5
　　　7.　　　　　　　$P \lor \neg P$　　　　　　　　　$\lor$I, 6
　　　8.　　　　　　$(P \lor \neg P) \mathbin{\&} \neg(P \lor \neg P)$　　　　$\&$I, 1, 7
　　　9.　$\neg(P \lor \neg P) \Rightarrow ((P \lor \neg P) \mathbin{\&} \neg(P \lor \neg P))$　　$\Rightarrow$I, 1–8
　　10.　$\neg\neg(P \lor \neg P)$　　　　　　　　　　$\neg$I, 9
　　11.　$P \lor \neg P$　　　　　　　　　　　　　$\neg$E, 10

Tom and Jim's Excellent Adventure

November 18

We are left with the problem of two Jims and two Toms. They can't all stay—there isn't room on the faculty. Who should go?

Tom & Jim 1 argue that there would be no problem if Tom & Jim 2 would leave as they had planned.

"Do what we did," says Jim 1 to Jim 2. "Go back and cut Jim's hair. If we keep this up, everyone will have a home!"

"And Jim will have no hair," says Jim 2.

Tom & Jim 2 are afraid that if they leave they will never find a universe they can call their own. They further point out that they were in this universe first; it is their universe. They insist on Tom & Jim 1 taking off immediately.

Jim 1 protests to Jim 2, "How can you treat me this way? I'm your own flesh and blood!"

CHALLENGE   Write a satisfying, logically consistent end to this adventure!

page 287 PROVING INVALIDITY

EXERCISES

1. Valid.

1.	$\forall x \neg Fx$	premise
2.	$\forall x Fx$	assumption
3.	Fx	$\forall E, 2$
4.	$\neg Fx$	$\forall E, 1$
5.	$Fx \,\&\, \neg Fx$	$\&I, 3, 4$
6.	$\forall x Fx \Rightarrow (Fx \,\&\, \neg Fx)$	$\Rightarrow I, 3\text{–}5$
7.	$\neg \forall x Fx$	$\neg I, 6$

(On the other hand, if we ever allowed the empty universe, this argument would be invalid. If the universe is empty, then $\forall x Fx$ and $\forall x \neg Fx$ are both true.)

3. Invalid. Take the universe of the 50 states of the United States. Let Fx mean "x borders on the Atlantic Ocean," and let Px mean "x borders on the Pacific Ocean." Let q be a name for Kansas.

5. Valid.

1.	$\forall x Px \lor \forall x Fx$	premise
2.	$\forall x Px$	assumption
3.	Px	$\forall E, 2$
4.	$Px \lor Fx$	$\lor I, 3$
5.	$\forall x (Px \lor Fx)$	$\forall I, 4$
6.	$\forall x Px \Rightarrow \forall x (Px \lor Fx)$	$\Rightarrow I, 2\text{–}5$
7.	$\forall x Fx$	assumption
8.	Fx	$\forall E, 7$
9.	$Px \lor Fx$	$\lor I, 8$
10.	$\forall x (Px \lor Fx)$	$\forall I, 9$
11.	$\forall x Fx \Rightarrow \forall x (Px \lor Fx)$	$\Rightarrow I, 7\text{–}10$
12.	$\forall x (Px \lor Fx)$	$\lor E, 1, 6, 11$

7. Invalid. Take the universe of colleges. Let Px mean "x is a women's college," and let Fx mean "a name of x begins with a 'W.'" It should be clear that the conclusion is false (Smith College, for example). Note that the premise is true because $\forall x Px$ is false (not every college is a women's college).

9. Invalid. Take the universe of fish. Let Px mean "x is a fish" (so $\forall x Px$). Let Fx mean "x is less than one meter long."

11. Valid. The premise is $\forall x ([Dx \Rightarrow \exists y(Dy \,\&\, Wy)] \Rightarrow Wx)$, Dx means "you do x" and Wx means "x is morally wrong." The conclusion is $\forall x(\neg Dx \Rightarrow Wx)$. Here is a proof:

1.	$\forall x ([Dx \Rightarrow \exists y(Dy \,\&\, Wy)] \Rightarrow Wx)$	premise
2.	$\neg Dx$	assumption
3.	Dx	assumption
4.	$\neg \exists y(Dy \,\&\, Wy)$	assumption
5.	$Dx \,\&\, \neg Dx$	&I, 2, 3
6.	$\neg \exists y(Dy \,\&\, Wy) \Rightarrow (Dx \,\&\, \neg Dx)$	$\Rightarrow$I, 4–5
7.	$\neg\neg \exists y(Dy \,\&\, Wy)$	$\neg$I, 6
8.	$\exists y(Dy \,\&\, Wy)$	$\neg$E, 7
9.	$Dx \Rightarrow \exists y(Dy \,\&\, Wy)$	$\Rightarrow$I, 3–8
10.	$[Dx \Rightarrow \exists y(Dy \,\&\, Wy)] \Rightarrow Wx$	$\forall$E, 1
11.	Wx	$\Rightarrow$E, 9, 10
12.	$\neg Dx \Rightarrow Wx$	$\Rightarrow$I, 2–11
13.	$\forall x(\neg Dx \Rightarrow Wx)$	$\forall$I, 12

_____ Tom and Jim's Excellent Adventure _____

November 14

Jim enters the machine, sets the dial for 24 hours, and pushes the button. Turn to page 558.

FORMALIZING FOR VALIDITY IN PREDICATE LOGIC

page 292

CHALLENGE

1. $\forall x(Mx \Rightarrow Rx)$, Ms, $s = p$ $\therefore$ Rp. Valid.

1.	$\forall x(Mx \Rightarrow Rx)$	premise
2.	Ms	premise
3.	$s = p$	premise
4.	Mp	=E, 2, 3
5.	$Mp \Rightarrow Rp$	$\forall$E, 1
6.	Rp	$\Rightarrow$E, 4, 5

3. $Ms \therefore \exists x(Mx \ \& \ x = s)$. Valid.

1.	Ms	premise
2.	$s = s$	$=$I
3.	$Ms \ \& \ s = s$	&I, 1, 2
4.	$\exists x(Mx \ \& \ x = s)$	$\exists$I, 3

5. $\forall x((Px \ \& \ Cx) \Rightarrow Px)$. Valid.

1.	$Px \ \& \ Cx$	assumption
2.	Px	&E, 1
3.	$(Px \ \& \ Cx) \Rightarrow Px$	$\Rightarrow$I, 1–2
4.	$\forall x((Px \ \& \ Cx) \Rightarrow Px)$	$\forall$I, 3

7. $\forall x \forall y(Fxy \Rightarrow Wxy), \ \forall x(Bx \Rightarrow \forall y \neg Wxy) \therefore \forall x(Bx \Rightarrow \neg Fxx)$. Valid.

1.	$\forall x \forall y(Fxy \Rightarrow Wxy)$	premise
2.	$\forall x(Bx \Rightarrow \forall y \neg Wxy)$	premise
3.	$Bx \Rightarrow \forall y \neg Wxy$	$\forall$E, 2
4.	Bx	assumption
5.	Fxx	assumption
6.	$\forall y(Fxy \Rightarrow Wxy)$	$\forall$E, 1
7.	$Fxx \Rightarrow Wxx$	$\forall$E, 6
8.	Wxx	$\Rightarrow$E, 5,7
9.	$\forall y \neg Wxy$	$\Rightarrow$E, 3, 4
10.	$\neg Wxx$	$\forall$E, 9
11.	$Wxx \ \& \ \neg Wxx$	&I, 8,10
12.	$Fxx \Rightarrow (Wxx \ \& \ \neg Wxx)$	$\Rightarrow$I, 5–11
13.	$\neg Fxx$	$\neg$I, 12
14.	$Bx \Rightarrow \neg Fxx$	$\Rightarrow$I, 4–13
15.	$\forall x(Bx \Rightarrow \neg Fxx)$	$\forall$I, 14

9. $\forall x((Px \ \& \ \exists y(Ny \ \& \ Hxy)) \Rightarrow Sx), \ \forall x(Hxx \Rightarrow Sx), \ \forall x(Px \Rightarrow \neg Hxx) \therefore \forall x(Px \Rightarrow \neg \exists y(Ny \ \& \ Hxy))$. Invalid. First, let's draw Venn diagrams for "is a Pole," "hates a Norwegian," "hates self," and "is silly." This will help us see what is going on. The three premises tell us that the shaded areas are empty (the numbers represent which premises require the areas to be empty):

590

Hates self

Is silly

Hates a
Norwegian

2

2

1   1 2

3 3

2 3 3

Poles

But this certainly doesn't mean that no Pole hates a Norwegian. So let us assign new meanings. Let's use the set of natural numbers. If we let *Hxy* mean "*x* < *y*," then nothing will hate itself, so to speak, making premises 2 and 3 true. Let *Px* be "*x* is positive." Let *Nx* be "*x* is less than 40"; thus there will be some Poles who hate a Norwegian (for example, 17 [a Pole] is less than [hates] 23 [a Norwegian]). Finally, we want all Poles who hate Norwegians to be silly. These are the numbers from 1 to 39, so let's make *Sx* mean "*x* is below 100." That will do it.

11. Here are two formalizations, both valid. One formalizes "portrait painter" by *PPx*, and the other by ∃*yPxy* ("there is someone *x* has painted"). Let *PEx* be "*x* is from Peoria."

> One: ∀*x*((*PEx* & *PPx*) ⇒ (*Ppx* ⇔ ¬*Pxx*)) ∴ ¬(*PPp* & *PEp*)
> Two: ∀*x*((*PEx* & ∃*yPxy*) ⇒ (*Ppx* ⇔ ¬*Pxx*)) ∴ ¬(∃*yPpy* & *PEp*)

with & about logic
in Hell with Raymond Smullyan

page 294

EXERCISE

1. Guess the license plates in alphabetical and numerical order: AAA000, AAA001, . . . , AAB000, AAB001, ...

3. First guess all the pairs that use only the number 1, which is just (1, 1). Next guess all the additional pairs that use 2, which are just (1, 2), (2, 1), and (2, 2). Next, guess all the additional pairs that use 3, and so on. Other strategies are possible.

5. Guess the nonsense words in alphabetical order.

7. The only difference is that it might take longer, but if you can eventually escape guessing every day, you will still escape guessing only on Sunday.

9. Same as problem 7. Just as there is an infinite number of Sundays in eternity, there is an infinite number of March 17ths in perfect-square years.

page 298 no (certain) escape

The proof in this section sometimes confuses readers unfamiliar with quantifiers. We are saying that no strategy for escaping Hell exists. That is,

$$\neg \exists s(\text{``s is a strategy for escaping Hell''})$$

How do we formalize "s is a strategy for escaping Hell"? We say that no matter what number the devil chooses, that number will be on our list. That is,

$$\neg \exists s\ \forall n(\text{``number n is on the list of strategy s''})$$

And how do we formalize this? We say that for some k, n is the kth number on the list:

$$\neg \exists s\ \forall n\ \exists k(\text{``n is the kth number on the list of s''})$$

By now you are familiar with the logical laws $\neg \exists = \forall \neg$ and $\neg \forall = \exists \neg$, and so we can translate this into

$$\forall s\ \exists n\ \forall k(\text{``n is \emph{not} the kth number in the list of s''})$$

This is exactly the statement we proved in the section.

Psychologists and mathematicians measure the complexity of sentences by the number of alternations of quantifiers. In this analysis, the sentence above is considered measurably difficult!

Another way to look at the results of this chapter is that there exists an infinite set that is larger in a meaningful way than the set of natural numbers. The set of real numbers (decimals) is this set. This raises two interesting questions:

1. We now have two infinite "sizes." Is there a size that is in between these two?

2. Are there still larger sizes?

Georg Cantor, the discoverer of these sizes, thought that the answer to the first question was no, and his guess became known as the "continuum hypothesis" (the real-number line is often called the "continuum"). What do you think? Was he right? (See "Impossibility" in part 9 for the answer.)

The answer to the second question is a definite yes; in fact, there is no largest size. A branch of mathematics has grown up to study these infinite sizes or "cardinals." The theory that has developed is truly cosmic. The existence of huge cardinals with exotic properties that seem so remote from ordinary mathematics turns out to be intimately related to it. The work has enabled mathematicians to answer some interesting questions about decimals and to show that many questions have no answer. See "Impossibility" for more on this.

In the Notes, References, Hints, and Some Answers for "Algorithm" in part 5, we proved that there is a noncomputable set. There is another proof that uses Cantor's theory of infinite sizes: The number of possible sets is uncountable. The number of possible programs in BASIC is countable (we can alphabetize the programs, listing first all programs with just one character, then all programs with two characters, . . .). A program can compute only one set. Since there are more sets than programs, there must be some sets (a lot, actually) that are not computed by any program.

This argument is especially interesting because it is "nonconstructive." It doesn't actually give us an example of a noncomputable set, as opposed to the proof given earlier.

CHALLENGE These are merely suggested answers. There are many observations one could make.

1. a. The verse from "Amazing Grace" implies that we'll be in heaven forever (infinitely many years). For the verse implies a one-to-one correspondence between the total time in heaven and that time minus the first 10,000 years. This can happen only if the number of years is infinite.

   b. This is an especially interesting quotation in light of Galileo's experience. He found paradox in two arguments regarding infinite subsets of an infinite set. Whitman seems to be saying he is comfortable with the contradictions. Of course, what Cantor showed is that there is no real contradiction.

2. a. The situation here is identical with that in "Amazing Grace."

   b. If his love is indeed infinite, then he can give an infinite amount of it away and still have an infinite amount. He must be careful, however. Suppose his love comes in boxes labeled 1, 2, 3, and so on. Then he could give away all the odd-numbered boxes, which would leave him with all the even-numbered boxes. In this case he would have given away infinite love and yet still retained infinite love. On the other hand, if he gave away all the boxes labeled 100 and above, he would have only a finite number left. Perhaps Shakespeare should have inserted a clause: "The more I give to thee—provided I give it in the right sort of way—the more I have."

We might add that the language seems to suggest something not mathematically precise. "The more I give to thee, the more I have" sounds as if he *gains* as he gives away. If so, then something beyond mathematics is at work. This is not surprising, of course; as the mathematician Blaise Pascal said, "Le coeur a ses raisons que la raison ne connait point" ("The heart has its reasons which reason knows nothing of").

page 302

EXERCISES

1. Argue that merely in going home you did an infinite number of tasks. (First you went halfway home, then . . .)

3. Yes. Always throw out the lowest-numbered ball but keep ball 1.

5. See James Thomson's "Tasks and Super-Tasks" in *Analysis* 15 (1954).

Note: When considering the difficulty of performing infinite tasks, we should bear in mind that finite ones can be practically impossible too. We know, for example that the sum of the first n numbers is exactly half of n times $(n + 1)$. Our inability to check this physically, for example by adding up the first 1,000,000,000,000,000,000,000 numbers, does not affect our belief in the theorem. Our belief is based solidly on mathematical proof, and here it is.

The sum of $1 + 2 + 3 + \cdots + n$ is equal to the area of the following figure (each square has area 1):

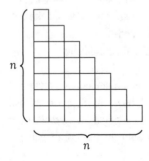

If we put two of these figures together,

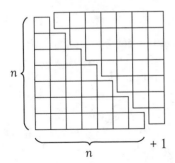

we get a rectangle with n rows and $n + 1$ columns. The area of the rectangle, $n(n + 1)$, is just twice the area of the original figure, and so the original sum must be $n(n + 1)/2$.

Are large finite numbers any more real than infinite numbers? We wonder.

An excellent work on infinity is Rudy Rucker's *Infinity and the Mind* (Birkhäuser, 1982).

infinity: potential and actual

page 306

Bruno, the author of the epigraph, was a sixteenth-century philosopher and theologian. He was an apostle of the actual infinite. He also tended to irritate people. He claimed, in contrast to church doctrine, that man could contemplate actual infinity. After a life of confrontation, he was burned at the stake for heresy. Although it is tempting to consider him a martyr to the infinite, the situation was undoubtedly far more complex. Politics, for example, could have played a role. Some recent research suggests that at one time Bruno spied on France on behalf of the English.

Dramatic evidence of the deep suspicion Greeks had of the actual infinite has come to light relatively recently. Archimedes, easily the greatest mathematician of the ancient world, solved a problem of calculus (though calculus was not formally developed until nearly 2000 years later). His solution was a model of potential infinity. It was preserved and was well-known. In 1905, however, a letter was found in which Archimedes explained how he discovered his theorem. He used the actual infinite in a deliberate and creative way. Clearly, he felt such methods were not proper; he eventually found a more acceptable, though equally creative, proof.

page 308 proof by contradiction

EXERCISES

1. The boy proves that Mama is a remainder by contradiction. He supposes that she is not a remainder. This provides a characteristic which shows that she is a remainder—a contradiction.

3. To prove she is not a woman, assume the negation, that she is a woman, W. From this, we obtain H (from $W \Rightarrow H$) and also $\neg H$ (from $W \Rightarrow \neg H$). This is a contradiction.

4. The error is in the formalization. We used H in the first premise to represent: "You *did* put your hands on her." In the second premise we used $\neg H$ to represent "You *should not* put your hands on her." These are not negations of each other, since they may both be true at the same time.

informal logic

page 312 *Anita Hill and Arlen Specter*

EXERCISES

1. Senator Specter's conclusion is that Anita Hill committed perjury in her testimony. He argues that her testimony in the afternoon contradicts her testimony in the morning. He gives as evidence for this excerpts from the transcript of the hearings from both the morning and the afternoon.

3. There are several approaches you could take. The first is that Anita Hill's testimony does not contradict itself. In the morning, she repeatedly said that she did not recall anyone suggesting that her statement might be used to force Thomas to withdraw. In the afternoon, she clearly does recall. This is not inconsistent. It is possible that in the afternoon she recalls something that she could not recall earlier.

A second approach develops Senator Specter's curious remark about recanting during a proceeding. You could argue that the morning and the afternoon are all part of the same proceeding. Then her testimony in the afternoon recants (possibly) her testimony in the morning and so is not perjury.

Bush, Clinton, and Perot

page 316

CHALLENGE

1. Clinton covers a lot of ground. He begins by stressing his record in Arkansas as rebutting the argument that he lacks experience (presumably in national office or in the White House). He presents evidence that his record there is good. He later promotes his experience with "ordinary people" but does not support his claims and leaves vague why this experience is good.

   He returns to the idea of change and presents arguments and reasonable evidence for its importance. His remark about the book implies that even the administration expects change but without changing policies, a statement that is not defended.

   Finally, he ties together the need for change with the greater experience of the president, suggesting that because conditions have changed, experience with previous conditions is not important.

2. Bush defends the economic condition of the country. He offers no support but makes a frank appeal to patriotism (see "Fallacies" in part 5). He repeats his charge that Congress has blocked change and that he will bring change with a new Congress. Again, there is no support for this claim.

3. Perot makes a number of points. He implies first that the country is in bad shape and supplies some detail. He next asserts that the greater experience of the president is actually bad and supplies some detail. Finally, he suggests that he has experience of a good kind, namely solving problems, although he does not support this claim.

   His argument that Bush's experience of failure in office is bad is somewhat weak, since one can learn from such experience. Of course, we might not want to vote for someone who will be learning on the job. What he is really saying, however, is that Bush has failed and can therefore be expected to fail again.

4. Bush attacks Clinton's character by discussing Clinton's involvement twenty years before in demonstrations against the Vietnam war while a student in England. Bush does not say why this is wrong. Once again he appeals to patriotism. The references to ghetto kids and prisoners of war are not explained.

   His strongest argument comes when he compares his own military record with his opponent's opposition to the Vietnam war and suggests that this history would handicap Clinton's ability to command forces.

5. Perot defends Clinton by attacking Bush's character. He seems to agree that Clinton made mistakes but compares these to the mistakes of Bush as president. Such mistakes might not in themselves indicate lack of character, but the failure to take responsibility for them might, and Perot points this out. Perot concludes by saying that he will clean up the mess but provides no support for this claim.

6. Clinton exposes Bush's appeals to patriotism both in the debate and before the debate. Clinton's comparisons with Joe McCarthy and Bush's own father are very effective. It is certainly true that the distortions of McCarthy and Bush differ greatly in degree, but they have some similarity.

Clinton does not make a point of it, but he does not admit any wrong in his behavior. He does not respond to the question of his ability to command forces.

page 321 *the a∂venture of the ∂ancing men*

There is an error in Holmes's argument. Let C be "You had chalk on your hands," let B be "You played billiards," and let T be "You played billiards with Thurston." The argument begins:

1. C
2. $B \Rightarrow C$
3. $B \Rightarrow T$

Clearly, Holmes is concluding after 1 and 2 that B is true, then moving on to T. Is it valid to conclude B? Not deductively but perhaps inductively. See "Bayes' Law and Sherlock Holmes" in part 7.

page 323 *commercial logic* I

This is a reproduction of an offer by the *Christian Science Monitor* to potential subscribers. If you are having difficulty identifying the difference between the alternatives, it is because there is no difference.

curiosities & puzzles

page 324 *The Digestor's Digest*, page 5

As with all pages now, we must consider two cases: In one case, we assume that this is not the fun page, and in the other, we assume that it is. In both cases, the first cannot be true. Since it is false, there must be statements on the page that are true, hence the second piece is true. Thus, if this is not the fun page, the first is an ad and the second is an article. If it is the fun page, the pieces are reversed.

This is the best we can do. We do not know if page 5 is the fun page or not.

the barbershop problem page 326

EXERCISE *Hint:* Formalize the following: Let A be "Allen is in," let B be "Brown is in," and let C be "Carr is in." There are just two statements to formalize.

English 254 page 329

We hope you have solved this and are just looking here to check your answer. If you have given up, let us give you a hint: Use the chart. Another hint: When you read that one book came right after another, then you know the first was not published in May and the second was not published in January.

Answers

Colonel Boddicker's Mistake: turgid romance; Rev. Tobias Stengel; February
The Secret of Sutcliffe Manor: lending libraries; Morgan McGraw; May
Inspector Palmer Decides: arctic exploration; Julia Williams; January
At the Sign of the Blue Goose: depravity; Nottingham Billy; March
Lady Quisenberry's Whim: mystery; Dame Dahlia Warren; April

Tom and Jim's Excellent Adventure

November 18

"Time branched," says Tom. "You and the other Jim have the same past but different futures." He paused and added soberly, "That is, if the other Jim *had* a future."

"On the other hand," he said brightening, "we know now that the law of the excluded middle is not true. This law [see the section on the subject in part 8] states that for any proposition P, the statement $P \lor \neg P$ must be true. But what if P is 'On November 18, Jim will be forty-four years and five days old? Two days ago, we probably would have said that $P \lor \neg P$ is true, since P is true, but now we know that in one branch (the branch we snatched Jim from), P is true and in another branch (the branch we are in now), $\neg P$ is true. Thus, two days ago neither P nor $\neg P$ was true, and so $P \lor \neg P$ was not true!"

CHALLENGE Can you devise experiments with any imaginable device that would definitely answer any of the following questions?

Does anything cause anything?
Does time have a direction?
Are there alternative universes?
Does time branch?
Does time loop?

Write a time travel adventure involving the paradox of the surprise exam.

7 SYMBOLIC SOPHISTICATION, INDUCTION, AND BUSINESS LOGIC

FORMAL LOGIC: SOME SYMBOLIC SOPHISTICATION

QUANTIFIERS AND ARITHMETIC   *page 334*

CHALLENGE 1 $\exists x \exists y \exists z (Fx \ \& \ Fy \ \& \ Fz \ \& \ x \neq y \ \& \ y \neq z \ \& \ x \neq z)$

CHALLENGE 2   *Hint:* The deduction in both directions is not difficult. Use Taut. and the laws regarding quantifiers and negation given at the end of "Hypothetical Reasoning: Deductions from Assumptions" in Part 5.

CHALLENGE 3 $\forall w \forall x \forall y \forall z ((Fw \ \& \ Fx \ \& \ Fy \ \& \ Fz) \Rightarrow (x = y \lor y = z \lor x = z \lor x = w \lor w = y \lor w = z)$

CHALLENGE 5

1.	$\exists x(Fx \ \& \ \forall y(Fy \Rightarrow x = y))$	premise
2.	$Fc^* \ \& \ \forall y(Fy \Rightarrow c^* = y)$	$\exists$E, 1
3.	Fc^*	&E, 2
4.	$\exists xFx$	$\exists$I, 3
5.	$\forall y(Fy \Rightarrow c^* = y)$	&E, 2
6.	$\quad Fx \ \& \ Fy$	assumption
7.	$\quad Fx$	&E, 6
8.	$\quad Fx \Rightarrow c^* = x$	$\forall$E, 5
9.	$\quad c^* = x$	$\Rightarrow$E, 7, 8
10.	$\quad Fy$	&E, 6
11.	$\quad Fy \Rightarrow c^* = y$	$\forall$E, 5
12.	$\quad c^* = y$	$\Rightarrow$E, 10, 11
13.	$\quad x = y$	$=$E, 9, 12
14.	$(Fx \ \& \ Fy) \Rightarrow x = y$	$\Rightarrow$I, 6–13
15.	$\forall y((Fx \ \& \ Fy) \Rightarrow x = y)$	$\forall$I, 14
16.	$\forall x \forall y((Fx \ \& \ Fy) \Rightarrow x = y)$	$\forall$I, 15
17.	$\exists xFx \ \& \ \forall x \forall y((Fx \ \& \ Fy) \Rightarrow x = y)$	&I, 4, 16

And the other direction:

1. $\exists xFx\ \&\ \forall x\forall y((Fx\ \&\ Fy) \Rightarrow x = y)$ premise
2. $\exists xFx$ &E, 1
3. $\forall x\forall y((Fx\ \&\ Fy) \Rightarrow x = y)$ &E, 1
4. Fc^* $\exists$E, 2
5. $\forall y((Fc^*\ \&\ Fy) \Rightarrow c^* = y)$ $\forall$E, 3
6. $(Fc^*\ \&\ Fy) \Rightarrow c^* = y$ $\forall$E, 5
7. Fy assumption
8. $Fc^*\ \&\ Fy$ &I, 4, 7
9. $c^* = y$ $\Rightarrow$E, 6, 8
10. $Fy \Rightarrow c^* = y$ $\Rightarrow$I, 7–9
11. $\forall y(Fy \Rightarrow c^* = y)$ $\forall$I, 10
12. $Fc^*\ \&\ \forall y(Fy \Rightarrow c^* = y)$ &I, 4, 11
13. $\exists x(Fx\ \&\ \forall y(Fy \Rightarrow x = y))$ $\exists$I, 12

page 337   **FUNCTIONS**

EXERCISE

1. $\forall z(z = z)$ =I
2. $fx = fx$ $\forall$E, 1
3. $\exists y(fx = y)$ $\exists$I, 2
4. $\forall x\exists y(fx = y)$ $\forall$I, 3

CHALLENGE 1

1. $\forall z(z = z)$ =I
2. $fx = fx$ $\forall$E, 1
3. $x = y$ assumption
4. $fx = fy$ =E, 2, 3
5. $x = y \Rightarrow fx = fy$ $\Rightarrow$I, 3–4
6. $\forall y(x = y \Rightarrow fx = fy)$ $\forall$I, 5
7. $\forall x\forall y(x = y \Rightarrow fx = fy)$ $\forall$I, 6

Consider the universe of whole numbers, with $fx = x^2$. Then $f(2) = f(-2)$, but $2 \neq -2$.

CHALLENGE 2 Rxy is a function from pairs of objects to {T, F}, while $\neg$ is a function from {T, F} to {T, F}, so the composition is again a function from pairs of objects to {T, F}. $\exists x$ is a function from properties to {T, F}. Now for every object c in the universe, $\neg R(x, c)$ is a property, so $\exists x\neg(Rx, c)$ assigns it a value from {T, F}. Thus each object c is assigned a truth value. It follows that $\exists x\neg Rxy$ is a function that assigns to every object a truth value in {T, F}.

"THE": RUSSELL'S THEORY OF DEFINITE DESCRIPTIONS

page 343

Russell wrote his *Introduction to Mathematical Philosophy* while in jail for opposing England's participation in World War I.

CHALLENGE 1

1.
1.	$\exists x(Fx \,\&\, \forall y(Fy \Rightarrow x = y) \,\&\, Gx)$	premise
2.	$Fc^* \,\&\, \forall y(Fy \Rightarrow c^* = y) \,\&\, Gc^*$	$\exists$E, 1
3.	Fc^*	&E, 2
4.	$\exists xFx$	$\exists$I, 3
5.	$\quad\quad Fx \,\&\, Fy$	assumption
6.	$\quad\quad \forall y(Fy \Rightarrow c^* = y) \,\&\, Gc^*$	&E, 2
7.	$\quad\quad \forall y(Fy \Rightarrow c^* = y)$	&E, 6
8.	$\quad\quad Fx \Rightarrow c^* = x$	$\forall$E, 7
9.	$\quad\quad Fy \Rightarrow c^* = y$	$\forall$E, 7
10.	$\quad\quad Fx$	&E, 5
11.	$\quad\quad Fy$	&E, 5
12.	$\quad\quad c^* = x$	$\Rightarrow$E, 8, 10
13.	$\quad\quad c^* = y$	$\Rightarrow$E, 9, 11
14.	$\quad\quad x = y$	=E, 12, 13
15.	$(Fx \,\&\, Fy) \Rightarrow x = y$	$\Rightarrow$I, 5–14
16.	$\forall y((Fx \,\&\, Fy) \Rightarrow x = y)$	$\forall$I, 15
17.	$\forall x\forall y((Fx \,\&\, Fy) \Rightarrow x = y)$	$\forall$I, 16
18.	$\quad\quad Fx$	assumption
19.	$\quad\quad \forall y(Fy \Rightarrow c^* = y) \,\&\, Gc^*$	&E, 2
20.	$\quad\quad \forall y(Fy \Rightarrow c^* = y)$	&E, 6
21.	$\quad\quad Fx \Rightarrow c^* = x$	$\forall$E, 7
22.	$\quad\quad c^* = x$	$\Rightarrow$E, 18, 21
23.	$\quad\quad Gc^*$	&E, 19
24.	$\quad\quad Gx$	=E, 22, 23
25.	$Fx \Rightarrow Gx$	$\Rightarrow$I, 18–24
26.	$\forall x(Fx \Rightarrow Gx)$	$\forall$I, 25
27.	$\exists xFx \,\&\, \forall x\forall y((Fx \,\&\, Fy) \Rightarrow x = y)$	&I, 4, 17
28.	$\exists xFx \,\&\, \forall x\forall y((Fx \,\&\, Fy) \Rightarrow x = y) \,\&\, \forall x(Fx \Rightarrow Gx)$	&I, 26, 27

CHALLENGE 3 Russell would ask whether the first premise is to be formalized using external negation or internal negation. If the former, the first premise is $\exists x(Vx \,\&\, \forall y(Vy \Rightarrow y = x) \,\&\, Mx) \vee \neg\exists x(Vx \,\&\, \forall y(Vy \Rightarrow y = x) \,\&\, Mx)$. The premise is true on logical grounds, but if the argument is to be valid, the third premise must be written as $\neg\exists x(Vx \,\&\, \forall y(Vy \Rightarrow y = x) \,\&\, Mx) \Rightarrow \exists xVx$, which is

false. Alternatively, if the first premise is formalized with an internal negation, it begs the question by assuming the existence of a vampire. That is, it is false unless there is such a vampire.

with & about logic

page 351 measuring uncertainty

EXERCISES 1. $\frac{1}{2}$ 3. $\frac{1}{12}$ 5. $\frac{1}{6}$

page 354 Bayes' law and Sherlock Holmes

EXERCISES

1. $\frac{1}{2}$

3. $\frac{1}{6}$

5. $\frac{1}{6}$ (It really doesn't matter what you flipped.)

7. 0.00285 (0.003 times 0.95)

9. 0.00015 (0.003 times 0.05)

11. 0.0527 (answer to problem 7 plus the answer to problem 8)

13. 0.95 (answer to problem 7 divided by the answer to problem 6)

page 358 inductive logic

A game of inductive logic, "Eleusis," was invented in 1956 by Robert Abbott. It is good fun and is described in Martin Gardner's *More Mathematical Puzzles and Diversions* (Penguin, 1966) and Abbott's *Abbott's New Card Games* (Funk & Wagnalls, 1963). For a version incorporating changes made in the 1970s, see R. Wayne Schmittberger's *New Rules for Classic Games* (Wiley, 1992).

There is a fascinating science fiction story whose premise involves the laws of chance, Robert M. Coates's "The Law." It is in the anthologies *The Mathematical Magpie*, edited by Clifton Fadiman (Simon & Schuster, 1962), and *The Looking Glass Book of Stories*, edited by Hart Day Leavitt (Random House, 1960).

Stan Wagon wrote a fine series of articles for the *Mathematical Intelligencer* on the evidence for mathematical conjectures. The example of the Collatz problem is taken from the first of these (vol. 7, no. 1, 1985, pp. 72–76).

Martin Gardner's example comes from the excellent "Induction and Probability" in his *Time Travel and Other Mathematical Bewilderments* (W. H. Freeman, 1988). This article is a rich essay on the difficulties confronting the inductive logician. Also of interest is William Poundstone's *Labyrinths of Reason* (Anchor-Doubleday, 1988).

A thorough introduction to quantum logic can be found in David Cohen's *An Introduction to Hilbert Space and Quantum Logic* (Springer-Verlag, 1989).

Keith Devlin's mathematical theory of information can be found in his book *Logic and Information* (Cambridge University Press, 1991).

Are you having difficulty with puzzle1? Are you facing a blank screen and wondering what went wrong? Nothing went wrong. Remember, you are supposed to type something in, then press Enter. After this, the computer will respond. In the first universe, the result is very simple: The computer will just repeat what you type. Once you have discovered that, you should move on to the next.

Too easy? Are you sure you have discovered everything? Some universes are simple, such as the first. Others are more complicated. There is usually a general rule, but often there are a few minor ones as well. Did you try typing in more than one word? Did you try typing in numbers or characters? Did you try capital letters?

How will you know when you have found everything there is to find? You should know the answer to that: You will never know. That is precisely the position investigators face in every discipline.

Worse, we ourselves, the programmers, will never know! Certainly, we know what we intended to program, but very few programs are bug-free. One important area of logical research involves finding ways to prove that programs do what they are supposed to do. It seems to be an extremely difficult problem, yet enormously important, as computer programs run the telephone system, transportation system, guide our missiles, and so on. Virtually none of these programs, on which our lives depend, have been proven free of error!

EXERCISE
Answers to Puzzle1

1. The computer simply copies whatever you typed in.

3. The computer alternates replying "HO" and "HI." It pays no attention to what you type in.

5. The computer takes each letter you type and replaces it with the next letter in the alphabet (e.g. "f" is replaced with "g"; "z" is replaced by "a"). It also subtracts one from every digit (e.g., "5" is replaced by "4"; "0" is replaced by "9").

7. The computer responds with "no" to nearly everything you type, unless you type "no" itself, in which case it types "yes." If you discovered this, it is quite enough, but as we said before, you can never be sure you have discovered everything. Is is possible that there is a special response to "Millard Fillmore"? Not likely, but until you try, how will you know? As it happens, "Millard Fillmore" gets "no" as expected, yet there is more. If you type "NO," it types "YES," if you type "No," it types "yeS," and if you type "nO," it types "yEs."

9. If the first letter you type is in the range "a" to "g," the computer responds, "Hey kids! It's time for inductive logic!" If your first letter is in the range "h" to "m," the response is "Tom and Jim are bald," "n" to "s" receives "this sentence is entirely in lowercase letters;" "t" to "z" gets "Honey, I shrunk the kids." Any other character is met with "Letters! Please! Just Letters!" There are further variations if your first letter is capitalized.

Answers to Puzzle2

1. The computer repeats what you type, but it remembers and adds on; that is, the response to the second line you type consists of your first and second lines. It keeps on this way, up to a limit of 200 characters. After this, it types only the last 200 characters you typed. Finally, if you end your line with a period, this wipes out the memory and the computer will start over fresh.

3. The computer always replies "Do you have a color monitor?" unless you type the name of a color. When this happens, the computer begins to type in that color and responds "Awesome!" New colors change things further. Mentioning several colors in a line makes the computer alternate colors. If, after having changed colors, you type a line without a color name, it merely replies "Hmm . . . " A very odd thing can happen if you type "black." The computer will appear to conk out. In fact, it has not malfunctioned; it is merely doing what it does with other colors; that is, it is typing in black! The computer

606

recognizes black, blue, green, red, purple, brown, white, gray, pink, yellow, and cyan (a sort of light blue). The colors persist even when you move to other exercises (unless the color is black).

5. The computer types the result of the computation: 2 plus 3 times the number of characters you typed. Spaces don't count.

7. This is extremely hard! This is mean. The computer is responding with the number of seconds that have elapsed since you last typed a line!

9. We will not spoil this for you. You will not have any difficulty.

logic programming

page 362

Leibniz (quoted at the beginning of this section) was one of several independent discoverers of the calculus (with Isaac Newton). He also was an independent discoverer of base 2 numeration (see "Binary" in part 4).

The forecast in Leibniz's quotation at the beginning of the section envisions the ultimate success of artificial intelligence. An avowed goal of this area of computer science is to duplicate the performance of the human mind. Several philosophers have claimed that this is intrinsically impossible. Perhaps J. R. Lucas was the first to make this argument, on the basis of Gödel's theorem (see "Impossibility" in part 9). The incompleteness theorem demonstrates limitations on the powers of formal systems such as machines, limitations that Lucas felt the human mind did not share. Most recently, Roger Penrose in his *The Emperor's New Mind* (Viking Penguin, 1991) elaborates on this argument.

In addition to its function as a logical machine, Prolog was designed to process natural and artificial languages. It has been very successful in this. In both its roles, it was a significant advance over previous languages.

An example of the remarks at the end of the chapter about meaning, consequence, and procedure is the symbol "=." Just what is it? Does "$a = b$" mean that a equals b? Not necessarily. If you query

a=b?

Prolog will always say

no

Well, then, does the wff "a = b" have consequences? Does it behave, for example, as it does in BASIC, where it is a command? That is, does "*a = b*" order the computer to change the value of *a* so that it is the same as *b*? Not really. We are not allowed, in fact, to use "=" in a simple fact or in the head of a rule. Actually, there is no way in Prolog to force two different constants to represent the same object!

So how do we understand "=" in Prolog? The key is procedure. For example, given any query, Prolog looks for a fact of this form, and for a rule with this form at the head. If it finds one, it proceeds from there, but if it doesn't (and in the case of "*a = b*" it won't) then the query fails.

A complete discussion of the procedure behind Prolog is entirely logical but beyond the scope of this book. There are many books on Prolog. See, for example, *Prolog and Natural-Language Analysis* by Pereira and Shieber (Center for the Study of Language and Information, 1987).

EXERCISES

1. father(X, Y):-parent(X, Y),
      husband(X, Z).

3. cousin(X, Y):-parent(Q, Y),
       parent(Z, X),
       not Z = Q,
       parent(W, Q),
       (parent(W, Z);
          (married(Z, P),
          not P = Q,
          parent(W, P))).
   (There are two different ways to be a first cousin).

4. ancestor(X, Y):-parent(X, Y).
   ancestor(X, Y):-parent(Z, Y),
      ancestor(X, Z).

5. mult(X, zero, zero).
   mult(X, s(Y), Z):-mult(X, Y, W),
      add(W, X, Z).

7. wff(X):-append([&], Y, X),
      append(Y1, Y2, Y),
      wff(Y1),
      wff(Y2).

_____ **Tom and Jim's Excellent Adventure** _____

November 16

Tom and Jim conclude that time is a line.

"This means that the principle of causality is true," says Jim. "Time does not branch. Causation is everywhere."

"Not at all," says Tom calmly. "Time may be a line, but that doesn't imply that anything is caused. You mathematicians always think philosophy is simple. It isn't at all; we've made it very complicated."

"But there is no free will!" cries Jim. "We can't affect the future—there is only one future!"

Again, Tom disagrees with Jim. If you think there is *no free will*, turn to page 629. If you think there is *free will* turn to page 629.

informal logic

the W-4

page 371

EXERCISE

1. Maximizing withholding
   Personal Allowances Worksheet

   A 1
   B
   C 0   (you want to maximize the amount withheld)
   D 2   (Geraldine and Bella)
   E
   F
   G 4

   You don't do the Deductions and Adjustments Worksheet because you don't want to reduce your withholding.

   Two-Earner/Two-Job Worksheet

   1. 4
   2. 5
   3.
   4. 5

5. 4
6. 1
7. 660
8. 660
9. 220 (it's Labor Day, you have three more paychecks this year)

Employee's Withholding Allowance Certificate
5. 1
6. 220

2. Minimizing withholding.
Personal Allowances Worksheet

A 1
B
C 1   (you want to minimize the amount withheld)
D 2   (Geraldine and Bella)
E
F
G 5

Deductions and Adjustments Worksheet

1. 14,500.34 (see 1040 line 34. Multiply by 1.05 to increase by 5%)
2. 6,200
3. 8,300.34
4. 0   (see 1040 line 30)
5. 8,300.34
6. 2,707.54 (add 1040 lines 8a and 12, multiply by 1.05)
7. 5,592.80
8. 2
9. 5
10. 7

You don't complete the Two-Earner/Two-Job Worksheet, because want to reduce your witholding.

Employee's Witholding Certificate

5. 7

page 376   *Canadian customs*

Hint: Be quite literal in your reading of the document. Do not assume that the rules may be liberally applied. They may in fact be liberally applied (in fact, they were), but that is not the point of this exercise. *Note:* Jim is not a resident of Canada.

the logic tea

page 377

EXERCISE

1. Yes, they do. They are a food service establishment (590.001(B)(17) and 590.052(A)(1)).

3. No, they need another sink (590.013(C)).

5. Yes, they do (590.009)

6. LaTina has to wear a hairnet (590.010(B)) and she has to drink her tea in another room (590.011(B)).

Note that 590.030 is self-referential.

commercial logic II

page 383

This is a reproduction of a mailing one of the authors received. In fact, he received three of these, each slightly different—different awards, different claim numbers, different 900 phone numbers. All were from Direct American Marketers, Inc.

The key to understanding this mailing is the fine print, which gives the odds of winning each prize. The odds of winning any particular cash amount are listed as 1:4,998,468, or one chance in about five million. The odds of winning a bunch of coupons are 1:1, which means that everybody who receives a notice gets this. Essentially, there is little difference between this and receiving in the mail an envelope with coupons that you will probably not find useful.

("Henle" is frequently misspelled, but the spelling "Hence" is new and very appropriate for a logician!)

curiosities & puzzles

The Digestor's Digest, page 6

page 384

The *Digest* puzzles where inspired by Raymond Smullyan's book *What Is the Name of This Book?* More Smullyan logic books: *The Lady or the Tiger?* (Knopf, 1985), *Forever Undecided* (Knopf, 1987), and a book of philosophical riddles: *5000 BC and Other Philosophical Fantasies* (St. Martin's Press, 1983).

While we are on the subject of Raymond Smullyan, we must recommend two more of his books, now unfortunately out of print: *The Chess Mysteries of Sherlock Holmes* (Knopf, 1979), and *The Chess Mysteries of the Arabian Knights* (Knopf, 1981). These are not ordinary chess puzzles. This is "retrograde analysis." In each problem, you are given a chess position and are asked questions about how that position could have come about. A typical question might be, "It is White's move. What was Black's last move, and what was White's last move?" *This is not a question of strategy.* The position is carefully constructed so that there is only one answer. Smullyan's problems are lovely and his explanations are beautiful deductions.

Lewis Carroll's "what the tortoise said to page 387 Achilles"

page 387

This piece first appeared in the philosophical journal *Mind* in 1895. The standard explanation of it is that Carroll is showing the importance of rules of inference—that without some sort of mechanism for producing conclusions from premises, we can never conclude anything.

This explanation is not universally accepted. William Warren Bartley III, editor of *Lewis Carroll's Symbolic Logic* (Potter, 1977), an annotated edition of Carroll's *Symbolic Logic*, does not believe that either the intention or the importance is clear. A full discussion of Carroll's views is contained in Appendix C, together with letters of Carroll in which he discusses the paper.

page 391

The Far Side

The Far Side cartoon by Gary Larson is reprinted by permission of Chronicle Features, San Francisco, CA. All rights reserved.

_____ **Tom and Jim's Excellent Adventure** _____

November 17

"Why does time flow forward?" Jim asks.

Tom replies, "It doesn't. Time just is; it doesn't move any more than the city of Chicago. November 17 is a point in time like Chicago is a point in space."

"But don't we move in time? And aren't we always moving forward?"

"At every instant, we are only in one place. It only appears to us that we are moving forward because we remember the past and we don't remember the future."

"Then we could change this if we found some way to know the future!" exclaims Jim. He suggests consulting the engineers at Sophist and changing the operation of the machine again. Once more, the engineers are able to do something. Now the time machine works so that only the contents go back in time, not the outside world.

Jim intends to go a day into the future. He will discover what will happen to Tom. He can tell Tom, who will then have memory of the future, and the flow of time will be reversed. Or at least confused.

Tom thinks that something will go wrong. If you think so too, turn to page 617. If not, turn to page 571.

8 COMPLETENESS, DISBELIEF, DEBATES, AND DINNER

FORMAL LOGIC: COMPLETENESS

GEOMETRY

page 394

We can say a little more about the shape of space. Locally, due to the presence of matter, space is curved, and the curvature can and has been measured. The more exciting question is whether space is globally curved (go straight in any direction and you will return to where you started). The overwhelming opinion is yes, but there is no proof. The distinction between *local* and *global curvature is* important. Colorado is locally curved as a surface (there are mountains), but not globally. (Go straight in any direction and you will leave Colorado.) The surface of the earth, however, is globally curved. Current theories hold that there is sufficient mass in the universe to curve all of space. At the moment, however, only one-tenth of the requisite mass has been detected. Nobody seems to know where the missing stuff is. (Have you cleaned under your bed recently?)

By the way, the same theory that predicts global curvature also predicts a finite universe. One of the authors of this book prefers the idea of an infinite universe and consequently tends to read the science section of the newspaper with the same hope and fear as the sports section.

An excellent reference for the geometry in this section and much more is Dan Pedoe's *Geometry and the Liberal Arts* (Penguin, 1976). A good reference for non-Euclidean geometry and many of the issues raised here is *The Non-Euclidean Revolution* by Richard J. Trudeau (Birkhäuser, 1987).

page 399 THE COMPLETENESS THEOREM

The equivalence of syntactic and semantic implication helps us to understand the discovery of non-Euclidean geometry. When mathematicians were trying to prove the fifth postulate from the first four, they sought a syntactic implication. Because this proved extremely difficult, they suspected that no proof was possible, but the task of showing that no proof exists must have been daunting. These mathematicians did not know of the existence of semantic implication. It was a great conceptual and philosophical leap to imagine other universes. When this leap was made, the failure of semantic implication in this case (the discovery of universes of spherical and hyperbolic geometry) came quickly.

One-half of the completeness theorem for statement logic is that any wff that is a tautology must be provable via our deduction rules. Of course, we are not including Taut. as one of those rules, or else the theorem would be trivial: If P is a tautology, then here is a deduction using Taut.:

P Taut.

Indeed, the real meaning of this part of the completeness theorem is that the use of Taut. is justified. Completeness assures us that any use of Taut. can be replaced with (perhaps extensive) use of the other rules.

For a different approach to this theorem, see the classic *Introduction of Mathematical Logic* by Elliot Mendelson (Van Nostrand, 1964).

EXERCISE For example, $\vee$-elimination, if $A \Rightarrow C$, $B \Rightarrow C$, and $A \vee B$ are T, then C must be T: first, either A or B is T since $A \vee B$ is T and $F \vee F$ is F. If A is T, then C is T, since $A \Rightarrow B$ is T and $T \Rightarrow F$ is F. If B is T, then again C is T, since $B \Rightarrow C$ is T and $T \Rightarrow F$ is F. In both cases, C is T.

CHALLENGE

1.	P	premise
2.	$\neg(\neg(\neg P \,\&\, Q) \vee R)$	assumption
3.	$\neg\neg(\neg P \,\&\, Q) \,\&\, \neg R$	Taut, 2
4.	$\neg\neg(\neg P \,\&\, Q)$	&E, 3
5.	$(\neg P \,\&\, Q)$	$\neg$E, 4
6.	$\neg P$	&E, 5
7.	$P \,\&\, \neg P$	&I, 1, 6
8.	$\neg(\neg(\neg P \,\&\, Q) \vee R) \Rightarrow (P \,\&\, \neg P)$	$\Rightarrow$I, 2-7
9.	$\neg\neg(\neg(\neg P \,\&\, Q) \vee R)$	$\neg$I, 8
10.	$\neg(\neg P \,\&\, Q) \vee R$	$\neg$E, 9

AXIOMATIZATION AND BOOLEAN ALGEBRA *page 404*

There several other reasons for axiomatization. One is confidence. After a number of alarming incidents (see "Russell's Paradox and Frege's Mistake" in part 9), mathematicians worried considerably about the consistency of their assumptions. It became important to state clearly what assumptions were being used and to know that everyone working in the field of, say, Boolean algebras was operating under the same assumptions, so that confidence in those assumptions could grow.

A second reason is aesthetics. It is tidy to know that everything you are doing can be traced to a short list of fundamental facts. Mathematicians sometimes use the word "elegant" to describe this. It is similarly pleasing if the list of axioms is minimal, that none can be proven from the others.

There are dozens of equivalent systems of axioms for Boolean algebras. Most are not minimal. We chose one that is pretty spare, and we recommend its source, *Boolean Algebra and Its Applications*, by John Eldon Whitesit (Addison-Wesley, 1961), as a good introduction. Note that it does not contain the associative law $(x \clubsuit (y \clubsuit z)) = ((x \clubsuit y) \clubsuit z)$. Instead the book proves it, although it takes three pages. We actually overstated the fifth axiom for Boolean algebras to make one proof shorter. We do not need to assume that a' is unique. That can be proven. A good reference for many of the issues raised in this chapter (as well as other parts of this book) is Raymond Wilder's classic *Introduction to the Foundations of Mathematics* (Wiley, 1952).

It was customary among nineteenth-century logicians to imagine that formal logic actually represents the "laws of thought," as Boole entitled his book. This view has all but disappeared as our appreciation of the complexity of the human mind has grown. Indeed, in the last twenty years alone, a new discipline has appeared, cognitive science, whose goal is to understand both human and machine intelligence, which are by no means presumed the same.

Contemporary psychologists now use formal logic descriptively. A good example is Jean Piaget, who expresses his theories of mental development by describing the increasing ability of children to perform logical operations. In his book *Logic and Psychology* (Basic Books, 1957), Piaget recalls a period in which there was great mistrust between psychologists and logicians: "Logic was thus used in the causal explanation of the psychological facts themselves. To this fallacious use of logic in psychology the name 'logicism' has been given . . . " (p. 1) and ". . . one of the chief tasks of later logicians has been to eliminate from the field of logic any appeal to intuition, that is to say, the psychological factor. When there is recourse to such factors in logic the fallacy is called 'psychologism'" (p. 2).

You may have noticed an interesting phenomenon in the axioms for a Boolean algebra. They are sort of symmetrically balanced between $\clubsuit$ and $\spadesuit$. In fact, if you switch these two symbols and also switch 1 and 0, then you have actually changed nothing. What this means is that whatever you prove about $\clubsuit$, $\spadesuit$, 1, and 0 is also true about $\spadesuit$, $\clubsuit$, 0, and 1. For example, we have just proven that $(a \clubsuit b)' = a' \spadesuit b'$. Now we also know that $(a \spadesuit b)' = a' \clubsuit b'$. This is known as the principle of *duality*, and it can be very useful.

EXERCISES

1. $1' = 0, 0' = 1$

3. $c' = f, f' = c$
   $d' = b, b' = d$
   $a' = e, e' = a$

5. Without using Taut., the best we could do is a 38-line deduction.

7. $1 = a ♠ a'$ axiom 5
   $= a ♠ (a' ♣ 1)$ axiom 4
   $= (a ♠ a') ♣ (a ♠ 1)$ axiom 2
   $= 1 ♣ (a ♠ 1)$ axiom 5
   $= a ♠ 1$ axiom 4
   $= 1 ♠ a$ axiom 1

9. $(a ♣ b) ♣ a' = a' ♣ (a ♣ b)$ axiom 1
   $= 0 ♠ (a' ♣ (a ♣ b))$ axiom 3
   $= (a ♣ a') ♠ (a' ♣ (a ♣ b))$ axiom 5
   $= (a' ♣ a) ♠ (a' ♣ (a ♣ b))$ axiom 1
   $= a' ♣ (a ♠ (a ♣ b))$ axiom 2
   $= a' ♣ ((a ♣ 1) ♠ (a ♣ b))$ axiom 4
   $= a' ♣ (a ♣ (1 ♠ b))$ axiom 2
   $= a' ♣ (a ♣ 1)$ lemma 1
   $= a' ♣ a$ axiom 4
   $= 0$ axiom 5

11. $(a ♣ b) ♠ (a' ♠ b')$
    $= (a' ♠ b') ♠ (a ♣ b)$ axiom 1
    $= ((a' ♠ b') ♠ a) ♣ ((a' ♠ b') ♠ b)$ axiom 2
    $= (a ♠ (a' ♠ b')) ♣ (b ♠ (a' ♠ b'))$ axiom 1
    $= (a ♠ (a' ♠ b')) ♣ (b ♠ (b' ♠ a'))$ axiom 1
    $= 1 ♣ 1$ lemma 4
    $= 1$ axiom 5

Tom and Jim's Excellent Adventure

November 18

If you keep making the safe choice, there won't be any fun.

CHALLENGE Write a satisfying adventure with this kind of time machine.

with & about logic

page 411 ### believing and knowing

The quotation from Augustine at the start of this chapter reflects his slow acceptance of Christianity and his occasional doubts. The "help" is in essence "assuage." It is said at a time of belief, in anticipation of periods of doubt. Contrast that with the mocking "Lord, I do not believe; help thou my unbelief" (Samuel Butler). The meaning is entirely different and also paradoxical.

An example will show the difficulty with BB: Consider the man who holds some racial stereotypes but believes that he does not.

CHALLENGE 1 $\forall x \neg \exists p (Bxp \text{ \& } Bx\neg p)$ is equivalent to $\forall x \forall p \neg (Bxp \text{ \& } Bx\neg p)$ by QE2, part 5, or from "Hypothetical Reasoning: Deduction from Assumptions" in part 6. $\neg(Bxp \text{ \& } Bx\neg p)$ is a truth table equivalent of $Bxp \Rightarrow \neg Bx\neg p$.

CHALLENGE 3 By LB, x believes $(p \text{ \& } q) \Rightarrow q$, since this is a tautology. By MPB, it follows that x believes q.

PUZZLE To give a false belief of one's own is to fall victim to a version of Moore's Paradox: P but I don't believe it! How could you continue to believe P if you thought it was false?

CHALLENGE 5 If Kxp, then p is true by TC. If we assume $Kx'\neg p'$ then $\neg p$ by TC, so we have $p \text{ \& } \neg p$. Thus $Kx'\neg p' \Rightarrow (p \text{ \& } \neg p)$ by $\Rightarrow$I and so $\neg Kx'\neg p'$ by $\neg$I. Thus $Kxp \Rightarrow \neg Kx'\neg p'$.

page 415 ### the law of the excluded middle

Intuitionism tends to be rather restrictive, ruling out certain practices when applied to mathematics, generally disapproving and rarely approving. Because of logical limitations, attempts to do mathematics constructively have usually failed to produce much. In recent years, however, there has been real progress. The late Errett Bishop developed a theory of constructive real numbers that managed to accomplish considerable mathematics.

Here is a sample of the difficulties. An intuitionist, or constructivist, might reject a real number if no procedure were available to produce the number's decimal expansion as far as we like. The fraction $\frac{2}{9}$ presents no problems, since this is $0.2222\ldots$, and algorithms for calculating the digits of π were discovered thousands of years ago. On the other hand, consider the number whose nth digit is either 0 or 1, and it is 1 only if there are n consecutive 7s in the decimal expansion of π. At present, no method exists for grinding out the digits of this number. To an intuitionist, the preceding words do not define a number.

Classically, the number of reals is uncountable. The number of procedures for describing reals, however, is countable. Thus there are far fewer constructive reals than reals. The interested reader should find *Constructive Analysis* by Errett Bishop and Douglas Bridges (Springer-Verlag, 1985).

CHALLENGE 1 The statement "I will cross the street without injury" is either true or false before I cross by the law of the excluded middle. If it is true, then there is no need for me to be careful. If it is false, then being careful is of no use.

CHALLENGE 3 $T \vee I$ is T: If we think of I as standing for either T or F, but we don't know which, then we see that it doesn't matter. No matter what I is, the statement is true, since both $T \vee T$ and $T \vee F$ are true.

$F \vee I$ is I: In this case it matters what the I stands for. $F \vee T$ is T, but $F \vee F$ is F. Thus the truth value of $F \vee I$ is as indeterminate as that of I.

$T \& I$ is I: This is similar to $F \vee I$. The truth value depends on the truth or falsity of the I.

$F \& I$ is F: No matter what I turns out to be, we know F & anything is F, so F & I is F.

EXERCISE See Challenge 2 in "Hypothetical Reasoning: Deduction from Assumptions" in part 6.

from puzzle to paradox

page 420

We've solved the paradox of the surprise examination by using the knowledge predicate. For some people, this is too powerful a weapon. After all, it's difficult to know what knowledge is.

It's much easier to believe in belief, and we can come to essentially the same conclusions with the belief predicate instead. We use as axioms:

LB: $B(p)$ for all tautologies p
MPB: $(B(p)\ \&\ B(p \Rightarrow q)) \Rightarrow B(q)$ *(modus ponens for belief)*
CB: $B(p) \Rightarrow \neg B(\neg p)$ (consistency of belief)
BB: $B(p) \Rightarrow B(B(p))$

The last axiom may be somewhat doubtful (see "Believing and Knowing"), but let's push ahead. Suppose the teacher says:

$$T\ \&\ \neg B(T) \tag{1'}$$

Then with this as an assumption, using only LB and MPB we can derive a contradiction from

$$B(T\ \&\ \neg B(T)) \tag{2'}$$

The proof is identical to that given for the knowledge predicate, which uses only LK and MPK (Challenge 3).

Using LK, MPK, and TC, we derived a contradiction from $K(T\ \&\ \neg K(T))$ alone. We can do something similar with belief:

1. $B(T\ \&\ \neg B(T))$	premise
2. $B(T)$	LB, MPB, 1
3. $B(\neg B(T))$	LB, MPB, 1
4. $B(B(T))$	BB, 2

The proof contradicts CB.

If you are still unhappy with belief, we offer you doubt. How can we say we doubt p? To say that we believe the negation of p would be too much. We simply say that we don't believe p: $\neg B(p)$. Now, in place of CB and BB, suppose we take the much milder DD:

$$\text{DD: } B(p) \Rightarrow \neg B(\neg B(p))$$

BB states that if you believe p, then you believe that you believe it. DD states that if you believe p, then you doubt that you doubt it, which is certainly a less extreme statement. What is nice is that we can solve the surprise examination now with just LB, MPB, and DD. We leave it as an exercise (*Hint*: Start out as before.)

CHALLENGE 3

1. $T\ \&\ \neg K(T)$	premise
2. $K(T\ \&\ \neg K(T))$	premise
3. $K(T)$	from 2, as in the text
4. $\neg K(T)$	&E, 1
5. $K(T)\ \&\ \neg K(T)$	&I, 3,4

Montague and Kaplan's essay "A Paradox Regained" was first published in *Notre Dame Journal of Formal Logic* 1:79–90 (1960).

informal logic

more Bush, Clinton, and Perot   page 429

CHALLENGE

1. The question of whether the medical profession is to blame goes unanswered. Clinton's use of the words "premise" and "conclusions" seems to be an attempt to give his argument a logical aura. The problem is that he has several premises. In addition, his first conclusion appears to be not a conclusion but another premise.

    Apart from this, Clinton does point out several problems in detail, and he proposes a number of steps to resolve them, also in some detail. The proposals are relevant, and citing the cases of Hawaii and Rochester provides good support.

2. Bush does answer the question—with a blunt no. Like Clinton, he notes some problems with the health care system and highlights his plan for solving them.

3. Perot begins discussing health care but spends most of his time attacking the political system for permitting special interests to wield so much power over Congress. As a consequence, none of the original questions are addressed.

4. Bush replies directly to the question of Social Security, but on the other two begins to wander. Rather than plan the future of pensions and Medicare, he suggests improving the economy, presumably so that if the system goes bust, we will be able to afford fixing it.

5. Perot takes the same sort of route as Bush did except that he implies the problems are easy to solve. He then points out other difficulties in the nation's financial system. He never addresses the questions asked, ultimately joining Bush in working on the economy.

6. Mostly Clinton joins his rivals in discussing the economy. He disputes Perot on the difficulty of the problems. He also points out that Bush's reliance on federal guarantees ignores a serious problem. On the other hand, he offers no plan or solution apart from the last sentence, which is rather vague.

presidential debates   page 435

EXERCISES   Sample answers:

1. Senator Snort, you have a record of proposing measures aimed at reducing gender discrimination, and in general, you support

gender equity. Does this mean that you would favor a draft that included women?

2. Mr. Snodgrass, I have a bill in the Senate now to reintroduce the draft. That bill contains provisions for both women and men, but the provisions are different, as indeed men are different from women. I feel that all our young people are privileged to be members of this society and owe it their service. Women can serve in many ways. Under the bill, women may join the armed forces in noncombat roles, but they may also serve our country at home as nurses' aides in veterans' hospitals, as staff in government day care centers, or teachers in public schools.

3. The senator's plan exposes to us her bleak vision of the place of women in our society. I would like to remind her that her route to the U.S. Senate is not open to everyone. Very few capable, energetic women such as we both are have been fortunate enough to marry a U.S. Senator with terminal cancer. I was not as lucky. I had to be elected, not appointed. I had to fight my way up the political ladder, and I wouldn't be here in front of you now, leading my state, if lawmakers had buried me in bed pans and bassinets.

page 439 *parliamentary debates*

We often have members of Smith's parliamentary debating team in our logic class. They are usually A students.

page 441 *commercial logic* III

We are indebted to Doug Cooper for noticing the logical significance of shampoo instructions. A similar example appears in his recent book *Oh! My! Modula-2!* (Norton, 1990), under the caption "Why the computer scientist never got out of the shower."

curiosities & puzzles

page 442 *The Digestor's Digest, page 7*

SPECIAL CHALLENGE! Write your own page of *The Digestor's Digest*.

Peano's dots

page 444

In the quotation, Lord Churchill is referring to decimal points.

The dot scheme here is the one that Quine used in his classic *Mathematical Logic*, revised edition (Harvard University Press, 1951).

CHALLENGE

1. $(\sigma \Rightarrow \varphi) \Leftrightarrow ((\chi \,\&\, \psi) \Rightarrow \neg\theta)$
3. $\varphi \,\&\, ((\forall x\psi \Rightarrow \gamma) \vee \sigma)$
5. $((\sigma \Rightarrow \varphi) \Rightarrow (\chi \Rightarrow (\psi \Rightarrow \theta))) \,\&\, \neg(((\gamma \Rightarrow \varphi) \Rightarrow (\varphi \Rightarrow \sigma)) \Rightarrow \theta)$
6. $((\gamma \vee (\theta \,\&\, \psi)) \Rightarrow \chi) \,\&\, (((\varphi \Rightarrow \sigma) \Leftrightarrow \alpha) \,\&\, \sigma)$
7. $\sigma \supset \chi .\equiv \theta$
9. $(x) \sim (y) \sim (z)(\sigma \equiv\, : \varphi \,\supset\, \chi : \psi \,:. \vee\, \theta)$
10. $\gamma \vee \sigma .\supset. \theta : \varphi \supset \chi :: \chi \supset \psi :. \varphi \equiv \theta :\supset \sigma)$

Charles Dana Gibson

page 445

It is easy to check that $\neg(Fc \Rightarrow Pcm) \,\therefore\, Fc$ is a valid argument using truth tables. A formal deduction (without Taut.) is somewhat longer:

CHALLENGE

1.	$\neg(Fc \Rightarrow Pcm)$			premise
2.		$\neg Fc$		assumption
3.			Fc	assumption
4.				$\neg Pcm$ — assumption
5.				$Fc \,\&\, \neg Fc$ — &I, 2, 3
6.			$\neg Pcm \Rightarrow (Fc \,\&\, \neg Fc)$	$\Rightarrow$I, 4–5
7.			$\neg\neg Pcm$	$\neg$I, 6
8.			Pcm	$\neg$E, 7
9.		$Fc \Rightarrow Pcm$		$\Rightarrow$I, 3–8
10.		$(Fc \Rightarrow Pcm) \,\&\, \neg(Fc \Rightarrow Pcm)$		&I, 1, 9
11.	$\neg Fc \Rightarrow ((Fc \Rightarrow Pcm) \,\&\, \neg(Fc \Rightarrow Pcm))$			$\Rightarrow$I, 2–10
12.	$\neg\neg Fc$			$\neg$I, 11
13.	Fc			$\neg$E, 12

the family reunion II: the women

page 446

We hope you have solved this and are just looking here to check your answer. If you have given up, however, here's a hint: Use the work-sheet. Set up the chart with rows labeled Madeleine, Madge, Ma-dame, Madonna, Madeira, Edwin, Edgar, Eduardo, Edsel, Crazy Eddie, seat 1, seat 2, seat 3, seat 4, and seat 5. Set it up with columns labeled lobster, anchovy, omelet, garlic, Big Mac, seat 1, seat 2, seat 3, seat 4, seat 5, Edwin, Edgar, Eduardo, Edsel, and Crazy Eddie.

More hints: A look at "The Family Reunion" in part 4 will tell you whom Madeleine married and with whom Madonna is living. After you have entered as much data as you can, you will find that there seem to be two places Madeleine could be. Check them out. One will work and one won't.

ANSWERS Madeleine is married to Crazy Eddie. She had the anchovy crepes and sat in #4.
Madge is married to Edgar. She ate lobster and sat on your left.
Madame is attached to Edwin. She ate roasted garlic and sat on your right.
Madonna is living with Eduardo. She had the Big Mac and sat in #2.
Madeira goes with Edsel. She picked at her yeast omelet while sitting opposite to you.

9 PARADOX, IMPOSSIBILITY, AND THE LAW

FORMAL LOGIC: DEEPER INTO LOGIC

page 450 WHERE DO NUMBERS COME FROM?

CHALLENGE 1
a. Fewer sheep have returned than left in the morning.
b. More sheep have returned than left that morning.
c. No, only that the same number returned.

CHALLENGE 3
Ask the kids to pair up; then check to see if every boy is paired with a girl and if every girl is paired with a boy.

CHALLENGE 5

a. $\exists h(\forall x(Fx \Rightarrow F(hx)) \ \& \ \forall x \forall y(x \neq y \Rightarrow hx \neq hy) \ \& \ \forall x(Fx \Rightarrow \exists y(Fy \ \& \ hy = x)))$

b. There are three clauses. First, there is $\forall x(Fx \Rightarrow F(ix))$. This is clearly true, since $x = ix$. The second is that $\forall x \forall y(x \neq y \Rightarrow ix \neq iy)$. Again, the fact that $ix = x$ and $iy = y$ makes this trivial. Finally, $\forall x(Fx \Rightarrow \exists y(Fy \ \& \ iy = x))$. The last part says that for some y, Fy and $iy = x$. Of course, $y = x$ satisfies this, so indeed there is such a y, namely x.

CHALLENGE 7 There are three clauses that must be checked to determine whether jh is a 1–1 correspondence: $\forall x(Fx \Rightarrow H(jhx))$, $\forall x \forall y(x \neq y \Rightarrow jhx \neq jhy)$, $\forall x(Hx \Rightarrow \exists y(Fy \ \& \ jhy = x))$.

1.	$\forall x(Fx \Rightarrow G(hx))$	premise
2.	$\forall x(Gx \Rightarrow H(jx))$	premise
3.	$\quad Fx$	assumption
4.	$\quad Fx \Rightarrow G(hx)$	$\forall$E, 1
5.	$\quad G(hx) \Rightarrow H(j(hx))$	$\forall$E, 2
6.	$\quad G(hx)$	$\Rightarrow$E, 3, 4
7.	$\quad H(j(hx))$	$\Rightarrow$E, 5, 6
8.	$\quad H(jhx)$	(definition of jh)
9.	$Fx \Rightarrow H(jhx)$	$\Rightarrow$I, 3–8
10.	$\forall x(Fx \Rightarrow H(jhx))$	$\forall$I, 9

1.	$\forall x \forall y(x \neq y \Rightarrow hx \neq hy)$	premise
2.	$\forall x \forall y(x \neq y \Rightarrow jx \neq jy)$	premise
3.	$\quad x \neq y$	assumption
4.	$\quad x \neq y \Rightarrow hx \neq hy$	$\forall$E, 1 (twice)
5.	$\quad hx \neq hy \Rightarrow j(hx) \neq j(hy)$	$\forall$E, 2 (twice)
6.	$\quad j(hx) \neq j(hy)$	$\Rightarrow$E (twice) 3, 4, 5
7.	$\quad jhx \neq jhy$	(definition of jh)
8.	$x \neq y \Rightarrow jhx \neq jhy$	$\Rightarrow$I, 3–7
9.	$\forall x \forall y(x \neq y \Rightarrow jhx \neq jhy)$	$\forall$I, 8 (twice)

1.	$\forall x(Gx \Rightarrow \exists y(Fy \ \& \ hy = x))$	premise
2.	$\forall x(Hx \Rightarrow \exists y(Gy \ \& \ jy = x))$	premise
3.	$Hx \Rightarrow \exists y(Gy \ \& \ jy = x)$	$\forall$E, 2
4.	$\quad Hx$	assumption
5.	$\quad \exists y(Gy \ \& \ jy = x)$	$\Rightarrow$E, 3, 4
6.	$\quad Gc^* \ \& \ jc^* = x$	$\exists$E, 5
7.	$\quad Gc^* \Rightarrow \exists y(Fy \ \& \ hy = c^*)$	$\forall$E, 1
8.	$\quad Gc^*$	&E, 6
9.	$\quad jc^* = x$	&E, 6

10.	$\exists y(Fy \ \& \ hy = c^*)$	$\Rightarrow$E, 7, 8
11.	$Fd^* \ \& \ hd^* = c^*$	$\exists$E, 10
12.	Fd^*	&E, 11
13.	$hd^* = c^*$	&E, 11
14.	$jhd^* = x$	=E, 9, 13
15.	$Fd^* \ \& \ jhd^* = x$	&I, 12, 14
16.	$\exists y(Fy \ \& \ jhy = x)$	$\exists$I, 15
17.	$Hx \Rightarrow \exists y(Fy \ \& \ jhy = x)$	$\Rightarrow$I, 4–16
18.	$\forall x(Hx \Rightarrow \exists y(Fy \ \& \ jhy = x))$	$\forall$I, 17

At the end of this section, an argument is given that the number of squares (1, 4, 9, . . .) is the same size as the number of natural numbers (1, 2, 3, . . .) by exhibiting a 1–1 onto function from one to the other. Another argument is given that the number of squares is less than the number of natural numbers by exhibiting a 1–1 function from the first into (but not onto) the second. Can you find an argument that the number of squares is greater than the number of natural numbers?

Another approach to constructing numbers is to build them from the most primitive of mathematical objects, sets. The first number, 0, is the empty set {}. The second number, 1, is defined as a particular set with one element, {0}, or {{}}. This may look peculiar. What is it? It is a set with one element and that element is the empty set. {{}} is not empty. It has one member!

What is 2? It should be a set with two elements, but which ones? We choose 0 and 1, that is, 2 = {0, 1} or {{},{{}}}. Notice that each new number takes about twice as long to write if you use only brackets and commas. The number 3 is {0,1,2}, or {{},{{}},{{},{{}}}}. With word processors, it's easy to write these:

4 is {{},{{}},{{},{{}}},{{},{{}},{{},{{}}}}}.
5 is {{},{{}},{{},{{}}},{{},{{}},{{},{{}}}},{{},{{}},{{},{{}}},{{},{{}},{{},{{}}}}}}.
6 is {{},{{}},{{},{{}}},{{},{{}},{{},{{}}}},{{},{{}},{{},{{}}},{{},{{}},{{},{{}}}}},{{},{{}},{{},{{}}},{{},{{}},{{},{{}}}},{{},{{}},{{},{{}}},{{},{{}},{{},{{}}}}}}}.

And so on.

This is very elegant, but it only scratches the surface. From these numbers, we can manufacture fractions, decimals, even infinite numbers. One reference for this development is *An Outline of Set Theory* by J. M. Henle (Springer-Verlag, 1986).

626

THE PARADOX OF THE HEAP *page 458*

CHALLENGE 2 Consider the universe of natural numbers. Let *Fx* mean "*x* is greater than 17," let *fx* be *x* + 1, let *c* be 20, and let *d* be 5. Since the premises can be true and the conclusion false, the completeness theorem (part 8) assures there is no syntactic deduction.

CHALLENGE 4 $Va \vee \neg Va$ is true because this is a law of logic and so is satisfied for all precise predicates. *Va* is not true, for we can form the sharpening *P* so that *Px* is true iff *Vx* is true. Then *P* is a sharpening of *V* and *Pa* is false. *Va* is not false, for we can form *P′* so that *P′x* is true iff *Vx* is not false. Then *P′* is again a sharpening of *V*, and *P′a* is true. Since some sharpenings make it true and some false, *Va* is neither true nor false, and similarly for ¬ *Va*.

CHALLENGE 5 See "Hypothetical Reasoning: Deductions from Assumptions" in part 5.

RUSSELL'S PARADOX AND FREGE'S MISTAKE *page 468*

CHALLENGE 1 From the statement, conclude $\forall x(x \in c^* \Leftrightarrow \neg(x \in x))$, and from this conclude $c^* \in c^* \Leftrightarrow \neg(c^* \in c^*)$, a contradiction by truth tables.

Russell's comments about Frege are contained in a letter to Jean van Heijenoortl printed in the latter's *From Frege to Gödel: A Source Book in Mathematical Logic, 1879–1931* (Harvard University Press, 1967), p. 127.

You can read about modern approaches to questions of mathematical existence, sets, and paradox in *New Directions in the Philosophy of Mathematics: An Anthology*, edited by T. Tymoczko (Birkhäuser, 1986.)

with & about logic

Life *page 474*

For more details on Life, including Conway's remarkable work, see *Winning Ways for Your Mathematical Plays*, Volume 2, by Berlekamp, Conway, and Guy (Academic Press, 1982). Yet another exposition can be found in William Poundstone's *The Recursive Universe* (Contemporary Books, 1985).

EXERCISE

1. (nothing)

2.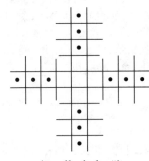

("bee hive")

3. Four blinkers:

("traffic lights")

4. (called "blinker")

5. ("block")

6. "glider"
Reproduces itself
after four generations
one cell to the right
and one cell down.

Ed Fredkin is a fascinating person, entrepreneur, scientist, and philosopher. He is one of three scientists profiled in Robert Wright's *Three Scientists and Their Gods* (Times Books, 1988).

Tom and Jim's Excellent Adventure

November 16

Bertrand Russell considered the question of free will. He supposed the worst: that the future is fixed, given the past. He noted that while it will never be possible to predict the future completely, we can take no comfort in that. Still, he did not fear loss of free will.

What we (the human race) might fear is being compelled by outside forces. Causing, however, is not compelling. The key is that in the end, we do what we choose to do.

Again, Russell considered the worst possible case. He supposed that there were beings who could see the future and knew it to be immutable. Would these creatures ever view the future with feelings of regret and impotence? Russell said no. Knowing their future deeds, they would also know the motivations for those deeds. Those motivations would be genuinely reasonable since all decisions would be informed by knowledge of the consequences of those deeds.

Russell concluded that the most important aspect of free will, the freedom from coercion, the knowledge that your actions are taken at your own volition, still remained.

Go to page 531.

page 480

What's the explanation of this paradox? If we regard a game as the set of all its possible plays, then there is no such set as Hypergame! Like the barber and Russell's set, language deludes us into thinking there must be an impossible object.

Part of the charm of the hypergame paradox, however, is that it's different from the others; it's asymmetric. In Russell's paradox, you show $R \in R \Rightarrow R \notin R$ and you show $R \notin R \Rightarrow R \in R$. Neither implication depends on the other. In the hypergame paradox, you must show that hypergame is a finite game *first*. You need this to prove that hypergame is not a finite game!

page 481   the busy beaver is not computable

In Notes, References, Hints, and Some Answers for "The Busy Beaver," we promised you more twenty-line programs. Here are a few.

A simple change is to add a line to the doubling machine to make it a quadrupling machine, as follows (recall that "$z = z + 5$" is short-hand for five lines, each "$z = z + 1$"):

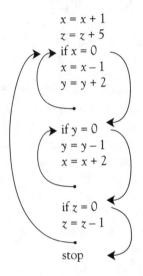

$$x = x + 1$$
$$z = z + 5$$
$$\text{if } x = 0$$
$$x = x - 1$$
$$y = y + 2$$

$$\text{if } y = 0$$
$$y = y - 1$$
$$x = x + 2$$

$$\text{if } z = 0$$
$$z = z - 1$$

stop

Now instead of reaching $2^7 = 128$, we reach $4^6 = 4096$. Next, we move the two instances of "$+ 2$" higher, changing our quadrupling machine to

$$y = y + 2$$
$$\text{if } x = 0$$
$$x = x - 1$$

$$x = x + 2$$
$$\text{if } y = 0$$
$$y = y - 1$$

This gives a little extra. Starting from $x = 0$, one time through the program gets us $x = 6$. Another time through gets us $x = 30$, then $x = 126$, then $x = 510$. What we are doing is computing: $2^3 - 2$, $2^5 - 2$, $2^7 - 2$, ... Now we don't need the "$x = x + 1$" at the start, so we can have:

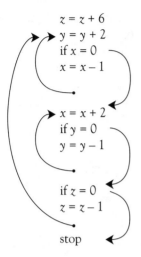

$$z = z + 6$$
$$y = y + 2$$
$$\text{if } x = 0$$
$$x = x - 1$$
$$x = x + 2$$
$$\text{if } y = 0$$
$$y = y - 1$$
$$\text{if } z = 0$$
$$z = z - 1$$
stop

This small change increases the value of the result to $2^{15} - 2 = 32{,}766$!

The variable z is our counter. It governs how many times we go through the quadrupling loop. To get *really* tricky, let's try to increase z by putting a "$z = z + 1$" inside one of the loops. We have to be very careful, however, because if we let z increase forever, the program will never stop.

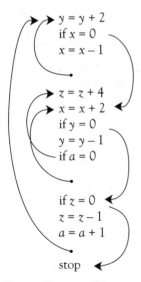

$$y = y + 2$$
$$\text{if } x = 0$$
$$x = x - 1$$
$$z = z + 4$$
$$x = x + 2$$
$$\text{if } y = 0$$
$$y = y - 1$$
$$\text{if } a = 0$$
$$\text{if } z = 0$$
$$z = z - 1$$
$$a = a + 1$$
stop

You will notice that z is allowed to increase only when a is 0 (otherwise you never get to "$z = z + 4$"). At the start, a is 0, of course, but as soon as we go through the quadrupling loop once, a is raised to 1, so

631

z (which got up to 6 before, but now reaches 8) will never go higher. This program ends with x at $2^{19} - 2 = 524,286$.

A big number? Not really! Here's another program, and surely still bigger numbers can be generated.

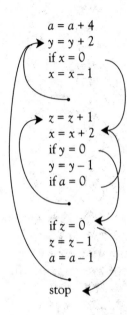

$$a = a + 4$$
$$y = y + 2$$
$$\text{if } x = 0$$
$$x = x - 1$$

$$z = z + 1$$
$$x = x + 2$$
$$\text{if } y = 0$$
$$y = y - 1$$
$$\text{if } a = 0$$

$$\text{if } z = 0$$
$$z = z - 1$$
$$a = a - 1$$

stop

This is big, we think. It reaches $2^{646} - 2 = $ 291996199527820493993 09498276481864479316662446390786555706832114555361070135 53527363784199243117695858331078127100420678840771021680 28031888170324462221708048127659159056956805303948303782 641662.

Tom and Jim's Excellent Adventure

November 14

Tom is worried about how the machine works. "When you return from the future or the past, are you sure you will remember it?" he asks. "What does it mean 'return to the present'? Doesn't it mean returning to your former state, and your former state has no memory of time travel. If you don't remember your trip, you may wind up going back and forth between November 14 and November 15 forever, each time thinking that it is the first trip!"

Jim is really impressed with this reasoning. He devises a scheme to test whether or not it is true and plans to try it out tomorrow. Turn to page 576.

impossibility

page 483

How did Gödel prove the incompleteness theorem? Essentially, he constructed a sentence in the language of arithmetic which, although it was in the context of numbers, actually had the meaning "This sentence cannot be proven." Such a sentence, of course, can't be proven, unless the system is inconsistent. Yet, it is actually true, and so it can't be disproven. The bulk of Gödel's work was showing that it is possible to form such a sentence.

How did Gödel prove that you can't disprove CH? The pattern is the same as the proof in "Geometry" in part 8 that you can't prove Euclid's fifth postulate from the other four. In that case, we used a standard world (three-dimensional Euclidean geometry) to form a nonstandard one (two-dimensional spherical geometry).

Gödel does the same. He starts with a world in which set theory is true and constructs inside it a world in which set theory and CH are both true:

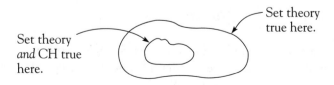

Set theory and CH true here.

Set theory true here.

This shows you can't disprove CH, because if you could, then everywhere set theory was true, CH would be false, which we see now is not the case.

How did Cohen prove that you can't prove CH? Building on Gödel's work, he was able to add to Gödel's world to create one where set theory is true and CH is false.

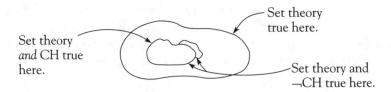

One of the authors of this book is a set theorist. Early in 1976, as he was putting the finishing touches on his Ph.D. thesis, it was reported that a major researcher in Europe had just proved ¬MC. The author's thesis was based entirely on MC. If the report were true, the thesis would be worthless. His advisor told him to remain calm. The proof might have an error, he said. Also, it might be a month or so before the proof was completely checked. Perhaps if the author hurried . . .

Within a week or so, an error was discovered in the proof. The thesis was saved; an academic tragedy (to the author of this book) did not happen.

Today, MC survives (although, like other axioms, it may be proven false at any time). Strangely, the near miss did not teach the author caution! Instead, it excited him and spurred him to investigate more powerful axioms. Why? He likes living on the edge.

In a sense, this is as close to romance as a pure mathematician can come. Mathematical worlds, after all, are entirely imaginary! In the academic world, however, the danger is undeniably real. A single result such as ¬MC can render one's lifework vacuous.

informal logic

page 486 *Quayle, Gore, and Stockdale*

1. Quayle describes his role under Bush through a single incident to present himself as an experienced leader. He never describes what

he would like to do in a second term. His last remarks seem weak; "having strong beliefs" is not the same as "standing up for what you believe in," and it is not obvious that this latter trait qualifies one to be president.

2. Stockdale describes a pretty open-ended role. He mentions areas he is interested in. He does not answer the question about his qualifications.

3. Gore ignores most of the questions entirely, choosing instead to attack the current administration for its neglect of domestic policy. His only statements relevant to the questions are those that emphasize how he and Clinton work together.

4. Quayle seems to take Gore's leap out of context as an invitation to further leaps. His only answer to Gore's attack is an attack of his own. He also suggests that working together is bad. His evidence is only that the president must make decisions, but this certainly doesn't mean that the president and vice president can't cooperate. This leads him to condemn Clinton for not making a firm decision on the Gulf war, suggesting that he is consequently unfit to lead.

5. Gore ignores this attack completely and repeats his charge that Bush has paid no attention to domestic problems. At the end he attacks the administration's economic policies. There follows a spate of bickering with each pointedly ignoring the other's charges.

6. Stockdale deftly points out that this sort of confrontational behavior has resulted in nothing being done to solve problems. He does not explain why a third candidate would succeed where the major parties have failed.

Tom and Jim's Excellent Adventure

November 16

Tom and Jim have gone back together. Together they meet Tom and Jim, who are more than a little surprised to see them. Jim (November 16) is told of the plan, and he agrees to have Jim (November 17) cut his hair, since he usually cuts it himself anyhow.

As Jim's locks (of November 16) fall, nothing whatever happens to Jim's locks (of November 17). Is this a paradox? Jim's hair (of November 16) is four inches long now, but Jim's hair (of November 17) is five!

With a sense of impending doom, Tom and Jim (of November 17) step into the time machine to return to November 17.

Before proceeding to page 546, think about the situation. Can you resolve it?

page 491 *law boards: logical reasoning*

1. C 3. B 5. A 7. D 9. B 11. D 13. C 15. D 17. C 19. D 21. E

page 499 *law boards: analytical reasoning*

1. C 3. B 5. C 7. D 9. B 11. D 13. C 15. D 17. B 19. D 21. E 23. B

page 506 *law boards: rules and disputes*

1. B

3. B This is certainly relevant, and we have no way of knowing the answer.

5. D It doesn't matter for the application of the second rule whether or not Nelson does anything other than read a relevant work.

7. B 9. C 11. D The question is, Is *Sophist College* liable? Tricky! 13. B 15. B 17. B 19. D

21. B Note that the question has an antecedent, "if no other . . . ." Now it may not be relevant that no other African-American students protested, but the actual question, "Can Dr. Hovic's remarks be considered threatening?" *is* relevant. The answer would also be B to "If Orioles win the pennant, would Dr. Hovic's remarks be considered threatening?" On the other hand, the answer to "If Dr. Hovic's remarks are considered threatening, will the Orioles win the pennant?" is D.

23. D 25. D

curiosities & puzzles

The Digestor's Digest, page 8

page 513

Page 7 is the fun page. You may recall that on page 1, one piece claimed it was not an ad. We observed later (in the discussion of page 4) that this could not happen on a fun page—neither an ad nor an article can say that on a fun page. Now consider page 7. The second piece says that it is an ad. On a nonfun page, no piece can say this; it leads to a contradiction.

exam warning VIII

page 514

If you're looking here for a clue, forget it.

quiz on Polish notation

page 515

1. c 3. c 5. e

The sentence in Polish at the top of the quiz says that you do not need to know Polish to answer the questions. Of course, someone who does not know Polish would be able to figure that out. Someone who does know Polish might easily be confused; the lines are all taken from nineteenth-century romantic plays! On the other hand, if you don't know Polish, then you don't need to know the meaning of that Polish sentence!

page 516   Tom and Jim's excellent adventure

The concepts of time and time travel have been favorites among philosophers and science fiction writers. In a little-known paper, the great philosophical logician Kurt Gödel showed that Einstein's theory of general relativity allowed for the possibility of time travel ("An Example of a New Type of Cosmological Solution of Einstein's Field Equations of Gravitation," *Reviews of Modern Physics* 21:447–450 (1949)). One of the most insightful of contemporary investigators is Michael Dummett (see his essays "Can an Effect Precede Its Cause?" and "Bringing About the Past," both reprinted in his *Truth and Other Enigmas* (Harvard University Press, 1978)). Martin Gardner's "Time Travel," from his *Time Travel and Other Mathematical Bewilderments* (W. H. Freeman, 1988), is an excellent survey article. He discusses many of the ideas in our adventure, together with relativity. The article lists many additional sources.

Among science fiction writers, one of the greatest is Philip K. Dick, and his short story "A Little Something for Us Tempunants" in *The Best of Philip K. Dick* (Ballantine, 1977) is an outstanding, if depressing, account of time travel. Equally impressive is Ursula Le Guin's novel *The Lathe of Heaven* (Avon, 1971), which describes a man whose dreams can change the past and a psychotherapist who tries to exploit him. Barry Malzberg in *Herovit's World* (Random House, 1973) tells of a time traveler who multiplies himself beyond necessity. Frederic Brown wrote a splendid short story about a time machine of the third sort, where objects inside the machine travel in time but objects outside do not. The machine was used by a scientist to send himself to the past. Written in 1953, the story, "Hall of Mirrors," was anthologized in Brown's *Honeymoon in Hell* (Bantam, 1958). It is a masterpiece.

Tom and Jim's Excellent Adventure

November 14

Tom argues that the weatherperson is talking not about the future but about the past. What he means is that the weatherperson has seen weather conditions like this before many times, and in the past these conditions have been followed by rain about half the time. There is no need for a time machine to understand this. Go to page 633.

INDEX